White Women,

Illicit Sex in the Nineteenth-Century South

Yale University Press New Haven and London

White Women, Black Men

For my father, Stuart
For my partner, Bruce

Contents

Acknowledgments

For generous support making possible invaluable periods of un-interrupted researching and writing, I thank the National Endowment for the Humanities, the American Council of Learned Societies, the Regents of the University of California, the Academic Senate of the University of California at Santa Cruz, the Whiting Foundation, the American Histori-cal Association, the North Caroliniana Society, the Princeton University Council on Regional Studies, and the Princeton University Program in Women's Studies. For graciously accompanying me in the search for evi-dence on a largely unindexed topic, I thank the archivists and librarians of the National Archives, the Maryland Hall of Records, the Maryland Historical Society, the Library of Virginia, the North Carolina Division of Archives and History, the Southern Historical Collection and the North Carolina Collection in the Wilson Library at the University of North Caro-lina, the William Perkins Library at Duke University, the Georgia De-partment of Archives and History, the Atlanta Historical Society, and the Schomburg Center for Research in Black Culture at the New York Public Library. The interlibrary loan staff at New York University's Bobst Library gave immeasurable assistance, providing me with a steady stream of elu-sive documents.

Christine Stansell was my greatest ally in this project's first incar-nation, consistently offering the most rigorous and enlightening criticism; I thank her also for her steadfast support ever since. Nell Irvin Painter from the beginning offered insights that illuminated enormous paths of inquiry, and every subsequent conversation with her has opened my eyes anew. James McPherson long ago demonstrated faith in this idea, and then showed me the best bicycling roads in the New Jersey countryside. Barbara Fields responded to a germ of a proposal with a very long let-ter that kept me from losing my way. Eva Moseley of Radcliffe College's Schlesinger Library on the History of Women set me on the path to be-coming a historian.

Bruce Dorsey read every word of the manuscript many drafts over and talked with me for uncountable hours about everything from the shad-ings of a word's meaning to the purposes of history. His inspirations have shaped much of my thinking on this project. Eleven more people read the entire manuscript at different stages. For their generous time and edifying commentary I am indebted to Edward Ayers, Thomas Bender, Nancy Cott, Hasia Diner, James McPherson, Kevin Mumford, Nell Irvin Painter, Jeffrey Sammons, Christine Stansell, Deborah Gray White, and an anonymous reader for Yale University Press. Other colleagues read particular portions of the manuscript and proffered crucial criticism in their special fields. I am grateful to Peter Bardaglio, Sharon Block, Kathleen Brown, Fitzhugh Brundage, Victoria Bynum, Laura Edwards, Drew Faust, James Goodman, Stephanie McCurry, David Roediger, and Bryant Simon. For commentary at conferences, colloquia, and seminars, I thank Victoria Bynum, Cornelia Dayton, David Garrow, Edith Gelles, Glenda Gilmore, Linda Gordon, Robert Gross, Suzanne Lebsock, Susan Levine, Stephanie McCurry, Melton McLaurin, Linda Reed, and Stephanie Shaw. Extra gratitude goes to Sharon Block and Fitzhugh Brundage for their generous sharing of archival material. I also thank participants in the Research Project in Southern History at the University of California at San Diego; the Bay Area Seminar on Early American History and Culture; the "Narrating Histories Workshop" at the California Institute of Technology; and the women's history reading group and cultural studies colloquium at the University of California at Santa Cruz. For indispensable assistance at the office, I am beholden to Sylvia Holmes in California and to Karin Burrell, Ben Maddox, and William Seward in New York. I thank Laura Jones Dooley for extremely keen copyediting. And knowing that Charles Grench was the editor of this book from its early stages has without fail eased my mind. I have not always agreed with or heeded the advice of readers and listeners, and I alone am responsible for the arguments herein.

For countless conversations that may have begun with scholarship but then ranged far and wide, I extend deep gratitude to Sharon Achinstein, Sharon Block, Wini Breines, Ada Ferrer, Miriam Formanek-Brunell, Dana Frank, Kristin Gager, James Goodman, James Green, Katherine Jansen, Walter Johnson, Jason McGill, Bryant Simon, Moshe Sluhovsky, and Judith Weisenfeld. For camaraderie and professional encouragement I am truly obliged to David Anthony, Thomas Bender, Robert and Jean Berkhofer, Yvonne Chireau, Lizabeth Cohen, Sophie de Schaepdrijver, Sarah Deutsch, Hasia Diner, Gregory Dowd, Lisa Duggan, Antonio Feros,

Lisbeth Haas, Ronnie Hsia, Robin Kelley, Yanni Kotsonis, Linda Lomperis, Louis Masur, Mary Nolan, Jeffrey Sammons, Jerrold Seigel, Sinclair Thomson, Joanna Waley-Cohen, Susan Ware, Louise Young, and Marilyn Young. The American Dance Festival at Duke University made summer Southern research a great deal more fun. And tremendous thanks to Marjorie Murphy and the History Department at Swarthmore College, who along with Harvard Avenue neighbors welcomed me during two years of unofficial residence. I finished this book to the rushing waters of Crum Creek.

Outside university walls, Jody Goodman and Marc Fisher genially opened their home to me during Washington research trips, thereby nourishing what will always be the longest friendship of my life; Duke Wiser forged an important friendship during the first draft; Sheba Veghte and Steven Fingerhood graciously kept a sun-filled room for me in San Francisco for whenever I needed a respite with good friends; Jamie Jamieson gave me precious companionship and ever-faithful friendship as she showed me the steepest canyons on our bicycle journeys in and around Santa Cruz; Becky Blythe and Peter Littman offered many warm dinners and at least one unforgettable adventure in the Santa Cruz mountains; and Sharon Achinstein became my best friend during the life of this project.

Also beyond the academy, I thank Stuart Hodes for his model of lifework as play and for his unwavering support; Linda Hodes for her vital model of independence and accomplishment; Ryn Hodes and Tal Ben-David for sisterhood in all its meanings: the sustenance is incalculable. Ryn, I would be happy if my work had one fraction of the effect on people's lives as yours does. Tal, you have walked with me along the rugged path of creative and ordinarily solitary work. I also thank Jack Gescheidt, who in the years of this project became a beloved soulmate; Chuck Choi, who was my first friend in Princeton and later became family; Steven Margolies, who offered abiding sympathy for the ways of academia; Rae Russell, who hosted our annual family gatherings with such a warm heart; Matthew Choi, who was born in the middle of this project, and Timothy Dorsey, who became a part of my life during it; and Kenneth Tosti, our family's best friend.

Any romantic motivations on the part of the protagonists in this book remain elusive in the archival documents; let me thus set down for the historical record my love for Bruce Dorsey, who walked into my life and broke through my efficient solitude and without whom this book would have been finished much sooner by a much lonelier historian. Bruce, you alone know the measure of the love.

1 Telling the Stories

A history of sex between white women and black men in the nine-teenth-century American South is also the history of a powerful category of illicit sex in the United States. When in 1967 the U.S. Supreme Court ruled that laws prohibiting marriage between people of different races were unconstitutional, sixteen states had such laws.[1] Decades later, the legacy of this history remains evident, notably in the modern-day annals of white violence, in both North and South. Researching this book, I never found whole stories in the archives. Rather, I found shards and bones, parts of conversations, and laconic responses to frightening questions. Sometimes I wondered, why not write a work of fiction on the same sub-ject? Why was I compelled to write history—to tell not just a story, but a true story? In fiction I could have dispensed with documentation and freely invoked imagination. But as I continued my research, I understood why I could not have undertaken this book as a work of fiction. As I began to write the history of sex between white women and black men in the nineteenth-century South, I realized I had found stories that did not con-form to what I had anticipated. This was a narrative that had to be told first as history.

The Historical Development of White Anxiety

White anxiety about sex between white women and black men is not a timeless phenomenon in the United States; rather, it is a historical development that evolved out of particular social, political, and economic circumstances.[2] Scholars agree that the most virulent racist ideology about black male sexuality emerged in the decades that followed the Civil War, and some historians have recognized that the lynching of black men for the alleged rape of white women was comparatively rare in the South under slavery. This book explains how whites in the antebellum South re-sponded when confronted with sexual liaisons between white women and black men, and how and why those responses changed with emancipation. Under the institution of racial slavery, I argue, white Southerners could respond to sexual liaisons between white women and black men with a measure of toleration; only with black freedom did such liaisons begin to provoke a near-inevitable alarm, one that culminated in the tremendous white violence of the 1890s and after. Two of the nation's foremost black activists, Frederick Douglass and Ida B. Wells, called attention to this transition as it occurred before their eyes in the post–Civil War South. Both observed that the accusation of rape of white women by black men was relatively uncommon in the slave South, as well as during the Civil War, when white men were absent from Southern homes. "The crime to which the Negro is now said to be so generally and specially addicted," stated Douglass at the height of the lynching era in 1892, "is one of which he has been heretofore, seldom accused or supposed to be guilty." During slavery and in wartime, Douglass noted, black men were "seldom or never . . . accused of the atrocious crime of feloniously assaulting white women." Or as Wells told her listeners that same year: "The world knows that the crime of rape was unknown during four years of civil war, when the white women of the South were at the mercy of the race which is all at once charged with being a bestial one."[3] Although white people in North America had professed beliefs about the greater sexual ardor of black men ever since the colonial era, and although black men had been accused and convicted of raping white women within the racist legal system of the slave South, Wells and Douglass were nonetheless correct that those ideas and inequities did not include relentless, deadly violence toward black men before the late nineteenth century.[4]

Sanctions against sex between white women and black men in the slave South must have accounted in part for the infrequency of such liaisons; yet my concern is not to point out that sex between white women and black men occurred with a particular frequency. Rather, my concern is to demonstrate that when such liaisons did occur, white Southerners could react in a way that complicates modern assumptions. Statistics are difficult to gather in part because sex between white women and black men did not enter the historical record under a uniform heading. Antebellum legal records do not employ any one word to define this particular transgression. The word *miscegenation* was invented during the Civil War, and until then liaisons between white women and black men went on record as a result of other crimes or legal disputes. Given the laws against marriage between blacks and whites, such liaisons could be prosecuted as fornication or adultery; if children were produced, the protagonists would be guilty of bastardy as well. Yet white women and white men were also routinely charged with fornication, adultery, and bastardy, demonstrating that Southern authorities did not simply target liaisons between white women and black men under the name of other sex crimes. A liaison between a white woman and a black man could also be revealed through rape charges, further clouding the possibility of straightforward statistics. Other liaisons entered the record under civil and criminal categories unrelated to sex crimes, including illegal enslavement, contested inheritance, libel, slander, and murder. Moreover, testimony in all such cases often made it clear that white neighbors had known about a liaison before (and often years before) it was revealed in a legal document, and therefore in the public record, for some other reason. For every liaison that unfolded in a county courtroom, there must have been others—it is impossible to say how many—in the antebellum South that never entered the record.[5]

White responses to liaisons between white women and black men differed markedly from the permissiveness displayed for sex between white men and black women, which most often involved the rape of female slaves by masters or other white men. Antebellum Southerners and their historians have written about the tacit acceptance on the part of whites for this phenomenon of slave society. Fugitive slave Harriet Jacobs told readers of her 1861 memoir that "if the white parent is the father, instead of the mother, the offspring are unblushingly reared for the market." Plantation mistress Mary Chesnut wrote in a now-famous diary entry of 1861 that "every lady tells you who is the father of all the mulatto children in everybody's household, but those in her own she seems to think drop from the clouds."[6]

That sex between white women and black men did not necessarily provoke white violence by no means implies its sanguine acceptance. There is a crucial nuance of language here: *tolerance* implies a liberal spirit toward those of a different mind; *toleration* by contrast suggests a measure of forbearance for that which is not approved. I use the term *toleration* to describe, in part, white attitudes toward sexual liaisons between white women and black men in the slave South. Yet the phenomenon of toleration, no matter how carefully defined, cannot convey the complexity of responses: white neighbors judged harshly, gossiped viciously, and could completely ostracize the transgressing white woman. As for the black man, it was the lack of sure violence that is historically significant, and this is difficult interpretive terrain: the evidence yielded striking absences, and absences are harder to interpret than their more tangible opposites. If a degree of local indifference is apparent at certain points in the stories that follow, the narratives also demonstrate that white toleration was mediated by limits of both patriarchy and class.

First, male authority and honor in white families and communities was a crucial component of the slave South, and patriarchal patience for illicit sex on the part of white girls and women was not forthcoming under any circumstances.[7] More specifically, Southern lawmakers had written statutes so that sex between white women and black men confounded the system of racial slavery and had entirely different consequences from sex between white men and black women. In the antebellum South, a child's legal status as slave or free followed the mother: if your mother was free, you were free; if your mother was a slave, you were a slave. Sexual liaisons between white women and black men therefore threatened racial slavery in a way that sex between white men and black women did not. When white women had children with black men, two important social categories were eroded: racial categories were eroded because the children would be of mixed European and African ancestry, and categories of slavery and freedom were eroded because free people of African ancestry endangered the equation of blackness and slavery. The possibility of white toleration for sex between white women and black men in the slave South sheds light on patriarchal power within white households and its crucial connections to the institution of racial slavery.[8]

Second, class boundaries played a role in white responses to sexual liaisons between white women and black men. The white population of the antebellum South ranged from wealthy plantation owners who commanded large slave-labor forces to work their substantial landholdings to yeoman farmers who strove for economic self-sufficiency, perhaps assisted by a modicum of slave labor, to poor whites who owned no slaves and little or no land. The economic status of any one family, especially outside the planter classes, might rise or fall over time with, for example, the purchase of a slave or the loss of property to debtors. The upcountry regions of the South were largely (though not exclusively) home to yeoman farmers and poor whites, while in lowcountry, tidewater, and blackbelt areas, small slaveholders and nonslaveholders coexisted with masters of large plantations. Distinct social tensions governed interactions among white Southerners of different classes. Such struggles can also be found in the stories of white women and black men narrated in these pages.[9] Specifically, dominant ideas about poor white women included convictions about their promiscuity and debauchery that could mitigate blame of a black man. As Nell Irvin Painter points out, "The stereotypes are centuries old and have their origins in European typecasting of both the poor and the black, for sex is the main theme associated with poverty and with blackness." And as Victoria E. Bynum writes, "Poverty defeminized white women much as race defeminized black women."[10] In the dominant visions of the antebellum South, then, black women seduced white men, and poorer white women were capable of seducing black men.

The danger of a liaison across the color line was graver for black men and elite white women because those women were at the center of white Southern ideas about female purity. Legal records concerning sex between white women and black men largely (although not uniformly) relay stories about white women outside the planter classes; it is difficult to know whether this was due to the greater surveillance of planter-class women by their families or whether it reflected the ability of wealthier white women and their families to keep sexual transgressions out of court and therefore out of the historical record. Dominant ideas about the sexuality of black men and white women were closely bound up with ideas about the sexual depravity of black women. All of these ideas were part of a system that ideally would permit white men to control all white women and all black people; the sexual abuse of black women by white men was the most extensive and gruesome component of this system.[11]

Third, the legal status of slave men as the property of white people, and the potential of free black men to become property or to be treated as such meant that white Southerners had a stake in protecting their human chattel from extreme violence or murder. White concerns about the preservation of slave property could therefore check violent reactions to a sexual transgression between a white woman and a black man.[12] The end of slavery also meant the end of property concerns and thus helps to explain the disintegration of restraints and the shift toward extreme white violence in the decades following emancipation. With the demise of slavery as a rough dividing line between black and white, the total separation of black people and white people became essential for whites who hoped to retain supremacy. White ideas about the dangers of black male sexuality were not newly formed after the Civil War, but white virulence reached a greater intensity with the transition from black slavery to black freedom. Beginning in the Reconstruction era, black men were terrorized and often murdered, and white women were subjected to extreme abuse, if they engaged or allegedly engaged in sexual liaisons across the color line. Furthermore, white Southerners explicitly conflated black men's alleged sexual misconduct toward white women with the exercise of their newly won political rights. Frederick Douglass and Ida B. Wells understood this phenomenon. Douglass directly equated accusations of sexual transgressions against white women with black men's newfound political power. "It is only since the Negro has become a citizen and a voter," he wrote in 1892, "that this charge has been made." Lynching, Wells wrote early in the twentieth century, was "wholly political, its purpose being to suppress the colored vote by intimidation and murder." [13]

Contradictions, Crises, Voices, Language

My purpose here is not to prove the existence of simple white toleration for sex between white women and black men in the antebellum South. Rather, I seek to uncover and explain how some white communities responded when such liaisons came to light and then to explore why, in the decades that followed emancipation, the majority of the white South became enraged about this particular category of illicit sex. Such explanations and explorations require a level of comfort with paradoxes; indeed, all answers to questions about societies that operated under human bondage include paradoxes. In fact, although Southern laws made liaisons between white women and black men dangerous to the institution of racial slavery, there was a contradictory lack of action in the face of such liaisons. In the antebellum South, white women and black men who engaged in illicit sex did not uniformly suffer swift retribution, for under slavery such liaisons did not sufficiently threaten the social and political hierarchy — as they would after emancipation. The roots of this strained toleration lie in two contradictory but coexisting factors: the insignificance of such transgressions in the face of the power of racial slavery versus the explosive nature of those transgressions, also in the face of racial slavery. For whites to refrain from immediate legal action and public violence when confronted with liaisons between white women and black men helped them to mask some of the flaws of the antebellum Southern systems of race and gender.

Yet paradoxically, any toleration of such transgressions meant that those flaws would also be exposed, especially in the evidence of free children of partial African ancestry—the free children of white women and black men. Indeed, in all the antebellum cases reconstructed in this book, it was the presence of free children that precipitated a local crisis, a crisis that ultimately intruded on local reluctance to prosecute or violently persecute. In the first story, the crisis concerned the enslavement of the descendants of a colonial marriage between a white servant-woman and a slave man. In the next story, the critical issue was the nature of the sex between a white servant-woman and a slave man after the woman had given birth and claimed rape. In the third, the fate of a white marriage was at stake after the wife had borne the children of a slave. In the last two antebellum stories, whites were in a quandary over whether people who might be the sons of white mothers and black fathers should inherit property. In each of these antebellum cases, the presence of children forced the liaison into court. Once there, testimony made it clear that whites had known about the liaison for quite some time. After that, the verdicts demonstrated that the law could tolerate a liaison between a white woman and a black man: the governor pardoned a black man initially convicted of rape, for example, and the legislature denied divorce to a white husband whose white wife had consorted with a black man.[14]

From the point of view of the transgressors rather than the authorities, the crises were very different, yet there are fewer sources to determine those contours. Throughout the antebellum documents, the voices of white men come through most clearly: as slaveholders, patriarchs, witnesses, jury members, and judges; next clearest are the voices of the transgressing white women, followed by the transgressing black men, who often had no opportunity to defend themselves or wisely chose to remain silent. Documents occasionally include the voices of neighboring white women and black men as observers of the transgressors. Black women, as mothers, wives, daughters, friends, or neighbors, undoubtedly often suspected or knew about liaisons between white women and black men, and they unquestionably were affected by and held opinions about those liaisons; yet black women's voices are the faintest in the antebellum historical record.[15] Following emancipation, the crises for all parties centered on the transition from slavery to freedom. White Southerners became more and more alarmed at the consequences of black freedom, and transgressors or alleged transgressors became increasingly fearful about the tremendous upsurge in white violence. The views of black women, who were also subject to tremendous white violence after the war, are finally discernible in testimony taken against the Ku Klux Klan in the 1870s. By the 1890s, the voices of educated black women formed a significant part of the growing protests against white violence.

The concept of communities is illuminating in regard to which voices are audible in the historical record: although the localities discussed in this book were home to blacks and whites whose lives were daily intertwined, sharp divisions of power also existed. The documents often (though not always) present Southern whites as living in a unified community, but that is only because select voices have been preserved. The phrases "white community" and "white Southerners" cannot therefore be wholly inclusive. For one thing, such phrases always exclude the transgressing white woman and any allies she may have had. For slave and free black communities in the antebellum South, historians can only speculate about unified or dissenting voices on the topic of sex with white women, for the records are nearly entirely silent on this matter. Sources are also largely quiet on the place of a transgressing black man within his own community. In many ways, then, the safest use of the word *community* is simply as a means to talk about some of the people who lived near one another. The boundaries of such an area would be as far as a person could travel in a day.[16]

Following from this understanding of intertwined white and black communities, the stories recounted here are also about problems of racial categorization for the descendants of white women and black men. If social and legal sanctions against sex between people of European ancestry and people of African ancestry had never existed, the categories "black" and "white" as they are known and used today would not exist either. W. E. B. Du Bois was among the first scholars to name and investigate this problem, partly through the mixture of "Africa and Europe" within his own family. More recently, Barbara J. Fields has eloquently supported the contention that race "is a product of history, not of nature." My corresponding view of race as a social construction creates attendant problems of description. Fields sums up such problems when she observes "the well-known anomaly of American racial convention that considers a white woman capable of giving birth to a black child but denies that a black woman can give birth to a white child." [17] In addition, Europe and Africa were not the sole categories, for some Southerners traced their ancestry to various combinations of American Indian, European, and African descent. In some of the stories that follow, all of these categories came into play in legal battles over marriage, freedom, and inheritance. I have used the terms *black* and *white* to denote people recognized locally as respectively African American and European American and have placed those words in quotation marks only to express ambiguities of identification among the historical actors themselves. I have echoed the phrase *person of color* when it appears in the documents. I do not use *mulatto* except when quoting sources, a word whose origins and definitions are both pejorative and murky. I similarly do not use *miscegenation,* a word coined during the presidential campaign of 1864 by the Democratic Party in order to cast aspersions upon Abraham Lincoln's Republican Party. Neither do I use the term *interracial,* because it it implies fixed categories of race and therefore an overly natural quality to those categories.

In the face of these convictions, as Evelyn Brooks Higginbotham points out, "To argue that race is a myth and that it is an ideological rather than a biological fact does not deny that ideology has real effects on people's lives." [18] Indeed, in the stories presented here, blackness was not the only category that mattered; ideas about whiteness, too, were important in the lives of transgressing white women, as well as in the lives of those who judged them. Whiteness in the slave South was every bit as much a constructed category as blackness, and the narratives presented in this book illuminate the ambiguities inherent in racial categorization. [19] In the same way, constructions of gender mattered not only in the lives of the white women but also in the lives of the black men.

A final note on language: for liaisons that came to pass in the slave South, I have used only the first names of the protagonists, because the last names of black men were seldom recorded. In post-emancipation documents, when black men's surnames begin to appear with greater frequency, I have shifted to the more conventional appellation.

The Stories

In Part I, I re-create individual liaisons between white women and black men in the South before the Civil War. To illuminate the roots of the problems of sexual liaisons between white women and black men under slavery, in Chapter 2, I present a case that spans the seventeenth and eighteenth centuries. In Chapters 3, 4, and 5, I relate antebellum stories in which the historical actors discuss such topics as fornication, cohabitation, rape, bastardy, adultery, divorce, and domestic violence. Changes over time within the antebellum South undoubtedly affected white responses to sexual liaisons between white women and black men. Intensifying criticism from Northern antislavery forces after 1830, coupled with the Virginia slave uprising led by Nat Turner in 1831, which convulsed the entire region, might well have restrained white forbearance.[20] Yet the scattered nature of the sources limits a definitive analysis of such a shift within the antebellum era, and in fact, the cases examined do not fit into before-and-after patterns. Records indicate that lynchings of black men for the alleged rape of white women increased beginning in the mid-1850s as white Southerners braced for sectional conflict over the institution of slavery. Still, such extralegal violence remained far from inevitable in the decade before the war broke out.

Transformations in white responses are most apparent in the evolution from black slavery to black freedom, and that is where I have focused my treatment of change over time. In the years during and after the Civil War, discussions about sex between white women and black men underwent a tremendous shift. In the slave South, people talked about such transgressions in their own communities, and documents tell largely of neighborhood dramas. With the outbreak of war, the demise of slavery, and the advent of black freedom, however, discussions about sex between white women and black men multiplied rapidly in the arenas of national political culture. The subject of sex between white women and black men could now be found with much greater frequency in, for example, government hearings and major Southern newspapers. Part Two opens with the Civil War years in Chapter 6; here, the voices of black men become more audible on the subject of sex with white women, and the subject of sex between white women and black men enters national politics for the first time in a sustained manner. The era of Reconstruction is the focus of Chapter 7, with white Southerners conflating sexual transgressions and politics with increasing directness and constancy. In Chapter 8 I take the history through the last quarter of the century, with the consolidation of white rage at sex between white women and black men. Here the story will sound more familiar than anything that has come before, with the recurrence of white people lynching black men for the alleged rape of white women.

A sexual liaison between a white woman and a black man was un-likely to be documented in any detail, and most references to such liaisons were brief and elusive, sometimes only a single line in a legal ledger. Hardly anyone wrote about such liaisons in letters, or even in diaries, at least not in any detail, and never in the first person. Very occasionally, personal papers (letters and diaries) or published sources (memoirs or travelers' ac-counts) mention a sexual liaison between a black man and a white woman, but the reference is never more than a sentence or two, and utterly lacking in detail. I thus selected cases for which there existed a considerable body of evidence, choosing to examine a small number of rich narratives for the pre–Civil War era, with each in-depth case study supported by numerous similar, though less well documented, scenarios. The chapters that rely on evidence from the Civil War, Reconstruction, and post-Reconstruction de-cades offer a larger number of briefer accounts. The cases investigated for this book, then, are by no means exhaustive. Readers who wish to know how I discovered the narratives I have re-created may turn to "Searching for Stories: A Note on Sources."

Each of the pre–Civil War case studies is documented primarily in legal records. As the historian Lawrence Stone has so aptly written, "People hauled into court are almost by definition atypical, but the world that is so nakedly exposed in the testimony of witnesses need not be so. Safety therefore lies in examining the documents not so much for their evidence about the eccentric behavior of the accused as for the light they shed on the life and opinions of those who happened to get involved in the incident in question."[21] This description well captures my methods and intentions. Courtroom testimony or legislative petitions are often the only window onto the lives of the transgressors; where judicial maneuverings mattered to the protagonists and their adversaries, I have incorporated them into the narrative. After emancipation, the provenance of the sources shifts. Reconstruction-era scenarios are grounded primarily in government investigations of the Ku Klux Klan, while cases in the 1880s and 1890s are found largely in newspapers, though also in some court proceedings. For the post-Reconstruction era, I have also invoked the writings of social commentators and activists, both black and white, on the newly urgent topics of rape and lynching.

A word about geography is also in order. The first story told here takes place in the colony of Maryland, in the region of earliest contact between Europeans and Africans in what would become the United States. The succeeding antebellum case studies take place in North Carolina, Virginia, and Georgia; the Civil War, Reconstruction, and post-Reconstruction documents encompass more of the South as a whole. Together, all the narratives (including the many supporting stories told within the major case studies) comprise a wide range of geographical areas, from the mountains and the upcountry to the coast and the cotton belt, although overall they favor states of the upper South. As any resident, traveler, or scholar knows, there has never been a monolithic South, and both the contours of Southern society and the institution of slavery differed considerably in different localities. At the same time, important continuities are apparent in the various stories I uncovered, and in light of those continuities as well as the scarcity of documents about sex between white women and black men, I chose to undertake a study that encompasses different parts of the South rather than one that scrutinizes a smaller region in greater detail. I have also chosen to omit South Carolina and Louisiana from this study: records relating to racial identity in these states are voluminous, and many such cases are connected to the urban cultures of Charleston and New Orleans. These two cities (along with Mobile, Alabama, and Savannah, Georgia, to some degree) more formally recognized an intermediate class between "black" and "white," thereby adding another and quite different dimension to the issue of sex across the color line. Stories about sex between white women and black men in South Carolina and Louisiana would doubtless introduce further complexities to the conclusions drawn here. Nonetheless, although the men and women involved in the stories I relate lived in various regions, there is no easily apparent pattern to determine a particular community's response to a liaison between a white woman and a black man. Some of the white women came from poor, landless families; others were members of the small-slaveholding yeomanry. Some of the black men belonged to wealthy masters, others belonged to masters who farmed with the assistance of a few slaves, and still others were free. A few of the white women hailed from families with considerable wealth, and one of the black men was himself a slaveowner in the midst of the black belt.[22]

Although each major case came to light as an isolated historical event, I have followed every discovery by researching the surrounding context through censuses, wills, inventories, local histories, and other relevant documents. Yet the records of all that came to pass before the transgressions were revealed in written documents are few to none. In order to re-create the worlds of the historical actors, then, I have had to ask and sometimes to beg men and women to reveal their lives through such elusive evidence as the self-righteous court testimony of racist villagers. In fiction, an author can alert a reader how to view a narrator, as in William Faulkner's Shakespearean reference to "a tale told by an idiot" in *The Sound and the Fury*.[23] County court records, however, do not come labeled with such clues as "a version told by the sanctimonious white elite townspeople." After coaxing information from the documents and casting a critical eye on different points of view, I had to refrain from smoothing over the inconsistencies—indeed the incoherence—in the stories I had heard. Hence the importance of the language of speculation, even uncertainty, in the writing of a social history such as this one. "Perhaps," "presumably," "possibly," "plausibly": these words have been constant companions, as have such phrases as "There is no way to know," "It has proven impossible to discover," "The evidence is not conclusive," and "If the story is true."[24]

As for true stories, I haven't assumed that only those historical actors with whom I sympathized were the truth tellers. Some who commanded my sympathy turned out to be liars. I have had to ask why a particular person told his or her story in a particular way; to do so, I have had to invert the narratives of the powerful to find the stories of the voiceless. For the most part, the powerless spoke only because they were forced to come forward, though not necessarily without a certain resistance that is evident in their very words. I have tried throughout to reconstruct the stories that various people told themselves and each other as events unfolded. Alongside the narratives of those who observed and judged the transgressors, I have attempted to discern the experiences of the white women and black men who defied taboos and the ways they sought to explain their actions. Because white people had courtroom privileges, and because black families were not legally recognized under slavery, antebellum cases were defined largely in terms of the white participants. Not only did the family status of the black men play no part in the outcome, but the lives of the men, except for their status as slave or free, are scarcely described in the documents. As for retelling the stories, historians must contend with the difficulties of memory and the reconstruction of even the near past. Sometimes the archival voices here belong to a participant or an eyewitness, though more often they belong to someone who conversed with an eyewitness or who had simply listened to local gossip. Rather than presenting verbatim disclosures and declarations, therefore, documents often reveal only what someone thought someone else had said. In turn, eyewitnesses could reshape what they had seen or heard according to new information, suasion, bias, forgetfulness, or any number of other influences. And of course my own standpoint has shaped the stories in these pages as well.[25]

Questions of motivations and emotions have ultimately proved the most resistant both to documentation and to imagination. It is not always clear, for example, whether sexual intimacy was brief or protracted; I therefore use the word *liaison* more often than *relationship,* because it allows for greater ambiguity of timespan, reasons, and feelings. (Although white Southerners sometimes referred to white women who had sex with black men as prostitutes, I have chosen to omit the formal category of prostitution, defined as a transaction of sex for material compensation.) The documents do attest to the fact that white women and black men who formed sexual liaisons, either ongoing or brief, were not always (or perhaps ever) forming alliances against the white patriarchs of the South. To be sure, there are records of white women and black men who talked back to authorities, professed love, and leveled counteraccusations at white men. Yet whether rebellion, revenge, defiance, strategy, desire, or love played a role, the dynamics of power between white women and black men were ultimately too complicated by race, gender, sexuality, and class to permit simple bonds against white men. White women, even very poor ones, had more choices than most black men, either slave or free, in the antebellum South, and this granted the women at least a small measure of power as well as a stake in racial slavery. More well-to-do white women, even those who may have despised the white men who ruled them, rarely, if ever, challenged the authority of whiteness, for they most certainly had a stake in the system. Indeed, some documents offer evidence that white women in the slave South, no matter what their class standing, could coerce black men into sex. In the post–Civil War cases, the problem of motivations and emotions takes on new contours: at that point, it is often impossible to distinguish between liaisons that had come to pass, alleged liaisons, and forced and false confessions. These questions raise related questions about agency. In sum, although the transgressors here may have demonstrated resistance, they were also often powerless. In lieu of clear evidence about motivations, emotions, and agency, I have instead tried to place the words and deeds of authorities, neighbors, and transgressors in dialogue with surrounding laws, taboos, culture, and history.[26]

What follows is intended to be inquiring and exploratory rather than definitive and conclusive, and more work remains to be done on the issues raised here. The stories told and retold in the following pages are not merely the miserable chronicles of obscure villages: the events may be compelling on their own, but they are also historically significant. These stories begin to illuminate the historical construction of a particularly powerful category of illicit sex in American history.[27]

Part One

Neighborhood Dramas

Because marriage between blacks and whites was prohibited or severely discouraged by law in the nineteenth-century American South, sexual liaisons between white women and black men took the legal form of fornication or adultery.[1] That had not been the case from the beginning of English settlement in the Southern colonies, for there was a time before the entrenchment of racial slavery when relationships between white women and black men could have the sanction of law. In 1681, a white servant named Eleanor Butler, called Irish Nell, and a black slave called Negro Charles married on the lower western shore of Maryland. The earliest mixing of Europeans and Africans in North America took place in the Chesapeake, the site of the first permanent English colonies across the Atlantic and the first in which the colonists wrote slavery into their laws. Because this story spans the seventeenth and eighteenth centuries, it serves well as a prologue to an investigation of sexual liaisons between white women and black men in the nineteenth-century South.[2]

The marriage of Nell Butler and Charles in the late seventeenth-century Chesapeake was much discussed by the couple's elite white neighbors, yet that discussion was most emphatically not about Charles's transgression with a white woman. Only after the Civil War would whites' ideas about the dangers of black male sexuality merge with their fears of political and economic independence for African-American men to produce a deadly combination. That was not at all the case for this servant-woman and slave man in the colonial Chesapeake. The consternation of local white people at the marriage of Nell and Charles centered on the consequences of the match. Why, they wondered, would a white woman marry a black man when the law stipulated that a white woman and all her children would become slaves by virtue of that marriage? Indeed, those circumstances were exactly what propelled the case into court nearly a century later.

When Nell and Charles married in 1681, no court case resulted. The story came to be told only in the following century, when two enslaved grandchildren of Nell and Charles filed a petition claiming their freedom on the grounds of descent from a free white woman. The story of Nell and Charles was then recounted by sixteen white witnesses, a fairly well-to-do group of neighbors; these witnesses were descendants of the white neighbors of Nell and Charles, and their knowledge of the unusual marriage was conjured up in the 1760s to resolve the legal status of the grandchildren. In order to reach a verdict, the court had to determine the legal status of Nell Butler after her marriage to Charles.[3] The sentiments of the colonial white neighbors, as refracted through the recollections of their descendants, illuminate connections between the development of racial slavery and the problem of sexual liaisons between white women and black men. The marriage of Nell and Charles would ultimately cross boundaries not only of the categories of English and African but also of the categories of white and black, free and enslaved.

Consequences of the Wedding

Here is the story of Irish Nell and Negro Charles as recounted by the eighteenth-century witnesses. Charles was a slave on the plantation of Major William Boarman. In 1681, when Nell Butler arrived in Maryland as the servant of the third Lord Baltimore, Baltimore boarded at Boarman's plantation. At the Boarmans, Nell washed, ironed, cooked, spun, labored in the fields, and performed the services of a midwife; after a short while, William Boarman purchased Nell's services from Lord Baltimore. Nell and Charles were to be married, but not before the servant-woman had a verbal spar with the lord. On the morning of the wedding day, Baltimore, who had been informed of the impending marriage, cautioned Nell against it, telling her that by such an act she would make slaves of herself and her descendants. Nell cried and told Lord Baltimore not only that this was her choice but also that she would rather marry Charles than marry Baltimore himself, and that she would rather go to bed with Charles than with Lord Baltimore. Unable to persuade her to change her mind, Baltimore cursed Nell and dismissed her.

The wedding ceremony was performed by a local Catholic priest at the Boarman plantation in the summer of 1681. Nell "behaved as a bride," and several people wished the couple much joy. A little white boy was urged to kiss the bride, or she wanted to kiss him, or did kiss him, and he ran away. Old Madam Witham, Old Mrs. Doyne, Old Ann Short, and Old Mrs. Ruthorn were all there. Someone said it was a fine wedding. Afterward, Nell and Charles acknowledged themselves as "man and wife," and people knew them as such. Nell called Charles her "old man," and Charles called Nell his "old woman." When William Boarman died in 1709, his wife, Mary, married John Sanders, and Nell and Charles went to the Sanders household. Nell also lived and worked for some time at the household of Leonard Brooke, who married one of the Boarman daughters. Nell and Charles had three or four children, all of whom were enslaved from birth. These children either lived at the Boarman plantation or were hired out or sold to other families. When Nell died, she was "much broken and an old woman."[4]

It is instructive to compare the marriage of Nell and Charles to liaisons between white women and black men that later came to pass in the antebellum South. Later liaisons would lack public ceremony and operate under at least a pretense of secrecy. In conjunction with those restraints, however, antebellum white neighbors could respond to such liaisons in ways that were not so very different from the responses of the white neighbors of Nell and Charles. This included expressions of apprehension at the liaison, pronouncements of judgment against the white woman, and the absence of violent retribution against the black man. Of course there were other liaisons between white women and black men in the colonial Chesapeake in which the participants did try for secrecy, notably those that took place outside of marriage, and these outnumber the incidences of matrimony. But the wedding of Nell and Charles is evidence of leeway for a union within the lowest ranks of society that was legally sanctioned by those in the highest. The marriage of Nell and Charles was a transgression, but not an illicit one.

The well-to-do white neighbors who watched Nell and Charles marry held more than enough social authority to take local matters into their own hands had they wished to do so. The masters of Nell and Charles were captains, commanders, and merchants in Maryland's Catholic community.[5] This was a community that relied on informal networks of friends and neighbors in the absence of extensive kin relations. Laws were enforced by county courts and magistrates, though citizens considered themselves responsible for the social order by keeping watchful eyes over neighbors and by seeing to the punishment of transgressors. These masters and their social equals did not fervently condemn Nell and Charles. Far from it, they attended the wedding, even as they judged Nell for her actions; the guests seem to have been drawn from the inner circle of white families that included the Boarmans and the subsequent masters of Nell and Charles.

Unfortunately, the documents contain almost no information whatsoever about the responses of less well-to-do white people or of neighboring servants and slaves.[6]

In certain ways, then, the marriage of this white woman and this black man in 1681 was not a cause for tremendous concern among those who held authority on Maryland's lower western shore. Several factors explain this relative equanimity: the blurred lines among classes of bound laborers; the probability of some acquaintance with other liaisons between white women and black men; and the absence of severe and violent white alarm over sex between white women and black men in the late seventeenth century. First, Nell and Charles had married in a society that did not distinguish a great deal between the conditions of servitude and slavery. Although the small number of Africans imported into the Chesapeake in the early seventeenth century may or may not have been slaves on arrival, they could be treated by their English masters in ways that differed little from the treatment of unfree English laborers. Living and working conditions on Maryland's lower western shore varied less between servants and slaves than among different households, and masters did not always perceive a great distinction in the respective situations of servants and slaves.[7] As a male slave, Charles would have worked in the fields cultivating tobacco. Female servants like Nell performed domestic labor, but masters did not keep them out of the fields, and Nell worked in both places. One witness, for example, recalled that Nell was "a hard laboring body and made good crops."[8] Charles's voice, except for calling Nell his "old woman," does not come through at all in the sources, but it is not unlikely that from his point of view, marriage to a white woman made some sense. Among blacks, as among whites, women were in short supply, and whereas white men who had finished their terms of servitude were free to move about in search of brides, enslaved men found no such freedom. Moreover, black women's chances of ill health and death, and their possible unwillingness to bring children into a world of enslavement and hard labor, made marriage to them more difficult.[9]

Second, the liaison between Nell and Charles was not a complete anomaly precisely because the lives of white and black laborers could be so closely intertwined in the colonial Chesapeake. The existence of other liaisons between white women and black men helps to explain the forbearance of white people, while at the same time those liaisons can be understood as a consequence of that forbearance. Other freedom suits on the western shore of Maryland, like the one brought by the descendants of Nell and Charles, attest to other marriages between white women and black men. A man named Basil Shorter, for example, won his freedom by proving that he was the great-grandson of a white woman and a black man, both of whom served the same master; Shorter produced a document stating that in 1681 (the same year in which Nell and Charles married), a priest "did join together in the holy estate of matrimony . . . a negro man named . . . Little Robin, to a white woman, whose name was Elizabeth Shorter." Likewise in another freedom suit, Louis Mingo proved he had been born in 1682, the son of a white woman and a black man; Mingo's parents had been "lawfully married according to the right and ceremonies of the Church of England." And a freedom suit in 1715 proved that a woman named Rose was the baptized daughter of a white woman named Mary Davis, who had been married to a black man named Domingo.[10]

Colonial Chesapeake marriages between white women and black men were also recorded in other kinds of documents. The marriage of a white servant-woman and a black man was noted in an inventory of 1713 that listed "One Irish woman named Grace married to a Negro man" as well as two "mulatto" children "born since their marriage." In a 1720 advertisement for a runaway slave, the owner described a male fugitive as "in company with a white woman named Mary, who't is supposed now goes for his wife."[11] Colonial marriages between white women and black men could also, however, be scrutinized by the courts, especially in the eighteenth century. In 1735, a "mulatto" man named Joseph Guy and a white woman named Bridget were convicted on the eastern shore of Maryland for marrying "contrary to the Act of Assembly." Both were sold to a master, presumably as slave and servant, respectively. And in 1742, the white Elizabeth Pearl was brought to court on the western shore for marrying "a mullatto, Daniel Pearl."[12]

Other freedom suits attest to liaisons between white women and black men without the benefit of marriage. Most such cases entered the historical record as unadorned accounts of evidence proffered and freedom granted. For example, a slave named Jonathan Glover petitioned for liberty when in his twenties, swearing in county court that he had been born in 1680 to a white woman named Sarah Smith who was not married to the petitioner's black father. Fornication and bastardy charges in

the court records of the colonial Chesapeake likewise attest to liaisons between white women and black men without the sanction of law. At least
until the 1660s, illicit liaisons between English and Africans had been
treated not unlike illicit liaisons between two English people.[13] Penalties
were intended to control reproduction among unmarried white women;
pregnancy and childbirth interfered with women's labor, and patriarchs
regulated reproduction whether the fathers were black or white. In most
such cases, the transgressing white woman was sentenced to become a servant; if she was already an indentured servant, her term would be increased
to make up for lost work time during pregnancy and childbirth. In addition, the illegitimate children of white women and black men were sentenced to terms of servitude for the first two to three decades of their lives.
Such a system of indenture protected white communities from having to
provide for the bastard children of free women. Still, punishments were
not uniform, and it is likely that some (or perhaps many) liaisons between
white women and black men went unrecorded, especially those that produced no offspring or involved white women above the servant classes,
whose labor was not coveted by anyone other than their own kinfolk.[14]

Pronouncements of social disapproval were by no means a uniform response to these liaisons, and where such disdain was documented,
the meaning is not always straightforward. In Virginia in 1681, a white
woman named Mary Williamson was convicted of "the filthy sin of fornication with William a negro" and fined five hundred pounds of tobacco.
Was fornication with "a negro" filthy, or was fornication alone worthy
of that description? William, who had also "committed fornication" but
had also "very arrogantly behaved himself," suffered thirty lashes. Were
the lashes administered for fornication alone, for fornication with a white
woman, for disrespectful behavior, or for some combination of those offenses? Other kinds of records occasionally hint at sentiments, such as
Thomas Plummer's petition in the mid-1690s protesting a fine; this white
man admitted that he "had one daughter, who unfortunately having too
much familiarity and commerce with a certain Negro man was supposed
by him to have a child, for which she is truly sorry." Most records, however, are entirely lacking in opinion beyond the fact of legal infraction,
such as the 1692 entry under breaches of law for the Grand Jury of Henrico County, Virginia, which stated only that "Maj. Chamberlyn's woman
servant Bridgett by name for bearing a base child by a Negro"; or a court

summons dating from the 1690s for a married white woman named Mary Oliver for "having committed adultery with a Negro"; or the notation of a sale in the late 1690s describing a master who sold a "Negro man slave," a "white woman," and a "mulatto child," the last of whom would be a servant "until it should arrive at the age of thirty one years." [15]

These chronicles of marriage, fornication, bastardy, servitude, fines, and court-ordered whippings attest to the absence of inevitably harsh legal consequences for black men who consorted with white women in the colonial Chesapeake, as well as the absence of deadly extralegal violence directed at the men alone. In fact, it was not uncommon for the black fathers of white women's illegitimate children to remain unnamed; apparently the authorities did not make a special effort to identify a black man if he was not mentioned or known from the start. Of course there is no way to know for sure what came to pass in a particular community in consequence of an individual liaison, but it is certain that any severe legal consequences would show up in court records, and that if white people continuously engaged in extreme violence, at least glimmers of those actions would appear in the documents. [16]

Indeed, third and finally, these annals of liaisons between white women and black men do not mention rape on any regular basis, either through the voices of the white women or through those of local authorities. Accusations against black men for the rape of white women were not unknown in the seventeenth- and eighteenth-century Chesapeake, and black men were more likely than white men to be convicted and sentenced to death for the rape of a white woman. [17] Yet that important information does not tell the whole story. An incident from tidewater Virginia in 1681, for example, indicates that swifter prosecutions and harsher convictions for black men could coexist with doubt about a black man's guilt. When Katherine Watkins, the white wife of a slaveowner, accused a black man of raping her, some of Katherine's white neighbors returned an accusation of her adulterous behavior with several black men, demonstrating that judgments upon a transgressing white woman, even one outside the servant classes, might override white suspicions about black male sexuality. One white witness recounted that when a black man named Dirke walked by Katherine, "she took up the tail of his shirt, (saying), Dirke thou wilt have a good long thing." Another described the same scene, quoting Katherine's words as "a good prick." Katherine, the first witness said, also flirted with another black man named Jack, claiming that she "put her hand on his codpiece, at which he smiled." Later, this witness continued, Katherine "took Mingo . . . about the neck," flung him on the bed, kissed him, and "put her hand into his codpiece." In addition, more than one white person testified that Katherine had been drinking and that she had confessed her love for "Mulatto Jack." On the other side, someone had seen "Katherine's mouth . . . torn and her lips swelled," along with the bloody handkerchief she said the alleged rapist had stuffed into her mouth; this witness said he had heard the accused confess to asking for Katherine's forgiveness and that Katherine's husband "bid him keep off his plantation or else he would shoot him." Thus did some white neighbors doubt and blame a white woman with a bad reputation, and the woman's own husband let the man off with only a warning. No verdict was recorded in the Watkins case, but other records document consequences far short of either lynching or court-ordered death for black men accused of raping white women. On the eastern shore of Maryland around 1699, a slave named Peter was sentenced to thirty-nine lashes for raping the white Hannah Johnson. The following year on the western shore, when a white widow named Mary Harris accused a slave named Sampson of raping her, both parties were held in the custody of the sheriff in order to ensure their appearances in court. Sampson was then acquitted.[18]

Racial discrimination can certainly be discerned in early American rape cases involving black men and white women, especially as the seventeenth century gave way to the eighteenth. In Virginia in 1701, a slave named Daniel was found guilty of raping a white woman and sentenced to death by hanging. The court ordered Daniel decapitated and his head displayed "to deter Negroes and other slaves from committing the like crimes and offenses."[19] While the phrase "Negroes and other slaves" here attests to the absence of an exclusive connection between black men and rape, various colonial laws did spell out both castration and the death penalty for black men convicted of sex crimes against white women. Whereas white men were seldom or never sentenced to castration for any crime, castration and death were stipulated for black men as the consequences of nonsexual crimes as well, including murder and arson, and some legal documents contain not only the words "Negroes and other slaves" but also specify other nonwhite men, such as "Indians."[20]

Evidence beyond legal codes also illuminates the fact that whites did not live in fear that black men would inevitably rape white women. In 1739, for example, whites claimed to have uncovered a conspiracy among slaves on Maryland's western shore, in which black men were supposedly about to massacre all whites except for the young women, "whom they intended to keep for their wives." When a female slave informed her mistress of the plot, the white woman dismissed the news; the lawyer who recorded the events commented of the mistress, "Foolish Woman! . . . perhaps she had a mind for a black husband." This white woman was not convulsed with fears of rape over this incident, and although the white man may have taken the threat more seriously, he also thought it perfectly possible for a white woman to desire a black man. Furthermore, judgments about the depravity of white women who, like Katherine Watkins, might fraternize with black men can also be discerned. In a defamation case that took place in 1694 in tidewater Virginia, one married couple accused another of slander, asserting that the accused wife had told stories about incest, abortion, and adultery as well as the fact that "Mrs. Hide was such a whore that she would lie with a negro."[21]

All of these factors—the blurred lines of servitude and slavery, the ongoing fact of other liaisons between white women and black men, and the absence of uniform and inevitable violent white anxiety about black male sexuality—help to account for the restraint on the part of the white neighbors of Nell and Charles. Yet at the very same time, although the marriage of Nell and Charles provoked no violence, elite whites were not wholly untroubled by it. Their vexation is apparent in the facts that everyone talked so much about the wedding and that Nell and Charles were condemned in gossip. The words "often heard" were repeated numerous times in the eighteenth-century testimony. Samuel Love said that as a boy he had "often heard" grown-ups "say that a negro man slave . . . was married to Eleanor Butler" and "often heard" that they "went as man and wife." Jean Howard "often heard" that Nell and Charles had slave children. And Benjamin Jameson "heard his mother say that she heard many people say" that Lord Baltimore had cautioned Nell against the marriage. Joseph Jameson recalled a scene in which Mrs. Doyne called on his father when Negro Charles had been there on an errand. Joseph's mother said to Mrs. Doyne, "There was Major Boarman's Charles, the husband of Eleanor Butler who Mrs. Doyne said she and Madam Witham saw married," at which point Mrs. Doyne launched into the story about Nell's encounter with Lord Baltimore. And of course the story of Nell and Charles was passed down for nearly a century. There was reason for all that talk.[22]

The Problem of the Marriage

For the elite white community on Maryland's lower western shore, the problem with the marriage of Nell Butler and Charles was less that Charles was a black man than that he was a slave. The marriage was a problem not so much because it transgressed boundaries of race but because it confused issues of freedom, slavery, and labor. Neighbors were concerned not so much because a white woman and a black man were sexual partners but because the mixture of European and African ancestry blurred the boundaries of freedom and bondage in a society that was beginning to stake its labor system on racial slavery. In the late seventeenth century, when whites were beginning to associate African ancestry and slavery exclusively with one another, sexual liaisons between Europeans and Africans would compromise the equations of blackness and slavery, whiteness and freedom. Such a liaison was, accordingly, more unsettling to the eighteenth-century descendants than to the seventeenth-century observers.[23]

These developments manifested themselves in the question of Nell's legal status as slave or free. Although Lord Baltimore wondered why Nell wanted to "go to bed" with Charles, he did not abuse her with a tirade about mixing European and African blood. Rather, Lord Baltimore chided Nell principally for the fact that by marrying a slave she would be enslaving her posterity and herself. Nell's status as slave or free was in fact the crucial issue when her enslaved grandchildren petitioned for liberty on the basis of descent from a free woman. The problem of Nell's status upon her marriage to Charles, and the ensuing freedom or bondage of their descendants, stemmed from colonial laws about the inheritance of slavery. People were confused because Nell and Charles had married in 1681, the year in which Maryland lawmakers had rewritten the statutes about marriage and the inheritance of slavery. Laws intended to control sex between servants and slaves, between English and African residents, between whites and blacks, were written to strengthen and maintain the developing system of racial slavery in the South. The early laws of Maryland, for example, indicate that slavery and freedom were not necessarily or absolutely correlated respectively with African and English identity: lawmakers used the two closely related phrases "Negroes or other slaves" and "Negroes and other slaves" in their statutes. The distinct categories were slave labor and free labor, and the intention was to keep the members of those two classes, whose lives could be quite similar, separate for the sake of the masters.[24]

Lawmakers in all Southern colonies wrote statutes that discouraged marriage or sex between English and Africans, servants and slaves, whites and blacks, from the late seventeenth century forward. Liaisons between white female servants and black male slaves amounted to enough of a problem that in 1664 the Assembly of Maryland passed a law to make it an undesirable choice for white women: free women who married slaves would be enslaved for the lifetimes of their husbands—meaning that a white person could become a slave—and the children of such liaisons would be enslaved for life. For example, when Mary Peters, who was white, married a slave in about 1680, she became the slave of her husband's master.[25] This was the law to which Lord Baltimore referred when he upbraided Nell on her impending marriage to Charles. When white Marylanders soon discovered, however, that such a law legally encouraged masters to force marriages between servant women and slave men in order to gain more slaves for themselves, the law was changed in 1681. Although their master, William Boarman, did not force Nell and Charles to marry each other, he may well have been perfectly pleased with the arrangement and its economic benefits to him.[26] The new law of 1681 stipulated that if a marriage between a slave man and a "freeborn English or white woman" who was a servant had been coerced or even simply permitted by the woman's master, the woman would be released from servitude and any children would be born into freedom. In fact, Lord Baltimore apparently had the law of 1664 changed specifically for the sake of Nell Butler, whose marriage to Charles was permitted, if not encouraged, by her master. Although this would seem to speak for Nell's ultimate freedom (and therefore for the freedom of her petitioning grandchildren), there was a problem of chronology: the marriage took place in August, and the law passed in September. If Lord Baltimore had pressed the change for Nell's sake, his actions may have come too late.[27]

Lawmakers also wrote statutes stipulating how the condition of slavery was to be inherited. Colonial inheritance laws, in contrast to English laws of patrilineal descent, were laws of *partus sequitur ventrem,* literally "progeny follows the womb": a child's legal status followed the condition of the mother, not the father, as slave or free.[28] Freedom suits from the late seventeenth century forward attest to the power of this law; partus sequitur ventrem meant that the children of an enslaved black woman would be slaves even if the father had been free. Keeping the children born of black women and white men in slavery worked to the advantage of masters in a number of ways. Masters could acquire more slaves through sexual exploitation; slaveholders could keep knowledge of this exploitation to a minimum in their own communities by keeping the offspring within the slave household; and the children, as slaves, could be raised by their mothers. Why colonial lawmakers did not write laws to enslave the children of any slave parent, whether the mother or the father, is open to speculation. Perhaps the most compelling reasons are the question of who would care for the enslaved children of a free white woman; the fact that paternity was too often difficult or impossible to prove; and the fact that such a law might encourage masters to coerce white women into sex with enslaved men in order to produce more slaves. Or perhaps such laws would have left too little distinction between white women and black women if either one could produce enslaved offspring.[29]

As the fundamental labor system of the South changed from white servitude to black slavery, the separation of Europeans and Africans became crucial to whites in order to sustain the institution of racial slavery. Once the law stipulated that a child's status as slave or free followed its mother, liaisons between white women and black men would render the equation of African ancestry and slavery ineffective, because such unions would produce free children of partial African ancestry; hence the enactment of laws that discouraged white women from choosing black partners. These transitions in labor and law help to explain the misgivings over the marriage of Nell and Charles in the late seventeenth century. The children of this union would erode the categories of slavery and freedom based on African and English, or "black" and "white," identity. With their marriage, the protagonists highlighted the potential for this erosion, causing unease at least among elite whites. Then, by their quest for freedom, the grandchildren of partial African ancestry brought the crisis beyond the local community, into the courts and the public record. That such a crisis did not arise when Nell and Charles were alive may be accounted for in part by the fact that their children had been legally enslaved in the late seventeenth century, thereby protecting the white community from having to provide for the offspring of a servant and a slave. Such children would become much more problematic for white Southerners as the nineteenth century unfolded.[30]

The language of late seventeenth- and early eighteenth-century statutes also betrays the anxiety of white lawmakers: it is difficult to disentangle the importance of keeping servants and slaves separate from the importance of keeping Europeans and Africans, and Christians and non-Christians, apart. This anxiety-laden language, moreover, contained distinct references to gender and sexuality. With regard to marriage, for example, the Maryland law of 1664 described "freeborn English women forgetful of their free condition" who, "to the disgrace of our nation, do intermarry with negro slaves." The same law also spoke of sanctions for "deterring such free-born women from such shameful matches." Of course the phrases "freeborn English women" and "negro slaves" make it difficult to pinpoint whether the disgrace stemmed from white women marrying black men, from freeborn women marrying enslaved men, or from a combination of the two. Maryland's law of 1681 referred to "freeborn English or white women" who married "negroes and slaves" as acting "always to the satisfaction of their lascivious and lustful desires, and to the disgrace not only of the English but also of many other Christian nations." A 1692 law included the same words about satisfying lascivious and lustful desires and disgracing English and Christian nations, and a law passed in 1715 referred to such sexual relations as "unnatural and inordinate copulations."[31] Although this language points to judgments upon the white (or freeborn or English or Christian) woman in a liaison with a black (or enslaved or African or non-Christian) man, the intent was largely to make those white women inaccessible to black men. The purpose of this injunction was, in part, to bar black men from the social, economic, and political rights of white men as racial slavery became the entrenched labor system of the South.[32]

Was Nell a Slave?

Nell and Charles had married before the new law about inheriting slavery through the mother took effect in 1681, but their children had been born after its enactment. Yet, in accordance with the earlier law, all

their children had been enslaved from birth. The eighteenth-century witnesses had varying memories as to the names, ages, and living quarters
of the progeny of Nell and Charles, but their collective memory clearly
spelled slavery as the descendants' lot. Thomas Bowling, for example, said
he "always understood the descendants of the said Irish Nell were held in
slavery." John Branson, who had worked for William Boarman, remembered a fellow laborer as "a mulatto man" who was "a son of a white
woman called Irish Nell" but was a slave "occasioned by his mother intermarrying with a slave." In Edward Edelon's version of the visit from Lord
Baltimore, the gentleman had reprimanded Nell with the words: "What
a pity so likely a young girl as you are should fling herself away so as to
marry a Negro," for, he warned her, "you'll make slaves of your children
and their posterity." Thomas Bowling also told the story of a "gentleman,
whether it was Lord Baltimore or any other person," who told Nell that
by marrying Charles she would enslave her children but that if she married
a white man her children "might be of credit in the world." [33]

In order to determine whether the petitioning grandchildren of Nell
and Charles should be freed, the court had to decide whether Nell, their
maternal ancestor, had herself been a slave. If Nell had in fact remained
free despite marrying a slave, then her descendants should be granted their
freedom. But the eighteenth-century witnesses disagreed as to whether
Nell had been enslaved on marrying Charles. Some were sure that she had
remained free. Ann Whitehorn, a woman near the age of one of Nell's
daughters ("They were girls together, and lived within two miles of each
other") and who knew Nell until she died, told the court that she "never
knew or heard that the said Eleanor Butler was in a state of slavery, that
she frequently used to come and see her children, and stay with them for
a month or longer at a time as other free people do." William McPherson said he "never knew of the said Nell being held as a slave." As he
remembered it, Nell acted as "a free woman." Though Nell lived among
slaves and labored in the fields, most remembered that she was not confined to the Boarman plantation. Over the years, when Charles was hired
out or passed on to other members of the Boarman family, Nell often went
with him.

Those who spoke of slavery as Nell's lot talked in abstract terms
only. Benjamin Jameson, for example, recounted that a county magistrate
had remarked that Nell and Charles "were married under a law that made

them slaves." And Samuel Abell had heard that Nell became a slave "by a law of this province whereby white women marrying of slaves should become slaves to the house of their husband's master." A number of witnesses also recalled Lord Baltimore's warning to Nell that by marrying Charles, she would enslave herself and her children. William Simpson remembered his father telling someone that Nell was "a foolish woman" for marrying Charles, because "it would make herself and her children slaves for ever after." Benjamin Jameson remembered Baltimore telling Nell that "if she married Negro Charles she would enslave herself and all her posterity." [34]

In the face of contradictory testimony, the inventory of Major William Boarman's goods and chattels taken after his death in 1709 offers a clue to Nell's legal status. At his death, Boarman owned "1 Elderly Negroe man named Charles." Below Charles were listed "1 old Negro man named Robert" and six named and unnamed "mallatto" slaves, two women, two girls, and two children of unspecified gender; some of these were surely the children of Nell and Charles. The final item on the list was "1 old Irish woman." Inventories were lists of saleable items; if Nell were not a slave, neither was she a free servant-woman. Slaves and indentured servants were listed in inventories; nonindentured servants were not, because they were not part of the master's property. At the very least, then, Nell was an indentured servant as long as Charles was alive. But Boarman's will offers a more definitive clue, one that the eighteenth-century court did not find. Boarman left three slaves to his wife with these words: "I give and bequeath unto my Dear and Loveing Wife Mary Boarman Three Slaves Namely Robt. Charles & Elliner." [35] It is clear from this inventory and will that Eleanor Butler, a white woman, was legally a slave of the Boarman family. The Boarmans no doubt allowed Nell a certain freedom of movement on and off their plantation, perhaps out of deference to Lord Baltimore, who had not wished to see Nell enslaved. But Nell's freedom of movement also suggests the possibility that although whites acknowledged Nell's legal status as a slave, they were unable to treat her fully as a slave as the institution of racial slavery became more entrenched toward the end of the seventeenth century. There is also the possibility that English people thought of Nell less as a white woman than as an Irish woman, with the "Irish" in Nell's name parallel to the "Negro" in Charles's, making it a racial designation rather than a national or ethnic one. [36]

In spite of parallels in the lives of servants and slaves in the colonial

Chesapeake, servitude and slavery were legally distinct categories in ways that would have mattered to Nell Butler. Although lawmakers often wrote statutes that applied to indentured servants and slaves alike (witness such titles as "An Act Concerning Servants and Slaves"), indentured servants were legally persons, with the ability to petition in court, a right denied slaves. Further, at the end of their terms of indenture, these servants assumed all the rights of free English people. When Nell came to the Chesapeake with Lord Baltimore, she was his indentured servant, and had she not married Charles, her term of servitude would have expired four or five years later.[37] Lord Baltimore probably expressed surprise at Nell's desire to marry Charles because had Nell wished to marry a white man she would not have had any trouble finding one: recall the surplus of white men and shortage of white women in the Chesapeake colonies.[38] Furthermore, the white men eligible to Nell could have offered her decent prospects, as the lower western shore of Maryland in the seventeenth century provided fair opportunities for white men who had finished their terms of servitude. If white men traveled overseas in hopes of attaining freeholder status, white women often made the passage in hopes of marrying a man with land. (Promotional literature even promised women marriage to wealthy planters.) True, opportunities declined for those whose terms ended after about 1680, but Nell could still have found a white husband among the as-yet-unmarried men who had arrived earlier or could have married a white man who, though not particularly prosperous, would not have caused her any notoriety either. This was why white neighbors talked. They could not imagine why Nell had chosen to marry Charles.[39]

The witnesses' accounts of the encounter between Nell and Lord Baltimore is one of the few places in which Nell's voice comes through in the testimony, though undoubtedly transformed by the visions of the story-tellers. According to Thomas Bowling, when Lord Baltimore reprimanded Nell, she insisted that the marriage was her choice and that she would rather have Charles than Lord Baltimore himself. In Benjamin Jameson's version, Baltimore "asked her how she would like to go to bed to a Negro," and "she answered him that she would rather go to bed to Charles than His Lordship." Just as evidence militates against a forced match, it also militates against pregnancy as the cause of the marriage: Samuel Love, for example, testified that he had "never heard" of Nell giving birth to any bastard children.[40] The descendants of those neighbors wove a narrative of Nell and Charles that could properly be called a love story. In Samuel Abell's words, "The said woman called Butler fell in love with" Charles "and wanted to marry him." Still, the motivations and emotions of the protagonists remain most elusive in the face of the consequences.[41] Nell Butler and Charles got caught on a rift in time. They were permitted to marry in what seems to have been a lovely wedding with the good wishes of their well-to-do white neighbors. Yet at the same time, gossip circulated, Nell was legally enslaved, and the children and grandchildren of Nell and Charles were enslaved from birth and treated as slaves. Not unlike later liaisons between white women and black men, the one between Nell and Charles provoked anxiety on the part of white people but did not threaten the foundations of their society.

The court at first agreed that because the children of Nell and Charles had been born after 1681, they should have been free and therefore that the petitioning grandchildren should be released from slavery. But their master (a grandson of William Boarman) appealed the decision and won on the grounds that Nell had in fact been a slave. Thus had her progeny inherited the condition of slavery, and thus would her grandchildren remain enslaved.[42] In 1787, however, the General Court of the Western Shore heard a petition for freedom presented by a great-granddaughter of Nell and Charles, and this time the petitioner won. Here the court ruled that in order to prove that Nell had been a slave, it would also have to be proven that she had been enslaved after marrying Charles. Without a record of such a sentence, the court reasoned, Nell could not legally have been held in slavery, and neither could her descendants. Because the county records had been destroyed in a fire, the court accepted hearsay evidence on this question. That evidence—the testimony of the sixteen witnesses in the 1760s—convinced the court that Nell had never been a slave. Not even the verdict of re-enslavement in the previous case swayed the court in the late 1780s. The master of Nell's newly freed great-granddaughter appealed, but freedom was affirmed.[43]

In fact, the two Butler cases together made an impression on other slaves, and many sought to claim descent from Eleanor Butler in an effort to gain their liberty. Shortly after the first case, for example, an artisan slave on the lower western shore by the name of Stephen Butler ran away, claiming his status as a relation of the original plaintiffs. Almost twenty years later, a Virginia slaveowner offered a reward for a runaway named

Jim, who "may pretend to be of the Butler family, who have lately obtained their freedom in the general court." In 1798, a Maryland newspaper notice described a "mulatto" named Ralph, who ran away "under pretence of going to the general court in order to procure his freedom, as one of the descendants of Nell Butler." Another notice said of mother and son run-aways, "It is supposed that they will make for Annapolis, as they pretend to be descendants of the famous Nell Butler." Ironically, then, although white people were apparently unable to envision Nell as a slave, the court decisions helped to free enslaved people of partial African ancestry.[44]

It is difficult to determine the motives that contributed to the verdicts of Maryland courts in the eighteenth century. The 1760s testimony, which played an important role in both cases, had been shaped by the world around those who were asked to narrate the story of Nell and Charles. In 1767, the year witnesses were first asked to recall the fateful marriage, it had been eighty-six years since the wedding, and the eldest witness was eighty-five years old. The recollections ranged from direct to quite indirect. Joseph Jameson, for example, had lived "within a mile" of and "knew Irish Nell very well," whereas Benjamin Jameson's information came from his late mother, who had gotten her information from a number of elderly women, all of whom had since died (his testimony began this way: "He has heard his mother, who is now dead, say that she has heard old Madam Witham, who is also dead, say . . ."). As one historian has noted, people construct memories in response to changing circumstances, and therefore "the important question is not how accurately a recollection fitted some piece of a past reality, but why historical actors constructed their memories in a particular way at a particular time."[45]

The late eighteenth-century white witnesses and judges who pondered the enslavement of Nell Butler were probably not entirely unfamiliar with liaisons between white women and black men either. In 1769, for example, when the white Mary Skinner deserted her white husband to live with a slave who was the father of her child, her husband published a notice in the *Maryland Gazette* proclaiming this fact. Freedom suits also continued to reveal such liaisons. Also in 1769, the enslaved Frances Peck won her freedom by demonstrating to the court that her mother, Mary Peck, was white. And in 1784, the enslaved Ann Gynn won her freedom when she convinced the court that she was "born of a free white married woman."[46] There is also evidence of white dismay at liaisons across the color line in the second half of the eighteenth century, although white women and black men were not necessarily targeted over white men and black women. One white Virginian observed in 1757, for example, that "the country swarms with mulatto bastards," each one of whom was the descendant of a "black father or mother" and who would then go on to marry another white person. Furthermore, a black man convicted of the rape of a white woman in the late eighteenth century could subsequently be treated with a modicum of justice. In 1770, after a slave named Abraham was sentenced to death for theft and rape, his master and both of his alleged victims successfully petitioned the governor for Abraham's pardon on the grounds that his confession had been extracted during a whipping. The rape victim, a white woman named Eleanor Bryan, also explained (perhaps she was coerced by the man's master, perhaps not) that she could "not swear to the identity" of her attacker.[47]

On one side, the Maryland judges may have been concerned about the property rights of slavemasters; on the other, they may have been influenced by revolutionary ideology about freedom. Yet as racial slavery took hold, eighteenth-century whites may well have been less familiar with the blurring of servitude and slavery than their seventeenth-century counterparts had been. Although white neighbors may have thought of Nell more as "Irish Nell" in her own lifetime, it seems that their eighteenth-century descendants thought of Nell more as a white woman. By the second half of the eighteenth century, when the descendants tried to resolve the dilemma of Nell's status as slave or free, they were largely unable to imagine a white person as a slave. That the ideology of the American Revolution ultimately equated freedom with whiteness worked in favor of Nell's descendants. The idea of Nell as a free woman swayed three of the four courts that heard the case in the eighteenth century. The one court that pronounced Nell to have been a slave centered its arguments on property rights.[48] In the story of Nell and Charles, as in the chronicles that follow, the children of a white woman and a black man precipitated a local crisis. In this case it was the offspring of a white woman and a black man (the enslaved grandchildren and great-grandchildren who petitioned for freedom) that forced the liaison into court and therefore into the world beyond one small Southern community. As people of mixed European and African ancestry, the descendants of Nell Butler and Charles defied not only racial categories but also the hardening categories of slavery and freedom; the petitioning descendants were people of partial African ancestry who claimed the right of freedom. As in the nineteenth-century stories to come, once the case was in court, testimony made clear that the liaison had not been a secret. And here, as in the cases that follow, white toleration for sex between a white woman and a black man also served paradoxically to expose imperfections in the system of racial slavery in the evidence of free children (and grandchildren and great-grandchildren) of partial African ancestry, in this case the freed descendants of Irish Nell and Negro Charles.

By the close of the seventeenth century, the transition from servitude to slavery was complete, and slavery rested upon racial foundations. As free people of African ancestry, the children of white women and black men would compromise the institution of racial slavery, and therefore sex between white women and black men posed a threat to Southern whites. And yet in the face of such a threat, local whites could still tolerate now-illicit liaisons between white women and black men. If this toleration resulted from the desire to avoid confronting the fallibilities of both racial slavery and patriarchy, the effect could be—where children were involved —to magnify those very fallibilities. White people did not react violently to the marriage of a white woman and a black man in the seventeenth-century Chesapeake, where such liaisons formed along with settlement. But in the late eighteenth century, in one of the Butler freedom cases, the Maryland court opined: "The assembly considered white women, who so debased themselves as to marry negroes, to be no better than negroes, and indeed they deserve less favor." [49]

Those sentiments lead perfectly into the story of Polly Lane and Jim in antebellum North Carolina, in which white people upheld the value of a slave man over the claims of a white woman who had, they discovered, chosen the black man as her sexual partner. In the antebellum narratives that follow, liaisons between white women and black men proceed without the legal sanction of marriage. But they continue to proceed with a measure of toleration, tempered by harsh judgment and ostracism, though not yet by inevitable white violence.

3 Bastardy *Polly Lane and Jim*

In Harper Lee's novel *To Kill a Mockingbird,* a poor white Southern woman named Mayella Ewell is caught flirting with a black man named Tom Robinson and is beaten by her father. When Mayella subsequently accuses Tom of violent rape, the narrator writes: "Tom was a dead man the minute Mayella Ewell opened her mouth and screamed." That scenario, of sure death for a black man falsely convicted of raping a white woman, is often thought of as timeless to the American South or as an accurate depiction of the white reaction to sex between white women and black men at least through the early twentieth century. In fact, the script of false conviction and sure death emerged and developed from the historical circumstances that characterized post–Civil War America and does not definitively represent the antebellum South.

In North Carolina in 1825, a poor white woman named Polly Lane who had consorted with a black man named Jim also opened her mouth and screamed, but the case of Polly and Jim was far different from the one portrayed in *To Kill a Mockingbird.* In slave-era North Carolina, white neighbors eventually maligned the white woman and rallied around the black man. Multifarious and entangled motives propelled the leaders of this crusade, including property rights, class-based ideas about female sexuality, and the problem of an illegitimate child who was free and yet of partial African ancestry. The matter of Polly Lane and "Slave Jim" entered the historical record as a rape case but soon thereafter began to be understood by authorities and neighbors alike as a case about bastardy.[1]

Conviction and Reconsideration

The account of Polly Lane and Jim came to be told in the autumn of 1825, when Polly, perhaps eighteen years old, accused Jim, a neighborhood slave, of rape. White people raised money to pay for a lawyer to prosecute Jim, because a "very high state of feeling . . . existed against him." Jim pleaded innocent. The twelve white men on the jury heard testimony from twenty witnesses; along with Polly, there appeared a number of the Lane family, as well as one of Jim's fellow slaves.[2] Some witnesses testified to seeing "marks of violence" and "bruises" on Polly's body, and some who had visited the scene of the alleged crime stated that "they saw marks which had the appearance of a person's heels being drawn along the ground." Jim was convicted, sentenced to death, and imprisoned.[3] What had come to pass in the months before the trial, however, and what would come to pass afterward, casts this sequence of events in a different light. If Polly Lane felt relief at the moment Jim's guilt was pronounced, it must have been her last such moment for a long time to come.

The story of Polly Lane and Jim is in part a continuation of the story of Nell Butler and Charles, in that the lives of a servant-woman and a slave man became intertwined in the household of one master. Polly, who usually lived with her parents, had been hired to work for Abraham and Roame Peppinger the previous summer, boarding with the elderly couple and their slaves, one of whom was Jim. Other than the Peppingers, Polly was the only white person in the household.

The Lanes and the Peppingers lived in Davidson County in the central piedmont of North Carolina. Planters there were less wealthy than their counterparts who dwelled on the superior soil of the coastal plain, and most settlers were yeoman farmers. Whites made up over three-quarters of the population, and many families, like the Lanes, owned no slaves. Yeoman families who owned land and could afford the labor to produce cotton or tobacco for sale could move beyond self-sufficiency to engage in the market economy. The Lanes, who had several children and no land, were among the poorest whites in the region: that a daughter of theirs worked as a servant was a mark of borderline poverty. Abraham Peppinger, in contrast, lived on a four-hundred-acre plantation and at his death owned ten slaves.[4]

The social world of white families in places like Davidson County centered on the household and immediate community, with the outer limits as far as a day's travel by horse. Along with election day and the annual militia muster, another important event for the exchange of community information was court week. Neighbors also commonly gathered at crossroad stores, taverns, mills, markets, and churches to exchange news about matters both trivial and grave. In the autumn of 1825, people were talking about Polly Lane and Jim; the two had probably been the subject of local gossip for quite some time.[5]

As the December date of Jim's execution approached, some white residents apparently began to feel unsettled about the verdict. Distrust of state power in antebellum Southern communities was strong, and citizens did not always allow courts the last word. Suspicion was sparked in white minds, when two months after the trial, Polly began to look pregnant. What followed over that winter and spring had white people arguing over both sex and race. Earlier, at the trial, Polly had sworn that as she was walking through the woods one August morning, "Jim overtook her on the road," dragged her into the woods, and forced her to ingest a dram of brandy. All day and until well after nightfall, said Polly, the two had remained in the woods, during which Jim raped her three times. According to Polly, she "did not holler until after it was dark, because he threatened her." Polly also swore that she had never "had carnal connection" with Jim "except by compulsion." When questioned, she "positively denied that she was pregnant."[6]

Dick, another slave in the Peppinger household, had testified at the trial that after nightfall on that same day in August, he had heard someone crying in the woods "as if in distress." Accompanied by a white boy, Dick ran into the woods to investigate, and when he and the white boy stopped to listen, they found themselves eavesdropping on a conversation. Dick saw his fellow slave and the servant-woman in the shadows, and overheard Jim say, "Polly don't cry so, they really will hear you." To this Polly had replied, "If I am left in the fire I am now in, I shall surely die." Dick then had made his presence known, recalling that Polly "appeared exhausted and required his assistance to get to the house." Dick had learned from Polly that Jim "had to do with her three times against her will," but Polly had implored him not to tell the Peppingers "that she and Jim had been out all day together." Polly had also confessed that "she was big"—pregnant—and had offered Dick money if he could "get her something to destroy it."[7] Although the court had called Dick to testify against Jim, Dick also recounted that he had often seen Polly and Jim in bed together in the Peppinger house "when all the white persons were asleep" (including, by his choice of words, the servant-woman with the slaves). Dick also had recently heard Jim tell Polly of his fears that she might be pregnant, to which Polly had replied that she "hoped not." Jim himself, for whatever it was worth in white minds, had confided to his lawyer that Polly had told him "she had missed one or twice of her monthly courses" and that both of them were "of opinion that she was pregnant by him a month or six weeks before the time of the alleged rape."[8]

Throughout the trial, local whites—including the jury—had believed Polly. Yet once Polly's pregnancy became visible, white neighbors became willing to reconsider the courtroom testimony. According to one white man who had watched the trial, the evidence pointed strongly to the fact that "an illicit intercourse existed between the plaintiff and defendant previous to the alleged commission of the rape." To begin with, Jim had admitted to an ongoing relationship with Polly when he explained that "he had kept her as a wife for several months before she accused him of the violence done her." Jim's lawyer had also introduced white witnesses to prove "that Jim and Polly Lane carried on an illicit intercourse with each other" before Polly ever accused Jim of rape. Some people, it now became clear, had even suspected Polly's pregnancy during the trial.[9]

The sexual liaison between Polly and Jim had clearly been a matter of local knowledge, and evidence reveals a measure of passivity on the part of those who were wise to it. One white man, for example, recounted to the court how he had once unintentionally surprised Polly and Jim outdoors when they were "near indecent." It had been a Sunday, and Thomas Briggs had watched the two before he let his presence be known. No further action was spelled out in a fairly detailed account, suggesting that this eavesdropper went on his way without reprisal. Others claimed to have seen the two together in "very suspicious circumstances," and another white man testified that there was "talk well known" to Polly's father that his daughter and Jim "were suspected of carnal intimacy." Polly's father had, this man said, "positively acknowledged it to me himself" and thought it likely that others knew as well.[10]

Up to a certain point, then, local whites had tolerated the liaison between Polly and Jim, at least to a degree. The two did not always succeed at privacy and secrecy, yet no white person expressed sentiments of rage or recounted deeds of revenge. This by no means implies a breezy acceptance; as one of the jurors explained, the court testimony demonstrated that "in that neighborhood, a greater intimacy existed between the blacks and whites than is usual or considered decent." And as a transgressor against societal codes of both gender and race, Polly Lane had likely been made to feel an outcast. Although it is impossible to know what Jim suffered for his transgressions, it is certain that no legal action had been taken before Polly told her story in court. Moreover, no violent acts are disclosed in any of the elaborate accounts of all that came before the trial.

Had vicious retribution against Jim taken place in Davidson County in the early 1820s, hints if not actual descriptions of that behavior would have appeared in documents that record far more mundane details.[11]

Whether other slaves judged Jim harshly is difficult to know; Dick obliquely defended him in the public tribunal, but from elsewhere in his own community, Jim may have suffered from gossip or ostracism. Antebellum Southern blacks, not unlike their white masters, could also subscribe to images of poor white women as depraved. In coastal North Carolina in 1827, for example, a free black woman named Mary Green was sentenced to six months in a dungeon for assaulting a white woman who associated with black men. Mary described the white woman as "of infamous character," and six whites corroborated, signing a petition for a lesser sentence. Mary's white allies called the woman "one of the lowest of this degraded class of white people" and asserted that Mary should not suffer any more than if she had assaulted another black person (thereby suggesting the equation in white minds between black women and depraved white women). Perhaps Jim's family and friends viewed his association with a white woman as doubly worthy of scorn because Polly was so lowly; perhaps they considered Jim the victim of Polly's dissolute advances.[12]

In leery white minds, it now seemed that Polly's pregnancy had precipitated her accusation of rape. Without the charge of rape, there would not have been so much trouble; without the pregnancy, there might have been no trouble at all. The white community members who acted on Jim's behalf claimed to be most offended by Polly's perjury when she insisted she was not pregnant on taking the stand. As one juror noted, "It cannot be supposed that a woman three months gone with child could be insensible of her own situation." Thus, he surmised, might not all of Polly's testimony have been as much a lie as this bit of it?[13] Others agreed, and for several weeks before Jim's scheduled execution, James Martin, the lawyer who had defended Jim, began to gather signatures on a petition to Governor Hutchins Gordon Burton. The petition requested that Jim be pardoned (or at least offered a reprieve until the birth of the child). John Motley Morehead, a distinguished criminal defense lawyer, was also instrumental in getting people to sign the petition and to write to the governor on behalf of the accused slave.[14]

Because the trial testimony has not been preserved, these letters, along with a number of depositions taken the following spring, comprise the body of documents through which the story of Polly, Jim, and their neighbors can be reconstructed. Both caution and speculation are required: the letters, though they relate some of Polly's words and actions, do so largely as recalled by those who condemned her, and reveal very little about the motives or sentiments of either Polly or Jim during the months of community upheaval. Further, although some of the witnesses at the trial were women, only men—most with some degree of standing in the community as slaveowners, county officials, or professionals—wrote letters.

From Polly and Jim's vantage point, of course, the story began not at the courthouse in Lexington but much earlier, in the household of Abraham Peppinger. Clues to this relationship are few and far between, and those that do exist illuminate more about Polly's circumstances than about Jim's. For example, at one point during her pregnancy, Polly mentioned that if the child were "black," it was begotten when Jim raped her, but if it were "white," its father was a man named Palmer. James Palmer was one of Abraham Peppinger's inheritors and an executor of his will; he had a son of the same name who in later years would be brought to court on charges of bastardy. Polly's words point to sex with one of the Palmers, men far above her in station, which in turn implies the possibility of sexual exploitation. Both Polly and Jim were also blamed for another crime involving one of these men. At some point before the rape accusation (the timing remains unclear), Polly and Jim together had been accused of stealing more than two hundred dollars from a Mr. Palmer who was visiting the Peppingers. Polly had been fired, and Jim was to be sold out of the county. Jim hid out in the woods in preparation for running away, and it was in those woods that the rape allegedly took place.[15]

Perhaps, then, Polly's liaison with Jim stemmed from a choice to take refuge in her fellow laborer in order to protect herself from the abusive friends of her elderly master. Jim's motivations are nowhere recorded, though an element of defiance cannot be ruled out. Perhaps the liaison was lonely and miserable for both. Perhaps it was less grim than that, although Polly did ultimately decide that she could stand to see Jim hanged rather than ruin whatever reputation she had left. Perhaps once Polly realized she was pregnant, she chose to pay the price of behaving like a white lady, which meant nothing less than Jim's execution. There is also the very real possibility that in the patriarchal and honor-bound culture of the slave South, Polly was persuaded, or more likely forced, by her family or other white people to press charges against Jim in order to salvage the Lanes' reputation. Perhaps the bruises and "marks of violence" that witnesses saw on Polly's body were inflicted by her father or her master as a consequence of her transgressions.[16]

At the same time, the rape charge raises the possibility that Polly had tried to end her relationship with Jim sometime before that night in the woods, and therefore that her accusation was truthful, though her testimony that she and Jim had never had sex before would not have been true. This seems to be the only scenario in which Polly emerges as anything more than a cruel-hearted young woman, and yet such a scenario is not without layers of its own. Might Polly have tried to break off the relationship once she ascertained that she was pregnant so that she could subsequently accuse Jim of rape? Sex may have been consensual sometimes, but not all the time; sometimes Jim may have forced Polly, and at other times Polly may have wielded her power as a white woman to coerce Jim, as was not unknown in the antebellum South.[17]

The relationship between Polly and Jim is so difficult to understand, not only because it was fraught with the complexities and ambiguities of any liaison between a poor white woman and a slave man in the antebellum South, and not only because their words have been filtered through partisan observers, but also because Polly's voice comes through only when she was forced to speak, while Jim's voice remains almost entirely obscured. Polly's version of events is recounted dozens of times, whereas there are only fragments of Jim's: that he and Polly had had an ongoing relationship at least since the preceding spring, that the two had admitted their fears to each other that she might be pregnant. Jim's voice also comes through in his imploring words asking Polly to keep quiet in the woods that night. Finally, Jim's lawyer would later express his pleasure that the facts "corresponded in a remarkable manner with the story which the negro told us."[18]

Two months after the trial, Jim received a reprieve from the governor until April, in order that "time might solve the doubt." In April, when Jim had been in prison for six months, the reprieve was extended until June. All during this time, white people tried to get Polly to confess. One man wanted her to sign the petition for Jim's pardon, but she refused, just as she refused to answer any questions whatsoever.[19] Jesse Hargrave, the county magistrate and a successful merchant who had helped found Davidson County, wrote up a bastardy warrant in an attempt to get Polly to make a "candid disclosure," thereby shifting the legal category of the crime from rape to illegitimacy and the burden of guilt from the black man to the white woman.[20] But when two men, one of them a county constable, knocked on the Lanes' door to arrest Polly for bastardy, she was missing. The investigators searched for Polly "all over the house" to no avail, and Polly's parents would not reveal their daughter's whereabouts. Polly had "fled from home," either to evade arrest or "for the purposes of delivery." Perhaps her censurers had hoped to elicit her confession about the baby's paternity during childbirth, a common practice in the colonial era. But Polly and her family apparently had allies, for the young woman stayed "at a private house" during some of the uproar, and long enough to give birth—revealing that the petitioners who narrated the story of Polly and Jim to the governor did not represent all of the neighborhood's white residents. Indeed, among those who were said to admit, however reluctantly, the advanced state of the pregnancy were Polly's "friends, and the friends of the negro."[21]

White neighbors were thus by no means unified, and even the designated storytellers could not agree on the facts. One magistrate who had been active in Jim's prosecution refused to sign the bastardy warrant. And although rape within a consensual sexual liaison was all but unimaginable in nineteenth-century law, such rigidity did not always operate in a local setting: the testimony about Polly's bruises convinced some people of Jim's guilt, and Dick's testimony about Polly's distress convinced others. In fact, thirty-nine white residents (six of whom had been present at the trial) signed a different petition to the governor insisting not only that Polly's testimony had been corroborated by that of righteous witnesses but also that Polly's character was "without blemish or reproach"; for some people, apparently, even the most destitute white woman could command respect in the face of alleged rape by a black man.[22]

If Polly was reprehensible to some—one letter-writer noted her "notorious bad character"—Jim was a good match, for Jim was no humble slave. More than one person said that Jim "always thought himself as good as any of the whites." And "many of the citizens of the county" were "anxious for his execution not because they believe his conviction rightful, but on account of general bad character." This argument, however, did not sway all. "Vile as he may be," one man said of Jim, "yet I believe the prosecutrix to have participated in his guilt by permitting his embraces, and that if executed he will suffer for that individual offense which he never committed."[23]

This was not a case of men maligning Polly Lane and women defending her, for opinions did not divide along such lines. Although the dialogue was conducted largely among men, those on record included a Mrs. Gregson, who testified that she had visited the scene of the alleged crime and had observed "no appearance of any scuffling," as well as two women who would declare that Polly's newborn was of "mixed blood," thereby contributing to Jim's vindication. And the thirty-nine petitioners who upheld Polly's good character were all men.[24]

In the months following the trial, then, Polly and Jim were each construed as both innocent and guilty. As time passed, however, the contention of Polly's guilt and Jim's innocence began to win out. At a certain point, of course, Polly was forced to change her story—namely, when those who had lately seen her noted that she was "far advanced in pregnancy and that the period of gestation cannot extend beyond the present month." Although Polly conceded pregnancy, she maintained that "the child was got at the same time the rape was committed." The issue then became whether Polly's child would be born earlier—seven months from the date of the alleged rape—or two months hence; and if the child were born soon, would it be premature? Most felt sure that a full-term child would arrive in late March, disproving Polly's version of events.[25]

Another assumption about female sexuality worked in Jim's favor as well. As Jim's lawyer suggested, "If impregnation follows, it is so far evidence of consent," and as another defender of the slave claimed, the coincidence of "the act of violence and procreation" was a "rare possibility." The idea that female sexual pleasure was necessary for conception went back in medical science to antiquity and was popular during the Renaissance.[26] The no orgasm–no pregnancy concept had begun to lose favor by the beginning of the nineteenth century, but such developments had not yet reached throughout the rural South. Dr. William Holt, a man whose medical training was considered the finest, agreed with Jim's lawyer: "It is the decided opinion of the medical faculty," he wrote, "that pregnancy cannot be produced when a rape is committed." But different people invoked medical science according to their own purposes, for at the same time, the thirty-nine supporters of Polly were convinced instead that conception had indeed taken place when Jim had "committed the crime."[27]

This question of pleasure and conception confused Governor Burton enough so that he sought additional opinions. Four doctors submitted the following half-authoritative, half-uncertain statement:

> It may be necessary to enquire how far her lust was excited, or if she experienced any enjoyment. For without an excitation of lust, or the enjoyment of pleasure in the venereal act, no conception can probably take place. So that if an absolute rape were to be perpetrated, it is not likely she would become pregnant.

The declaration was described as emanating from "the *highest authority* on medical jurisprudence," and the doctors who signed it assured the governor not only that it corresponded with the opinion of other medical men but also that it was "induced by their own observations." Their view won out. The late eighteenth-century reinterpretation of female orgasm was tied up with politics as much as with science, emerging from developing ideas about the moral nature of women. With the older view prevailing in Polly Lane's community, and with the seeming proof by pregnancy that she had enjoyed sex with Jim, Polly's culpability seemed certain.[28]

Although the sexual liaison between Polly Lane and Jim did not by itself unduly threaten the white community, the birth of a "black" child to a white woman would be more problematic. Precisely because no one had stopped Polly and Jim early on, a white woman was about to produce offspring that would make all too apparent some of the flaws in the system of racial slavery. As the offspring of a white woman and a black man, that child's existence would erode the power of patriarchy as well as the racial categories of "black" and "white." As a free child of partial African ancestry, its existence would erode categories of slavery and freedom based upon race. All together, it was the problem of the child that brought the illicit liaison into the public realm beyond the confines of gossip and scandal: first by way of Polly's accusation of rape once she became pregnant, and then by way of the child's status as both free and, as would be determined upon its birth, as "black."

The Crimes and Choices of Unmarried White Women

The liaison between Polly Lane and Jim was not an anomaly in the antebellum South. Polly and Jim had met as laborers in the same household, and other lowly white women also consorted with black men, both slave and free. It is impossible to know how many other cases of fornication between white women and black men never entered the public record, especially those that left no proof by pregnancy and childbirth. Some white Southern communities could evidently live with such transgressions as long as they were not flaunted and did not cause undue upheaval. Owing to a dispute over a sale of cattle in eastern North Carolina, for example, it came to the attention of the county court in 1827 that a free "mulatto" man named John Weaver and an unnamed white woman were cohabiting. The legal issue here was the financial transaction; people discussed the illicit liaison only insofar as it affected the sale. In spite of laws to the contrary, witnesses said it was "generally reported" of the woman that John Weaver "was married to her," and the judge instructed the jury that "they were at liberty from reputation and cohabitation to infer a marriage."[29] Also most likely referring to common-law marriage, the federal census of 1830 for one tidewater Virginia county reveals two households headed by free black men, followed by the phrase "and white wife."[30] In North Carolina in the 1830s, marriage between free people of color and whites was more explicitly prohibited, yet such alliances did not cease.

Most liaisons between white women and black men in the antebellum South came to light during the prosecution of other criminal or civil offenses, but in some cases the protagonists were directly targeted for having crossed the color line.[31] In western North Carolina, for example, a free man of color named Alfred Hooper and a white woman named Elizabeth Suttles were prosecuted almost a decade after they married in 1832. The couple had "lived together and cohabited as man and wife" before the court declared their union void. In 1841, in eastern North Carolina, a "free person of color" named Joel Fore and a white woman named Susan Chesnut, who "bedded and cohabited together as man and wife, and had one child," were each fined two hundred dollars. Even so, prosecutors had not caught up with the couple right away: a county clerk had issued a marriage license the previous year, and the census taker in 1840 had recorded Fore's household as consisting of one white female and one free man of color. In 1843, William Watters argued unsuccessfully before a western North Carolina court that his marriage to the white Zilpha Thompson was legitimate because he was not of African descent. And in 1848 in east Tennessee, when a white woman named Louisa Scott and a "mulatto" man named Jesse Brady were brought to court for living together "as man and wife," the court found Louisa guilty but pronounced Jesse innocent, noting that the law against white-black cohabitation specified only the white person as the "offending party."[32]

Whites might also neglect a liaison between a free black man and a white woman if the couple lived within a black community and therefore outside the bounds of white society. The cohabitation of Griffin Stewart and Penny Anderson in eastern North Carolina came to light in 1849 only when Griffin was convicted of murdering Penny. A neighbor testified that Griffin and Penny "had been living together, though unmarried, as man and wife for many years." Penny had worn a plain gold ring, and the couple had resided on good enough terms with their free black neighbors, attending corn shuckings and borrowing items back and forth. Or a white community might be unable to prohibit a liaison between a white woman and a black man, even a slave, if together the transgressors outwitted white authorities. In 1825, a slave named Delks Moses was causing tremendous consternation among whites on the Virginia coast. Delks was abusive to his master, had run away more than once, carried a gun, and shot at white people. He had also "taken up and cohabited with a base white woman" named Catharine Britt, and there seemed to be little anyone could do about it.[33]

Although elite white families may have been better able to guard their daughters and wives, poor white women were not the sole female transgressors on this terrain. Still, concealment of wayward behavior was less formidable for those whose families held social authority, and accordingly the evidence for liaisons involving more well-to-do white women is slighter. One official who toiled in the same county as Polly and Jim noted that cases of bastardy were brought before the court at almost every session and that the illegitimate children were "by no means exclusively" white. "Mulattoes are not a rare article," this man remembered, "and wives and daughters of slaveholders are oftener the mothers of them, than are poor women." This particular observer's antislavery sentiments may well have prompted exaggeration, but he did offer concrete examples. A Mrs. James Howard, who "bore a mulatto child, sired, as was supposed by her own negro slave Henry," did not escape a hearing before the law, but Catharine Beck had an easier time of it. Catherine gave birth to the child of a family slave, but "before a knowledge of the color of the child extended beyond the bounds of the family, a messenger was dispatched for two justices of the peace" who took the new mother's bedside oath that the child's father was a white man. Clearly it suited the purposes of these planter-class families to smooth over any cracks in the Southern system of patriarchy and racial domination. The fate of the black fathers in these liaisons remains undocumented.[34]

Polly Lane's family did not command the social standing to hush up Polly's liaison with Jim, and neither of the protagonists had been artful enough to keep it a secret, even before the pregnancy. The Lanes had the same aspirations to conceal sexual transgressions as any other white family, though less power to protect their honor. Planter-class women were subject to control by their fathers or husbands; indeed, in many ways, they were the property of these men. In contrast, although Polly's father had known about the liaison with Jim, it was difficult for him to exercise authority over her because she worked in someone else's household. To at least some extent, Polly became the property of her employers. Her parents could not control her, so instead they defended her: they may well have convinced or forced their daughter to charge Jim with rape, and neither one would disclose Polly's whereabouts when she hid from the constables waving the bastardy warrant at their door.[35] Once Polly discovered she was pregnant, however, she had to make—or agree to—a decision. Simply by virtue of being white, the indigent servant-woman commanded a tenuous measure of power, apparent in meager gestures of defiance; for example, Polly would hide her newborn child when neighbors came to investigate. Moreover, she and her family did have a number of choices, no matter how grim. Among those choices was the power to make a grave accusation that for a brief time rescued the young woman from complete wretchedness.

Polly's first thought had been abortion. Recall that she had offered money to Dick if he could "get her something to destroy" the pregnancy. Rumors circulated on this point as well: "I have heard it repeatedly said," claimed Dr. William Holt, "that she has used various means for effecting abortion" (Polly had apparently jumped from heights and tried to make herself bleed). Polly was not the only white woman in the antebellum South to contemplate abortion before leveling an accusation of rape. Nancy Wallis, from the North Carolina piedmont, pleaded with a local doctor to help end her pregnancy in 1838. Nancy explained that the man "had done it 'partly against her consent.'" Holding to the idea that rape could not result in pregnancy, the doctor told Nancy that such "could not be the case or she would not be in her present condition." When Nancy later gave birth to a "black" child, she accused an elderly slave of rape.[36]

Alternatively, if Polly had had relatives or friends elsewhere, she could have tried to conceal the pregnancy and send the baby away at birth. Or Polly could have tried to conceal the birth as well as the pregnancy, and then murdered the newborn infant. There had even been speculation to this effect: as one of Jim's lawyers wrote to the governor, "Nor should I be surprised if the birth was concealed." This was rumored to have been the case in western North Carolina in 1832, when the white Lucretia Scroggins gave birth to a child whose father was clearly black; the child, it was recounted, was "removed to Tennessee, and is either dead or continues there." Perhaps Polly hoped that Jim would offer to help her in such a mission. In 1821 in piedmont North Carolina, a coroner's jury convicted the white Betsey Crabtree and the black Harry Wall of murdering their infant "by drowning, smothering, or some other improper means." Or Polly might have thought to escape all together; in Tennessee also in 1821, a white woman had disappeared from a roadside inn during the night, leaving her illegitimate "mulatto" infant son behind.[37]

Concealing pregnancy and birth was accomplished more easily by women who were not required to show up at work outside their own households, or who had relatives elsewhere with the resources to pay for travel and then to support a child, or perhaps whose own fathers could sell the child away as a chattel, or at least send it up North. The fugitive slave Harriet Jacobs, in recounting the story of a North Carolina planter's daughter who sustained a sexual liaison with a slave man, noted: "In such cases the infant is smothered, or sent where it is never seen by any who know its history."[38]

Had Polly succeeded in abortion, concealment, or infanticide, she might have had to contend only with local tattling about her illicit behavior. In 1818, a white farmer nailed a notice to a tree in the North Carolina piedmont declaring that he had come upon a white woman named Betsey Holt "busily engaged" with a black man. Enduring rumors were also the fate of a Mrs. Horton, another white woman from the North Carolina piedmont. Also in 1818, a white neighbor claimed that Mrs. Horton, "while single, had sexual intercourse with a negro," insisting that "there was a report in the neighborhood" that she "had had connection with a man of the wrong color." A married white woman in western Kentucky also lived among such gossip: "There was an old report in circulation in the neighborhood" that a grown "mulatto" woman was Mrs. Middleton's daughter from an earlier liaison with a black man. One white resident claimed in 1820 that "he had heard it from Mrs. Stuart, and other respectable persons and old settlers." Similarly, in Georgia's cotton belt in 1858, the white Martha Kelly was confronted with the information that she "had a negro child" and that black men had "been with" her. (In the subsequent slander suit, one county judge opined that "to call a woman a whore in Georgia is actionable where the charge has reference to white men" because it would amount to adultery but that this did not apply to white women who consorted with black men.) And in 1859, rumors circulated as to the paramours of an unmarried white woman named Candace Lucas, also in the North Carolina piedmont. One person named the slave "Wesley-Dean's Pete" as Candace's "new sweet-heart," at the same time naming two other neighborhood slaves as previous lovers; local whites also believed that Candace had "two or three black children." Each of these incidents went on record as part of a slander suit, indicating that although the transgressors were the targets of local disdain, they were not the targets of legal action. Rather, it was the gossip-mongering white neighbors who had to answer to the courts. Moreover, had those gossipers resorted to any sort of violent retaliatory actions, at least a breath of that information would have shown up in the detailed narratives recounted in court.[39]

Had Polly Lane had a white sweetheart, she might have prevailed upon him to get married before her pregnancy became visible. Then she would have hoped no one could tell that the child was not his. Indeed, when Polly was brought before the court on the bastardy warrant six weeks after she gave birth, she still denied that Jim was the father.[40] The ruse might have worked, but then again it might not have. Four months after Elizabeth Morris married Dabney Pettus in the Virginia piedmont in 1801, she gave birth to a "mulatto" baby. When Elizabeth confessed that "it was begotten by a negro man slave in the neighborhood," her husband divorced her. Similarly, Benjamin Butt was granted a divorce in tidewater Virginia in 1803 when Lydia Butt confessed that the baby she conceived just before her marriage "was the child of a Negro man slave named Robin." (Lydia maintained that the illicit liaison came to pass when Robin performed magic intended to compel Benjamin to marry her.) Likewise, when Peggy Jones from Virginia's eastern shore delivered a child nine months after her marriage in 1812, she was forced to "acknowledge that the father" was "a negro." With that information "notorious in the neighborhood," the Joneses were divorced. Abraham Newton also filed for a Virginia divorce when his wife delivered a "mulatto" child five months after they married in 1815 and "acknowledged that a Negro fellow in the neighborhood was the father." Nancy Newton and her mother left the Virginia piedmont for Ohio, and Abraham was granted a divorce.[41] Two North Carolina cases from the 1830s echo these circumstances. When Lucretia Scroggins gave birth to a "mulatto" baby five months after her marriage and sent the child off to Tennessee, her husband asked for a divorce. And in eastern North Carolina, Jesse Barden thought his fiancée was pregnant with his child before their wedding day, but "soon after the marriage he discovered that the child was a mulatto" and divorced his wife.[42]

Travelers to the slave South also commented on liaisons between unmarried white women and black men. As one visitor to the Georgia piedmont recounted: "A young girl of the neighbourhood had been recently married . . . and the rumour had gone abroad that the first offspring of this young mother, produced after seven months' gestation, was 'a mule!' . . . a 'coloured child.'" A traveler in southwestern Virginia recorded a conversation about the white daughters of one family as follows: "This countryman said—nay, I saw one of them myself, with a black child—'that there were several instances of their having children by black men.'" Later in the century, a white writer recalled of antebellum North Carolina (no doubt overestimating) that "hardly a neighborhood was free from low white women who married or cohabited with free negroes."[43]

Barring abortion, concealment, infanticide, running away, or marriage to a white man, Polly Lane could have owned up to her deeds. Perhaps she wished to do so but was prevented from such bold actions by her parents. Had Jim been free, Polly might have been able to prevail upon him to support the child, as did the white Lydia Roberts in piedmont North Carolina in 1850, where the court ordered that free black men were "bound to support their bastard children, whether begotten upon a free white woman or a free black woman." Had Polly protected Jim by forfeiting rape charges, she could have been immediately subject to bastardy fines. Of course, Polly's family was too poor to pay, and if the Peppingers had not paid for her, someone might have gone to jail.[44] But Polly did not confess or own up to anything, and her baby girl, named Candas, was born on April 7 "of full size and health," within a few days of the date Jim had predicted and almost six weeks too early for the conception to have taken place at the alleged mid-August rape. White neighbors then seized on the color of Polly's baby as a means to determine that Jim had been Polly's lover, hoping to use this evidence, to prove not Jim's guilt in the crime of sex with a white woman but instead to prove his innocence. It was Polly's guilt they hoped to prove.[45]

The uncertainty that next ensued on the question of Candas Lane's ancestry illuminates the potential instability of racial categories in the antebellum South. At this point, Jim's lawyer urged "those who had taken an interest in the negro's fate" to view the child and write up statements about her color. White neighbors and county residents dutifully trooped to the Lane household, but Polly was as stubborn as ever. One day, a month after Candas was born, Polly was standing in her doorway when she saw two men approaching. She hurried inside, got into bed, and covered up the infant beside her. "We told her we came to see the child, as it had been reported to have been a colored child," the uninvited guests recounted. But Polly, they admitted, "positively refused to let us see it." Four more neighbors were subject to the same treatment, reporting that when they made their housecalls, Polly "covered the child up." Several intruders somehow got their way, but when they managed to see the baby they disagreed over her ancestry. As one man put it, "Some think the child is black, and a number think it is white." Another noted that "there was a diversity of opinions as to its color." Still another proclaimed in consternation that "it appears to me as other white children, but I don't say it is not a colored child, but if it is, it must alter from what it is now." Two women and a man who had glimpsed Candas's face and head pronounced her to be of "mixed blood." A woman who was able to examine the baby's "neck, legs, arms, and body" made the same proclamation. And a man who had "inspected it very closely" had no doubt that the child was "colored," but he admitted that "a superficial observer might possibly on slight examination doubt it." This observer, who poked and pulled at the baby girl, offered the following statement: "My reason for deciding it to be a colored child is from the deep yellow color of the fingers near the roots of the nails, and the darker color of the upper lip near the nose, the very black cast of its eyes and hair, and the retraction of the hair when stretched, and the figure of the nose, and from the unusually large size and clamminess of the feet." Eventually, a consensus emerged. William Holt and Jesse Hargrave, doctor and magistrate respectively, stated of Candas Lane that, according to most observers, if her mother was a white woman, then her father must be a black man.[46]

Candas Lane, her lineage declared, was a source of anxiety to the white community. The baby was free, of course, following the status of her mother, and this was precisely why sex between white women and black men was problematic in the slave South. A child such as Candas Lane not only defied categories of "black" and "white," but as a free person of partial African ancestry, she also defied the equation between African ancestry and slavery. Here is where local authorities could intervene to try to repair the social structure. In the Davidson County census of 1840, the census taker recorded one free person of color between the ages of ten and twenty-four in the Lane household, no doubt Polly and Jim's daughter. As a child, then, Candas lived in the Lane household. But ten years later, Candas Lane was listed in the county census with the unusual designation "m" (for "mulatto") in the column denoting color (almost all county residents were either "w" or "b"), living in the household of a white farmer named Daniel Wilkerson with his wife and young daughter.[47] Another North Carolina case offers a clue here. In 1855, a coastal county court ordered two "colored base born children" of a white woman named Nancy Midgett bound out as apprentices to a white man. The man had proven that Nancy was the mother of five bastard children, some of whom "were by a negro father." Although Nancy contended that she "lived respectably and worked," she lost by the invocation of a statute that all "free base-born children of color are liable to be bound out as apprentices." This was also the fate of Candas Lane, perhaps by economic necessity as much as by legal coercion, and it points to the indenture system as one way to police the lives of free people of African ancestry, including the free children of white women and black men.[48]

With the birth and inspection of the baby, the guilt of Polly Lane, the white woman, had been proven to the satisfaction of white neighbors. Jim would not be put to death for rape, and Polly was culpable of fornication, bastardy, and perjury. Governor Burton issued a pardon for Jim in May 1826, a little more than seven months from the day Jim had been jailed. This must have been Jim's moment of relief.[49]

The Pardoning of Black Men

Although Polly Lane commanded a small degree of power, Jim was the one who truly lacked choices. Jim was the one who spent months in the county jail, probably chained to a filthy, cold floor, thinking about mounting the gallows. Whether Polly chose to accuse Jim of rape of her own accord or under pressure, the charges indicate that an accusation of rape directed toward a black man carried the potential to clear the reputation of a pregnant, unmarried white woman in the antebellum South.[50] It is crucial to remember that when Polly had first implicated Jim, the case had proceeded in her favor; recall that money had been raised to prosecute Jim owing to the "very high state of feeling" against him. One white man had noted of Jim: "Public opinion and popular prejudice were at the time of his conviction very much excited against him, and I must confess myself that my prejudices were roused in a very high degree against him." Jim had been sentenced under a state law of 1823 stipulating that black men convicted of raping white women were subject to capital punishment, a harsher penalty than was meted out to white men for the same crime.[51] Indeed, if antebellum white Southerners could display a measure of toleration for sexual liaisons between at least certain white women and black men, that stance existed alongside currents of white anxiety over the rape of white women by black men. Property rights and the value of slave labor, an alleged victim's moral reputation, and white fears about black male sexuality—all of these could create community tension when a white woman claimed rape by a black man.

Black men convicted of raping white women in the antebellum South could legally be treated with brutality. In 1801, for example, when a slave was sentenced to death in western North Carolina, the court ordered the man decapitated and his head displayed to deter "evil doers and all persons in like cases offending."[52] When neighbors judged a white woman's character to be above reproach, that factor could help determine a black man's guilt. In coastal North Carolina in 1838, for example, a white observer described the rape trial of a black man, calling the white woman "respectable," the alleged crime "revolting to human society," and the defendant a "monster in the shape of a black negro" and a "vile devil." The convicted man was hanged.[53] Neither would maligning the white woman's character necessarily preclude a guilty verdict for a black man accused of rape. When the white Amy Baker accused a slave named Lewis in southside Virginia in 1829, Amy used uncommonly graphic language, recounting that Lewis had "said he would stick his dick in her if she attempted to escape" and that "he came for *cunt*, and *cunt* he would have." But one white man testified that he himself had "been to the house of Mrs. Baker for the purpose of unlawful intercourse with females" and had "known others to do so," and another had likewise "seen four negro men" at Amy's house "at one time, and three negro men there at another time." In spite of this damaging information, Lewis was executed.[54] Finally, although the castration of a black man convicted of sexually assaulting a white woman in the South had largely been superseded by the death penalty by the early nineteenth century, court-ordered mutilation was not unknown. In piedmont Georgia in 1827, for example, a black man found guilty of raping a white woman was sentenced to castration, although a local newspaper afterward condemned the action.[55]

For black men in the antebellum South, the law did not always prevail when a white woman made an accusation of rape. In the Maryland piedmont in 1823, a black man declared innocent in court was left to dissatisfied whites and "beaten so severely, as almost to deprive him of life." A traveler to the South in the early nineteenth century was told of a coastal North Carolina planter who offered a doctor one hundred dollars to castrate a slave he considered dangerous to white neighborhood women. The doctor refused payment for the mutilation, and the castrated man was informed that "he had received the punishment due for his abuse and insults to white women." Whites might also threaten to lynch a black man acquitted of raping a white woman, and this course of action became increasingly common (though by no means inevitable) by the 1850s as white Southerners confronted ever-increasing sectional conflict over slavery. During a rape trial in tidewater Virginia in 1856, white people displayed "a general determination" to hang an accused black man "notwithstanding his supposed acquittal." The man was convicted after all. Likewise, a North Carolina newspaper noted in 1859 that an accused black man in the piedmont "would have been shot before he left the prisoner's box" had he been acquitted. In some instances, lynching was carried out. The same Southern traveler also heard about a North Carolina slave who allegedly broke into a white family's house and raped the daughter; local whites went after the man, "tied him to a tree, collected wood around him, and immediately consumed his body to ashes." And in Georgia's plantation belt in 1861, as a slave named George awaited trial on charges of raping a white woman, white neighbors who "could not content themselves with the law's delay" broke into the jail and burned the man to death.[56]

At the same time, however, other scenarios were possible. Once a black man was convicted in county court for the rape or attempted rape of a white woman, for example, his case could be appealed, and the state supreme court could reach a different verdict. Defendants might be acquitted, released, or awarded a new trial for a variety of reasons, including insufficient evidence, lack of force in an assault, or improper legal language in court papers. In one case, a free black man was acquitted because the Supreme Court of Virginia contended that while the man had indeed climbed into the woman's bed and awakened her by pulling up her clothes, no actual force had been used, thereby eluding the legal definition of rape.[57] Or a black man could be convicted and then, like Jim, pardoned. A pardon, of course, was an act of amnesty that confirmed the man's guilt, and pardoned slaves were usually sold out of the county. In the case of Polly and Jim, perhaps their incensed white neighbors could hold in their minds two contradictory facts: Jim was in some measure guilty, but Polly was entirely at fault.[58] Much of the concern for Jim's pardon stemmed from the economic interests of his master and the related interests of the master's friends. Lawyers like the ones who defended Jim were hired not so much to protect the rights of a slave but to protect the rights of the slave's owner. A conviction followed by a pardon therefore advanced two purposes: the conviction controlled slaves' behavior, while the pardon served the retention of property in slaves. As one man explained to the governor, "Mr. Peppinger had given the negro to" the lawyers "provided they got the negro pardoned."[59]

Indeed, the problem of slaves in the criminal justice system of the antebellum South turned on their dual identity as property and human; the law had to take into account both market relations and master-slave relations.[60] Masters and mistresses made clear their economic interests in no uncertain terms when their male slaves were accused or convicted of rape. In the Virginia piedmont in 1803, for example, a master's wife became extremely "irritated" when the timing of rape charges interfered with crop production. When Jack was apprehended, the mistress "made use of illib-

eral language towards those who had taken up the fellow" and expressed
hope that legal proceedings could be "suspended a few days longer until
harvest was over." Proving the power of wealth, she assured the other
slaves ("never mind boys, said she") that their master had "money enough"
to protect them all. In an 1831 petition on behalf of a North Carolina
piedmont slave named Sam, a white man pleaded that the mistress was in
financial straits and "would very severely feel the loss of the slave." Similarly, on Virginia's eastern shore in 1859, sixty-five white petitioners asked
that a convicted slave's life be spared "in consideration of the poverty
and large family of the owner," for "the loss of the slave will be severely
felt by him." [61] If the treatment of accused slaves adhered to the letter of
the law, then, it was at least partly because slaves were the property of
white people. That fact also accounts in part for the rarity of the lynching
of black men in the antebellum South.[62] In fact, in the lynching of the slave
George in 1861, the master brought suit against the lynchers.[63] Even as
slavemasters defended their interests in human chattel, they did not hesitate to inflict violence upon those valuable slaves. In 1832 a black man in
southside Virginia received 150 lashes at the hands of a white man whose
daughter the man had allegedly raped. Another slave "received 120 lashes
from his master for an attempt on a girl" in southwestern Virginia in 1829.
Slaveowners might also try to allay the legal loss of a slave (through execution or transportation) by offering to appease the white woman who had
made a rape accusation. In the Virginia tidewater in 1856, for example, a
slavemaster proposed to pay the woman ten dollars, along with having the
man "whipped to her satisfaction." [64]

To complicate the issue further, some of Jim's white neighbors quite
skillfully presented themselves as motivated by sympathy and justice (recall the man who wrote of Jim that "if executed he will suffer for that
individual offense which he never committed"). Other evidence, however,
reveals that some of those who invoked humanity and justice were writing
in direct response to accusations of economic self-interest. Of Jim's lawyers, one man noted: "I cannot believe that these gentlemen would make
an effort to save his life did they think him guilty." Dr. William Holt felt
it "an act of justice to make the following statement respecting the guilt
of said slave" and then invoked "the truth of the facts" as crucial to Jim's
pardon. The lawyer John Morehead also wrote to disabuse the governor
of the notion that he and James Martin were "interested in the value of the

negro," adding, "But I *do assure* your Excellency that that interest would not weigh with me a feather"—the word "not" was first omitted, then inserted—"did I believe him a fit victim to the offended laws of the county." The lawyer expounded upon his certainty of Jim's innocence even before he had become the defense counsel, claiming that he "thought the rights of humanity required some effort to be made to respite his punishment." Another white man felt compelled to petition for the pardon in light of available information, "fearing that the life of a poor ignorant slave without any power to defend himself even if innocent . . . should suffer death at the expense of humanity, by a false prosecution." [65]

It is not clear who exactly had brought charges of insincerity against these doctors, lawyers, and their associates, but at least one man who was approached to sign the petition contended that Jim had always been "protected by some trifling white people" and that because Abraham Peppinger had no children, he had instead "several friends for his property, which is considerable." [66] Indeed, a number of those who pressed for Jim's pardon hailed from the county's wealthiest sector and enjoyed social ties with one another. John Morehead was a college chum of William Holt, the Hargraves were among the county's largest slaveholders, the Holts and Hargraves were neighboring farmers in the 1820s, and Jesse Hargrave named John Morehead the guardian of his two youngest sons.[67] Jim's master and his allies may also have appealed to white neighbors of lesser means to write on behalf of his slave, for others who petitioned for Jim were not slaveowners. Whether these people acted of their own accord or under the persuasion or coercion of those whose land and slaves endowed them with local authority is difficult to say.[68] Still, alignments were not entirely predictable by class standing. Reuben Holmes, a large slaveowner and near neighbor to Abraham Peppinger (he had purchased land from him), was among the few to sign a statement calling Jim "a very troublesome and bad Negro." Two others of lesser means joined that wealthy man to malign Jim's character.[69]

As in the case of Polly Lane and Jim, requests for mercy on behalf of slaves convicted of rape could be accomplished in part by invoking the white woman's bad reputation, thereby demonstrating that a poor and transgressing white woman could be worth less to elite whites than the profitable labor of a slave. In the 1800 pardon of two slaves convicted of raping a white widow in tidewater Virginia, the woman's testimony was contradictory, and white neighbors claimed that by the "common and general talk and opinion of the neighborhood," she was considered to be infamous, vile, bad, abandoned, loose, and "in habits of intimate intercourse with Negroes." In 1803, also in tidewater Virginia, a slave named Carter was pardoned for the rape of the white Catherine Brinal after citizens declared Catherine "a woman of the worst fame," proven by her "three mulatto children, which by her own confession were begotten by different Negro men." Catherine, moreover, had permitted Carter "to have peaceable sexual intercourse with her, before the time of his forcing her." In southside Virginia in 1807, when a slave named Jerry who was convicted of raping the white Sarah Sands continued to assert his innocence, one citizen requested a pardon because, he wrote, "The woman, I learn from a variety of sources, is under a very infamous character." This man maintained that Sarah had "lived as a concubine" with a white man "in whose house this negro I am informed was as intimate as any white person." Jerry was granted a reprieve. The next year in tidewater Virginia, a slave was convicted of attempting to rape a white woman and sentenced to castration; those who petitioned the governor for a pardon maintained that the woman was "a common strumpet" and "a common prostitute" who admitted to being the mother of several illegitimate children. Eighty-three county freeholders signed the petition. When a slave named Gabriel was brought to trial for rape in southwestern Virginia in 1829, the character of the alleged victim, eleven-year-old Rosanna Green, was maligned by her adoptive parents, her schoolteacher, her white neighbors, and Gabriel's fellow slaves. (One slave woman had heard that "Rosanna had behaved badly with a black boy in the neighborhood." And a white neighbor had heard that Rosanna had "had intercourse with a negro boy in the neighborhood.") Gabriel, too, was pardoned. When in 1856 a white woman accused a slave of attempting to rape her in eastern North Carolina, a white man testified that "the general character of Elizabeth Sikes was bad for want of chastity, drinking, for illicit intercourse with negroes, and for truth." The man's death sentence was reversed on appeal.[70]

Yet such matters were often more complex than simply defaming a white woman in order to pardon a black man, for as in the case of Polly Lane and Jim, white neighbors were not always in accord. In 1825 in the North Carolina piedmont, a slave named Warrick was convicted of raping a white woman named Mary Dunn. The ten white men who drew up the petition for pardon feared "that the jury were excited by that honest indignation with which our white population views the slightest impertinence of a slave to them or any approach towards a connection with a white woman even by her consent." Strong words, and yet Mary's sexual reputation held greater sway than that indignation. White neighbors had testified at the trial that they had seen Mary alone with Warrick, that Mary and Warrick were "too thick," and (expressing intertwined sentiments about the sexuality of both white women and black men) that they knew Mary "would get debauched by a negro" if she did not change her ways. Mary's door had not been broken down, witnesses claimed, and the nature of the lock was such that only someone from the inside could have unlatched it. Mary denied intimacy with Warrick but eventually expressed regret at her decision to prosecute, for she "believed that her character would be ruined in consequence of it." She also wished "for Warrick to get away and not be hanged," and indeed, Warrick was pardoned.[71]

Community tensions could be even more acute, with dissenting whites expressing anger and anxiety on the subject of black men, white women, and rape, in the face of a request for pardon. In the North Carolina piedmont case of 1831 in which the slave, Sam, had been sentenced to death for raping a white woman, "the public mind" was "considerably excited" during the trial, likely due to the Virginia rebellion of slaves led by Nat Turner over the summer. Although some whites believed "the woman prevaricated," one man noted that "prudential mothers have withheld their signatures" from the pardon petition and that a counter-petition was circulating. In the Virginia piedmont in 1831, after a slave named Dick was convicted of raping a married white woman named Pleasant Cole, white people also divided on the slave man's fate. While Dick's lawyer and another prominent white man requested a commuted sentence (the lawyer noted "indiscretion" on the part of the woman), three men who claimed to speak for "a *large* majority of the people" dissented, explaining to the governor that "it was a most aggrieved and outrageous case" and that Dick's brother had previously been pardoned on charges of barn-burning. Were Dick now to be pardoned, they maintained, "there is no telling where crime is to end among that class of our population." Such language implied fear for white women, though in the context of more general fears about slave crime. Those who opposed the pardon also took care to uphold the reputation of Pleasant Cole despite her indigence, describing her as one who "tho' in the humble vale of poverty sustained an unblemished character." This fact was also marshaled to make a point about the safety of poor white women, singling out "females in the humble walks of life, who have not thrown around them the protection of wealth and of influential friends." [72]

Loyalties were also divided in the 1838 North Carolina case in which Nancy Wallis asked a doctor for an abortion and subsequently accused an elderly slave of rape. Nancy maintained that Juba had dragged her from the road and assaulted her for over an hour while she screamed "the whole time." After Juba was convicted, petitioning citizens pointed out that no one had heard the screams and that no "marks of violence" were found on Nancy's body. Juba's supporters further pointed out that Nancy had told no one of the assault until she had given birth to "a black child" nine months later, and besides, Juba could not even walk without a cane. Invoking "humanity" and "justice," these citizens wrote of "an odious *illicit* intercourse this unfortunate base woman has had with another negro." On the other side, however, Nancy's supporters countered that Juba had previously assaulted white women and had threatened to kill Nancy (a woman of good character, they said) with his iron-pointed walking stick. According to the white woman's defenders, Juba's master was poised to sell the slave for $250 to a man active in the pardon request. [73]

Some whites who dissented from slave pardons could barely disguise resentment of their wealthier neighbors. After the conviction of a slave for the attempted rape of a white woman in 1859, sixty-eight Davidson County citizens requested a pardon based on the young man's age, while one angry citizen thought it wrong that "our wives and our daughters are to be insulted and injured by every Buck Negro upon the high ways," just because of "a few *speculators who care* more for a few *hundred dollars* than they do for the safety of the females of their county." The governor declined to issue the pardon. [74]

Requests for a slave's pardon cannot be reduced simply to the value of personal property, for the reputations of white women could also come into play where an accused black man was free. In Richmond, Virginia, in 1854, when a free black man was charged with the attempted rape of a white woman, one newspaper opined: "If the charge be true, the black imp deserves to be hung, without judge or jury," but added that because the woman associated with "the lowest and most debased free negroes in the valley," it would "be a difficult job to induce them to believe a single sentence uttered by her," adding, "The white woman may have told the truth, but very few who know her believe it."[75]

Community tensions could also surface in cases involving free black men. In tidewater Virginia in 1834, for example, a black laborer named Caleb Watts was convicted of raping a poor, eleven-year-old white girl named Jane Barber. In hopes of securing a commuted sentence, one of Caleb's lawyers informed the governor that Jane and her mother were both "of the lowest order of society." Another lawyer noted that Jane had been "raised with an aunt who has given birth to several bastard children." The petition, bearing nearly a hundred signatures, described Caleb Watts as honest, humble, industrious, and upright, perhaps indicating the value of a free black man's low-wage labor. Yet Caleb's supporters battled strong neighborhood opposition: one of the lawyers described "prejudice against the defendant," "eagerness for his condemnation," and "a strong popular prejudice and excitement against the prisoner." In the end, Caleb was denied a pardon.[76]

Prosecuting and convicting a black man for the sexual assault of a white woman, then, was a process that involved various factors, including racial control and economic interests, patriarchy and class control, and concerns for at least the image of Southern justice. White anxiety about black male sexuality was neither uniform nor inevitable and could well be tempered by both economics and ideology. White Southerners viewed black women as licentious and promiscuous, in part in order to deny sexual exploitation by male slaveholders. White women were also supposedly endowed with dangerously strong sexual desires; because they were white, however, their desires required control, if not by a woman's own accord, then by her father, husband, or community. Elite white Southerners considered poor white women especially prone to sexual depravity and dishonor.[77] Polly Lane's father had been forced by poverty to relinquish his authority when his daughter went to labor in someone else's household. Although Abraham Peppinger might have filled that gap as Polly's employer, he did not succeed in policing his servant-woman's sexual activity. White people considered Polly Lane degraded because she consorted with someone beneath her own lowly station, a black man and a slave. But it also mattered that Polly's family was indigent and that the child she had out of wedlock disproved her courtroom testimony. That Polly Lane might have been telling the truth when she accused Jim of rape only reinforces the fact that many whites believed poorer and supposedly depraved white women unable to be raped by any man, black or white. This in turn reinforces the fact that white ideas about the dangers of black male sexuality did not inevitably overwhelm all other factors in a rape case. White Southerners did express suspicion and a measure of fear about black men and rape. Yet at the same time, neither death sentences nor lynchings were anywhere near inevitable in the event of a black man accused of raping a white woman in the antebellum South, most especially if the woman's family were poor, landless, non-slaveholding people.

Polly Lane's cries that summer night in the woods had been, according to one of the petitioners, a "lamentation concerning her deplorable condition." In this scenario, the accusation against Jim was "brought forward to screen the unhappy girl from the reproach of being found alone with him in private, lamenting her sad fate of pregnancy and disgrace with Jim."[78] Perhaps Polly and Jim had fought with each other in the woods. Or perhaps Polly was trying to create a disturbance loud enough that her subsequent accusation of rape would be believed. Or maybe Polly had heard Dick in the woods and feared being caught by a white person, and only then had cried out. In any case, Polly and Jim had had sex some months before Polly's accusation of rape, a liaison that defied Southern rules of race and gender.

The liaison between Polly and Jim did not by itself threaten white neighbors. It was the free child of partial African ancestry that threw the case into the spotlight and caused so much trouble. A liaison between a white woman and a black man made apparent that whites and blacks, the free and the unfree, could not be kept utterly separate. It also made clear that white women and black men could transgress the rules of both racial hierarchy and patriarchy. The liaison between Polly and Jim therefore made clear that the codes preserving slavery and patriarchy were not absolutely enforceable or infallible. Such a transgression, while it might not always elicit rage or violence, would certainly unsettle hierarchies of race and gender at the local level. Taking no further action than maligning and ostracizing the white woman could serve the interests of white people with a stake in those hierarchies. But the birth of Candas Lane, the free child of partial African ancestry, gave the lie to the infallibility of the Southern social structure. Polly and Jim's liaison may have threatened the Southern racial hierarchy, but local whites did not put a stop to it; only the rape charge forced them to discuss the liaison in a public forum. The community's keepers of order were forced to confront the liaison first through the death sentence of a valuable slave and then through the life of a free child of African ancestry. Had Polly given birth without benefit of the rape accusation, the local court may have invoked the indenture system just the same, though with less drama, for the existence of the free "black" child intruded on the reluctance of white people to take action against a sexual liaison between a white woman and a black man.

Perhaps what people had heard that August night in 1825 was Polly sobbing about her dismal future. Jim had been trying to quiet her down, lest she attract too much attention, and so had said, "Polly, don't cry so, they really will hear you," to which Polly, the unmarried white servant-woman pregnant by a slave, had replied, "If I am left in the fire I am now in, I shall surely die." After Jim was pardoned, Polly lived in her parents' household for the next fifteen years or so, and perhaps married later in life than did most white women in the nineteenth-century South. Following the pardon, Jim was likely sold out of the county, as had been promised and was customary. When Jim was transported, he would have left friends such as Dick, as well as his daughter. Perhaps he also left parents, brothers, sisters, or other loved ones. Candas Lane remained a servant in the Wilkerson household at least until the Civil War broke out, living there with a son of her own. After the war, Candas kept her own house; her son was a farm laborer, and both passed as white.[79]

Less than a year before Polly leveled her rape accusation at Jim, a white yeoman farmer in the Virginia piedmont accused his white wife of an adulterous liaison with a neighborhood slave. The response of that community, in the story that follows, also points to a measure of toleration on the part of white society for liaisons between white women and black men.

4 Adultery *Dorothea Bourne and Edmond*

If a married white woman in the antebellum South gave birth to a child whose father was presumably black, she was likely to be the subject of considerable scrutiny and judgment. Even without pregnancy and childbirth, suspicion of a white woman's adulterous liaison with a black man could become a fervid topic of local conversation. The seriousness of the matter and the actions taken, however, would depend more upon the woman's white husband. If he chose to remain silent, there might be talk but no concerted effort either to prove the transgression or to put a stop to it. If, instead, the white husband presented himself as a wronged man, friends and neighbors would be apt to cooperate in the legal investigation to support his claims. A white husband who proved his wife guilty of adultery with a black man was usually granted the divorce he requested, precisely because authorities had been swayed that the white wife was at fault. Yet white husbands were not guaranteed divorces under such circumstances. The gravity of breaking up a white family through divorce could outweigh the gravity of illicit sex between a white woman and a black man. Regardless of the verdict, antebellum divorce cases and other recorded instances of adultery based on the transgressions of white wives with black men confirm a marked absence of white outrage and violent retribution toward the participating black man, whether slave or free.

In 1824, an elderly white man named Lewis Bourne asserted publicly that his much younger wife, Dorothea, also called Dolly, made a habit of associating with black men in their Virginia piedmont neighborhood and specifically that she had been sexually involved with Edmond, one of John Richardson's twenty-five slaves, for the past six or seven years. Thus sex between a white woman and a black man entered the historical record as an offense of adultery. There were no accusations of rape, either by Dorothea, her husband, or any other white person, and unlike in the case of Polly Lane and Jim, white neighbors blamed the white woman from the beginning. Dorothea was both bullied and shunned, yet in the end the circumstances were not grave enough to permit Lewis a divorce. The story of Dorothea and Edmond presents another case of white people's uneasy endurance of a sexual liaison between a white woman and a black man in the slave South. Their story, too, involves dominant ideas about the sexuality of marginal white women, the precedence of a slaveowner's property rights over any other white person's reaction to the sexual transgressions of a valuable slave man, and the problem of free children of partial African ancestry.[1]

As in the case of Polly Lane and Jim, the evidence from Dorothea and Edmond's neighborhood reveals local knowledge of the illicit liaison. Many whites testified to familiarity with Dorothea Bourne's transgressions with more than one black man, but especially with John Richardson's slave Edmond. According to Dorothea's husband, there was "no room to doubt that an illicit intercourse" was "regularly kept up between them," precisely because so many "respectable persons" knew about it. Indeed, people said that Dorothea had "taken up with" a black man, "was intimate with" other men, and had been seen "in company with" Edmond. Others noted that she had children "by a slave" or that some of her children were "mulatto."[2] The Bourne and Richardson families resided in the southeastern corner of Louisa County and the bordering western section of Hanover County, a region that contained both farms and plantations. Unlike Polly Lane's family, Lewis Bourne could count himself among the small property-holding yeomanry. Like many of his neighbors, he was a farmer who depended little on the market economy of the slave South.[3] Lewis's father had divided his land between two of his four sons, and Lewis was one of the lucky heirs. For the last fifteen years of his life, Lewis owned seventy-five acres of land, placing him squarely among the county's middling folk. Just before he married Dorothea in 1812, he had been able to purchase one slave, though economic straits later forced him to sell his chattel and move in with a brother. By contrast, the Richardsons, who lived within half a mile of the Bournes, owned more than four hundred acres of land in addition to their many slaves.[4]

The white people whom Lewis Bourne selected to tell the story of Dorothea and Edmond agreed on its broad outlines. The blacksmith Peter Wade, for example, noted of Dorothea that "she generally keeps the company of Negro slaves." Nathan Ross similarly testified that Dorothea kept "the company of negro slaves as often or perhaps oftener than any other company." The narrators also agreed that Dorothea consorted in particular with Edmond. Richard Woodson had "witnessed considerable intimacy" between Dorothea and Edmond, and Edmond's master himself believed that Dorothea had "quit" her husband and taken up with Edmond because the slave man was younger and more handsome than her spouse. Dorothea and Edmond had even been caught in the act. One winter's night in 1823, Lewis's brother and his servant-woman had found Dorothea and Edmond in bed together on the Bourne property. Dorothea and Edmond also carried on their illicit liaison in Edmond's quarters and had been caught there, too. John Richardson's wife, Judith, said she had "often seen Dolly Bourne lurking about her negroes' houses."[5]

Neighbors had also witnessed affection, at least on the part of Dorothea. When Daniel Molloy hired Edmond to travel to another town, he observed Dorothea's sorrow at the separation. Thomas Pulliam, who had known Lewis for twenty years, averred that Edmond and Dorothea "live together almost as man and wife." Another witness used the same phrase, adding that Dorothea washed and mended for Edmond in her own home. Dorothea had in fact ceased to cohabit with Lewis, and resided instead in a dwelling "on a corner of his land." Some white people believed that Lewis consented to this arrangement so that Dorothea "might have it in her power to have a more uninterrupted intercourse" with Edmond. Finally, the storytellers largely agreed that Edmond was the father of some of Dorothea's children; one of these had died in 1823 at about age three, and rumors of others had made their way around the neighborhood. Peter Wade had "seen the children of Dolly Bourne" and had "no doubt of some of them being colored." Joseph Perkins swore that Dorothea had "children by a slave," adding that "no person in the neighborhood doubts it." John Richardson believed that Dorothea's last child was "by my man, Edmond." Such statements were echoed by others, including relatives of Lewis and a man who testified that he had made a coffin for the deceased child.[6]

As with Polly Lane and Jim, then, the liaison between Dorothea and Edmond was tolerated by white neighbors to a point. There is no way to know whether, if Dorothea's husband had never spoken up, the liaison might have continued without entering the annals of the antebellum South. But because Dorothea and Edmond had a living child or children, Lewis Bourne ultimately decided to seek a divorce from his wife. In the case of the unmarried Polly Lane and the slave Jim, local authorities had seized responsibility and bound out the free child of color; but any offspring of Dorothea, including any by a man other than her husband, would have been a burden to Lewis, for the children of adulterine bastardy were the responsibility of the spurned husband. Advising Lewis on the divorce proceedings, the county sheriff had pointedly told him: "You had better do it, Lewis, otherwise you will have them mulatto children to support all your life."[7] The presence of one or more children believed to belong to Dorothea and Edmond thus sparked Lewis's plea for divorce, thereby precipitating a local crisis. Only after Lewis decided on that course of action did a group of white neighbors confront the fact of the illicit liaison in a unified and zealous manner. As in the case of Polly and Jim, it was the guilt of the white woman they set out to prove, this time from the start.

When Lewis presented his divorce plea before the Virginia legislature in 1824, he had already been gathering depositions about his wife's transgressions for almost two years. The story of Dorothea Bourne and Edmond came to be recorded in that collection of narratives, and once again caution and speculation are required in the re-creation of events and sentiments. It is not possible to know all that occurred before Lewis Bourne began to gather his sworn statements intended to justify the legal dissolution of the marriage. In a divorce petition such as Lewis filed, the voice of the wronged husband is easily discernible, and the voices of those who sided with him ring equally clear. Almost none of the witnesses who spoke on behalf of Lewis owned as many slaves as John Richardson, but for the most part, neighbors of good economic standing and status came forward to support a man of precariously middling circumstances. The voices of the transgressors themselves come through haltingly, if at all.[8] The lone person who defended Dorothea was a midwife named Keziah Mosely, a woman who headed her own household. Although Keziah claimed to have delivered all of Dorothea's children and asserted that none had a black father, her testimony was refuted by three men who either countered that Keziah had previously pronounced one of Dorothea's children to be "black" or insisted that Keziah had not been present at every birth. The other six women who filed depositions sided with Lewis, as did the twenty-nine men who gave sworn testimony (there was also one anonymous witness).[9] Of course, because Lewis was the gatherer of the depositions, it is impossible to determine how many white neighbors may have defended Dorothea in their own minds. Dorothea commanded no power to call her own defense both because she was female and dependent and because she had transgressed too many boundaries. In any event, local authorities would likely have considered any supporters unrespectable outcasts. Opinions of the other slaves in John Richardson's household or in the neighborhood are equally difficult to discern. Those who knew the facts may have admired Edmond's defiance or held him in contempt for stooping to consort with a white woman.

In the process of proving himself wronged, Lewis Bourne ran into some trouble, for his wife did not wish for the divorce. And although Lewis was able to gather a considerable party of supporters, not all of their recollections worked in his favor. Lewis's probable violent treatment of Dorothea was crucial to the outcome, even though most petitioners painted a favorable portrait, proclaiming Lewis peaceable, honest, industrious, and "never . . . disposed to use his wife badly." One such speaker was the public notary, Anderson Bowles, who had been Lewis's neighbor for twenty-nine years. Another was Joseph Anderson, who had known Lewis from "infancy." Lewis was said to provide adequately for his family —he and Dorothea had one or two children of their own—except that Dorothea supposedly gave away food and clothing to the black men with whom she fraternized, leading the Bournes into poverty.[10]

But Thomas Anderson, who lived within a few miles of the Bournes, also stated of Lewis, "I believe had he married a virtuous woman, he would have made as kind a husband as any man," thereby implying that Lewis did not always treat Dorothea with complete forbearance. Other notes of suspicion also crept into the testimony, echoing this observation. Hannah Bourne, Lewis's niece who lived next door, said that her uncle "never was disposed to be unfriendly to his wife until she had taken to such an infamous course." Joseph Perkins, who had known Lewis for forty years, agreed that Lewis "would have made his wife a good husband . . . if she had conducted herself tolerably well." When Joseph Anderson testified to Lewis's good behavior as a husband, he pointed out that Lewis hadn't known Dorothea was "a strumpet" until after their marriage. Finally, eleven men, all neighbors of the Bournes, came forward on behalf of Lewis to opine: "We . . . think the many indignities offered Lewis Bourne by his wife has been sufficient to produce one of the few causes in which a husband might feel justified in whipping his wife." It is clear that at least some of the white neighbors considered domestic violence an appropriate course of action for a white husband whose white wife dishonored him by carrying on an affair with a slave, though there is no reason to believe that such violence would not also have been sanctioned if Dorothea had consorted with a white man.[11]

Although divorce in the nineteenth-century South was neither a common nor a swift process, adultery was one of the grounds for which most state legislatures and courts considered the proceeding justifiable. Yet despite evidence about Dorothea's sexual transgressions with a black man, despite the serious charge of adultery, and despite Virginia laws prohibiting sex between white women and black men, Lewis Bourne was denied his divorce.[12] Lewis's inability to control his wife in spite of his probable violent behavior seems to have settled the matter in his wife's favor. If the beatings had stopped Dorothea's transgressions, there might have been no divorce plea; because they did not, Lewis became the party at fault.[13]

Other cases bear out this interpretation. Mistreatment was likely the deciding factor in the case of Lucy Whittington of the North Carolina piedmont, who leveled counteraccusations of physical abuse and abandonment at her husband. According to the husband, Andrew Whittington, Lucy had deserted him a month after their wedding in 1823 and after returning had "indulged in criminal intercourse with both whites and mulattoes." Andrew claimed that Lucy's three children were illegitimate and that one of them was "colored." But in Lucy's version, Andrew "accused her of having unlawful intercourse with a negro slave" without a shred of evidence and "inflicted a most cruel whipping upon her." After a second severe beating, she asserted, Andrew had promised good behavior, only to desert Lucy shortly thereafter. The county and appellate courts alike ruled that Lucy was indeed guilty of adultery, but only after she had been abandoned, and therefore denied Andrew a divorce.[14]

Two additional cases from the North Carolina piedmont are instructive. In 1832 Peggy Johnson pled for a divorce after sixteen years of marriage, claiming that her husband, John, beat her in "drunken frolics," deserted her, and left her destitute (a neighbor vouched that John had kicked Peggy in the face and thrown wood at her). Although John Johnson countered that Peggy had formed a relationship with a free black man, he was not granted his divorce.[15] And in the case of Elizabeth Walters, the courts were more interested in her sufferings at the hands of her husband than in proof of her adulterous liaison with a black man. According to Hardy

Walters, Elizabeth "lived in illicit carnal cohabitation with a negro slave, became pregnant by him, and had a negro child." Hardy drew up a divorce petition, and the messenger who delivered it inquired if the charges therein were true. Elizabeth "held up the child and said it would show for itself." Hardy never followed through, and when he died in the early 1850s, Elizabeth hoped to collect her widow's dower. The men defending the deceased Hardy called Elizabeth "a lewd woman" and a "strumpet," but the judges gave greater weight to Elizabeth's assertions that Hardy had seduced her while married to another woman. Elizabeth won the case.[16]

The reasoning of legal authorities has not been preserved in other antebellum Southern cases of liaisons between black men and married white women in which divorce was denied. It is clear only that, for example, about a year after their marriage in the Virginia piedmont in 1806, William Howard learned that his wife, Elizabeth, "was engaged in the most brutal and licentious connections, having no regard to persons of color." (One night William had found Elizabeth "undressed and in bed" with Aldredge Evans, "a man of color.") Although Elizabeth continued "to pursue her accustomed vicious and licentious course of life," William's divorce plea was rejected.[17] Similarly, even though Tabitha Hancock of piedmont North Carolina purportedly lived "at a Negro quarter among Negroes" and had "children of various colors and complexions," her husband was denied a divorce in 1813.[18] In the case of John and Elizabeth Dever, the two had married in eastern North Carolina in the early 1800s, but within a few years Elizabeth had "suckled at her breast an infant bearing the most certain marks of a colored father." Elizabeth had (like Dorothea) "resided under the roof of a slave" for two years, and yet John was denied divorce in 1813.[19] In eastern North Carolina in the same year, James Hoffler's divorce plea was rejected even though Deborah Hoffler lived with a black man with whom she had a child.[20] Thomas Culpeper of tidewater Virginia claimed that within six months of his marriage in 1831, his wife had "sacrificed her virtue on the altar of prostitution" and was having "carnal intercourse with black men or negroes." Caroline Culpeper presented a different version of the facts, and Thomas lost his case.[21]

Neither were white husbands guaranteed divorce on the grounds that their wives had consorted with black men before marriage. True, the husbands of Elizabeth Pettus, Lydia Butt, Peggy Jones, Nancy Newton, and Ann Barden, all of whom accused their wives of having sex with black men before marriage, were granted divorces. But when Marville Scroggins of western North Carolina claimed that his wife, Lucretia, had conceived the child of a black man before their wedding, the Supreme Court of North Carolina would not grant a divorce, declaring Marville at fault "in marrying a woman whom he knew to be lewd." There was, however, a fascinating connection between the Scroggins and Barden divorce cases, both of which reached the state supreme court in 1832. After Marville Scroggins was denied divorce, the public outcry forced the court to hand down a different verdict in the eastern North Carolina case of Jesse Barden. In the words of the chief justice: "This is a concession to the deep-rooted and virtuous prejudices of the community upon this subject." Although both cases entered the record as adultery, the crime of sex between a white woman and a black man mattered explicitly in the Barden case precisely because the judges had not especially considered it in the Scroggins case. True, Marville Scroggins's lawyer had argued that "imagination can scarcely conceive a case which is calculated to awaken a larger share of sympathy in the human bosom," though to no avail for his client. In this instance, white Southerners forced a judge to rethink his ruling on the subject of sex between white women and black men, perhaps due to the increasing militancy in support of racial slavery after 1830 in response both to the Nat Turner rebellion in 1831 and to the growing ire of Northern antislavery forces. Although the judge in the Scroggins case may have thought the legal breakup of white families more dangerous than sex between a black man and a married white woman, other white people wanted it on record that such adulterous liaisons should not be idly overlooked.[22]

Additional clashes between law and community also testify to the potentially volatile nature of sex between black men and married white women in the antebellum South. In 1809 an anonymous citizen of North Carolina expressed consternation in a letter to the editor citing the case of a man whose wife "left him and attached herself to a free Negro, by whom she then had several children" but whose divorce plea was rejected. The writer also cited a married white woman who delivered a "mulatto" child a few months after marrying a white man and whose husband was denied divorce. Such circumstances warranted the legal dissolution of marriage, the writer insisted, for the cases were "as plain as the blaze of day."[23]

In the eyes of Lewis Bourne's friends, too, the disgraceful conduct of his wife justified whatever abusive behavior he may have displayed, and made Lewis entitled to divorce. To the Virginia legislature, however, Lewis's abuse was at least as reprehensible as Dorothea's transgressions. Perhaps legal minds reasoned that breaking up a white family could only magnify weaknesses in Southern hierarchies of gender and race, hierarchies that were not so gravely threatened by a liaison between a white wife and a black man, at least as long as patriarchal authority still operated to some degree within the household, and especially as long as the institution of slavery remained intact. The institution of marriage thus might on occasion require legal preservation to shore up the structure of patriarchy that undergirded racial slavery.[24]

Divorce laws were liberalized in the first half of the nineteenth century in the South, principally through a more flexible interpretation of what made a marriage unendurable and a broader definition of what constituted cruelty. This was fostered largely by the development of an ideology that cast women as more virtuous than, but physically inferior and legally subordinate to, men and therefore potential victims of their husbands. Divorce laws were formulated largely with the protection of women in mind, and most divorces in the antebellum era were requested by wives.[25] Dorothea Bourne, Lucy Whittington, Peggy Johnson, Elizabeth Walters, and perhaps the other white women whose husbands lost their cases were understood by the law to be victims of their husbands' abusive treatment, a circumstance that was apparently more dangerous than their own adulterous behavior, even with black men. The view that it was a husband's duty to control his wife—which contradictorily could also sanction the physical abuse of wives—was also central to these verdicts. In the Scroggins case, the chief justice invoked the marriage vow of "for better, for worse," noting that "nothing would be more dangerous" than to permit one spouse to claim that the other was "worse than was expected." Lucretia Scroggins had, it seemed, not matched the ideal of a virtuous woman, and thus the judge opined: "He who married a wanton, knowing her true character, submits himself to the lowest degradation, and imposes on himself."[26] At the same time, the fact that many white husbands whose white wives had transgressed with black men were indeed granted divorces indicates that convictions about white female virtue and victimization were never uniformly entrenched in antebellum culture, for those convictions did not always or necessarily apply to white women outside the planter classes or to white women who consorted with black men. Thus if the white wife were judged to be depraved, the husband might win; but if the wife were depraved and at the same time experienced severe abuse in her marriage, the husband could lose. Or to put it another way, if a severely abusive husband was unable to halt such depravity, he could be denied a divorce.

Although Lewis and his friends made Dorothea suffer for her transgressions, Lewis had also relinquished more than a measure of his patriarchal authority over his wife. Just as Polly Lane's father was too poor to control his daughter, Lewis Bourne may have been too elderly and infirm to control his wife, who was after all part of his property. Whatever children belonged to Dorothea and the enslaved Edmond certainly threatened both the community's racial categories and its racial hierarchy, especially given that white people already considered Edmond to be a very light-complexioned slave. Dorothea's liaison with Edmond might not by itself have mattered to Lewis Bourne in any degree that made it worth his while to seek a divorce from her, especially in light of his ostensible exercising of disapproval through domestic violence. But the "black" children born to Dorothea, who required Lewis's economic support, forced him to take legal action and therefore put the case on record. As with Polly Lane and Jim, precisely because no one had stopped Dorothea and Edmond early along, they had produced offspring that made apparent some of the fallibilities of the larger slave society within which they all lived. Like Candas Lane, the children of Dorothea and Edmond illuminated an erosion of patriarchy as well as an erosion of the racial categories of "black" and "white": free children of partial African ancestry eroded categories of slavery and freedom based upon race.

This time, too, the problem of the children had brought an illicit liaison between a white woman and a black man out of the realm of gossip and scandal and into the realm of law. Yet ultimately Virginia legal authorities understood Lewis to be at fault. Lewis's inability to govern as a patriarch, they may have reasoned, had produced free children of partial African ancestry. Although the presence of such children created problems for a society based on racial slavery, perhaps the judges felt that to leave Dorothea Bourne with no husband would allow her only to cause more trouble both within her community and in Southern society as a whole.

The Crimes and Defiance of Married White Women

Although white women's requests for divorce in the antebellum South were usually based on charges of cruelty or desertion, white men's were usually based on charges of adultery or premarital sex. Lawmakers were more likely to consider a middling or well-to-do woman requesting divorce to be the victim of her husband's ill treatment, and more likely to deny a poorer woman such a ruling. As one legal scholar sums it up, "A divorce decree was, in theory, a reward for an innocent and virtuous spouse, victimized by an evil partner." For divorces initiated by white husbands in adultery cases, that was certainly so.[27] Just as the liaison between Polly Lane and Jim was not an anomaly in the antebellum South, neither was the liaison between Dorothea Bourne and Edmond. It is impossible to know how many other cases of adultery between white women and black men were never recorded because white husbands took no legal action. Moreover, a liaison that involved a well-to-do white woman was likely to be documented by way of a slander suit rather than in a divorce record.

For those white husbands who did act against transgressing wives, the petition for divorce followed a particular script: first the man enumerated the good qualities of the woman he had once chosen to be his bride (he might note her industrious nature and would be certain to describe her as virtuous). There followed a description of the harmonious marriage that had ensued, including the husband's unfailing fulfillment of his duties. Astonishment came next, when the husband learned of his wife's egregious conduct, in these cases either the birth of a child whose father was black, or the rumor or discovery of illicit congress with a black man or men. In language filled with pain ("he has experienced the heart-rending mortification of the most certain evidence of infidelity," for example) the husband would name the newly discovered flaws of his wife: she was lewd, licentious, depraved, corrupt, profligate, even notorious in the neighborhood. Sometimes this description was followed by a sketch of the husband's futile suggestion for his wife's reform or of his own attempts at reconciliation. At the end, the plea for divorce was put forth. In all, the men's language gave explicit agency to their wives. Soon after their marriage in the early 1800s, for example, Hezekiah Mosby of the Virginia piedmont suspected that his wife, Betsy, "was not only not faithful to the marriage bed, but moreover, that she bestowed her favors on men of a different color from herself."[28]

Although Lewis Bourne was unable to convince the legislature that he was the victim of his straying white wife by invoking this formula, other white men in the antebellum South had greater success. In many cases of adultery with black men, courts or legislatures were persuaded of the wife's depravity, and on those grounds granted divorces to the pleading husbands. In 1794 in the North Carolina piedmont, when Isaac Cowan's wife, Sarah, gave birth to a baby whose father appeared to be "a negro or person of color," Isaac was incredulous. Although it was "evident to the whole neighborhood" that the child was "of African blood," Isaac refused to acknowledge the facts "until the birth of a second child, of the same hue with the first." Isaac was granted a divorce.[29] In the winter of 1809, when Nancy Owen of piedmont Virginia gave birth to "a black male child," her husband felt that this fact alone justified divorce: "Such a horrid violation of the marriage bed," he asserted, excused him from commenting further, though he did bring five witnesses before the legislature to confirm that Nancy had had a "black child." Leonard was granted a divorce.[30] When in 1810 Elizabeth Cook of southwestern Virginia gave birth to "two mulatto children" after several years of marriage, John Cook stated only that fact and requested a divorce. Two witnesses, one a midwife, confirmed the birth and color of Elizabeth Cook's children, and John's divorce was granted.[31] In the case of David Parker, his first wife had deserted him, and his second marriage to Jane Miller in 1820 proved troublesome as well. Overlooking any possible fault on the part of David, tidewater Virginia witnesses condemned Jane, whom David described as "guilty of acts of the greatest lewdness, immorality and vice." His wife, David said, had "frequently had criminal intercourse with slaves or persons of color" and had one or more children whose fathers were black. The divorce was granted.[32] Jacob Johnson of the North Carolina piedmont pled for a divorce in 1823, claiming that his wife, Hannah, had "distinguished herself as an abandoned woman in points of morals and chastity by having been delivered of a colored child" the previous year. Jacob's plea was successful.[33] William Pruden of tidewater Virginia described his wife as "a notorious whore." Not only had Louisa Pruden had a child by a black man, but William had, he avowed, once found her "engaged in illicit intercourse with a negro man at my own house, and on my own bed." In 1841 William, too, got his divorce.[34] Thirteen years after her marriage to Bryant Rawls, Rachel Rawls left her husband in tidewater Virginia and was "delivered of a colored child." Thereafter Bryant, whose character and conduct were judged acceptable by witnesses, refused to recognize Rachel as his wife, and kept their three legitimate children with him. In spite of his warnings, Bryant asserted, Rachel continued "indulging in illicit intercourse." The couple was divorced on the same day as the Prudens.[35] Finally, Jacob Plum from western Virginia earnestly wished to "disconnect" his daughter, "now arriving at womanhood," from her mother, Mary Jane, who had been "caught in the act of adultery with a colored man," who had a "mulatto" child, and who lived "in open adultery" with a black man. Jacob was granted his divorce in the 1840s.[36]

Ending a marriage—even an abusive one—had serious consequences for white women in a society in which there existed few alternatives, either social or economic, to the family and household.[37] Most married white women who entered into liaisons with black men must have attempted secrecy at first, and those who succeeded also kept their actions out of the historical record. But secrecy was not always possible, especially in small, tightly knit communities, and evidence from other cases reveals that sex between a married white woman and a black man sometimes (as with Dorothea and Edmond) achieved the status of general knowledge. When a married North Carolina woman accused a neighbor of stealing one of her slaves in 1810, for example, the neighbor retaliated by publishing a notice in the local paper stating: "In regard to Mrs. Hoffer, it is a matter well known, and which I am always ready to prove, that whilst she was the wife of Mr. Hoffer, she took up with a mulatto man and lived with him 12 months, and in the time had a child, which was generally believed to be the child of the said mulatto." After estrangement from her husband, Sarah Hall of the Virginia piedmont lived in poverty with the three "colored" children she had had after her marriage in 1829. One day when Sarah was visiting her mother-in-law with one of them, the elder Mrs. Hall presented the child to another visitor and "asked as to its being a white or colored child." The visitor thought the child was "colored" and later testified that "it is generally understood and believed in the neighborhood" that Sarah Hall had two other such children.[38]

Married women from the planter classes might also find themselves the subject of such gossip. In the 1840s, a rumor circulated in eastern North Carolina about one Mrs. Reid, whom a visiting neighbor claimed to have surprised in bed with one of her husband's slaves. When the neighbor had come to Mrs. Reid's door at night, the man "jumped out of her bed and sprang through the window carrying sash and all." The news went around at gatherings of the elite, "in the midst of convivial conversation in the social circle around the fireside," though one person thought it was all "too bad to talk about." White people disagreed as to whether the man had left on his own accord or had been "put out of the bed through the window." When Mr. Reid sued for slander, his lawyer spoke of the "virtue and innocence" of Mrs. Reid, a woman "of high standing." The Reids were awarded five hundred dollars in damages and a request for appeal was denied. Thus did this case, or the rumor of it, go on record as slander.[39]

Although the choices for a married white woman who engaged in an illicit liaison with a black man were few, there were nonetheless various points at which she could decide among different courses of action. In spite of the hard fact that Dorothea Bourne had been caught (both with Edmond and by virtue of offspring to prove the liaison), her first recorded response was simple denial. In January 1824, a white man named David Johnson, upon entering Lewis's home during the night with the motive of catching the white woman and the slave, found Edmond "undressed . . . either going to bed or retreating from there." Late one night in November of the same year, Dorothea was discovered by neighbors and forcibly removed from a bed in the Richardson slave quarters. When one of the men in the party told her to run, she followed his advice, only to be overtaken and detained in the house of another neighbor. There the barefoot Dorothea, who also lacked hat or cape, claimed that she had not in fact been in bed with Edmond but, when threatened with appearance before a magistrate, relented and "promised to quit her bad practices." She then signed a statement admitting that "I was caught in a Negro quarter of John Richardson, in bed with one of his Negroes." The purposes of Lewis's allies had been accomplished, and more supporting depositions for the divorce petition could thenceforward be gathered. All this suggests that Dorothea and Edmond had been observed together before, since neighbors knew where to find them; indeed, John Richardson's wife had admitted as much when she confessed that she had "often seen Dolly Bourne lurking about her negroes' houses."[40]

It is impossible to know what other courses of action Dorothea may have taken before her rather pathetic attempt at denial. Like an unmarried white woman who transgressed across the color line, a married one might also try to terminate a pregnancy, especially if she were certain that the child was not her husband's. Foregoing that route, or failing at it, she might resort to infanticide. Hezekiah Mosby, for example, brought "respectable ladies of the neighborhood" into his wife's birthing chamber in order to ensure that someone saw Betsy Mosby's child "before any accident could happen to it," for Hezekiah believed that the birth would disclose Betsy's adulterous liaison with a black man, and feared that his wife would attempt to destroy the fruits of the crime, thereby destroying his case for divorce.[41] If a transgressing white woman had financial resources or relatives willing to come to her aid, she might flee the community. A deserting wife may have been acting out of humiliation and ostracism or in order to escape an unhappy or abusive marriage; alternatively, she may have been acting on orders from her husband, who would later cast himself as a victim. Jane Parker deserted David, and Elizabeth Howard moved to the next county. Similarly, in the summer of 1804 Tabitha Tatham of Virginia's eastern shore took her child, "which was obviously the issue of an illicit intercourse with a black man," and left her husband and one legitimate child; a neighborhood report had it that she fled to Philadelphia. In the 1840s, Elizabeth Rucker gave birth to a "mulatto" child, and moved from southwestern Virginia to Ohio.[42]

If a white woman caught in an adulterous liaison with a black man had nowhere to go or no means to get there, she might own up to her actions and amend her ways. If her husband subsequently took no legal action, the woman's misdeeds would never go on record. One such case did, however, enter the record in the memoir of two black women, who recounted this story from southside Virginia: "A fellow named John Logan, who was white, was an army officer called away to fight during the War of 1812. While he was gone, his wife took up with a Negro slave on their plantation. She was already the mother of seven daughters by her husband, and her romance with the slave produced two more daughters. When the husband returned, he forgave his wife—*forgave her!*—and adopted the two mulatto girls as his own. They even took his last name, Logan. . . . This slave and this white woman were our great-great grandparents." How many other such anecdotes exist in the privacy of family histories remains unknown.[43]

Alternatively, an adulterous white woman could own up to her actions and, rather than seek forgiveness, present herself with a measure of defiance. After her lame denial when caught in Edmond's quarters, Dorothea Bourne chose this course by offering an alternative set of facts about her husband's motives and the motives of other witnesses who supported his allegations. Though Dorothea was unhappy with Lewis and very possibly abused by him, she hoped to remain married at least for the sake of her economic well-being. Dorothea accused Lewis's brother, William, of instigating the divorce proceedings and charged Lewis with selling off her dower (including land and livestock) to William in order to maintain himself and their legitimate children on the money. "The deep interest then which William Bourne feels in this question of divorce between my husband and myself is so palpable," noted Dorothea in a petition of her own (written out by someone else and signed with an "x"), that she felt William's testimony should not be admitted in the case, and neither should that of his "poor laboring dependent" servant-woman, Pleasants Proffit. Dorothea made a final and significant plea: in addition to two children she claimed were by Lewis, she had a third child, a babe in arms (she did not name the father), and she trusted that the legislators would not permit her to go unprovided for. Thus while Lewis did not want to support another man's children, Dorothea successfully invoked the lives of her children without specifying paternity in order to move the legal proceedings in her favor. If Lewis did not support Dorothea and the children, the burden would presumably fall on the community.[44]

Other white women who carried on adulterous liaisons with black men demonstrated decidedly more defiance than Dorothea Bourne. There were those who talked back, professed love for black men, and leveled more severe counteraccusations, though they did not always succeed in their endeavors. Betsy Mosby, for one, voiced her disapproval of a moral double standard. One day, when a visitor stood talking with Hezekiah Mosby, Betsy came to join the two men, holding her newborn. The visitor, later called to file a deposition, had "no doubt" that the child "was begotten by a black man" and perhaps he said as much to Betsy when she answered "that she had not been the first, nor would she be the last guilty of such an act, and that she saw no more harm in a white woman's having a black child than in a white man's having one, though the latter was more frequent."[45] In the case of Elizabeth Walters, she spoke of her black partner to the messenger who delivered the divorce petition, confiding that "she loved him better than anybody in the world."[46] And Sarah Gresham

Yet it is crucial to realize that even when legal authorities and white communities alike understood dishonorable white wives like Dorothea Bourne to be the victims of abusive white husbands, neither the law nor the white neighbors cast those adulterous white women as the victims of the black men with whom they had sex.

The Silence and Defiance of Black Men

The liaison between Dorothea and Edmond was common knowledge, but only when Dorothea's husband entered a divorce plea did his friends and neighbors act. Their purpose was to prove Dorothea's guilt, and although this was readily accomplished, the Virginia legislature denied Lewis Bourne his divorce. While there was no doubt that Dorothea had carried on a liaison with a black man, there was sufficient suspicion that Lewis had abused a wife he was unable to control, and that factor outweighed other evidence. This reiteration of facts is to say that the contest was between the transgressions of Dorothea, the white wife, and the transgressions of Lewis, her white husband. The behavior of Edmond, the black man, was not a factor in the minds of either local or legal authorities.

The fates of some of the black men in adulterous liaisons can be gleaned, but their motivations and sentiments are more difficult to discern. Dorothea had a petition of her own among the collection of documents on the Bourne divorce case. Edmond's voice is a great deal more elusive. Because black men in such circumstances were not called upon to explain their transgression in any public forum, they wisely offered nothing to white people. Within his own family or community, Edmond surely dealt with the consequences of a liaison with a white woman, but just about the only thoughts attributed to Edmond (or any black person) in the documents come from his master, John Richardson, who recounted: "I have good reason for believing this man of mine has been disposed to forsake this woman, which has produced considerable discontent in her, and has been the cause of her often visiting my negro houses and staying all night in the quarters." If this story is true, Edmond was less than a completely willing partner in the liaison with Dorothea, and Dorothea imposed herself on Edmond at least some of the time.[52] Not only is it impossible to trace events on this point, but Dorothea and Edmond themselves probably understood the circumstances of their liaison in different ways. From

Edmond's point of view, consenting to sex with a white woman may have contained an element of defiance. No matter what various people thought had transpired over the two years or longer in which Dorothea and Edmond had sex, Edmond was likely neither a complete victim nor as an enslaved black man in the antebellum South could he have been a free agent. For Edmond, too, the liaison with Dorothea may have been one choice among bleak and limited choices. Perhaps he deemed an enduring relationship with a black woman too risky, for example, entailing the possibility of separation through sale, or of his own powerlessness in the face of white sexual abuse or violence toward her.[53]

A clue may lie in two depositions filed on behalf of Lewis Bourne, if taken in conjunction with John Richardson's story that Edmond at some time wished to "forsake" Dorothea's affections. First, the eleven neighbors who felt Lewis was justified in beating his wife came forward to refute rumors that Lewis had once ordered Dorothea whipped by a black man. Second, Joseph Perkins, who had known Lewis for two decades, recalled hearing of a fight that took place a few years past between Dorothea and a slave belonging to Lewis's brother, in which Dorothea came away with "some bruises."[54] These witnesses wished to assert that Lewis had never set a slave violently upon his wife, opening up the possibility that the elderly Lewis had done exactly that in his efforts to get his aberrant wife to obey him. But it is also conceivable that this testimony points to a scenario of conflict between Dorothea Bourne and another slave man in the neighborhood, thereby possibly backing up John Richardson's version of the liaison between Dorothea and Edmond. Edmond's master had good reason to paint Dorothea as the perpetrator, leaving his slave property safe from a bad reputation, but it is not completely out of the question that the slave who beat Dorothea had been coming to the defense of Edmond or trying to put a stop to unwanted advances toward himself. All that is certain is that Dorothea suffered in some measure, perhaps severely, as a result of the liaison, and that Edmond himself may have suffered a great deal as well.

Edmond's voice may remain largely inaudible on the dynamics of this liaison, but in a few other antebellum cases the voices of black men, both slave and free, have been preserved. In these instances the level of defiance matches that of some of their partners. In 1847 in the North Carolina piedmont, a slave named George was charged with the murder of a white man named James Meadows. George had not only stabbed and beaten James but also, "with both his hands . . . fixed and fastened about the penis and testicles" of James, he "did violently squeeze." James's wife was named an accessory in the crime, and witnesses noted that Mary Meadows had shown "hostility to her husband" and that there was evidence of "a guilty connexion" between Mary and the slave man. George was sentenced to death in county court, but on appeal the judgment was reversed on technicalities regarding the evidence of a conspiracy between Mary and George.[55] The case of Redding Evans in southern Georgia in the volatile late 1850s reveals a stark example of defiance on the part of a black man who entered into an adulterous liaison with a white woman. Redding was a free man of color who kept the company of a woman named Mrs. Smith, who lived apart from her husband, James. Redding Evans and James Smith had an antagonistic relationship "on account of Evans' criminal intimacy with Smith's wife." When James Smith complained that Redding Evans's chickens were eating his corn, for example, Redding told the white man to leave those chickens alone or he might kill him. On another occasion, Redding promised to cut the white man's throat "if he bothered him." One day when Redding Evans and Mrs. Smith were in bed together, James Smith ordered the black man out of the house. Failing in this demand, James Smith departed, but Redding Evans "followed him and knocked him down, and made him come back in the house and sit down, and Evans went back to bed with Smith's wife, in the presence of Smith and his children." Another morning James Smith tried to retrieve his children, because he had heard that Redding Evans "was going to run away with his wife." At the same time, the black man was approaching the house. The white man pulled his shotgun and fired at the black man; Redding Evans, wounded, then fired at James Smith five times, killing him.[56] In these two cases the black men were on trial, not for sex with a white woman, but for violence toward a white man. Although that may not have differed had the black men been white men, the conscious resistance to white authority behind the actions of these transgressing black men caught in an already dangerous endeavor is significant if not remarkable. The slave, George, was allowed to live, almost certainly because of his value as property. The free man, Redding Evans, was convicted of murder in 1861, as white Southerners clamped down on free people of color with the coming of war. The execution was presumably carried out.

As for local white people's reactions to black men who consorted with married white women, neither indignity nor outrage are detectable in the documents. To be sure, white husbands in some of the divorce cases explicitly indicated that adultery with a black man was more deplorable than the same crime with a white man. Joseph Gresham, for example, proclaimed that his wife's adulterous behavior was "aggravated by the fact that it was committed and carried on with a man of color." Thomas Cain from Virginia's Shenandoah Valley charged his wife with adultery "of the most aggravated character," because she had twice "become the mother of black children who could not be other than the fruits of an adulterous intercourse with a negro." Other white husbands no doubt assumed that lawmakers and judges would find adultery with a black man extremely offensive. Some took pains to state this explicitly in order to bolster their cases; Isaac Fouch, for example, first wrote about his wife's illicit partner by name and later inserted the words "a man of color," indicating the salience of race to his quest for divorce.[57]

Nonetheless, taking offensiveness for granted did not warrant violent reprisal toward black men who were sexually involved with white women. Recall the winter's night scene in 1823 in which white neighbors ensnared Dorothea and Edmond in Edmond's slave quarters. Not only was Dorothea the target of the trap, but capturing Edmond did not concern those who participated in the vigilante episodes that followed: no mob went after the slave man. When Dorothea was forced from Edmond's bed in the Richardson slave quarters, it was she who was chased and captured, precisely because her husband hoped to use the evidence for his divorce plea. That the neighbors chased Dorothea into the night indicates that they were not seeking out Edmond for punishment, at least not at that moment, nor at any other moment recorded over two years in all the descriptions of that illicit liaison. Of course, because Edmond was the property of another white person, neither Lewis nor anyone else could take revenge without intruding on John Richardson's rights, and it is certainly possible that Edmond suffered violence at the hands of his master, even though John Richardson would later defend his slave by blaming Dorothea for the liaison. Still, the detailed narratives in the many depositions contain no hint of any public or private violent retribution toward Edmond, nor of white neighbors' wishes for violent retribution to be carried out by Edmond's master. Nor do the documents contain the least expression of white outrage, nor even a glimmer of the most casual disapproval toward the slave man for his liaison with a white woman.[58]

Indeed, other black men were named in their antebellum Southern communities as transgressors with white women, and as with Edmond there is no record of white people seeking these men out for violent revenge. The partner of the defiant Elizabeth Fouch, for example, was identified as James Watt, a free man of color whom one witness had known "from his infancy." When Isaac Fouch finally left his wife, Elizabeth set off with the remaining household possessions loaded onto a wagon, and James Watt "followed her in a little time after." The two were followed in turn by a constable, but all he wanted was a portion of the Fouch property that Isaac owed someone.[59] In the case of Rebecca Baylis, also of the Virginia piedmont, her husband proclaimed her to be guilty of living "in open adultery with a free man of color named Wilford Mortimer," with whom she continued to live after her husband sought a divorce. William Howard of the Virginia piedmont had found his wife "undressed and in bed with a certain Aldredge Evans, a man of color." In the piedmont Virginia divorce case of Daniel and Henrietta Rose in 1806, the father of Henrietta's child was recognized as a slave belonging to Henrietta's grandfather. In 1813 in eastern North Carolina, James Hoffler pled that his wife "did take up with a man by the name of John Lowance, a person of color by whom she . . . had a child."[60] The 1824 petition of shoemaker Lewis Tombereau in eastern North Carolina told of finding his wife, Peggy, cohabiting "with a certain mulatto barber named Roland Colanche then living in Williamston," with whom she had one child. Rather than describing a violent conflict, however, the cobbler explained how his own poverty prevented him from exacting any redress without making a fool of himself. In the 1832 petition of John Johnson, the white husband claimed that his wife had "formed an attachment" with a free black man with whom he farmed in the North Carolina piedmont.[61] The foregoing documents indicate unequivocally that the black men in these adulterous liaisons were named and known. Other black men are not identified by name in the documents but were clearly known to cohabit with white women, for example those who lived with Louisa Pruden (whose husband found them in bed together), Mary Jane Plum, Tabitha Hancock, and Elizabeth Walters. On the other side, it seems that if no one beyond the white woman herself knew which black man had been her illicit partner, white neighbors made no attempt to identify or find the male transgressor. Although Elizabeth Walters told the messenger who delivered the divorce petition that "she was not the first or only white woman that that negro . . . had taken in," no white reactions of fury to that statement are on record.[62]

It is not possible to know all that came to pass prior to the recording of any liaison, yet not a shadow of an enraged white person, not an inkling or an intimation of vigilante violence, not a faint or distant echo of a call to physical revenge appears in any of the recorded cases. If the man were enslaved, white people probably considered his offenses to be within the purview of his master, and some of these men may well have suffered within their own quarters. Again, it is impossible to know if John Richardson beat Edmond on discovering his liaison with Dorothea Bourne or threatened to sell away loved ones or tormented him in some other way. At the same time, because the white women in these cases were married, the matter of the transgressing man was likely considered to be within the purview of the white husband, and black men (like white men who had sex with married white women) may have suffered at the hands of angry white patriarchs, although once again no evidence whatsoever exists to support that conjecture. Although white Southern men did not take the matter of adultery between a white woman and a black man lightly or in stride—just as they did not take any sexual transgression of white women in stride—neither did rage and retribution, based on the race of the man, inevitably follow from local knowledge. In the case of free black men who transgressed with white women, a clue may be taken from antebellum rape cases. The lack of inevitable white violence in cases of adultery with white women may have stemmed in part from the value of free black men as low-wage workers. The execution of the free Redding Evans (who owned at least his own chickens) indicates that white people considered free black men who enjoyed some economic independence more dangerous; in fact, Redding's death sentence foreshadows the fate of black men after the Civil War, when whites conflated black male autonomy with sexual transgressions across the color line.[63]

Finally, because these white women were married, local authorities were less concerned with the support of bastard children. Instead, the white husbands would have to take responsibility, as did Lewis Bourne, whom the sheriff warned about having to care for "them mulatto children" for the rest of his life. Such a problem could plague white men even after death; in 1858 in tidewater Virginia, a white man's executor sought to cut out of the man's will "three negro children born," presumably to his wife, "between the date of his will and the time of his death." At least some of the free black men who engaged in liaisons with white women became the children's caretakers, either voluntarily or by legal order. The illegitimate child of Louisa Pruden, for example, lived "with the reputed father, a free negro." The illegitimate child of Rachel Rawls lived "as a pauper in the house of a free negro" by an order of the county overseers of the poor.[64] This measure may have been the equivalent of bounding out the children of unmarried white women as apprentices, a way to control the comings and goings of free people of partial African ancestry, and therefore a way to minimize disruptions to the equation of African ancestry and slavery. Although Edmond was not free, one of the white witnesses had heard Dorothea tell Edmond that "he must take the child she had and provide for it, as it was his child." Edmond's voice emerges here, for he agreed to do so if Dorothea "would tell him it was his child," meaning if Dorothea were absolutely sure that the child was not her husband's. Of course, as a slave, it is hard to know how Edmond could have provided for a child; perhaps Dorothea imagined the child being raised in the slave quarters and cared for by the Richardsons.[65]

There were, then, black men in the antebellum South who participated in liaisons with married white women, who lived with married white women or with their illegitimate children by those women, or who ran away with married white women. Only if a black man took revenge on a white husband in the form of violence (as the enslaved George and the free Redding Evans had done) were they sure to be called into court. Even then, the cause of that court appearance would be violence toward a white man. Although they consorted with white women, these black men were not automatically assumed by their white neighbors to be rapists or even seducers of white women. They were not systemically sought out in a white frenzy if no one knew their identity, and they did not suffer public retribution if anyone (or everyone) did. In the recollection about a white soldier in the War of 1812 who forgave his wife for her affair with a black man, the family's descendants wrote: "No one remembers what happened to the slave, except he must've left town in a big hurry." Perhaps the man did run away, or perhaps no one could remember because the man was simply not the focus of local attention.[66]

When Lewis Bourne filed for divorce, his major concern was the support of children not his own. Lewis's ineffective control over Dorothea illuminated an imperfectly functioning patriarchy, which in turn produced free children of partial African ancestry, children who then served to expose some of the imperfections of racial slavery. White neighbors and acquaintances all along cast Dorothea Bourne as the guilty party, but the Virginia legislature did not agree with that judgment. Although white community members had judged Dorothea to be the victim only of her own depraved sexual nature, legal authorities viewed her also as the victim of her white husband. Neither local nor legal authorities cast Dorothea as the victim of Edmond, the black man. And although Lewis did not get his divorce, white husbands under the same circumstances were often granted their wishes precisely because their white wives were understood to be so degraded. That a white woman's illicit partner was a black man in no way indicated to white authorities that she had been forced into the crime.

Far fewer questions emerge about what came to pass between Dorothea Bourne and Edmond than about the circumstances of Polly Lane and Jim's liaison. Whereas Polly repeatedly refused to name Jim as the father of her child, it took little to scare Dorothea into signing a statement that implicated Edmond. True, just as Polly's father could not control his daughter, Dorothea's husband could not control his wife; yet a major difference between the two cases lay in the accusation of rape. The life of a valuable slave was at stake in the case of Polly and Jim but not in the case of Dorothea and Edmond. In the case of Polly and Jim, the black man was on trial; in the case of Dorothea and Edmond, the black man was never asked to tell his story and never as much in need of the defense of powerful white people. No white person ever considered taking the life of John Richardson's valuable slave because he had had sex with a disreputable white woman in the neighborhood. In the case of Dorothea and Edmond, all that was at stake was the financial situation of a white husband who had long ago relinquished his honor, as well as his authority, over his transgressing white wife. Still, as in the liaison between Polly and Jim, the consequences of the liaison, rather than the liaison by itself, spurred local whites to action. Those consequences were the offspring of a white woman and a black man. That is not to say that white husbands tolerated their wives' affairs with black men (nor with white men) if no children were produced.

But when children were born to a white woman and a black man, there was so much more at stake. No one had stopped Dorothea and Edmond until Dorothea's husband decided he didn't want to support another man's children. Dorothea and Edmond's liaison did not stir up white rage, but it did unsettle the local social order. Like Candas Lane, the children of Dorothea and Edmond gave the lie to the infallibility of the Southern social structure.

Because Lewis Bourne was not granted a divorce, Dorothea's life with her husband probably continued much as it had before. The liaison with Edmond may have continued, or perhaps once the community became enmeshed in the scandal, it came to an end. Or if John Richardson was correct, perhaps Edmond was an agent in ending the liaison. Whatever sentiments Edmond may have had toward his children went unrecorded. After Lewis's death in the mid-1830s, Dorothea and her children surely suffered economically. In his will, Lewis left all his land to his son, Thomas, the only child he called his own. Lewis referred to each of the two other children, Fanny and Mary Bourne, as "my wife's daughter which I do not believe to be my child," and left each girl a dollar. Dorothea inherited nothing. The census of Louisa County taken in 1850 lists Dolly Bourne as the sixty-year-old head of a household, living with her daughter Mary Bourne, thirty years old, and perhaps two grandchildren. She had no occupation and no property.[67]

There is a final twist to the story of Dorothea and Edmond. Like his children with Dorothea, Edmond was of mixed African and European ancestry. Although some white people described Edmond as "Negro," "mulatto," or a man "of color," other descriptions reveal more ambiguous white perceptions.[68] One man called Edmond "a remarkable white slave," and another concurred that Dorothea had "taken up with a white slave." John Richardson described Edmond as "as white as any white men generally are." [69] In spite of this perception, however, the same witnesses were certain that the father of Dorothea's illegitimate children was "Negro" or "black" and that the children were of partial African ancestry. One person, for example, was sure that one of the children "must have had a black father," and another said the children were "by a black negro." One neighbor stated that Dorothea's last child "although to all appearances white, is by a slave." [70] Many described the illegitimate children as of "dark complexion," "colored," "mulatto," "black," and "Negro." [71]

Thus although Edmund appeared remarkably "white," he was thoroughly understood to be "black" within the confines of his own locality. His enslaved status served to identify him as a "black Negro," because slavery was synonymous with blackness, at least ideally. Edmond's appearance may have unsettled the rigidity of racial categories, but his status as a slave placed him firmly in the social hierarchy of the antebellum South. After all, everyone who passed him in the neighborhood knew that he lived in John Richardson's "Negro houses."[72] In Edmond's children with a white woman, however, the effort to keep people of African ancestry in slavery was unsuccessful. Their existence eroded not only categories of race based upon color but also categories of slavery and freedom based upon racial designations. Everyone in town knew that those children were of partial African ancestry (they were "colored," "mulatto," "black," and "Negro"), and yet they were free. As such, they were troublesome to whites in a way that the enslaved children of a white man and a black woman could never be. And yet ultimately it did not matter so much, except for those who wished to help out Lewis Bourne, because the institution of slavery for the most part kept people of African ancestry in slavery—even where that ancestry might be invisible. Again, the contradiction: the liaison between a white woman and a black man did not sufficiently threaten the institution of racial slavery, but the production of children made apparent defects in the Southern social structure.

In the case of Dorothea Bourne and Edmond, there was no argument about whether a white woman and a black man had carried on an illicit liaison, however subjectively those racial categories were construed: the woman was white and the man was a slave, even if a "remarkable white" one. In the stories that follow, however, it becomes clear that in other cases involving white women and black men in the antebellum South, questions of race and color could prove to be major points of contention.

The children of white women and black men presented antebellum white Southerners with complexities and confusions of racial categorization. Because Southern statutes stipulated that a child's legal status as slave or free followed the mother, the children of white women and black men were of partial African ancestry but also free, thereby violating the equation of blackness and slavery. Recall that the marriage of Nell Butler and Charles in the late seventeenth-century Chesapeake was problematic because the mixture of European and African ancestry blurred boundaries of freedom and unfreedom in a society that was beginning to stake its labor system on racial slavery. In the late eighteenth century, when descendants of that marriage challenged their bondage, whites were forced to grant freedom to African Americans. Recall that after Polly Lane was served with a bastardy warrant in piedmont North Carolina in 1825, white neighbors speculated in consternation about the ancestry of her daughter, who, it turned out, was of partial African ancestry yet free like her white mother. Recall that at the same time in the Virginia piedmont, Dorothea Bourne's husband was advised to seek a divorce so as to avoid supporting his white wife's free "mulatto" children for the rest of his life. The children of white women and black men—these free children of partial African ancestry—made illicit sex across racial boundaries visible to white Southerners, and notably more visible than the children of white masters and enslaved women, who could legally be kept among the slave population, thereby preserving the equation of African ancestry and slavery. The children of white women and black men increased the problematic population of free people of color in a society based on racial slavery. Along with reminding white Southerners of transgressions against the authority of fathers and husbands, therefore, the free children of white women and black men also exposed the potential difficulties of sustaining racial boundaries in a society predicated upon just such distinctions.[1]

Racial categorization can be based upon rigid criteria of ancestry or upon more flexible criteria of appearance. *Prima facie* means "at first view, before investigation." In the antebellum South, laws about prima facie slavery and freedom (slavery and freedom based upon appearance) as

well as laws defining racial status by degrees of ancestry brought both factors into play. In theory, degrees of ancestry could be legally defined and
proven, but in reality this was hardly possible in every case, leaving those
with an interest in racial stratification groping for solutions at least some of
the time. This was as true for census takers as it was for the courts. In addition to ancestry and appearance, then, community knowledge was crucial
in determining racial status in the slave South. The way white people described people of African ancestry not only identified individuals by sight
but also signified slavery. The matter was far from straightforward. When
the District of Columbia abolished slavery in 1862, for example, masters
filled out forms that required a description of each former bondperson,
and the notations there included the following: dark black, quite black,
light black, dark brown, light brown, chestnut, dark chestnut, copper-
colored, dark copper, light copper, yellow, dark yellow, bright yellow, pale
yellow, very light, and nearly white.[2]

Cases involving the descendants of white women and black men
were among a variety of legal disputes in which racial identity proved
troublesome in the antebellum South. It was precisely the unstable correspondence of blackness with slavery, and whiteness with freedom, that was
at issue. Some of these cases involved enslaved people who were light in
color; although in many such cases the fathers were white, some protagonists claimed non-African maternal ancestry in an effort to gain freedom.
Other cases involved dark-complexioned free people who were forced to
convince authorities of their entitlement to liberty; some of these claimed
English maternal ancestry while others claimed descent from Spanish, Portuguese, or American Indian kin. Questions of racial identity could also be
crucial to legal authorities in cases concerning the inheritance of property.
Two Georgia court cases commencing in the 1850s illuminate some of the
ways racial status could be disputed both legally and locally. Each case
involved the son of a white mother, and in both cases white community
members offered conflicting testimony as to whether the fathers had been
men of African descent. Sex between white women and black men either
came to pass in each case or people assumed it had, yet that transgression remained largely peripheral to the court proceedings. In both cases,
once legal authorities intervened to resolve the inheritance dispute, it became clear that white neighbors had long been cognizant of the illicit or

alleged liaisons. In both cases, the intrusion of the market forced the issue of racial identity where it might otherwise have remained unresolved with a degree of community toleration.

As sons of white women, Joseph Nunez and Franklin Hugly were free in antebellum Georgia. Census takers in Georgia in 1860 decided that 8 percent of slaves, and 57.2 percent of free African Americans should be classified as "mulatto" rather than "black." In Georgia, as elsewhere in the slave South, there was never an absolutely strict two-tier system of racial identification. Rather, whites informally recognized a category in between "black" and "white," and some white Georgians treated some people of partial African ancestry as if they had no African ancestry at all, especially if they were among the very few free people of color who themselves owned slaves. Free blacks made up no more than 1 percent of the population of antebellum Georgia.[3]

Joseph Nunez was a slaveowner, and when his case reached the Supreme Court of Georgia in 1856, he had died without descendants. Franklin Hugly, who had died at the age of six, had come into an inheritance of land and slaves; his case reached the Georgia Supreme Court in 1858. The late 1850s could be perilous years for free black people, with the sectional conflict over racial slavery simmering all around them. In each case, for the purposes of distributing property, the judges needed to determine degrees of African ancestry. In each case, economic quarrels led to debates about race and racial categories. The real dramas in each story took place at the local level, where the county courts called on the respective communities of Joseph Nunez and Franklin Hugly to help determine the racial status of each deceased person. What emerges so strikingly in these cases is the ability of white people residing in such close proximity to live with enormous contradictions. Although the law insisted on formal categories of race, white neighbors were willing not only to determine racial status on an ad hoc basis but also to disagree among themselves on such matters.[4]

Who Was Joseph Nunez?

Where degrees of ancestry could not be proven and where a person's appearance prompted too many different opinions, courts seeking to classify a person by race had to investigate the person's entire way of living. This meant inquiring into comings and goings, his or her companions, reputation, treatment by neighbors, and manner of self-presentation. It meant, in short, inquiring into a person's precise footing in a community. Such was the case for Joseph Nunez. The Nunez family had lived within the profitable slave economy of Burke County in Georgia's black belt, where in 1860 slaves formed 70 percent of the population.[5] The court had to determine whether Joseph had possessed the legal right to sell (or even to give away) six slaves together worth between nine thousand and seventeen thousand dollars. These were a woman named Patience and her five children, three boys and two girls. To do this, the court needed to ascertain Joseph's racial status: if Joseph were found to possess at least an eighth of "African blood" he would be legally classified as a "free person of color" and would not have been lawfully permitted to sell his slaves.[6] But white people who had known the Nunez family told remarkably conflicting stories about them. Listening now to what neighbors remembered about Joseph Nunez and his parents, it appears that the family resided in an ambiguous and perhaps shifting (though not marginal) place in their Savannah River settlement, somewhere amid the status of free blacks, Indians, and whites. The ease with which white community members believed varying perceptions is startling. Unfortunately, evidence of how the Nunez men thought of themselves can be gleaned only in white people's descriptions of their actions and behavior; there are no further clues as to their self-perceptions.

No one questioned that Joseph Nunez was the son of a white woman named Lucy. Other white women in the neighborhood had known and socialized with Lucy. Mary Rogers, for example, who described Lucy as a very pretty "free white woman" with fair skin, blue or gray eyes, and light hair, told the court that she had "always treated" Lucy "as a white woman; been to her house and ate with her and associated with her as a white woman," and that "other white women in the neighborhood treated her as such." Harriett Kilpatrick also remembered Lucy as "a free white woman," though with "straight, smooth, black hair." Harriett, too, had "stayed in her house many a night."[7] The relationship between Lucy and Joseph's father was less clear, however. One man who had lived about a mile from the Nunez family and was "intimately acquainted" with Joseph also described Lucy as "a free white woman," naming her as Lucy Anderson, "afterwards called Lucy Nunez," implying marriage at least in the eyes of the community. Joseph's parents, this neighbor said, had "lived together as husband and wife." At the same time, three men of the Cosnahan family who had "always understood" that Lucy was white claimed that they did not know her personally but that they did know Joseph's father, perhaps indicating that the couple did not live together continuously. More concretely, Mary Harrel offered that the father lived in Burke County "though he was very often over in South Carolina, and sometimes stayed there a month or two or three months."[8]

Because Joseph Nunez's mother was white, Joseph was unequivocally a free man, but this did not mean that he was a white man. The key question for the court was the ancestry of Joseph's father, James Nunez, and it was here that the instability of racial categories made apparent the near-futility of this legal quest for racial precision. White witnesses described the appearance of Joseph Nunez and his father in detail, offering an array of impressions about ancestry and racial status. On one side, some neighbors felt sure that neither man had any African ancestry. Joseph Bush and Mary Rogers, for example, contended at first that both Joseph Nunez and his father were free people of color, but Bush changed his mind and said that Joseph Nunez's father was American, whereas his grandfather was a Portuguese who "passed as a white man." (Opposing the categories of "free person of color" and "American" conflated nationality and color. Asserting that a Portuguese person could pass for white could also indicate a conflation of nationality and racial categories.) Other witnesses alternatively introduced the possibility of American Indian ancestry. Mary Rogers also changed her mind, saying that Joseph Nunez's father "was of mixed Indian and white blood." The absence of "negro blood" was evident, she pointed out, by the man's "mighty red face." Harriett Kilpatrick described the father as of "dark" complexion but admitted the inconclusiveness of this by adding that she had "seen some white men darker than he was"; she, too, thought the father was "partly Indian and partly white" without "any negro blood." And Stephen Newman and Mary Harrel, who had also known the father, thought his hair was "straight, black and smooth," and that he was "of a white and Indian extraction."[9]

But other white neighborhood residents quite literally saw things differently, claiming that both Joseph Nunez and his father were in fact people of partial African ancestry. One of the Cosnahan men remembered the father as "not much brighter than a half-breed white and negro."

Another Cosnahan (who knew the Nunez family "as he would any close neighbors in a thinly settled country" and "was often with them") remembered the father as "quite dark" and felt that the family's "general appearance indicated them as mulattoes." The third Cosnahan called the father a "dark mulatto," and described Joseph as a "mulatto" who had "negro, Indian and white blood in him." Charles Ward (who had known Joseph "from his infancy till a few years before his death") also called Joseph a "mulatto" and concluded of the Nunez family that they all "showeth the negro in their features." It is worth wondering: Before the court case, had there existed an ongoing division and tension within the community as to how whites should interact with the Nunez family? Had white neighbors found occasion to argue their differences either mildly or heatedly? Or perhaps the whites had assumed consensus where none existed, or simply had not troubled themselves about the matter. Still, it is difficult to imagine how these various perceptions coexisted in one small place, for beyond appearance and ancestry, white neighbors also recounted the treatment and self-presentation of Joseph Nunez and his father in their community in ways that were decidedly contradictory.[10]

In the view of some whites, the Nunez men were treated in every way as people without a trace of African ancestry—although not the same as white people. At one extreme, Stephen Newman and Mary Harrel thought that no one in the neighborhood regarded the father "as a negro" and offered supporting details of frequent interaction. They recalled the man as a graceful dancer and noted that "many persons tried to catch his step, and nearly all admired its style" (that "there was no clumsiness about him" would have further marked him in white eyes as a person without African ancestry). Both remembered "that whenever Jim Nunez was staying in this neighborhood, at a Mrs. Holmes, he was always received as a respectable person." He had "never kept low, trifling or rakish company," had "associated with respectable whites in the neighborhood," and "fellowshipped with the whites"—was in fact "often at their balls and parties, assemblies and little gatherings, where no free negro was allowed to associate with the whites, and dined with the whites just the same as any gentleman would have done." Both of these witnesses claimed to have attended neighborhood balls and "seen him dancing there." (Mary Harrel had "danced on the same floor with him," though "not as a partner" as far as she could remember.) Both said they "never knew of Jim Nunez associating with negroes, free or slave, or of his being regarded by his neighbors as having any negro blood in him." [11]

Other witnesses agreed that the father was treated the same as a white person. Mary Rogers remembered that he "was always among respectable white people in the neighborhood, in their dances, parties, &c., and was received by them as on a footing with whites." No "free negro," she said, had ever been "received and treated in that way by the neighborhood." As for his son, Joseph, she "never knew of Joe's calling or considering himself a free negro." This woman did, however, recall that free blacks associated with the Nunez family, and this she attributed to the fact that "Joe had a negro for his wife." Indeed, Joseph Nunez's "wife" was Patience herself, one of the slaves over whom the parties in the courtroom were fighting; the other slaves in dispute, Patience's five children, were presumably the sons and daughters of Joseph Nunez. That Joseph had had children with one of his slaves might have proven to some white people that he himself was white, though this fact did not sway others. [12]

Some whites skirted the confusion of "Negro" and "white" by believing that the Nunez men had been treated as American Indians. According to Harriett Kilpatrick (who claimed to know Joseph Nunez well), neither Joseph nor his father "were regarded as free negroes, nor," she added, "did either regard himself as such or act as such." Although neither man was a voter, this woman insisted that they were not "mulattoes" either. Rather, she said, the father was a "three-quarter blood Indian." Mary Rogers likewise recalled that the father "was always treated and regarded in the neighborhood as not a negro, or having any negro blood in his veins, but as a respectable Indian and white blooded man." If all of these observations were true, then the Nunez men either genuinely believed that they were not the descendants of African ancestors or felt at ease allowing white people—in whose circles they apparently moved—to believe that fact. [13]

Again, however, other whites saw things very differently, and here the dissonance is most striking, for this other contingent of white neighbors believed that the Nunez men were actually treated by whites as if they were unmistakably people of African ancestry. One of the Cosnahans stated unequivocally that whites associated with the Nunez men "as if they were free negroes." Another Cosnahan had never known the Nunez men to exercise the rights of white citizens, and although the father "was an educated man and mixed sometimes with white men," even those friendly whites had "regarded them as mulattoes." What was more, in this opinion the Nunez men "regarded themselves as free mulattoes." The third Cosnahan agreed that the family were "reputed mulattoes in the neighborhood" who were "treated as free negroes." And according to Charles Ward, the family was "regarded as free negroes," and Joseph Nunez "regarded himself as a free negro." If these alternative observations were true, then the Nunez men embraced their African ancestry.[14]

White members of a single community thus constructed diverse and contrasting visions of race by combining highly subjective physical descriptions with broad speculations about ancestry and then mixing those two factors with personal recollections about community status. Although the disagreements about appearance and ancestry are intriguing, it is the lack of consensus on the reception and self-presentation of the Nunez men that is more perplexing and that best illuminates the potential for intense ambiguities of race in the antebellum South. The categories of slave and free were clearly of greatest import, and there was no question that the Nunez family was free. Unlike the categories of slave and free, however, color and race must have been less urgent to white neighbors. The law needed the facts, but the neighborhood had never agreed on the matter. While different views of the Nunez family may have stemmed from varying interests regarding the purchase of Joseph Nunez's slaves, it is clear that different white people felt justified in swearing to very different accounts of the Nunez family's appearance, reception, and self-definition in a single neighborhood. Only with the advent of conflicts over property did this knowledge carry weight. Witnesses had, of course, been produced by plaintiff and defendant to support their respective contentions—the white administrator of Joseph Nunez's estate had sued to recover slaves sold to another white man—but the major witnesses on each side did not break down by class status in any significant way. It would be instructive to know how other free families of color (who comprised less than 1 percent of the population of Burke County) might have perceived and received the Nunez men, but no such witnesses were called. The knowledge and opinions of Patience and her five children also remain unrecorded, as do the insights of other slaves who lived nearby.[15]

According to the census takers in decades past (whose perceptions cannot be considered any more precise than those of any other white people), the Nunezes were slaveowning free people of color.[16] Certainly the Nunez family occupied an unusual place in the community: a white woman and a free man of equivocal racial status cohabited at least some of the time, and some whites considered them married. At other times, the white woman lived without this man and received, and was received by, other neighborhood white women without hesitation. The man came and went in the neighborhood, and when present was welcomed on an equal footing by some whites, though not by others. He did not vote, but he did own slaves and mix with whites on the dance floor. The couple's son, Joseph, had inherited slaves from his father, and Joseph had, like many white men in the slave South, fathered children by one of his female slaves. Within these various and contradictory facts lay the multilayered ambiguities inherent in any free person whom whites did not fully consider to be one of their own in the slave South. The free child of a white woman and a black man would be part of that troublesome population.

The county court instructed the jury to decide the Nunez case by weighing "the testimony of all the witnesses, so as to impute perjury to none." Indeed, each witness was likely convinced of the truth of his or her own version of the family's standing. In 1856, the Supreme Court of Georgia ruled that testimony about "general reputation," "public rumor," and "general notoriety" counted as original evidence instead of hearsay, and at least in part on that basis the judges decided that Joseph Nunez had at least an eighth of "African blood." Joseph Nunez therefore had not possessed the legal right to sell Patience and her children.[17] Although the ruling was at odds with so much of the local testimony, the interest of legal authorities in pronouncing the Nunez men to be people of African ancestry may have stemmed from the desire to erase racial ambiguities: better such a liminal family be "black" than "white." Moreover, better that anyone whom even some whites considered not white should be deprived of the rights of white people, especially when slavery, and therefore racial hierarchy itself, seemed endangered by mounting tensions between white Southerners and their Northern enemies. Ironically, the same ruling also acknowledged the existence of a population of free people of color, which in itself confounded the equation of African ancestry and slavery, not to mention that these were slaveowning African Americans as well. Indeed, census takers had dutifully recorded the existence of the free and slaveholding Nunez family members for decades. There was just no way to make all white people free and all black people slaves since, even on the level of "close neighbors in a thinly settled country," white people could not always agree on matters of color and reputation, and therefore of race.

The Nunez case went to trial again in the middle of the Civil War and reached the Supreme Court of Georgia in the spring of 1864, closing its eleven-year journey through the legal system. This also brought the case to just a few months before General William Tecumseh Sherman and his Union army would begin their fierce Atlanta campaign; Atlanta would fall at the end of that summer. Slaves throughout the South continued to seize their freedom whenever possible, especially as Union soldiers marched through their homes, but both sides in the Nunez case persevered. This time, old witnesses offered new descriptions of the Nunez men—for example that Joseph's father had straight dark hair "which he wore in plaits, tied at the end with ribbons." At the same time, each party offered new evidence as well. On one side, three new witnesses came forward to testify that Joseph Nunez was "a free white citizen," specifically a Portuguese man. On the other side, the 1785 will of Joseph's paternal grandfather, Moses Nunez, was produced to indicate that James was the manumitted son of the white Moses Nunez and a "mulatto" woman named Rose. While this contradicted the testimony of witnesses who claimed that Joseph had no African ancestry, it did not solve the dilemma of the "fractions" of African ancestry in regard to the "mulatto" grandmother.[18]

And indeed, the judges did not change their minds about Joseph Nunez's status as a free man of African ancestry who lacked the right to sell his slaves. Chief Justice Joseph H. Lumpkin freely admitted that "there never was a fairer case for doubt," commenting: "Is it strange that persons should have mistaken the blood of James and Joseph Nunez? It is done daily in our midst." The justice's words at times dripped with sarcasm (he summarized portions of the testimony by noting that Joseph Nunez's father "acquired some notoriety at dances for the grace and agility with which 'he tripped the light fantastic toe,'" for example). Posing the semi-rhetorical question, "What was Moses Nunez?" he supplied the answer: "Probably a Portuguese, as his name imports, from a left-hand marriage with a mulatto by the name of Rose." And of this union: "The father had eaten sour grapes, and the children's teeth were on edge." After that, James Nunez had "intermarried with a very pretty white woman" and thus were the Nunezes a "mongrel family."[19]

Such were the consequences when white patriarchs (whether fathers, husbands, or lawmakers) failed in their efforts to prohibit a white woman like Lucy Anderson from having a child with a man of color like James Nunez. The class standing of Lucy's own family remains unknown; one of the two white women who claimed to have socialized with her was a slaveholder in 1850, while the other was a pauper. It is also impossible to know which patriarchal authority would have been responsible for Lucy's actions and how her transgressions played out among her kin. And nothing whatsoever in the documents reveals the motivations or sentiments of either Lucy Anderson or James Nunez themselves. Because the court proceedings were not about their liaison, no witness took the time to attribute intentions or emotions to them. It is apparent only that the result of that mysterious liaison was a child whose racial identity and status confounded both court and community throughout his life and even more so after death.[20]

As Justice Lumpkin noted, similar circumstances in other antebellum Southern families were not uncommon. In determining racial identity, courts could be forced to give considerable weight to hearsay evidence, precisely because degrees of ancestry were difficult or impossible to prove. In coastal North Carolina in 1845, for example, when a man named Whitmel Dempsey was indicted for possession of a shotgun under a law that free people of color must be licensed to carry weapons, the court needed to determine whether Whitmel was indeed "of color." Hearsay evidence determined that four generations of Dempsey men had had children with white women: Whitmel's great-great-grandmother, great-grandmother, grandmother, and mother were all white. On the other side of the family tree, one witness described Whitmel's great-grandfather as "a coal black negro," while others had observed the same person to be "a reddish, copper colored man, with curly red hair and blue eyes." Whitmel Dempsey was declared to be "in the fourth generation from negro ancestors" and found guilty.[21]

An Alabama case from the 1840s offers an interesting twist on marriage across lines of racial categories. Girard Hansford was a free man of color who sought to divorce his wife, Maria, whom court documents allowed was "not described as colored." The two had presumably been married about twenty years, but when Maria gave birth to a child "pronounced by individuals to be white, with blue eyes," she admitted adultery: now it seemed that a white woman and a black man had in fact married contrary to law. When the court awarded custody of the children to Girard, Maria appealed and both sides invoked race to support their contentions. Maria argued that because she was white, the marriage should have been void to begin with; Girard countered that both he and his wife were "colored." The Supreme Court of Alabama preferred Girard's portrait of the union, and affirmed both the marriage and the custody ruling. Perhaps the judges wished to explain away the marriage of a white woman and a black man—and to erase racial ambiguity—by hastily agreeing that the woman was not really white at all.[22]

As for Joseph Nunez and his parents, the record of white perceptions in plantation Georgia in the 1850s and 1860s reveals the inherent contradictions of racial slavery and the vagaries of color and ancestry. Yet despite the details recounted in the reputation and reception of the Nunez family, no white witnesses told any stories with even the faintest glimmer of a clue that they or other white neighbors had reacted with anger or violence toward the white woman and the man of color who had at times lived together as husband and wife. On the contrary, a number of witnesses told stories of accepting both Lucy Anderson and James Nunez into their circles. Although that acceptance was presumably predicated upon the conviction that James was not "black," even those who felt sure that James was a man of African ancestry did not relay stories of outrage or express shock either at the liaison or at the couple's acceptance by white neighbors. The transgression entered the historical record only when a sale of slaves was in dispute. Perhaps that was the only time it mattered.

This is not to say that Lucy Anderson never suffered from gossip, or that some contingents of the white community did not refuse her company, or that white neighbors were not incensed by the behavior of James Nunez. But if any of that came to pass, it would have coexisted with the reactions of other white people who kept the company of Lucy Anderson and socialized with James Nunez. Might the white people on record have tolerated such a liaison in part so as to banish from scrutiny (including their own scrutiny) those ever-troublesome broken rules in the slave South's gender and racial systems? Who could help but notice that not all white women upheld the rules of patriarchal society, including rules against sex between white people and black people? The consequences could be frustrating, even infuriating, but not necessarily intolerable in a society in which racial slavery functioned largely to the satisfaction of whites, especially in a region with such a minuscule proportion of free people of African ancestry. In turn, of course, any degree of toleration (including refraining from retribution) only exposed little cracks in the Southern racial hierarchy by producing free children of partial African ancestry. In the case of the Nunez family, both the ancestry and social status of the descendants was a mire of contradictions. Legal authorities made a ruling on that vexing question, but that did not change what had come before. No legal pronouncement could change how the Nunez family had interacted with their neighbors of various colors for decades before the court classified them as people of African ancestry.

A liaison between a white man and his slave (Moses Nunez and Rose) in the eighteenth century had perhaps started the trouble, especially when their son (James Nunez) was set free by the father. When this son produced a child (Joseph Nunez) with a white woman (Lucy Anderson), not only were categories of race further confounded, but so were categories of slavery and freedom that were meant to be based upon race. A white woman had produced a child who was both free and of partial African ancestry. And yet all of those complications could be safely disregarded or endured until it came time for local white people to argue among themselves about the inheritance of property. Perhaps most ironic, that property was not in the form of land or money but in the form of human beings enslaved due to their African ancestry.

Who Was Franklin Hugly?

Witnesses had known and associated with Joseph Nunez for many years, but when the main character in an inquiry about racial identity was an orphaned and dead six-year-old boy whose parents had moved away, neighbors could offer only visual conjurings and remote recollections. Also in Georgia's cotton belt, this time in 1860, neighbors and friends came into county court to describe the appearance of Caroline Hugly and her family, Amos Hugly and his family, and the young Franklin Hugly, as well as the behavior of Caroline and Amos toward the boy. But although the Hugly case involved an accusation of a white woman's adulterous liaison with a black man, the testimony focused barely at all on Caroline's probable transgression. Rather, her own and her husband's racial status were of paramount importance because the law was concerned with Franklin's ancestry. Even though Franklin's appearance had years earlier set off local gossip about his mother's illicit behavior, the gossip entered the historical record only with the later financial quarreling of relatives.

Franklin Hugly's parents, Caroline Sullivan and Amos Hugly, were both children of the first white settlers of the Stroud Community, a locality populated largely by yeoman farmers but in the state's plantation belt. Yet both families were prosperous slaveholders, adding a fascinating dimension to the case: in 1850, Caroline's father owned thirty-four slaves and Amos's father owned fifty-seven. Caroline and Amos married in 1840 and later moved away to the mountains of Georgia's northwest corner. When Amos died, he left half his estate to Caroline and half to the son, Franklin. Caroline died soon thereafter, and in 1851, at age six, Franklin died, too. The boy had no will, and in 1858 fourteen cousins on both sides claimed to be the heir to Franklin's estate, worth more than ten thousand dollars and including land, slaves, money, livestock, and cotton. This property lay in the hands of Caroline's father, who maintained that relatives from Amos's side were not entitled to Franklin's estate. Franklin, "although born in the wedlock of persons of the free white race," he proclaimed, "was the adulterine bastard child of Caroline . . . and was a half breed of the African race." In other words, Caroline's own father maintained that because Franklin was the bastard child of Caroline by an unnamed black man, no one on Amos's side could claim an inheritance. This man's financial interests apparently outweighed the stigma of notifying the court—and reminding the community—of his daughter's adulterous liaison with a black man, a fact that would also have highlighted his own inadequacy as a Southern patriarch and a member of the community's higher ranks at that. Thus in 1860, fifteen years after Franklin's birth, a trial was held to determine whether Franklin Hugly was the legitimate son, and therefore an heir, of Amos Hugly.[23]

White witnesses came into court to testify about the racial status of Caroline and Amos and to consider whether Franklin resembled his parents. Witnesses generally agreed that Franklin did not resemble his parents, at least not in the realm of racial classification. Benjamin Zelner (county judge and another descendant of the community's first white settlers) thought that Caroline's family was "of dark complexion," though Caroline was "more fair" than the others. In spite of dark freckles, Amos was undoubtedly white, with his "fair skin," "thin sharp nose, high cheek bones, high broad forehead," and "long chin, just like a white man." Leonides Alexander agreed that Amos was red-haired, freckled, and fair skinned, though he added that "on looking on the side of Amos' face it made him think of a negro." This he amended, perhaps hastily, with: "not that Hugly himself was a negro." Watson and Margaret Crawford, who had lived next door to the Hugly family, also described Amos as a fair-skinned and freckled redhead; Caroline, they recalled, was fair-skinned with rosy cheeks. But both thought little Franklin "the darkest child they ever saw born of a white woman." Margaret said that "from the dark color of Franklin Hugly and his curly black hair, and low forehead, she would say he was one half negro." Watson concurred that Franklin was "one half of the negro race." Dr. Dudley W. Hammond, a physician of thirty years' experience, described both Amos and Caroline as fair but recalled their new baby as "of dark complexion" and therefore "a mulatto or in other words half negro—an adulterine bastard." According to the doctor, the midwife who attended Franklin's birth had pronounced the baby a "mu-latto," and the doctor added that one could infer Franklin's bastardy from the fact that Amos and Caroline "lived together for many years before this child was born, and several years afterwards, and had no other." When questioned, then, white neighbors agreed that although both of Franklin's parents were white, the child seemed to display some African ancestry.[24]

But neighbors also agreed that (as the Crawfords put it) "Amos Hugly treated Franklin as his own," although rumors had circulated on whether the little boy did in fact belong to Amos. Benjamin Zelner had once spoken with Amos when Amos was "very mad" because people were saying that Franklin was "a negro child." If that were so, Amos fumed, "he would make more fuss about it than any body else, and would discard or leave his wife." Of course it is impossible to say whether Amos was furious because he knew the rumors were false, or because he wanted to cover up the truth, or even because he did not himself know the truth. As for the identity of the rumored black father, Amos had once told Watson Crawford that "whenever he went from home, he directed a negro man to sleep in the house where his wife slept." Could this man—mentioned only this once and this sketchily in all of the neighbors' testimony—have been the father of Franklin Hugly? There is no further information about Caroline Hugly and any black man, no echo of this man's voice, no further clue about the motivations or agency of either Caroline or the unnamed man, and no mention whatsoever about any suspicion of rape. The documents indicate only that the white woman appeared guilty to her white neighbors. Some offered that Amos was not a very bright man and therefore presumably (like Dorothea Bourne's husband) unable to control his wife. The Crawfords said he was mentally deficient and "easily imposed upon." Dudley Hammond thought Amos an "imbecile" and a "simpleton." As in the Nunez case, no documents reveal what any local slaves or free people of color might have known or thought about a sexual liaison between Caroline Hugly and a black man.[25]

Amos, Caroline, and little Franklin eventually moved away, suggesting that they could not continue to live with community suspicion or knowledge of Caroline's adulterous behavior with a black man; it is possible, in fact, that their families sent them away. Indeed, both Caroline and Amos were respectively removed from the annals of their fairly prominent families. Spencer Sullivan did not mention his daughter in his will, nor did Zachariah Hugly name his son in his. If Caroline's name had been erased for dishonorable deeds, perhaps Amos's was erased both for his mental deficiency and for the dishonorable deeds of his wife. (Or perhaps Amos Hugly was himself the manumitted child of his father by a slave woman, or even the free child of a white mother and a black father: recall Leonides Alexander's words that "on looking on the side of Amos' face it made him think of a negro.") Caroline and Amos both suffered from harsh judgment and ostracism; Dr. Hammond had "examined the child at different times 'closely, for the purpose of ascertaining whether it was a white child or a mulatto,'" perhaps indicating an ongoing local scandal. And yet there is, as in the Nunez case, no shred of a hint pointing to white outrage or retribution toward a black man who in this case people were saying committed adultery with a white woman from a well-to-do family. Although the Huglys may well have been forced to pack up and move to the poorer upcountry, and although there is no way to know for sure what may have befallen a black man who consorted with Caroline, it is also true that not one word about threats or violence, escapes or searches, in regard to any slave or free black man made its way into any of the stories told by white neighbors.[26]

Perhaps most significant in terms of racial classification, none of the Huglys' upcountry neighbors thought there was (in the words of the court) "anything strange or peculiar in the appearance of the child, or that it was of negro descent." When questioned, one of these new neighbors noted that Amos always treated Franklin "very kindly" and that both Caroline and Amos "frequently claim him and say he was their child." In the absence of community knowledge to the contrary, then, Franklin appeared to be the legitimate child of both parents, and the family suffered no more. Without community knowledge of what had come before, the problem of racial identity vanished.[27]

The white neighbors' recollections of appearances were impressionistic, but the court also heard a lecture on racial theory that was intended to be much more precise. Although Enlightenment and Revolutionary thought had supported the view that social conditions rather than natural traits accounted for varying levels of human achievement, by the mid-nineteenth century the idea of a single human species had been largely replaced by theories that distinguished sharply among races. In the South, this was partly the result of a growing need to defend the institution of slavery. Such theories not only were discussed in scholarly circles but enjoyed wide exchange and acceptance throughout white society. The works of Josiah Nott, who put forth a theory of "polygenesis," or the separate creation of different races, for example, were widely read and discussed beginning in the 1840s, in both the South and the North, as well as in Europe.[28]

These scientific theories of race made their way into Southern courts as well, and indeed, Dudley Hammond offered a science lesson about Franklin Hugly's racial identity. This boy, the doctor said, "differed from the pure white race in several particulars." The lecture began: "The Caucasian or white variety, as a general rule, is characterized by a fair white skin, red cheeks, soft, flowing hair, generally curled or waving, ample broad forehead, small, oval and straight face, with features distinct, large elevated cranium, narrow and prominent nose, small mouth, and projecting chin." Contrary to the intimations of another witness, the doctor thought that both the Hugly and the Sullivan families were "characterized by the above indications of purity." Hammond continued: "The Ethiopian or negro variety, on the other hand, is characterized by dark skin, black, short woolly hair, compressed skull, and elongated anteriorly, forehead low, narrow and receding, cheek bones broad and prominent, so as to render the upper front teeth oblique, as projecting, usually, as to extend beyond a straight line dropped from the end of the nose to the chin, eyes full, nose broad and flat, lips (especially the upper) thick, facial angle deficient." Invoking both appearance and ancestry, the doctor thought the Hugly child "departed, or was wanting in many developments existing in its parents, or the white race, and instead, was indelibly impressed with those pertaining to the negro variety." In short, "the whole contour of the child's countenance or appearance would at once impress upon the mind that it was the offspring of a negro." [29]

Yet all of this man's scientific rhetoric did not persuade the court. In the Nunez case there had been no issue of preserving a white family since the Nunez men were not white. In the Hugly case, however, the verdict of the county court illuminates the interest of legal authorities in sanctifying the institution of the white family: the jury concluded that it had heard no convincing evidence that Franklin Hugly was not the legitimate child of Amos Hugly. Spencer Sullivan appealed, but the Supreme Court of Georgia upheld the ruling in 1861.[30] As one of the judges wrote, "the repose of families and the tranquility of marriages" was to be "presumed in all its force, unless combated by proofs stronger and more convincing." Such proofs were not to be found even in racial theory. Dudley Hammond may have been "a scientific and learned gentleman on the subject of the races," but his observations were not "infallible." As one judge wrote, "We constantly see departures in the negro and white races, from the peculiar and natural characteristics of these respective varieties, more glaring and striking than those pointed out by these witnesses." As for the testimony of the midwife, now dead, it was "nothing but an opinion," and hearsay at that.[31]

In the face of all the testimony, and despite the widespread dissemination of racial theory at midcentury, the court's ruling was based on the words and deeds of Amos Hugly, husband and self-proclaimed father. Any evidence that "the husband could not, by the laws of nature, be the father of the child" (in other words, that Franklin's father must have been black because his mother was white) was outweighed by Amos Hugly's "declaration" that "the child was his." According to the court, a husband's judgment on the question of a child's legitimacy should surpass any other pronouncements. Addressing the question of Caroline's transgressions, the court opined that there was "no evidence of any kind, either directly or indirectly, that the wife was guilty of adultery at all" and ruled "in favor of the innocence of the mother." And so, Franklin Hugly was the legitimate heir, Carolina Hugly was blameless, and so was any black man who may have had sex with her. So, too, was Amos Hugly pronounced a blameless patriarch, a man capable of controlling his wife. Science and community knowledge alike were simply too ambiguous, or so the courts maintained in their efforts to keep the white husband and wife an intact family.[32] Perhaps once again a sexual liaison between a white woman and a black man was best overlooked. And again, it was precisely such disregard that may have permitted the production of children like Franklin Hugly in the first place, children whose very existence could challenge the racial and gender systems of the slave South. As in divorce cases where legal authorities deemed the consequences of breaking up a white family more serious than an adulterous liaison between a white wife and a black man, the same could be true for the rulings in inheritance cases. Again, legal men decided that sundering white families would jeopardize Southern social hierarchies that functioned reasonably well under a broad community-wide patriarchy and as long as racial slavery held firm. In the Hugly case, the reasoning differed from the Nunez case, turning on the racial identity of the male heads of household. James and Joseph Nunez were men of color, and the court had declared the family to be of African ancestry. But Amos Hugly was a white man, and thus did the court declare the whole family "white." Another consideration may have been the increasing endangerment of racial slavery at the opening of the 1860s: the court may have decided that as long as the child of disputed identity was ensconced in a family of two white parents, better to pronounce that child white, if the alternative meant he would be "black" and free.

The Hugly case was not the only inheritance dispute in the antebellum South in which evidence was weighed in this manner. In tidewater Virginia in the 1830s, the issue of family sanctity had also been invoked in such a case. In question was the racial status of a child named William, whose mother was a white woman married to a white man. A daughter of the white couple claimed William to be an illegitimate "mulatto" and therefore not entitled to any of the bequest. But the court took the other side, noting that a child should be presumed legitimate if born while his mother and father were married, cohabited, "and had opportunities of sexual intercourse." By this reasoning, bastardy could be proven only by definitive evidence that the white husband had been impotent or absent, and the indignant sister was thus not permitted to submit scientific testimony declaring the impossibility of a white man and a white woman having a "mulatto" child. Such unyielding reasoning about marriage and cohabitation, of course, left no room for the possibility of adulterous behavior on the part of the white wife as long as her white husband was present at home—and as long as he did not make the claim himself. Here, as in the Nunez case, "some of the witnesses thought the defendant William a mulatto, others thought him a white person." Coming down on the side of white family stability, the lawyer defending William's inheritance asked how such contradictory testimony could be invoked to bastardize a person. He then suggested the folk belief that if a white woman cast a glance on a black man during pregnancy, "a child procreated by white parents might have the appearance of a mulatto," a convenient explanation for offspring who defied the rules of patriarchy and racial hierarchy.[33]

In an inheritance case from Alabama in the 1850s, a white man on his deathbed bequeathed his entire estate to a man he named as his child. But according to others, Gustavus Florey "was under an insane delusion as to Edward G. being his son." Witnesses testified that both Gustavus and his wife "were white persons" and that the heir "was of mixed blood" and "exhibited, plainly, the peculiar marks of the negro in his person—that his color was that of the mulatto, and his hair woolly." The Supreme Court of Alabama conceded the "physiological fact, that a white man cannot be the father of a mulatto child by a white woman." Yet although it admitted that Gustavus was indeed under the illusion that Edward was his son, the court nonetheless upheld the will, offering a legal technicality as explanation.[34] Here, as in the Hugly case, the declarations of the white husband prevailed. Evidence of any defiance of patriarchal authority—even such defiance as a white wife committing adultery with a black man—counted for little in the face of the husband's insistence on unchallenged power. The white wife's dishonorable behavior may have defied gender conventions, but the white husband's denial of that defiance dismissed it in one stroke, even if that particular husband was understood to be a man suffering from insane delusions or, like Amos Hugly, was an outcast imbecile. Again, it was advantageous for white men with an interest in the social order to endure the occasional defiance of patriarchal authority and the sporadic transgression across racial categories. Again, it was precisely that willful inaction that illuminated imperfections in the social structure in the form of children of partial African ancestry whom, in these cases, courts insisted were the offspring of two white parents.

As in the case of the Nunez family, in the Hugly family the probable sex between a white woman and a black man that produced free offspring intensified the inconsistencies of antebellum Southern racial categories. Yet here as there, in recounting recollections of appearance and status, no white witnesses embellished their testimony with stories of outraged violence. Even though Caroline and Amos were effectively removed from their respective family histories and may well have been forced to move away, the supposed black partner of Caroline Sullivan was barely mentioned by the white neighbors; when he was mentioned, no one pursued the facts. Furthermore, if Franklin Hugly were indeed a free child of partial African ancestry, produced by Caroline and an anonymous black man, no white person in the Huglys' new neighborhood would ever have known save for the suit brought after the death of the entire family. The transgressions of this family, too, entered the historical record only when an inheritance of wealth was in dispute. Perhaps that was the only time it, too, mattered. Perhaps it had not mattered before because Southern patriarchy and racial slavery for the most part kept order. In the end, the law ruled on Franklin Hugly's ancestry in such a way as to cover over any possibility of illicit sex between a white woman and a black man. Even if Franklin Hugly were indeed a free person of color, the court decided that to recognize that identity would be entirely too problematic. As in the Nunez case, the ruling did not likely alter the opinions of the Huglys' cotton-belt neighbors, who had always believed that Franklin was the child of a white woman and a black man, and who had blamed and shunned the white woman for the transgression. In the end, neighbors could safely overlook the possibility of such transgressions with the sanction of the state's highest court.

The Problem of Racial Categories

Recall that in the case of Polly Lane and Jim, white neighbors inspecting Polly's child could not at first agree on whether the father was a black man; likewise, the white voices in the Nunez courtroom sharply disagreed about the racial status of the Nunez men. Recall that in the case of Dorothea Bourne and Edmond, neighbors noted that a stranger would take Edmond, the slave, to be a white man; likewise, the Huglys' new neighbors in northwest Georgia did not think twice about Franklin being the white child of white parents. As one legal scholar of the antebellum South notes, "slave law" would have been synonymous with "black law" except for "problems in determining race when it mattered." Southern law rejected the line of slavery and freedom as its sole categorizing device because lawmakers could not abide by treating free blacks as the equals of whites. And yet when lawmakers attempted to embrace race as the categorizing device, they encountered the problem of individuals in "intermediate categories." The manumitted children of slave women and white masters contributed to this problem, and to this must be added the free children of white mothers and black fathers. As part of the free "black" population of the slave South, these offspring complicated racial categories.[35] In eastern North Carolina in the 1830s, for example, Ann Barden at first convinced her husband that the child she delivered was the result of their premarital courtship; only later did her husband decide that the child was a "mulatto" and file for divorce. A state supreme court justice noted that "color is an object of the senses," adding, "In so young an infant, whose mother was white, it might not be in the power of an ordinary man, from inspection of the face and other uncovered parts of the body, to discover the tinge." The court ruled that Ann's husband was entitled to divorce if he could prove that at first "the real color" of the child "was not so obvious as to be detected by . . . a person of ordinary diligence and intelligence."[36]

In short, because the children of white mothers and black fathers were of partial African ancestry but were not slaves, they confounded legal and social presumptions of prima facie slavery and freedom. Indeed, children of white mothers and black fathers were sometimes held illegally in bondage in the nineteenth century, as had been the case for the descendants of Nell Butler and Charles in the eighteenth century. In piedmont Virginia in 1835, for example, the enslaved William Hyden maintained that he had been "born free" in New York, "the son of a white woman." Passing through Virginia without documentation of his free status, he had been captured and treated as a runaway slave. In Georgia in 1843, a boy named Erasmus won his freedom on the grounds that he was the son of a white woman, even though some witnesses claimed that it was his father who was the white parent.[37] Not all cases were resolved to the advantage of the enslaved, especially by the late 1850s. In 1859, a slave named Dick at first won his freedom in western Florida by claiming that "his mother was a white woman." But when Dick's owner appealed, the state supreme court noted that Dick's "color . . . showing that he is of the African race, is *prima facie* evidence that he is a slave and puts the onus on him to prove that he is free." Reversing the initial decision, the court commented: "This is one of the hardships of his condition."[38] While color should have formally indicated slavery or freedom, then, both free blacks and slaves who contested their bondage rendered that rule problematic. Those populations included the children of white mothers and black fathers.

Other cases involved issues lesser than freedom but nonetheless illuminate ambiguities of color for the children of white women and black men. In the Virginia piedmont in the 1840s, for example, two brothers who were the victims of a robbery had trouble in court because of their racial status. The indicted white thief objected to their testimony since they were, he said, "mulattoes." The court determined that the victims' grandfather, who had died in the American Revolution, "was spoken of as a respectable man, though probably a mulatto." Evidence on the maternal side was contradictory; their grandmother was "probably white," their mother "certainly" so. In the end, they were deemed competent witnesses. In upcountry Georgia in 1851, Jacob Yancy protested the legal requirement that he register himself as a free man of color. In court, whites agreed that Jacob "was of dark complexion" but that he was also "the son of a white woman." To no avail, Jacob claimed that "as the child of a white woman, he was presumed to be a white person until found otherwise" (meaning, of course, that he was presumed to be a free person until found otherwise).[39]

Trouble ran the other way, too. Slaveowners considered slaves who might pass for white to be risky property, for (like Edmond) their bondage depended upon community knowledge and could be challenged beyond community confines. White Southerners were thus wary of purchasing slaves who might cross the line from slavery to freedom on account of European (or less often, American Indian) ancestry, and this included enslaved people who claimed descent from white women. William Hyden, the slave who claimed his mother was a white New Yorker, was not easy to sell. In 1835, no one would buy this man "at any price, on account of his color," for he was "too white." William could "too easily escape from slavery and pass himself as a free man," which he should in fact have been if his mother was white.[40]

Ancestry that might render a person's complexion dark but was not owing to African forebears also created difficulties. Recall that one neighbor had described Joseph Nunez's grandfather as a "Portuguese" who "passed as a white man." Debates over nationality and color also came into play when slaves claimed Spanish, Portuguese, or other such ancestry to prove their free status. Anthony Boston was granted his freedom on Maryland's western shore in the 1790s by proving that he was the descendant of "a yellow woman being a Portuguese" who was in turn the descendant of a free "Spanish woman." Also on the western shore of Maryland in the late eighteenth century, a slave named Eleanor Toogood won freedom on the grounds that her mother was a free woman who had been married by a Catholic priest to a slave named Dick. Eleanor's grandmother was also free, her great-grandmother was a white woman, and Eleanor's father was described as an "East India Indian who became a free mulatto."[41] Recall the 1843 western North Carolina case in which the state declared the marriage of William Watters, "a man of color," and Zilpha Thompson, "a white woman," void. When a neighbor accused the couple of an illicit liaison, William called this "false, scandalous, and malicious libel" and contended that he was "descended from Portuguese, and not from Negro or Indian ancestors." Some witnesses thought that William's father was "a white man, but of dark complexion," and that one of his grandmothers "was not as black as some negroes." But another swore that the grandparents were "coal black negroes," and some said that William's mother was "a bright mulatto, with coarse straight hair." William attempted to prove that one of his grandfathers was white, but the court rejected the evidence.[42]

Questions of color and status also arose in antebellum Southern rape cases. In 1850 in Alabama's cotton belt, for example, a man named Thurman was indicted for raping a white woman under a law that stipulated that every "slave, free negro, or mulatto" convicted of the rape or attempted rape of a white woman was to be executed. The question was whether the indicted man, the son of a white woman and a "mulatto" man, could himself be categorized as "mulatto." Counsel for Thurman contended that "a mulatto is to be known, not solely by color, kinky hair, or slight admixture of negro blood . . . but by reputation, by his reception into society, and by the exercise of certain privileges." The state countered that a "mulatto" was a person of "any admixture of the white and African race," prompting one judge to query: "If the statute against mulattoes is by construction to include quadroons, then where are we to stop? If we take the first step by construction, are we not bound to pursue the line of descendants, so long as there is a drop of negro blood remaining?" Although that would be closer to the situation in the South in the decades following emancipation, a white lawmaker in the slave South construed this possibility as absurd. The state supreme court decided that the alleged rapist was not in fact a "mulatto."[43]

The presence of free people of African ancestry, and of slaves who might pass into freedom because of their appearance, rendered unreliable the equations of blackness and slavery, and of whiteness and freedom. Into this category fell the children and descendants of white women and black men. Georgia plantation mistress Ella Gertrude Clanton Thomas recorded "a singular little circumstance" in her 1858 diary that illuminates the quandaries of racial categories. When a man at the front gate informed Thomas that her husband had sent him, she worried that he might not be a white man but did not wish to "insult him if he was." At dinner, the man commented that he could not vote, and Thomas asked if that was " 'in consequence of your mother or father.' " The visitor, it turned out, was the son of a white woman and a black man. Thomas refrained from informing him that the same law that prohibited voting also " 'did not allow him to sit at a white lady's table' " but later noted that she "felt sorry for the poor fellow—He may indeed merit the expression of *base* born."[44] Free African Americans were troublesome to white Southerners throughout the antebellum era, but the children of white women and black men carried in their identity the added burden of displaying defiance not only of race and status but also of the rules of patriarchy: whether with direct intention or not, white women had defied white men, and black men had defied white men. As one white person noted in 1859, "As long as there are Negro slaves in Virginia, and bad white women, we shall have a mulatto population free."[45] That population relentlessly troubled Southern slavery.

Even the growing authority of racial theory in both intellectual and popular circles by the mid-nineteenth century could not solve the problems of slavery, freedom, and ancestry, for much could depend, as in the cases of Joseph Nunez and Franklin Hugly, on perceived local appearance, treatment, reputation, and self-presentation. One's daily life in a Southern community could defy the precision of abstract racial categories, while at the same time that life could be lived in a remarkably ambiguous manner. Some neighbors thought that Joseph Nunez looked and acted like a white man, while others thought he looked and acted like a black man. Neighbors suspected that Franklin Hugly's father was a black man, but no one knew for sure. Because Southern laws decreed that a child's status as slave or free followed the mother, sanctions against sex between white women and black men helped to ensure the perpetuation of slavery based on race. Once that law was in place, beginning in the colonial era, white Southerners constructed laws and taboos against sexual liaisons between white women and black men, in part to avoid augmenting a class of free people of African ancestry residing in a society based upon racial slavery.[46] Yet fornication and adultery between white women and black men, as well as legal marriages between people of ambiguous ancestry, produced free children of African ancestry in the South from the colonial era through the Civil War. White communities coped with such liaisons in different ways. In the absence of children and heirs, white Southerners reacted to at least some of those liaisons with a degree of equanimity. The female transgressors were judged and ostracized and may have suffered violence at the hands of fathers and husbands, though not necessarily or markedly more than would a white woman who had transgressed with a white man. The men may have suffered violence at the hands of their masters or other white citizens, but not because whites leapt to conclusions about rape.

Where children and heirs were involved, the circumstances could be more dire: the enslaved children of Nell and Charles claimed freedom; Polly Lane and Dorothea Bourne had children who had to be supported; the Nunez neighbors wanted to purchase slaves; and Sullivan and Hugly relations wanted an inheritance. Thus were sexual liaisons between white women and black men brought into the legal arena. Had the buyers of Joseph Nunez's slaves given up on the purchase, or had the relatives of Franklin Hugly decided to let the inheritance alone, white people would not have had a chance to tell their stories of racial perception. As it turned out, each of these stories came to be told because of the legal and social difficulties inherent in the offspring of a white woman and a black man in the slave South. And in each story, white neighbors revealed a concern for the specific consequences of the liaison between a white woman and a black man more than any concern at the fact of the liaison by itself. Although silence in the historical records of the antebellum South does not by itself indicate the absence of white outrage at sexual liaisons between white women and black men, it is significant that when such liaisons were in fact recorded, the outrage of whites formed no part of that record. Only with the demise of slavery as keeper of the social order would white Southerners react almost uniformly to sex between a white woman and a black man with lethal fury.

Although the "mixed" offspring of people of European ancestry and people of African ancestry indicate clearly that race is far from a transhistorical phenomenon, to nineteenth-century Southerners race was a very real category. Polly and Jim's child, Dorothea and Edmond's children, Joseph Nunez and probably Franklin Hugly—each of these people, and others like them, were the products of sex between white women and black men, and as free people of African ancestry each one therefore brought confusions of color and status to antebellum Southern communities. Yet as long as the mighty institution of slavery remained in place, so, too, did a mostly satisfactory, if at times unreliable, system of stratification. That was all soon to change, however, with the Civil War and emancipation.

Part Two

Escalating Violence

The four years of upheaval that the Civil War brought to Southern communities also brought significant changes in the meaning of sexual liaisons between black men and white women. Accordingly, the focus must shift from the outbreak of the war forward: the consequences of such liaisons would no longer play out solely as community dramas of gossip, disapproval, and anguish. With black freedom came new fears and brutalities on the part of white people, and local stories concerning practical life in small communities now fade in favor of larger social and political chronicles. Sex between black men and white women now became a frequent and direct topic in the arena of national politics. Indeed, the invention of the word *miscegenation* in 1864 was the strategy of one political party against another. At the same time, wartime documents shed new light on the dynamics of sexual liaisons between black men and white women as they had come to pass under slavery, for during the war the voices of black men emerge for the first time.

Recall that when a white community in the antebellum South confronted a sexual liaison between a black man and a white woman, the man rarely had a chance to tell his story for the historical record. The voices of Southern white men have been most clearly audible in the stories of sex between black men and white women thus far recounted. Documents offer the versions of local authorities like Jesse Hargrave, the county magistrate who wrote up a bastardy warrant for Polly Lane; of well-to-do slaveowners like Edmond's master, John Richardson, who protected his slave; of professionals like Dr. Dudley W. Hammond, who lectured on the science of racial categorization. The voices of white men of lesser standing have also been perceptible: struggling farmers like Lewis Bourne or poorer men like Polly Lane's father, who refused to divulge his daughter's whereabouts. Voices of transgressing white women have also come through, often (though not always) mediated through someone else's story. There is Nell Butler's retort to Lord Baltimore, Polly Lane's testimony on the witness stand, and Dorothea Bourne's petition of grievances. There are also white women's versions of other people's transgressions: those who recounted the wedding of Nell and Charles, neighborhood women who guessed at the race of Polly's baby; the midwife who defended Dorothea

Bourne; the women who claimed to have danced on the same floor as James Nunez; and those who offered opinions on Franklin Hugly's racial status.

By contrast, white people attributed only two words to Charles, in their recollections that he referred to Nell as his "old woman." Jim's lawyers referred to "the story which the negro told us," though only fragments of that story were recorded. Edmond's voice was recorded only in the master's story that the slave had tried to "forsake" the white woman, and in the story that Edmond agreed provisionally to provide for one of the children. White people who recounted the story of James Nunez did not attribute one word or thought to this black man. And although Amos Hugly once confided in a neighbor that a black man slept in his house when he was absent, that man was never again mentioned, let alone named, nor were any words or thoughts attributed to him. Only the actions and words of a few black men have allowed a glimpse of defiance on the subject of sex with white women in the antebellum South. Recall the slave, Delks Moses, who eluded authorities in Virginia by violently threatening white people and living with a white woman. Recall the slave George, who assaulted and murdered a white man in North Carolina, and the free Redding Evans of Georgia, who taunted and murdered a white man.

In contrast to all that has come before, then, the middle of the Civil War brought a moment in which the voices of black men were set on record, not in county archives but in the chronicles of the national government. The tellers were mostly white men who had spoken with black men, and thus the voices remain mediated through those who held greater power. At the same time, because black men were the original storytellers, the voices of the transgressing white women are, for once, mediated through those of their male partners. And in some instances black men did speak directly on the subject of sex with white women.

Wartime Stories

"I will tell you a fact that I have never seen alluded to publicly, and I suppose a man would be scouted who should allude to it publicly," stated Captain Richard J. Hinton, "but my relations with the colored people have led me to believe that there is a large amount of intercourse between white women and colored men." So Captain Hinton, an ardent white abolitionist who commanded black troops during the Civil War, testified in

1863.[1] Hinton spoke before the American Freedmen's Inquiry Commission, which had been formed under the War Department to foster the incorporation of emancipated slaves into American society. The AFIC, composed of three white antislavery men, would ultimately propose the establishment of the Freedmen's Bureau to assist former slaves in their transition to free labor. Although the word *intercourse* was often used in the nineteenth century to mean conversation or interaction, Hinton's later testimony makes his particular meaning clear.[2] And Hinton was not the only witness to retell the stories of black men on the subject of sex with white women. The indexer for the wartime commission saw fit to make entries under the letter "I" for "Illicit intercourse between white women & black men not uncommon" and "Intercourse between white women and colored men common — Instances of." [3]

James Redpath, another white abolitionist and a self-described revolutionary, had traveled through the South during the 1850s to talk with black residents. Testifying before the AFIC, Redpath first elaborated on the depravity of white men who sexually exploited slave women, which prompted one commissioner to ask: "Well sir, among such a universal system of libertinage what is the effect upon white women?" Speaking of his black informants, Redpath answered: "I have often heard them talking and laughing about the numerous cases that have occurred in which white women have had colored children." One black man told Redpath that "it was just as common for colored men to have connection with white women, as for white men to have to do with colored women." Another said that "it was an extremely common thing among all the handsome mulattoes at the South to have connection with the white women." Redpath relayed an episode, told to him by a black man, about a white woman "of good family" in Mobile, Alabama, who carried on an affair with a slave, had sex with him on the morning of her wedding, and bore his child nine months later. Redpath concluded: "There is a great deal more of this than the public suspect." [4] Another white man, Samuel B. Lucille, who had lived for two years on a cotton plantation near Natchez, Mississippi, likewise told the wartime commission that "the cross between a white woman and a black man" was "not uncommon," adding: "I knew well a ferry man on the Wachita River, whose mother was a white woman and his father a black man. He was a free voter, but it was notorious in the neighborhood that he was a half-blooded negro." [5] Likely giving a more accurate perspective to the question of frequency, a freedman named J. W. Lindsay who had lived in Tennessee, North Carolina, Georgia, and Alabama told the commission, "There are very few mulattoes that come from pure white women, though I have known some cases of that kind." [6] The testimony of Major George L. Stearns, a white abolitionist who led recruitment efforts for black Union soldiers throughout the North before he organized black troops out of Nashville, told the commissioners: "I have often been amused that the planters here in Tennessee have sometimes to watch their daughters to keep them from intercourse with the negroes. This, though of course exceptional, is yet common enough to be a source of uneasiness to parents." [7]

The rarity of such information becomes apparent in the trajectory of James Redpath's testimony. Although Redpath told the commission about sexual liaisons between black men and white women in considerable detail, he had withheld such knowledge from the public just a few significant years earlier. In a collection of his dispatches from the South published in 1859, Redpath "most solemnly" declared "that in no one instance have I sought either to darken or embellish the truth—to add to, subtract from, or pervert a single statement of the slaves." Yet with one brief exception Redpath had in fact omitted information about sexual liaisons between black men and white women from the book, instead extolling the chastity of Southern white women and sympathizing with them for the immoral conduct of their white husbands, fathers, and brothers. Perhaps Redpath had understood (along with his publisher) how dangerous to the cause of abolition would be any disclosure of sex between black men and white women in the volatile years before the outbreak of war. Four years later, Redpath, Richard Hinton, and a few others seized on the wartime juncture of social and political upheaval to quote the stories they had heard from black men, and some black men themselves spoke publicly about white women and sex. As it turned out, the officers of the AFIC suppressed all of these stories. Only in the brief interval of wartime disruption were the voices of black men given credence in a public arena.[8]

Significant notes of defiance can be detected in the voices of the black men recorded by white abolitionists during the war. The wartime testimony before the AFIC offers a glimpse of well-guarded circles of black men, both free and slave, as one setting in which they could speak boldly about sex with white women. Listen to Patrick H. Minor, a black man who had worked as a steward on the Mississippi River. Minor, later a commissioned officer in the war, told Hinton that black men who worked on the river shared information among themselves about the desires of certain white women to "sleep with them." Recall James Redpath's words about his black informants: "I have often heard them talking and laughing about the numerous cases that have occurred in which white women have had colored children." Even if Hinton and Redpath were embellishing their stories, there is no reason to doubt that black men traded information and laughed together about the scorning of social and legal injunctions.[9]

If black men who had sex with white women (or who speculated on that possibility) bragged among themselves, the wartime dialogues also reveal evidence of stern disapproval within their own communities. The sentiments of a black man who had fled the South for Canada were likely shared by others; the town's white mayor reported to the wartime commission: "A colored man ran away with a white girl, and a colored man, speaking of the affair, said 'I always looked upon him as a respectable man. I didn't think he would fall so low as to marry a white girl.' "[10] Indeed, the wartime testimony illuminates ideas within black communities about the depravity of all white women. Unlike white Southerners, black Southerners did not necessarily make distinctions of virtue based on class. Even approval on the part of black communities indicates suspicions about the decency of any white woman. A black Methodist bishop who had also left the South for Canada told the commissioners that when a black man and a white woman got married, "If the man is an upright man, and the woman an upright woman, they treat them as if they were both colored." This man also mentioned two black men, a grocery keeper and a house plasterer, both married to white women; those women, he said, were accorded as much respect as "any black woman." (Perhaps not surprisingly, in the AFIC report incorporating this testimony, Commissioner Samuel Gridley Howe altered this—whether unwittingly or not—to read that the wives were "as much respected as any white woman.")[11] Other black refugees from the South to Canada offered similar opinions about relationships with white women while talking to the government in 1863. A barber named John Kinney commented: "I want to have a woman I am not ashamed to go into the street or into company with, and that people won't make remarks about." A white teacher named Mr. Sinclair similarly recalled: "Quite a noise was made about the marriage of a black man to a white woman, about four years ago, and the blacks seemed as much displeased as the whites."[12] Susan Boggs, who had escaped from slavery in Virginia and may have been the only woman to speak to the commission on this subject, recounted: "My son married a white woman. Not that his marrying a white woman made it any better for me."[13]

The voices of the black men in this wartime testimony also offer a narrative about sex with white women heretofore unilluminated. Along with registering a measure of defiance on the part of the men, the wartime narratives also reveal the possibility of sexual coercion by white women, and the dangers of resistance, especially for a black man who had sex with a white woman of the planter classes. The accounts of black men recorded in the wartime testimony moreover include information about illicit liaisons with planters' daughters or plantation mistresses—information rarely if ever recorded in detail before the war.[14]

Black men told Richard Hinton in no uncertain terms that some white women in the South sought out sex with them. Hinton recounted a conversation he had had with the black steamboat steward, Patrick Minor, who informed Hinton of the women of a particular white family; according to Minor, "the colored men on that river knew that the women of the Ward family of Louisville, Kentucky, were in the habit of having the stewards, or other fine looking fellows, sleep with them when they were on the boats." Minor also relayed a personal anecdote about a Ward woman who, when on Minor's boat, had offered him five dollars to arrive at her house in Louisville at a particular time. Minor waited for the woman until he had to return to work, and although the rendezvous never took place, the black man "had no doubt that she wanted him to have connection with her."[15]

James Redpath heard similar stories. One black informant, when pressed on how liaisons with a white woman came to pass, said: " 'I will tell you how it is here. I will go up with the towels, and when I go into the room the woman will keep following me with her eyes, until I take notice of it, and one thing leads to another. Others will take hold of me and pull me on to the sofa, and others will stick out their foot and ask one to tie their boot, and I will take hold of their foot, and say "what a pretty foot!' " " Thus did the black men inform their white Northern listeners that a white woman from a planter family could force a black man to have sex. "I have never yet found a bright looking colored man, whose confidence I have won," Hinton testified, "who has not told me of instances where he has been compelled, either by his mistress, or by white women of the same class, to have connection with them." Hinton also recounted a conversation with a white Kansas doctor who knew "from his experience in Virginia and Missouri, that a very large number of white women, especially the daughters of the smaller planters, who were brought into more direct relations with the negro, had compelled some one of the men to have something to do with them." A former slave likewise told Hinton about his experience with his forty-year-old widowed mistress. The man, who had been "brought up in the family," said that he had "never had anything to do with his mistress until after her husband died" but that almost a year into her widowhood, the woman "ordered him to sleep with her, and he did regularly." [16]

It is imperative to approach the wartime testimony of white abolitionists recounting the stories told by black men with caution. White Northern ideas about race, gender, and sexuality were no more straightforward than white Southern ideas. Richard Hinton, for one, simultaneously invoked and contradicted the impression of black men as especially sexual. Hinton spoke of black men as reluctant to comply with the sexual aggressions of white women while simultaneously holding to the idea of black male sexual ardor. When Hinton told the AFIC a story about a white woman who pressed a black man into having sex with her, one commissioner commented, "He didn't need much persuasion, did he?" Hinton answered, "I have generally found that, unless the woman has treated them kindly, and won their confidence, they have to be threatened, or have their passions roused by actual contact, which a woman who goes as far as that would not hesitate to give." Yet elsewhere Hinton put forth ideas about black male potency, though he never attributed violent lust to black men. For example, he concluded a story about white frontier women who wished to "give loose to their passions" by saying, "And I suppose, as the negro is very strongly amative, that the gratification of passion would be greater with them than with a white man." [17]

If these Northern abolitionists thought black men capable of greater passion, they also believed the white women of the South, often without distinction of class, to be downright corrupt. The theme of profligacy among Southern white women and men of all classes was common in Northern antislavery thought, and whites who testified before the AFIC unmistakably drew upon this tradition. Hinton's portrayal of all Southern white women as totally licentious no doubt served his political convictions. "The complete demoralization of the South is astonishing," he told the commissioners. "I have seen white women who call themselves ladies, stand on the street and call minor officers, as they were passing by, 'sons of bitches,' 'God damn' them, and use all such phrases; and I have never been to any locality where the officers and men, who were so disposed, did not sleep with all the women around." [18] Another Northern white man, who had spent two winters in the Gulf states, divided the Southern white population into "two classes, slave and nonslaveholding," commenting that "females of both classes . . . resign themselves to folly and degrada-tion." Of all poorer whites, he said, "a more degraded, profligate, ignorant and sinful race cannot easily be imagined." [19] Some such pronouncements included inferences about sex between black men and white women, for example Hinton's story about the Missouri frontier where white settlers from North Carolina and Tennessee had accumulated wealth. The daugh-ters in these families, he said, "knew that their brothers were sleeping with the chambermaids, or other servants, and I don't see how it could be otherwise than that they too should give loose to their passions." [20] In one published report, Commissioner Howe wrote, "It is certain that the inevi-table tendency of American slavery is not only to bring about promiscuous intercourse among the blacks, and between black women and white men, but also to involve white women in the general depravity, and to lower the standard of female purity." He continued, "The subject is repulsive, but whoever examines critically the evidence of the social condition of the Slave States, sees that the vaunted superior virtue of Southern women is mere boast and sham." [21]

For their part, white Southerners entered into this national dialogue by counteraccusing Northern white women of having sex with black men, fastening particularly on those who came South to teach in the freed-people's schools during the war. One Southern white army captain wrote in 1864 about "Yankee 'School marms' who philanthropically miscege-nate as well as teach," noting sarcastically "the prolific birth of mongrel babies by these worthy school mistresses." And a Southern newspaper re-ported shortly after the war that white abolitionist Harriet Beecher Stowe would open a school in Georgia for "mulatto children that have been born in the South since its invasion by Yankee schoolmarms." [22]

The stories of black men who confided in white abolitionists, then, were filtered through white Northern ideas about sex and sexuality in the slave South, as well as through an antislavery and anti-South agenda that included free elaboration of white Southern depravities. Other cautions are also in order. Perhaps the white men were so surprised by what a few black men told them about sexual coercion that they repeated the startling scenarios with exaggeration. Perhaps they were exaggerating their roles as white insiders among black people or as Northern insiders among Southerners. Or exaggeration may have been spurred by their own anxieties at the thought of white women desiring black men. It is also possible that the black informants themselves had recast their experiences with white women in their conversations with Northern white men, crafting their narratives as stories of coercion in order to present themselves as innocent participants in such potentially dangerous transgressions. Combine this with the possibility of male boasting about illicit sexual conquests, and it is indeed difficult to decipher the various perceptions of what had come to pass between these black men and the white women about whom they spoke.[23]

At the same time, however, the possibility that white men like Hinton and Redpath wholly invented their testimony before the AFIC, or that the black men fabricated the stories they told to white abolitionists, is contradicted by a more direct, if rarer, record of a black woman's voice. In her 1861 autobiography, fugitive slave Harriet Jacobs indicated that black women knew about white women coercing black men into sex in the antebellum South. Of planters' daughters, Jacobs wrote unambiguously: "They know that the women slaves are subject to their father's authority in all things; and in some cases they exercise the same authority over the men slaves. I have myself seen the master of such a household whose head was bowed down in shame; for it was known in the neighborhood that his daughter had selected one of the meanest slaves on his plantation to be the father of his first grandchild." Jacobs further pointed out that this white woman "did not make her advances to her equals, nor even to her father's more intelligent servants." Rather, she "selected the most brutalized, over whom her authority could be exercised with less fear of exposure."[24]

A few antebellum legal documents also support the wartime stories about sexual coercion by white women of slaveowning families. A central Kentucky court rendered a ruling in 1841, for example, that acknowledged such powers of a white woman over a black man. The woman, named Thomason Grady, "cohabited with a black man named James Hog and sometimes called James Grady." When Thomason tried to sell some of her land, she was stopped by the laws of coverture on the grounds that she was married to James. Although the court found "abundant proof" of cohabitation (apparently tolerated), it also declared that because "James was a slave" whom the white woman *"sometimes threatened to sell,"* that fact "would alone be sufficient to repel the presumption of marriage." Instead, the court proclaimed, "the presumption should be, that the relation between the black man slave and free white woman, was that of *concubinage* rather than *marriage*." Although this reveals nothing about the relationship from the perspectives of Thomason and James, the jurists recognized that a relationship between a male slave and female slaveholder could not embody the mutuality that marriage was meant to imply. Suspicions about the desires of elite white women even occasionally crept into the musings of Southern patriarchs. In 1858, a white Georgian wrote disdainfully of supposed Northern marriages between black men and white women, adding, "Do not many of our pretty white girls even now, permit illicit negro embrace at the South. . . . We have as many of these black devils to manage now, and *keep from our women,* as we can." [25]

Antebellum documents also support the fact that white women from poorer families could attempt to coerce black men into sexual liaisons. Recall the words of John Richardson, who thought that his slave Edmond had "been disposed to forsake" Dorothea, which had in turn "been the cause of her often visiting my negro houses and staying all night in the quarters," indicating that Edmond may not have been a completely willing partner.[26] Those words remain elusive, yet at least one antebellum document is explicit enough to lend a good dose of credibility to the wartime stories about the coercion of black men by white women. In 1813 in Virginia's Shenandoah Valley, a slave named David twice broke into the home of the white Getts family and went on violent rampages, swinging an ax, throwing rocks, and threatening to kill either Mr. Getts or his daughter, Dolly. After David's sentencing, a number of white citizens asked the governor for a pardon: Dolly and David, it seemed, had sustained "a considerable intimacy" for at least three years, for which Dolly had received "a severe whipping" from her father "for keeping company" with David. One petitioner, who had caught the two together more than once, claimed that Dolly "admitted to me that his (David's) improper conduct arose from her persuasions" and that she had often pleaded with him "to run off with her which he, for some length of time, refused to accede to." Dolly had "earnestly entreated David to go to her father and tell him they were married, and perhaps they might then be permitted to remain together," but David "refused and wept, charging her with having brought him into this unpleasant situation." Economic motives certainly influenced the decision to seek a pardon (another petitioner described David as "a very likely young Negro man, perfectly sound"); still, in the end, Dolly "confided the truth of the charge." Perhaps Dolly had hoped to escape with David in order to free herself from her father's violence, suggesting the possibility that a white woman who suffered at the hands of a male relative used whatever social authority she could draw upon to flee from an abusive household. To David, however, the impossibility of such an escape, as well as lack of interest in Dolly, may have turned the idea of a tryst into cruel coercion that drove him to retaliate.[27]

The wartime testimony reveals that a liaison with a planter-class white woman was more dangerous for a black man, for the woman could more readily invoke images of chastity in order to allay trouble for herself. Although the sexual coercion of black men could take place among all classes of white women, the white woman's status influenced how local authorities treated the black man. Whites were more likely to blame the man if the woman belonged to an elite family; indeed, the poorer status of women like Dorothea Bourne and Dolly Getts contributed to the vindication of Edmond and David, respectively. Just as dominant ideology held that black women seduced white men, it also held that poor white women could coerce black men. Even as wealthier white women held the real power of coercion, they were protected from censure by those who held authority in their communities and by dominant ideas about white female virtue. And in such equations of seduction and coercion, only "seduced" white men were wholly innocent. In the wartime testimony, a black underground railroad agent and recruiter of black Union soldiers, William D. Matthews, told Richard Hinton about another black man who relayed that "a young girl got him out in the woods and told him she would declare he attempted to force her, if he didn't have connection with her." Patrick Minor told Hinton "several cases of the same kind." Although the class status of these particular women remains unspecified, poorer white women might not have attempted such a threat, or if they had, might have found themselves discredited and maligned.[28]

Questions about agency and consent are difficult to untangle, but black men's own accounts of their instrumentality in liaisons with elite white women offer some clues. James Redpath asked one man who had spoken of such liaisons: " 'Do you dare to make advances?' " to which the man replied: " 'No, we know too much for that.' " Another of Redpath's informants pointed out, " 'If I have connection with a white girl she knows that if she takes precautions she is safe, for if I should tell I should be murdered by her father, her brother, or herself.' " These words point to black men's fears of violent retribution should those men engage in sex with elite white women in the slave South. Redpath in fact told the commission that he had "heard of half a dozen cases in which colored men have been killed because of their intimacy with white women." Likewise pointing to the power of white women in his discussion of Missouri frontier daughters, Richard Hinton observed: "It was a great deal safer for them to have one of these colored fellows than a white man." If a black man in the slave South complied with a white woman either willingly or against his will, that compliance would also in some measure have been strategic. Like Edmond in his liaison with Dorothea Bourne, the men who told their stories to Hinton and Redpath would have been neither simply victims nor simply assenting partners. Just as some black women were able to risk fending off white men, some black men who were propositioned must also have risked refusal. Yet in a liaison with an elite white woman, it was not only more dangerous for a black man to consort, but also more dangerous for him to resist or refuse.[29]

The wartime stories also illuminate the problem of an elite white woman producing a child whose father was black. The black men who spoke to white abolitionists pointed out that a planter-class white woman was more likely than her poorer counterparts to have access to effective birth control, indicated by the words of Redpath's informant about taking "precautions." The man who had been ordered to sleep with his widowed mistress told Hinton that the woman had "procured some of those French articles, that are used to prevent the consequences of sexual intercourse," a reference to condoms. Another man told Redpath that white women (of better-off families) and black men had sex "because the thing can be so easily concealed." He explained: "The woman has only to avoid being impregnated, and it is all safe." And of the white Mobile woman who apparently conceived a child with a black man on her wedding morning, the black narrator told Redpath, "That was not the first time, but she had taken no precautions on that occasion." [30]

Of course, contraceptive measures did not always succeed, and in such cases a wealthier woman confronted the same choices as a poorer one in her attempts to protect herself, her family's honor, and perhaps her black partner. During Hinton's testimony, one of the commissioners prompted him: "But the consequences are terrible to the negro if found out?" When Hinton agreed, the commissioner asked, "What are the consequences to the woman if found out?" to which Hinton replied, "They generally brush it up." Like poorer transgressors, a well-to-do white woman might resort to infanticide or try to send the child away. A black man told Hinton about a planter's daughter in Missouri who had given birth to a "black child" and refused to reveal the father's name until the man escaped to Kansas. "The child was reported to have died," Hinton said, "but the man believes it was killed." That scenario is supported by fugitive slave Harriet Jacobs, who added to her portrayal of a planter's daughter bearing the child of a slave: "In such cases the infant is smothered, or sent where it is never seen by any who know its history." [31] If unmarried, a planter-class white woman could also resort to marrying a white man, hoping that no one could tell the ancestry of her child; perhaps this is what really came to pass in the episode Redpath told of the Mobile woman who had given birth to a black man's child nine months after her wedding. A planter-class patriarch whose daughter transgressed could also send the child into the slave quarters, an option unavailable to poorer white families. As freedman J. W. Lindsay told the wartime commission: "A colored child wouldn't be treated any better, if from a white woman, than one from a black woman by a white father." [32]

The exercise of racial domination by elite white women might also be mixed with romantic emotion, at least for the women. Lindsay also told the commission of "cases where white women fall in love with their servants," though he did not mention whether the black men returned such sentiments. That testimony is also supported by earlier documents; an antebellum traveler to Virginia heard of an instance in which "a planter's daughter having fallen in love with one of her father's slaves, had actually seduced him." [33] Later documents concur, for the descendants of such liaisons told stories about illicit love between black men and planter-class white women. Millie Markham, born in North Carolina about 1855, told the story of her parents, a planter's daughter and a slave. Her mother, a white woman named Tempie James, "lived on her father's big plantation on the Roanoke River" and "fell in love with" Squire James, the family's black coachman. Tempie's parents "raved, begged and pleaded," the daughter recalled, until Tempie insisted: " 'You haven't given me Squire. He's all I do want.' " Squire's master sold him, but according to the story, Tempie ran away, bought and freed the man, and changed his name to Squire Walden. Tempie then drank a cup of whiskey mixed with Squire's blood before she "swore she had Negro blood in her" and the two were married. Tempie James's family disowned her, and the couple had fifteen children. Indeed, Squire Walden is listed in the census of 1850 as a laborer, along with his wife, Temperance, and eight children. If the story is true, Tempie James had altered her racial identity in order to marry a black man: the census taker designated both Squire and Temperance as "mulatto."[34] Adora Rienshaw told a similar tale about her grandparents. Her grandmother was a white woman married to a white man on a Mississippi plantation when she came to "fall in love" with her coach driver, "a coal-black nigger man." According to the recollection, the driver comforted the white woman who often confided in him about her unhappy marriage. When the woman got pregnant, her white husband nearly "went crazy" with fury, and the baby was bound out for twenty-one years. That child was Rienshaw's father.[35]

In the wartime testimony describing sex between black men and white women, white abolitionists thus reversed both gender and racial stereotypes by painting the white women as aggressive and the black men as reluctant. Although white men of the planter classes ruled in the slave South, white women of slaveholding families also commanded power over slaves, both female and male, as well as over free blacks. While those white women may have suffered from and lamented the abuses of the patriarchs who ruled their households, they generally did not challenge that authority. White men of the slaveholding and nonslaveholding yeomanry, and even those of the lowest social ranks of Southern society, also shared a measure of this power by virtue of their membership in the racial category "white." White women outside the planter classes could likewise draw upon that power, if not always successfully.[36] Where a white woman, whether rich or poor, threatened to cry rape (or tried to threaten, or experimented with threatening), the black man must have responded with some combination of disdain, anger, and fear. In such scenarios, it is not difficult to see how the two parties could later arrive at different accounts of the sex that may have ensued. The very institution of racial slavery recast and distorted traditional Southern gender hierarchies by allowing some women (white and free) power over some men (black and especially enslaved).

Stories of reluctance and resistance that black men told to white abolitionists, even if crafted for white ears—and then magnified by the white men who retold the stories—could not have been fabricated out of imagination alone. Rather, the black men would have been drawing on dynamics they knew to exist between black men and white women in the slave South. It is revealing that stories about coercion were often set on record by abolitionists: not only Union men like Richard Hinton and James Redpath but also the fugitive slave Harriet Jacobs. The details of such stories may have been enhanced for the sake of antislavery propaganda, yet abolitionists may also have been among the few to describe the reality of the coercion of black men for the public record.[37] Never before the Civil War had the words of black men on the subject of sex with white women been set down in so sustained a manner. Although there is no way to know how common or uncommon were scenarios such as those the black men described to white Northerners, their voices as recorded during the war years uncover a consequence of Southern slave society that lurked as a possibility regardless of how frequently it came to pass.

Sex and Politics during the War

Whether liaisons between black men and white women occurred less often or more often during the social upheaval of the Civil War is impossible to measure. Wartime conditions meant that fewer white fathers, husbands, and local officials were present to watch over their families and police their communities. At the same time, for both black and white Southerners on the homefront there were the most pressing concerns of food to eat, the destruction of property, and the fate of the Confederacy.[38] Evidence indicates only that sexual liaisons between black men and white women did not cease in wartime. In western North Carolina in 1862, for example, a white man named Jesse Black assaulted his white wife, Tamsey, after discovering her liaison with a black man. The white man, not the unnamed black man, was on trial, and the county court pronounced him guilty of assault. The higher court subsequently ruled that because a husband was "responsible for the acts of his wife," Jesse was permitted to use force to make Tamsey "behave herself." In southern Alabama in 1865, the white Martha Smith was charged with "adultery or fornication" with one of her former slaves, Joe. Martha Smith, not Joe, was on trial, and witnesses testified that the two had been caught in bed together in Martha's room in the house where she boarded.[39] But there is also evidence that Southern authorities tried to crack down on such homefront liaisons just before and during the war. In late 1860 in piedmont North Carolina, for example, N. J. Steward and Matilda Leonard, a free black man and a white woman, were indicted for fornication and adultery. In early 1865, a slave in Richmond, Virginia, was sentenced to two doses of thirty-nine lashes for "associating and cohabiting with his mistress, Delia Mack, a white woman."[40] Liaisons between black men and white women also occurred away from the homefront. For example, a white Northern soldier in Missouri recorded in his 1862 diary that there was "some excitement this morning on account of the disappearance of one of the girls who worked in the factory. She had run away it was said with a negro or mulatto." The record is vague, but it seems the man was caught and tied to a tree, then "delivered to a man . . . who had hired him," possibly a former slavemaster. The young woman came into camp a few days later, offering "ill treatment from her father" as her "reason for running away as she did." She was subsequently "left against her will at the house of a stranger."[41]

Although white Southerners lived in fear of slave uprisings during the war, white women were not necessarily engulfed by sexual alarm when white men went off to war and left them alone with slave men. In 1864, a white Virginia woman described "500 negroes . . . going throughout the county, robbing at every house they stopped at and committing every crime that can be imagined," without any overt expression of panic about rape. Likewise, a white schoolteacher wrote in her Tennessee diary about a group of armed black men being mustered out of service in 1865: "If these corrupted negroes are to be turned loose among us," she commented in a manner that can hardly be characterized as terrified, "I do not know what will follow, but evidently no great amount of good." And a white Georgia woman expressed fear of black men outnumbering white men, but only in regard to insurrection. Even if fears of sexual violence could have been

implied in such words as "crime" and "insurrection," there is a considerable difference between such oblique references and the frenzied ravings
of white women about black male sexuality that would so often be heard
in the post-emancipation South.[42]

Wartime trials of slaves accused of the rape of white women reveal, as in the antebellum years, masters invoking economic interests and
putting forward technical arguments to protect their property, even in the
face of—or likely more vehemently in the face of—the ongoing destruction of slavery. When a slave boy named Sam was accused of raping a
four-year-old white girl in piedmont North Carolina in 1864, the courts
agreed that despite evidence of "an emission of seed," Sam was innocent
on the grounds that someone under age fourteen could not "commit an
assault with intent to commit a rape," thus indicating that concern for the
master's property took precedence over any alarm at the alleged crime.
Yet at the same time, there is evidence of harsher consequences for black
men accused of raping white women during the war. Also in piedmont
North Carolina in 1864, a slave named Wesley McDaniel was sentenced
to death for the attempted rape of a white woman named Mary Boyd and
subsequently pardoned; unlike in antebellum pardons, however, this one
came with the provision that the man receive two whippings of thirty-nine
lashes apiece. And wartime masters, like their antebellum counterparts,
were not always successful in attempts to preserve their human chattel. In
early 1865, when a slave named Elias was convicted of attempting to rape
the white Martha Burton, his master sought a pardon, suggesting that he
would "put him in the army" if the man were allowed to live. Elias was
executed.[43]

Rape trials of black Civil War soldiers also reveal complexities in
wartime white responses. Black women were most often the rape victims
of white soldiers during the Civil War, whether the men were from Union
or Confederate armies, and most wartime rapes, no matter who the victim, must have gone unreported. As for crimes on record, although both
black and white soldiers were tried and executed for rape during the war,
the alleged victims were always white women. Moreover, black men were
brought to trial and executed out of proportion to their numbers, indicating that white men more often got away with the crime. Nonetheless,
when a black soldier was tried for the rape of a white woman, the court did
not consider the man's guilt a foregone conclusion.[44] Dandridge Brooks

and John Shepperd, for example, were part of a group of men from the Thirty-eighth U.S. Colored Infantry who left camp near Richmond, Virginia, one night in 1865 and landed themselves in a courtroom, on trial for rape. Four men had returned to camp early, sensing what was to come; as one of them put it, "I didn't go there for no sick purpose. . . . I didn't want nothing like that at all." But along with two other soldiers, Brooks and Shepperd broke into a house outside the city and among the four of them raped the white Mrs. Fanny Crawford and her fourteen-year-old niece, Eliza Woodson. According to fellow black soldiers, the men had "boasted freely of their crime in conversation with the soldiers of their regiment." The dialogue that ensued between the court and these fellow soldiers (all of whom testified against Brooks and Shepperd) was filled with colloquial language on both sides. One soldier quoted Brooks as saying that he "fucked the young woman." Another heard Brooks say that "he got some, from the young gal." Here, the judge asked, "Did he say he fucked the young gal?" to which the witness replied, "He didn't call out fuck." Likewise at Shepperd's trial, the court queried one of the witnesses as to whether either of the women tried "to prevent him from fucking them?" To another, the court asked, "How many times did the prisoner say he fucked the woman?" The women used different words in their testimony, and the court followed suit in those dialogues. Eliza Woodson relayed that the men had "done violence" to her, and Fanny Crawford allowed that they had "violated my person."

The court rigorously questioned the accusers before arriving at a verdict. Lawyers asked Woodson why she had opened the door in the first place, whether she was dressed when the men knocked, whether a soldier had pulled her dress up or she had done so herself, what she had done "to prevent his putting you on the bed," whether she was "screaming all the while," if she had resisted once on the bed, whether she had struggled as he entered her, and exactly how she had struggled. (When asked "What did he enter your person with?" she answered, "I should think you might know.") Crawford was subjected to equally rigorous questioning, including, "How did the prisoner force your legs apart when he used one hand to hold you down, and the other held the pistol?" Dandridge Brooks's only defense was "I was not in the house," and John Shepperd likewise stated, "I was not at the house that night." Both men were hanged. Just as in the antebellum South, then, black men accused of raping white women were

more likely to be convicted and sentenced to death than white men accused of the same crime. At the same time, whites had not immediately
assumed guilt when white women leveled accusations of rape.[45]

The legal mutilation of black men was also not unknown during
the Civil War. In 1864, two doctors in Georgia's cotton belt carried out
a sentence of castration on a slave convicted of the attempted rape of
a white woman, and one newspaper commented that the action would
rightly "operate as a terrible warning." And in the wartime South as in the
antebellum South, it was not unknown for a black man accused of raping
a white woman to be lynched. Near Athens, Georgia, in 1862 there was
"considerable excitement" over the arrest of a slave accused of attempting to rape a white woman whose husband was away in the army. After
the man's arrest, and despite pleas from various white authorities, a group
of whites "overpowered the Sheriff and his Deputy," took the man a mile
out of town, and hanged him. A crowd of whites from surrounding communities sang and yelled as they followed the vigilantes. Still, two Athens
newspapers denounced the lynching (one editor opined, "Is it not absurd,
then, while our noble army is in the field battling for law and order, that
we at home should be trampling them under foot?").[46]

Wartime liaisons, rape trials, and infrequent lynchings all reveal
points of continuity with the slave South. Black men might suffer harsh
consequences, yet white women could also be blamed for liaisons across
the color line, and black men were not instantly assumed guilty by white
authorities. At the same time, however, with the destruction of slavery and
the seizing of freedom by African-American men and women, the subject
of sex between black men and white women began to acquire new import and urgency among whites. During the Civil War, the issue directly
entered into the arena of national politics in a concerted manner: black
men's hopes for and insistence on equality brought public expressions of
fear from white Southerners, and those fears included direct references
to white women and sex. White concerns over such transgressions now
moved well beyond the realm of neighborhood consternation.

Black men, both Northern and Southern, equated their experiences
as Civil War soldiers with "manhood," connoting the rights of citizenship and equality as well as autonomy. Former slave and acting chaplain
Thomas Long sermonized to the men of his black regiment that serving
as soldiers kept freedom forever in their grasp "because we have showed

our energy and our courage and our naturally manhood." Another former slave similarly assessed his experience as a soldier with these words: "This was the biggest thing that ever happened in my life. I felt like a man with a uniform on and a gun in my hand." Indeed, witnesses before the American Freedmen's Inquiry Commission told of the equation not only between military experience and black manhood but also between newly found freedom and manhood. George Ross, a headwaiter born a slave in Maryland, spoke on this point. "It is a pleasure to a man to work for his own living and pay his own way through the world," he said. "I know what it is to be a man—that is the idea exactly." Sympathetic white men concurred. General John Eaton, superintendent of freedmen in Tennessee, told the commission how the arming of men who had once been enslaved promoted their "manhood," and a superintendent of contrabands told how both military experience and independence allowed black men a sense of "manliness."[47] But white men of the Confederacy sounded alarm at these impending developments. In 1860, a Baptist minister contemplated the end of slavery and speculated on what would happen when "every negro" in the South "will be the equal to every one of you." As he told his fellow citizens: "If you are tame enough to submit, Abolition preachers will be at hand to consummate the marriage of your daughters to black husbands."[48]

The subject of sex between black men and white women explicitly entered the arena of national politics during the Civil War in the presidential election campaign of 1864. It was at this political moment that the Northern Democratic party coined the pejorative term *miscegenation* (from the Latin *miscere,* to mix, and *genus,* race) and asserted that Lincoln's Republican party advocated sex and marriage across the color line. Posing as Republicans, two Northern Democrats distributed an anonymous booklet advocating political and social equality, and specifically the mixture of blacks and whites. The authors wrote that although the "frenzy of love in the white Southern woman for the negro" was rarely acted on, plantation mistresses had a stake in slavery because it permitted them sexual access to black men. Yet until racial prejudice was overcome, the authors maintained, the "full mystery of sex—the sweet, wild dream of a perfect love . . . can never be generally known," and thus should white women be entitled to black husbands. The Democratic posers also wrote about the desire of black men for white women, contending: "Our police courts give painful evidence that the passion of the colored race for the white is often so uncontrollable as to over come the terror of the law." The publication was ignored or renounced by Republicans, and most readers viewed it with suspicion; but the fears on which its white Northern authors played would be expressed with great seriousness by white Southerners beginning in the Reconstruction era and continuing into the twentieth century.[49]

With utmost solemnity, Democratic politicians brought the specter of sex between black men and white women into wartime congressional debates over racial equality, whether discussing integrated transportation and schools or the advent of black suffrage.[50] In an 1864 Senate exchange about the exclusion of blacks from railroad cars in Washington, D.C., one Maryland Democrat introduced the point that a white woman marrying a black man would provoke a "trembling, anxious, depressing, harassing, crushing fear" on the part of the woman's male family members. Less than a year after the war ended, a Democratic senator from Kentucky announced that any further empowerment of the Freedmen's Bureau would mean that black men could marry white women in violation of his state's laws. Another Southern senator pronounced that "miscegenation would be encouraged" if whites were "cut off from position and office and political power" and blacks were to become "the ruling power of the country." Although this man did not specifically define "miscegenation" as sex between black men and white women (as opposed to black women and white men), he implied as much in his portrait of politically powerful black men. White Republicans joined in this dialogue about race, politics, and sex by pointing out the absurdity of conflating black suffrage with sex across the color line. A Pennsylvania Republican wondered in 1866 how anyone could believe that marriage with a white woman would result "because a colored man is allowed to drop a little bit of paper in a box." For their part, black men countered by reminding white men of their own participation in such transgressions. "The white man says he don't want to be placed on equality with the negro," said North Carolina leader Abraham H. Galloway just after the war. "Why, Sir," he pronounced, "if you could only see him slipping around at night, trying to get into negro women's houses, you would be astonished."[51]

Thus did white Southern politicians begin during the Civil War to conflate the possibility of freedom and rights for black men with a fear of widespread sex between black men and white women. With emancipation and the end of the war, Southern whites who sought to maintain the racial hierarchy would begin systematically to invoke the idea that free and newly empowered black men would inevitably desire sex with white women. At first, Southern whites focused their fears largely on marriage and consensual liaisons. The threat of rape, though present in some measure in wartime and Reconstruction white rhetoric, would be much more blatantly emphasized and much more violently acted on in the last decades of the century.

Black men's stories of defiance, danger, and coercion recorded during the Civil War got no farther than the government commission. In the end, except for expounding upon the depravity of Southern white women, the American Freedmen's Inquiry Commission kept the testimony it had heard about sex between black men and white women a secret from Congress and the public. Richard Hinton's testimony covered thirty-two pages, with the information about black men and white women occupying the last six of those pages. On the cover sheet someone had penciled: "This paper can be printed as far as this mark × on page 27. The remaining portion should be suppressed." The "x" marked Hinton's disclosure about sex between black men and white women. The AFIC's final report did not address the subject of sex between black men and white women; the commission had clearly judged it too controversial to let any readers believe that emancipation would bring sex between black men and white women in its wake, especially if such liaisons could not be written off as the province of the poorer classes of white women.[52]

In the Civil War years, Southern dialogues on sex between black men and white women moved beyond the realm of village crossroads and into the arena of sectional and national politics. White Southerners now began to alter their strategies in responding, not only to such liaisons, but also to the idea of such liaisons. Under slavery, sex between black men and white women violated the rules of patriarchy and racial hierarchy, and yet had never overwhelmingly threatened either system. With the demise of slavery, however, evolving—or devolving—white ideas about the dangers of black male sexuality would become intimately intertwined in the violent politics of the Reconstruction South.

Black freedom brought a marked shift away from uneasy white toleration for sex between black men and white women, and a move toward increasingly violent intolerance. In the antebellum South, the dividing line of black slavery and white freedom had sufficiently if imperfectly sustained racial hierarchy, but with the demise of slavery, the maintenance of this hierarchy through other means became essential to white Southerners. Thus did the "mixture" of European and African ancestry come to be a much more serious taboo than ever before. Whereas in the antebellum South racial hierarchy had rested on the categories of "black" and "white" as well as on the categories of slavery and freedom, now categories of color bore the entire burden of upholding the racial hierarchy. The new freedoms claimed by black men and women were extremely troubling to whites, but it was the newfound autonomy of the men among the former slaves that carried the gravest danger, especially in the eyes of white patriarchs. Because it was the men of the free black population who now gained formal political power and began to achieve economic independence, it was they who had enormous potential to destroy the South's racial caste system. Intertwining these unfamiliar dangers—the possibility of blurring the categories of "black" and "white" in a world without racial slavery, and the alarm of diminishing white supremacy—white people fastened on the taboo of sex between black men and white women with newfound urgency.[1]

More concretely, the vanquished white patriarchs of the Old South feared the loss of control over sex between blacks and whites. Under slavery, that control had permitted unchecked sex between white men and black women. Indeed, Southern patriarchs would soon devise a rationale by which they could retain their power of sexual exploitation over black women while claiming that sex between black men and white women would destroy the white race. After emancipation, expressions of white anxiety about sex between black men and white women reached an unprecedented intensity. "Americans are not squeamish as to jokes; but you must not jest in their society about the loves of black men for white women," observed a British traveler to the South in 1867. "Merely for paying a compliment where it is thought he should not, a negro would be flogged and tarred and hung. No punishment would be deemed brutal and fierce enough for such a sinner."[2] The early years of Reconstruction marked the beginning of an era of terrorism in the American South. Those vanquished patriarchs and their sympathizers replaced slavery with lethal violence in an effort to maintain control over the political, economic, and social activities of freedpeople, including control over the sexual agency of black men and women. At the same time, following the social upheaval of wartime, they sought to reassert control over white women.

The intertwining of politics and sex in the minds of white Southerners is betrayed throughout testimony taken in the congressional investigation of the Ku Klux Klan in 1871. In these years, the Klan's actions represented the common concerns of whites who hoped to retain a racial hierarchy without the institution of slavery.[3] In justifying violence, Klansmen and their supporters conflated the recently won political and economic authority of black men with alleged sexual liaisons with white women. And although the Klan purported to protect "white womanhood," in fact only certain white women were accorded that protection. The dialogues that ensued between congressmen and the black and white witnesses called before them differed markedly from the neighborhood conversations about sex between black men and white women that had come to pass in antebellum communities. White neighbors no longer merely quarreled among themselves over the innocence or guilt of the transgressors. Now conflicts over sex between black men and white women were played out violently by a regionwide white supremacist organization that directed terrorist tactics at entire black communities. And the subject of sex between black men and white women came to matter beyond community boundaries. Such liaisons were no longer solely local problems about illegitimate children, dishonored white husbands, or neighborhood identity. The subject now gained a place in wider ideological dialogues over sectional struggles. Sex between black men and white women now mattered not only locally but also nationally. At the same time, community responses to such liaisons more frequently came to pass outside the realm of law.

Terrorizing Black Men

After the war, Southern states set out to renew laws that prohibited marriage across the color line. Although many freedpeople looked down on marriage to whites, most emphatically did not wish to see it criminalized, knowing that statutes would be enforced largely against black men without protection for black women compelled into concubinage. The annals of Reconstruction document both legal and extralegal liaisons between black men and white women, but the frequency of such liaisons remains difficult to determine.[4] The record makes clear only that black men and white women who wished to marry each other encountered both legal and social obstacles, including white violence. In Virginia in 1866, for example, a black man failed to appear at his wedding to a white woman after he learned that local whites "had made preparations to treat him to a coat of tar and cotton." When Jackson Hayley and Susan Fly applied for a marriage license in Virginia in 1867, the clerk cited a law against "such unnatural affiliations." Hayley expressed indignation and invoked his civil rights to no avail.[5] In Tennessee in the late 1860s, a woman was "warned by the police that she must not live with her husband because he is black." The woman appealed to the Freedmen's Bureau by attempting to prove that she was "in reality a colored woman"; although this may have been the case, it might also have been a tactic to ensure the couple's safety.[6] An Alabama judge refused to issue a marriage license to the white Stella Cusack for marriage to a black man in 1872, though the two were "anxious to be 'joined in matrimony.' " The man was skeptical of help from the Freedmen's Bureau "in this case because of its character." In Mississippi in 1874, a freedman who was serving in the state legislature married a white woman. There was "a good deal of talk," and the woman's father mentioned murder, though black neighbors "threatened to burn the town and wreak vengeance on the people if a hair of that negro's head was harmed." The couple fled, and when a black man publicly named the white woman's family, rumors flew that the informer had advised other black men to pick their white wives "from the best families in this State."[7] Those who did marry could be convicted of fornication on the grounds that the union was legally void. Such was the fate of Aaron Green and Julia Atkinson, who wed in Alabama in the summer of 1876 only to find themselves arrested shortly thereafter. Atkinson served two years in prison. When Robert Hoover determined that "it was lawful for him to marry a white woman" in Alabama, a minister married him to Betsey Litsey. Less than a year later, in 1876, the two were charged with living in a one-room house, even though they "recognized each other as husband and wife." Hoover was convicted and then pardoned on the condition that he cease "this very gross offence against morals and decorum."[8]

Some couples tried to avoid the dangers of legally sanctioned marriage all together. In 1866, a discharged Union soldier named Ben Leslie ("a very black negro") and a white woman named Mollie Furlow "were disturbed from their sweet slumbers" by Mississippi authorities who sought proof of their sleeping in the same bed in order to make an arrest. One newspaper predicted that "the sable lover and his white paramour, will be assigned lodgings in the Penitentiary for a term of years." Couples might also leave town, though not without consequences for their families. In Virginia in 1870, after a black man eloped with his white employer's daughter, a shoot-out ensued between relatives of the runaways.[9]

White women also continued to resort to desperate measures if they found themselves pregnant by a black partner. When one "new-born male mulatto infant, born seemingly alive," was found in 1866, a Virginia paper reported that an "alarming" number of black infants were turning up dead. The editors made disparaging comments about black mothers, but it is possible that white women were among the guilty. As one Alabama newspaper reported in 1867: "A white woman was arrested by the Police yesterday, on the charge of strangling a colored infant, to which she gave birth last Thursday."[10]

As in antebellum cases, the motivations of Reconstruction-era transgressors remain elusive, with few defiant voices on record. Freedman Richard Hill recounted a white woman saying that "if she felt disposed to fall in love with or marry a black man, it was nobody's business but hers." Countering the views of many black leaders, Hill added that "if the colored race get all their rights, and particularly their equal rights before the law," such a union "would not hurt the nation or trouble the nation." A letter to the Freedmen's Bureau in 1867 more directly reveals the sentiments of a transgressing white woman. Carrie and Sandy Hall had been married by an ordained minister in Georgia but lived apart while Sandy labored on an Alabama plantation. Carrie Hall described how a number of years ago she "became very much attached to this colored gentleman . . . and my whole desire was to choose him for my companion and husband through life," for "he was the only one on earth that I desired for a husband." If not for whites who eventually threatened them, Carrie was certain they would be "one of the happiest couples in the world." Carrie took responsibility for "charging" Sandy to marry her, perhaps in an effort to protect her black husband, and vowed to "stand up in any crowd to save him." [11]

Still, such statements are rare, and the enigmas of choice and volition deepen with the increasing threat and reality of deadly white violence resulting from sex between black men and white women. For along with the possibility of arrest and prosecution there now came a form of terrorism that included the maiming and murder both of black men and, to a lesser extent, of white women. In his 1867 diatribe on white supremacy, the venomously racist nonslaveholder of the antebellum South, Hinton Rowan Helper, denounced black suffrage, citizenship, and education, pronouncing: "If the negro marries an outcast white woman—of course no white woman who is not an outcast of the worst possible sort would ever think of marrying him—both he and she ought to be hung three minutes after the conclusion of the ceremony, or as soon thereafter as the necessary preparations could be made." [12]

White Southerners conflated the political rights of black men with sexual transgressions in justifying the Klan-led violence that terrorized freedpeople between 1868 and 1871, coinciding with the organization of the Republican party in the defeated Confederacy. Although the Ku Klux Klan victimized white supporters of freedpeople's rights, the greatest violence was reserved for black men and women. Six young returning Confederate officers had organized the Ku Klux Klan as a secret social club in Pulaski, Tennessee, in 1865 or 1866; the name probably derived from *kuklos,* Greek for "circle." The Klan's activities soon encompassed the harassment of freedpeople, and by 1868 branches had been established at least for some time in all Southern states, occasionally under other names that denoted secrecy, white supremacy, or both. Although patterns varied across the South and are difficult to schematize with precision, the Ku Klux Klan gathered where black or Republican populations approximated white or Democratic populations, and it was generally most active in areas of greatest economic equality between blacks and whites. Klan membership included all classes of white Southerners, but leaders were largely drawn from among the more well-to-do. The former Confederate general Nathan Bedford Forrest became the Klan's first leader, or Grand Wizard, and state leaders included lawyers, businessmen, journalists, former governors, and future U.S. senators among their ranks. [13]

Although the Klan lacked central control, its methods were consistent. The majority report filed by Congress in 1871 concluded that "we see, from Maryland to Mexico, the same general spirit of spite against the freedman, and determination to keep him down and use his labor without compensation." [14] Tactics ranged from the destruction of property to whipping, torture, castration, rape, and murder. Because Klan participants early on realized the power of operating underground, there were few public signs of their existence. Attacks usually took place in isolated rural areas at night. Attackers disguised themselves and might number about a dozen, though mobs of fifty or a hundred also launched raids. Klansmen were motivated by the goal of white supremacy, manifested most concretely in white control of formal politics. Members claimed to guard against insurrection by freedpeople, deter crime, punish corruption, and protect against "lawlessness." White Southerners who disagreed with Klan tactics largely remained silent. Black men and women, given the threats they faced, showed tremendous resistance, perhaps most especially in the act of testifying before Congress. [15]

In the spring of 1871, a joint committee of Congress embarked on an investigation of Klan violence. Republicans, the party of antislavery Northerners and of virtually all blacks in the Reconstruction South, outnumbered Democrats, the majority party of white Southerners. For months, testimony was taken in Washington, D.C., as well as in North Carolina, South Carolina, Georgia, Mississippi, Alabama, and Florida. The committee discovered that those in greatest danger of attack were black men—and their families—who defied white efforts to retain racial hierarchy. This included men who were voters, political leaders, labor activists, those who displayed economic independence, and those who crossed boundaries of the color line in acts that ranged from talking back to sex with a white woman. Among whites, Klansmen targeted Republican officers, teachers of the freedpeople, Northerners ("carpetbaggers"), and white Southern Republicans ("scalawags"). [16] Congressmen listened to both victims and perpetrators, though Klansmen and their sympathizers were evasive and claimed ignorance, aided immeasurably by the underground nature of the organization. When asked about an organization of disguised harassers in his Mississippi community, for example, one white witness said: "If there is, I don't know it, and never heard of it, sir; that is, to know it to be a fact, or ever to have heard of its being a fact." A white Alabama man likewise averred: "I will state my theory about the Ku-Klux organization. Of course I know no Ku-Klux; I never consciously saw one in my life."[17]

The victims, black and white, male and female, had much more to say, though they could not always speak forthrightly. Notably, stories about black men and white women were often told by white witnesses, some of whom sympathized with Klan victims and some of whom did not. Because both sympathizers and enemies commonly relayed secondhand accounts, it is impossible to separate fabricated accusations from observed transgressions and to distinguish false admissions given under threat or torture from truthful confessions. Yet what comes through consistently in the testimony is how white anxiety over sexual liaisons between black men and white women was linked to both party politics and successful crops. Indeed, black victims and witnesses alike made that connection, whether cautiously or candidly, in their testimony before Congress.[18]

Two narratives of Klan violence illustrate this link. Jourdan Ware, a freedman whom the Klan assaulted and later murdered in Georgia's upper piedmont, told the white postmaster of his town that the first aggression against him was "on account of his politics" and an effort by whites "to get possession of his place." Ware, who tended about thirty acres of land and worked for a local white woman, was "fixed very comfortably." His attackers told him to leave the area and "not vote the radical ticket any more." Even though Ware moved away, disguised Klansmen beat him to death the next time they found him. The sympathetic postmaster agreed that Ware was "a leading man, a prominent man among the colored people." An unsympathetic white farmer described him as "a big, mighty forward, pompous negro," adding, "I think they whipped him more for that than anything else. . . . he pushed about among white men too much." Moreover, a white lawyer thought Klansmen had attacked Ware because they believed he "had made some insulting remark to a white lady." Although "lady" signified a well-to-do white woman, whites may also have described any alleged victim of a black man as such, without regard to her actual class standing, in an effort to justify violence.

When the investigating committee pressed on—"Let me understand the character of the allegation against him. You say that he made some insulting proposal to a white lady?"—the lawyer answered, "O, no; that he had just made some insulting remark. He remarked, 'How d'ye, sis,' or something of that kind, as the young lady passed down the road." A white blacksmith had also heard that Ware "had some slight talk to a gentleman's wife, a white lady, and called her 'sis,' or 'wife,' or something of that sort, one day when she was passing along the road." Again, the phrase "gentleman's wife" marked the woman's status. In the most incriminating version, a white editor heard that Ware "had made lecherous advances to the lady. . . . He called her 'wife,' and thrust out his tongue at her. The lady ran away very much frightened." Because such "propositions" were of a "grossly indecent character," this man felt, Ware's death was justified, for "the lady was spared the mortification and shame of appearing in court in connection with a cause that the delicacy of any lady would shrink from in terror." The development of an increasingly rigid and violent system of deference and stricter rules about interaction between black men and elite white women is apparent in the ordeal of Jourdan Ware, and in Jourdan Ware's murder it is clear that in combination with political and economic independence, any remark toward a white woman deserving of the title "lady," even a daytime greeting, could be construed by whites as a threatening sexual overture deserving of death.[19]

The ordeal of Henry Lowther, a husband, father, and freedman in Georgia's cotton belt, also reveals how white anger about the political and economic power of black men merged with accusations of sexual misconduct toward elite white women. Like Jourdan Ware, Henry Lowther had done well for himself. Twenty disguised Klansmen came to the Lowther home on horseback one night, but Lowther managed to elude them and got up a "company" of black men to serve as protection. "They said I had taken too great a stand against them in the republican party," Lowther recalled. "I worked for my money and carried on a shop. They all got broke and did not pay me, and I sued them." Lowther concluded, "They have been working at me ever since I have been free. I had too much money." Lowther was jailed on charges of conspiring to murder another black man and was denied trial. A white man who came to warn Lowther of trouble asked him whether he would be "willing to give up your stones to save your life," indicating castration. As Lowther remembered the scene, almost two hundred Klansmen arrived in the middle of the night, and twenty of them carried him away to a swamp. "The moon was shining bright, and I could see them," Lowther testified. All the men were Democrats. (Before he was blindfolded, Lowther recognized one of his attackers as "a man I thought a heap of . . . a nice young man," whom Lowther suspected was forced to participate.) "They asked me whether I preferred to be altered or to be killed. I said I preferred to be altered. After laying me down and getting through they said: 'Now, as soon as you can get to a doctor go to one . . . ' I asked how long it would take to get well, and they said five or six weeks. I was naked and bleeding very much." Dressed again yet nearly frozen and sure he would die from loss of blood, Lowther dragged himself to a white doctor's home, but no one came to the door; Lowther believed the doctor had participated in the attack. A number of black women "came to see me," Lowther said, "and told me that the blood was all over town."

The congressmen who questioned Lowther also understood the interchangeable nature of political and sexual offenses. Did Lowther know the reason for the attack, "any offense against the law, any breach of the peace, any violence, any insult to any white woman, or anything of that kind?" asked one. "No, sir; I never insulted any white woman," Lowther answered. "They said I was getting to have too much influence in the republican party there." When pressed, however, Lowther relayed that his attackers "said I was going to see a white lady"—again the class-designation mattered—but pointed out that the charge was untrue. The woman in question had hired Lowther to tend her land, but this charge had not been made the first time Klansmen had come for him. According to a white Republican judge, once Lowther had been assured that "he would not be compelled to criminate himself before the court," he admitted "that he had had connection with that white woman." This white man expressed consternation over any political charges: "I do not believe, and I cannot believe," he said, "that the maltreatment of Henry Lowther was owing to his politics."[20] Yet in the castration of Henry Lowther and in other cases in the early years of Reconstruction, white Southerners invoked charges of illicit sexual behavior toward or with white women deemed respectable in white eyes, together with charges of Republican activism or successful crops—that is, of political and economic independence.[21]

Henry Lowther's was not the only case of sexual torture by the Klan. When a black man and a white woman were accused of cohabitation in Georgia, a doctor recalled that "the colored man was taken out into the woods, a hole dug in the ground and a block buried in it, and his penis taken out, and a nail driven through it into the block; that a large butcher or cheese knife, as they call it, very sharp, was laid down by him, and light-wood piled around him and set on fire; the knife was put there so that he could cut it off and get away, or stay there and burn up." The man chose to escape. Klansmen could in fact resort to sexual mutilation for any act that struck them as demonstrating too much authority, whether or not they tacked on an accusation of sexual misconduct. In North Carolina, for example, a black man named Nathan Trolinger was "made to mutilate his own private parts with his pocket-knife" after a severe whipping. The cause was a labor dispute. An investigator for the Department of Justice reported the cases of two black ministers in Georgia: one of the men "was taken just as he finished preaching one night and his privates were cut 'smooth off.'" The other "was strapped across a log and his 'stones' whipped out with a buggy trace." The victims were "Republicans and men of influence," the investigator wrote, "and on that account undoubtedly they were thus treated by disguised men, known as the Klux."[22]

It is significant that those who sympathized with Henry Lowther's tormenters did not characterize his alleged bad behavior toward the white woman as rape. A black man could be tortured or murdered in the Reconstruction South even if a liaison with a white woman was acknowledged by whites to be consensual, as was the case for the Georgia man accused of cohabitation and mutilated with a butcher knife. In Tennessee in 1869, Klansmen abducted a black man from the sheriff's custody, lifted him off his feet with a rope around his neck, doused him with turpentine and set him afire, and finally shot him to death as they let him run. The man had "recently eloped with the white daughter of his employer."[23] A consensual liaison could alternatively result in a legal death sentence. A black man named George Alford returning from the army to his old neighborhood in Kentucky ended up convicted of killing his former slavemaster. Evidence pointed to a consensual liaison with the white man's wife as the cause of the murder (had the white woman "permitted this bloody-handed wretch to occupy her husband's bed?" queried one reporter). Alford remained silent on the question and was executed in 1874. In 1876 in North Carolina, one judge reasoned that a jury could infer the intention of rape from the fact that a black man had run after a white woman who accused him of attempted rape, "considering that he was a negro" and "considering the repugnance of a white woman to the embraces of a negro." The man was found guilty. Reconstruction judges also alluded to lynching when they wrote opinions in rape cases involving black men and white women.

When a rape conviction was upheld in Georgia in 1873, one judge opined that the man had "no right to complain where both the law and an outraged family spare his life." Likewise when a death sentence was upheld in a Texas rape case in 1876, the judges closed their opinion with smug congratulations for white neighbors who refrained from lynching, noting the people's "spirit of tolerance" in the face of "this vile outrage."[24]

Whites did not uniformly level rape accusations at black men in the early years of Reconstruction, though they began to put forth the idea that such a crime was becoming more frequent. A white man from Georgia, for example, told the congressional committee that the rape of white women by black men was "vastly more frequent now" than during slavery, though he could not cite any actual cases.[25] At the same time, an accusation that concerned the rape of a "respectable" white woman could lead to lynching. Charles Clarke of Georgia's cotton belt, for example, was charged with raping the white daughter of a Methodist preacher and jailed by Klansmen. The judge found the evidence insufficient for conviction, and Clarke was returned to jail (guarded by black men), supposedly pending further investigation. A black man overheard that Clarke "never would come out of that jail alive," and indeed, thirty-six undisguised Klansmen shot him dead. Similarly, a white businessman in Georgia described a case in which a black man was accused of raping a sixteen-year-old white girl: "They caught that negro, tied him to a stake, and burned him in the day time before, I suppose, a thousand people," the man recalled. "They never had any trial, or proof, or anything of that sort, and they never gave the name of this girl, so far as I ever knew."[26]

The respective murder and torture of Jourdan Ware and Henry Lowther illuminate the connections between newly won political and economic standing for black men and the taboo of sex with white women. Political power, economic success, and sex with a white woman—all such actions on the part of a black man confounded the lines of racial categories in a South without slavery, and therefore became unforgivable transgressions in the eyes of whites. Without the legal status of slavery and freedom as a dividing line, white Southerners had to rely on the fickle categories of "black" and "white" to define white supremacy. The color line, therefore, had to be fixed in two ways. It had to be established first by stricter racial definitions, which would come to fruition in the late nineteenth century with a codified "one-drop rule." It also had to be established by distinct political, economic, and social castes for white men and black men, a task that required constant vigilance on the part of white people in order to ensure that no black man crossed over into the territory of political power, economic independence, or social authority. When black men did cross those lines, as they did during Reconstruction, white men reacted with threats and acts of lethal violence.

Men like Jourdan Ware, Henry Lowther, and the other victims of Klan violence were nobody's property; they did not merit white protection from mutilation or murder. In part due to their subjugated status as slaves, Abraham Peppinger's Jim and John Richardson's Edmond, along with numerous others, had not suffered castration or death for their liaisons with white women in the antebellum South. In the post-emancipation South, by contrast, no white person needed to be compensated and no one needed to fight for the pardon of a transgressing black man. As one white observer from the North noted just after the war, "The pecuniary value which the individual negro formerly represented having disappeared, the maiming and killing of colored men seems to be looked upon by many as one of those venial offences which must be forgiven to the outraged feelings of a wronged and robbed people." Black antilynching activists would in fact make the same point later in the century.[27] In the antebellum South, neither had free black men like James Nunez suffered mutilation or murder for their liaisons with white women. But with emancipation and the demise of racial slavery, free black men, now exercising political power and demonstrating economic self-sufficiency, were infinitely more dangerous to whites who sought to maintain racial supremacy.

In tandem with political and economic strength so infuriating to white people, freedmen who consorted with white women (or who were accused of such behavior) became transgressive in a way they had never been under the oppressive regime of slavery. Less than a year after the Civil War, a Virginia newspaper issued a warning to a girl from a well-to-do white family who had gone horseback riding with a black man as her guard. "Under our ancient institutions there would have been no impropriety in this," the white editors explained, "as the distinction between the two races was then too marked to admit of any misconstruction." But now, with the lurking shadow of racial equality, they advised, "we think it would be more appropriate for ladies to refrain from equestrian exercise unless they can obtain an escort of their own color." And now, as part of this relentless resolve to preserve the racial hierarchy, Klansmen and their supporters also subjected transgressing white women to violence heretofore unknown.[28]

Protecting and Abusing White Women

Some white Southerners blamed the Civil War for liaisons between black men and white women. A white man in Virginia spoke with disgust about a white woman who had "a nigger husband" and associated with black people, and mistakenly believed that such an event could never have occurred under slavery. Other white Americans misguidedly believed that a liaison between a black man and a white woman was too unspeakably horrid and absurd ever to come to pass in the Reconstruction South. J. H. Van Evrie, a proslavery New York physician who was widely read and admired among white Southerners, wrote of the South in 1868 that "such a thing is altogether impossible, for the woman would not alone be driven from the society of her own race . . . but she would not be permitted (if known) to live even among negroes!" [29]

Although the Reconstruction-era Klan excluded women from membership, scattered evidence indicates that white women took part in racial violence or Klan activities. In Kentucky, for example, a white woman stabbed a black woman in the neck "for giving water to a Union soldier." More commonly, wives, mothers, sisters, and daughters sewed Klansmen's costumes, either voluntarily or on orders. As North Carolina Klansman John Long said of the costumes: "We got our wives to make them." One white man felt sure that the Klan had "its strongest support among the women of the country," offering as evidence the fact that "these women manufacture the disguises worn by the Klan, which are in some instances quite fancifully trimmed." Other women lent their own clothing as disguises. One Georgia victim who had recognized an attacker said: "Wilson had on his wife's dress. My wife is well acquainted with them, and she knew that he had on his wife's dress." At least some white women urged their husbands not to join in. Long's wife, for one, pleaded with him not to go out on a raid, and a few expressed their apprehensions more directly. A white woman in North Carolina "said the 'Yankees' were gentlemen compared to these Ku-Klux," and a white woman in Alabama was whipped and thrown into a ravine (and later died of the injuries) for informing on Klansmen.[30]

Albion Tourgée, the white Northerner who served as a judge in North Carolina during Reconstruction, observed that Klan victims were either black men, white men in political sympathy with black men, or "renegade" Klan or Democratic party men. What he omitted were the women, both black and white.[31] As a male-only organization, one of the Klan's stated purposes was that "Females, friends, widows, and their households shall ever be special objects of our regard and protection." The Klan's intentions to protect women never applied to black women, and as part of their violent rampages Klansmen routinely assaulted and raped black women.[32] Not all white women merited protection either. As in the antebellum South, dominant ideology about the purity of white women continued to rest on class standing. As in the case of Jourdan Ware, Klansmen took offense when a black man acted in a manner they judged even mildly insulting to a white woman deemed worthy of the title "lady." As for the definition of insulting behavior, one white Northerner observed that a black man was "called insolent whenever his conduct varies in any manner from what a southern man was accustomed to when slavery existed." [33]

In the case of Sandy Sellers in North Carolina, twenty or so disguised Klansmen entered his home, wrenched him out of bed, tore off his shirt, tied his hands around a tree, whipped him, and then rubbed his lacerated back with a rough stick. One raid participant claimed that "it was for cursing a white woman" whose cattle had trampled on the corn of the white man for whom Sellers sharecropped. But the Klansman soon changed his story to say that they had beat Sellers "because he made an insulting proposal to a white woman," that he "wanted to sleep with her," and that "when she would not consent, he complained of her hogs getting into his wheat." One of the attackers later claimed to remember only that "we told him never to talk about white ladies the way he had, or something about some stock—was said." Sellers maintained that he had not made any propositions, but he was forced to promise not to order white women around. Although the class status of this woman was not specified, she probably belonged to a family that commanded social authority, for poorer white women were not often regarded as capable of being insulted.[34]

Indeed, in numerous other narratives, the allegedly victimized white

women were "ladies." A Klan attack on a black man in Georgia was attributed to the fact that he "had used this saucy expression to a white lady."
Another white Georgian said that freedmen "were abusive to ladies." In
Mississippi, a black man was assaulted for using "some improper language
in regard to some white ladies of the neighborhood." [35] In North Carolina, one black man was hanged because "he was a great terror to white
ladies and impudent to them," another because he made "a bad proposition to a very respectable young lady." [36] Whites also consistently invoked
the term "lady" when a black man was accused of raping a white woman.
In Virginia in 1869, for example, Jesse Edwards was hanged for the alleged
rape and murder of "Miss Susan Hite, a respectable young lady." White
people in North Carolina severely beat a black man for allegedly assaulting "a respectable young lady." And as Grand Wizard Nathan Forrest put
it: "Ladies were being ravished by some of these negroes, who were tried
and put in the penitentiary, but were turned out in a few days afterward."
(When pressed for details, Forrest admitted only hearsay and claimed lack
of recollection.) [37]

Like black women, white women of the lower classes, and especially
those who defied the rules of patriarchy, could not count on ideology
about female purity to absolve them of alleged illicit sexual activity. Poorer
white women whom Klansmen and their sympathizers judged to be lacking in virtue were subject to abuse that ranged from insulting language to
rape. After Georgia Klansmen shot a black man " 'living in adultery with
a white woman,' " they " 'strapped the woman across a log, and whipped
her so severely that she could not sit up yesterday.' " Klansmen also sexually mutilated white women who lived outside the boundaries of sexual
propriety. In the Georgia case of cohabitation in which the black man was
castrated with a butcher knife, a witness recounted (perhaps exaggerating, perhaps not) that Klansmen "took the woman, laid her down on the
ground, then cut a slit on each side of her orifice, put a large padlock in
it, locked it up, and threw away the key, and then turned her loose." In
North Carolina, a white girl with a bad reputation was assaulted by the
Klan; one witness testified that "they took her clothes off, whipped her
very severely, and then lit a match and burned her hair off, and made her
cut off herself the part that they did not burn off with the match." [38]

Sometimes black men and white women were simply accorded the
same treatment. In Georgia, angry whites "burned three colored men, and

three white women, alive, because they lived together." The North Carolina case of Mary Gappins reveals white men's casual attitude toward white women whom they suspected of moral depravity. Gappins's house, which she denied operating as a brothel, had been torn down by seven disguised Klansmen. When her white Southern interrogators asked how many "colored" children she had, Gappins admitted to one. The men laughed, and then laughed again when she explained, "It was a darkey who took me in some way and got me where I could not help myself," leaving the question of rape ambiguous. Markings in the transcript indicating "[Laughter]" make clear that no white man was outraged by the possibility of a white woman forced into sex with a black man if that white woman ran a whorehouse and had a "black" child. Gappins added, perhaps hastily, "I have as much objection to white folks and darkies mixing up as anybody." [39]

The reputations of white women were continually assessed by white Southerners in the Klan testimony, with the congressional committee participating in such dialogues. Questioning a witness about the lynching of Charles Clarke for alleged rape, for example, the committee asked, "Was she a respectable girl?" Voluntary association with a black man immediately implied depravity for a white woman. The white farmer who testified about the murder of Jourdan Ware had heard that Klansmen had been on the lookout for "a sort of low character of a white woman" who "harbored about his house." When asked by the committee if she were a "low-down white woman," the farmer replied, "Yes, sir, one of the meanest you ever saw in the world, so mean that she ought to be hung." This apparently was not the "lady" whom Ware supposedly insulted. Similarly, when questioned about the reputation of the white woman with whom Henry Lowther allegedly had sex, a white judge thought that she was "one of those low-down tramps which are scattered about the country"—not a "lady" after all. Both of these white women had, significantly, been honored with the designation of "lady" when painted by white people as the victims of black men. [40]

Comparable descriptions of "bad" white women abound. In another Georgia case, a white man testified that Klansmen beat a black man who had asked a white woman "to copulate with him." The woman had refused, and when questioned as to her character, the witness answered, "I suppose it was fair, because if she had been a common whore or strumpet,

I do not suppose they would have paid any attention to it." When a black Georgian accused of attempting to rape a white woman was left alone, the committee asked a white witness, "What was there about that case that mitigated it; was the woman of bad character?" The man answered that the woman's character was good but that she was "a woman of low position in society, and such a proceeding would not have been so great a shock to her, perhaps, as to one of higher refinement," thus indicating the presumed equation between poorer women and a base lack of sensitivity. A white witness who told the committee about a black Alabamian shot by Klansmen because his wife was white, added: "I suppose she was a low woman." Poorer white women were also excluded from those who supposedly lived in fear of black men. Speaking of such fears, Grand Wizard Forrest remarked that "in the poorer neighborhoods I do not think that insecurity was felt."[41] Whites continued as well to recognize the possibility of sexual coercion by white women. One white witness in whom Henry Lowther confided relayed that the white woman in question had followed Lowther into the woods and asked for sex. The witness said, "The inference I drew was that she was a very bad, abandoned character, from the circumstance that she voluntarily followed him into the woods, and, as I supposed from his language, solicited him to have intercourse with her."[42]

Black men and women used the same language when they described white women to the congressional investigators, though with less rigid distinctions of class and status. Henry Lowther called the white woman with whom he was accused of fraternizing a "lady" in one sentence and a "bad character" in the next. In the murder of freedman John Walthall in Georgia, a black neighbor, Maria Carter, identified four white sisters with whom, she said, Walthall had had sex before his marriage. When the committee inquired whether these were "women of bad character," Carter replied, "Yes, sir; worst kind." According to Carter, it was "well known" that Walthall "had been living with these low white women," but she had also heard that Walthall "could not get rid of them to save his life." Black women could also seek revenge in such matters. In Virginia in 1868 when a black man left his black wife to "live with the white woman," the wife assaulted the white woman for "having stolen the affections of her husband."[43]

Talk of party politics also entered into discussions of "bad" white women, and again the congressional investigators participated. A dialogue with a white North Carolina man illustrates the intertwining of the moral reputations and political leanings of white women:

Q: Were the women whipped because they were republicans?

A: That I cannot answer; I can only make the statement that in every instance—

Q: You said they were women of low character.

A: Some of them were; others were of good character.

Q: The most of them were women of low character?

A: Yes, sir.

Q: What do you mean by women of low character?

A: I mean base women.

Q: Do you mean strumpets and unchaste women?

A: Yes, sir; of course women have been whipped who were not of that character. . . .

Q: I understood you to say that men were whipped at the same time?

A: I said this, that when women were whipped the men who lived at the place were republicans. They have whipped one woman where there was no man at all.

Q: That was a woman of bad character?

A: Yes, sir.[44]

A former North Carolina Klansman likewise testified that a white widow had been harassed because "she believed with the radical party" and at the same time "had been accused of having black men lying around there and staying." Alabama Klansmen whipped a white woman, "a loose character," because "it was thought she wasn't keeping a nice house"; the committee then asked whether the woman was "a radical," a "Union woman." In Georgia, Klansmen assaulted a white woman for boarding a white Republican at her home. Her enemies threw rocks at the woman's son and, when she tried to protect him, taunted her with the words: " 'well, s'posing we do kill him, there will be one radical less to grow up.' "[45]

For Klansmen and their supporters, then, only certain white women merited the supposed benefits of male protection. There were few accusations of the rape of white women who did not qualify as "ladies," and just as in the antebellum South, when poorer white women consorted with black men, their actions only proved their degradation. Transgressing white women like Polly Lane, Dorothea Bourne, and Caroline Hugly had suffered gossip, persecution, and ostracism in the slave South, but none had suffered extreme violence outside the bounds of their families. Beginning in the years after the Civil War, white women who consorted with black man were subject to whipping, maiming, and murder by the Ku Klux Klan. Moreover, in the post-emancipation South, the supposed sexual immorality of transgressing white women could be linked to party politics through the activism of the men with whom they may have kept company. For Klansmen, transgressing white women, too, were potentially threatening to white men's quest to retain their power in the face of political and economic advances being made by freedpeople. As in the antebellum South, some of these white women defied the patriarchal tenet that their sexuality was the exclusive property of white men. As serious a trespass as that had been in the slave South, such defiance now became grounds for organized retributive physical atrocities. With slavery demolished, fault lines in the racial and gender hierarchies had to be repaired and then guarded. In this endeavor by white Southerners came the terrorization of black men and some of the white women who consorted with them.

The Sexualization of Reconstruction Politics

The issue of sex between black men and white women held a significant place in the formal political debates of Reconstruction. After emancipation, freedmen and freedwomen expressed their newly won status in multiple ways. They chose new names and daily refused to defer to whites; they established schools and independent churches; they sought to control their own labor; they demanded their own land. Within families, freedmen assumed authoritative roles that had been difficult or impossible to fulfill under the domination of white slaveholders, and some freedwomen withdrew from labor outside their homes, at least for a brief period. And beginning with radical Reconstruction directed by the Republican party in 1867, black men registered to vote, held public office, and participated in political meetings, rallies, debates, and protests. Black women also wielded significant political influence within their communities. To white people, black male suffrage was the most galling of all seizures of power.

For black men, suffrage was the most radical and radicalizing departure from their former status as slaves. As one black man put it in 1869, "the loss of suffrage" would be equal to "the loss of freedom."[46]

Throughout Reconstruction, black men continued to connect civil and politics rights to ideas about manhood. When the minister Henry McNeal Turner was barred from his seat in the Georgia state legislature on the grounds of race in 1868, he intoned: "I am here to demand my rights and to hurl thunderbolts at the men who would dare to cross the threshold of my manhood." Directly linking manhood with political rights, Turner asked, "Am I a man? If I am such, I claim the rights of a man. . . . I want to convince the House today that I am entitled to my seat here." Turner reinforced this point with the warning that "if, tomorrow, a war should arise, I would not raise a musket to defend a country where my manhood is denied." Joseph H. Rainey, congressman from South Carolina, also unmasked the connection between political rights and black manhood in a congressional debate of 1873. Southern white men, Rainey declared, wished to withhold citizenship from the black man because such actions as suffrage "had a tendency to make him feel his manhood," which in the eyes of white men was "asking too much." Rainey observed: "Just as soon as we begin to assert our manhood and demand our rights . . . we become objectionable, we become obnoxious, and we hear this howl about social equality." Alabama congressman James T. Rapier likewise equated manhood with the right to vote, announcing in 1874 that "nothing short of a complete acknowledgment of my manhood will satisfy me."[47]

The Southern state constitutional conventions held between 1867 and 1869 uniformly provided civil and political rights for black men. Yet what Rainey referred to as "social equality" was a point of contention among delegates, many of whom were Southern white Republicans. "Social equality" was a nebulous term referring largely to integration. Mingling with black people was often acceptable to white people where only one sex prevailed. Black and white women could cook in the same kitchen, and black and white men could drink at the same bar. Arenas frequented by both sexes, such as schools and streetcars, by contrast, were thought by whites to be dangerous to white girls and women. To some white Southerners, then, "social equality" meant fostering conditions that would lead to sex between black men and white women.[48] Some white Southerners thus understood political rights as a certain prelude to sexual

intimacy. In Virginia just after the war, a white man debating Negro suffrage fretted that black men would "vote themselves white wives." A Richmond newspaper likewise mixed politics and sex when criticizing the Republican state convention of 1867 (in which black delegates outnumbered
whites and thousands of freedpeople attended), noting that sympathetic
whites "would rather miscegenate than democratize." The North Carolina constitution of 1868 included one resolution stating all at once that
"intermarriages and illegal intercourse between the races should be dis-
countenanced, and the interests and happiness of the two races would be
best promoted by the establishment of separate schools."[49]

Dialogues about politics and sex, begun in the halls of the federal
government during the Civil War, thus continued into the Reconstruction
years. Recall that white wartime politicians had brought fears of sex between black men and white women into congressional debates about black
rights; now again, according to an Arkansas Democrat in 1868, to give a
black man the vote meant that "he would be taken into the parlors of all
that vote for him—to marry their daughters, and, if necessary, hug their
wives!" (In the same year, a Northern white Republican asked if those
who professed such fears would feel obliged to arrange a social visit "because your ballot and theirs had been mingled in the same box?" And,
he elaborated, "should your ballot and that of a black man happen to be
placed in juxtaposition," did that mean you had "to give your daughter in
marriage to the 'American citizen of African descent?' ")[50] In 1875 in Mississippi, a book entitled *Sister Sallie* warned white Southerners that their
own wretchedness would be final with "the *marriage* of their sister—their
own, deah sister Sallie, to a buck negro." A white Northerner commenting
on the book felt that it was impossible "not to see in all these preparations
a settled purpose" on the part of white Southerners "to take possession of
the government by force if necessary."[51]

It was the equation of political rights and black manhood that became so central to Reconstruction conflicts. The idea of manhood, which
had long implied the rights and responsibilities of citizenship in American
political thought, now assumed connotations in white minds of black men
engaging in sex with white women. Black spokesmen in turn perceived
the connection in white minds. One black writer noted in 1866 that "the
cry is loud and long when there is a prospect, through the agency of new
born freedom, of a man with a *dark skin* leading to the altar a woman with

a *white skin,*" adding that the white man "seems to be afraid that some of his daughters may do what a good many of his sons and himself has done time and again." Henry McNeal Turner challenged the notion that free black men desired marriage to white women. That "was another foolish dream," Turner scoffed, asking, "What do we want with their daughters and sisters?" He added, perhaps ominously to white ears, "*All we ask of the white man is to let our ladies alone,* and they need not fear us." [52] Black protestors not only challenged white fears of marriage between black men and white women but also confronted white Southerners about their articulated fears of rape. One "Colored Citizen" from Georgia reminded white men in 1866 that during the war black men "not only protected their wives and children, but tilled their fields and fed their armies," pointedly asking, "Did we, at any time rise against their helpless families . . . ? . . . Ladies of Georgia! can you now fear us who were courteous to you while your husband, father, and brother were absent? Is it not ungenerous now to manifest such distrust, simply because we are free?" At the Arkansas constitutional convention in 1868, black delegate James T. White similarly pointed out: "In the late bloody war, these gentlemen left their wives and daughters in the care of colored men for four years, and I defy the gentleman to cite me a single instance where they have failed to live up to their integrity." Black protestors would continue to invoke this argument to the end of the century. [53]

Grand Wizard Forrest claimed that his organization "had no political purpose," and the Democratic members of the congressional committee agreed, denying "any political significance" to the violence. Of course, politics could be defined narrowly, as it was in the mind of a white North Carolinian who assessed a Klan attack by saying, "I suppose this grew out of some prejudice against the race, not out of politics." [54] Those who took a broader view, however, linked Klan assaults for sexual misconduct to Reconstruction politics, whether that misconduct was fabricated, rumored, or real. A lawyer who renounced his membership in the North Carolina Klan readily acknowledged connections between political and sexual transgressions. "In a great many instances, where negroes were whipped," this man said, they had been accused of, among other things, "insults to white ladies." As for the truth of such charges, no one bothered to find out, because violence "had the effect . . . to intimidate a number of negroes into voting the Democratic ticket, and also preventing a number from voting at all." Likewise in Alabama, a mob of Klansmen fired into a black settlement, supposedly because there was "a negro man living in marital relation with a woman thought to be of the white race"; but one witness averred that it was "only a pretext for maltreating the colored people . . . and the determination of driving them away." Others seem to have been less conscious of the links they made between politics and sex. A white lawyer from North Carolina described the Klan to his diary as "a Political society, based on the Supremacy of the White race" that seemed "to abhor miscegenation, and to protect female virtue from negro violence or his embraces." [55]

Witnesses also offered theoretical interpretations about politics and sex, and these mirrored the "social equality" debates taking place in Congress. When the investigating committee asked a North Carolina Klansman about the purpose of the organization, he said, "It was to keep down the colored un's from mixing with the whites." And by what means would this be accomplished? "To keep them from marrying, and to keep them from voting," he answered. Another white North Carolina man said, "The common white people of the country are at times very much enraged against the negro population. They think that this universal political and civil equality will finally bring about social equality," adding, "There are already instances . . . in which poor white girls are having negro children." A white postmaster in Mississippi thought whites believed that "putting colored men into office, in positions of prominence, will gradually lead them to demand social equality, and to intermingle by marriage with the whites." A white lawyer in Mississippi thought poorer whites were "induced to believe that republicanism means social equality; that, if a man is a republican, he must necessarily be in favor of white people and negroes marrying and associating on terms of perfect equality in the social circle." As a white tax collector in Georgia explained, white Southerners "take the question of equality in its broadest sense." That is, "If you talk about equality, they at once conclude that you must take the negro into your parlor and into your bed." He added, "It is a very unfortunate thing to have mixed up in politics." [56]

A British traveler to the Reconstruction South wrote of the lynching of black men accused of raping a white woman and relayed that "an experienced judge told me he had known many accused and many hanged, but none convicted on trial." This writer astutely included these observations under the heading "The Political Situation in the South." Members of the congressional committee also chose sides on the links between Klan violence, sex, and politics. One Democratic interviewer offered a white witness the following hypothetical scenario, presumably in an effort to deflate the idea that murder for alleged rape was in any sense a political act: "Well, sir," he said, "suppose that a man were killed in your town to-day, and it were known that he were killed by ten republicans, and that the man happened to be a democrat, and had been guilty of a rape upon the wife of one of those republicans, and he should be killed whilst being conveyed to jail; would you say that was political . . . ?" On the other side, a Republican committee member tried to get a white witness to admit that politics did indeed play a role in casting aspersions upon Northerners. "Do you know a single northern person, male or female, who has come down into this country and taken an interest in your political affairs, who has not suffered in character; who has not been maligned?" he asked. "Has not some fault been found with their personal character, invariably?" In 1871, Robert Elliott, a black representative from South Carolina, spoke for "nearly every Southern state" when he described Klansmen as "seeking revenge for political power lost" in all their violence toward black men.[57]

The volatile intertwining of sex and politics in the Reconstruction South brought in its wake violence directed at any person who transgressed traditional moral boundaries. In spite of their own violent actions, sexual and otherwise, Klansmen in the Reconstruction South took upon themselves the monitoring of sexual conduct beyond transgressions between black men and white women. A white man whose politics were in accord with the Klan was likely to be left alone if he engaged in a liaison with a black woman. Indeed, some Klansmen themselves sought black mistresses; in Georgia, for example, a white witness thought that black men had frequently been whipped "for keeping a mulatto girl that some white man wanted."[58] And yet Klansmen searched out white men who were their political enemies and whom they purportedly suspected of sexual liaisons with black women. The Klan also targeted those who formed sexual liaisons across the Mason-Dixon line. A white Northerner who worked for the Freedmen's Bureau had his horse disfigured for marrying a Southern woman, and a white Southern woman was whipped for "marrying a Union man."[59]

There were also numerous Klan offensives for adultery and fornication between whites and between blacks, and charges of wife abuse and child abuse could precipitate Klan violence. One Alabama victim assaulted for "cruelty to his wife," for example, was warned to practice "more proper customs in his domestic habits." [60] A North Carolina witness recalled a rare instance in which a Democrat was targeted by the Klan, noting that the attackers "were scourging him for being a very dissipated man, for having maltreated his wife, and for having associated with bad persons." And like white women, white men could be described as "bad" or "low" for illicit actions that ranged from running houses of prostitution to having children with black women. Accusations of incest or rumors of abortion could also prompt a Klan attack. Nor did Klansmen confine themselves to strictly sexual or domestic misconduct. Drunkenness or the illegal distilling of liquor could be cause for an assault.

Thus while Klansmen committed sexual depredations across the color line and practiced extreme violence on men and women both black and white, they attempted a retrenchment of authority on the part of Southern white men, assuming the role of sexual and moral arbiters and taking it upon themselves to police all conduct in the post-emancipation South. (That Klansmen on their rampages sometimes dressed in frocks that resembled women's clothing prompted one investigator to remark: "They seem to have a nice sense of morality, these gentlemen who wear this peculiar dress." [61]) Moreover, all of these moral transgressions—not only liaisons between black men and white women—were bound up with politics in dialogues about Klan violence. A white man in Georgia, when asked why a particular "mulatto" man was whipped, said: "I heard some people allege that there was a feeling against Colby for living with a near relative of his, I think his daughter, as his wife." Did he mean incest? "Yes, sir;" the witness answered. "I heard that alleged against him; I also heard other people, white men, say that there was nothing against Colby except his politics. Both of these things were stated to me." [62]

The conflation of sex and politics, the terrorization of black men, the abuse of white women, and the violent condemnation of any behavior deemed morally transgressive—these were interlocking elements in the broader sexualization of politics in the Reconstruction South. Every form of power exercised by freedmen meant a parallel loss of power for white men. That included newfound authority over black women in the domestic sphere, as well as any invented or observed agency or aggression in relation to white women, whether in the form of marriage, cohabitation, fornication, adultery, familiarity, brazenness, harassment, sexual assault, or rape. But Klansmen and their sympathizers usually invoked the latter categories (from familiarity to rape) subject to the white woman's class standing and moral reputation.

Although the geography of Klan violence during the first half of Reconstruction is difficult to plot with certainty, it is clear that Klansmen worked their violence in areas of the South where whites had previously contended with sex between black men and white women without such violence. Klan activity in North Carolina, for example, centered in the piedmont area around Greensboro, just north and west of Davidson County, the home of Polly Lane and Jim. Rowan County (out of which Davidson had been carved in 1822) was also the scene of Klan violence by the early 1870s.[63] In Georgia, Burke County experienced terrible violence against voting freedmen; this had been the home of the Nunez family, and it was here that Klansmen shot a black man for living with a white woman and beat the woman " 'so severely that she could not sit up yesterday.' " It was also in Burke County that whites burned three black men and three white women alive for cohabiting. A white man from Augusta also recalled an "open and notorious case of adultery" between a black man and a white woman on the Burke County line that "outraged the community very much." Both were arrested, with neighbors paying for a lawyer to prosecute them. Chattooga County in northwest Georgia was also the venue of tremendous Klan violence a little more than ten years after the Huglys moved there to escape the gossip about Caroline's probable adulterous affair with a black man. The murder of Jourdan Ware took place just south of Chattooga, in Floyd County.[64] These and numerous other counties in which whites had once confronted sex between black men and white women with a measure of toleration, or had treated rape charges without lethal alarm, became areas of tremendous Klan violence after the Civil War.[65] Virginia, though largely free of the Klan, was by no means exempt from white violence during Reconstruction. In 1866 a Northern teacher in the tidewater recorded that "the Ku Klux have been in our neighborhood, and we have received notice that they intend giving us a call." She heard they had "a desire to frighten the negroes from voting the Republican ticket" and that they committed acts of violence to this end.[66]

Ultimately, the Klan offered white Southerners a new language of

sexualized politics. This language moved away from the white-only democratic and republican rhetoric that had justified the coexistence of black
slavery and white liberty in the antebellum South to issue ominous warnings about the political and sexual perils of racial equality in the postwar
South. Speaking before the congressional committee, a white Republican
whose father had been a slaveowner put it this way about "the negro":
"When he was a slave they looked upon him as a chattel. . . . Now they
look upon him as something worse than a chattel—more like a bad animal, that they must fear."[67]

Klan victims had no effective legal recourse until as late as 1871.
Anti-Klan laws passed by state governments proved nearly impossible to
enforce, though the use of military power was slightly more effective. On
the national level, President Ulysses S. Grant's determination to control
the Klan from 1868 (the year in which the violence reached its pinnacle)
did not succeed in arrests and convictions until 1871. By the national election of 1872, the state governments of Virginia, Tennessee, North Carolina, and Georgia (and, briefly, Alabama) had been returned to Democratic rule or, in the language of white Southerners who despised both
black and white Republicans, had been "redeemed." Now white Southerners in the remaining Republican-controlled states began to change their
tactics, moving away from undercover attacks on individuals and toward
violence openly sanctioned by the Democratic party with the specific aim
of winning elections. Although a great many undeterred freedmen continued to vote Republican, the Democratic party brought good numbers
of new white voters to the polls. The Klan had been broken as an undercover organization, but the violence perpetrated from the end of the Civil
War until 1871 had played at least some part in the ultimate demise of Reconstruction. With or without the Ku Klux Klan, such violence escalated
as the end of the century approached.[68]

Throughout the South, the end of racial slavery spelled the end of
a secure racial hierarchy for white people. At least some idealistic black
people believed that the demise of slavery would mean the demise of racial
distinctions, or as a black teacher wrote in his diary in 1868: "I heard a
white man say, today is the black man's day. Tomorrow will be the white
man's. I thought, poor man—Those days of distinction between colors is
about over in this (now) free country."[69] In 1872, when a black minister

was asked how many white men were members of a Florida organization in support of freedpeople, he declined to answer, saying, "We do not count noses, black or white; we take men." The white interviewer persisted: "I am asking you a fact; men are white or colored, one of the two, although some of them are pretty well mixed," and reiterated, "How many men of the white race are members of this organization?" With a measure of defiance, the minister replied, "I cannot tell." But white people needed to tell and could not have disagreed more with the idea that black and white were "all one color now." [70]

After the war, in order to preserve racial hierarchy, whites set out to fashion a more rigid dividing line based upon stricter racial categories. One of the most certain ways to sustain the racial categories of "black" and "white" was to make sure that people of African ancestry and people of European ancestry did not have children together. Of course, white men had been largely responsible for the mixture of European and African ancestry throughout the era of slavery, and their power of sexual coercion had stemmed precisely from their political, economic, and social authority in Southern society. With emancipation, black men now possessed a measure of power that white people feared might include access to white women, and white Southern men and women conflated that power with a newly alarmist set of ideas about sex between black men and white women. Armed with such ideology, they hoped to halt the disintegration of their racial caste system as well as any political, economic, and social authority within communities of freedpeople.

In the antebellum South, the children that had resulted from illicit sex between black men and white women had spurred white neighbors to action, and in the postbellum South reproduction mattered, too. But the intertwining of power and sex—"social equality"—was also very much at the center of white concerns. Whether whites truly believed that black male suffrage would inevitably mean sex between black men and white women is difficult to determine. In the world of the slave South, voting had connoted manhood and citizenship, which in turn had represented patriarchal power. That power entailed control by white men over black men and women, as well as over white women. Extralegal control in the form of lethal violence now seemed the only way to retain that power. White men may have been the major actors in such violence, but white women would become their partners and accomplices as the century drew to a close.

The ramifications of the sexualization of Reconstruction politics would be fully realized toward the end of the century when the conflation of politics and sex transformed into the conflation of politics and rape. When lynching reached its height in the 1890s, white apologists invariably invoked the rape of white women as justification for extralegal execution. As the post-Reconstruction era began, white people more and more often named the political rights of black men as catalyst to the rape of white women.

8   Murder   *Black Men, White Women, and Lynching*

As the history of sex between black men and white women reaches the last decades of the nineteenth century, the stories become a series of false accusations of rape followed by certain, violent death for the man. Thus the historical record here accords most closely with modern assumptions about the past treatment of transgressors. At the same time, the relation between rape accusations and lynching in the post-Reconstruction South was a sinister one. Lynching was relatively rare before the Civil War, but between 1882 and 1900 more than a thousand people in the South were killed by whites who took the law into their own hands. Lynchings peaked in 1892, and in all years the overwhelming majority of victims were black men. Whites routinely claimed that the rape of white women was the prime cause, yet this oft-repeated statement was untrue in two senses. Not only was there no postwar wave of such sexual assaults, but rape was not in fact the cause white Southerners recorded most frequently when justifying specific lynchings. In spite of these two facts, white apologists relentlessly named the rape of white women as the reason for murdering black men, and fully intended the lynching of black men to sustain an atmosphere of terrorism that was in turn intended to maintain the racial hierarchy that emancipation and Reconstruction had begun to destroy.[1]

Lynchings differed from Klan assaults in that the perpetrators were largely undisguised and the murder was open to the public. When a black man was lynched for the alleged rape of a white woman, the execution was likely to be carried out by mass mob.[2] Vivid descriptions were frequently printed in the national press. In a composite portrait of the most gruesome (though not atypical) such lynching, the appointed victim might be a neighbor or a stranger; the charge might be suspected or wholly fabricated. Capture might involve white people taking the man forcibly from the street, his workplace, or his home. If a man was already under arrest, it meant taking him forcibly from the local jail with little or no objection from the white jailer or sheriff. White people of all classes came from miles away to participate in the spectacle, sometimes with their children and picnic supplies in tow. (Notices might be printed in local papers, railroad companies might add extra cars or run special trains, and children might be given the day off from school to attend.) The crowd could be composed of hundreds or thousands, including local officers of the law. The method of murder might include mutilation, castration, skinning, roasting, burning, hanging, and shooting. Afterward the audience might gather souvenirs, including rope, ashes, buttons, toes, fingers, ears, teeth, and bones. Shopkeepers might display small body parts in their windows, and photographers might sell picture postcards of the event. Even as the newspapers published detailed accounts from the mouths of eyewitnesses, the coroner or his jury would name the cause of death as "at the hands of persons unknown."[3] As black bishop Henry McNeal Turner observed in 1893, the local papers "can advance what they are going to do, how and when it was done, how the rope broke, how many balls entered the Negro's body, how loud he prayed, how piteously he begged, what he said, how long he was left hanging, how many composed the mob, the number that were masked, whether they were prominent citizens or not, how the fire was built that burnt the raper, how the Negro was tied, how he was thrown into the fire, and the whole transaction; but still the fiendish work was done by a set of 'unknown men.' "[4] The unrecorded or silenced voices of the victims, along with the deliberate anonymity of lynchers, makes it difficult to re-create historical events. When the victim "is dead and silent, and the murderer is alive and at large," Frederick Douglass observed in 1892, the killer "can tell any story he may please and will be believed." In the words of Ida B. Wells: "Dead men tell no tales, and living ones will not voluntarily do so when it means an exposure of their crimes."[5]

Beginning about the last decade of the century, white Southerners began to tell themselves and each other powerful stories about black men and white women—stories that invariably expounded upon the twin themes of rape and lynching, and that continued to equate black men's political power with sexual transgressions across the color line. In an effort to maintain the rigid racial categories of "black" and "white" that were vital to racial hierarchy, whites argued as well for the purity of white women in a way that began to cut more thoroughly across class lines. All of these narratives reveal an alarmingly vituperative strain of racism, a monstrous incarnation of proslavery thought.[6] At the same time, black Southerners and their Northern allies called attention to the political purposes of lynching. A few outspoken black Southerners also told entirely different stories about black men and white women, for in spite of the convictions of white apologists that a consensual liaison between a black man and a white woman was an impossibility, documents reveal that such liaisons continued to form in the decades after Reconstruction. Antilynching protesters drew on this fact, and accordingly offered their own interpretations of white violence in the late nineteenth-century South.

The Agency of White Women

There were cases in the late nineteenth-century South in which there had been no contact whatsoever between the alleged victim of rape and the victim of a lynching. Still, black antilynching protesters did not proclaim the innocence of every black man accused of raping a white woman. Frederick Douglass maintained that he had never "raised a finger or uttered a word in defense of any one really guilty of the dreadful crime now in question." Ida B. Wells knew that "individual Negroes commit crimes the same as do white men." Protesters focused solely on the injustice of lynching and on the notion that "the Negro race is peculiarly given to assault upon women." Wells noted that after a man was lynched there would "always be doubts as to his guilt," whereas there would be "no doubt whatever as to the guilt of those who murdered and tortured and burned alive this victim of their blood lust."[7]

Alternatively, then, the white woman could be a transgressor against the patriarchs of her family and community, taking cover under the cloak of victimization when discovered. If her parents, husband, or other relatives had been unaware of her illicit liaison with a black man, they could do the work for her, assuming her to be prey and then presenting her as such without dissent. If the family had suspected or known of illicit behavior, they could bury that knowledge in criminal charges, again with the woman's consent. The categories of consent and rape may in fact have become confused to the woman herself, especially after being held before her family and community as a violated female; as victim, she could in some measure be exalted. Refusal to cooperate could also result in violence at the hands of white patriarchs.

Part of the problem lay in the fact that whites now more often claimed consensual sex between a black man and a white woman to be unimaginable, expounding upon white women's revulsion at the thought. "Wealth, character, abilities, accomplishments and position, have no effect to modify this aversion of the white woman to a negro-marital alliance,"

Alabama senator and former Confederate general John T. Morgan reported in 1890, adding that "the snows will fall from heaven in sooty blackness, sooner than the white women of the United States will consent to the maternity of negro families." Frederick Douglass dispensed with such pronouncements, pointing out that "if the thing is impossible to happen no one should be afraid that it will happen."[8] Although some blacks defied whites by supporting marriage across the color line, others responded with disdain to such liaisons. "We don't want any white wives," Virginia editor John Mitchell announced. "Colored ones are good enough for us." John Edward Bruce, a journalist who had been born a slave in Maryland, made a note to himself in the corner of a letter from another black man that read: "A foxy half breed and trouble maker professional Negro, for revenue only married a second rate white woman."[9]

The ever-present threat of lynching proscribed consensual liaisons between black men and white women in the late nineteenth-century South. "With the Southern white man," Ida Wells wrote in 1895, "any mesalliance existing between a white woman and a colored man is a sufficient foundation for the charge of rape." Wells believed that "four-fifths of the cases of so-called assault of white women by black men would be called adultery" were it not for the factor of race. There were, however, instances in which families could not cover over the transgressions of a white woman. Such cases, though rare (when Ida Wells published her lists of alleged causes for lynching, only a handful out of hundreds appeared under the heading "miscegenation"), shed light on the dynamics of sexual liaisons between black men and white women in the post-Reconstruction South. Exactly why a white woman or her family would be unable to conceal an illicit liaison by conjuring rape charges remains obscure.[10]

The story of Ida Abercrombie and Peter Stamps in a small town west of Atlanta in Georgia's upper piedmont reveals possible complications. Peter Stamps, a married black man in his forties with seven children, worked for James M. Abercrombie, a white man from a prominent local family. A Civil War veteran and member of the Baptist church, Abercrombie owned a mill and a brickyard and played an active role in county development and local Democratic politics.[11] After rape charges were brought against Stamps, the newspapers described him as "a large black negro." On a summer night in 1885, Stamps was arrested at the Abercrombie farm and taken to jail. Hundreds gathered as the details of the alleged crime leaked out, and by the next afternoon a mob of five hundred was "ready to swing the negro from a tree." Into the night, the town was "wild," its streets clogged with white people "discussing the terrible story." The men carried shotguns, marginally disguising themselves with hats and bandannas. To no avail the sheriff apparently tried to avoid the gathering forces, but the mob (perhaps fifty, perhaps four hundred) caught up and in the middle of the night hanged Stamps from a bridge railing in the center of town. People then vanished but by daybreak returned to observe the suspended body. If the papers are to be believed, the crowd moved back as Peter Stamps's wife stared at her husband, cradling her newborn in her arms. The morning train was crammed with white sightseers hoping for a glimpse of the dead man. Not surprisingly, before the jury turned Stamps's body over to his wife, they pronounced that he had been hanged "by unknown parties."

What Peter Stamps had done was called "revolting, disgusting and deplorable," and it involved a white girl just thirteen years old. Ida Abercrombie was the daughter of Stamps's well-to-do employer and "pretty as a picture." She had a "wreath of golden hair," "drooping lashes," and "evenly shaped features." She was a good student, "the idol of her home," and the "favorite" of all who knew her. And yet, although (according to the papers) not one word of evil had ever been spoken against Ida Abercrombie, Peter Stamps was not charged with rape. The story was bigger than that. In the summer of 1885, Ida's stepmother could no longer ignore her suspicions that the child was pregnant (this "discovery which shocked her" was never named directly). When grown-ups questioned Ida, her answers were both perplexing and frightening. James Abercrombie immediately sent for two doctors who confirmed the stepmother's suspicions. When questioned a second time, the girl "told a most shocking story." It seemed that on a winter's night seven months earlier, Peter Stamps had "caught her" at the farmhouse and that "at subsequent times the same act had been repeated." Grieving and shamed, the father was assisted by friends who "advised the instant arrest of the negro." Before that could happen, however, Ida Abercrombie and Peter Stamps allegedly met one more time. A few nights later, Ida informed her father that she was going to die, and a quarter of an hour later she expired. This time the doctors determined that Ida had died of poisoning. It was after Ida's funeral that white people began to gather in the streets of Douglasville.

The public story relayed by white voices about Ida Abercrombie was thereafter a story about purity. Ida's responses to the inquiring adults had been "innocent answers"; she had had "no conception of what had transpired," had displayed complete "ignorance of the great wrong done her," and "though she did a great sin she was sinless." In short, Ida had been "too pure minded to know her sin." The girl's death could not possibly have been suicide, for Ida "had not realised her sin." Rather, Peter Stamps had handed the poison to Ida just before his arrest, "telling her that it would hide her shame." (The few white folks who held out for suicide concluded that Ida had sought "peace in death.") With a hint of puzzlement, an *Atlanta Constitution* reporter added, "It seems strange that a girl with a bright mind at her age should be so deluded, but no other story will ever be believed by the people of Douglasville." Any such doubts were cleared in the white newspaper's obligatory final statement: "While the people very much regret the circumstances causing the lynching, and the necessity for it, and do not openly advocate lawlessness, still they tacitly approve of what was done." As for Peter Stamps's version, the paper reported that his confession was "identical with the story of the girl." He had been kind to Ida Abercrombie when she was little, thereby winning her confidence; he "denied having overcome the girl," and he denied the poisoning. There is no other record of his voice.

The vagueness and unreliability of the account make it difficult to discern the nature of the liaison between Ida Abercrombie and Peter Stamps. Because the family did not bring rape charges, it seems likely that it was in some measure consensual and that other people knew of the consensual liaison—although in theory this should not have precluded a false accusation. Perhaps Ida's visible pregnancy (at seven months) had helped Stamps on this point. Perhaps townspeople knew that the circumstances were rather different from what the papers reported and that the news story was intended simply as a record for outsiders and posterity. Ida Wells would later uncover lynching accounts in which the victim's age was revised far downward, but this was not the case here; census records confirm that Ida Abercrombie was thirteen in 1885.[12] Perhaps she was a lonely or abused young woman who took refuge in Peter Stamps, who in turn took advantage of her. Perhaps she was a rebellious youth, and never-recorded gossip contradicting the newspaper account raged for weeks or months following the lynching. Perhaps the local black community knew the real story. Perhaps her father and stepmother had known of the liaison but cared to say nothing unless word got out, in the interest of preserving the family's reputation. Perhaps Peter Stamps was a valuable or irreplaceable laborer in the Abercrombie business (records indicate that although he was an agricultural worker, he may also have been a skilled blacksmith). Perhaps Ida's father and stepmother simply did not care. Much about the liaison remains elusive, yet the response of the white family reveals that at least in the mid-1880s, whites were unable to present every liaison between a black man and a white woman (or even a white girl) as unequivocal rape. The Stamps-Abercrombie affair demonstrates also that even when whites acknowledged such a liaison to be in some measure consensual, the woman could still be considered innocent and the black man murdered for the mutual transgression.[13]

Two briefer cases shed a dim beam of light on the circumstances that led to the lynching of Peter Stamps. In the Virginia piedmont in 1880, Arthur Jordan was taken from jail by a mob of perhaps fifty men in the middle of the night, tied, gagged, and hanged from a tree in a nearby cemetery. The coroner's jury determined that Jordan had died "at the hands of parties unknown," though people seemed to agree that the men came from Nathan Corder's neighborhood. The charge against Jordan was not rape but rather seduction, abduction, "influencing," and in some versions "marrying" the white Elvira Corder, the twenty-five-year-old daughter of Nathan. Jordan, a married man, lived with the Corders as a laborer for two years before he and Elvira tried to run away together; the two were caught in Maryland, where Jordan was arrested and brought back to a Virginia jail. Perhaps it was the too-public nature of the liaison, including the attempt to escape together, that precluded rape charges. Such local knowledge may thus have figured as well in the case of Peter Stamps and Ida Abercrombie. Another clue lies in the description of Elvira: although she was an "attractive" and "respectable" girl, she was also "of weak intellect," "half-witted," and "of unsound mind." In such cases whites may have felt it necessary to describe daughters from respected families as not entirely responsible for their own actions. In fact, although reporters described Ida Abercrombie as smart and studious, the overall effect conveyed nearly the opposite: a young girl so naive as to border on feeble-minded.[14]

Nearly a decade later, in Georgia's northern mountains in 1889, a band of disguised men broke into the home of John Duncan. They told the black man to get out of bed and pray, but before he could do so someone fired a shot and killed him. Like Peter Stamps and Arthur Jordan, Duncan lived on the farm of a white man, and like the other two, he was described as married. Duncan had once been "considered an inoffensive, harmless negro" until it came to light that "a white woman lived in the same house with him and his children." The identity of the white woman was never revealed and her character never assessed, but the two were clearly cohabiting, and for this the man was lynched. Perhaps, then, at least some whites in the Abercrombies' neighborhood had understood the newspaper account of the Stamps lynching as at least in part invented.[15]

The violent revenge of white patriarchs did not always take the form of mob lynching. There were times instead when male relatives intervened individually and went on record for it, and such a case sheds another thin ray of light on consensual liaisons between black men and white women in the late nineteenth-century South. In the East End neighborhood of Richmond, Virginia, in 1897, a young black man named Paul Davis was shot as he moved from jail to courthouse to stand trial for rape. The man who intended to kill Davis was Carlos Twitchell, a white farmer of little means who had recently employed Davis and who claimed that Davis had raped his daughter, Cora. Paul Davis, who was gravely wounded by the shooting, had once lived with the Twitchell family, sharing meals and sleeping in their one-room dwelling. Cora's father was prompted to vengeance by his wife's news that his daughter was "in a delicate condition" due to Paul's assault. When a doctor confirmed the pregnancy, the father "became nearly crazy with anger" and had the black man arrested. Carlos Twitchell swore at first that his daughter was fourteen when Davis raped her, but when he learned that a death sentence could be handed down for the rape of an underage girl, he changed his mind and swore that she had been thirteen. Cora's father justified violence the same way elite white apologists did. "The idea of a man's daughter being ruined and by a 'nigger' at that," he said. "I did no more than any other man would have done." Although Richmond's black newspaper described the Twitchell family as of "little or no social standing in the community," a white reporter called Cora Twitchell the "daughter of respectable white parents," indicating that the designation of respectability could have less to do with class standing and more to do with allegedly suffering rape at the hands of a black man. Just as the Atlanta papers had described Peter Stamps as a "large black negro," false pictures of Davis had been published to make him look darker. Black editor John Mitchell believed that such images had been circulated in an effort to "prejudice public sentiment against him." Mitchell thus called attention to white apologists' purposes in equating blackness with crime in an effort to differentiate supposedly threatening black men from supposedly trustworthy white men.

Richmond's black weekly told a story quite different from the one Cora Twitchell's father relayed. Under such headlines as "Woman's Love: A Strange Infatuation of a White Girl for Paul Davis," the *Planet* reported how the two had often walked toward school together, separating where the roads diverged to their respective destinations, and how Cora visited Paul after he had stopped working for the Twitchell family. In a rare instance of a black man's first-person account, Paul Davis told a *Planet* interviewer how Cora "used to come over there after me," "stay all day sometimes," and send notes "two and three times a week" asking to meet with him. When Cora implored Paul to run away with her, he refused. "I told her I couldn't go," he remembered. "She said she was coming after me to go with her anyway." The girl's father "tried to get her to say that I ravished her," Davis explained, "and she wouldn't do it." [16]

The ensuing progression of Cora Twitchell's testimony, confessions, and refutations reveals something of the experience of a white girl pursuing a relationship with a black man in the late nineteenth-century South. At the trial Cora concurred with her parents that Paul Davis had raped her and that she had been underage. Davis "had first had intercourse" with her "in the kitchen about the middle of June, 1896," she testified, "and at another time in the woods" when she was "watching the cows." A child was born in March of the following year. Paul Davis was convicted and sentenced to nine years in prison (Carlos Twitchell was acquitted for the shooting). But a month later, Cora changed her mind. Wishing "to repair the wrong I did to Davis," as she said, she went back to county officials to swear that the liaison had been consensual ("One was as much to blame as the other!"), that she had not in fact been underage, and that she had testified "from fear of my parents." [17] But after another month passed, Cora was back refuting that confession: everything she had said in court was true after all. "I am not in the least afraid of my parents," she asserted, but rather had reversed the testimony under pressure from Paul Davis's mother, who tearfully "begged" Cora "to do something for her son." [18]

Evidence, however, points to the truth of parental pressure and coercion. The lawyer who defended Paul Davis contended that Cora had visited his office after the trial. "I want you to get Paul Davis out of jail," Cora had commanded, explaining, "It is my fault that he is in there." She then invented a scenario in accordance with her own wishes: "I was engaged to be married to him," she stated, "and we intended to run away and be married, if mother had not found out how matters stood between us." Cora then confided that she had left home in fear that she would "be either killed or cruelly beaten or driven from home by my parents." (Cora's mother herself later visited the lawyer "in a towering passion" and "a violent rage.") Moreover, Paul's mother told her own story of how Cora had come to her home to apologize, offering hopes that the new information she had given would "do Paul good." On the strength of this evidence, Paul Davis was granted a new trial and then set free when the state declined to prosecute any further.[19]

Preserved with the court testimony is a packet of letters from Cora Twitchell to Paul Davis, written as her pregnancy was advancing. Though brief and cryptic, these notes offer a rare glimpse of emotions. The girl's affection was apparent. "I would like to see you before you go," she wrote one day. "But I do not want you to go, for I will be alone. . . . Stay home for me. . . . I am afraid I might not see you any more." In another letter, she wrote jealously: "Did you have a good time with that girl you was telling me about? . . . I know you want to see her again." But the letters also reveal Cora's futile determination to extract promises from Paul in the face of her dire circumstances, and illuminate the potentially coercive powers of a white woman in the post-Reconstruction South. "I want to see you Sunday, up you know where we was before," she told her lover. "Do not forget what you told me you would do." Every letter contained some such instructions, though Paul Davis clearly held his own. "I want you to stay with me Sunday, for I will be alone," she wrote another time. "Do as I tell you. About nine o'clock I will be up you know where." Only once did Cora allude more directly to pregnancy, expressing fear that her mother would "find it out," and begging Paul, "don't show this to no one." Cora had apparently told her mother about "Paul's intimacy with her" once she was questioned, and some believed that her father "knew of the intimacy," as well. The knowledge may have been more widespread, for Cora stated that "no one complained to her parents because she associated with a colored person." In an echo of antebellum cases, it was only with the birth of a child to prove the liaison that the white family took action.[20]

Carlos Twitchell's attempt at violent revenge failed, and with a defiant daughter he could not invoke purity and respectability to rally local forces behind him. Perhaps then, in the case of Ida Abercrombie and Peter Stamps, Ida's father and stepmother, too, had begged her to confirm rape charges to no avail. Although the wealthy and admired Abercrombies were able to invoke the veil of purity even in the absence of rape charges—remember that Ida had sinned but remained innocent—the poorer Twitchell family could not make that leap. Neither Ida Abercrombie nor Cora Twitchell had played their proper roles as white women, yet Ida's class standing allowed her to retain the chivalric protection of white men. But this was also possible because Ida was dead; Cora, in contrast, was a troublemaking white woman with an illegitimate "black" child in her arms. And while Peter Stamps had been silenced and killed, Paul Davis remained alive and gave his own story to the press. It is not entirely out of the question, then, that Ida Abercrombie's own father had poisoned her in order to silence his daughter and tell the story his own way. That story included memorializing Ida Abercrombie as a pure and innocent white girl.

Clues to consensual liaisons between black men and white women at the end of the century are scarce. On occasion white women spoke out to prevent lynching, but the circumstances remain shrouded. In the Tennessee mountains around the turn of the century, a freedman named Alf Cannon and a white servant-woman had a child. When a mob came for Cannon, the woman declared herself at fault with more courage than Cora Twitchell, convincing the white men that Cannon "didn't rape her." Cannon's former masters drove off the mob. Alf Cannon was an angry loner with few friends, and the entire incident was later mentioned only rarely and with the direst warnings about secrecy.[21] But for every white woman who crossed her male relatives by remaining silent like Ida Abercrombie, by attempting to run away like Elvira Corder, by cohabiting with a black man like John Duncan's anonymous partner, by trying feebly to speak forthrightly like Cora Twitchell, or by contradicting a mob like Alf Cannon's lover, hundreds of others consented to fables about rape. Here was a significant change from the antebellum South, where white relatives and neighbors did not so swiftly assume or invoke sexual violence.

In 1894, an anonymous North Carolinian who had left the South described a presumably representative scenario as follows: "Very frequently a Negro will secretly visit some white woman, and for a time the intercourse not be known; but should it be suspected to any extent, the safest thing for him to do would be to 'light out' the first dark night; for he will be watched, and when found going to see his paramour word is given and he is caught." Up to this point, this had indeed been the fate of Peter Stamps, Arthur Jordan, John Duncan, and Paul Davis. In the typical case, this nameless writer continued, the white woman "denounces him as having assaulted her, and proclaims her virtue and innocence. The poor darkey is strung up, and his voice is silenced."[22] Although that was not precisely what had come to pass for Stamps, Jordan, Duncan, and Davis, three of those men were murdered and the fourth was meant to be. This, too, marked a significant change. According to some forthright black anti-lynching activists in the South, the deaths of a great many other black men fit that anonymously detailed outline perfectly. When these activists attempted to talk about the agency of white women in liaisons with black men, the consequences were extremely grave.

Alternative Stories About Lynching

Ida B. Wells was the most outspoken of these activists, but she was neither the first nor the last to offer stories about white women's voluntary participation in sexual liaisons with black men and their subsequent capitulation to lynchers. Sometime in the mid-1880s, an obscure black newspaper out of Atlanta, Georgia, carried the following editorial:

> The constant reports of white women in the South being raped by colored men has become a stale old lie. It does seem that a great many of them get off in lonesome places with colored men in a surprising degree. This is a sort of predestination, but there seems to be a great spirit of watchfulness on the part of the white men, who somehow don't seem to trust their white sisters with the Negro. These white girls want watching as well as the Negroes. The whole thing looks like a partnership business until somebody is caught."[23]

The writer here likely knew at least a few cases in which black men had been lynched for "partnerships" with white women, and felt the need to bring the possibility of such scenarios to light. But if this editor was too obscure to reach many white readers, that was not the case for the politically active Jesse Duke of Alabama.

Jesse C. Duke, a leader in both the Republican party and the black Baptist church, had witnessed a brutal lynching in the summer of 1887. The alleged crime was rape, and Duke addressed himself to the subject in his own weekly, the *Montgomery Herald*. "Every day or so we read of the lynching of some negro for the outraging of some white woman," began his editorial. Shifting the burden from black men to white women, he asked: "Why is it that white women attract negro men now more than former days?" Duke offered his own interpretation of this change. "There was a time when such a thing was unheard of," he wrote. "There is a secret to this thing, and we greatly suspect it is the growing appreciation of the white Juliet for the colored Romeo, as he becomes more and more intelligent and refined." Duke struck here at the heart of white fears that independent black men would achieve so-called social equality.

If Duke thought that white people did not read his paper or would pay little attention if they did, he was wrong. The outcry was swift and angry. Seventy-five whites attended a public meeting and passed a resolution declaring Duke's words "an intolerable insult." Another resolution declared Duke himself "a vile and dangerous character, who seems bent on inculcating doctrines among his race that are a menace to society and to every white woman in the land." Yet another called him "a scoundrel who has crossed the limit of toleration." More than two hundred white men signed the declarations, giving Duke eight hours to leave town "or take the consequences." Either fortuitously or speedily, Duke had departed for a Sunday School convention, and his wife could not or would not reveal his whereabouts. (When word came that he had been spotted in a restaurant, a delegation rushed to bully him, only to find him gone; a committee of ten met each train at the station to no avail.) White leaders proffered Duke's words in an effort to halt the construction of a recently approved black college in Montgomery. "We deprecate any further efforts being made to introduce any such 'Educated' Romeos in our midst," they intoned. One white man saw proof in Duke's words that a schooled black man became "an unmitigated fool with unparalleled effrontery," prompting him to ask: "What State had the honor of educating this brute?" Irate whites continued "a sharp lookout" for Duke through the night and into the following day, as more than a hundred people again gathered to put a stop to the college.

Although white reporters commented smugly on the orderliness of these events (with descriptions of seemingly quiet meetings issuing thoughtful resolutions), the response of the black community belies that version. Prominent black men in Montgomery called their own meeting, not to protest but to figure out how best to protect themselves from white fury. The convener, James Hale, presented whites with a statement "disclaiming sympathy with Duke or his paper and condemning in the strongest terms" the offending commentary. Whites targeted other prominent black men, too. A lawyer suspected of prior knowledge of the editorial was handed train fare and told to leave "in all possible haste." Assuring his enemies that "he had had nothing to do with Duke's article," this man also revealed "very ill and unpleasant treatment at the hands of some of our white citizens." Whites next accused a black doctor of preaching "that the negro is as good as the white man and should assert himself," forcing the man to offer an "emphatic disclaimer of any connection with Duke." Though it was never reported in the newspapers, the white men also pounded on the door of the Duke home and broke windows as his wife and children took refuge in the cellar.

White Alabama newspapers spewed forth venom. One described Jesse Duke as "the insolent negro" whose "foul insult" excused "the outraging of white women by negroes." To let him escape without at least a tarring and feathering would constitute "violence to the women of Montgomery and of the entire country," and, readers were warned, "your wife, your sister, and your daughter, are objects of this animal's attack." Another editor added formal politics to the brew, noting that Duke came from "the class of negroes that the Republicans sought to force upon the South" during Reconstruction, adding, "No wonder the whites became solid for Democracy." Finally, a white man wrote to endorse the swift reaction to Duke's editorial. "You will preserve the purity and integrity of your race if you have to kill every negro that exists in your midst," he cheered. In the middle of the night, a black messenger delivered Duke's apology to the offices of the white newspaper: his editorial had been "unfortunate," and he had intended no offense, he said; he was "very sorry, indeed," and would "never" do such a thing "any more." Reminding his tormentors of his status as "a poor man" with a family to support, Duke signed off "Very Respectfully." The presses of Duke's *Montgomery Herald* were spared from destruction only because they were owned by a white man.

When the commotion died down after several days, it remained certain that "Duke must stay away." The family left Alabama for Arkansas, where Jesse Duke continued his career in journalism. From outside the state, he sent a letter to Montgomery both disavowing any intention of maligning white women and denouncing journalistic intolerance. Duke claimed that he had written the editorial in a state of "impassioned indignation at the repeated and increasing lynching of my race."[24] The Reverend T. W. Coffee of the African Methodist Episcopal church, who edited a newspaper out of Birmingham, subsequently defended Jesse Duke with the question: "Is it not possible that white women could love colored men; what is there inhuman about this?"[25] Jesse Duke, T. W. Coffee, and the editor of the obscure Atlanta newspaper understood the possibility of consensual sex between black men and white women in the post-Reconstruction South, but whites would not hear it.

In the early 1890s, Ida Wells, co-editor and part owner of Memphis's black weekly newspaper, embarked on a mission to tell the world about consenting white women. Wells, born a slave in Mississippi during the war, investigated more than seven hundred lynchings, published her findings in a black-owned New York newspaper and a fifteen-cent pamphlet financed by Northern black women, and became the foremost antilynching activist in the United States. She criticized racist whites and silent blacks, took her campaign to England, and remained a pioneer of the antilynching crusade until well into the twentieth century, especially following the death of Frederick Douglass in 1895.[26] Her investigations brought to light liaisons between black men and white women that had been, in her words, "voluntary, clandestine and illicit." In 1892, Wells published a now-famous editorial in her *Memphis Free Speech*. "Nobody in this section of the country believes the old thread bare lie that Negro men rape white women," she wrote. "If Southern white men are not careful, they will over-reach themselves and public sentiment will have a reaction; a conclusion will then be reached which will be very damaging to the moral reputation of their women." Memphis whites were as incensed as Montgomery whites had been five years before, and whether on purpose or by chance, Wells was up north when the piece ran. This time there was no pretense of order. White people called a meeting and burned the presses. They threatened Wells's life and kept watch over incoming trains and Wells's home. One editor warned of "no mercy for the negro rapist and little patience with his defenders." Another, who assumed the editorial's author to be male, suggested castration: "Tie the wretch who utters these calumnies to a stake," he directed, "and perform upon him a surgical operation with a pair of tailor's shears." Wells never returned home, her business manager fled, and whites assaulted a black man who had once owned the paper, forcing him at gunpoint to sign a statement condemning the words as "slander on white women."[27]

Ida Wells continued her reporting from the North, where she worked for T. Thomas Fortune's black newspaper, the *New York Age*. Like Jessie Duke before her, Wells placed the burden of agency on white women. There were "many white woman in the South," Wells declared, "who would marry colored men" if they could do so without shame. "White men lynch the offending Afro-American," she wrote, "not because he is a despoiler of virtue, but because he succumbs to the smiles of white women." The facts alone, Wells believed, would defend "the Afro-American Sampsons who suffer themselves to be betrayed by white Delilahs." Relentlessly Wells sounded the theme of mutuality. "Why should it be impossible to believe white women guilty of the same crime for which Southern white men are notorious?" Wells asked in the early 1890s. "In numerous instances where colored men have been lynched on the charge of rape," she wrote in 1895, "it was positively known at the time of lynching, and indisputably proven after the victim's death, that the relationship sustained between the man and woman was voluntary and clandestine." Lynchers knew this all too well, she contended. "Such cases are not rare," Wells insisted, "but the press and people conversant with the facts, almost invariably suppress them."[28]

Employing the strategy that whites were best condemned with their own words, Ida Wells gathered much of her information from the white press, often quoting verbatim. In Memphis alone, Wells unearthed six voluntary liaisons between black men and white women. In one, a white woman named Sarah Clark "loved a black man and lived openly with him." When indicted for "miscegenation," the woman "swore in court that she was *not* a white woman," thereby absolving herself. In another, a white woman living on Poplar Street was "discovered in intimate relations" with a black man named Will Morgan. The woman helped Morgan escape to the North and joined him there. In another, the seventeen-year-old white Lillie Bailey ran away from home only to end up in the Women's

Refuge, where she gave birth to a child whose father was black. Bailey refused to reveal the father's identity, moving one white reporter to speculate on "some very nauseating details in the story of her life." In other Memphis cases, black men were lynched for liaisons they claimed had been voluntary. Just before Richard Neale was lynched in front of two hundred people, for example, he warned other black men away from the "blandishments" of white women. According to a report in a white paper, the alleged rape victim, Mrs. Jack White, asked the constable to no avail "if he could not save the Negro's life."

What was true of Memphis, Wells felt sure, was "true of the entire South." In Natchez, Mississippi, a well-to-do white woman named Mrs. Marshall delivered a child whose complexion gave pause to family and friends before the baby was "traced to some brunette ancestor." When the second baby was too dark, the Marshall's coachman left town and Mrs. Marshall followed soon thereafter. In Indianola, Mississippi, the papers reported a lynching for the rape of the sheriff's eight-year-old daughter; according to Wells's investigation, the daughter "was more than eighteen years old, and was found by her father in this man's room, who was a servant on the place." In a case on the Arkansas-Texas border, an investigation into the lynching of Edward Coy determined that the white woman had been "a willing partner" and "publicly reported and generally known to have been criminally intimate" with the man for more than a year. Thus did Ida Wells conclude that there was "hardly a town in the South" free of a "well-known" liaison between a black man and a white woman. For each case Wells reported with confidence, she must have been stymied by a great many others. In one instance she wrote, "We feel this to be a garbled report, but how can we prove it?"[29]

Wells was adamant that her declarations did not malign white women; when so accused she reiterated that her aim was only to prove the injustice of assuming rape and the dire necessity for fair trials. Yet Wells also uncovered cases in which whites described a known relationship as rape, thereby proving the hopelessness of a fair trial. In Alabama, for example, when a white woman gave birth to a child whose father was black, Daniel Edwards was jailed and lynched in a crowd of a hundred. Yet the woman's mother had known that the "relationship had been sustained for more than a year," and the lynchers pinned a notice to Edwards warning black men who were "too intimate with white girls," thereby acknowledging the relationship. The papers later claimed that "Edwards was lynched for rape." [30]

Neither Jesse Duke nor Ida Wells elaborated on the motives of prevaricating white women, but one of Wells's reports offers an important clue. In the lynching of Edward Coy in 1892, an investigation undertaken by a Chicago newspaper revealed that the white woman had been "paraded as a victim of violence" and "compelled by threats, if not by violence, to make the charge against the victim." If white women sometimes took the initiative in claiming rape in order to save their reputations, they could also be threatened into sustaining charges of rape. That is what Cora Twitchell's father had hoped to accomplish when he discovered his daughter's liaison. Perhaps that is also what Ida Abercrombie's father had hoped to accomplish. Yet although Cora Twitchell and Ida Abercrombie thwarted such plans, many other white women concurred in naming their black partners as rapists. Some of those women must have been coerced into concurring, and in those cases, marks of violence on their bodies were likely sustained at the hands of white fathers or husbands. Those markings could then be displayed as evidence of rape by a black man. A white woman in Virginia, for example, "finally broke down and confessed that she had told her story in order to conceal her own shame, and the bruises on her throat were made by her indignant husband because of her infidelity." [31]

At century's end, a third black activist spoke from the South about the agency of white women. Alexander Manly was the editor of a North Carolina black newspaper, the *Wilmington Daily Record,* when he penned a response to a speech given by the inflammatory white Southerner Rebecca Latimer Felton. Felton, who had grown up in a well-to-do slaveowning family, carried the figure of the subordinate but protected plantation mistress with her into the uncertainties of the post–Civil War era. When she began to lecture to rural whites in the 1890s, she expounded often upon white farm women and their fears of black men. Speaking before the Georgia Agricultural Society in 1897, Felton delivered what would become a famous announcement: "If it needs lynching to protect woman's dearest possession from the ravening human beasts—then I say 'lynch;' a thousand times a week if necessary." [32]

In the summer of 1898, Alexander Manly challenged Felton's ideas about black rapists. Addressing himself to white men, Manly wrote: "You leave your goods out of doors and then complain because they are taken away. Poor white men are careless in the matter of protecting their women, especially on farms." Manly offered an alternative version of events: "Our experience among poor white people in the country," he wrote, "teaches us that the women of that race are not any more particular in the matter of clandestine meetings with colored men, than are the white men with colored women." He elaborated, "Meetings of this kind go on for some time, until the woman's infatuation or the man's boldness bring attention to them and the man is lynched for rape." Manly then broadened his narrative to include elite white women: "Every negro lynched is called a 'big, burly, black brute,' when in fact many of those who have thus been dealt with had white men for their fathers, and were not only not 'black' and 'burly,' but were sufficiently attractive for white girls of culture and refinement to fall in love with them, as is well known to all." Finally, Manly appealed to white women to tell their men "that it is no worse for a black man to be intimate with a white woman than for a white man to be intimate with a colored woman." [33] Predictably now, the white reaction was instant and furious. All other news, according to one observer, "was crowded out to afford room for daily repetitions of the Negro editor's defamatory article." A white man declared that Manly "ought to be food for catfish in Cape Fear River." A white woman invoked politics as she "urged the white voter to save her sex from outrage." A Democratic spokesman later remembered how Manly's words "went like wildfire from house to house, particularly in the rural districts. The women and their husbands were righteously indignant." [34]

The timing of Manly's editorial, less than three months prior to North Carolina's 1898 elections, caused an explosion. Four years earlier, a "fusion" of Republicans and Populists had put the Democrats out of power, and the party was determined to regain control with as much violence as necessary. Here the conflation of black men's political rights with sexual transgressions across the color line reached perhaps its highest pitch of the century. Manly's assessment of white women's agency soon became central to white supremacist Democrats in statewide campaigns, and Democratic newspapers reprinted a hundred thousand copies of the editorial for the upcoming election. One of North Carolina's major papers led the attack, thundering, "Read the following, white men of North Carolina, and see one of the effects of Russellism and Butlerism in your State"—referring to Republican governor Daniel Russell and Populist senator Marion Butler. In case the meaning was lost on any reader, the paper explained, "Republican rule bears the fruit of insult and outrage to white women of the South always and everywhere that it gains control in the Southern States." The most sensational headline summarized Manly's editorial as follows: "White Women Slandered. A Leading Negro Republican Newspaper Excuses Rapists. Declares that Attractive White Girls of Culture Fall in Love With Negroes, and the Assaults Committed are the Result of Mutual Love and Not of Violence—The Poor White Women are Charged With Secret Meetings With Negro Men and With Being Infatuated With Them."[35] The chain of events was a severe setback for black and white Republicans and Populists, who "saw at once what a terrible political blunder had been made" and took pains to assure whites that they considered the editorial "base libel" and Manly "an irresponsible upstart." Manly also made enemies among Wilmington's leading black citizens, a number of whom hoped he would cease publication for the sake of peace. One black government official thought that the editorial "lost the two parties 25,000 votes among the poorer whites who were slandered."[36]

In the days before the election of 1898, a story appeared in a Democratic newspaper that intertwined sex and politics at every turn. Maggie Brewer, a white woman married to a "prominent" white farmer, had run away from her home in Chapel Hill with a black man named Manly McCauley, the family's hired laborer. The paper informed readers that Maggie had been "brought up by a Republican father" who associated with black people and that Maggie's husband was a Republican who had "been seen hanging around among the negroes." The reporter warned "fellow Democrats and white people" that this was "an index of how things will be if negroes are allowed to predominate," using the occasion to urge Democrats to "vote for white supremacy." Indeed, Maggie's white husband "announced that in the future he will vote the Democratic ticket," for he had realized "in his own home the horrible effects of the social equality teachings of the Republican party." The story's political twist may have been fabricated, but a search party captured the couple, and two days before the election the body of Manly McCauley was found hanging from a tree. Around the same time, a white Wilmington paper ran a story about a black man who reportedly told a white woman that he would be her "fellow." The editors warned that "the greatest forbearance" prevented a lynching of "this brute" and named the fusionist politicians as the cause of black men thinking themselves "as good as the 'poor white man.' "[37]

The lynching of Alexander Manly was averted in part by Wilmington's black police officers, but white leaders were also eager to keep the volatile issue of the editorial—and therefore Manly himself—alive throughout the campaign. Manly had no choice but to smooth over his militant statements as the election approached. "The whole trouble at Wilmington was caused by the misconstruction of an article in my paper," he announced in the fall. "Flaming mutilations of this article were published all through the South, and I was charged with slandering the virtue of white women. Such a thought never entered my head." Rebecca Felton was quick with a doubly violent rejoinder, blaming the political rights of black men for "trembling and afraid" white women and exclaiming, "when you take the negro into your embraces on election day to control his vote" and "make him believe he is a man and your brother," so long would lynching continue. The cause of lynching, Felton predicted, "will grow and increase with every election." (Here she reiterated her call to action: "If it requires lynching to protect woman's dearest possession from ravening, drunken human beasts, then I say lynch a thousand negroes a week, if it is necessary.") Themes of race and manhood are not difficult to discern in these dialogues. While Alexander Manly criticized white men for their supposed inadequate protection of their women ("You leave your goods out of doors and then complain because they are taken away"), Rebecca Felton warned white men that to permit a black voter to feel like "a man and your brother" would incite the rape of white women.[38]

Guided by well-planned statewide corruption and violence, Democrats regained control of the state, though not the city of Wilmington, in November. Just after the election, hundreds of armed white men (Wilmington's "very best citizens," according to one Democrat) met to demand suspension of Manly's paper and threatened to expel Manly "by force" should he not leave the county. The following day a group of men demolished the presses and burned the building. A committee of whites forced fifteen black leaders to submit their approval of the press's destruction; after that, many others had no choice but to denounce the outspoken editor. Manly left the city, and whites later blamed him for the riot. Between ten and twenty black residents were killed, many more were wounded, and thousands fled, their homes and property seized or destroyed by marauding whites. According to a black Baptist pastor in Wilmington, "All the better class of the colored citizens were driven from the city, showing to the world that they were not after the criminal and ignorant class of Negroes, but the professional and business men."[39] Two years later, when black North Carolina congressman George H. White refuted the idea that rape was the major cause of lynching, he was denounced by a Democratic editor for his "Manleyism." Decades later, a white man remembered that Manly's "base slander of the white womanhood of the South" had "directly started" the white uprising of 1898.[40]

Jessie C. Duke, Ida B. Wells, and Alexander Manly—no doubt along with other more obscured black voices—told alternative stories about black men and white women in the late nineteenth-century South, speaking in some measure for the silenced victims of lynching. At the same time that these protesters criticized white women, black antilynching activists also knew that those same women were crucial to their struggle. "But what a tremendous influence for law and order, and what a mighty foe to mob violence Southern white women might be," wrote Mary Church Terrell in 1904, "if they would arise in the purity and power of their womanhood to implore their fathers, husbands and sons no longer to stain their hands with the black man's blood!"[41] The edge in Terrell's reference to white women's "purity and power" is unmistakable. In one sense, Southern white women of any class commanded power: as long as they feared black men or said that they did, as long as they consented to transforming a liaison into rape, as long as they called for the lynching of black men, the dominant narrative would retain its strength. Of course, there were white women who defied Southern patriarchs, but neither their numbers nor their power was great enough to cause the disintegration of white-told tales about the rape of white women by black men. Neither were the tactics of Duke, Manly, and Wells embraced by all blacks; some felt that the incendiary stories did more harm than good.[42] But white listeners would most especially hear none of it, for the stories told by crusading black journalists in the post-Reconstruction South clashed with changing ideas about the purity of white women that were crucial to the larger purposes of disempowering black people after the Civil War.

On the Purity of White Women and the Danger of Black Men

The construction of white female purity in the post-Reconstruction South was dependent upon images of black men as bestial, and a white woman's innocence was contingent upon assault by a black man rather than a white man. At the same time, the purity of white women was also dependent upon images of black women as depraved. White constructions of black women as lustful had served slavemasters' purposes, and such ideas continued to serve whites after emancipation. Black women in the late nineteenth-century South were also the victims of lynch mobs, but more often they were subject to assault and rape by white men, a form of sexual violence that provoked neither legal nor extralegal retribution on the part of white people.[43] Black women figured in all kinds of derogatory ways in the stories white Southerners told about lynching in the late nineteenth century. Among the most common was the idea that black women were responsible for the supposed criminality of their sons and husbands. According to Philip Alexander Bruce, whose father had owned hundreds of slaves in Virginia, a black man was "so accustomed to the wantonness of the women of his own race" that it was no wonder he was "unable to gauge the terrible character of this offense against the integrity of virtuous womanhood." A North Carolina lawyer likewise decided that the "want of virtue" among black women caused their men to retaliate by "the commission of rape upon the white women, which is sure to be followed by a lynching."[44] Black protesters told their own stories about the relation of black women to lynching. The founding of the National Association of Colored Women in 1896 by elite black women was prompted in part by the desire to challenge both the lynching of black men and the defamation of black women. Ida B. Wells castigated white men for a chivalry that, as she put it, "confines itself entirely to the women who happen to be white." Alexander Manly mocked the hypocrisy of white men, writing, "You cry aloud for the virtue of your women, while you seek to destroy the morality of ours." As activist Nannie Burroughs pointed out, "The same man who will join a mob to lynch a Negro for committing an outrage upon a white woman will outrage a black or white woman any time he makes up his mind so to do."[45]

Dominant ideas about white women, black women, and purity were part of a larger scheme of ideas that grew out of the transition from black slavery to black freedom. The racial caste system that emerged in the post-Reconstruction South was neither slavery nor equality but rather a system of racial subordination based on an ever more rigid color line. Whites ultimately preserved racial hierarchy with the "one-drop rule," whereby anyone with any known African ancestry was classified as "Negro." As early as 1876 a black man had observed, "They call everybody a negro that is as black as the ace of spades or as white as snow, if they think he is a negro or know that he has negro blood in his veins." Whereas the institution of slavery had satisfactorily preserved the equation of blackness and slavery, the one-drop rule was the next best solution in a world that lacked legal bondage. But to preserve racial hierarchy in the absence of slavery, white people had to guard the categories of "black" and "white," entailing more vigilant surveillance of the mixture of European and African ancestry in order to be able to tell who belonged on which side of the color line. By this logic, white men should have made sure that no black women bore their children, and some whites did worry tangentially about this phenomenon. H. S. Fulkerson, for example, expressed anxiety that white women might follow in the footsteps of their immoral brothers: would white men "yield their fair sisters to the embrace of the lustful black?" he asked. "If not, then let them beware of their own lusts." For the most part, however, white men turned a convenient ideological somersault to justify their own access to black women while furiously denouncing sex between black men and white women on the grounds of racial purity.[46]

In the antebellum South, the children of slave mothers and white fathers had reinforced the social order by producing enslaved children of African ancestry. In the post–Civil War South, it likewise mattered not at all if a black woman gave birth to a child of partial European ancestry, for any child born of a black woman was, according to the one-drop rule, fully "black" regardless of paternity. In the antebellum South, white women who gave birth to children of partial African ancestry had confounded racial slavery, yet such imperfections in the social structure had not significantly threatened racial hierarchy. But the case was different for white women after the Civil War. With only the one-drop rule to guard white supremacy, all white women had to give birth to all-white children. As a result, no white person ever challenged sex between a white man and a black woman with anything more than verbal condemnations, and here is where the ideological somersault came into play. Charles Carroll, a writer intent on proving scientifically that black people were not human beings, defined "amalgamation" as solely the result of sex between black men and white women. Because white women were "the great stronghold, the vital point" of creation, he explained, the white race would not be "absorbed and destroyed by amalgamation" as long as white women confined themselves to white men. The illustrations accompanying Carroll's treatise depict a white woman cuddling an apelike black baby; a fashionably dressed white couple with a very dark little girl walking between them (here the man casts the woman a suspicious glance as she stares coldly ahead); and two white parents at the bedside of three children, one of whom is black, with the subtitle, "Will Your Next Child Be a Negro?" Likewise, white writer William Smith reasoned that the transgressions of white men were "individual and limited," whereas those of white women struck "mortally at the existence of the family itself." True, it was disgraceful that white men had already mixed African and European "blood," yet those transgressions could not "even in the slightest conceivable degree" make a difference, for (according to Smith) women alone were the carriers of racial identity. The "blood" of white women remained "absolutely pure," he insisted, "and it is the inflexible resolution of the South to preserve that purity, no matter how dear the cost."[47]

The one-drop rule was codified in *Plessy v. Ferguson,* the Supreme Court decision of 1896 that established segregation by the doctrine of "separate but equal." Homer Plessy, who had challenged a Louisiana law requiring separate railway cars for "white" and "colored" people, described himself as seven-eighths white and one-eighth black. Plessy's lawyer asked rhetorically: "Why not count every one as white in whom is visible any trace of white blood?" Part of the answer lay in the determination to preserve white supremacy through a rigid color line constructed so as to dismiss the depredations of white men upon black women while requiring the strict surveillance of black men and white women. Recall that Jim Crow laws allayed white anxieties about the integration of blacks and whites in places frequented by both sexes, and that white Southerners invoked the dreaded idea of "social equality" to connote conditions that could result in sexual contact between black men and white women.[48]

Lynching not only terrorized black men and women, but it also subordinated white women. White women's fear was in fact a favorite theme of lynching apologists, both male and female. Southern academic George

Winston thought that white women alone in their farmhouses shuddered in "nameless horror" at a knock on the door. "The black brute is lurking in the dark," he lectured, "a monstrous beast, crazed with lust." North Carolina editor Clarence Poe believed that "for every negro who is disturbed by fear of the mob, a hundred white women are haunted by the nameless dread." White women themselves made the same point. "Even in small towns the husband cannot venture to leave his wife alone for an hour at night," writer Corra Harris stated in 1899. "At no time, in no place, is the white woman safe from the insults and assaults of these creatures." Another white woman portrayed a similarly threatening atmosphere: "Hovering over women in their country homes is a cloud of fear blacker than a starless night," she declared. Perhaps some of this dread on the part of white women stemmed from what they knew would be the violent reaction of their male relatives if a liaison across the color line came to pass or was suspected. These fears—of both black men and white men—enabled white men to hold fast to their roles as protectors of white women. Such protection was, as before, a bargain: to earn the guardianship of white men against the presumed danger of black men, a white woman had to abide by certain rules. Just as white ideas about the dangers of black men intensified after emancipation, so, too, did white ideology about the purity of white women.[49]

Such ideas would never cut entirely across white class lines, but in the late nineteenth century, convictions about the sexual depravity of poor white women began to command less power. Dominant ideas about white female purity now came to include poor women more overtly, as those who expounded upon the threat of black men took care to include lower-class women in their most sweeping statements. "This proneness of the negro is so well understood," wrote Philip Bruce, "that the white women of every class, from the highest to the lowest, are afraid to venture to any distance alone, or even to wander unprotected in the immediate vicinity of their homes." Maligning Alexander Manly, one North Carolina newspaper commented that his offending editorial was "a sweeping insult to all respectable white women who are poor" and that it slurred "every white wife in the South whose condition is poor as to this world's goods." There were also cases to prove that neither a white woman's poverty nor her supposed depravity would particularly benefit a transgressing black man. Cora Twitchell's well-known liaison with Paul Davis first nearly cost Davis his life and then cost him nine years in prison, and Cora's father was not convicted for shooting the black man. When the lynching of Edward Coy in 1892 was found to rest upon a yearlong liaison with a white woman, the fact that the woman was judged to be "of bad character" did not stop the lynchers.[50]

To white Southerners who wished to preserve racial hierarchy in the absence of slavery, it was crucial that both elite and nonelite white women minded the boundaries of the color line and gave birth only to white children. Without slavery to differentiate blacks from poor whites, it was equally important that ideas about the purity of white women included poor women. For to characterize all white women as pure had an important effect: it made sex between a black man and a white woman by definition rape, because a "pure" white woman, no matter how poor, could not possibly (in white minds) desire sex with a black man. As Frederick Douglass told an audience in Washington, D.C., in 1894: "An abandoned woman has only to start the cry that she has been insulted by a black man, to have him arrested and summarily murdered by the mob." Ida Wells likewise observed that no black man was "safe from lynching if a white woman, no matter what her standing or motive, cares to charge him with insult or assault." Such had not been the case in the South before the Civil War. And yet at the same time, inclusion in the category of those deserving protection still remained precarious for white women outside the ranks of the elite. Philip Bruce contradicted himself when he wrote that the "few white women who have given birth to mulattoes have always been regarded as monsters; and without exception, they have belonged to the most impoverished and degraded caste of whites, by whom they are scrupulously avoided as creatures who have sunk to the level of the beasts of the field." In the end, the designation of white female purity remained ambiguous on the matter of class. Still, endlessly repeated stories about rape—told by white men and women alike—warned all white women away from transgressive behavior and impressed upon them (or themselves) the proper behavior required for male protection.[51]

In the post-Reconstruction South, the threat and reality of lynching alerted black men and white women to the newly rigid boundaries of the color line. In the last decades of the century, whites accused black men of rape more than at any time before or since, and black men could be lynched for all manner of objectionable behavior toward white women. As antilynching protesters knew, rape could be defined so broadly that an insult, a grimace, an unwanted glance, or an accidental touch might be transformed in white minds into sexual violence. Proposing marriage or writing a letter could count, too.[52] Jesse Duke cautioned his readers as early as 1887: "If something is not done to break up these lynchings, it will be so after awhile that they will lynch every colored man that looks at a white woman with a twinkle in his eye." A black minister likewise warned his listeners in 1892: "If one of our men look at a white woman very hard and she complains he is lynched for it." Black protesters repeatedly reminded their enemies of a crucial change since the war. Recall the words of Ida Wells in 1892: "The world knows that the crime of rape was unknown during four years of civil war, when the white women of the South were at the mercy of the race which is all at once charged with being a bestial one." Recall the observation of Frederick Douglass two years later that before the end of the war, black men were "seldom or never . . . accused of the atrocious crime of feloniously assaulting white women." Such statements, continued from Reconstruction-era dialogues, were intended to call attention to the falsity of the charges now so frequently brought against black men. In 1893, Henry McNeal Turner described enslaved black men as "the virtual custodian of every white lady and child in the South." Likewise Professor Kelly Miller of Howard University wrote in 1899, "When the care and safety of the white women of the South were entrusted to the keeping of the slaves, they returned inviolate all that had been entrusted to their hands."[53]

The theme of safe white women in bygone days was not the sole province of antilynching activists. White Southerners made the same point —but instead to justify lynching. Bishop Atticus Green Haygood of Georgia wrote of rape in 1893: "This particular crime was practically unknown before Emancipation. Only one case I heard mentioned from my childhood till after the War." Georgia columnist Charles Henry Smith agreed, writing, "Before the War, there was seldom a personal outrage of the kind indicated, from the Potomac to the Rio Grande." Publisher Walter Hines Page believed that slavery had restrained black men from sexual assault, writing of "a social crime that was unknown and impossible in slavery, and that was very infrequent as long as the manners and traditions of slavery survived." White women, too, lifted their voices in accord. In 1897, Rebecca Latimer Felton lectured, "When I recollect that the crime of rape on white women was almost unknown among negro slaves before the war,

I ask myself, why has the crime assumed such proportions in the years following the war?" Such remembrances offered a wistful portrayal of loyal and submissive slave men who had taken no part in seizing their freedom. If only, former Georgia governor William J. Northen lamented in 1899, white Southerners had erected a monument to wartime slaves "for their unceasing devotion to our homes and the gallant protection they gave the women and children of the South all during the dark days of our bloody civil strife." A white woman likewise reminisced about "faithful slaves who were the only protectors of our mothers and the little children while our fathers were in the war." [54] The difference between the white story and that of black protesters lay in the respective comparisons with the 1890s. While protesters invoked the former paucity of rape charges in order to prove the ulterior motives of lynchers, apologists invoked nostalgia for a once-enslaved and harmless generation of black men as a preface to warnings about a supposedly new generation of criminals. Protesters capitalized on this white narrative about loyal black men, ignoring the truth of slaves' wartime betrayal and escape in an effort to catch white Southerners in their lies. "It is improbable," Frederick Douglass wrote in 1892 of black men, "that this peaceful and inoffensive class has suddenly and all at once become changed into a class of the most daring and repulsive criminals." Yet that was exactly what whites argued by century's end. [55]

The story white people told themselves about the security of slavery days served as a lead-in to their most important defense: the rape of white women justified the lynching of black men. "The lynching of such a monster," Charles Henry Smith wrote in 1893, "is nothing—nothing compared with what he has done. . . . there is no torture that could suffice." Sometimes this conviction was leavened with an acknowledgment of lynching's barbarity, though still followed by warnings that nothing would change until black men ceased to rape white women. A Georgia editor maintained in 1894, for example, that his reporters "never failed to condemn" lynching, but then cautioned: "When they stop making assaults upon helpless women the crime of lynching will stop." [56] In such defenses, whites commonly expressed distrust of the Southern legal system, claiming that ineffective courts required vigilante justice. Still, whites who pled for effective courts gave no thought to the impossibility of fair trials (potential jurors no doubt took part in lynchings, as did sheriffs and judges). In fact, many white advocates first called for fair trials, then proceeded to assume a lynched black man guilty even though no trial—much less a fair one—had taken place. Atticus Haygood's denunciation of one lynching was typical of this reasoning; "it was horrible to torture the guilty wretch," he wrote.[57] White Southerners also repeatedly expressed special horror at the thought of a white woman testifying in court on the subject of rape, and some endorsed lynching on those grounds alone. One black dissenter unmasked such pleas, pointing out that "testimony given to the mob is the same as testimony given in the court," noting that an alleged rape victim "testified before the mob of three thousand men, women and children."[58]

Black protesters continued to demonstrate that when whites recorded their reasons for specific lynchings, the cause most often named was not rape but murder. No one was more prominent in this task than Ida B. Wells, prompted to action after the murder of her dear friend Thomas Moss in 1892. Moss, along with two other black men, had opened the successful People's Grocery in Memphis, thereby taking black business away from a nearby white-owned store. When the men armed and defended themselves against the threat of attack, they were arrested and jailed, then seized and shot to death in the middle of the night. Moss and his colleagues had been lynched, but they had not been accused of rape. "This is what opened my eyes to what lynching really was," Wells wrote later. In her subsequent investigations, Wells found that only a third of the victims had even been charged with rape.[59] In spite of her tireless work, white people who had no use for such facts paid her no mind, and even those who meant well did not always comprehend her larger point. When the Chicago reformer Jane Addams condemned lynching without challenging statistics on rape, Wells responded angrily. "This record, easily within the reach of every one who wants it," she wrote, "makes inexcusable the statement . . . that negroes are lynched only because of their assaults upon womanhood."[60]

Indeed, whites continued to invoke the political rights of black men as the catalyst of alleged sexual transgressions against white women. Charles Henry Smith believed that in order to halt "crime and outrage," blacks would "have to be disfranchised." Rebecca Latimer Felton thought that "so long as your politics takes the colored man into your embraces on election day to control his vote . . . so long will lynchings prevail because the causes of it grow and increase." Corra Harris described black men as lustful savages, concluding: "To him liberty has always meant license of one sort or another. Is it any wonder North Carolina, Mississippi and Louisiana have passed laws virtually disfranchising him?"[61] Antilynching protesters called attention to this conflation of political rights and rape in an effort to lay it bare. Frederick Douglass explicitly located rape accusations with the advent of black political power. "It is only since the Negro has become a citizen and a voter," he wrote in 1892, "that this charge has been made." This was an "invention," with "a well defined motive," Douglass contended, "a means of paving the way for our entire disfranchisement." Ida Wells, too, believed that rape charges were a means to wrest political and economic power from black men, arguing that lynching could be "explained" by white Southern resentment at "giving the Afro-American his freedom, the ballot box and the Civil Rights Law." For W. E. B. Du Bois, the black historian who was born during Reconstruction, terrorism, lynching, and disfranchisement formed a triad. Lynching, he believed, was "an attempt to terrorize . . . and grew directly out of the disfranchisement of 1876."[62] Antilynching activists also continued to invoke the idea of black manhood, equating it as before with freedom, economic independence, citizenship, and political rights. "We are men and our aim is perfect manhood, to be men among men," wrote Douglass in an 1892 denunciation of lynching. In an effort to invert dominant ideas that equated black people with savagery and white people with civilization, Wells implored black men to defend their "name and manhood from this vile accusation," declaring that whites were "wedded to any method however revolting, any measure however extreme, for the subjugation of the young manhood of the race."[63]

Even as white people most often named murder as the cause of lynching, then, their stories about the rape of white women continued to serve them best in their postwar quest for racial supremacy.[64] This was a discourse that at once glorified slavery and presented black autonomy and authority as lethal to white people. "In the time of slavery if a Negro was killed, the owner sustained a loss of property," Douglass wrote in a pamphlet distributed by the thousands at the Chicago World's Fair in 1893. "Now he is not restrained by any fear of such loss." Ida Wells reiterated the same point: "The slave was rarely killed, he was too valuable," she wrote in 1895. "But Emancipation came and the vested interests of the white man in the Negro's body were lost." Three days after the Wilmington riot in 1898, an anonymous black woman ("I cannot sign my name and live," she noted) made the same point in a letter to President William McKinley. "When our parents belonged to them, why, the Negro was all right," she wrote. "Now, when they work and accumulate property they are all wrong." [65] By the 1890s, whites had transformed ideas about the agency of white women in an effort to reinforce new ideas about the dangers of empowered black men. Now sex between a white woman and a black man was met with near-inevitable and public white violence, directed largely at the black man, who was almost certain to be branded a rapist.

Lynching deterred black men and white women from forming sexual liaisons in a world without racial slavery. To whites, such liaisons put black men and white men on a too-equal footing, illuminated the fact that white men could not always control white women, and blurred the lines of racial categories that were so crucial to maintaining the racial hierarchy previously sustained by slavery. It was in the face of this overwhelming violence that black protesters told alternative stories about the agency of white women and exposed the politics of lynching. But exposing those facts remained a perilous endeavor. On a spring Sunday in the last year of the nineteenth century there occurred one of the most notorious public murders in Southern history. Sam Hose, accused of killing a white man in Georgia's cotton belt and assaulting the man's white wife, maintained that he had acted in self-defense and had never touched the woman. Hose was tied to a pine tree and burned to death before two thousand people. Morning worshipers had heard the news at church, and many white spectators and participants arrived on two special trains that ran from Atlanta. "For sickening sights, harrowing details and bloodcurdling incidents," the white Atlanta papers observed, the lynching of Hose was "unsurpassed." Afterward spectators "eagerly snatched" bones, carried away pieces of flesh, and fought over the ashes. The only arrest made was that of a white man charged with disputing Hose's guilt and thereby "using language which was likely to cause disorder or a riot." The subsequent editorial in the *Atlanta Constitution* encompassed the major themes of the decade: black manhood was equated with aggression in the new and "insolent" generation of black men; the alleged rape victim was a farm wife who stayed at home filled with dread over black men; her "chastity would be cross-questioned if the case was taken into court"; and Hose was assumed unequivocally guilty.[66] W. E. B. Du Bois, who lived in Atlanta at the time, later recalled how shortly after Hose's murder he had started over to the offices of the *Constitution* to "try to put before the South what happened in cases of this sort." On his way, he came upon a meat market in which, he later recalled, "they were exhibiting the fingers of Sam Hose." Du Bois turned back, understanding the futility and the danger of his mission.[67]

Epilogue

The haunting walk that W. E. B. Du Bois took through the streets of Atlanta in 1899 stands as a marker for the twentieth-century legacy of the history of sex between black men and white women in the American South.[1] On that spring day in the last year of the nineteenth century, Du Bois set out to explain to white Southerners that Sam Hose, though already lynched, was innocent of rape. It is not surprising that he turned back after discovering the dead man's severed fingers on public display in the neighborhood. Nor would it surprise modern-day readers if Du Bois had taken a different route, missed the gruesome display, and yet turned back nonetheless. White violence in response to sex between black men and white women, whether the sex was consensual, imagined, or trumped-up rape, is a familiar story. But if what made Du Bois turn back is familiar, what first made him set out is less so. Du Bois started out to the offices of the white newspaper with the conviction that rational explanation would prevent future travesties of justice. That in turn suggests Du Bois's understanding that lethal white violence in response to sex between black men and white women was a recent phenomenon, and therefore a phenomenon with a history.[2]

The stories told in this book have illuminated the historical development of white alarm about sexual liaisons between black men and white women in the South. A white woman and a black man married in 1681 in the colonial Chesapeake, the first site of contact between Europeans and Africans in what would become the United States. Although elite white neighbors who attended the wedding of Nell Butler and Charles were not untroubled by the union, it did not present white Southerners with the same complications as the illicit liaisons between white women and black men that would come to pass in the antebellum South. Yet at the same time, the sexual liaisons between Polly Lane and Jim, Dorothea Bourne and Edmond, Lucy Anderson and James Nunez, and Caroline Hugly and an unnamed black man—along with other white women and black men before the Civil War—were never as troublesome to white Southerners as those that transpired after the advent of African American freedom and the claiming of citizenship by black men.

"Negro suffrage," W. E. B. Du Bois wrote at the dawn of the twentieth century, "ended a civil war by beginning a race feud." Du Bois and other black protesters had quickly come to realize that this feud included the sexualization of politics. "The charge of rape against colored Americans was invented by the white South after Reconstruction to excuse mob violence," wrote Du Bois in 1919, naming such violence as "the recognized method of re-enslaving blacks." Decades later, when Du Bois recalled his mission to explain the truth about Sam Hose in the spring of 1899, he did not condemn his own callow visions of justice. It had been, he wrote, "but a young man's idealism, not by any means false, but also never universally true."[3]

Many colleagues, friends, and readers have asked about the process, or ordeal, of finding the evidence for this book. No archive contained any sort of index on the topic of sex between white women and black men, and only rarely did a card catalog heading for "miscegenation" or "interracial marriage" lead to one or two brief references. For the most part I gathered my cases from a variety of leads, both textual and conversational. On my first visit to the Maryland Hall of Records, the archivist Phebe Jacobsen listened to a description of my project and led me to the long, handwritten transcripts about the colonial marriage of Nell Butler and Charles. Later I found the case mentioned in a number of published works.[1] For the story of Polly Lane and Jim, I came across a reference in Guion Griffis Johnson's 1937 work, *Ante-Bellum North Carolina,* and followed that lead to the North Carolina Division of Archives and History. There I found the cited document in a large scrapbook of letters to the governor. When I turned the pages, I found more letters about Polly and Jim, and when I turned the pages back the other way, there were still more letters. Again, I later found more recent published references to this case.[2] For the story of Dorothea Bourne and Edmond, I went to the Library of Virginia armed with references gleaned from James Hugo Johnston's 1970 compendium of cases, *Race Relations in Virginia and Miscegenation in the South.* There I searched until I found a case with sufficient documentation for a detailed study.[3] I first came across the Nunez and Hugly stories in Helen Tunnicliff Catterall's five-volume series from the 1920s and 1930s, *Judicial Cases Concerning American Slavery and the Negro.* From there, I found the printed court transcripts from the Georgia Supreme Court, which I then followed backward to the manuscript county court records in the Georgia Department of Archives and History.[4] The American Freedmen's Inquiry Commission testimony from the Civil War years came from a lead in Herbert G. Gutman's 1976 book, *The Black Family in Slavery and Freedom.* When I followed several intriguing footnotes to the National Archives in Washington, D.C., I found documents that illuminated much of what I had found for the antebellum era. In addition, an assortment of sources, including court cases, personal papers, newspapers, pamphlets, and congressional records, charted wartime changes in white responses.[5] My principle documents for the Reconstruction years were the thirteen printed volumes of testimony taken by the federal government about the Ku Klux Klan, as well as a number of other government reports that included testimony from black and white Southerners. For the last decades of the nineteenth century, I began with references from W. Fitzhugh Brundage's 1993 work, *Lynching in the New South,* followed by a long and profitable conversation with Professor Brundage. After reading the newspaper accounts of the liaisons between Peter Stamps and Ida Abercrombie, and Paul Davis and Cora Twitchell, along with a few briefer cases, I tracked the protagonists through censuses and local histories and, for the Davis-Twitchell case, searched for the original court papers at the Library of Virginia. The papers (including an envelope with Cora's penciled love letters crushed inside) were tied with brittle cloth ribbons and had not been uncreased since 1897. It was not difficult to consult the voluminous outpouring (from both sides of the color line) of published articles, essays, and commentaries addressing directly or obliquely the issue of sex between white women and black men, including the alternative stories told by Jesse C. Duke, Ida B. Wells, and Alexander Manly.[6]

The stories I mention more briefly throughout the chapters derive from any number of sources. Some came to light through references in other history books, ranging from early twentieth-century works to the most recent scholarship on the South. Some came from colleagues who were aware of my topic of inquiry and generously sent me documents they had found in the course of their research. Many I came across while searching for something else, for example in folders of pardon papers to antebellum governors, in county court documents, in newspapers, or in travelers' accounts. Still others were offered by people who befriended me at the archives. On one memorable day, an older white woman who was a professional genealogist led me to a case of a white woman who had murdered the child she had borne by her father's slave. The genealogist had found the document while researching a white family but had omitted the information from her notes because, she told me, "they wouldn't want to know." All professional librarians and archivists of all colors were without exception immensely helpful, though not all fellow researchers were so forthcoming. In one instance, a white woman told me that I would never find anything on the topic. When I told her that I already had, she admonished me to "make sure you say they're trash" about the white women involved, thereby helping to prove the legacy of part of my argument.

Notes

Abbreviations

AHS	Atlanta Historical Society, Atlanta, Ga.
GDAH	Georgia Department of Archives and History, Atlanta
LLP	Legislative Papers, Petitions
LVA	Library of Virginia, Richmond
MHR	Maryland Hall of Record, Annapolis
MHS	Maryland Historical Society, Baltimore
NA	National Archives, Washington, D.C.
NCC	North Carolina Collection, Wilson Library, University of North Carolina, Chapel Hill
NCDAH	North Carolina Division of Archives and History, Raleigh
SCRBC	Schomburg Center for Research in Black Culture, New York Public Library, New York
SHC	Southern Historical Collection, Manuscript Department, Wilson Library, University of North Carolina, Chapel Hill
SSCMR	State Supreme Court Manuscript Records
SSCOP	State Supreme Court Original Papers
WPL	Manuscript Department, William R. Perkins Library, Duke University, Durham, N.C.

I have corrected and modernized the spelling and punctuation in the manuscript documents for the sake of readability, with the exception of capital and lowercase for the words Negro and negro and except where indicated otherwise.

Chapter 1 *Telling the Stories*

1. The case of 1967, *Loving v. Virginia,* 388 U.S. 1 (1967), concerned a white man and a black woman; see Drinan, "Loving Decision"; Lombardo, "Miscegenation, Eugenics, and Racism"; and Wadlington, "*Loving* Case." Over time, 41 states had laws against sex or marriage across color lines. In the nineteenth century, 38 states had such laws; 9 states repealed those laws during the Civil War era. For states with such laws in 1967, see Applebaum, "Miscegenation Statutes," 50.

2. On change over time in the phenomenon of racism, see Holt, " 'Empire over the Mind,' " 307.

3. Douglass, "Reason Why," 473–74. Wells, *Southern Horrors,* 5. For further discussion of Douglass and Wells, see chap. 8, below.

4. On the colonial and antebellum eras, see Brown, *Good Wives, Nasty*

Wenches, chap. 6, for the most complex and nuanced examination; Schwarz, *Twice Condemned,* 21–22, 72, 82–84, 150–52, 155–64, 179–80, 205–10, 291–95; and Jordan, *White over Black,* 32–43, 150–63, 398–99, 578–79. Eugene D. Genovese and Elizabeth-Fox Genovese point out that the idea of black male hypersexuality fully formed in white minds only after emancipation; see Genovese, *Roll, Jordan, Roll,* 422, 461–62; and Fox-Genovese, *Plantation Household,* 291. See also Sommerville, "Rape Myth." On the frequency of antebellum lynching, see chap. 3, n. 62, and chap. 8, n. 1, below. For an intriguing parallel, in a different time and place, of "marked dissonance between local *social patterns* and translocal *ideology,*" see Bender, *Community and Social Change,* 76–77.

5. It is difficult to quantify the cases of liaisons between white women and black men uncovered in this book. For example, a case that entered the record as rape may have been a rape but may alternatively have been a voluntary liaison that subsequently involved rape, or a voluntary liaison covered over by rape charges. There is also no way to quantify sex that may have transpired against the will of the black man. It is also difficult to quantify mentions of liaisons in such nonlegal sources as this white man's declaration in 1833: "Were it necessary I could refer you to several instances of slaves actually seducing the daughters of their masters! Such seductions sometimes happen even in the most respectable slaveholding families" (Rankin, *Letters on American Slavery,* 69). In any event, the argument here does not depend upon frequency.

6. Jacobs, *Incidents,* 52; Chesnut, *Mary Chesnut's Civil War,* 29. See also Painter, "Journal of Ella Gertrude Clanton Thomas," 45–46, 50, 58–59, 64–65. On sex between black women and white men, see Clinton, "Caught in the Web"; Clinton, *Plantation Mistress,* 210–22; Clinton, "'Southern Dishonor,'" 60–68; Genovese, *Roll, Jordan, Roll,* 413–31; Getman, "Sexual Control," 142–51; Gutman, *Black Family,* 83–84, 388–93; Jennings, "'Us Colored Women,'" 60–66; Johnston, *Race Relations,* chap. 9; Lecaudey, "Behind the Mask"; McLaurin, *Celia;* Painter, "Soul Murder," 134–39; Powell, "Remembrance of Mira"; Stampp, *Peculiar Institution,* 353–61; Steckel, "Miscegenation and American Slave Schedules"; Stevenson, "Distress and Discord," 112–15, 121–22; Stevenson, *Life in Black and White,* 193–94, 236–41; White, *Ar'n't I a Woman?* 33–46, 78–79; and Wyatt-Brown, *Southern Honor,* 296–98, 307–15, 318–24. For primary sources, see Jacobs, *Incidents,* and Thomas, *Secret Eye,* 167–69, 319–22, 329, 332.

7. See Wyatt-Brown, *Southern Honor,* chap. 12; Clinton, *Plantation Mistress,* chaps. 5, 6; Fox-Genovese, *Plantation Household,* chap. 4 passim; and Scott, *Southern Lady,* chaps. 1–3.

8. On inheritance of slavery through the mother, see Patterson, *Slavery and Social Death,* chap. 5; see also chap. 2, below. On white responses to free people of African ancestry, see Williamson, *New People,* 65–71.

9. On white class relations in the antebellum South, see McCurry, *Masters of Small Worlds,* the most nuanced study, and the first to incorporate gen-

der; Ford, *Origins of Southern Radicalism;* Genovese, "Yeoman Farmers"; Hahn, *Roots of Southern Populism;* Harris, *Plain Folk and Gentry;* Watson, "Conflict and collaboration"; and Wright, *Political Economy of the Cotton South,* chaps. 2, 3.

10. Painter, "Hill, Thomas, and the Use of Racial Stereotype," 206; Bynum, *Unruly Women,* 7.

11. See Painter, "Of *Lily,* Linda Brent, and Freud," 97; Bynum, *Unruly Women,* 10; and Getman, "Sexual Control," 133–34.

12. On the status of free blacks, see Roark and Johnson, "Strategies of Survival." On the mistreatment and murder of slaves, see Genovese, *Roll, Jordan, Roll,* 37–43.

13. Douglass, "Reason Why," 474; Wells-Barnett, "Lynching: Our National Crime," 261.

14. G. R. Quaife writes of six ways in which illicit sex can become public: "suspicious company, suspicious circumstances, caught in the act, confessing the deed, consequences of the act, and cracks in the curtain of initial concealment." See Quaife, *Wanton Wenches and Wayward Wives,* 48.

15. Citing a Northern example, Mary Frances Berry and John W. Blassingame write: "Traditionally, the major opposition to intermarriage in the black community was expressed by black women"; see *Long Memory,* 139. On the voices of black women as "distinguishable from both white women and black men," see Higginbotham, "Beyond the Sound of Silence," 54. Although slaves were not legally permitted to marry, I use the terms *husband* and *wife,* from their own point of view.

16. On communities, see Bender, *Community and Social Change,* 5–11, 61–108.

17. Du Bois, *Dusk of Dawn,* 103; Fields, "Ideology and Race," 152, 149. On the social construction of race, see ibid.; Fields, "Slavery, Race and Ideology"; Omi and Winant, *Racial Formation in the United States,* chaps. 1–4; Outlaw, "Toward a Critical Theory of 'Race,' " 58–68; Smedley, *Race in North America;* Spickard, "Illogic of American Racial Categories"; Winant, *Racial Conditions,* chap. 2; and Zack, *Race and Mixed Race,* chaps. 1–4. See also Walker, "How Many Niggers Did Karl Marx Know?"

18. Higginbotham, "African-American Women's History," 255 (quotation); see 253–56 on defining race. On the word *mulatto,* including an assessment of the theory of its origin from the word *mule,* connoting hybridity, bastardy, and servitude, see Forbes, *Black Africans and Native Americans,* chaps. 5, 6, 8; see also Williamson, *New People,* xii–xiii; and Mills, "Tracing Free People of Color," 263–66. On the word *miscegenation,* see chap. 6, below; and Zack, *Race and Mixed Race,* chap. 15.

19. Barbara J. Fields writes: "Americans regard people of known African descent or visible African appearance as a race, but not people of known European descent or visible European appearance" ("Slavery, Race and Ideology," 97–98). See also Roediger, *Abolition of Whiteness,* Introduction.

20. On antislavery forces, see Walters, *Antislavery Appeal*. On the aftermath of Nat Turner, see Oates, *Fires of Jubilee*, pt. 4.

21. Stone, "Revival of Narrative," 22. Peter Burke likewise notes that historians attempt "to reconstruct ordinary, everyday assumptions on the basis of the records of what were extraordinary events in the lives of the accused" and "to reconstruct what ordinary people thought on the basis of what the accused, who may not have been a typical group, were prepared to say in the unusual (not to say terrifying) situation in which they found themselves." See "Overture: The New History," 12.

22. The upper South encompasses Washington, D.C., Delaware, Maryland, Virginia, North Carolina, Kentucky, Tennessee, and Missouri. On South Carolina (which did not legally prohibit marriage across the color line), see, e.g., Johnson and Roark, *Black Masters*; Wikramanayake, *World in Shadow*. On Louisiana, see, e.g., Berlin, *Slaves Without Masters,* chap. 4; Domínguez, *White By Definition*; and Hirsch and Logsdon, eds., *Creole New Orleans*. On upper versus lower South, see Morton, "From Invisible Man to 'New People,'" and Williamson, *New People*, 2–3, 14–24, 33–42. See also Mills, "Miscegenation and Free Negro," for evidence to support the phenomenon of toleration in antebellum Alabama.

23. Riggan, *Pícaros, Madmen,* 10; Bleikasten, *Most Splendid Failure,* 67.

24. See Ginzburg, "Checking the Evidence," 90.

25. See Thelen, "Memory and American History." Simon Schama notes that "even in the most austere scholarly report from the archives, the inventive faculty—selecting, pruning, editing, commenting, interpreting, delivering judgments—is in full play"; see *Dead Certainties*, 322. See also White, *Tropics of Discourse*, chaps. 1, 2, 5. As Robert Berkhofer, Jr., so wisely noted in a Cultural Studies Colloquium at the University of California–Santa Cruz in 1993, historians cannot be true to the times we write about because we know the future.

26. Kathleen M. Brown writes of the colonial South: "The truth of many interracial relationships may lie somewhere between consent and exploitation, with individuals making choices in a context warped and circumscribed by slavery"; see *Good Wives, Nasty Wenches,* 237. For a more optimistic view, see Aptheker, *Anti-Racism in U.S. History,* chap. 4; but see also Solomon, "Racism and Anti-Racism in U.S. History," 76. On the political dimension of slaves' transgressive behavior, see Schwarz, "Forging the Shackles," 127. On lack of agency among slaves, see Walker, *Deromanticizing Black History,* Introduction; Wyatt-Brown, "Mask of Obedience"; Shore, "Poverty of Tragedy"; and Kolchin, "Reevaluating the Antebellum Slave Community," 579–601. On plantation-class women's stake in slavery, see Fox-Genovese, *Plantation Household,* 97–98, 145, 192–93, 242–43, 334; Rable, *Civil Wars,* esp. chap. 2; and Scott, "Women's Perspective on the Patriarchy in the 1850s," 86.

27. "Miserable chronicles of obscure villages" is from Burke, "History of Events," 241, quoted from A. Asor Rosa, ed., *Letteratura Italiana* (Turin, 1986),

224. See also Stone, "Revival of Narrative," 22. A sampling of related scholar-ship includes Bardaglio, "Rape and the Law" and *Reconstructing the Household;* Block, "Coerced Sex"; Brown, *Good Wives, Nasty Wenches;* Brundage, *Lynching in the New South;* Buckley, "Unfixing Race"; Edwards, "Sexual Violence, Gender, Reconstruction" and *Gendered Strife;* Gilmore, *Gender and Jim Crow;* Goodman, *Stories of Scottsboro;* Hall, *Revolt Against Chivalry;* Painter, " 'Social Equality' "; Pascoe, "Miscegenation Law" and "Race, Gender, and Intercultural Relations"; Rosen, "Struggles over 'Freedom' "; Smith, "Split Affinities"; Sommerville, "Rape Myth"; and Williamson, *New People.*

Chapter 2 *Marriage*

1. Such laws began in the late seventeenth century, as discussed later in the chapter; marriages could be declared null and void or result in punishments such as fines. On laws in the antebellum South, see Grossberg, "Guarding the Altar," 200–203, and *Governing the Hearth,* 126–29. See also Bardaglio, *Reconstructing the Household,* 48–64.

2. The marriage took place in Charles County. On this region, see, e.g., Horn, "Adapting to a New World." On slave law, see Alpert, "Origin of Slavery."

3. The manuscript and printed records for this case are: *William Butler and Mary Butler v. Richard Boarman,* Provincial Court Judgments, vol. D.D., no. 17, vol. 61, pt. 1, 1770–71, pp. 233–44, MHR (hereafter *Butler v. Boarman,* MHR), and *William and Mary Butler v. Richard Boarman,* 1 Md. Harris & McHenry 371 (1770). Spellings of witnesses' names vary; I have used one version throughout.

Some of the witnesses appear in rent rolls, congregation lists, militia and voter lists, marriage and baptism registers, and lists of subscribers to oaths of allegiance; see O'Rourke, ed., *Catholic Families of Southern Maryland.* For marriages among these families, see, e.g., *Maryland Marriages: 1778–1800,* 66; and Carr, Menard, and Walsh, *Robert Cole's World,* 244–45. The recollections of the witnesses also attest to intermarriage among the families of owners; see *Butler v. Boarman,* MHR. See also Burnard, "Tangled Cousinry?" Seven of the witnesses were listed in the 1790 census. William Simpson owned 10 slaves; Edward Edelon owned 11 slaves; Benjamin Jameson owned 15 slaves; Samuel Love owned no slaves; William McPherson owned 11 slaves; Thomas Bowling owned 2 slaves; and Samuel Abell owned 11 slaves. See *Heads of Families at the First Census,* 12, 49, 51, 52, 93, 106; and Owings, *His Lordship's Patronage,* 171. Nine of the 12 men signed their testimony; none of the 4 women did (*Butler v. Boarman,* MHR).

4. The narrative is taken from the 1760s testimony in *Butler v. Boarman,* MHR; all quoted testimony is from this document and cited by names only. Three witnesses mentioned a Catholic priest named Hubbert as the officiator; see testimony of Thomas Bowling, William Simpson, and Joseph Jameson. The

Boarman plantation had a chapel on its property; see "Genealogy of Boarman Family," 15. The ages of Nell and Charles at the time of the wedding (or at any other time) are never mentioned.

5. The masters of Nell and Charles (the Boarman, Sanders, and Brooke families) were among a handful of wealthy Catholics from England's gentry who were part of Maryland's original settlers. Though a numerical minority, their status was enhanced by alliances with Lord Baltimore, the Catholic proprietor of the province; most lived in Charles and St. Mary's Counties, forming a cohesive community. On the Boarman family, see Howard, "Early Colonial Marylanders"; "Genealogy of Boarman Family"; Thomas, *The Boarmans;* and Parran, *Register of Maryland's Heraldic Families,* 24. On Maryland's Catholic community, see Dolan, *American Catholic Experience,* chap. 3; and Reavis, "Maryland Gentry and Social Mobility." The Boarman land was in or around present-day Bryantown, Charles County; see "Genealogy of Boarman Family," 15.

6. On local authority, see Carr, "Foundations of Social Order"; Graham, "Meeting House and Chapel"; Horn, "Adapting to a New World," 170–74; and Walsh, "Community Networks." For recollections of the wedding ceremony and guests, see testimony of Nathaniel Suit, Benjamin Jameson, William Simpson, and Joseph Jameson. John Branson's testimony is the only voice outside the ranks of the elite, and offers only facts.

7. See Morgan, *American Slavery,* 319, also 327; Breen, "Changing Labor Force"; and Main, *Tobacco Colony,* chap. 3.

8. Testimony of Mary Crosen; also testimony of John Jordan Smith, Ann Whitehorn, Samuel Abell, and William McPherson. On labor, see also *Archives of Maryland,* 15:339; Carr and Walsh, "Planter's Wife"; Menard, "Maryland Slave Population," 36; and Walsh, "Slave Life, Slave Society," 177.

9. Kulikoff, "'Prolifick' People," 396–400; Menard, "Maryland Slave Population," 33–35; Walsh, "Slave Life," 171. Charles spoke at least some English; he may have arrived on the Boarman plantation via the West Indies rather than directly from Africa; see Menard, "Maryland Slave Population," 31; and Kulikoff, "'Prolifick' People," 392. Two witnesses used the phrase "salt water Negro," meaning those who came to America directly from Africa (testimony of William Simpson and Samuel Abell); see Johnson, *Shadow of the Plantation,* 22–23.

10. *Basil Shorter v. Henry Rozier,* 3 Md. Harris & McHenry 238 (1794), 239 (St. Mary's County); also *Shorter v. Boswell,* 2 Md. Harris & Johnson 359 (1808), and *Sprigg v. Negro Mary,* 3 Md. Harris & Johnson 491 (1814). Charles County Court, vol. E, no. 2, 1711–15, p. 307, and Provincial Court Judgements, vol. V.D., no. 1, 1713–16, pp. 150–52, MHR (Mingo case). Anne Arundel County Court Judgments, vol. V.D., no. 1, 1714–16, pp. 93, 178, 244–46, MHR (Rose case).

11. Inventory of Edmund Howard, Charles County Prerogative Court Inventories and Accounts, vol. 35, 1713–14, p. 248, MHR. *Philadelphia American*

Weekly Mercury, Aug. 11, 25, Sept. 1, 1720 (Queen Anne's County). For other accounts of seventeenth-century Chesapeake marriages between black men and white woman, see Morgan, *American Slavery,* 334; Brown, *Good Wives, Nasty Wenches,* 126; and Deal, "Race and Class in Colonial Virginia," 265, 273, 277, 315–16, 332–33, 385–86, 420. T. H. Breen and Stephen Innes understand some of these as fornication; see *"Myne Owne Ground,"* 96, 107.

12. Queen Anne County Court Judgment Record, 1732–1735, p. 526, MHR; Prince George's County Court, vol. AA, 1742–43, p. 191, MHR.

13. Charles County Court Proceedings, vol. A, no. 2, 1701–4, p. 251, MHR; Kimmel, "Slave Freedom Petitions," 19 (Glover case). For other such cases through the mid-eighteenth century, see: Provincial Court Judgments, vol. T.L., no. 1, pt. 5B, 1694–96, pp. 700–701, MHR; Charles County Court, vol. K, no. 2, 1720–22, p. 236, MHR; Prince George's County Court, vol. X, no. 12, 1738–40, p. 109, MHR. See also Alpert, "Origin of Slavery," 211–12; Breen and Innes, *"Myne Owne Ground,"* 94, 95; Higginbotham, *Matter of Color,* 42; Morgan, *American Slavery,* 333; and Morgan, "British Encounters," 172.

14. Kathleen M. Brown found harsher consequences for sex between white women and black men in the last quarter of the seventeenth century, stemming from new concerns to discourage white and black laborers from joining forces against white masters; see Brown, *Good Wives, Nasty Wenches,* chap. 6, also chap. 4. See also Deal, "Constricted World," 277–78. For Maryland laws, see *Archives of Maryland,* 1:533–34 (1664), 7:203–5 (1681), 13:546–49 (1692), 30:289–90 (1715). For Virginia, see Hening, ed., *Statutes at Large,* 8:134. See also Higginbotham and Kopytoff, "Racial Purity," 1994–97, 2004–7. For North Carolina, see Clark, ed., *State Records of North Carolina,* 23:65. On bastardy law, see Grossberg, *Governing the Hearth,* 197–200; and Wells, "Illegitimacy and Bridal Pregnancy."

For a sampling of other Maryland cases of fornication and bastardy between white women and black men through the mid-eighteenth century, in which penalties included whipping, fines, and servitude, see: Jane Hudleston and Gye (Talbot County Court Judgments, 1682–85, p. 22, MHR); Ann Butler and Emanuel (Somerset County Judicial Record, 1689–90, pp. 36–37, 53, 60, MHR); Elizabeth Cobham and Robert Butchery (Dorchester County Court Proceedings, 1690–92, in Dorchester County Land Records, vol. 4 1/2, pp. 176, 165, 157, 156, MHR); Jane Shoard and Grinedge Hormely (Talbot County Judgments, 1691–98, in Talbot County Land Records, vol. A.B., no. 8, pt. 2, p. 524, MHR); Ann Hazelwood and unnamed man (Charles County Court Proceedings, vol. S, no. 1, 1692–94, pp. 116–17, MHR); Elinor Atkins and unnamed man (Charles County Court Proceedings, vol. V, no. 1, 1696–98, pp. 161, 372, and vol. X, no. 1, 1698–99, p. 340, MHR); Mary Walker and Lawrence (Somerset County Judicial Record, 1698–1701, p. 508, MHR); Ann Dazey and unnamed man (Queen Anne County Court Judgment Record, 1718–19, fifth unnumbered page of writing, MHR); Mary Turner and Peter Smith (Prince

George's County Court, vol. O, 1728-29, pp. 344-45, MHR); Margaret Lang and unnamed man (Queen Anne County Court Judgment Record, 1730-32, pp. 160-61, MHR); Elizabeth Green and unnamed man (Queen Anne County Court Judgment Record, 1730-32, pp. 161-62, 264, MHR); Mary Wedge and Daniel (Prince George's County Court, vol. N, 1726-27, pp. 358-59; vol. S, 1732-34, pp. 297-98; vol. V, 1734-35, pp. 108, 410; vol. W, 1735-36, p. 504; and vol. X, 1738-40, p. 192, MHR); Joanne McDonnald and unnamed man (Queen Anne County Criminal Record, June 1753, n.p., MHR). For a Virginia case, see Ann Wall and unnamed man (Elizabeth City County Deeds, Wills, and Orders, 1684-99, p. 83, LVA). See also Breen and Innes, *"Myne Owne Ground,"* 96, 107; Brown, *Good Wives, Nasty Wenches,* 197-206; Johnston, *Race Relations,* 175-76; Madden, *We Were Always Free,* 2-5; Morgan, *American Slavery,* 336; Nicholls, "Passing Through," 54; and Smith and Crowl, eds., *Court Records of Prince George's County,* 130-31, 294, 369.

15. Lower Norfolk County Order Book, 1681-86, p. 139, LVA, cited in Billings, ed., *Old Dominion,* 161 (Mary Williamson and William). *Archives of Maryland,* 8:352 (Anne Arundel County, Plummer case). Henrico County Records, May 16, 1692, pp. 321-22, LVA (Bridgett case). York County Deeds, Orders, Wills, No. 9, 1691-94, ms. p. 332, LVA (Mary Oliver case). *Archives of Maryland,* 23:508 (Anne Arundel and St. Mary's Counties, sale record).

16. On the absence of legal consequences for slave men in liaisons with white women, see Higginbotham and Kopytoff, "Racial Purity," 2000-2002. For unnamed black men, see n. 14, above.

17. On the unequal treatment of black and white men accused of rape or attempted rape, see Block, "Coerced Sex," chap. 4; Brown, *Good Wives, Nasty Wenches,* 207-10; and Higginbotham and Kopytoff, "Racial Purity," 2008-12.

18. Henrico County Deed Book, 1677-1692, pp. 192-96, LVA; also in Billings, ed., *Old Dominion,* 161-63 (Watkins case). Somerset County Judicial Record, 1698-1701, p. 92, MHR (Hannah Johnson and Peter case). Charles County Court Proceedings, vol. Y, no. 1, 1699-1701, pp. 110-11, and Provincial Court Judgments, vol. W.T., no. 3, 1699-1702, pp. 624-25, 628, MHR (Mary Harris and Sampson case). For a North Carolina adultery case between a white woman and a slave man in 1726, see Saunders, ed., *Colonial Records of North Carolina,* 2:711 ("Several persons among us of their own knowledge say that she left her husband and for some years cohabited with a Negro man of Captain Simon Jeffries"), also 704.

19. Colonial Office, Class 5, no. 1312, pt. 2, pp. 22-24, Virginia Correspondence, Board of Trade, October 1701, Virginia Colonial Records Project, LVA. Philip J. Schwarz writes that this punishment was "a stark reminder of what awaited slaves accused of aggression," highlighting the fact that rape may not have been the only problem; see *Twice Condemned,* 72. See also Block, "Coerced Sex," 172-74.

20. For castration, see Hening, ed., *Statutes at Large,* 8:358 (1769); Bar-

daglio, "Rape and the Law," 752–53; and Block, "Coerced Sex," 170. For black men sentenced to castration for non-sexual crimes, see Trial of Prymus, Craven County Court Minutes, Aug. 15, 1761, NCDAH; and Rutman and Rutman, *Place in Time,* 176–77. See also Jordan, *White over Black,* 154–58; and Fredrickson, *White Supremacy,* 105. For several rape cases in late eighteenth-century Virginia in which black men were ordered castrated, whipped, and hanged, see *Twice Condemned,* 150–52, 158–59.

For the death penalty, see *Archives of Maryland,* 40:93 (1737); the law stipulated death for "Negroes and other slaves" for the rape of white women; other crimes carrying the death penalty included rebellion, murder, and arson. See also Schwarz, *Twice Condemned,* 83–84; and Brown, *Good Wives, Nasty Wenches,* 209. A 1758 North Carolina law stipulated the death penalty for murder and rape by slave men and castration for other capital crimes by slave men; see Clark, ed., *State Records of North Carolina,* 23:489. See also Crow, *Black Experience,* 26; and Spindel, *Crime and Society,* 109. For a North Carolina rape case in which a slave was sentenced to death, see Trial of Titus, Aug. 25, 1777, Onslow County Criminal Actions Concerning Slaves, NCDAH. A 1770 Georgia law stipulated the death penalty for slave or free black men, and other nonwhite men convicted of the rape or attempted rape of a white woman; see Marbury and Crawford, eds., *Laws of Georgia,* 430. On rape in the antebellum South, see chap. 3, below.

21. For the supposed conspiracy (Prince George's County), see Stephen Bordley to Matthias Harris, Stephen Bordley Letter Book, 1738–40, Jan. 30, 1739, pp. 56–58, MHS; see also Schwarz, *Twice Condemned,* 164. For the slander, see York County Deeds, Orders, Wills, no. 10, 1694–97, June 25, 1694, ms. pp. 9–13 (quotation on 12), LVA.

22. Testimony of Samuel Love, Jean Howard, Benjamin Jameson, and Joseph Jameson; also testimony of Thomas Beach. On gossip, see Norton, "Gender and Defamation"; and Walsh, "Community Networks," 236–37.

23. On race and the origins of American slavery, see Breen and Innes, *"Myne Owne Ground";* Brown, *Good Wives, Nasty Wenches* (an analysis incorporating gender); Campbell and Oakes, "Invention of Race"; Davis, *Problem of Slavery in the Age of Revolution,* 299–306; Fredrickson, *White Supremacy,* chap. 2, and *Arrogance of Race,* chap. 13; Jordan, *White over Black,* 583–85; and Morgan, *American Slavery,* chaps. 15–18. For debates on the chronology of slavery and racism, see Billings, "Cases of Fernando and Elizabeth Key"; Evans, "From the Land of Canaan to the Land of Guinea"; Huggins, "Deforming Mirror of Truth," 32–37; and Vaughan, "Origins Debate" and "Blacks in Virginia."

24. See Fredrickson, *Arrogance of Race,* 196; see also Alpert, "Origin of Slavery," 209. On laws glossing over white men who produced children with black women, see Getman, "Sexual Control," 115, 126, 142–51. Kathleen M. Brown proves overall that the regulation of white women's sexuality was central to the entrenchment of racial slavery; see *Good Wives, Nasty Wenches.*

"Other slaves" could refer to American Indians; see Alpert, "Origin of Slavery," 191. By the same token, rather than specifying "white," lawmakers wrote of "freeborn English women" (1664), "any freeborn English or white woman" (1681), and "freeborn English and white women" (1692). By 1715, lawmakers also used the phrases "white person," "white woman," and "white man" and wrote of a "negro or other slave or free negro." See *Archives of Maryland*, 1:533-34 (1664), 7:203-5 (1681), 13:546-49 (1692), 30:289-90 (1715).

25. Provincial Court Judgments, vol. 4, D.S.C., 1692-93, p. 241, MHR (Mary Peters case). Peters went to court when the 1692 law was passed, but because she had been married under the 1664 law, she remained enslaved. The 1664 law (*Archives of Maryland*, 1:533-34) was part of the same law that made Africans slaves *durante vita* (for life). *Butler v. Boarman*, 1 Md. Harris & McHenry 371 (1770), 371, refers to this law as dating from 1663. Liaisons between whites and blacks had not been prohibited in English law; see Applebaum, "Miscegenation Statutes," 50.

26. Nothing in the sixteen versions of the story alludes in any way to this scenario. Carter G. Woodson read the printed court cases to mean that William Boarman had forced Nell's marriage to Charles in order to produce more slaves for himself; see "Beginnings of Miscegenation," 340, and *Negro in Our History*, 111. Karen A. Getman writes of Nell that her master "married her to" Charles ("Sexual Control," 128), and Bell Hooks writes that Nell's master "encouraged" Nell to marry Charles (*Ain't I a Woman?* 16). The court document reads: "In 1681 she married, and the repealing law was passed in the month of August, immediately after the marriage, and his Lordship interested himself in procuring the repeal with a view to this particular case. The act of 1663 [meaning 1664] was repealed *also* [emphasis added], to prevent persons from purchasing white women and marrying them to their slaves for the purpose of making slaves of them." See *Butler v. Boarman*, 1 Md. Harris & McHenry 371 (1770), 376. The eighteenth-century testimony, as well as the word "also," does not support these readings.

If an indentured servant-woman married a free man before the expiration of her term, her husband was required to purchase her time from her master in order to secure her freedom (Carr and Walsh, "Planter's Wife," 72), something Charles could not have done as a slave.

27. For the 1681 law, see *Archives of Maryland*, 7:203-5, also affirming durante vita. See also Fredrickson, *Arrogance of Race*, 196-97; and Getman, "Sexual Control," 128-29. The 1692 law penalized all liaisons between blacks and whites without regard to gender; see *Archives of Maryland*, 13:546-49. For the timing of the marriage, see n. 26, above.

Laws did not always differentiate between marriage and fornication. A 1691 Virginia law penalized sex between blacks and whites regardless of gender but was likely intended to control white women; see Hening, ed., *Statutes at Large,* 3:87 (1691), also 453–54 (1705), 6:361–62 (1753); Brown, *Good Wives, Nasty Wenches,* 197–201; and Higginbotham, *Matter of Color,* 44–45. A 1701 Virginia law fined ministers who "shall presume to marry white people and black together"; see McIlwaine, ed., *Journals of the House of Burgesses,* Aug. 25, 1701, p. 266; see also Apr. 28, 1704, p. 56. North Carolina followed in 1715, with penalties for white women who either married black men or bore their children; see Clark, ed., *State Records of North Carolina,* 23:65, also 106, 160, 195. For a 1725 indictment of a minister for marrying "a mulatto man to a white woman," see Saunders, ed., *Colonial Records of North Carolina,* 2:591, 594, 602. Georgia followed in 1750 (when blacks were first permitted into the colony); all marriages between blacks and whites were forbidden, and all parties were subject to fines or whippings; see Candler, ed., *Colonial Records of Georgia,* 1:59–60. Colonial South Carolina also prohibited marriages between blacks and whites; see Higginbotham, *Matter of Color,* 158–59.

28. See *Archives of Maryland,* 1:534 (1664), 7:204 (1681); see also *Mary Butler v. Adam Craig,* 2 Md. Harris & McHenry 214 (1787), 220; Patterson, *Slavery and Social Death,* 138. For later laws affirming this principle, see *Archives of Maryland,* 13:546–49 (1692), 30:289–90 (1715). The children could be subject to a term of servitude. Virginia made slavery inheritable through the mother in 1662; see Hening, ed., *Statutes at Large,* 2:170, 5:548 (1748); and Guild, ed., *Black Laws of Virginia,* 23–24. On *partus sequitur ventrem,* see Brown, *Good Wives, Nasty Wenches,* 128–35; Patterson, *Slavery and Social Death,* 139–41; and Wiecek, "Statutory Law," 262. By the nineteenth century, this was taken for granted; e.g., lawmakers in North Carolina in 1835 wrote of the pre-Revolutionary era: "The few free men of color that were here at that time, were chiefly mulattoes, the children of white women, and therefore unquestionably free, because their mothers were so." See *Proceedings and Debates of the Convention of North-Carolina,* 351.

29. See Brown, *Good Wives, Nasty Wenches,* 134; Carby, *Reconstructing Womanhood,* 31; Fields, "Slavery, Race and Ideology," 107; Getman, "Sexual Control," 125–26; Hall, *Magic Mirror,* 131; Higginbotham and Kopytoff, "Racial Purity," 2005–6; Moore, "Slave Law and Social Structure," 186; and Wiecek, "Statutory Law," 262–63. The judges in *Butler v. Boarman,* 1 Md. Harris & McHenry 371 (1770), wrote: "The holding of the mother in slavery would be burthensome to the master, if the issue were not also to be held in slavery" (375).

30. On the transition from servitude to slavery, see Alpert, "Origin of Slavery"; Galenson, *White servitude,* chap. 9; Kulikoff, *Tobacco and Slaves,* 37–44; Main, "Maryland and the Chesapeake Economy" and *Tobacco Colony,* chap. 3; and Menard, "From Servants to Slaves."

31. *Archives of Maryland,* 1:533–34 (1664), 7:204 (1681), 13:547 (1692), 30:290 (1715); see also Fields, "Slavery, Race and Ideology," 107. On the distinction of Christianity, see Brown, *Good Wives, Nasty Wenches,* 108, 135–36; see also Fredrickson, *White Supremacy,* 99–108; and Epperson, " 'To

Fix a Perpetual Brand.'" Because a Catholic priest married Nell and Charles, whites probably considered Charles a Christian.

32. Brown, *Good Wives, Nasty Wenches,* 181, 196–201. See also Wood, *Black Majority,* 236–37.

33. For the timing of the marriage and the births, see *Butler v. Boarman,* 1 Md. Harris & McHenry 371 (1770), 372. For the enslavement of the children, see testimony of Thomas Bowling and John Branson; see also testimony of Jean Howard, Samuel Abell, Nathaniel Suit, William McPherson, Joseph Jameson, and Elizabeth Warren. For the names and ages of the children, see testimony of John Jordan Smith, Jean Howard, Thomas Beach, Ann Whitehorn, William McPherson, Thomas Bowling, William Simpson, Joseph Jameson, Mary Crosen, Elizabeth Warren, and John Branson. William Boarman's 1709 inventory and John Sanders's 1730 inventory both list slaves with names that match the children and grandchildren of Nell and Charles; see Inventory of Major William Boarman, Charles County Inventories and Accounts, vol. 30, 1709–10, pp. 60–63, also in Charles County Inventories, 1677–1717, pp. 258–61, both MHR; and Inventory of John Sanders, Prerogative Court Inventories, 1729–30, pp. 634–38, MHR.

For the visit, see testimony of Edward Edelon and Thomas Bowling; also testimony of Joseph Jameson, who remembered Baltimore's surprise because Nell "was likely enough to marry someone of her own color." Bowling's words, "whether it was Lord Baltimore or any other person," imply that the personage of Lord Baltimore may have been apocryphal.

34. Testimony of Ann Whitehorn, William McPherson, Benjamin Jameson, Samuel Abell, and William Simpson.

35. Inventory of Major William Boarman, pp. 60–63, and Will of William Boarman, Charles County Wills, vol. J.C. & W.B., no. 2, 1706–9, pp. 108ff., second run of numbered pages, both MHR (spellings as in originals). When Mary Boarman remarried, her property passed to her second husband John Sanders, and Charles appears in the 1730 inventory of John Sanders as "1 Negro Charles very old & lame" (Inventory of John Sanders, Prerogative Court Inventories, 1729–30, pp. 634–38, MHR). In his 1730 will, Sanders left to Mary "my Negro Charles" (Will of John Sanders, Charles County, vol. C.C., no. 2, pp. 892ff., MHR).

36. On English views of the Irish, see Canny, *Elizabethan Conquest of Ireland,* 123–36; see also Breen and Innes, *"Myne Owne Ground,"* 97; Ignatiev, *How the Irish Became White;* Rutman and Rutman, *Place in Time,* 174. At the same time, according to the lawyer who argued for the Butlers in 1787, Nell was "an English subject, and as such entitled to all the privileges of an English subject"; see *Butler v. Craig,* 2 Md. Harris & McHenry 214 (1787), 233.

37. Hurd, ed., *Law of Freedom and Bondage,* 1:220; Alpert, "Origin of Slavery," 191–93, 202–4, 211; *Butler v. Boarman,* 1 Md. Harris & McHenry 371 (1770), 376.

38. Carr and Menard, "Immigration and Opportunity"; Horn, "Servant Emigration"; Kulikoff, *Tobacco and Slaves,* 32–36; Menard, "Immigrants and Their Increase"; and Moller, "Sex Composition."

39. Campbell, "Social Origins," 73–75; Horn, "Servant Emigration," 64–65; Menard, "British Migration," "From Servant to Freeholder," and "Immigration and Opportunity"; Walsh, "Servitude and Opportunity."

40. Testimony of Thomas Bowling, Benjamin Jameson, and Samuel Love; Samuel Abell and Joseph Jameson also remembered that Nell said she would rather marry Charles than Lord Baltimore. The Virginia planter Robert Carter wrote: "A Domestic Nell Butler informed her Master that she proposed to marry a black man a slave in Maryland" and that "Nell Butler married her lover"; see Letterbook IX, Sept. 17, 1789, p. 25, Robert Carter Plantation Records, WPL. Servant-women who became pregnant and were not purchased by the fathers of their children were often fined or whipped, and no such events appear in the testimony; see Carr and Walsh, "Planter's Wife," 72–73.

41. Testimony of Samuel Abell. The eighteenth-century testimony conforms to the development of romantic love that some scholars believe accompanied the consolidation of patriarchy; see Kulikoff, *Tobacco and Slaves,* 167–74, 183; Lewis, *Pursuit of Happiness,* 188–208; and Smith, *Inside the Great House,* chap. 4. Likewise, changing demographics in the late eighteenth century brought about more settled slave families, and white witnesses may have depicted a more stable family life for Nell, Charles, and their children than existed in the late seventeenth century; see Kulikoff, *Tobacco and Slaves,* 335–51, 358–71; and Menard, "Maryland Slave Population," 35–38.

42. *Butler v. Boarman,* 1 Md. Harris & McHenry 371 (1770), 374–76. A note following the verdict discusses the process of replacing one law with another, and the property rights of the master in such a case; the commentator noted: "For what was the true intent and purpose of the act of [1664]? To make the issue of these unnatural marriages, and their mothers, slaves. How is that intent and purpose answered, if immediately upon the repeal they are manumitted? . . . This construction is good in a political point of view. Many of these people, if turned loose, cannot mix with us and become members of society" (381, 382).

43. The manuscript and printed records for the second case are: *Mary Butler v. Adam Craig,* 2 Md. Harris & McHenry 214 (1787), in which the 1791 decision is recorded at the end, and *Adam Craig v. Mary Butler,* Court of Appeals, Judgments no. 3, June 1791, MHR (hereafter *Craig v. Butler,* MHR). There is no printed record of the 1791 case. Spellings of witnesses' names vary; I have used one version throughout. The 1791 records from the Court of Appeals contain the records of the 1770 Provincial Court case, which contain the testimony from the 1760s. Opinions were divided in the General Court; see *Butler v. Craig,* 2 Md. Harris & McHenry 214 (1787), 226–31. For the technical argument about replacing one law with another in relation to the timing of the marriage and the birth of the children, see 218–26.

It seems unlikely that a conviction for Nell existed in the burned court records; the 1681 corrective makes clear that the 1664 law was troublesome precisely because no official conviction or punishment was expected for a white woman and a black man who married; rather, they would suffer only the pronouncement of the master that the woman was to be enslaved. Moreover, no witnesses mentioned such a conviction.

44. *Maryland Gazette,* Feb. 14, 1771, Apr. 9, 1772, from Charles County (the master was Leonard Boarman of the same family); *Fredericksburg Virginia Herald,* July 8, 1790; *Maryland Gazette,* Aug. 27, 1798. Samuel Abell mentioned 120–300 slaves "of that family" and recounted that the master of Nell's descendants asked him not to talk about it, probably in the hopes of not encouraging other slaves to seek freedom; according to another man, however, it was no secret, as the master "had told it to fifty people"; see testimony of Samuel Abell.

45. Thelen, "Memory and American History" (quotation on 1125). For example, because the story of the actual wedding celebration had been passed down for almost a century before the witnesses were called upon, eighteenth-century Marylanders may have added touches according to their own experiences; see Kulikoff, " 'Throwing the Stocking.' " Two of the witnesses were in their eighties, five were in their seventies, and three apiece were in their and sixties, fifties, and forties.

46. *Maryland Gazette,* Oct. 12, 1769 (Mary Skinner). Talbot County Civil Judgments, 1768–70, June Court, n.p., MHR (Frances Peck case). *Ann Gynn v. James West,* Anne Arundel County Court Judgments, 1783–84, pp. 203–4, MHR. See also the conviction of Eleanor Graham and an unnamed black man for "mulatto bastardy" (Prince George's County Court, June 1769, p. 206, MHR). In 1794, Robert Thomas won his freedom when a Mrs. Smith testified that Robert's mother had been a free white woman; the slaveowner had attempted to discredit this testimony "by proving to the jury that the said Mrs. Smith was a woman, who, by general reputation of the neighbourhood, associated and kept company with negroes"; see *Robert Thomas v. Henry Pile,* 3 Md. Harris & McHenry 241 (1794), no county noted. A 1794 advertisement described a runaway as "a negro man" who "hath a white wife" in Anne Arundel County; see *Maryland Gazette,* July 31, 1794; see also Smith and Wojtowicz, *Blacks Who Stole Themselves,* 30–31, 50 (1749 and 1761; the 1761 advertisement specified that the man "pretends to be married" to a white woman). For other freedom suits involving the descendants of white women and black men, see "Abstracts from Records of Richmond County, Virginia" (Order Book No. 2, Oct. 7, 1767), 75; *Gwinn v. Bugg,* 1 Va. Jefferson 87 (1769); *Howell v. Netherland,* 1 Va. Jefferson 90 (1770); *Richard Higgins v. Nathaniel Allen,* 3 Md. Harris & McHenry 504 (1796); *Allen v. Higgins,* Court of Appeals, June 1798, Judgment no. 28, MHR; J. Prentis and Wm. Nelson to Governor James Wood, Jr., Executive Papers, Letters Received, Apr. 4, 1798, LVA. Freedom claims based on a white mother continued into the nineteenth century; see Manumission and

Emancipation Record, 1821–62, labeled "Slave Manumission Records," 1:134, 274–75, 385, 391, 414–15, 465, 476, 479, 482, 488, 537–38, 555, 559, 2:10, 40, 109, 168, 224, 225, 231, 275, 291–92, 333, 430, 430–31, 435, 3:78, 373, 451, 497, RG 21, NA; *Hezekiah Wood v. John Davis*, 11 U.S. 271 (1812); *John Davis v. Wood*, 14 U.S. 6 (1816); *U.S. v. Richard Davis*, 4 D.C. Cranch 606 (1835); Brown, *Free Negroes in the District of Columbia*, chap. 4. For antebellum freedom suits, see also chap. 5, below.

In 1755, free black men in three North Carolina counties protested paying taxes on their white wives noting that the act compelled them to "intermarry with those of their own complexion"; see Saunders, ed., *Colonial Records of North Carolina*, 5:295. In 1772 in North Carolina, a married white woman fractured the skull of her three-day-old infant, whom she admitted was the son of "Will, a Negro fellow belonging to her father." See *King v. Sarah Wiggins*, Secretary of State Court Records, Box 312, April–May 1772, Dobbs County, NCDAH. See also Hazard, "Journal," 376, in which a traveling merchant observed that a white man's daughter "was delivered of a Mulatto Child" and that neighborhood women "talked freely of it"; Wood, trans., and Ezell, ed., *New Democracy*, 14, in which a traveler observed that the white daughter of a Revolutionary general had "two sons by one of the Negro slaves" in North Carolina.

47. Peter to Moses Fontaine, Mar. 30, 1757, in Fontaine, *Memoirs of a Huguenot Family*, 350. *Archives of Maryland*, 32:368–70 (St. Mary's County).

48. In paraphrasing the 1664 law, the court used the word "white" in place of the law's wording "freeborn English" women and likewise shortened "negro slave" to "negro"; see *Butler v. Craig*, 2 Md. Harris & McHenry 214 (1787), 217, 228; *Archives of Maryland*, 1:533–34. On whiteness and freedom, see Davis, *Problem of Slavery in the Age of Revolution*, chaps. 6, 7; and Roediger, *Wages of Whiteness*, 27–40.

49. *Butler v. Craig*, 2 Md. 214 (1787), 228. This was one judge's gloss on the 1715 law imposing penalties for sex between white women and black men in *Archives of Maryland*, 30:289–90.

Chapter 3 *Bastardy*

1. Lee, *To Kill a Mockingbird*, 244 (quotation).

2. In 1825, Polly was between ages 14 and 21; Jim could have been anywhere from a young teenager to age 50. See 1820 census, Rowan County, N.C., 362 (Lanes), 330 (Peppingers); Davidson County was carved out of Rowan in 1822. The case was *State v. Jim*, Davidson County Court Minutes, October 1825, NCDAH. I have used the spelling "Peppinger" throughout.

For Jim's prosecution, see Jesse Hargrave to Governor Hutchins G. Burton (hereafter HGB), Letter Books, Governor's Papers, Mar. 24, 1826, NCDAH; see also deposition of William Holt, General Assembly Session Records, Miscellaneous Court Cases [ca. March–May 1826]. Hereafter, all correspondence and depositions are cited by names and dates only. In North Carolina, slaves could not legally testify against white people but could testify against other slaves; see *Revised Laws of North Carolina*, 1821, 1:300; and Flanigan, "Criminal Procedure," 556, 557.

3. Jno. Smith to HGB, Mar. 23, 1826; Alexander Gray to HGB, Dec. 8, 1825, Mar. 24, 1826. *State v. Jim* and *State v. Negro Jim*, case #15, Davidson County Superior Court Recognizance Docket, October 1825, all NCDAH. The date of execution was set for Dec. 23, 1825; see six signers to HGB, Dec. 8, 1825. To protect both the interests of slaveholders and the slave standing trial, North Carolina law required jurors to be slaveholders; see Flanigan, "Criminal Procedure," 550–51.

4. In 1820, Polly's parents had four children under age 16 (1820 census, Rowan County, N.C., 362). The Lanes were one among 31 families out of 91 in their district who owned no land; see Davidson County Tax List, 1827, p. 2, NCDAH (the earliest tax list available). In 1820, 20.3% of Rowan County's population were slaves and 0.5% free people of color (1820 census, Rowan County, N.C., 408). In 1830, 14.3% of Davidson County's population were slaves and 1.1% free people of color (1830 census, Davidson County, N.C., 261). For Polly as the only white laborer, see six signers to HGB, Dec. 8, 1825. On poor whites in the North Carolina piedmont, see Bolton, *Poor Whites,* chaps. 1, 2; Cecil-Fronsman, *Common Whites,* 12–18; Leonard, *Centennial History,* 25, 72–73; and Tullos, *Habits of Industry,* chap 2.

For Abraham Peppinger, see Reeves and Shoaf, *Will Summaries,* 48; he died in the early 1830s. In 1827, he owned 600 acres of land and three taxable slaves; see Davidson County Tax List, 1827, p. 6, NCDAH. In 1820 and 1830, Abraham Peppinger owned nine slaves (1820 census, Rowan County, N.C., 330; 1830 census, Davidson County, N.C., 230).

5. On rural antebellum Southern communities, see Johnson, *Ante-Bellum North Carolina,* 90–113, 613; Cecil-Fronsman, *Common Whites,* 152. One day's travel would be about 35 miles; see Tullos, *Habits of Industry,* 56.

6. On distrust of state power, see Cecil-Fronsman, *Common Whites,* 138; Watson, "Conflict and collaboration," 283; and Wyatt-Brown, *Southern Honor,* 391–92, 400–401. For Polly's sequence of events, see six signers to HGB, Dec. 8, 1825; see also Alexander Gray to HGB, Dec. 8, 1825; and Jno. Smith to HGB, Mar. 23, 1826. For "carnal connection" and the pregnancy denial, see Alexander Gray to HGB, Dec. 8, 1825; and A. W. Shepperd to HGB, Mar. 24, 1826; see also Alexander Gray to HGB, Mar. 24, 1826.

7. Six signers to HGB, Dec. 8, 1825; Alexander Gray to HGB, Dec. 8, 1825.

8. For Dick, see six signers to HGB, Dec. 8, 1825. For Jim, see James Martin to HGB, Mar. 24, 1826; Jesse Hargrave to HGB, Mar. 24, 1826; see also A. W. Shepperd to HGB, Mar. 24, 1826.

9. For "illicit intercourse," see deposition of William Holt [ca. March–

May 1826]; see also Alexander Gray to HGB, Dec. 8, 1825. For Polly as Jim's "wife," see Robert Moore to HGB, [ca. April–June] 1826. For Jim's lawyer, see Alexander Gray to HGB, Dec. 8, 1825. "Her appearance on the trial seemed to call in question the correctness" of her testimony, said A. W. Shepperd to HGB, Mar. 24, 1826.

10. Six signers to HGB, Dec. 8, 1825. Jesse Hargrave to HGB, Mar. 24, 1826 (the testimony of others who had witnessed suspicious circumstances was discredited due to character attacks on these witnesses); Robert Moore to HGB, [ca. April–June] 1826.

11. Alexander Gray to HGB, Dec. 8, 1825 ("greater intimacy").

12. Philip J. Schwarz writes: "A good many slaves lived within supportive communities whose members would cover up running away and other behavior proscribed by whites"; see "Forging the Shackles," 138. *State v. Mary Green*, Craven County Court Minutes, Nov. 15, 1827; Petition of Mary Green, Governor's Papers, Nov. 16, 1827, both NCDAH. On slaves' attitudes toward poor whites, see Genovese, " 'Rather be a Nigger' "; Rawick, ed., *American Slave*, 16:8, 40; suppl. 1, vol. 8, pt. 3:1221–22.

13. Alexander Gray to HGB, May 18, 1826; on people changing their minds, see deposition of William Holt [ca. March–May 1826]; Jesse Harper (a juror) to HGB, Mar. 25, 1826; Robert Moore to HGB, [ca. April–June] 1826]; J. M. Morehead to HGB, May 19, 1826; and William Holt and Jesse Hargrave to HGB, May 19, 1826.

14. Morehead later served two terms as governor of North Carolina (as a Whig) in the 1840s; see Konkle, *John Motley Morehead;* Connor, *Ante-Bellum Builders,* chap. 5; Morehead, *Morehead Family,* chap. 6; and Sink and Matthews, *Pathfinders,* 56 (Morehead, "when in Lexington, stayed at the home of his friend, Dr. W. R. Holt, and was often employed by the Hargraves for their most important legal work"). On lawyers representing slaves on trial, see Flanigan, "Criminal Procedure," 553–56.

15. J. M. Smith to HGB, May 6, 1826; six signers to HGB, Dec. 8, 1825. See also Robert Moore to HGB, 1826 [ca. April–June] 1826. Polly had testified against Jim in the burglary case; see case #19, Davidson County Superior Court Recognizance Docket, October 1825, NCDAH. For the Palmers, see Reeves and Shoaf, *Will Summaries,* 48; and Davidson County Bastardy Bonds and Records, 1832, NCDAH.

16. On motivations for slave crime, see Schwarz, "Forging the Shackles," 129. On community influence in a woman's decision to bring rape charges, see Block, "Coerced Sex," chap. 3. On honor, see Wyatt-Brown, *Southern Honor,* chap. 12.

17. On coercion by white women, see chap. 6, below.

18. Jesse Hargrave to HGB, Mar. 24, 1826; James Martin to HGB, Mar. 24, 1826; A. W. Shepperd to HGB, Mar. 24, 1826; Robert Moore to HGB [ca. April–June] 1826; James Martin to HGB, Mar. 24, 1826.

19. For the reprieve, see HGB Letter Books, ca. Dec. 14, 1825; *State v. Jim*. See also James Martin to HGB, Mar. 24, 1826; 39 signers to HGB, Mar. 25, 1826. For Polly's silences, see deposition of John Turner, Mar. 23, 1826; James Martin to HGB, Mar. 24, 1826. James Goodman writes of one of the women who falsely accused the Scottsboro Boys of rape in 1930s Alabama: "She charged rape and forever after stuck to her story with the tenacity of a person who believed what she said. Perhaps she believed it from the moment she said it. More likely . . . she came to believe it over time"; see *Stories of Scottsboro*, 192.

20. Jesse Hargrave to HGB, Mar. 24, 1826; see also deposition of Jack Sullivan and David Owen, Mar. 23, 1826; James Martin to HGB, Mar. 24, 1826; A. W. Shepperd to HGB, Mar. 24, 1826; William Holt and Jesse Hargrave to HGB, May 19, 1826; J. M. Morehead to HGB, May 20, 1826. Hargrave was also a founder of Lexington; members of the Hargrave family were state senators throughout the antebellum period; see *Heritage of Davidson County*, 245; Leonard, *Centennial History*, 26; and Sink and Matthews, *Pathfinders*, 37, 44, 401. In 1830, Jesse Hargrave owned 28 slaves (1830 census, Davidson County, N.C., 192).

21. Deposition of Jack Sullivan and David Owen, Mar. 23, 1826. Deposition of William Holt [ca. March–May 1826]. W. R. Holt and Jesse Hargrave to HGB, May 19, 1826. Jesse Hargrave to HGB, Mar. 24, 1826. For Polly's friends, see also Robert Moore to HGB, [ca. April–June] 1826. On confession during childbirth, see Ulrich, *Midwife's Tale*, 147–53.

22. J. M. Morehead to HGB, May 20, 1826. Thirty-nine signers to HGB, Mar. 25, 1826. See also Block, "Coerced Sex," chap. 4.

23. M. L. Henderson to HGB, Dec. 6, 1825. Deposition of Elizabeth Lane (apparently not related to Polly, and called a "creditable witness"), May 6, 1826; A. W. Shepperd to HGB, Mar. 24, 1826. Elizabeth Lane also described Jim as a "thief" and a "rogue."

24. Six signers to HGB, Dec. 8, 1825; deposition of Leah and Ruth Peacock, May 5, 1826. Thirty-nine signers to HGB, Mar. 25, 1826.

25. A. W. Shepperd to HGB, Mar. 24, 1826 ("far advanced"); see also deposition of William Holt [ca. March–May 1826]; Robert Moore to HGB, [ca. April–June] 1826; J. M. Morehead to HGB, May 19, 20, 1826. Jno. Smith to HGB, Mar. 23, 1826 ("the child was got"); James Martin to HGB, Mar. 24, 1826; Jesse Hargrave to HGB, Mar. 24, 1826; J. M. Morehead to HGB, May 20, 1826.

26. James Martin to HGB, Mar. 24, 1826; A. W. Shepperd to HGB, Mar. 24, 1826. On conception and female orgasm, see Laqueur, *Making Sex*, 99–103, 161–63, 181–92.

27. Deposition of William Holt [ca. March–May 1826]; 39 signers to HGB, Mar. 25, 1826. On Holt (the father of 14 children), see Ashe, Weeks, and Van Noppen, eds., *Biographical History of North Carolina*, 7:171–80; Leonard,

Centennial History, 162–66; and Sink and Matthews, *Pathfinders,* 341–43, 401. In 1830, Holt owned seven slaves (1830 census, Davidson County, N.C., 192).

28. Four doctors to HGB, Mar. 27, 1826, emphasis in original. The statement was lifted from a 1785 text in which the author wrote that "without an excitation of lust, or enjoyment in the venereal act, no conception can probably take place." See Samuel Farr, *The Elements of Medical Jurisprudence* (London, 1785), 42–43, cited in Laqueur, *Making Sex,* 161.

29. *John Weaver v. George Cryer and Samuel Moore,* Hertford County, SSCMR #1510, NCDAH, and 12 N.C. 337 (1827), 208. See also *Voss v. Howard,* 1 D.C. Cranch 251 (1805); this was an assault case in which the slave was described as living "with his own wife, a free white woman," a circumstance unrelated to the assault. Marriage between blacks and whites was illegal in North Carolina; see *Revised Laws of North Carolina,* 1821, chap. 23 (130).

30. In Nansemond County, 2 of 48 households of slaveholding blacks were listed as such; see Woodson, *Free Negro Owners of Slaves,* vi–vii, 39. Woodson writes: "Others reported with white wives were not slaveholders" (vii).

31. See *Laws of North Carolina,* 1831, chap. 4 (9–10); *Revised Statutes of North Carolina,* 1836–37, 1:386–87; *Laws of North Carolina,* 1838–39, chap. 24 (33). For tolerated marriages between white women and black men, see Bynum, *Unruly Women,* 99; Stevenson, *Life in Black and White,* 43, 304–5; see also Mills, "Miscegenation and Free Negro."

32. *State v. Alfred Hooper and Elizabeth Suttles,* Rutherford County, SSCMR #3545, NCDAH, and 27 N.C. 201 (1844). *State v. Joel Fore and Susan Chesnut,* Lenoir County, SSCMR #3002, NCDAH, and 23 N.C. 378 (1841), 379, 380; 1840 census, Lenoir County, N.C., 25. The crime went on record as "fornication and adultery" because the marriage was considered null and void. Curiously drawing on a technicality in the indictment, the defense pointed out that Susan was not necessarily female because no gender pronouns were used to describe her. *State v. William P. Watters,* Ashe County, SSCMR #3540, NCDAH, and 25 N.C. 455 (1843); Watters argued that "he was descended from Portuguese, and not from Negro or Indian ancestors" (456). *State v. Brady,* 28 Tenn. 74 (1848), 74, 75; the judges were probably intent on exempting slaves in order to protect masters' property. See also *State v. Diana Wharton and Negro George,* Pasquotank County Superior Court Docket, March 1814, NCDAH, in which the couple was indicted for fornication. In east Tennessee in 1852, a free man of color married a white woman from a laboring family; the case came to light only when the woman's uncle assaulted the man's brother. The uncle was found guilty, and the court addressed the question of the marriage only to note that the black man was "within the degrees prohibited by the statute from intermarrying with white persons." See *James Bloomer v. State,* 35 Tenn. 66 (1855), 67 (Hawkins County). See also Cecil-Fronsman, *Common Whites,* 90–92, on sexual relationships between poor whites and blacks.

33. *State v. Griffin Stewart,* Nash County, SSCMR #4749, NCDAH, and

31 N.C. 342 (1849). On the two marriages of the free Robert Wright to white women in antebellum Virginia, see Buckley, "Unfixing Race." For Delks Moses, see Silas Summerell to Governor James Pleasants (Southampton County), Executive Papers, Letters Received, Apr. 6, 1825, LVA. As in the colonial era, advertisements for runaway slaves testified to possible liaisons between white women and slave men; see, e.g., *Raleigh Register and North Carolina State Gazette,* Feb. 23, 1802, in which a slave ran away with a white woman in piedmont Franklin County.

34. Benjamin Sherwood to "B. S. Hedrick and family," copy of speech delivered in Iowa, Apr. 7, 1860, Benjamin Sherwood Hedrick Papers, WPL. See also Mills, "Miscegenation and Free Negro," 23.

35. See Cecil-Fronsman, *Common Whites,* chap. 5. On privacy and class status, see Painter, "Of *Lily,* Linda Brent, and Freud," 97. On the idea that white women's bodies belonged to white men, see Bardaglio, "Rape and the Law," 754; and Bynum, *Unruly Women,* 109.

36. Deposition of William Holt [ca. March–May 1826]; James Martin to HGB, Mar. 24, 1826. Abortion before "quickening" (about three months) could be a less serious offense in antebellum America than the attempt to cover up a sexual transgression such as fornication; see Gordon, *Woman's Body, Woman's Right,* 49–60; and Mohr, *Abortion in America,* chap. 2. For Nancy Wallis (Orange County), see Letters and Petitions to Governor Edward B. Dudley, Apr. 3–7, 1838; quotation from J. W. Norwood to Governor Edward B. Dudley, Apr. 7, 1838, Governor's Papers, NCDAH; her name was also spelled "Wallace."

37. James Martin to HGB, Mar. 24, 1826 ("birth was concealed"). *Marville Scroggins v. Lucretia Scroggins,* Buncombe County, SSCMR #2140, NCDAH, and 14 N.C. 535 (1832). *Hillsborough (N.C.) Recorder,* Sept. 5, 1821. (Paris, Ky.) *Western Carolinian,* Aug. 9, 1823.

38. Jacobs, *Incidents,* 52 (Chowan County). A black man in Kansas told of a similar case in a planter family (probably in Missouri) in which the child "was reported to have died, but the man believes it was killed"; see testimony of Captain Richard J. Hinton, New York City, Dec. 14, 1863, American Freedmen's Inquiry Commission, Letters Received by the Office of the Adjutant General, M619, reel 201, file #8, RG 94, NA.

39. The accused slanderers usually won such cases on appeal. See *State v. Neese,* 4 N.C. 691 (1818), 692 (Orange County). *Horton and wife v. Reavis,* 6 N.C. 380 (1818) (Granville County). *James Calloway v. Robert Middleton and wife,* 9 Ky. 372 (1820), 372, 373 (Warren County). *Ezra Castleberry and wife v. Samuel S. Kelly and wife,* Warren County, SSCOP, RG 92, #A-2725, GDAH, and 26 Ga. 606 (1858). *Candace Lucas v. Gilbert R. Nichols,* Montgomery County, SSCMR #7901, NCDAH, and 52 N.C. 32 (1859). In western North Carolina in the 1820s, a white man gossiped that a white woman was pregnant by his slave; see *Mary Watts v. John M. Greenlee,* 12 N.C. 210 (1827), and 13 N.C. 115

(1829). See also *Hudson v. Garner and wife*, 22 Mo. 423 (1856). For a South Carolina example, see McCurry, *Masters of Small Worlds*, 80, 89. See also King, "Constructing Gender," 77–78.

40. William Holt and Jesse Hargrave to HGB, May 19, 1826.

41. Dabney Pettus Divorce Petition, Fluvana County, Dec. 13, 1802, #A6138, LPP, LVA; *Journal of the House of Delegates*, Dec. 21, 1802. Benjamin Butt Divorce Petition, Norfolk County, Dec. 7, 1803, #4594, LPP, LVA; *Journal of the House of Delegates*, Dec. 9, 1803; *Laws of Virginia*, December 1803, chap. 6 (26). Richard Jones Divorce Petition, Northampton County, Nov. 28, 1814, #6364, LPP, LVA; *Journal of the House of Delegates*, Nov. 28, 1814; *Acts of the General Assembly*, 1815, chap. 98 (145). Abraham Newton Divorce Petition, Fauquier County, Nov. 16, 1816, #6729, LPP, LVA; *Journal of the House of Delegates*, Nov. 27, 1816; *Acts of the General Assembly*, 1817, chap. 120 (176).

42. *Scroggins v. Scroggins*. *Jesse Barden v. Ann Barden*, Wayne County, SSCMR #5554, NCDAH, and 14 N.C. 548 (1832). See also General Assembly Session Records, Senate Bills, Dec. 15, 1821, NCDAH, in which Caleb Miller's wife had a "black" child after six months of marriage; and letter from "A Citizen of Richmond," *Raleigh Register and North Carolina State Gazette*, Nov. 30, 1809, in which a white man claimed that a few months after his 1807 marriage, his white wife "was delivered of a Mulatto child."

43. Buckingham, *Slave States*, 1:240; [Royall], *Sketches of History*, 31; Dodge, "Free Negroes of North Carolina," 29. See also Glascock County Superior Court Minutes, June 29, 1858, GDAH, in which the white Rebecca Scarber was accused of "fornication with one free man of color known by the name of Sterling Shelton." For two more records of white women bearing children by black men, see Dickenson, comp., *Entitled!* 2, 12.

44. *State v. Williamson Haithcock*, Orange County, SSCMR #6830, NCDAH, and 33 N.C. 32 (1850). See also General Assembly Session Records, Miscellaneous Petitions, Nov. 29, 1820, and House Committee Reports, Dec. 6, 1820, NCDAH, for a western North Carolina case in which the free Samuel Love petitioned for the legitimation of his son in order to pass property to him. White neighbors contended that Samuel was an "industrious and good citizen," but authorities countered that "the petitioner is quite a black man, and the mother of his son a white woman" and objected to encouraging "licentious intercourse between persons of opposite colors." Bastardy laws were passed in 1741, 1799, and 1814; see *Revised Statutes of North Carolina*, 1836–37, 1:89–92. See also Grossberg, *Governing the Hearth*, 200–218; and Smith and Hindus, "Premarital Pregnancy," 549–54.

45. For dates of birth and conception, see Robert Moore to HGB, [ca. April–June] 1826, June 6, 1826. See also J. M. Smith to HGB, May 6, 1826; William Holt and Jesse Hargrave to HGB, May 19, 1826; and J. M. Morehead to HGB, May 20, 1826. The name of the child appears only in a later census; see n. 47, below.

46. J. M. Morehead to HGB, May 20, 1826 ("the negro's fate"). For Polly's refusals, see deposition of J. Kinney and John Turner, May 8, 1826. Depositions of George Gregson, Reuben Shepherd, Barberry Holloway, and Rachel Cross, May 5, 1826; Gregson had been a witness at the trial; see *State v. Negro Jim*. For the child's color, see J. M. Smith to HGB, May 6, 1826 ("some think"); also J. M. Morehead to HGB, May 20, 1826. For other quotations, see Alexander Gray to HGB, May 18, 1826; J. M. Smith to HGB, May 6, 1826; depositions of Leah and Ruth Peacock, and Willy Northern, May 5, 1826; deposition of Jacob Miller (about his wife), May 8, 1826; Robert Moore to HGB, [ca. April–June] 1826; and William Holt and Jesse Hargrave to HGB, May 19, 1826.

47. 1840 census, Davidson County, N.C., 288. Polly and Jim's child had either escaped the notice of the 1830 census taker or was recorded as white (1830 census, Davidson County, N.C., 205). 1850 census, Davidson County, N.C., 358, household #626; the age was noted as 22, close enough to confirm her as the child.

48. *Nancy Midgett v. Willoughby McBryde*, Currituck County, SSCMR #4944, NCDAH, and 48 N.C. 22 (1855). For a similar North Carolina case in 1861, see Bynum, *Unruly Women*, 88–93, see also 99–103. For an example of the child of a white woman and a black man who continued residing with his white mother in western North Carolina, see George Junkin Ramsey Papers (Burke County), Legal Papers, Mar. 12, 1845, WPL; here petitioners swore that a 23-year-old man was the son of a white woman and that "Jackson Wilder and his mother have always resided in this county." See also Mills, "Miscegenation and Free Negro," 23–24. On apprenticeship, see also Grossberg, *Governing the Hearth*, 259–68; and Stevenson, *Life in Black and White*, 258–59.

49. HGB Letter Books, May 23, 1826 (recorded on same page as reprieves, ca. Dec. 14, 1825). Bertram Wyatt-Brown notes that "governors acted only after all local parties had an opportunity to voice their opinions, so that, in effect, he often served as representative of the local elite or of the 'general opinion' of the entire community"; see "Community, Class, and Snopesian Crime," 194.

50. On executions and jails, see Johnson, *Ante-Bellum North Carolina*, 677–82. On the credibility of white women charging slaves with rape, see Schwarz, *Twice Condemned*, 162, 206–7; see also Clinton, " 'Southern Dishonor,' " 60; and Mills, "Miscegenation and Free Negro," 28.

51. Jesse Hargrave to HGB, Mar. 24, 1826. Deposition of William Holt [ca. March–May 1826]. *Laws of North Carolina*, 1823, chap. 51 (42); *Revised Laws of North Carolina*, 1823, chap. 1229 (131). Punishments for white men convicted of raping white women were eased over time from the death penalty to prison terms; see Bardaglio, "Rape and the Law," 755; and Wriggins, "Rape, Racism, and the Law," 106. On the different treatment of black and white men accused of rape, see Block, "Coerced Sex," chap. 4; Partington, "Incidence of the Death Penalty," 50–51; and Sommerville, "Rape Myth," 492–93.

52. *State v. Negro Liberty,* Rutherford County Court Minutes, Dec. 16, 1801, NCDAH. For other cases of the death penalty, see *Raleigh Register and North Carolina State Gazette,* Sept. 14, 1802 (Wake County); *Niles' Weekly Register,* July 13, 1822, p. 320, and Sept. 14, 1822, p. 18; Trial of Moses, 1828 (Lincoln County), File II, RG 4, Box 83, folder marked "Negroes—Slave Trials," GDAH; *New Orleans True Delta,* June 21, 1859 (for a Virginia execution); Edwards, "Slave Justice," 265–68; Harris, "Rowdyism," 21–22; and Shingleton, "Trial and Punishment," 68–69, 71–72.

53. William D. Valentine Diaries, Feb. 17, Apr. 20, 1838, SHC; see also Bertie County Superior Court Minutes, March 1838, NCDAH. In Davidson County in 1859, when a slave was sentenced to death for attempting to rape a white woman, the court wrote: "The character of the female was proved to be very good for truth and chastity"; see *State v. Elick,* Davidson County, SSCMR #8014, NCDAH, and 52 N.C. 68 (1859), 69.

54. June 13, 1829, Executive Papers, Letters Received, Box 311 (Mecklenburg County), emphasis in original; Auditor of Public Accounts, Entry 756, Condemned Blacks Executed or Transported, Aug. 4, 1829 (executed July 24), LVA.

55. *Macon (Ga.) Daily Telegraph,* July 16, 1827. For other cases in which black men were sentenced to castration for the rape of white women, see Chesterfield County Court Order Book, July 12, 1802, pp. 301, 306, LVA, cited in Egerton, *Gabriel's Rebellion,* 209, n. 35; Executive Papers, Letters Received, folder marked "Pardon Papers, 1803," Box 128, LVA, re: Nancy Lacy and Jack; and *State v. Anderson,* 19 Mo. 241 (1853), in which the jury was instructed that if convinced, they could not acquit the man even if they believed the woman was "of bad character for virtue, or that she associated with negroes" (242). On castration as a legal consequence, see Bardaglio, "Rape and the Law," 752–53; see also Jordan, *White over Black,* 154–58, 473.

56. *Niles' Weekly Register,* Nov. 15, 1823, p. 176 ("beaten"), from Frederick, Md. Janson, *Stranger in America,* 386–87 (castration), from Chowan County. George E. Tabb to Governor Henry A. Wise, Sept. 10, 1856 (Mathews County), Executive Papers, Letters Received, Box 436, LVA (lynching threat). *North Carolina Weekly Standard,* Dec. 7, 1859 ("would have been shot"), from Rowan County. Janson, *Stranger in America,* 386 ("consumed his body"). For the second burning, see *Columbus (Ga.) Daily Sun,* Feb. 22, Mar. 2, 29, 1861; *John A. Middlebrook v. Abel Nelson,* Harris County, SSCOP, RG 92, #A-3916, GDAH, and 34 Ga. 506 (1866).

When a white girl accused a black man of raping her near Raleigh, one newspaper called the incident "almost too shocking for recital," and asked for "the punishment his villainy merits," but those words do not reveal whether the writer meant punishment by the law or outside of it; see *Star and North Carolina State Gazette,* July 17, 1834. For a Tennessee case of burning at the stake for murder and the alleged rape of a white woman (the man was tortured until he confessed), see *New York Daily Tribune,* July 4, 11, 1854. See also Dyer, " 'Most Unexampled Exhibition.' "

57. *Commonwealth v. Fields,* 31 Va. 648 (1832), 649. For similar circumstances, see *Charles v. State,* 11 Ark. 389 (1850) 409; *Wyatt v. State,* 32 Tenn. 394 (1852); and *Lewis v. State,* 30 Ala. 54 (1857), in which a slave tried to have sex with a white woman by pretending he was her husband. For reversed convictions due to insufficient evidence, see *Peter v. State,* 24 Tenn. 436 (1844), and *Major v. State,* 34 Tenn. 11 (1854), 36 Tenn. 597 (1857). In *Sydney v. State,* 22 Tenn. 478 (1842), the indictment was set aside because the alleged victim was a six-year-old girl and therefore not "a woman, within the meaning of the statute"; but see *Commonwealth v. Watts,* 31 Va. 672 (1833), for similar circumstances, with conviction of a free black man affirmed. In *Commonwealth v. Jerry Mann,* 4 Va. 210 (1820), conviction was reversed because the indictment failed to state that the woman was white; the same occurred in *Grandison v. State,* 21 Tenn. 451 (1841); *Henry v. State,* 23 Tenn. 270 (1843); and *State v. Charles,* 1 Fla. 298 (1847). In *State v. Martin,* 14 N.C. 329 (1832), and *Joe Sullivant v. State,* 8 Ark. 400 (1848), conviction was reversed due to incorrect legal language; see also *State v. Jim,* 12 N.C. 142 (1826). In *Thurman v. State,* 18 Ala. 276 (1850), and *Dick v. State,* 30 Miss. 631 (1856), new trials were granted on technicalities of legal racial definitions. In *Lewis v. State,* 35 Ala. 380 (1860), a new trial was granted due to technicalities in the legal concept of "attempted" rape. In *State v. Phil,* 1 Stewart Ala. 31 (1827), the man was released because the trial had been delayed too long. In *Day v. Commonwealth,* 44 Va. 629 (1846), a new trail was granted to a free black man because one of the jurors "was not a freeholder" in the county. In *Green v. State,* 23 Miss. 509 (1852), a new trial was awarded because the alleged assault was not committed within the county stated. In *Pleasant v. State,* 13 Ark. 360 (1853), 15 Ark. 624 (1855), a new trial was awarded due to various errors of the court. In *State v. Henry,* 50 N.C. 65 (1857), a new trial was awarded due to an erroneous statement made by the judge to the jury. See also Coulter, "Four Slaves Trials," 244–45; Higginbotham and Kopytoff, "Racial Purity," 2012–15; and McPherson, "Documents: Slave Trials," 273–84.

For appellate courts affirming the guilt of black men convicted of rape, see, e.g., *State v. Washington,* 6 N.C. 100 (1812); *Thompson v. Commonwealth,* 31 Va. 652 (1833); *State v. Jesse,* 19 N.C. 297 (1837), in which conviction was reversed, but followed by 20 N.C. 95 (1838); *Dennis v. State,* 5 Ark. 230 (1843); *Bill v. State,* 24 Tenn. 155 (1844); *Wash v. State,* 22 Miss. 120 (1850); *Ellick v. State,* 31 Tenn. 325 (1851); *Stephen v. State,* 11 Ga. 225 (1852); *Smith v. Commonwealth,* 51 Va. 734 (1853); *Isham v. State,* 33 Tenn. 111 (1853); and *State v. Tom,* 47 N.C. 414 (1855). On the judicial handling of rape cases by appellate courts in the antebellum South, see also Bardaglio, "Rape and the Law" and *Reconstructing the Household,* 64–78; and Morris, *Southern Slavery and the Law,* chap. 14.

58. On pardoning, see Clark, "Aspects of North Carolina Slave Code,"

153; Johnson, *Ante-Bellum North Carolina,* 509; Schwarz, *Twice Condemned,* 155–64, 205–6, 293; and Sommerville, "Rape Myth." For Jim being sold beyond the limits of the county, see six signers to HGB, Dec. 8, 1825. In Virginia in 1817, a free black man was convicted of raping a white woman, but when the woman gave birth to a child conceived before the alleged rape, the man chose a pardon application over a new trial in order to avoid more prison time; see H. Holmes to Governor James P. Preston, Executive Papers, Letters Received, Oct. 23, 1817, re: John Holman and Susannah Baughman (Shenandoah County), LVA. For a case of a slave sold "beyond the limits of the United States" after conviction for the rape of a white woman, see Executive Papers, Letters Received, July 30, 1856, Box 435, papers re: "Mrs. Lucy Scott's Negro, Robert Bruce" (Powhatan County), LVA.

59. Jno. Smith to HGB, Mar. 23, 1826. Even if Jim were already about to be sold out of the county for theft, his master clearly felt he would benefit more from a sale than from compensation for Jim's execution. On the purposes of pardoning black men convicted of rape, see also Bardaglio, "Rape and the Law," 768; and Getman, "Sexual Control," 136, 137.

60. On dual identity, see Tushnet, *American Law of Slavery,* esp. 90–121 on North Carolina. See also Fox-Genovese and Genovese, "Jurisprudence and Property Relations"; Higginbotham and Kopytoff, "Property First, Humanity Second"; Nash, "Reason of Slavery"; and Wiecek, "Statutory Law," 264–67.

61. For Jack (Goochland County), see affidavit of William Saunders, Sept. 17, 1803, and affidavit of Samuel Gathright, Sept. 24, 1803, both in Executive Papers, Letters Received, folder marked "Pardon Papers, 1803," Box 128, LVA. For Sam (Rowan County), see W. L. Henderson to Governor Montfort Stokes, Governor's Papers, Oct. 15, 1831, NCDAH. For the 65 petitioners (Northampton County), see Jas. W. Newsom et al. to Governor John W. Ellis, 1859, Letter Book 1859–61, p. 74; the pardon was denied, with the governor replying that "the administration of the criminal laws ought not to depend upon the pecuniary circumstances of the owners of slaves" (p. 75), NCDAH. Petitioners maintained that Elizabeth agreed to the request for mercy, indicating either her own remorse at a false accusation or the coercion of more powerful white neighbors.

In 1813 in Norfolk, Virginia, whites commended a white woman for killing a neighborhood slave whom she claimed was about to rape her; at the same time, the slave's master remarked "'that he was sorry to lose such a fellow.'" See *Niles' Weekly Register,* Dec. 25, 1813. Charges could be dropped if a master entered bond for an offending slave; see *State v. Negro Charles,* Pasquotank County Court Minutes, June 1834, in which a white man posted bond for $500 for Charles to behave, "especially toward Polly Benton." In *Pleasant v. State,* 13 Ark. 360 (1853), the court opined that a jury could infer "that it was not worth the forfeit of a human life"—that is a slave—if the white woman's reputation cast doubt on a rape accusation (378). When a slave was convicted of raping a white woman in tidewater Virginia in 1856, the master's daughter requested a pardon, informing the governor that the man was "young and valuable"; see Elizabeth F. Borum to Governor Henry A. Wise, Executive Papers, Letters Received, Aug. 29, 1856 (in September folder), Box 436, LVA. In 1856 in eastern North Carolina, a petitioner pointed out that an accused slave's master was "a very worthy old man" who would "lose greatly by losing Jim"; see Letter to Governor Thomas Bragg, Apr. 1, 1856 (Johnston County), Governor's Papers, NCDAH.

62. On fair and unfair treatment of slaves, see Ayers, *Vengeance and Justice,* 134–37; Morris, *Southern Slavery and the Law;* Flanigan, "Criminal Procedure"; Genovese, *Roll, Jordan, Roll,* 25–49; and Nash, "More Equitable Past?" and "Fairness and Formalism." On North Carolina, see Holt, *Supreme Court of North Carolina;* Taylor, "Humanizing the Slave Code"; and Watson, "North Carolina Slave Courts." See also Oakes, *Slavery and Freedom,* 56–78. Some scholars have assumed that antebellum white Southerners nearly always lynched black men accused of sexually assaulting white women; see, e.g., Bardaglio, *Reconstructing the Household,* 77; Stampp, *Peculiar Institution,* 190–91; and Wyatt-Brown, *Southern Honor,* 388. But on the rarity of such lynching, see Genovese, *Roll, Jordan, Roll,* 33–34; and Jordan, *Tumult and Silence,* 150 n. 1. See also chap. 8, n. 1, below.

63. The master withdrew charges due to "infirmity and age," but when the war ended he and a white man who had hired George's labor argued over compensation, highlighting the economic interest of white Southerners in preventing lynching. See *Columbus (Ga.) Daily Sun,* Feb. 22, Mar. 2, 29, 1861; and *John A. Middlebrook v. Abel Nelson,* Harris County, SSCOP, RG 92, #A-3916, GDAH, and 34 Ga. 506 (1866).

64. *Niles' Weekly Register,* Mar. 10, 1832. Alexander Smyth to Governor William B. Giles, June 28, 1829 (Wythe County), Executive Papers, Letters Received, Box 311, LVA. *Commonwealth v. George,* Aug. 11, 1856 (Mathews County), Executive Papers, Letters Received (in September folder), Box 436, LVA (the woman refused the offer, saying she would still not be safe). In the Virginia piedmont in 1803, a white woman who accused a black man of rape "said she did not know that the law would take any action, and she assumed Jack would just be whipped for raping her"; see affidavit of Samuel Gathright (Goochland County), Executive Papers, Letters Received (folder marked "Pardon Papers, 1803," Box 128, LVA, re: Nancy Lacy and Jack). For a case in which the white woman's family and the black man's master discussed payment and whipping as incentives not to prosecute, see *Pleasant v. State,* 13 Ark. 360 (1853), and 15 Ark. 624 (1855). See also Higginbotham and Kopytoff, "Racial Purity," 2000–2001.

65. A. W. Shepperd to HGB, Mar. 24, 1826. Deposition of William Holt [ca. March–May 1826]. J. M. Morehead to HGB, May 20, 1826, emphasis in original. Robert Moore to HGB, [ca. April–June] 1826; this man later implored

the governor not to mention his name in connection with the defense of Jim, again implying local conflicts; see Robert Moore to HGB, June 6, 1826.

66. J. M. Smith to HGB, May 6, 1826. This letter was notably less literate than any other sent to Governor Burton on Jim's behalf, actually reading as follows: "The negro Jim is all ways Bin purtected by som trifling white people and is yet Sir Mr. Peppenger has got no Child and He has seaverl friends for his property which is Considerable." He added: "Wont the precident inger the publick more than it will do [the lawyers] good." For a case in which a master attempted secretly to sell a slave accused of rape in order to preserve his investment, see *Ingram v. Mitchell*, 30 Ga. 547 (1860).

67. On Holt, Morehead, and the Hargraves, see Raynor, *Piedmont Passages*, 35. According to one Davidson County source, "The majority of slaves were owned by the three Hargrave brothers," of whom Jesse was one; see Williams and Ellis, "Blacks of Yesterday," 66. For Hargrave's will, see Reeves and Shoaf, *Will Summaries*, 30–31. In 1820, Jesse Hargrave had purchased 1,300 acres of land in Davidson County for $16,000; see deed of land to Jesse Hargrave, June 16, 1820, Skinner Family Papers, SHC. In 1830, John Morehead owned 11 slaves (1830 census, Guilford County, N.C., 137). Another of Jim's defenders, Robert Moore, was also a neighborhood doctor and farmer; see Raynor, *Piedmont Passages*, 35. Other defenders of Jim were also slaveowners: James Martin, Jim's lawyer, owned 12 slaves (1820 census, Rowan County, N.C., 280, and 1830 census, Rowan County, N.C., 402); Jacob Miller, whose wife had examined Polly's baby, owned 14 slaves (1820 census, Rowan County, N.C., 332).

68. Nonslaveowners in the 1820 and 1830 censuses who petitioned for Jim included the Gregsons (1820 census, Orange County, N.C., 384); J. Kinney, one of the six signers (1830 census, Davidson County, N.C., 193); David Owen, who came with the bastardy warrant (1820 census, Rowan County, N.C., 336, and 1830 census, Davidson County, N.C., 189); members of the Peacock family (1830 census, Davidson County, N.C., 199–201); Willy Northern (1830 census, Davidson County, N.C., 204); Reuben Shepherd (1820 census, Rowan County, N.C., 330, and 1830 census, Davidson County, N.C., 195, 203; and John Turner (1830 census, Davidson County, N.C., 199). Alexander Gray owned one slave (1830 census, Guilford County, N.C., 167).

69. Deposition of Reuben Holmes and Samuel Hamilton, May 8, 1826. In 1820, Holmes owned 24 slaves (1820 census, Rowan County, N.C., 330) and in 1830, 36 slaves (1830 census, Davidson County, N.C., 205). He had purchased 240 acres of land from Abraham Peppinger in 1794; see Linn, *Holmes Family*, 1, 14; this local historian notes: "The only person who died in Davidson County during the time-period 1823–1846 naming more slaves in his will than Reuben Holmes was Jesse Hargrave" (5). See also Reeves and Shoaf, *Will Summaries*, 36. Those who maligned Jim were Elizabeth Lane, who owned no slaves (1830 census, Davidson County, N.C., 194), and Samuel Hamilton, who

owned one slave (1820 census, Rowan County, N.C., 330). The page number of the 1820 census indicates that Samuel Hamilton lived very near to Reuben Holmes; they signed the same deposition.

70. For the 1800 pardon (Westmoreland County), see Letters to Governor James Monroe, Executive Papers, Letters Received, October 1800, re: *Commonwealth v. Dennis and Winkey,* LVA. For Catherine Brinal and Carter (King and Queen County), see Petition, May 9, 1803, Executive Papers, Letters Received, folder marked "Pardon Papers, 1803," Box 128, LVA. On the trial transcript was written: "Reprieved for 12 mos. & transported." See also Auditor of Public Accounts, Condemned Slaves, Entry 756, 1803. For Sarah Sands and Jerry (Henry County), see Executive Papers, Letters Received, June 4, 20, 1807, LVA; Jerry was pardoned. For the 83 signers (Hanover County), see petition to Governor William H. Cabell, Executive Papers, Letters Received, October 1808 re: Patsey Hooker and Peter, LVA. For Gabriel (Wythe County), see Trial of Gabriel, June 20, 1829, Executive Papers Letters Received, Box 311, LVA. For Elizabeth Sikes, see *State v. Jim,* Johnston County, SSCMR #3631, NCDAH, and 48 N.C. 438 (1856) and petitions to Governor Thomas Bragg, Apr. 1, 1856, Governor's Papers, NCDAH. For extended debates over the virtue of a married white woman who accused a black man of rape, see *Pleasant v. State,* 13 Ark. 360 (1853), 15 Ark. 624 (1855). For a case in which fellow slaves testified against an accused rapist, see Executive Papers, Letters Received, Nov. 19, 1808, re: Sally Briggs and Dick, and Auditor of Public Accounts, Entry 756, Condemned Slaves Executed or Transported, 1808 (noting Dick's execution), LVA. See also Morris, *Southern Slavery and the Law,* 313–15.

71. For Mary Dunn and Warrick, see Petition to HGB, Governor's Papers, Mar. 24–Apr. 13, 1825 (Anson County), NCDAH. A slave in coastal North Carolina accused of attempting to rape a seven-year-old white girl in 1828 was granted a new trial in the appellate court despite outrage among whites, in part because the only eyewitness was a white woman described by others as "a common strumpet, a woman of the town"; see *State v. Jim,* Brunswick County, SSCMR #1628, NCDAH, and 12 N.C. 509 (1828). In 1860 in North Carolina, a slave was convicted of raping a thirteen-year-old white girl, but the girl was asked whether she and Peter had been "friendly" before and why she had waited three weeks to tell her father; see *State v. Peter,* New Hanover County, SSCMR #8218, NCDAH, and 53 N.C. 19 (1860). In *Cato v. State,* 9 Fla. 163 (1860), the appellate court awarded the black man a new trial because he had used "persuasion" rather than "force" (the woman was cast as a prostitute). See also Johnston, *Race Relations,* 262–63. On granting new trials to black men convicted of rape, see Bardaglio, "Rape and the Law," 762. For parallels in rape cases involving working-class white women in the antebellum North, see Stansell, *City of Women,* 23–27, 85; and Arnold, " 'Life of a Citizen.' "

72. For Sam (Rowan County), see W. L. Henderson to Governor Montfort Stokes, Governor's Papers, Oct. 15, 1831, NCDAH. In 1800, word of slave

insurrection included fear that black men would murder white men and "take possession of the houses and white women"; see *Kentucky Gazette,* Oct. 6, 1800. For Pleasant Cole and Dick (Loudoun County), see letters and petitions in Executive Papers, Letters Received, July 1831, Box 320, LVA, emphasis in original. Dick was executed; see Auditor of Public Accounts, Entry 756, Condemned Blacks Executed or Transported, Dec. 19, 1831. In the 1829 case of 12-year-old Rosanna Green and Gabriel, a white man urged the governor not to heed the pardon petition, pointing out that the orphaned Rosanna had no father to protect her; see Alexander Smyth to Governor William B. Giles, along with enclosed clipping about the case, June 28, 1829, Executive Papers, Letters Received, Box 311, LVA.

73. Petitions and letters to Governor Edward B. Dudley, Governor's Papers, Apr. 3–7, 1838, NCDAH, emphasis in original. There is no documentation of Juba's pardon or execution. Though elderly, Juba worked in a blacksmith shop, indicating valuable skills. In an 1856 Virginia tidewater case, one man thought that a pardon petition "must have had a very limited circulation" either to friends of the master or to those opposed to capital punishment; see George E. Tabb to Governor Henry A. Wise, Executive Papers, Letters Received, Sept. 10, 1856 (Mathews County), Box 436, LVA. These were the same people who threatened lynching on acquittal.

74. Sixty-eight signers to Governor John W. Ellis, April 1860, Letter Book 45, pp. 226–27, NCDAH; also in Governor's Papers 149, folder marked "1860"; Henry Hege to Governor John W. Ellis, Apr. 17, 1860, Governor's Papers (numerous misspellings corrected), emphasis in original. Ellis to High Sheriff, Apr. 23, 1860, Letter Book 45, p. 226, all at NCDAH. See also *State v. Elick,* Davidson County, SSCMR #8014, NCDAH, and 52 N.C. 68 (1859); the letter from Henry Hege to Ellis was endorsed by 14 others, including three Hargrave men. In 1804, a North Carolina slave named Peter was sentenced to death for the attempted rape of a married white woman, and pardoned only after the woman's husband and "a large number of respectable citizens" made the governor promise that Peter would be transported out of state; see *Raleigh Register and North Carolina State Gazette,* Oct. 22, 1804.

75. *Richmond Daily Dispatch,* Apr. 27, 1854. For two more pardons of free black men for rape convictions, see Executive Papers, Letters Received, May 29, 31, July 7, 1827, re: Henry Hunt (Southampton County), LVA; Executive Papers, Letters Received, May 5, 1831, Harry Carroll (Wake County), LVA.

One case demonstrates the lesser value of a free black man's life. Alexander Hooker, a poor white man in the North Carolina piedmont, accused the free John Chavis of seducing his sister and forcing her to live in a brothel, and killed him. After Alexander's conviction, white neighbors requested and received a pardon. See *State v. Alexander Hooker,* Randolph County Criminal Action Papers, Fall 1856; petitions and letters to Governor Thomas Bragg, Sept. 26–27, Oct. 2–3, 1856; and Pardon of Alexander Hooker by Governor

Thomas Bragg, Oct. 1, 1856, all in Governor's Papers 141, NCDAH. On sex between white women and free black men, see also Higginbotham and Kopytoff, "Racial Purity," 2016–19.

76. Edward B. Wood to Governor Littleton W. Tazewell, June 26, 1834; W. F. Sturman to Tazewell, June 11, July 9, 1834; and petition for pardon of Caleb Watts, July 12, 1834, all in Executive Papers, Letters Received, Box 338, LVA; Jane described herself as poor in her testimony accompanying these papers. Penciled on the back of the petition were the words: "Advised that the Executive do not interfere with the sentence of the Court." See also *Commonwealth v. Caleb Watts,* Oct. 16, 1833, Westmoreland County Superior Court Orders, pp. 163–65 (for a record of trial), and Apr. 18, 1834, pp. 183–84; *Commonwealth v. Watts,* 31 Va. 672 (1833). For another case of a pardon denied, see *Commonwealth v. Peter,* Executive Papers, Letters Received, June 1834, Box 338, LVA.

77. On white Southern ideology about black women, see White, *Ar'n't I a Woman?* chap. 1. Karen A. Getman notes that views of black women were "applied to white women who had sexual relationships with Black men" ("Sexual Control," 117). Ideas about Southern white womanhood differed from Northern middle-class ideas, especially in the absence of the conviction of female "passionlessness." On the North, see Bloch, "Gendered Meanings of Virtue"; and Cott, "Passionlessness." On Southern ideas, see Clinton, *Plantation Mistress,* chaps. 5, 6; Fox-Genovese, *Plantation Household,* chap. 4; Friedman, *Enclosed Garden;* Scott, *Southern Lady,* chap. 1; and Wyatt-Brown, *Southern Honor,* 50–55, 293–94. For the most nuanced analysis about race, see Carby, *Reconstructing Womanhood,* chap. 2.

78. Robert Moore to HGB, [ca. April–June] 1826, June 6, 1826.

79. For Polly, see 1830 census, Davidson County, N.C., 205, and 1840 census, Davidson County, N.C., 288. Polly Lane does not appear in any of the Lane households in the 1850 census of Davidson County. In 1842, a woman named Polly Lane married a John Vick (Dec. 19, 1842, Statewide Index to Marriages, NCDAH); all other Polly Lanes married before 1825. No Vick households in later censuses yield any further clues. For Jim's sale, see J. M. Morehead to HGB, May 20, 1826. When Abraham Peppinger died in 1832, Jim was of course not among his property; see Reeves and Shoaf, *Will Summaries,* 48. In 1860 the Wilkersons kept a boardinghouse in which both Candas and her son were listed as "mulatto" servants; see 1860 census, Davidson County, N.C., 961, household #797. In 1870 the two lived near other members of the Lane family, and both were designated as white; see 1870 census, Davidson County, N.C., 104, household #72 (Candis Laine).

Chapter 4 *Adultery*

1. Lewis Bourne (sometimes spelled Louis) petitioned for divorce twice, signed two notices warning his wife that he would be taking affidavits as evi-

dence for divorce, and placed three advertisements about the petition in the newspaper. See Lewis Bourne Divorce Petition, Louis County, Dec. 16, 1824, #8218, LPP, LVA; and statements of Lewis Bourne, Dec. 25, 1823, Jan. 17, 1825, and receipt for advertisements, Sept. 10, 1824, in Lewis Bourne Divorce Petition, Louisa County, Jan. 20, 1825, #8305, LPP, LVA. All depositions, statements, and notices are from petition #8305, unless otherwise indicated. Spellings of names vary; I have used one version throughout. In 1820, John Richardson owned 25 slaves (1820 census, Hanover County, Va., 67). Upon his death later in the decade, he owned between 30 and 40 slaves and slightly over 400 acres of land; he and his wife had no surviving children, but John had an illegitimate white daughter; see Cocke, ed., *Hanover Wills,* 118.

2. Bourne Divorce Petition #8218; Depositions of Joseph Anderson, Jan. 22, 1824; Thomas Pulliam, Jan. 29, 1824; [no name], Jan. 20, 1825; Anderson Bowles, Jan. 6, 1824; and Joseph Perkins, Jan. 17, 1824. Numerous petitioners referred to Dorothea's children as "mulatto."

3. 1820 map of Hanover County, Virginia, LVA; Lancaster, *Sketch of Hanover County,* 61. More than half of Louisa County's white residents in the early nineteenth century lived on small farms, owned livestock and one or a few slaves, and produced food crops for subsistence and perhaps tobacco for cash. Less than 5% resided on plantations of 1,000 acres or more with between 20 and 80 slaves who produced tobacco and wheat as cash crops. See Harris, *History of Louisa County;* Hart, "Louisa County"; Shifflett, *Patronage and Poverty,* 4–11; and True, "Louisa Economy." On the market economy, see Genovese, "Yeoman Farmers"; and Watson, "Conflict and collaboration."

4. Lewis Bourne first appeared in the land tax book for 1820, owning 75 acres worth $10 per acre; this remained largely unchanged until 1831, when Lewis had given 25 acres to William Bourne. He last appeared in 1835, where it was noted that Thomas Bourne owned the 50 acres of land he inherited from his deceased father, Lewis. See Louisa County Land Tax Books, 1820A–1835A. This final figure contrasts with Lewis Bourne's will, in which he left 75 (not 50) acres to his son; see will of Lewis Bourne, Louisa County Will Book #9, Nov. 10, 1834, pp. 174–75, LVA. Using the 1824 land tax book, Lewis Bourne's land value was at the high end of those who owned land valued at under $1,000. Lewis's father owned one slave on his death in the 1780s; see will of William Bourn [sic], June 27, 1781, Louisa County Will Book 2, pp. 404–5, LVA. For Lewis's status, see also deposition of Thomas Anderson, Jan. 23, 1824. Dorothea Woodall was born into a family of similar economic status as the Bournes; her father owned no slaves when she married Lewis and later acquired one slave for a short time. See 1810 census, Hanover County, Va., 53; 1820 census, Richmond City, Va., 196; and 1830 census, Richmond City, Va., 405. For her unmarried name and the date of the marriage, see Bourne Divorce Petition #8218. Lewis also did not appear in the Virginia census of 1810. For John Richardson, see Hanover County Land Tax Book, 1824A, 1825A, LVA.

For the proximity of the Bourne and Richardson houses, see deposition of John Richardson, Jan. 18, 1825; will of Lewis Bourne.

5. Depositions of Peter Wade, Mar. 26, 1823, and Nathan Ross, Dec. 26, 1823; also Thomas Anderson, Jan. 23, 1824 (company of slaves); Richard Woodson, Jan. 28, 1824, and John Richardson, Jan. 18, 1825 (Dorothea and Edmond); William Bourne and Pleasants Proffit, Nov. 25, 1823 (being caught); Judith Richardson, Dec. 26, 1823; also [no name], Jan. 20, 1825 (Edmond's quarters).

6. Depositions of Daniel Molloy, Jan. 28, 1824 (affection); Thomas Pulliam, Jan. 29, 1824, and [no name], Jan. 20, 1825 ("man and wife"); Thomas Anderson, Jan. 23, 1824 (Dorothea's house); Hannah Bourne, Dec. 25, 1823; Thomas Anderson, Jan. 23, 1824; John Conway and Daniel Molloy, both Jan. 28, 1824; Thomas Pulliam, Peter Wade, and Stephen Pulliam, all Jan. 29, 1824; John Richardson, Jan. 18, 1825 (all re: dead child); Peter Wade, Mar. 26, 1823 (quotation); Joseph Perkins, Jan. 17, 1824; and John Richardson, Jan. 18, 1825 (children by a black man). For echoes of these statements, see depositions of George Bourne (a brother of Lewis) and Eliza Bourne, both Nov. 25, 1823; Hannah Bourne, Dec. 25, 1823; Judith Richardson, Ezekiel Perkins, Nathan Ross, and Mary Ross, all Dec. 26, 1823; Anderson Bowles, Jan. 16, 1824; 11 men, Jan. 20, 1824; Joseph Anderson, Jan. 22, 1824; Thomas Anderson, Jan. 23, 1824; Wilson Sayne, D. B. Johnson, William and John Shelton, John Conway (the coffin maker), and Daniel Molloy, all Jan. 28, 1824; Thomas Pulliam (who also mentioned a slave named Jack as the father of one of Dorothea's children) and Thomas Sayne, both Jan. 29, 1824; and [no name], Jan. 20, 1825. Lewis said that he allowed Dorothea to live "in a house upon his own land" (Bourne Divorce Petition #8218).

7. Deposition of William Bourne, speaking about Lewis's conversation with "Old Mr. Geo. Fleming," Jan. 16, 1824; see also statement of Lewis Bourne, Jan. 16, 1824. George Fleming, county justice and sheriff, owned 1,000 acres of land; see Chisholm and Lillie, *Old Home Places,* 19. Lewis noted one living child and one deceased child belonging to Edmond (Bourne Divorce Petition #8218). On white women giving birth to children whose fathers were presumably black, see also Higginbotham and Kopytoff, "Racial Purity," 1997-98.

8. Joseph Anderson owned 10 slaves (1830 census, Hanover County, Va., 216); Anderson Bowles owned 18-25 slaves (1820 census, Hanover County, Va., 67, and 1830 census, Hanover County, Va., 216); David B. Johnson owned 16 slaves (1820 census, Louisa County, Va., 54); Ezekial Perkins owned 16 slaves (1820 census, Louisa County, Va., 58); Joseph Perkins owned 13 slaves (1820 census, Louisa County, Va., 58); Stephen Pulliam owned 5 slaves (1830 census, Hanover County, Va., 237); Thomas Pulliam owned 13-25 slaves (1820 census, Hanover County, Va., 67, and 1830 census, Hanover County, Va., 216); Peter Wade owned 9-15 slaves (1820 census, Hanover County, Va., 67, and 1830 census, Hanover County, Va., 216); and Richard Woodson owned 1 or 2 slaves

(1820 census, Hanover County, Va., 67, and 1830 census, Hanover County, Va., 216). See also Chappelear, ed., *Hanover County Census Records,* 41, 28, 46; and Cocke, ed., *Hanover Wills,* 114–15. On the Perkins family, see Chisholm, "Wyndcroft." Shandy Perkins was a merchant of Hanover County; see Cocke, ed., *Hanover Wills,* 120. On the Sheltons, see Bagby, "Shelton Family"; and Harris, *History of Louisa County,* 410–11. Chisholm and Lillie, *Old Home Places,* discuss members of the Bowles, Kimbrough, Shelton, and Richardson families; see 5, 32, 37, 38, 53, 55. On the Kimbroughs, see also Harris, *History of Louisa County,* 371. Members of the Bowles, Perkins, Wade, Richardson, and Shelton families were related through marriages and had business ties; see also *Hanover Wills,* 118.

Nonslaveholding witnesses included John Conway (1820 census, Louisa County, Va., 47, and 1830 census, Louisa County, Va., 27); Delphy Hooker (1820 census, Hanover County, Va., 67); Keziah Mosely (1820 census, Hanover County, Va., 68, and 1830 census, Hanover County, Va., 216).

9. Depositions of Keziah Mosely, Jan. 27, 1824; and Peter Wade and Stephen Pulliam, both Jan. 29, 1824. For the Mosely household, see 1820 census, Hanover County, Va., 68 (listed as "Heziah"), and 1830 census, Hanover County, Va., 216. Depositions of Keziah Mosely, Jan. 27, 1824; and Thomas Sayne, Peter Wade, Stephen Pulliam, all Jan. 29, 1824 (all re: Keziah's midwifery).

10. Depositions of Judith Richardson, Dec. 26, 1823 ("never disposed"); Anderson Bowles, Jan. 20, 1823, Jan. 16, 1824; Joseph Anderson, Jan. 22, 1824; Thomas Anderson, Jan. 23, 1824, and Thomas Pulliam, Jan. 29, 1824 (providing adequately). See also Ezekial Perkins, Nathan Ross, and Mary Ross, all Dec. 26, 1823; Joseph Perkins, Jan. 17, 1824; 11 men, Jan. 20, 1824; Thomas Anderson, Jan. 23, 1824; Richard Woodson, D. B. Johnson, and William and John Shelton, all Jan. 28, 1824; Thomas Pulliam and Thomas Sayne, both Jan. 29, 1824; and John Richardson, Jan. 18, 1825.

11. Depositions of Thomas Anderson, Jan. 23, 1824; Hannah Bourne, Dec. 25, 1823; Joseph Perkins, Jan. 17, 1824; Joseph Anderson, Jan. 22, 1824; and 11 men, Jan. 20, 1824. See also Bourne Divorce Petition #8218. On the dishonor of adultery, see Stevenson, *Life in Black and White,* 151–52; and Wyatt-Brown, *Southern Honor,* 298–307.

12. On divorce and adultery, see Phillips, *Putting Asunder,* chap. 4, and 344–54, 439–61; Hindus and Withey, "Husband and Wife"; Censer, " 'Smiling Through Her Tears' "; and Bardaglio, *Reconstructing the Household,* 32–34. Specifically on antebellum Virginia, see Stevenson, *Life in Black and White,* chap. 5. South Carolina was the sole antebellum state that did not permit divorce; see Salmon, *Women and the Law of Property,* 64–65. The first bills for divorce in both Maryland and Virginia passed due to a white wife's adulterous liaison with a black man. In Talbot County, Md., in 1790, after John Sewell won an annulment, Eve Sewell and her illegitimate child were sold into servitude. See *Laws*

of Maryland, November 1790 sess., chap. 25. In Virginia, the case was that of Benjamin and Lydia Butt (in chap. 3, above); see Salmon, *Women and the Law of Property,* 211 n. 29.

On the Virginia laws, see Hening, ed., *Statutes at Large,* 3:453-54; 6:361-62; 8:134; Woodson, "Beginnings of Miscegenation," 342-45. In Virginia until 1827, divorce was granted by the state legislature, which would pass an act naming the individuals; see *Acts of the General Assembly,* Feb. 17, 1827, chap. 23. On divorce procedures in antebellum North Carolina, see McBride, "Divorces and Separations," 43, 44; and McBride, "Divorces, Separations," 43.

13. On the outcome of the Bourne case, see *Journal of the House of Delegates,* Jan. 26, 1825, p. 184. *Acts of the General Assembly* between the years 1825 and 1835 contain no act granting Lewis Bourne a divorce. See also Buckley, "Assessing the Double Standard"; and Wyatt-Brown, *Southern Honor,* 304.

14. *Andrew Whittington v. Lucy Whittington,* Caswell County, SSCMR #2491, NCDAH, and 19 N.C. 64 (1836).

15. Petitions of Peggy Johnson and John Johnson, Orange County, General Assembly Session Records, Propositions and Grievances in Senate Committee Reports, Nov. 23, 1832, NCDAH. The committee refused to take action, suggesting that the couple take their case to court; at no time in the next five years did they do so, according to the Orange County Superior Court Minute Docket, NCDAH.

16. *Elizabeth Walters v. Clement Jordan,* Person County, SSCMR #6458, NCDAH, and 34 N.C. 170 (1851), 35 N.C. 361 (1852).

17. William Howard Divorce Petition, Amherst County, Dec. 6, 1809, #5370, LPP, LVA; *Journal of the House of Delegates,* Feb. 5, 1810.

18. Joseph Hancock Divorce Petition, Wake County, December 1813, and Committee of Divorce and Alimony in House Committee Reports, November-December 1813, both in General Assembly Session Records, NCDAH.

19. Committee of Divorce and Alimony report re: John Dever Divorce Petition, Duplin County, and Bill of Divorce in House Bills, Nov. 30, 1813, General Assembly Session Records, NCDAH.

20. James Hoffler Divorce Petition, Gates County, General Assembly Session Records, 1813, NCDAH. In 1818, James was finally granted his divorce; see *Session Laws of North Carolina,* 1818, p. 34; see also *Session Laws of North Carolina,* 1807, chap. 109 (40). Two other Virginia husbands who claimed desertion by wives who lived openly with black men and had children by those men, were initially denied divorces but granted them later; see William Baylis Divorce Petition, Fairfax County, Dec. 8, 1831, #9781, LPP, LVA; *Journal of the House of Delegates,* Dec. 13, 1831; *Acts of the General Assembly,* 1834, chap. 267 (315-16); and see Jacob Plum Divorce Petition, Preston County, Dec. 9, 1841, #13261, LPP, LVA; *Journal of the House of Delegates,* Dec. 31, 1841; *Acts of the General Assembly,* Jan. 11, 1848, chap. 372 (351).

21. Thomas Culpeper Divorce Petition, Norfolk County, Dec. 9, 1835, #10943, LPP, LVA; *Journal of the House of Delegates,* Feb. 13, 1836.

22. *Marville Scroggins v. Lucretia Scroggins,* 14 N.C. 535 (1832), 547 (Buncombe County), and 537 for the words of Marville's lawyer; also 540. *Jesse Barden v. Ann Barden,* 14 N.C. 548 (1832), 550 (Wayne County). On the Pettus, Butt, Jones, Newton, and Barden cases, see chap. 3, above.

23. *Raleigh Register and North Carolina State Gazette,* Nov. 30, 1809.

24. On the reluctance of judges to dissolve marriages in the early nineteenth century, see Griswold, "Doctrine of Mental Cruelty" and "Law, Sex, Cruelty."

25. Censer, "'Smiling Through Her Tears'"; Griswold, "Divorce and Legal Redefinition"; Hindus and Withey, "Husband and Wife"; Wyatt-Brown, *Southern Honor,* 286–87.

26. *Scroggins v. Scroggins,* 545, 546.

27. Friedman, *History of American Law,* 207 (quotation); Censer, "'Smiling Through Her Tears,'" 35, 36–37, 46; Hindus and Withey, "Husband and Wife," 134; Thomas, "Double Standard," 199–202. For a comparison with cases in which antebellum Southern white men committed adultery with black women, see Buckley, "Assessing the Double Standard."

28. Daniel Rose Divorce Petition, Prince William County, Dec. 9, 1806, #5021, LPP, LVA ("heart-rending mortification"). Hezekiah Mosby Divorce Petition, Powhatan County, Dec. 6, 1815, #6428, LPP, LVA. For Lewis Bourne's rendition of this formula, see Bourne Divorce Petition #8218.

29. Isaac Cowan Divorce Petition, Rowan County, Senate Bills, General Assembly Session Records, Nov. 24, 1802, NCDAH.

30. Leonard Owen Divorce Petition, Patrick County, Dec. 11, 1809, #5424, LPP, LVA; *Journal of the House of Delegates,* Dec. 23, 1809.

31. John Cook Divorce Petition, Boutetout County, Dec. 2, 1812, #6014, LPP, LVA; *Journal of the House of Delegates,* Dec. 9, 1812.

32. David Parker Divorce Petition, Nansemond County, Dec. 8, 1826, #8683, LPP, LVA; *Journal of the House of Delegates,* Dec. 22, 1826; *Acts of the General Assembly,* Jan. 17, 1827, p. 126.

33. Jacob Johnson Divorce Petition, Chatham County, and report of Committee of Propositions and Grievances, House Bills, all in General Assembly Session Records, Dec. 26, 1823, NCDAH.

34. William Pruden Divorce Petition, Nansemond County, Dec. 14, 1840, #13024, LPP, LVA; *Journal of the House of Delegates,* Jan. 5, 1841.

35. Bryant Rawls Divorce Petition, Nansemond County, Dec. 14, 1840, #13025, LPP, LVA; *Journal of the House of Delegates,* Jan. 5, 1841.

36. Jacob Plum Divorce Petition, Preston County, Dec. 9, 1841, #13261, LPP, LVA; *Acts of the General Assembly,* Jan. 11, 1848, chap. 372 (351).

37. Phillips, *Putting Asunder,* chap. 10. On the resistance of yeoman wives, see McCurry, *Masters of Small Worlds,* 89–90.

38. *Edenton (N.C.) Gazette,* Nov. 23, 1810. Richard Hall Divorce Petition, Orange County, Jan. 29, 1838, #11955, LPP, LVA.

39. William D. Valentine Diary, Oct. 12, 1846, and "Wed. 10 o.c.," SHC; *William L. Reid and wife v. Edmund B. Skinner,* Gates County Superior Court Minute Docket, October 1846, NCDAH.

40. Depositions of D. B. Johnson, Jan. 28, 1824; and Anderson Bowles, Delphy Hooker, and Shandy Perkins, all Jan. 18, 1825; statement of Dorothea Bourne, Nov. 7, 1824 (signed with an "x" and by four witnesses, including Anderson Bowles); deposition of Judith Richardson, Dec. 26, 1823.

41. Mosby Divorce Petition.

42. Ayres Tatham Divorce Petition, Accomack County, Dec. 13, 1805, #4888, LPP, LVA. Ayres was granted a divorce; see *Journal of the House of Delegates,* Dec. 23, 1805. William Rucker Divorce Petition, Alleghany County, Mar. 5, 1849, #16648, LPP, LVA. William was granted a divorce; see *Journal of the House of Delegates,* Mar. 16, 1849.

43. Delanys, *Having Our Say,* 28.

44. Petition of Dorothea Bourne, n.d.; deposition of William Bourne and Pleasants Proffit, Nov. 25, 1823. In Lewis Bourne's will, he noted one child as his own and two as illegitimate; see will of Lewis Bourne.

45. Deposition of Thomas Miller in Mosby Divorce Petition. Hezekiah was granted a divorce; see *Journal of the House of Delegates,* Dec. 14, 1815.

46. Deposition of Henry Satterfield in *Walters v. Jordan,* SSCMR.

47. Joseph Gresham Divorce Petition, James City County, Dec. 10, 1833, #10403, LPP, LVA; *Journal of the House of Delegates,* Dec. 30, 1833.

48. Statement of Caroline Culpeper in Culpeper Divorce Petition.

49. Isaac Fouch Divorce Petition, Loudoun County, Dec. 22, 1808, #5321A, LPP, LVA; *Journal of the House of Delegates,* Jan. 28, 1809.

50. *State v. Jefferson,* Mecklenburg County Superior Court, SSCMR #3699, NCDAH, and 28 N.C. 305 (1846).

51. Deposition of Henry Satterfield in *Walters v. Jordan,* SSCMR.

52. Deposition of John Richardson, Jan. 18, 1825. On coercion by white women, see chap. 6, below.

53. On slave crime and risk, see Schwarz, "Forging the Shackles," 129.

54. Deposition of 11 men, Jan. 20, 1824; this incident was denied by Thomas Anderson, Jan. 23, 1824, and by William and John Shelton, Jan. 28, 1824. Deposition of Joseph Perkins, Jan. 17, 1824.

55. *State v. George,* Granville County, SSCMR #4188, NCDAH, and 29 N.C. 321 (1847).

56. *Redding Evans v. Georgia,* 33 Ga. 4 (1861), from Miller County.

57. Gresham Divorce Petition. Thomas Cain Divorce Petition, Frederick County, Jan. 9, 1841, #13079, LPP, LVA. Fouch Divorce Petition; Fouch also had witnesses testify to the fact that the man's mother was a woman of color

(depositions of James McNeilege and Ann McNeilege, Colmore Brashears, Jan. 9, 10, 1809).

58. On harsher consequences for whites involved in liaisons across the color line, see Higginbotham and Kopytoff, "Racial Purity," 2000–2001.

59. Depositions of Colmore Brashears (who said "it is generally believed" that James Watt "had a criminal commerce and intrigue with Elizabeth Fouch"), James and Ann McNeilege, and Jane Campbell, in Fouch Divorce Petition. Jane said she "heard they were followed by a constable and more [property] taken from them the same day near Leesburg."

60. Baylis Divorce Petition; the divorce was granted; see *Acts of the General Assembly,* 1834, chap. 267 (315–16). Howard Divorce Petition. Rose Divorce Petition; the divorce was granted (*Journal of the House of Delegates,* Dec. 22, 1806). Hoffler Divorce Petition, 1813.

61. Lewis Tombereau Divorce Petition, Martin County, Nov. 19, 1824, General Assembly Session Records, 1824–25, NCDAH (outcome not recorded). Petitions of Peggy Johnson and John Johnson, Orange County, in Propositions and Grievances in Senate Committee Reports, General Assembly Session Records, Nov. 23, 1832, NCDAH.

62. Pruden Divorce Petition; Plum Divorce Petition; Hancock Divorce Petition; *Walters v. Jordan,* SSCMR.

63. Ten years before he was executed in Georgia, Redding Evans was in a Florida jail on charges of kidnapping and homicide. He was listed along with four other men, suggesting the possibility of an attempted uprising. See 1850 census, Jefferson County, Fla., 1; Redding was listed as a Georgia-born 32-year-old laborer. On the post–Civil War conflation of black male autonomy and sex with white women, see chaps. 7, 8, below.

64. *Richmond Enquirer,* Aug. 17, 1858 (Henrico County); verdict of jury, Pruden Divorce Petition; Rawls Divorce Petition.

65. Deposition of William Kimbrough, Nov. 25, 1823.

66. Delanys, *Having Our Say,* 28.

67. Will of Lewis Bourne. 1850 census, Louisa County, Va., household #377, p. 385. Lewis does not appear in the 1830 census, and Dorothea does not appear in the 1830 or 1840 censuses. The 1840 census lists Mary Bourn as between 20 and 30 years old, living alone in Amherst County and designated as white; the 1850 census lists her as a 32-year-old "mulatto" head-of-household with four children aged 2 to 11. This could be Dorothea and Edmond's daughter, born about 1818; see 1840 census, Amherst County, Va., 205; 1850 census, Nelson County, Va., 239. Nelson and Amherst Counties are adjacent to one another, south and west of Louisa. There is no listing for a Fanny Bourne.

68. "Negro": depositions of John Richardson, Nov. 25, 1823; and [no name], Jan. 20, 1825. "Mulatto": depositions of William Kimbrough, William Bourne and Pleasants Proffit, and George Bourne, all Nov. 25, 1823; and Thomas

Anderson, Jan. 23, 1824. Man "of color": deposition of Joseph Anderson, Jan. 22, 1824; and statement of Dorothea Bourne, Nov. 7, 1824.

69. Depositions of Thomas Pulliam, Jan. 29, 1824; Wilson Sayne, Jan. 28, 1824; and John Richardson, Jan. 18, 1825. See also depositions of Richard Woodson, Jan. 18, 1824; Joseph Anderson, Jan. 22, 1824; Thomas Anderson, Jan. 23, 1824; Daniel Molloy, Jan. 28, 1824; and Thomas Sayne, Jan. 29, 1824.

70. Depositions of Daniel Molloy, Jan. 28, 1824; Thomas Anderson, Jan. 23, 1824; and Richard Woodson, Jan. 18, 1824. See also depositions of John Conway and D. B. Johnson, both Jan. 28, 1824; Thomas Pulliam, Jan. 29, 1824; and [no name], Jan. 20, 1825.

71. "Dark complexion": depositions of Richard Woodson, Jan. 28, 1824; [no name], Jan. 20, 1825; and Thomas Pulliam, Jan. 29, 1824. "Colored": depositions of Peter Wade, Mar. 26, 1823; Eliza Bourne, Nov. 25, 1823; Hannah Bourne, Dec. 25, 1823; Judith Richardson, Ezekial Perkins, and Mary Ross, all Dec. 26, 1823; William and John Shelton, Jan. 28, 1824; Richard Woodson, Wilson Sayne, William and John Shelton, and Daniel Molloy, all Jan. 28, 1824; and Stephen Pulliam, Thomas Pulliam, and Peter Wade, all Jan. 29, 1824. "Mulatto": depositions of William Bourne and Pleasants Proffit, George Bourne, Eliza Bourne, and John Richardson, all Nov. 25, 1823; George Fleming in deposition of William Bourne, Jan. 16, 1824. "Black": depositions of Thomas Sayne, Jan. 29, 1824; and John Richardson, Jan. 18, 1825. "Negro": depositions of Hannah Bourne, Dec. 25, 1823; and Ezekial Perkins, Nathan Ross, and Mary Ross, all Dec. 26, 1823.

72. Depositions of Judith Richardson, Dec. 26, 1823; John Richardson, Shandy Perkins, and Anderson Bowles, all Jan. 18, 1825; and [no name], Jan. 20, 1825; also statement of Dorothea Bourne, Nov. 7, 1824. On male "white slaves," see also Stevenson, *Life in Black and White,* 181.

Chapter 5 *Color*

1. On free blacks in the slaveholding South, see Berlin, *Slaves Without Masters;* Johnson and Roark, *Black Masters;* Madden, *We Were Always Free;* Stevenson, *Life in Black and White,* chaps. 9, 10; and Warner, *Free Men in an Age of Servitude.* On Georgia, see Alexander, *Ambiguous Lives;* Flanders, "Free Negro in Ante-bellum Georgia"; Sweat, "Free Blacks in Antebellum Atlanta"; and Young, "Racism in Red and Black." See also Leslie, *Woman of Color.*

2. On racial categorization, see McFerson, "'Racial Tradition'"; and Toplin, "Between Black and White," esp. 187. For the descriptions, see Emancipation Papers Resulting from the Act of Apr. 16, 1862, Records of the United States District Court for the District of Columbia Relating to Slaves, M433, RG 21, NA. After the Civil War, authorities listing the former slaves of Dr. William Holt (from the case of Polly Lane and Jim) used the words "dark," "mulatto," "black," "yellow," "copper" and "dark copper"; see "Names of Negro Families,

Davidson County, North Carolina, formerly owned by Dr. W. R. Holt, December 1865," Records Relating to Court Cases, Records of the Assistant Commissioner for the State of North Carolina, M843, reel 31, RG 105, NA.

3. For percentages, see Berlin, *Slaves Without Masters,* 178; and Sweat, "Free Blacks in Antebellum Atlanta," 64. On Georgia's racial system, see Small, "Racial Differentiation," esp. 198, 258, 267, 271.

4. On the travails of free people of color in the 1850s, see Ira Berlin, *Slaves Without Masters,* chap. 11; and Johnson and Roark, *Black Masters,* chaps. 5–7.

5. Hillhouse, *History of Burke County,* 89; four slaveowning Nunezes are noted for 1830 on p. 92. Baldwin and Hillhouse, *Guide to Burke County,* chap. 5. Burke County was home to several plantations of the wealthy, white slaveowning Thomas family described in Thomas, *Secret Eye.*

6. Joseph Nunez died in 1846 or 1847, and the case came about when his white administrator sued to recover the slaves sold by Nunez (or his guardian) to a white man. The lower court proceedings were held in Houston County (also in the cotton belt), where the plaintiff who had purchased Nunez's slaves resided; see *Seaborn C. Bryan v. Hughes Walton,* April 1851, October 1851, April 1852, October 1852, April 1853, August 1853, October 1853, April 1854, October 1854, April 1855, April 1856, Houston County, SSCOP, RG 92, #A-1836; and Houston County Superior Court Minutes, October 1851, April, October 1853, April 1856. Spellings vary; I have used "Nunez" throughout.

The case came to the Supreme Court of Georgia in 1853. The parties argued over possession of Joseph's slaves, but Joseph's racial status was not questioned; the court ruled that as a free person of color, Joseph did not have the right to sell his slaves; see *Seaborn C. Bryan v. Hugh [sic] Walton,* 14 Ga. 185 (1853). The next state supreme court case was 20 Ga. 480 (1856), after which the case appeared in the Houston County Superior Court Minutes for April 1857, October 1858, April 1859, October 1860, April 1862, October 1862, and August 1863 and as a dismissed writ of error in 30 Ga. 834 (1860). The case's final state supreme court appearance was 33 Ga. suppl. 11 (1864).

For the estimated value of the slaves, see Petition of Walton in SSCOP; and 33 Ga. suppl. 11 (1864), 12. For Georgia statutes regarding the ability of free people of color to own slaves as it relates to this case, see *Bryan v. Walton,* 14 Ga. 185 (1853), 204–5, 20 Ga. 480 (1856), 511–12; see also Rogers, "Free Negro Legislation," 31–32.

7. *Bryan v. Walton* (also printed as Watson), 20 Ga. 480 (1856), 491, 492, 494. The 1856 testimony also appears in SSCOP in much the same form.

8. *Bryan v. Walton,* 20 Ga. 480 (1856), 491, 499, 500, 502, 497. Marriage between blacks and whites was illegal in Georgia; see chap. 2, n. 1, above. The chief justice of the Supreme Court of Georgia affirmed this (without specific reference to Lucy Anderson and James Nunez) in *Bryan v. Walton,* 14 Ga. 185 (1853), 200.

9. *Bryan v. Walton,* 20 Ga. 480 (1856), 481, 491, 494, 496. James Nunez

died between 1809 and 1813; see *Bryan v. Walton*, 14 Ga. 185 (1853), 188; 20 Ga. 480 (1856), 482, 490, 491.

10. *Bryan v. Walton*, 20 Ga. 480 (1856), 498, 499, 501, 500.

11. Ibid., 496, 497. "Mrs. Holmes" may have been Jane B. Holmes, possibly the widowed sister of a wealthy planter in Burke County (at age 50 she resided in the household of 49-year-old James W. Jones, who owned $21,000 worth of real estate; see 1850 census, Burke County, Ga., 272).

12. *Bryan v. Walton*, 20 Ga. 480 (1856), 492. For Patience as Joseph's wife, see 500; on Joseph living as "man and wife" with one of his slaves, see also *Bryan v. Walton*, 33 Ga. suppl. 11 (1864), 16. Slaves in the antebellum South could not legally marry.

13. *Bryan v. Walton*, 20 Ga. 480 (1856), 493, 494.

14. Ibid., 498–99, 501, 500. Witnesses also had different ideas about the appearance of Patience; several described her as "light," but another described her as "dark"; see 484, 485, 488, 495.

15. Mary Rogers (who hoped to see the sale declared legal) had hired out a slave from James Nunez, had been given two slaves by Joseph Nunez for life, and later bought the hired slave; see ibid., 482, 484, 502. One side offered evidence that Joseph Nunez had never registered as a free person of color in Burke County; the other, that he had petitioned the court to appoint him a guardian as free people of color were required to do; see ibid., 498, 502–3. On percentages of free blacks, see Hillhouse, *History of Burke County*, 105.

According to the 1850 census of Burke County, Ga., for the witnesses in the 1856 case: of those claiming that Joseph Nunez was not of African ancestry, Joseph Bush owned six slaves; Mary Rogers was a 62-year-old head of household who owned $800 worth of real estate (p. 295) and 8 slaves; Harriett Kilpatrick was a 58-year-old head of household and a pauper (p. 317); Mary Harrel was a 44-year-old head of household who owned $1,600 worth of real estate (p. 293); and Stephen Newman is not listed. Of those who claimed that Joseph Nunez was a person of color, Thomas Cosnahan was a 50-year-old farmer who owned $2,700 worth of real estate (p. 316) and 25 slaves; Charles Ward was a 42-year-old farmer who owned $2,100 worth of real estate (p. 275) and 9 slaves; and the other Cosnahans are not listed. For slave ownership, see 1850 slave schedule, Burke County, Ga., 4, 51, 109.

16. Between 1830 and 1840, Joseph Nunez owned six to eight slaves; other family members were also listed as free "colored" people or as "mulattoes," some of whom owned slaves. See 1830 and 1840 censuses, Burke County, Ga., both 140; 1850 census, Burke County, Ga., 277, 278, 295, household #124, 133, 376; 1850 slave schedule, Burke County, Ga., 47; *1850 Federal Census, Agricultural Schedule*, 143; 1860 census, Burke County, Ga., 922, household #409. For an illuminating study of Southern slaveholding blacks, see Johnson and Roark, *Black Masters*.

17. *Bryan v. Walton*, 20 Ga. 480 (1856), 505, 509, 512.

18. *Bryan v. Walton,* 33 Ga. suppl. 11 (1864), 15, 19, 13, 16. The other side maintained that the will was a false document. The original document indicates that Joseph's father had been emancipated by his slaveowner-father and given slaves of his own. Moses Nunez had fathered three sons by "Mulatto Rose," one of his slaves, all of whom (along with Rose) Moses emancipated upon his death (he also bequeathed land and slaves to each one). One of these sons was James Nunez, Joseph's father. See will of Moses Nunez (spelled "Nunes"), Oct. 14, 1785, Chatham County Court of Ordinary, Wills, vol. C, pp. 436–43, GDAH.

19. *Bryan v. Walton,* 33 Ga. suppl. 11 (1864), 22–25. On the ambiguity of race, the judge asked: "Which of us has not narrowly escaped petting one of the pretty little mulattoes belonging to our neighbors as one of the family?" (24).

20. For the white women who socialized with Lucy (Mary Rogers and Harriet Kilpatrick) see 1850 census, Burke County, Ga., 295, 317. Both were likely widows; see 1830 census, Burke County, Ga., 139, 140. In the only reference to Lucy Anderson's family, Harriett Kilpatrick said that she "knows nothing of her father or mother"; see *Bryan v. Walton,* 20 Ga. 480 (1856), 494. The name does not appear in any Georgia census between 1820 and 1850.

See Buckley, "Unfixing Race," for the story of Robert Wright, the emancipated son of a slave woman who became a slaveowner in the Virginia piedmont in the early 1800s. Wright married and divorced one white woman, then married another, and evidence indicates that both unions were accepted by the women's families as well as by neighboring white slaveholders. Buckley posits that class rather than race determined the identity of Robert Wright.

21. *State v. Whitmel Dempsey,* Bertie County, SSCMR #4723, NCDAH, and 31 N.C. 384 (1849), 384–85. North Carolina marriage records for Whitmel Dempsey's father and grandfather do not indicate "col." (for colored) beside the grooms' names; see July 25, 1781, and June 17, 1801 (in printed index) or 1806 (in ms. records), Marriage Bonds and Statewide Index to Marriages, NCDAH.

Hearsay evidence and ancestry were also discussed in regard to the children of white women in *Pricilla Queen v. Francis Neale,* 2 D.C. Cranch Circuit Court 3 (1810); *Hezekiah Wood v. John Davis,* 11 U.S. 271 (1812); *John Davis v. Wood,* 14 U.S. 6 (1816); *Gregory v. Baugh,* 25 Va. 611 (1827), 29 Va. 665 (1831). See also *State v. Norton,* 60 N.C. 303 (1864). For a case in which people of partial African ancestry were "treated and received into society" as free and white, see "Statement concerning Turner and Hussey families whose ancestor was a mulatto," Montgomery County Miscellaneous Records, 1860, NCDAH.

22. *Hansford v. Hansford,* 10 Ala. 561 (1846), no county specified. Maria Hansford also argued that the children should not be taken from their mother.

23. Caroline and Amos Hugly lived in Upson County, adjacent to Monroe County but with a smaller slave population in the late antebellum decades. On the Hugly and Sullivan families, see *Forsyth-Monroe County,* 28; and Worsham, *Stroud Community,* esp. 1, 2, 8, 9, 26, 27. On Chattooga County, to

which Caroline and Amos moved, see Baker, *Chattooga County*. For the marriage, see Monroe County Court of Ordinary, Marriages, 1824–45, Book A, January 1840, p. 163, GDAH. For slave ownership, see Spencer Sullivan and Zachariah Hugly in 1850 slave schedule, Monroe County, Ga., 313, 315. According to the 1850 slave schedule, Chattooga County, Ga., Amos (recorded as "A. F. Heugley") owned ten slaves. On his death in 1851, Amos's estate included eight slaves worth $3,900, as well as livestock, furniture, and household items. It was appraised at the time at just over $5,000 (half the amount claimed by the various parties in the court case); see Chattooga County Inventories and Appraisements, Annual Returns and Vouchers, Sales Bills, Book B, Jan. 27, 1851, pp. 27–28, 95, 279–80, 351, GDAH.

All the cousins were minors. Caroline's father was Franklin's court-appointed administrator, and the lawsuit had been brought against him for allegedly lending the money, selling off the land, and hiring out the slaves for his own profit. Quotation from statements of Spencer Sullivan, Mar. 3, 4, 1859, in *Spencer Sullivan v. Anderson Hugly, et al.*, 1858–60, Monroe County, SSCOP, RG 92, #A-3518, GDAH. The state supreme court case is *Spencer Sullivan v. Anderson Hugly et al.*, 32 Ga. 316 (1861). I have used the spelling "Hugly" from the printed case.

24. All testimony is from *Hugly v. Sullivan*, Monroe County, August 1860, SSCOP, RG 92, GDAH; this testimony appears in abbreviated form in the printed state supreme court case, *Sullivan v. Hugly*, 32 Ga. 316 (1861). On the Zelner family, see Worsham, *Stroud Community*, 2, 14; and *Forsyth-Monroe County*, 8, 60. In 1850, Benjamin Zelner owned four slaves and Leonides Alexander owned nine slaves. On Dudley Hammond, see Board of Physicians Registry of Applicants, 1826–81, p. 10, and Board of Physicians Minutes, 1826–81, p. 198, GDAH; in 1850, he owned nine slaves. For slave ownership, see 1850 slave schedule, Monroe County, Ga., 283, 311, 319.

25. *Hugly v. Sullivan*, August 1860, GDAH.

26. Ibid., and *Sullivan v. Hugly*, 32 Ga. 316 (1861), 323 ("examined the child"). Spencer's will names neither a Caroline nor a Sarah (her full name was Sarah Caroline) under the listing of his children; see *Monroe County Georgia, A History*, appendix A–1, abstracts of wills, p. 473. In the 1958 work of local historian Nannie Worsham (the Worshams were also founding white families of the community), there is no mention of a Caroline or a Sarah in the list of Spencer's children (see *Stroud Community*, 27). For the Huglys, see Monroe County Court of Ordinary, Estate Records, Will Book B, pp. 268–69, GDAH. In the manuscript transcription of the testimony, the following words were crossed out: "Zachariah Hugly, the father of the said Amos, believed the child to be the offspring of a negro" (testimony of Dr. Dudley W. Hammond, *Hugly v. Sullivan*, August 1860, GDAH). There is also no mention of Amos as a son of Zachariah Hugly in Worsham's history, though the Hugly family is discussed at length.

Worsham notes that "The Huguley [sic] place is now on an off road, and is owned mostly by colored people" (Worsham, *Stroud Community,* 8).

27. *Hugly v. Sullivan,* August 1860, GDAH, and *Sullivan v. Hugly,* 32 Ga. 316 (1861), 323. This was the testimony of James Harlow ("Harlon" in the printed case), who also served as witness to Amos's last will and testament and as executor and administrator to Amos's estate. For maneuverings of the administration and executorship of Amos's will and estate between James Harlow and Spencer Sullivan, see Chattooga County Ordinary Inferior Court Minutes (Ordinary Purposes), Jan. 13 (p. 151), 27 (p. 154), Mar. 3, 1851 (pp. 162–63), March 1852 (p. 168), November 1853 (p. 201), February 1854 (p. 204), and Chattooga County Administrators and Guardian Records, January 1852, March 1852, GDAH.

28. On racial theory, see Fredrickson, *Black Image,* chap. 3; Gossett, *Race,* chaps. 3, 4; Horsman, *Race and Manifest Destiny,* chaps. 6–8; and Stanton, *Leopard's Spots.* On Nott, see Horsman, *Josiah Nott,* chap. 4.

29. *Hugly v. Sullivan,* August 1860, GDAH, and *Sullivan v. Hugly,* 32 Ga. 316 (1861), 319.

30. *Hugly v. Sullivan,* August 1860, GDAH, and *Sullivan v. Hugly,* 32 Ga. 316 (1861), 325.

31. *Sullivan v. Hugly,* 32 Ga. 316 (1861), 322, 323, and on the midwife, 320.

32. Ibid., 324, 325.

33. *Watkins and wife v. Carlton,* King and Queen County Circuit Superior Court of Law and Chancery Order Book, 1831–58, LVA, and 37 Va. 560 (1840), 564, 569. The white husband had omitted both his wife and this child from his will, but the county court reserved land and slaves for the child. See also *Julius A. Howell et al. v. Henry Troutman,* 53 N.C. 304 (1860) from Rowan County, in which a white man claimed the child of his white housekeeper as his own, even though others thought the baby's father was black. The white man "accounted for the color from a fright which" the housekeeper "had received" while pregnant" (305). In the dispute over the white man's will, the judge noted that the woman may have "made him believe that he had begotten a child by her, which everybody, but himself, could see was a mulatto" (307).

34. *Florey's Executors v. Florey,* 24 Ala. 241 (1854), 245, 248, 250 (from Shelby County). See also *Dinah Carter v. W. J. Montgomery and others,* 2 Tenn. Chancery 216 (1875); and *F. T. Warlick v. Peter White and wife,* 76 N.C. 175 (1877). For a case decided in favor of illegitimacy, see *Ursin Raby v. Jacob Batiste and wife,* 27 Miss. 731 (1854), no county specified, in which one son claimed that another son had been fathered by a black man. This parallels the Nunez case in that the court listened to much conflicting testimony about racial status and decided on the presence of African ancestry.

35. On slave law, see Tushnet, *American Law of Slavery,* 139–56, and

"American Law of Slavery," 169–75. Tushnet does not discuss the children of white women and black men.

36. *Jesse Barden v. Ann Barden*, 14 N.C. 548 (1832), 549, 550 (Wayne County).

37. Basil Brawner Petition, Prince William County, Feb. 20, 1835, #10906, LPP, LVA. *Jacob R. Davis, Guardian of Erasmus v. Executors of Samuel Hale*, 2 Ga. Decisions 82 (1843), no county specified. For another case involving a white mother and a dispute over enslavement, see *Gilbert Cone v. Charles Force*, Floyd County, SSCOP, RG 92, case #A-3444, GDAH, and 31 Ga. 328 (1860). See also *Richmond Enquirer*, June 12, 1855, and *Crawford v. Ripley*, Boutetout Circuit Court Common Law Minute Docket, May 29, 1855, LVA, in which the daughter of a white woman was freed after more than fifteen years of slavery. For Georgia's prima facie laws, see Prince, ed., *Laws of Georgia*, 446; and Clark, Cobb, and Irwin, *Code of Georgia*, 319.

Proof of descent from an American Indian mother could also grant freedom. In Virginia in 1806, generations of slaves won liberty by tracing their ancestry to a woman named Butterwood Nan; see *Hudgins v. Wrights*, 11 Va. 134 (1806), 140. For American Indian maternal ancestry and freedom, see also *Coleman v. Dick and Pat*, 1 Va. 233 (1793); *Pegram v. Isabell*, 11 Va. 387 (1807), 12 Va. 193 (1808); *Gregory v. Baugh*, 25 Va. 611 (1827), 29 Va. 665 (1831); and Petersburg Hustings Court Minute Book, 1851–53, pp. 323–34, LVA. For cases debating slave or free status based on appearance, see *Hook v. Nanny Pagee and her children*, 16 Va. 379 (1811); *Gobu v. Gobu*, 1 N.C. 188 (1802); *Samuel Scott v. Joseph Williams*, 12 N.C. 376 (1828); *Alfred Nichols v. William F. Bell*, 46 N.C. 32 (1853); and *State v. Alford*, 22 Ark. 386 (1860). See also Higginbotham and Kopytoff, "Racial Purity," 1983–88.

38. *William Clark v. Thomas N. Gautier, in behalf of Dick*, 8 Fla. 360 (1859), 361, 366 (Jackson County).

39. *Dean v. Commonwealth*, 45 Va. 541 (1847), from Culpeper County. *Jacob Yancy v. Ezekiel Harris*, February 1851, Forsyth County, SSCOP, RG 92, case #A-175, GDAH, and 9 Ga. 535 (1851), 536. See also *John Beckley, Jr. v. United States*, 1 D.C. Hayward & Hazelton 88 (1842).

40. Basil Brawner Petition. The 1850 slave schedule of Burke County, Ga., listed three slaves as "white negroes from black parents" (p. 82). The figure of the "white slave" made an appearance in abolitionist literature, presumably to alert white audiences that people like themselves could be held in bondage in the South. See, e.g., Chambers, *American Slavery and Colour*, 3; and [Newcomb], "Negro Pew," 2, 67, 78.

41. *Gassaway Rawlings v. Anthony Boston*, 3 Md. Harris & McHenry 139 (1793), from Anne Arundel County. *Upton Scott v. Eleanor Toogood*, Court of Appeals, Judgments no. 15, May 1783, MHR, and *Eleanor Toogood v. Doctor Upton Scott*, 2 Md. Harris & McHenry 26 (1782), from Anne Arundel County. Of course not all such suits were successful for the enslaved; see, e.g., *Milly*

Ogleton v. Oswald Boone, Prince George's County Court Papers, "Blacks," 1700–1851, folder 16, Sept. 5, 1811, MHR.

42. *State v. William P. Watters,* Ashe County, SSCMR #3540, NCDAH, and 25 N.C. 455 (1843), 456.

43. *Thurman v. State,* 18 Ala. 276 (1850), 278, 277, 279 (Russell County). For two other rape cases involving legal technicalities of color though not the offspring of a white mother and a black father, see *Dick v. State,* 30 Miss. 631 (1856); and *State v. Anderson,* 19 Mo. 241 (1853), in which the defense argued unsuccessfully that "the court erred in telling the jury they might find that the prosecutrix was a white female, from seeing her on the witness stand, and that the defendant was a negro, from seeing him in court," for "such questions are often of the greatest difficulty, requiring for their solution scientific skill" (243).

44. Thomas, *Secret Eye,* 161.

45. *Richmond Enquirer,* Feb. 24, 1859.

46. As Hazel V. Carby writes, the laws "necessitated the raising of protective barriers, ideological and institutional, around the form of the white mother, whose progeny were heirs to the economic, social, and political interests in the maintenance of the slave system"; see *Reconstructing Womanhood,* 31.

Chapter 6 *Wartime*

1. Testimony of Captain Richard J. Hinton, New York City, Dec. 14, 1863, American Freedmen's Inquiry Commission, Letters Received by the Office of the Adjutant General, M619, RG 94, NA (hereafter AFIC), reel 201, file #8. Hinton also served as an officer in a black Kansas regiment, was an army correspondent in Kansas, Missouri, and Tennessee, wrote Abraham Lincoln's campaign biography, and organized the Kansas Emancipation League in 1862 to aid 4,000 former slaves; see Berlin, ed., *Black Military Experience,* 335–36; and McPherson, *Struggle for Equality,* 20, 170, 424.

2. The AFIC was set up in March 1863 in New York City. The commissioners were Robert Dale Owen, Indiana Congressman and advocate of birth control and sexual equality (chairman); Samuel Gridley Howe, Boston physician and advocate for the blind and deaf; and James McKaye, a New York antislavery activist. On the purposes of the commission, see *War of the Rebellion,* ser. 3, 3:73–74. For recommendations of the commission, see Owen, McKaye, and Howe to Stanton, June 30, 1863 (preliminary report), and "Final report of the American Freedmen's Inquiry Commission to the Secretary of War," May 15, 1864, ibid., ser. 3, 3:430–54, 4:289–382; McPherson, *Struggle for Equality,* 182–87; and Sproat, "Blueprint."

3. Indexes to files #7, 8, AFIC, reel 201; in the general index appeared the category "Intercourse between white women and col'd men common, instances of" (reel 200).

4. Testimony of James Redpath, Boston, Mass., Dec. 24, 1863, AFIC,

reel 201, file #9. Redpath visited the South three times in the 1850s and published a compilation of dispatches from Virginia, North Carolina, South Carolina, Georgia, Alabama, Louisiana, and Missouri; see Redpath, *Roving Editor*. See also McKivigan, "James Redpath."

5. Testimony of Samuel B. Lucille, Louisville, Ky., Nov. 19, 1863, AFIC, reel 201, file #7 (perhaps referring to the Washita River in Oklahoma). Lucille also said: "I believe the instances at the South where a yellow woman breeds with a full-blooded black man are fewer than where a black man has breeded on a white woman."

6. Testimony of J. W. Lindsay, St. Catharine's, Canada West, Nov. 6, 1863, AFIC, reel 201, file #10; also in Blassingame, ed., *Slave Testimony*, 400. Canada West is present-day Ontario. "Pure" here most likely refers to women of exclusive European ancestry, rather than to moral virtue. Lindsay was born free and kidnapped into slavery before escaping to Canada as a grown man. On the probable truthfulness of black witnesses' testimony before the AFIC, see Blassingame, ed., *Slave Testimony*, lix–lx.

7. Testimony of Major George L. Stearns, Nashville, Tenn., Nov. 23, 1863, AFIC, reel 201, file #7. On Stearns, see Berlin, ed., *Black Military Experience*, 9, 75–76, 90–92, 97–98, 98–101, 113, 123, 124–25, 172–73, 173–74, 176–80; Glatthaar, *Forged in Battle*, 32, 55, 59, 87, 199; McPherson, *Struggle for Equality*, esp. 208–10; and Quarles, *Negro in the Civil War*, 8–9, 184, 195.

8. Redpath, *Roving Editor*, 2, 184, 257–58. Redpath relayed a story told by a former slave named Malinda Noll whose sisters were sold to a man in Platte County, Mo. Of this white man, Noll said: " 'his daughter bore a child to one of his slaves. The boy was frightened, and ran away to Kansas, but was brought back in chains and sold" (316).

9. Hinton testimony, AFIC. Redpath testimony, AFIC. Hinton referred to Minor as "a graduate of Oberlin College." Slaveholders were known to send the children they had fathered by slave women North to Oberlin, and Minor was one of those children; see Fletcher, *History of Oberlin College*, 2:528. In 1864 and 1865, Minor served as lieutenant (one of three commissioned officers, all black men) of an independent battery raised at Leavenworth, Kans.; see Berlin, ed., *Black Military Experience*, 311n; Cornish, *Sable Arm*, 215–16; Dyer, *Compendium of the War of the Rebellion*, 3:1723. On the sexual boasting of slave men, see Stevenson, *Life in Black and White*, 241–43.

10. Testimony of Mayor Cross, Sept. 11, 1863, Chatham, Canada West, AFIC, reel 201, file #10. Such sentiments had been published in the antebellum North, for example, by black antislavery agitator David Walker, who wrote in 1829 that he "would not give a *pinch of snuff* to be married to any white person I ever saw in all the days of my life"; see *David Walker's Appeal*, 9. Cross himself noted that "it is only the most abandoned whites" who married blacks, and "it is a very good trait in the character of the people, that they do not regard it as any honor to marry a white person." Another white man commented: "They don't

marry much with whites. It is looked down upon with such dreadful contempt by all classes—even by the negroes themselves. The respectable colored people don't like it to have one of their color marry a white whore—for a woman is nothing else when she comes into such a connection as that. The white women are broken down outcasts when they come to that." See Testimony of E. W. Stephenson, St. Catharine's, Canada West, Sept. 17, 1863, AFIC, reel 201, file #10.

11. Testimony of A. R. Green, Windsor, Canada West, Sept. 14, 1863, AFIC, reel 201, file #10. For Howe's version, see "The Self-Freedmen of Canada West, Supplemental Report A," May 14, 1864, AFIC, reel 199; and the published report (almost the same), Howe, *Refugees from Slavery*, 30–31. (Much of the Canada West testimony can also be found in Howe's published report.) A prominent white educator in Canada told the commission: "There is one very curious thing—the number of white women who marry black men; they make better husbands. That is remarkable here. No white men marry black women"; see testimony of Rev. Dr. McCaul, Toronto, Canada West, Sept. 5, 1863, AFIC, reel 201, file #10.

12. Testimony of John Kinney, St. Catharine's, Canada West, Sept. 17, 1863, and Mr. Sinclair, Chatham, Canada West, Sept. 11, 1863, both AFIC, reel 201, file #10. See also testimony of the white Rev. William King, Buxton, Canada West, Sept. 12, 1863, who commented on "marriage of black men to white women," saying "the women are not respected by the blacks"; testimony of the white Dr. Andrew Fisher, Malden, Canada West, Sept. 14, 1863; and testimony of the black livery stable keeper, Mr. Foster, Malden, Canada West, Sept. 14, 1863, all reel 201, file #10.

13. Testimony of Susan Boggs, St. Catharine's, Canada West, Nov. 8, 1863, AFIC, reel 201, file #10; also in Blassingame, ed., *Slave Testimony*, 420.

14. According to Bertram Wyatt-Brown and Catherine Clinton, women of the planter classes were under too much scrutiny to be able to commit sexual offenses; see Wyatt-Brown, *Southern Honor*, 298; and Clinton, *Plantation Mistress*, 72–73, also 209. See also Fox-Genovese, *Plantation Household*, 208, 241; and Freehling, *Road to Disunion*, 56. On white Southern ideology about female purity, see, e.g., Clinton, *Plantation Mistress*, chap. 5; Fox-Genovese, *Plantation Household*, 109, 202–3, 210, 235–36; Scott, *Southern Lady*, chap. 1; and Wyatt-Brown, *Southern Honor*, chap. 9.

15. Hinton testimony, AFIC; the class status of the Ward women remained unspecified.

16. Redpath testimony, AFIC. Hinton testimony, AFIC. Incidentally, the confession of the Mobile woman who had intercourse with her slave on her wedding day included the information that the man "came up to tie her boots the morning of her marriage, and had connection with her before the ceremony."

17. Hinton testimony, AFIC. White abolitionists' ideas about black women were similarly convoluted; for example, along with acknowledgment

that black women were often powerless to resist the sexual exploitation of white men, James Redpath put forth such negative images as the lack of chastity and virtue and the desire to have sex with white men; see AFIC, reel 201, file #9. In the general index to the testimony, the entry, "Women, consider it an honor to have connection with white men" is followed immediately by, "Women, punished for not submitting to lust of masters" (reel 200). On the racism embedded in the AFIC, see Fredrickson, *Black Image,* 164. On contradictory characteristics attributed to black men by whites in the slave South, see Blassingame, *Slave Community,* 224–35; and Fox-Genovese, *Plantation Household,* 291. See also Jordan, *White over Black,* 32–43, 150–63, 398–99, 578–79.

18. Hinton testimony, AFIC. On Northern ideas about the depravity of white Southerners, see Walters, *Antislavery Appeal,* chap. 5. Some elite white women joined in the chorus of voices about the depravity of Southern white men; see Chesnut, *Mary Chesnut's Civil War,* 29–31, 168–69; Thomas, *Secret Eye,* 147, 167–69; and Painter, "Journal of Ella Gertrude Clanton Thomas," 45–46, 50, 58–59, 64–65.

19. L. B. Cotes to AFIC, Batavia, N.Y., Oct. 31, 1863, American Freedmen's Inquiry Commission Papers, bMS Am 702, Houghton Library, Harvard University, Cambridge, Mass., by permission of the Houghton Library, Harvard University.

20. Hinton testimony, AFIC. A white physician in Canada told the commission of "several Irish women here living with black men," and expressed puzzlement that "the low Irish, who have such a strong prejudice against the colored people, are the very ones who take up with black men"; see testimony of Dr. James H. Richardson, Toronto, Canada West, Sept. 5, 1863, AFIC, reel 201, file #10. See also testimony of Dr. Litchfield in "Self-Freedmen," AFIC, reel 199.

21. Howe, *Refugees from Slavery,* 94; "Self-Freedmen," AFIC, reel 199.

22. John C. Gorman Diary-Memoir, 1864, ts. p. 55, WPL ("mongrel babies"). Gorman was later involved in one of North Carolina's Klan-like organizations during Reconstruction; see Trelease, *White Terror,* 114. *Atlanta Constitution,* June 27, 1868 ("Yankee schoolmarms"). Debates about the sexual morality of Southern white women during the war also ensued among elite Southerners. One Mississippi plantation mistress wrote to her husband in 1864: "I am not astonished to hear of Gen. Sherman saying he could buy the chastity of any Southern woman with a few pounds of coffee," adding, "God though so many have gone beside themselves there are still many virtuous women in the Confederacy." See Matilda Champion to Sydney S. Champion, June 14, 1864, Sydney S. Champion Papers, WPL.

23. Redpath in particular seemed to be quite a boaster. In his AFIC testimony he bragged, "I have talked with at least five or six hundred slaves, perhaps with a thousand; have had long talks with them about slavery, just as you and I would talk, confidentially, in Virginia, North and South Carolina and Georgia, particularly" (AFIC, reel 201, file #9).

24. Jacobs, *Incidents*, 52. In 1837, a white antislavery minister from Ohio observed of slaveholding families that father and son alike "are involved in one common ruin," adding, "nor do the daughters always escape this impetuous fountain of pollution. Were it necessary I could refer you to several instances of slaves actually seducing the daughters of their masters! Such seductions sometimes happen even in the most respectable slaveholding families"; see Rankin, *Letters on American Slavery*, 69.

25. *Armstrong v. Hodges*, 41 Ky. 69 (1841), 69–70 (from Franklin County), emphasis in original; the court noted that the marriage was prohibited by state law. John Jacobs Flournoy to Robert F. W. Allston, Athens, December 1858, quoted in Easterby, ed., *Papers of Robert F. W. Allston*, 146. A commonly expressed idea was that the availability of slave women to white men kept Southern white women pure. In the words of pro-slavery writer Chancellor Harper, for example: "And can it be doubted, that this purity is caused by, and is a compensation for the evils resulting from the existence of an enslaved class of more relaxed morals?"; see Elliott, ed., *Cotton Is King*, 583.

26. Deposition of John Richardson, Jan. 18, 1825, Lewis Bourne Divorce Petition, Louisa County, Jan. 20, 1825, #8305, LPP, LVA. Recall also the possibility of Dorothea Bourne's coercing a second slave man; see Deposition of eleven men, Jan. 20, 1824, in Bourne petition, and chap. 4, above.

27. Letters to Governor James Barbour, Rockingham County, Oct. 5, 1813, Executive Papers, Letters Received, LVA. It seems that Dolly's father let Dolly and David sleep in the same bed upon occasion. David belonged to Zachariah Shackleford, a man who owned six other slaves as well; see 1810 census, Rockingham County, Va., 140. Philip Getts is not listed in the 1810 Virginia census. A white North Carolina man who harbored antislavery sentiments recalled in 1860 "Two cases where young white girls enduced Negro slaves to steal horses and run away with them, wishing to find a place where they could live together as husband and wife"; see Benjamin Sherwood to "B. S. Hedrick and family," copy of speech delivered in Iowa, Apr. 7, 1860, Benjamin Sherwood Hedrick Papers, WPL.

28. Hinton testimony, AFIC. Captain William D. Matthews, another of the commissioned officers of the Kansas battery (along with Patrick H. Minor), was born free in Maryland and moved to Kansas in the 1850s to assist freedpeople; see Berlin, ed., *Black Military Experience*, 69–70, 309, 311n, 335–36; Quarles, *Negro in the Civil War*, 126; Ripley, ed., *Black Abolitionist Papers*, 5:287n. Catherine Clinton writes: "The penalty attached to violation of sexual taboos was so severe for white women that a 'cry-rape' syndrome evolved"; see " 'Southern Dishonor,' " 60.

29. Redpath testimony, AFIC. Hinton testimony, AFIC.

30. Redpath testimony, AFIC. Hinton testimony, AFIC. On "French articles," see Gordon, *Woman's Body, Woman's Right*, 44.

31. Hinton testimony, AFIC; this took place in Platte County, Mo. Jacobs,

Incidents, 52. For a wartime case of a poor white woman convicted of murdering her child by a black man in South Carolina's upper piedmont, see *New York Times,* Nov. 9, 1866; though suspected of being an accessory, the man was acquitted for lack of evidence. For an earlier case of planter-class infanticide, see *King v. Sarah Wiggins,* Secretary of State Court Records, Box #312, April–May 1772, Dobbs County, NCDAH. Here, in eastern North Carolina a married white woman fractured the skull of her three-day-old infant whom she later admitted was the son of "Will, a Negro fellow belonging to her father."

32. Benjamin Sherwood to "B. S. Hedrick and family," 1860. Lindsay testimony, AFIC; also in Blassingame, ed., *Slave Testimony,* 400.

33. Lindsay testimony, AFIC; also in Blassingame, ed., *Slave Testimony,* 400. Neilson, *Recollections of a Six Years' Residence,* 297.

34. Rawick, ed., *American Slave,* vol. 15, pt. 2, pp. 106–8. 1850 census, Northampton County, N.C., 52, household #858. In subsequent censuses, Squire and Temperance Walden and their children were also designated as "mulatto"; see 1860 census, Northampton County, N.C., 155, household #387; 1870 census, Northampton County, N.C., 649, household #151 (in which Squire was listed as a "ditcher" and Tempie as "keeping house"). Squire Walden also appeared as a free man of color with a family (members unspecified) in the 1840 census of Northampton County, N.C., 104. The 1850 slave schedule of Northampton County, N.C., listed a Temperance Jaymes as the owner of eight slaves (12). Other evidence is equally vague: the Northampton County censuses listed no James family as large slaveowners. The Walden household also contained an elderly "mulatto" man who owned property, possibly Squire's free father. Tempie James may have been a free person of color all along, the daughter of a free woman of color; a Charlotte James (the name Markham gave for Tempie's mother) was listed as a "mulatto" woman living alone in the 1840 and 1850 censuses, Wake County, N.C., censuses, 126, 274, household #314, old enough to be Tempie's mother. Millie Markham or her parents may have made up the story. For an 1886 recollection of a white woman drinking blood to marry a black man, see Dodge, "Free Negroes of North Carolina," 29.

35. Rawick, ed., *American Slave,* vol. 15, pt. 2, pp. 213–14. The storyteller did not know the plantation's location or her grandmother's first name. In another recollection, a former slave named William Scott remembered that his grandfather was "born of a white woman"; see ibid., vol. 15, pt. 2, p. 260; see also vol. 10, pt. 5, suppl. ser. 1, p. 2269.

36. On planter-class women's stake in the Southern hierarchy, see Bleser, "Southern Planter Wives and Slavery"; Fox-Genovese, *Plantation Household,* 49, 145, 192–93, 243, 334; and Rable, *Civil Wars,* esp. chap. 2. On the stake of non-planter-class white men in the Southern hierarchy, see Cecil-Fronsman, *Common Whites,* chap. 3; Fredrickson, *Arrogance of Race,* chap. 2; Hahn, *Roots of Southern Populism,* chap. 2; Harris, *Plain Folk and Gentry,* esp. chap. 3; and McCurry, *Masters of Small Worlds.*

37. The other antislavery thinkers who relayed stories of coercion were John Rankin and B. S. Hedrick; see nn. 24, 27, above.

38. On the upheavals of the Southern homefront, see, e.g., Bynum, *Unruly Women*, chap. 5; Faust, "Altars of Sacrifice" and *Mothers of Invention;* Rable, *Civil Wars*, chap. 5; Roark, *Masters Without Slaves*, chap. 2.

39. *State v. Jesse Black*, Ashe County, SSCMR #8716, NCDAH, and 60 N.C. 262 (1864), 263. *Smith v. State*, 39 Ala. 554 (1865), from Butler County. The court described Joe as the property of either an unknown person or of Martha Smith (554). See also Burton, *In My Father's House Are Many Mansions*, 189.

40. *State v. Matilda Leonard and N. J. Stewart*, Orange County Criminal Action Papers, 1861, NCDAH; see also Bynum, *Unruly Women*, 124–25. *Richmond Enquirer*, Mar. 15, 1865.

41. Diary of Eugene Marshall, ts., Eugene Marshall Papers, Oct. 1, 4, 6, 1862, WPL.

42. Mary T. Hunley Diary, Mar. 19, 1864, SHC; see also May 13. Abbie M. Brooks Diary, May 9, 1865, AHS. Ann Bridges to Charles E. Bridges, July 17, 1865, Charles E. Bridges Papers, WPL. See also Grace B. Elmore Diary, Oct. 1, 1865, SHC, in which a white South Carolina woman described fears of insurrection and murder without mention of rape. On the trust of a white woman for a slave man while the woman's white husband was away at war, see Cashin, "'Since the War Broke Out,'" 205, 207, 209. Winthrop D. Jordan recounts white women seeking out slave men to protect them from Northern white men; see *Tumult and Silence*, 100, 171. Jordan also writes here about accusations of rape in tandem with a plot for an 1861 Mississippi slave uprising, which resulted in hangings (see esp. chap. 9 and 377–79). On Jordan's reading of the men's confessions, see Davis, "Terror in Mississippi," who writes: "For their part, as Jordan notes, white women never seemed to share this sexual phobia, at least in the pre–Civil War period, and they seldom if ever made allusion to black rapists in their letters and diaries" (11). But for evidence of white women's expressions of sexual fear of slave men during the war, see Faust, *Mothers of Invention*, 57–60.

43. *State v. Wesley McDaniel*, 60 N.C. 248 (1864), from Montgomery County; for the pardon, see Governor Zebulon B. Vance Letter Book, 1862–64, p. 567, 1863–65, p. 243, both NCDAH. *State v. Sam*, Davie County Miscellaneous Records, "Slaves, Criminal Actions," 1864, Box 7, NCDAH, and 60 N.C. 300 (1864), 301. *State v. Elias* and letter from Christopher Stephens, Mar. 7, 1865, both in Orange County Criminal Action Papers, 1864–65, NCDAH. See *Edward A. Lewis v. State*, 41 Miss. 686 (1868), from Greene County, for a case in which Union soldiers released a slave who was in jail for the attempted rape of a white girl.

44. On the rape of black women, see Faust, *Mothers of Invention*, 200; Jordan, "Sleeping with the Enemy," 57–58; Mitchell, *Vacant Chair*, 106–9. Of

the 267 Northern soldiers executed during the Civil War, 21 were found guilty of rape; of these, 10 were white and 11 black; see List of U.S. Soldiers Executed by United States Military Authorities during the Late War, 1885, in Proceedings of United States Army Courts-Martial and Military Commissions of Union Soldiers Executed by United States Military Authorities, 1861–66, M1523, NA. Most of these records are part of RG 153; some are part of RG 94. See also Glatthaar, *Forged in Battle*, 118; and Mitchell, *Vacant Chair*, 109–10.

45. For the trials, see Records of the Office of the Judge Advocate General (Army) Court-Martial Case Files, M1523; trial of Dandridge Brooks, #MM1972, reel 1; trial of John Shepperd, #MM-2006, reel 7. For other cases of black men tried for the rape of white women, see, e.g., Spencer Lloyd, #CMSR-2, reel 2; James Gripen, #MM-3184, reel 2; and Benjamin Rudding (alias Ben Redding), #MM-3184, reel 7.

46. *Macon (Ga.) Daily Telegraph*, Feb. 4, 1864 (castration); *Athens (Ga.) Southern Watchman*, July 16, 23, 1862 (lynching); *Athens (Ga.) Southern Banner*, July 23, 1862 (denunciation). On wartime lynchings, see also Brundage, *Lynching in the New South*, 6; Cashin, "Lynching in War-Time Carolina"; and Faust, *Mothers of Invention*, 126. For a case of a black man legally hanged for the rape of a white girl, see *Columbus (Ga.) Daily Sun*, Dec. 5, 1861.

47. Higginson, *Thomas Wentworth Higginson*, 245. Rawick, ed., *American Slave*, 19:179–80. Testimony of George Ross, St. Catharine's, Canada West, Nov. 6, 1863, AFIC; also in Blassingame, ed., *Slave Testimony*, 408. Report of John Eaton, Department of Tennessee, Memphis, Apr. 29, 1863, AFIC, reel 200, file #6; testimony of B. K. Lee, Jr., Department of the South, 1863, AFIC, reel 200, file #3. For black men positing slavery as the opposite of manhood, see Blassingame, ed., *Slave Testimony*, 134, 135, 144, 152, 192. See also Berlin, ed., *Black Military Experience*, 1–34, chap. 11; Berry, *Military Necessity*, chaps. 3–7; Blight, *Frederick Douglass' Civil War*, chap. 7; Cullen," 'I's a Man Now' "; Glatthaar, *Forged in Battle*, 107–8, 123, 138, 160, 167, 168, 172, 181; Quarles, *Negro in the Civil War*, esp. 199–213, 296–311; and Whites, "Civil War as a Crisis in Gender," 10. See also Horton, *Free People of Color*, chap. 4; and Black, " 'I Am a MAN, a BROTHER Now.' "

48. Letter to the Citizens of South Carolina from James Furman et al., *Spartanburg Spartan*, Nov. 22, 1860, quoted in Channing, *Crisis of Fear*, 287.

49. [Croly and Wakeman], *Miscegenation*, 43, 44, 28 (quotations); some of this may have been a parody of free-love language. The word *miscegenation* subsequently came to replace the older term *amalgamation*. On the pamphlet's history, see Fredrickson, *Black Image*, 171–74; Kaplan, "Miscegenation Issue"; McPherson, *Battle Cry of Freedom*, 789–91; Roediger, *Wages of Whiteness*, 155–56; and Wood, *Black Scare*, chap. 4. Other pamphlets whose titles revealed a similar spirit were: *Lincoln Catechism, Wherein the Eccentricities and Beauties of Despotism Are Fully Set Forth; A Guide to the Presidential Election of 1864;*

L. Seaman, *What Miscegenation Is! What We Are to Expect Now That Mr. Lincoln Is Re-elected;* and *Miscegenation Indorsed by the Republican Party.*

50. In 1798, while debating the wisdom of the Alien and Sedition Acts in Virginia's House of Delegates, Federalist George K. Taylor had summoned a scene of the French inciting insurrection among American slaves, warning that white men would witness "their wives and daughters torn from their arms, with naked bosoms, outstretched hands, and dishevelled hair, to gratify the brutal passion of a ruthless negro, who would the next moment murder the object of his lust"; see *Virginia Report of 1799-1800,* 37. See also Saillant, "Black Body Erotic," 424.

51. *Cong. Globe,* 38th Cong., 1st sess., pt. 2, Mar. 17, 1864, p. 1157 ("trembling"). Ibid., 39th Cong., 1st sess., pt. 1, Jan. 25, 1866, p. 418 (marriage). Ibid., Jan. 16, 1866, p. 251 ("political power"). Ibid., Jan. 10, 1866, p. 180 ("paper in a box"). *New York Times,* Sept. 17, 1865 ("slipping around").

52. Hinton testimony, AFIC. For the commissioners' discussion of the problem of "amalgamation," see "Final report," 375, 377, 378; see also Fredrickson, *Black Image,* 124.

Chapter 7 *Politics*

1. On black autonomy and white fears of "miscegenation," see, e.g., Grossberg, *Governing the Hearth,* 136; Shapiro, *White Violence,* 13; and Wyatt-Brown, *Southern Honor,* 453–54. See also Wiegman, "Anatomy of Lynching."

2. Dixon, *New America,* 2:335–36.

3. Foner, *Reconstruction,* 425; Rable, *But There Was No Peace,* 95.

4. On postbellum legal developments, see Bardaglio, *Reconstructing the Household,* 176–89; Grossberg, "Guarding the Altar," 203–5, and *Governing the Hearth,* 136–38. See also Hamilton, "Miscegenetic Marriages." On black views, see, e.g., Palmer, "Miscegenation as an Issue in the Arkansas Constitutional Convention"; Gutman, *Black Family,* 399–402; and Schultz, "Interracial Kinship Ties."

Some scholars have argued that liaisons between black men and white women increased after the war because of the shortage of white men. That argument rests on the white woman's point of view and fails to take into account the diminished coercive powers of white women. On the frequency of sex across the color line after the war, see Ayers, *Promise of the New South,* 152–53; Berry and Blassingame, *Long Memory,* 120–21; Clinton, *Plantation Mistress,* 210; and Williamson, *New People,* 88–91. For an 1870s observation of diminishing liaisons between blacks and whites, see King, *Great South,* 784–85.

5. *Daily Richmond Enquirer,* Sept. 13, 1866 ("tar and cotton"). *Richmond Enquirer,* Feb. 15, 1867 (Hayley and Fly); the paper called the man a "modern Othello" and the woman a "meek Desdemona." The same imagery was invoked

in another Virginia case in which the "modern Othello" was arrested and the "weeping Desdemona" released to her father; see *Richmond Enquirer*, Jan. 30, 1875.

6. Trowbridge, *The South*, 343. For another case in which a woman insisted she was black in order to marry a black man, see *Richmond Daily Dispatch*, Feb. 3, 1873; the couple was indicted and jailed.

7. J. P. Southworth to George H. Williams, Mobile, Ala., Mar. 12, 27, 1872, M1356, reel 6; Letters Received by the Department of Justice from the State of Alabama, Register of Letters Received, Mar. 12, 27, 29, 1872, M1356, reel 1, both RG 60, NA (Cusack case). *Denial of elective franchise in Mississippi*, 159, 191–92, 1312–13, 1367 (Mississippi case). In Alabama, a judge refused a marriage license to a black man in jail for a liaison with a white woman who was his employer; see Bill Wyrosdick to Wager Swayne, Crenshaw County, May 22, 1867, Alabama Letters Received, cited in Kolchin, *First Freedom*, 62. A Freedmen's Bureau agent in South Carolina in 1866–67 wrote: "It is true that there are a few marriages, and a few cases of illegal cohabitation, between Negro men and the lowest class of white women. For example, a full-blooded black walked twenty miles to ask me if he could have a white wife, assuring me that there was a girl down in his 'settlement' who was 'a-teasin' every day about it.'" See De Forest, *Union Officer*, 132; see also 138. For a black man's recollection of an 1866 Tennessee marriage of a black soldier to a white woman, see Rawick, ed., *American Slave*, 18:123.

8. *Green v. State*, 58 Ala. 190 (1877); the opinion here referred to the case of *Thornton Ellis v. State*, 42 Ala. 525 (1868), in which a black man and a white woman were granted a new trial only because the lower court had not prescribed harsh enough penalties. *Hoover v. State*, 59 Ala. 57 (1877). See also *State v. Wesley Hairston and Puss Williams*, 63 N.C. 451 (1869); *State v. Alexander Reinhart and Alice Love*, 63 N.C. 547 (1869); *James and Mollie Robeson v. State*, 50 Tenn. 266 (1871); *Doc Lonas v. State*, 50 Tenn. 287 (1871); *State v. Pink Ross and Sarah Ross*, 76 N.C. 242 (1877); *State v. Isaac Kennedy and Mag Kennedy*, 76 N.C. 251 (1877); and *Richmond Dispatch*, Apr. 6, 1878. For a discussion of appellate cases about marriage across the color line after the Civil War, see Bardaglio, *Reconstructing the Household*, 181–89, also 233. Mary Frances Berry found that "more often than not in miscegenation cases, convictions were upheld. The sex of the black and white partners made little difference in the reversal rates." With the exception of Louisiana, "Reconstruction judges upheld the relationships, and the judges after Redemption did not"; see "Judging Morality," 839, 854. For an elite white woman's view in 1869, see Thomas, *Secret Eye*, 322.

9. *Jackson (Miss.) Daily Clarion*, June 14, 1866; *Hinds County (Miss.) Gazette*, June 22, 1866 (Leslie and Furlow case). *Richmond Daily Dispatch*, Nov. 29, 1870 (shoot-out); according to the Democratic newspaper, the man "became desperately in love" with the woman, "which was mutual," and "seduced her," a result of the white family's support of the "Radical negro-equality

party." For other cases of escaping couples, see *Daily Richmond Enquirer*, Feb. 22, 1867; and *Richmond Daily Dispatch*, Dec. 2, 1874. A white Virginia woman who lived with a black man was tarred and feathered before being ordered to leave the neighborhood; see *Richmond Daily Dispatch*, June 14, 1871.

10. *Richmond Enquirer*, May 12, 1866. *Montgomery (Ala.) Advertiser*, May 16, 1867. A South Carolina farmer wrote to his brother: "relative to John H. Lipscomb's daughter having Negro children, I am forced to answer in the affirmative no doubt but she has had two, and no hopes of her stopping"; see Edward Lipscomb to Smith Lipscomb, Goucher Creek, June 19, 1874, Lipscomb Family Papers, SHC.

11. *Report of the Joint Committee on Reconstruction*, 56 (Richard Hill). Carrie Hall to Christian Raushenberg, Aug. 1, 1867, enclosed in Raushenberg to John R. Lewis, Sept. 13, 1867, Letters Received, ser. 693, Subordinate Field Offices (Albany, Ga., Subassistant Commissioner), RG 105, NA; also published with valuable annotations in Formwalt, "Case of Interracial Marriage." The couple's fate is unrecorded.

12. Helper, *Nojoque*, 218; see 85–86 on denouncing white men who had sex with black women.

13. On the nineteenth-century Klan, the most thorough work is Trelease, *White Terror*. See also Foner, *Reconstruction*, 425–44, 454–59; Franklin, *Reconstruction*, chap. 9; and Rable, *But There Was No Peace*, 69–80, 92–100. On the geography of the Klan, see Perman, "Counter Reconstruction," 128–29, and Trelease, *White Terror*, 64. On the participation of all white classes, see Foner, *Reconstruction*, 432; Rable, *But There Was No Peace*, 94; and Trelease, *White Terror*, 51. On white violence in general during Reconstruction, see Carpenter, "Atrocities in the Reconstruction Period"; Du Bois, *Black Reconstruction*, 670–84; Foner, *Reconstruction*, 119–23; Litwack, *Been in the Storm So Long*, 274–82; and Rable, *But There Was No Peace*. Kentucky was the only state outside the former Confederacy in which Klan violence was extreme; see Wright, *Racial Violence in Kentucky*, chap. 1.

14. *Report of the Joint Select Committee to Inquire into the Condition of Affairs in the Late Insurrectionary States* (hereafter *KKK Report*), 1:270. See also *Cong. Globe*, 42d Cong., 1st sess., Appendix, Apr. 4, 1871, p. 298 ("from Virginia to Texas, from the Potomac to the Rio Grande").

15. On resistance, see, e.g., Shapiro, "Afro-American Responses to Race Violence." For an example of 19 black men banding together to retaliate against the Klan in North Carolina by burning barns, see *Cong. Globe*, 42d Cong., 1st sess., Appendix, Mar. 31, 1871, p. 102.

16. On the committee (13 Republicans and 8 Democrats), see Trelease, *White Terror*, 391–98. Black activist T. Thomas Fortune called the volumes of testimony a "merciless chronicle of murder and outrage, of defiance, inhumanity and barbarity on the one hand, and usurpation and tyranny on the other"; see *Black and White*, 99–100.

17. *KKK Report,* 12:623, 8:431.

18. Peter H. Wood found that whites in colonial South Carolina grew increasingly anxious about the rape of white women by black men at the same time that blacks "were threatening to compete too successfully economically" with white men; see *Black Majority,* 236. Kathleen M. Brown found that after Bacon's Rebellion in colonial Virginia, black men were denied "the privileges of white manhood that hard experience had already shown to be dangerously empowering and conducive to rebellion," including "access to white women"; see *Good Wives, Nasty Wenches,* 108–81.

19. For Ware (Floyd County), see *KKK Report,* 6:44–46, 66, 74–75, 404–5, 7:885, 900, 913, 920–21; see also 6:21–22, 30–31, 98–99, 130. On the class status of women who brought rape charges, see Edwards, "Sexual Violence," esp. 250. Occasionally, a white person would note that a "respectable" person was also "poor"; see *KKK Report,* 7:1190.

20. For Lowther (Wilkinson County), see *KKK Report,* 6:356–63; for the judge's version, see 6:426, 430–31, 443; see also 7:1036. For a retelling that describes Lowther as a blacksmith and "the most influential negro in the county," see J. E. Bryant to Attorney General Akerman, Washington, D.C., Oct. 31, 1871, Letters Received, Source Chronological Files, Georgia, Box 690, folder 5, RG 60, NA. Despite the immensity of the ordeal, Lowther proceeded (to no avail) to file charges, though the Klan threatened him for doing so (*KKK Report,* 6:361–62); rumors later circulated that Lowther had been castrated by black people for raping his step-daughter (7:973).

21. Among other examples are the following: John Walthall was accused of sleeping with white women and murdered in Georgia; a black neighbor believed the accusation was the consequence of a labor dispute between Walthall and his white employers (*KKK Report,* 6:407–8, 411–14, 471–77, 544, 547, 7:1010). Joe Kennedy was shot by Georgia Klansmen; in one version it was for marrying a "mulatto" woman who was too white, but in another version, white men threatened Kennedy, saying, "You damned niggers are getting too big anyway, and it is time you should seek some other business or get out of the country" (6:45, 75, 94). James Hicks was whipped by a mob in Mississippi, charged with insulting a white woman or boasting about sexual intimacy with a white woman, but Hicks believed it was because of his successful crop. Hicks and his wife, who was also whipped, were left without any property (for Hicks's version, see 12:891–93; see also 11:417–18, 445, 12:671–72, 704, 707, 720, 727, 776, 894, 1038, 1046–47, 1081–83). Caswell Holt was brutally assaulted in North Carolina; in testimony taken during the governor's impeachment trial, Holt was asked, "Did they ever talk to you about their politics?" and then a few minutes later, "Did they say that night that they whipped you for your behaving indecently to white women?" See *Trial of Holden,* 1311–25; see also *Third Annual Message of Holden,* 156–57, 179, 224.

22. *KKK Report,* 7:1120 (butcher knife). *Select Committee to Investigate*

Alleged Outrages in Southern States (hereafter *Outrages*), lxvi; *Third Annual Message of Holden,* 155–56, 198–200; *Trial of Holden,* 2007, 2009; testimony of John W. Long, Ku Klux Klan Papers, WPL (all on Trolinger). Bryant to Akerman, Department of Justice Letters (ministers); see also *KKK Report,* 6:359. For the castration of a white man, see 6:360.

23. *Greensboro (N.C.) Patriot,* Jan. 28, 1869. For mentions of Klan violence precipitated by accusations of a sexual liaison between a black man and a white woman, see also *KKK Report,* 2:213, 227, 539, 583, 586, 8:476, 12:1144.

24. *Louisville (Ky.) Commercial,* May 3, 1874; the white woman was also to stand trial. *State v. Neely,* 74 N.C. 425 (1876), 429; a dissenting judge offered harsh criticism of this reasoning (429–32). *Bib Sharpe v. State,* 48 Ga. 16 (1873), 20. *Wesley Jones v. State,* 1 Tex. App. 87 (1876), 89. See also *Patrick Carter v. State,* 35 Ga. 263 (1866), in which conviction was upheld; *Joe Wharton v. State,* 45 Tenn. 1 (1867), in which the black man was released (the court was under Republican control); *Boxley v. Commonwealth* 65 Va. 649 (1874), in which a new trial was granted partly due to inconclusive evidence.

For black men on trial for the alleged rape of white women, see also *KKK Report,* 2:315, 8:242, 11:364, 12:879; Report of Francis M. Bache to A. S. Webb, Raleigh, N.C., Sept. 7, 1865, Letters Received by the Office of the Adjutant General, M619, reel 331, file #1370A, RG 94, NA; "Semi-Monthly Report of Outrages by Whites against Blacks in the State of North Carolina," Fayetteville County, Feb. 13, 1867, Records of the Assistant Commissioner for the State of North Carolina, M843, reel 33, RG 105, NA; Wright, *Racial Violence in Kentucky,* 43–46, 54–56.

25. *KKK Report,* 6:124. For general statements about black men raping white women, see 2:142, 6:275, 8:446; *Cong. Globe,* 42d Cong., 1st sess., Appendix, Mar. 20, 1871, p. 23. On the lack of Reconstruction-era lynching statistics, see Rable, *But There Was No Peace,* 98; see also Brown, *Strain of Violence,* 323.

26. *KKK Report,* 7:655–66, 720, 725, 723, 726, 1061 (Clarke); the testimony was interspersed with discussions of the county's political leanings. Ibid., 6:214 (burning). For other cases of black men lynched (or nearly lynched) for alleged rape or attempted rape of white women or girls, see 2:8, 6:574, 575, 577–78, 7:611, 1190–91, 12:642–46. See *Baltimore American and Commercial Advertiser,* June 15, 1875, for such a lynching near Annapolis.

27. Schurz, *Report on the Condition of the South,* 20. For black activists' statements, see chap. 8, below.

28. *Daily Richmond Enquirer,* Sept. 6, 1866.

29. Trowbridge, *The South,* 111. Van Evrie, *White Supremacy,* 154; this was a reissue of an 1853 work with a different title, demonstrating the existence of this erroneous or disingenuous belief in the antebellum South.

30. *KKK Report,* 1:264 (Kentucky example). Testimony of John W. Long,

Ku Klux Klan Papers, WPL; *Third Annual Message of Holden,* 147 ("wives"); Charles H. Morgan to Adjutant General, Raleigh, N.C., June 18, 1871, Letters Received, M666, reel 12, file #1612, pp. 318–19, RG 94, NA ("fancifully trimmed"). *KKK Report,* 6:519 (Wilson's dress), 2:100, 8:157–58 (apprehension). On costumes and Klansmen dressing in women's clothing, see Fry, *Night Riders,* 122–35; and Trelease, *White Terror,* 53–54. See also *KKK Report,* 2:87, 473, 7:955, 9:813.

31. Tourgée, *Invisible Empire,* 37.

32. For statement of protection, see *KKK Report,* 2:364, repeated or paraphrased passim. For the assault and rape of black women by Klansmen, see, e.g., ibid., 2:99–100, 148, 6:375–77, 387, 8:547, 553, 9:930, 1188, 1189, 11:38–39, 12:1084; "Semi-Monthly Report of Outrages by Whites against Blacks in the State of North Carolina," Alamance County, Mar. 9, 1867, Records of the Assistant Commissioner for the State of North Carolina, M843, reel 33, RG 105, NA; J. C. Brubaker, Harper's Ferry, W. Va., Sept. 25, 1867, Reports of Operations, Records of the Assistant Commissioner for the District of Columbia, M1055, reel 13, RG 105, NA. In North Carolina, a black woman struck disguised attackers with an axe as they entered her house; see *Outrages,* lxvi, 43. See also Brown, "Negotiating and Transforming," 112; Clinton, "Bloody Terrain"; Edwards, *Gendered Strife,* chap. 5; and Rosen, "Struggles over 'Freedom.' "

33. Schurz, *Report on the Condition of the South,* 31.

34. Testimony of Sandy Sellers and John W. Long, Ku Klux Klan Papers, WPL; *Outrages,* lxvi; *Third Annual Message of Holden,* 141–43, 156, 157, 201–6; *Trial of Holden,* 1996–97.

35. *KKK Report,* 6:86 ("saucy"), 7:1166 ("abusive"), 11:417 ("improper language").

36. *Outrages,* 191. Another executed black man "was charged with making some bad proposition of some kind to some white woman," but a white witness admitted that he may have been "killed on account of his politics" (ibid., 45).

37. *Greensboro (N.C.) Patriot,* June 24, 1869 (Edwards). *Wilmington (N.C.) Daily Journal,* Mar. 28, 1869 ("respectable"). *KKK Report,* 13:7, 15 (Forrest).

38. *KKK Report,* 7:1096 ("across a log"), 7:1120 ("padlock"), 2:37 ("burned"). For similar treatment see 2:49, 7:1022; see also 2:4, 371–72, 7:1007, 8:476, 549, 550–51, 9:771, 956, 12:652, 13:137. In North Carolina, a woman and her two daughters were "thrown out of their house and whipped, and one of them made to exhibit her person, while the fiends proceeded to inflict blows upon her private parts." No race was specified in the report, but either black or white women could have been subjected to such treatment; see *Outrages,* lxvi.

39. Stearns, *Black Man of the South,* 409. *Trial of Holden,* 1397–1402; see also 1516–17.

40. *KKK Report*, 7:723 (Clarke), 920–21 (Ware), 6:431 (Lowther).

41. Ibid., 6:125 ("common whore"), 291–92 ("low position"), 10:1854 ("low woman"), 13:14 (Forrest); see also 6:82. On the ever-invoked phrase "bad character," see Edwards, "Sexual Violence," 243–44. A Mississippi newspaper described a white woman arrested for living with a black man as "a slovenly piece of humanity, and not a fit companion for a respectable negro"; see *Jackson (Miss.) Daily Clarion*, Aug. 26, 1866.

42. *KKK Report*, 6:431.

43. Ibid., 6:362 (Lowther), 413 (Walthall). James Johnson to O. Brown, Fredericksburg, Va., Jan. 31, 1868, Records Relating to Court Cases Involving Freedmen, Records of the Assistant Commissioner for the State of Virginia, M1048, reel 61, RG 105, NA (revenge); the black woman was bound over to the court. In 1866 in South Carolina, a black woman who accused her husband of "having illicit intercourse with a worthless white woman" assaulted the white woman and was subsequently beaten by the husband; see *Charlotte Brown v. George Brown* in Sterling, ed., *We Are Your Sisters*, 340–41.

44. *KKK Report*, 2:196.

45. Ibid., 2:233 ("radical party"), 9:733, 772–73 ("Union woman"). Stearns, *Black Man of the South*, 408; and *Condition of Affairs in Georgia*, 108 ("one less radical").

46. *Testimony Taken by the Sub-Committee of Elections in Louisiana*, 181. On assertiveness and community-building, see Foner, *Reconstruction*, 79–81, 88–110. On the new roles of black men and women, see ibid., 84–88; Giddings, *When and Where I Enter*, chap. 3; and Jones, *Labor of Love*, 58–68. On suffrage and political participation, see Foner, *Reconstruction*, 281–91. On black women's political participation, see Brown, "Negotiating and Transforming the Public Sphere."

47. Turner, "I Claim the Rights of a Man," 358, 360, 364. *Cong. Rec.*, 43d Cong. 1st sess., pt. 1, Dec. 19, 1873, p. 344 (Rainey). Ibid., 2d sess., pt. 5, June 9, 1874, p. 4784 (Rapier). For a nuanced analysis of conceptions of manhood, see Edwards, *Gendered Strife*, chaps. 3, 4.

48. On the conventions, see Foner, *Reconstruction*, 316–33; Hume, "Negro Delegates." On "social equality," see Litwack, *Been in the Storm So Long*, 255–61; Painter, " 'Social Equality' "; and Wood, *Black Scare*, chap. 7.

49. Dennett, *South As It Is*, 31. *Richmond Southern Opinion*, Aug. 3, 1868; on this convention, see Foner, *Reconstruction*, 304. *Constitution of the State of North Carolina*, 122.

50. *Debates of Convention at Little Rock*, 637 ("hug"). *Cong. Globe*, 40th Cong., 2d sess., pt. 2, Mar. 18, 1868, p. 1970 ("juxtaposition). Republicans countered Democratic offensives with several arguments (none of which included defenses of marriage across the color line). They asked why Democrats felt such a strong need for laws restraining them from marrying blacks (ibid., 42d Cong., 2d sess., pt. 1, Feb. 5, 1872, p. 821); they pointed out that chil-

dren of Democrats "had the same nurse" as slave children and "sometimes had the same father" (*Cong. Rec.,* 43d Cong., 1st sess., pt. 1, Jan. 7, 1874, p. 457); and they noted that children of black women and white men proved "social equality" had existed under slavery (2d sess., pt. 2, p. 1006, Feb. 4, 1875).

51. Morgan, *Yazoo,* 455–56 (quotation on 456). In 1873, a Kentucky Democrat warned that a white woman might be arrested and imprisoned if she refused a marriage proposal from a black man (*Cong. Rec.,* 43d Cong., 1st sess., pt. 1, Dec. 19, 1873, p. 343). Commenting upon one state's laws prohibiting marriages across the color line, a Tennessee Representative mixed his gendered metaphors when he said that the state "wisely declines to allow her manhood to be emasculated by the degeneracy which always marks a mongrel race" (ibid., Jan. 7, 1874, p. 453).

52. *Colored American,* Jan. 6 ("loud and long"), 13 (Turner), 1866.

53. Ibid., Jan. 6, 1866. Arkansas Constitutional Convention, 1868, quoted in Du Bois, *Black Reconstruction,* 549.

54. *KKK Report,* 13:6 (Forrest), 1:292 (minority report), 2:241 (North Carolinian).

55. *Outrages,* 20 (North Carolina). *KKK Report,* 9:1210 (Alabama). David Schenck Books, Dec. 18, 1869, ts. 6:153, SHC ("abhor"). In his autobiographical novel of 14 years in post–Civil War North Carolina, Albion W. Tourgée had his protagonist record the following anecdote: "James Leroy was hanged by the Ku-Klux on Tuesday night. . . . He was *accused* of having slandered a white woman. The truth is, he was an independent colored man . . . who could read and write, and was consequently troublesome on election-day, by preventing fraud upon his fellow"; see *Fool's Errand,* 173.

56. *KKK Report,* 2:434 ("marrying"), 318 ("poor white girls"), 11:76 ("intermingle"), 310 ("social circle"), 6:529 ("parlor"). See also 11:558–60.

57. Campbell, *White and Black,* 171–72 ("many hanged"). *KKK Report,* 12:710, 870 (congressional committee). *Cong. Globe,* 42d Cong., 1st sess., pt. 1, Apr. 1, 1871, p. 392 (Elliott). On the Klan as broadly political, see Foner, *Reconstruction,* 425, 428–30.

58. *KKK Report,* 6:172; see also 6:79, 9:1390–91. "Semi-Monthly Report of Outrages by Whites against Blacks in the State of North Carolina," Bladen County, Feb. 3, 1867, Records of the Assistant Commissioner for the State of North Carolina, M843, reel 33, RG 105, NA.

59. Both black and white witnesses acknowledged sexual liaisons between white men and black women, and described Klan violence directed toward both parties involved; see *KKK Report,* 2:134, 229, 6:184, 187, 274, 362–63, 7:1204, 8:429, 445–46, 9:1297–98, 10:1440–41, 1485, 1492–93, 1523, 11:226–27, 12:623–24, 632, 701, 879. Liaisons between white men and black women could also prompt freedmen to assault or kill the white man; see 7:611, 776, 10:1511–12, 13:222. Ibid., 9:926–27, 947 (Mason-Dixon line).

60. Ibid., 8:611 ("cruelty"). For fornication and adultery, see 2:270,

546–47, 6:310, 7:642, 1044, 9:1143, 1361. In North Carolina, four "loose women" (race unspecified) were run out of town and the white boys who visited them were whipped; see *Outrages*, 194. For domestic violence or desertion, see also *KKK Report*, 2:502, 556, 9:987, 10:1808, 11:361, 13:13, 48.

61. *KKK Report*, 2:104, 137, 167 (Democrat), 2:78, 6:280, 9:1070, 1107, 12:849 ("bad" white women), 11:420, 12:849, 921, 1153 (incest), 11:126 (abortion), 11:330, 7:1126 (alcohol), 8:476 (costumes). One victim in South Carolina described the Klansmen who attacked him as wearing padding "under their breeches to make them look big—bulging out" (3:521).

62. Ibid., 7:1114.

63. On North Carolina, see Olsen, "Ku Klux Klan"; Trelease, *White Terror*, chaps. 12, 13, 21; on Rowan County, see 206. Rowan was also the venue of the pardon of the slave Sam after his mistress pleaded financial hardship in 1831; see chap. 3, above. On Klan violence in Davidson County, see also *Outrages*, 109. Other North Carolina counties in which whites had previously tolerated liaisons between white women and black men, or had not demonstrated violent alarm over rape accusations, were also arenas of Klan violence. Joel Fore and Susan Chesnut, a free man of color and a white woman lived together in Lenoir County; the free black Henry Carroll was pardoned for rape in Wake County; Nancy Wallis, whom some white neighbors claimed had falsely accused an elderly slave of rape, lived in Orange County (see chap. 3, above). Lucy Whittington, the white woman whose husband was denied divorce despite her adulterous liaison with a black man, lived in Caswell County; Elizabeth Walters, the white woman who professed love for a black man and whose husband was also denied divorce, lived in Person County; Peggy Johnson, whose husband was denied divorce despite her liaison with a free black man, lived in Orange County (see chap. 4, above). A slave named Sam had been acquitted of rape in Davie County during the war (see chap. 6, above). For Klan violence, see Trelease, *White Terror*, 189–91 (Lenoir County); 114, 206, 224, 336 (Wake County); 192, 195–96, 206 (Orange County); 192, 198, 206, 211–15, 222–23 (Caswell County); 206 (Person County); 206 (Davie County).

64. On Burke County, see Stearns, *Black Man of the South*, 287, 409; *KKK Report*, 7:1096, 6:274. On Chattooga County, see Trelease, *White Terror*, 64, 239–40, 325, 329–30. Warren County in Georgia's cotton belt also saw tremendous Klan violence (ibid., 64, 118, 119, chap. 14). There in 1858, when a white woman brought a slander suit against her accusers, the county judge had dismissed the case, noting that "to call a woman a whore in Georgia is actionable where the charge has reference to white men," but that it did not apply to white women who consorted with black men (see chap. 3, above).

65. In Franklin County, Ky., the court had found "abundant proof" of cohabitation of a white woman and a black man in 1841, but the only issue on trial had been a land dispute (see chap. 6, above). In Butler County, Ala., a white woman was accused of "adultery or fornication" with a former slave in

1864, but the man had not been mentioned (see chap. 6, above). Both of these areas were now arenas of Klan violence; see Trelease, *White Terror,* 246; and Wright, *Racial Violence in Kentucky,* 38, 59. In Alabama, Tuscaloosa and Calhoun Counties were also venues of Klan violence (Trelease, *White Terror,* 246, 269, 271). These were areas in which Gary B. Mills found toleration for liaisons between white women and black men in the antebellum era; see "Miscegenation and Free Negro."

66. On Virginia, see Thorpe, "Life in Virginia," 202–3; Trelease, *White Terror,* 63–64; and *Cong. Globe,* 42d Cong., 1st sess., Appendix, Apr. 4, 1871, p. 285. The Klan was also extremely active in South Carolina and Louisiana; see Saville, *Work of Reconstruction,* 127, 129–30, 181–82, 190; Trelease, *White Terror,* 92–98, chaps. 8, 22, 23.

67. *KKK Report,* 6:528.

68. Although the Congressional proceedings broke the organization, few Klansmen were brought to justice; see Rable, *But There Was No Peace,* 103–10; Trelease, *White Terror,* chaps. 24, 25. On violence during the second half of Reconstruction, see Perman, "Counter Reconstruction," 130–35 and *Road to Redemption,* chap. 7. On the deterioration of Reconstruction from 1871 forward, see also Foner, *Reconstruction,* chaps. 9–12. Historians disagree about Klan violence as a cause of the demise of Reconstruction; see Ayers, *Vengeance and Justice,* 163; Foner, *Reconstruction,* 442–44; Perman, "Counter Reconstruction," 129; Rable, *But There Was No Peace,* 101, 110–11; and Trelease, *White Terror,* 419.

69. Robert G. Fitzgerald Papers, SCRBC; on Fitzgerald, see Murray, *Proud Shoes.*

70. *KKK Report,* 13:173. Racial categories could still be ambiguous of course; see 1:265, 6:75, 94, 567, 7:850, 990; and *Trial of Holden,* 1694–95. But see also Williamson, *New People,* 92. In 1869, a senator from Delaware had his fellow congressmen laughing in a debate about whether the Fifteenth Amendment should include a clause that stated, "There never shall be hereafter any distinction of color." The senator suggested appointing a special committee "to devise a plan of doing away with the color white, and the color black, and so mix them up that it shall present blue, and have all mankind of a blue color." See *Cong. Globe,* 40th Cong., 3d sess., pt. 2, Feb. 17, 1869, p. 1310. (One colleague thought this as funny as an amendment stating that there should be no legal distinctions based on gender, and joked: "We can devote ourselves to those great interests common to a blue people and a people without sex.")

Chapter 8 *Murder*

1. On the relative rarity of the lynching of black men before the Civil War, see Belknap, *Federal Law and Southern Order,* 2–4; Brundage, *Lynching in the New South,* 5–6; Williamson, *Crucible of Race,* 183; see also chap. 3,

n. 62, above. Statistics are from Tolnay and Beck, *Festival of Violence,* 271; see also 259–67. The exact number is 1,165, counting Alabama, Arkansas, Florida, Georgia, Kentucky, Louisiana, Mississippi, North Carolina, South Carolina, and Tennessee (but omitting Virginia, Delaware, Maryland, Missouri, and Texas); see also Ayers, *Promise of the New South,* 495–97. On the geography of lynching, see ibid., 156–58; Brundage, *Lynching in the New South,* chaps. 4, 5; McMillen, *Dark Journey,* 230–32; National Association for the Advancement of Colored People, *Thirty Years of Lynching,* Appendix II; and Tolnay and Beck, *Festival of Violence,* 34–39, 49.

2. On alleged rape and mass mobs, see Brundage, *Lynching in the New South,* 37, 64; on different types of lynchings, see ibid., chap. 1. See also McMillen, *Dark Journey,* 240–45.

3. For descriptions of mass mob lynchings, see, e.g., Brundage, *Lynching in the New South,* 36–45; Shapiro, *White Violence,* 30–31; and Williamson, *Crucible of Race,* 186–89. For contemporary accounts, see, e.g., Cook, "New Black Codes," 36–40; Presley, *Negro Lynching,* 14–16, chap. 4; Wells, *Red Record,* esp. 25–29, 50–57; and Wells-Barnett, *Mob Rule,* 42–46. On the motivations of different classes, see Brundage, *Lynching in the New South,* 25–26; Hall, *Revolt Against Chivalry,* 132, 139–40; and McMillen, *Dark Journey,* 238–39. Elite whites often described lynching participants as lower class; see "Negro Problem . . . to a Southern White Woman," 2226; Poe, "Lynching," 161. But see also Terrell, "Lynching from a Negro's Point of View," 861; and Williamson, *Crucible of Race,* 291–95.

4. Turner, "Emigration Convention," 153.

5. Douglass, "Reason Why," 473. Wells, "Bishop Tanner's Ray of Light," 1045. On the historiography of causes, see Brundage, *Lynching in the New South,* 8–15; and Hall, *Revolt Against Chivalry,* 137–38. For economic explanations, see Ayers, *Vengeance and Justice,* 250–52; Tolnay and Beck, *Festival of Violence,* 69–75, chap. 5, 256–57; and White, *Rope and Faggot,* chap. 5. For cultural explanations, see Fredrickson, *Black Image,* 272, 282; and Wyatt-Brown, *Southern Honor,* chap. 16. For psychological explanations, see Ayers, *Vengeance and Justice,* 240–44; Hall, *Revolt Against Chivalry,* chap. 5; and Williamson, *Crucible of Race,* esp. 306–10. But see also Harris, "Etiquette, Lynching," 389. Links between formal black political power and lynching can be tenuous when scrutinized statistically; see Ayers, *Vengeance and Justice,* 238–40; Finnegan, "Lynching and Political Power"; and Tolnay and Beck, *Festival of Violence,* 66–69, chap. 6.

6. On the virulent racism of the 1890s, see Fredrickson, *Black Image,* chap. 9; Gutman, *Black Family,* 531–44; Litwack, " 'Blues Falling Down' "; and Williamson, *Crucible of Race,* chap. 4. The two most important portraits of the post-emancipation South are Woodward, *Origins of the New South;* and Ayers, *Promise of the New South.*

7. Douglass, "Lessons of the Hour," 591. Wells, *Mob Rule,* 47–48; Wells,

Crusade for Justice, 84–85. For similar expressions, see Grimké, *Lynching of Negroes,* 25–27, 40; and "Frightful Experience," 58–59. For an example of no contact, see ibid., 43–55. For an analysis of Wells's implied belief that no white women were the victims of black rapists, see Smith, "Split Affinities," 273–74.

8. Morgan, "Race Question," 395; for similar sentiments, see Avary, *Dixie After the War,* 394; and Simmons, *Solution of the Race Problem,* 30. Frederick Douglass, "Negro Problem," 450; see also White, *Rope and Faggot,* 66–81. Douglass had married the white Helen Pitts in 1884 and claimed that he neither advocated nor deprecated such marriages; see Douglass, "Future of the Colored Race." Writing to her daughter decades later, white Southern activist Jessie Daniel Ames wrote: "I have always been curious about the male mentality— white male, which as far back as I remember assumes that only segregation and the law against intermarriage are all that have kept white women from preferring the arms of negro men than those of white men." See Jessie Daniel Ames to Lulu Daniel Ames, July 3, 1965, Jessie Daniel Ames Papers, SHC.

9. *Richmond Planet,* May 24, 1890. Henry Johnson to John Edward Bruce, Nov. 24, 1893, reel #1, mss. autograph letters #98, Bruce Papers, SCRBC. See also John C. Dancy to John Edward Bruce, Jan. 30, 1899, Salisbury, N.C., reel #1, mss. autograph letters #311, Bruce Papers, SCRBC, in which T. Thomas Fortune "was mad because I would not support his attitude in favor of mixed marriages." For black support of marriage to whites, see, e.g., Cooper, *Voice from the South,* 221–22; Turner, "Emigration to Africa," 56; see also Gatewood, *Aristocrats of Color,* 177–80.

In the 1880s and 1890s, black men and white women (as well as black women and white men) could be indicted for marriage. For convictions, see, e.g., *Kinney v. Commonwealth* 71 Va. 858 (1878); *Pace and Cox v. State* 69 Ala. 231 (1881); *State v. Jackson* 80 Mo. 175 (1883); *Dodson v. State* 61 Ark. 57 (1895). See also *McAlpine v. State* 117 Ala. 93 (1897) in which a "miscegenation" conviction was overturned on a technicality. In 1882, the Supreme Court found that state laws forbidding intermarriage were not in conflict with the Fourteenth Amendment because the consequences to "each offending person, whether white or black" was the same. See *Pace v. Alabama* 106 U.S. 583 (1883), 585; the case involved a black man and a white woman convicted of "adultery or fornication"; see also *Plessy v. Ferguson* 163 U.S. 537 (1896), 545. On appellate court cases about marriage across the color line after the Civil War, see Bardaglio, *Reconstructing the Household,* 181–89, 232–33.

10. Wells, *Red Record,* 11; Wells quoted in "Anti-Lynching Crusade," 421; Wells-Barnett, "Lynching and the Excuse for It," 1134. See also Brundage, *Lynching in the New South,* 270–83.

11. For the Abercrombies, see Davis, *Douglas County,* 147, 181, 232, 393, 456; see also 80, 83, 105, 219–20, 242, 454 passim. For Stamps, see 1880 census, Douglas County, Ga., e.d. 49, p. 30. A white Stamps family also figured in the history of Douglas County, and Peter may once have been their slave; see

Davis, *Douglas County,* 103, 104, 146, 351. On local black families, see ibid., chap. 10, a short sketch that bypasses both slavery and racism.

12. The 1880 census lists nine-year-old Ida Abercrombie as the daughter of James M. Abercrombie; see 1880 census, Douglas County, Ga., e.d. 49, p. 30. The father can be found as Marion Abercrombie 10 years earlier (the ages match) in a nearby county, a married farmer with $700 worth of personal and real estate; see 1870 census, Campbell County, Ga., 43, household #139.

13. For the Stamps-Abercrombie case (Douglas County), see *Atlanta Constitution,* July 25, 26, 29, 1885; the news account is not always clear as to the timing of each event. In 1870 Stamps's occupation was listed as "work in blacksmith shop"; see 1870 census, Coweta County, Ga., 355, household #145. In 1880, Stamps was listed as a "farm laborer," an occupation also claimed by his wife and three of their seven children; see 1880 census, Douglas County, Ga., e.d. 49, p. 30. I thank W. Fitzhugh Brundage for uncovering this case (noted in *Lynching in the New South,* 62), along with the Jordan-Corder case, the Duncan case, and the Davis-Twitchell case (all discussed below), and for very generously sharing newspaper citations and his thoughts with me.

14. For the Jordan-Corder case (Fauquier County), see *Baltimore Sun,* Jan. 20–22, 1880; *Richmond State,* Jan. 19, 1880; *New York Times,* Jan. 20, 1880; and Brundage, *Lynching in the New South,* 62. No one was charged with murder. The paper gave no age for Elvira, but she was 15 years old in 1870; see 1880 census, Fauquier County, Va., 589. For Jordan, one year older than Elvira and listed as a laborer, see 585. In the 1880 census, taken in June, Elvira was no longer living in her father's household; see 1880 census, Fauquier County, Va., e.d. 40, p. 10. Fauquier County was the site of the 1815 case in which Abraham Newton divorced Nancy Newton after she gave birth to a "mulatto" child, and Nancy fled to Ohio. Abraham "acknowledged that a Negro fellow in the neighborhood was the father"; see chap. 4, above.

15. For the Duncan case (Murray County), see *Atlanta Constitution,* Oct. 1, 1889; *Dalton North Georgia Citizen,* Oct. 3, 1889; and Brundage, *Lynching in the New South,* 334 n. 68. The employer, John L. Edmondson, was a married farmer with one live-in white laborer and nine children; see 1880 census, Murray County, Ga., e.d. 153, p. 49. For a similar case of elopement and lynching in Texas, see *Richmond Daily Dispatch,* Apr. 16, 1878.

16. *Richmond Planet,* Jan. 16, 23, July 24, Oct. 30, Nov. 13, 1897. The Twitchells (also spelled Twichell) had moved South from upstate New York and probably moved again, as they were not listed in the 1900 census of Richmond. Paul's father, Henry Davis, was listed as a farmer living with his wife and two sons who were farmhands; see 1900 census, Henrico County, Va., e.d. 33, p. 31. He was also listed in the 1897 *Directory of Richmond* as a laborer (251). On Mitchell, see Brundage, " 'To Howl Loudly,' " and Alexander, "Black Protest in the New South," esp. chap. 4.

17. Affidavit of Cora Twitchell, Aug. 12, 1897, *Commonwealth v. Paul*

Davis, July 1897, County Court, Ended Cases, LVA. Davis's lawyer also presented Cora Twitchell's birth certificate from Buffalo, N.Y., to prove she had been fourteen. Buffalo's mayor wrote to Davis's lawyer: "This will be good news to your client, but in my opinion he ought to have his neck broke anyway." See Mayor Edgar B. Jewett to George W. Thomas, Buffalo, N.Y., Aug. 16, 1897, and transcript of birth records, Aug. 19, 1882, in ibid. See also affidavit of T. F. Taylor, Oct. 13, 1897, who testified to examining Cora's birth certificate in Buffalo and speaking with the attending physician who said Cora's mother and grandmother had both asked him to alter her birthdate; all in ibid. For Carlos Twitchell's trial, see *Commonwealth v. Carlos A. Twichell,* Richmond City Hustings Court, Ended Cases, Oct. 1897, Box 183, LVA.

18. Statement of Cora Twitchell, Sept. 14, 1897, in *Commonwealth v. Paul Davis.* Cora's parents simultaneously stated that they had never coerced her, and reiterated her later birthdate; see statement of Carlos and Helen A. Twitchell, Sept. 14, 1897, in ibid.

19. Affidavit of George W. Thomas, Oct. 18, 1897; affidavit of Anna Davis, Oct. 16, 1897, in which she testified that Cora also said: "Mrs. Davis, it was not my fault that Paul was shot. I tried to see Paul and let him know that my father intended to shoot him, but I was so closely watched that I had no opportunity to do so," both in *Commonwealth v. Paul Davis.*

For the trial and subsequent events, see Henrico County Court, Minute Book No. 67, pp. 200, 201, 219, 338, 339, 340, 345, 359, 381, and Minute Book No. 68, pp. 12, 22, LVA; *Commonwealth v. Paul Davis; Richmond Planet,* Jan. 16, 23, July 24, Oct. 30, Nov. 13, 1897; *Richmond Dispatch,* Jan. 12, July 15, 16, Oct. 27, 28, 1897; and Brundage, *Lynching in the New South,* 319 n. 39. I thank W. Fitzhugh Brundage for bringing the *Richmond Planet* account to my attention.

20. Cora Twitchell to Paul Davis, September–October 1896, in *Commonwealth v. Paul Davis;* Cora's spelling was poor, and her letters contained little punctuation. *Richmond Planet,* Jan. 16, July 24, 1897. For a case in which a black man in Virginia was jailed for the seduction of a white girl, see *Louisville Courier-Journal,* Oct. 9, 1894; the white reporter wrote, "The girl seems to have a peculiar infatuation for Watson, as is shown by letters she had written him." For another instance of individual violence, see the 1887 quoted account in Fulkerson, *Negro: As He Was,* 79, in which a black Alabama educator in the 1880s "became attentive to a young white girl, a Miss Ina Jones, daughter of the wealthiest planter in the county." When the two eloped, the girl's father and a party of white men overtook them and killed the man.

21. Green, *Ely: Too Black, Too White,* 104–5, 120–28 (quotation on 127). Perhaps in keeping with his loner status, Alf Cannon does not show up in the census records, 1900–1920. Green, who played with Alf's Cannon's son as a child, was the son of a black woman and a white man; see pp. ix–x on the veracity of Green's memoirs.

22. "Lynching: Its Cause and Cure." In an 1899 Washington, D.C., sermon, black minister Francis Grimké spoke of a Southern white woman "who frankly admitted that she knew, and that others knew that some of these alleged cases of rape were not rape,—the relation between the parties being well understood. . . . The cry of rape is raised, and the Negro brute, as he is called, is riddled with bullets, or is strung up to a tree. That is the real history of some of these so-called cases of rape"; see *Lynching of Negroes,* 36–37.

23. Quoted in Fulkerson, *Negro: As He Was,* 85–86, and attributed to *Herald of United Churches,* "a colored paper, published in Atlanta, Ga.," n.d.

24. *Montgomery (Ala.) Herald,* Aug. 13, 1887 (Duke's editorial), reprinted with news stories in *Montgomery (Ala.) Advertiser,* Aug. 16, 1887; additional stories in *Advertiser,* Aug. 17–18, 1887. Editorials from other white papers, reprinted Aug. 18, are in *Birmingham Age, Macon Telegraph* (quoted here), *Tuskegee News, Birmingham Herald, Selma Times, Alabama Baptist, Mobile Register* (quoted here), and *Selma Mail,* plus letter from Col. J. J. Abercrombie ("kill every negro"). Fulkerson, *Negro: As He Was,* 54 ("unmitigated fool"). *Montgomery (Ala.) Advertiser,* Aug. 21, 1887 (Duke's last word). See also Wells, *Southern Horrors,* 5–6; and for facts not reported in the white newspapers, see Jones, "Black Press in the 'New South.'"

25. *Washington Bee,* Sept. 10, 1887, quoting Coffee's *Birmingham Era;* see also Sept. 3, 1887, for an assessment of Duke's response as cowardly (the *Bee* was a black newspaper).

26. On Wells's life, see, e.g., Wells, *Crusade for Justice;* Giddings, "Ida Wells-Barnett" and *When and Where I Enter,* chap. 1; Schecter, "Unsettled Business"; and Thompson, *Ida B. Wells-Barnett.* On her militant strategies and outsider status in black protest circles, see Holt, "Lonely Warrior." On Douglass's post-Reconstruction career, see Blight, *Frederick Douglass' Civil War,* chap. 10; Martin, *Mind of Frederick Douglass;* and McFeely, *Frederick Douglass,* chaps. 22–29.

27. Wells, *Red Record,* 81 ("voluntary, clandestine, and illicit"). *Memphis Free Speech,* May 21, 1892 (editorial), reprinted in Wells, *Southern Horrors,* 4; *Red Record,* 11–12; and (mostly the same) *Crusade for Justice,* 65–66. For subsequent events, see ibid., 61–63; and Wells, "Lynch Law in All Its Phases," 177–80, and *Southern Horrors.* Quotations from *Southern Horrors,* 4, 5, and "Lynch Law in All Its Phases," 179. See also Aptheker, "Suppression of *Free Speech*"; Giddings, "Ida Wells-Barnett," 376–78; and Tucker, "Miss Ida B. Wells." Much of *Southern Horrors* was first printed in the *New York Age,* June 25, 1892, in response to the *Free Speech* editorial.

28. Wells quoted in "Anti-Lynching Crusade," 421; Wells, *Southern Horrors,* 6, 5, and *Red Record,* 11, 58. For the dissemination of facts as antilynching strategy, see Wells, *Red Record,* 97–99, 101, and *Southern Horrors,* 22–24. Black Bostonian Archibald Grimké wrote in 1915: "Has it ever been seriously considered that like father may occasionally produce like daughter in the South? . . .

The sons are like their fathers in respect to their fondness for colored women, why may not one daughter in, say, ten thousand, resemble those fathers in that same shameful, though not altogether unnatural respect?"; see "Sex Question," 21.

29. For quoting verbatim, see Wells, *Red Record*, 15, 71. Gail Bederman notes that this tactic sidestepped charges that it was unladylike to discuss sex and rape; see *Manliness and Civilization*, 63. For the cases, see Wells, *Red Record*, chap. 6, and *Southern Horrors*, 7–11, 19, 20–21; also Wells, *Crusade for Justice*, 65. For other quotations, see *Southern Horrors*, 9 ("true of the entire South"), 11 ("hardly a town"), 24 ("garbled report"). A 40-year-old, single, childless, white servant named Sarah Clark lived on Memphis's small Poplar Street in 1900; see 1900 census, Shelby County, Tenn., e.d. 116, p. 2. Some of Wells's evidence was not in and of itself proof of a voluntary liaison, e.g., a white woman giving birth to a child whose father was black.

30. Wells, *Red Record*, 81, also 12 (not maligning), 65 (Edwards case).

31. *Southern Horrors*, 10–11 (Coy). The investigation was reported in Albion W. Tourgée's column in the Chicago *Inter-Ocean;* see also Graham, "Some Facts About Southern Lynchings," 615. *Cong. Rec.,* 56th Cong., 1st sess., pt. 3, vol. 33, Feb. 23, 1900, p. 2152 (Virginia case).

32. *Atlanta Journal,* Aug. 12, 1897 (Felton speech), repeated in slightly different forms Nov. 15, 1898, and in *Atlanta Constitution,* Apr. 23, 1899; see also Dec. 22, 1898. On Felton, see Whites, "Rebecca Latimer Felton and the Problem of 'Protection' " and "Rebecca Latimer Felton and the Wife's Farm."

33. "Mrs. Felton's Speech," originally published in *Wilmington Daily Record,* Aug. 18, 1898 (photograph of mutilated original in NCC); reprinted in *Raleigh (N.C) News and Observer,* Aug. 24, 1898 (in part); *Atlanta Constitution,* Nov. 11, 1898; "Race Troubles," 623–24.

34. West, "Race War," 588–89. Daniels, *Editor in Politics,* 287. See also *Raleigh (N.C.) Progressive Farmer,* Aug. 30, 1898.

35. *Raleigh (N.C.) News and Observer,* Aug. 24, 28, 1898; see also Aug. 25, 26, 1898. John C. Dancy to John Edward Bruce, Jan. 30, 1899, Salisbury, N.C., reel #1, mss. autograph letters #311, Bruce Papers, SCRBC (on reprinting the editorial). For attacks on Manly that conflate Republican politics with endangered white women, see *Wilmington (N.C.) Messenger,* Aug. 21, 23–27, 1898; see also Oct. 22, Nov. 1–5, 1898.

36. *Atlanta Constitution,* Nov. 11, 1898 ("political blunder"). *Raleigh (N.C.) News and Observer,* Aug. 26, 1898 ("libel"); John C. Dancy to John Edward Bruce, Jan. 30, 1899, Salisbury, N.C., reel #1, mss. autograph letters #311, Bruce Papers, SCRBC ("25,000 votes").

37. *Durham (N.C.) Daily Sun,* Oct. 29, Nov. 2, 4, 5, 7, 1898. The *Sun* reported that Maggie's father had once defended a black man accused of rape by

contending that "force was not necessary" in order for him to have sex with a white woman. In 1880, Manual McCall was a 46-year-old black farmer living with his wife and seven children; see 1880 census, Bladen County, N.C., e.d. 20, p. 19. In 1900, Milton G. Brewer was a 34-year-old farmer married to his wife of 12 years, Maggie, age 28; see 1900 census, Orange County, N.C., e.d. 65, p. 16. It may be significant that Manual McCall went by the name of (or that white reporters called him) "Manly." *Wilmington (N.C.) Messenger,* Nov. 3, 1898 ("fellow"). These parallel the 1870 Virginia elopement in which a Democratic newspaper attributed the liaison to the white family's support of the "Radical negro-equality party"; see *Richmond Daily Dispatch,* Nov. 29, 1870; chap. 7, n. 9, above.

38. "Race Troubles," 625 (Manly's words and Felton's response); see also *Atlanta Journal,* Nov. 15, 1898. *Raleigh (N.C.) News and Observer,* Aug. 25, 1898 (averted lynching). One white man remembered that Manly's life was saved in order not to "discredit" the white community; see Thomas W. Clawson, "The Wilmington Race Riot of 1898: Recollections and Memories," 5, in Thomas W. Clawson Papers, SHC, and Louis T. Moore Collection, NCDAH.

39. On the foregoing events, see *Wilmington (N.C.) Messenger,* Nov. 10–15, 1898; *Atlanta Constitution,* Nov. 11, 1898 (which states incorrectly that blacks were permitted to vote in the election); "Race Troubles," 623–25; *Durham (N.C.) Daily Sun,* Nov. 10, 1898; Kirk, *Bloody Riot in Wilmington,* NCC (pastor's account). For recountings by white Southerners, all of which include the intertwining of Democratic politics with the protection of white women, see Bourke, "Committee of Twenty-Five"; Clawson, "Wilmington Race Riot" (written in the 1940s); Hayden, *Story of The Wilmington Rebellion;* Meares, "Wilmington Revolution," NCDAH; McKelway, "Cause of the Troubles"; "North Carolina Race Conflict"; George Rountree, "My Personal Recollections of the Election of 1898," n.d., in Henry Groves Connor Papers, SHC; Waddell, "North Carolina Race War"; and for an account critical of fellow whites, Jane Cronly, "Account of the Race Riot in Wilmington, N.C., Nov. 10, 1898," in Cronly Family Papers, WPL.

For secondary accounts, see Anderson, *Race and Politics,* chap. 14; Ayers, *Promise of the New South,* 299–304; Edmonds, *Negro and Fusion Politics,* chaps. 10, 11; Escott, *Many Excellent People,* chap. 10; Prather, *We Have Taken a City;* and Williams, *Crucible of Race,* 195–201. For an analysis that incorporates gender, see Gilmore, *Gender and Jim Crow,* 105–18, also 82–89, 91–104. The massacre was fictionalized by two black writers; see Thorne, *Hanover* (1900), and Chesnutt, *Marrow of Tradition* (1901); see also Sundquist, *To Wake the Nations,* chap. 4. The white writer, Thomas Dixon, Jr., also fictionalized these events in his bestselling novel, *The Leopard's Spots* (1902). On these fictionalized accounts, see Gunning, *Race, Rape, and Lynching,* 29–43, 62–76, 89–96.

40. *Cong. Rec.,* 56th Cong., 1st sess., pt. 2, vol. 33, Feb. 5, 1900, p. 1507.

Clawson, "Wilmington Race Riot," 1, 8. Manly later worked as a painter in Philadelphia and for a time passed for white in order to get work (Prather, *We Have Taken a City,* 159–60).

41. Terrell, "Lynching From a Negro's Point of View," 862. Terrell also described "the white women who apply flaming torches" to the "oil-soaked bodies" of black men (861) and called white women and children "savages" (866).

42. See, e.g., Riley, *Philosophy of Negro Suffrage,* 48, in which he discussed Wells's "uncalled-for crusade . . . resulting in more harm and permanent injury to us."

43. For black protests against ongoing rape of black women by white men, see Year File 1898-17743, Box 1117A, RG 60, NA. On sexual violence against black women after the Civil War, see Bardaglio, *Reconstructing the Household,* 195–97; see also Brown, "Negotiating and Transforming the Public Sphere," 139–41. On the lynching of black women, see Brundage, *Lynching in the New South,* 80–81. On ties between the rape of black women and the lynching of black men, and between the protection and oppression of white women, see Hall, " 'The Mind That Burns in Each Body' " and *Revolt Against Chivalry,* xx–xxi, 155–56. On the rape of white women by white men, see Hall " 'Mind That Burns in Each Body,' " 336; and Brundage, *Lynching in the New South,* 94.

44. Bruce, *Plantation Negro as Freeman,* 84. Simmons, *Solution of the Race Problem,* 21. For a black woman's refutation, see Cooper, *Voice From the South,* 9–47. See also Gaines, *Uplifting the Race,* chap. 5; Guy-Sheftall, *Daughters of Sorrow,* esp. chap. 3; and Higginbotham, "African-American Women's History," 261–62, 263–66.

45. Wells, *Red Record,* 13. *Wilmington (N.C.) Record,* Aug. 18, 1898, reprinted in *Atlanta Constitution,* Nov. 11, 1898 (Manly). Burroughs, "Miss Burroughs Replies," 107. For similar expressions, see, e.g., Huntington, "Negro Womanhood Defended," 280; "Race Problem," 587; and Terrell, "Progress of Colored Women." For a nuanced interpretation of late nineteenth-century black clubwomen countering negative stereotypes, see Hine, "Rape and the Inner Lives of Southern Black Women," 185–89.

46. *Denial of elective franchise in South Carolina,* 234 ("negro blood"); on the one-drop rule, see Myrdal, *American Dilemma,* 113–17; and Williamson, *New People,* chap. 2. Fulkerson, *Negro: As He Was,* 78 ("fair sisters").

47. Carroll, *Negro a Beast,* 187; illustrations on 74, 196, 226. Smith, *Color Line,* 10, 14–15. See also Hoffman, *Race Traits,* 177. For a gloss on this logic, see Myrdal, *American Dilemma,* 589–90.

48. *Plessy v. Ferguson* 163 U.S. 537 (1896); Brief for Homer A. Plessy by Albion W. Tourgée (1895), in Olsen, ed., *Thin Disguise,* 85. On segregation and gender, see Ayers, *Promise of the New South,* 140.

49. Winston, "Relation of the Whites to the Negroes," 108–9. Poe, "Lynching: A Southern View," 156. Harris, "Southern Woman's View," 1354.

Gordon, "Symposium." On gender and white supremacy, see Gilmore, *Gender and Jim Crow*, chap. 4; Hall, *Revolt Against Chivalry*, 149–55; Painter, " 'Social Equality.' "

50. Bruce, *Plantation Negro as Freeman*, 83. *Wilmington (N.C.) Messenger*, Aug. 21, 1898. Wells, *Southern Horrors*, 10 (Coy). See also *Wilmington (N.C.) Messenger*, Nov. 3, 1898, in which a white woman insulted by a black man was described as the daughter of "a very poor and humble, but respectable white man." In a change from many antebellum cases, the Supreme Court of Alabama ruled in an 1887 rape case involving a black man and a white woman that the jury could convict the man "on the uncorroborated testimony of the prosecutrix, although she be impeached for ill-fame in chastity, or otherwise; provided they be satisfied, beyond a reasonable doubt, of the truth of her testimony"; see *Barnett v. State* 83 Ala. 40 (1887), 45.

51. Douglass, "Lessons of the Hour," 579. Wells, "Lynch Law in America," 18. Bruce, *Plantation Negro as Freeman, 55*. See also Bardaglio, *Reconstructing the Household*, 197–98.

52. On the alleged actions that provoked lynching, see Ayers, *Promise of the New South*, 158; Brundage, *Lynching in the New South*, chap. 2, 270–83; Hall, *Revolt Against Chivalry*, 145–49; Shapiro, *White Violence*, 32; Tolnay and Beck, *Festival of Violence*, 46–50, 92; Wells, *Red Record,* chaps. 2, 5, 9; and *Cong. Rec.*, 56th Cong., 1st sess., pt. 3, vol. 33, Feb. 23, 1900, p. 2152. See also McMillen, *Dark Journey*, 23–28, 235–36. Alleged causes unrelated to white women included murder, assault, arson, robbery, burglary, poisoning, looting, pillage, child abuse, trespass, slander, fraud, and gambling, as well as voting, arguing with or insulting a white man, boasting, talking too much, asking for respect, wanting work, using obscene language, and vagrancy.

53. *Montgomery (Ala.) Herald*, Aug. 13, 1887, reprinted in *Montgomery (Ala.) Advertiser*, Aug. 16, 1887 (Duke). A. N. Jackson to Albion W. Tourgée, Lafayette, Ala., Mar. 23, 1892, quoted in Olsen, ed., "Albion W. Tourgée," 195 (minister). Wells, *Southern Horrors*, 5. Douglass, "Reason Why," 474. Turner, "Emigration Convention," 148. Miller, "Possible Remedies," 419.

54. Haygood, "Black Shadow," 172. Smith, "Have American Negroes Too Much Liberty?" 182. Page, "Southern Bully," 303. Speech in Rebecca Latimer Felton Papers, Special Collections, University of Georgia Libraries, quoted in Whites, "Rebecca Latimer Felton and the Wife's Farm," 370. Northen, "Negro at the South," 5–6; he was governor 1890–94. Gordon, "Symposium." On the theme of harmless slaves, see also Sommerville, "Rape Myth in the Old South," 486–87.

55. Douglass, "Lynch Law in the South," 23. Whites' usual explanations were relapse to barbarism or revenge. For similar alarm over the difference between generations of black men, see Bruce, *Plantation Negro as Freeman, 84*; Haygood, "Black Shadow," 173–74; and Page, *The Negro*, chap. 6. A common argument put forth by whites, ignoring or dismissing the racism of the criminal

justice system, was the number of blacks in prison as compared to the number of whites; see Fulkerson, *Negro: As He Was,* 46–52; and Smith, "Have American Negroes Too Much Liberty?" 177–78. On the alleged increase in black criminality, see Du Bois, "Negro and Crime." See also Ayers *Promise of the New South,* 153–54.

56. Smith, "Have American Negroes Too Much Liberty?" 182. *Augusta Chronicle* reprinted in "Miss Wells' Crusade," 366. For further justifications, see Avary, *Dixie After the War,* 382–83, 387; Haygood, "Black Shadow," 168; Northen, "Negro at the South," 15; Poe, "Lynching: A Southern View," 160–61; and Page, *The Negro,* 111, 115.

57. Haygood, "Black Shadow," 171. For the impossibility of fair trial, see Douglass, "Lessons of the Hour," 585–86; Wells-Barnett, "Lynch Law in America," 19; and "Negro Problem . . . to a Southern Colored Woman," 2223. For supposedly ineffective courts, see Clark, "True Remedy for Lynch Law"; and Poe, "Lynching: A Southern View," 158–59. See also Ayers, *Vengeance and Justice,* 245–47; Bardaglio, *Reconstructing the Household,* 214–22; and Tolnay and Beck, *Festival of Violence,* 60–65; chap. 4.

58. "Black Crime of Europa," 304 (quotation). Douglass also condemned "mock modesty" as "absurd and shameless" ("Lessons of the Hour," 585). On white women testifying, see Page, *The Negro,* 98; Poe, "Lynching: A Southern View," 159; and Somerville, "Some Co-operating Causes," 511–12. For blacks' views, see Smith et al., "Is the Criminal Negro Justly Dealt With?" Recall the testimony of a white man that Jourdan Ware's death was justified because "the lady was spared the mortification and shame of appearing in court" (chap. 7, above). Peter W. Bardaglio found that when rape cases involving black men and white women did go to court, the judicial treatment of the defendants "reflected the intensification of hostile racial attitudes in the postwar South"; see *Reconstructing the Household,* 190–95 (quotation on 193).

59. Wells, *Crusade for Justice,* 64 (quotation). Wells told the story of Moss and her investigations in ibid., chap. 6; "Lynch Law in All Its Phases," 173–76; *Red Record,* 73–74; and *Southern Horrors,* esp. 18–19. See also Aptheker, "Suppression of *Free Speech*"; and Tucker, "Miss Ida B. Wells." For Wells's statements about rape not being the leading cause, see "Lynch Law in America," 20–21; "Lynch Law in All Its Phases," 182–83; *Mob Rule,* 48; *Red Record,* 20, 59; and *Southern Horrors,* 14. See also Bruce, "Blood Red Record," 71; and Terrell, "Lynching From a Negro's Point of View," 854. In her autobiography, Wells wrote that she had once accepted the notion that black men deserved lynching for "the terrible crime of rape"; see *Crusade for Justice,* 64.

60. Addams, "Respect for Law"; Wells-Barnett, "Lynching and the Excuse for It" (quotation on 1134). See also Aptheker, ed., "Lynching and Rape."

61. Smith, "Have American Negroes Too Much Liberty?" 182. *Atlanta Journal,* Aug. 12, 1897 (Felton). Harris, "Southern Woman's View," 1355. For similar connections between politics and rape, see Avary, *Dixie After the War,*

377, 384; Carroll, *Negro a Beast,* 280, 292; Northen, "Negro at the South," 16; Page, *The Negro,* 95, 112; and Somerville, "Co-operating Causes," 509. Philip Bruce put the topic of rape and lynching in a chapter entitled "Political Condition"; see *Rise of the New South,* 438–39.

62. Douglass, "Lessons of the Hour," 588. Wells, *Southern Horrors,* 13. Du Bois, *Black Man and Wounded World,* 37. See also Bruce, "Blood Red Record," 82. On Wells's connections between sex and politics, see Carby, *Reconstructing Womanhood,* 107–14, and " 'On the Threshold of Woman's Era.' "

63. Douglass, "Reason Why," 477. Wells, *Red Record,* 11. See also Bederman, "Ida B. Wells's Antilynching Campaign" and *Manliness and Civilization,* chap. 2. On lynching as a form of control and terrorism, see Ayers, *Promise of the New South,* 157; Belknap, *Federal Law and Southern Order,* 7–8; Brundage, *Lynching in the New South,* 6; Davis, *Women, Race, and Class,* chap. 11; Hall, " 'The Mind That Burns in Each Body' " and *Revolt Against Chivalry,* 141; McMillen, *Dark Journey,* 28–32; Tolnay and Beck, *Festival of Violence,* 19–24, 57–60; and Wyatt-Brown, *Southern Honor,* chap. 16. For a cautionary view against reducing lynching to a monolithic model of successful social control, see Brundage, "Varn Mill Riot of 1891."

64. Any dissenting white voices were subject to extreme public attack. Two much-discussed articles by more liberal whites were Sledd, "The Negro: Another View," (1902); and Bassett, "Stirring Up the Fires of Race Antipathy," (1903). For an attack, see Felton, "The Negro, as Discussed by Mr. Andrew Sledd." See also Reed, "Emory College and the Sledd Affair." On less virulent strains of white racism, see Williamson, *Crucible of Race,* chaps. 3, 8. On the lack of recorded opposition to lynching by Southern whites, see McMillen, *Dark Journey,* 245–51.

65. Douglass, "Reason Why," 473; on the pamphlet, see Wells, *Crusade for Justice,* 115–17. Wells, *Red Record,* 7. Year File 1898-17743, Box 1117A, folder 2, Wilmington, Nov. 13, 1898, RG 60, NA (anonymous).

66. For the Hose lynching (Coweta County), see *Atlanta Constitution,* Apr. 24, 1899; *New York Times,* Apr. 24, 1899; *Atlanta Constitution,* Apr. 25, 1899 (editorial). See also NAACP, *Thirty Years of Lynching,* 12–13; Terrell, "Lynching From a Negro's Point of View," 859–860; Wells-Barnett, *Lynch Law in Georgia,* chaps. 2–4, and *Mob Rule,* 3, 45; speech of Congressman George H. White in *Cong. Rec.,* 56th Cong., 1st sess., pt. 3, vol. 33, Feb. 23, 1900, 2151; Brundage, *Lynching in the New South,* 82–84; and Ellis, " 'Rain Down Fire.' "

67. "Reminiscences of W. E. B. Du Bois," 148. Du Bois maintained that after Hose shot his employer, "in order to arouse the neighborhood to find this man, they brought in the charge of rape." See also Du Bois, *Dusk of Dawn,* 67. In other versions, Du Bois turned back after he heard that the fingers were on display farther down the street; see "Pageant in Seven Decades," 254; and *Autobiography,* 221–22.

Epilogue

1. For reflections on the legacy, see, e.g., DeSantis, *For the Color of His Skin;* Didion, "Sentimental Journeys"; duCille, "Blacker the Juice,"; Franklin, *"The Birth of a Nation";* Goodman, *Stories of Scottsboro;* McGovern, *Anatomy of a Lynching;* Morrison, ed., *Race-ing Justice;* Rise, *Martinsville Seven;* Smead, *Blood Justice;* Walker, "Advancing Luna—and Ida B. Wells"; and Whitfield, *Death in the Delta.*

2. On rationality in relation to Hose, see "Reminiscences of W. E. B. Du Bois," 148–49; *Dusk of Dawn,* 67–68; "Pageant in Seven Decades," 254; and *Autobiography,* 221–22.

3. Du Bois, *Souls of Black Folk,* 28. "Rape," 12; he added that "in less than *one-quarter* of the cases of lynching Negroes has rape been even *alleged* as an excuse." *Dusk of Dawn,* 68.

Searching for Stories

1. The case of Nell Butler and Charles is mentioned in Berlin, *Slaves Without Masters,* 33–34; Catterall, ed., *Judicial Cases,* 4:2–3; Getman, "Sexual Control," 128; Hooks, *Ain't I a Woman?* 16; Kimmel "Negro Before the Law," 44–46; McCormac, *White Servitude in Maryland,* 68–69; Morgan, "British Encounters," 172; Woodson, "Beginnings of Miscegenation," 340, and *Negro in Our History,* 111; and Wright, *Free Negro in Maryland,* 28.

2. The case of Polly Lane and Jim is mentioned in Cecil-Fronsman, *Common Whites,* 89; Franklin, *Free Negro,* 37; Johnson, *Ante-Bellum North Carolina* 71; and Wyatt-Brown, *Southern Honor,* 317–18.

3. The case of Dorothea Bourne and Edmond is mentioned in Johnston, *Race Relations,* 254–55; and Williamson, *New People,* 52.

4. Catterall, ed., *Judicial Cases,* 3:33, 50–51, 87–88 (Nunez), 81–82 (Hugly).

5. Gutman, *Black Family,* 82n, 560–61 n. 21, 612–13 n. 9.

6. Brundage, *Lynching in the New South,* 62 (Stamps, Jordan), 319 n. 39 (Davis), 334 n. 68 (Duncan).

Bibliography

Manuscripts

Atlanta Historical Society, Atlanta, Ga.

Abbie M. Brooks Diary

Georgia Department of Archives and History, Atlanta

Board of Physicians:
    Minutes
    Registry of Applicants
Chatham County Court of Ordinary Records
Chattooga County:
    Administrators and Guardian Records
    Inventories and Appraisements
    Ordinary Inferior Court Minutes
Georgia Supreme Court Original Papers (Record Group 92):
    Superior Courts of Floyd, Forsyth, Harris, Houston, Monroe, Sumter, and Warren Counties
Glascock County Superior Court Minutes
Houston County Superior Court Minutes
Monroe County Court of Ordinary Records
"Negroes—Slave Trials" (Record Group 4)

Houghton Library, Harvard University, Cambridge, Mass.

American Freedmen's Inquiry Commission Papers

Library of Virginia, Richmond

Auditor of Public Accounts
Boutetout Circuit Court Common Law Minute Docket
County Court, Ended Cases
Elizabeth City County Deeds, Wills, and Orders
Executive Papers, Letters Received
Hanover County:
    Land Tax Books
    Maps
Henrico County:
    Court Minute Books
    Deed Books
    Records
King and Queen County Circuit Superior Court Order Book

Legislative Papers, Petitions
Louisa County:
  Land Tax Books
  Will Books
Petersburg Hustings Court Minute Book
Richmond City Hustings Court, Ended Cases
Virginia Correspondence, Board of Trade, Virginia Colonial Records
Project
York County Deeds, Orders, Wills

Maryland Hall of Records, Annapolis

Anne Arundel County Court Judgments
Charles County:
  Court Proceedings
  Inventories and Accounts
  Wills
Court of Appeals Judgments
Dorchester County Court Proceedings in Dorchester County Land
Records
Queen Anne County:
  County Criminal Record
  Court Judgment Record
Prerogative Court Inventories
Prince George's County:
  County Court Papers, "Blacks"
  Court Records
Provincial Court Judgements
Somerset County Judicial Record
Talbot County:
  Civil Judgments
  Court Judgments
  Judgments in Talbot County Land Records

Maryland Historical Society, Baltimore

Stephen Bordley Letter Book

National Archives, Washington, D.C.

Record Group 21. Records of the District Courts of the United States
Record Group 60. Records of the Department of Justice
Record Group 94. Records of the Adjutant General's Office
Record Group 105. Records of the Bureau of Refugees, Freedmen and
Abandoned Lands

Record Group 153. Records of the Office of the Judge Advocate General (Army)

North Carolina Division of Archives and History, Raleigh

Bertie County Superior Court Minutes
Craven County Court Minutes
Davidson County:
  Bastardy Bonds and Records
  Court Minutes
  Superior Court Recognizance Docket
  Tax Lists
Davie County Miscellaneous Records
Gates County Superior Court Minute Docket
General Assembly Session Records:
  Committee of Divorce and Alimony
  Committee of Propositions and Grievances
  House Bills
  House Committee Reports
  Miscellaneous Court Cases
  Miscellaneous Petitions
  Senate Bills
  Senate Committee Reports
Governors' Papers and Letter Books:
  Thomas Bragg, Hutchins G. Burton, Edward B. Dudley, John W. Ellis, Montfort Stokes, and Zebulon B. Vance
Orange County:
  Criminal Action Papers
  Superior Court Minute Docket
Marriage Bonds
Montgomery County Miscellaneous Records
Louis T. Moore Collection
Onslow County Criminal Actions Concerning Slaves
Pasquotank County:
  Court Minutes
  Superior Court Docket
Rutherford County Court Minutes
Secretary of State Court Records
Edmund Smithwick and Family Papers
State Supreme Court Manuscript Records:
  Superior Courts of Ashe, Bertie, Buncombe, Caswell, Currituck, Granville, Hertford, Lenoir, Mecklenburg, Montgomery, Nash, Orange, Person, Rutherford, and Wayne Counties
Statewide Index to Marriages

Schomburg Center for Research in Black Culture,
New York Public Library, New York

John Edward Bruce Papers
Robert G. Fitzgerald Papers

Southern Historical Collection, Manuscript Department, Wilson Library,
University of North Carolina, Chapel Hill

Jessie Daniel Ames Papers
Thomas W. Clawson Papers
Henry Groves Connor Papers
Grace B. Elmore Diary
Mary T. Hunley Diary
Lipscomb Family Papers
David Schenck Books
Skinner Family Papers
William D. Valentine Diaries

William R. Perkins Library, Manuscript Collection,
Duke University, Durham, N.C.

Charles E. Bridges Papers
Robert Carter Plantation Records
Sydney S. Champion Papers
Cronly Family Papers
John C. Gorman Papers
Benjamin Sherwood Hedrick Papers
Ku Klux Klan Papers
Eugene Marshall Papers
George Junkin Ramsey Papers

Census Records

Chappelear, Nancy, ed. *Hanover County, Virginia, 1810 and 1820 Census Records.* Washington, D.C.: Chappelear, 1966.
Heads of Families at the First Census of the United States Taken in the Year 1790, Maryland. Baltimore: Genealogical Publishing, 1972.
U.S. Bureau of the Census. Manuscript Census Schedules.
   Third through Twelfth Censuses. 1810–1900.
———. Slave Schedules. Seventh Census. 1850.
———. *1850 Federal Census, Agricultural Schedule.* Burke County, Ga.

Newspapers
Athens (Ga.) Southern Banner
Athens (Ga.) Southern Watchman
Atlanta Constitution
Atlanta Journal
Baltimore American and Commercial Advertiser
Baltimore Sun
Colored American (Augusta, Ga.)
Columbus (Ga.) Daily Sun
Daily Richmond Enquirer
Dalton North Georgia Citizen
Durham (N.C.) Daily Sun
Edenton (N.C.) Gazette
Fredericksburg Virginia Herald
Greensboro (N.C.) Patriot
Hillsborough (N.C.) Recorder
Hinds County (Miss.) Gazette
Jackson (Miss.) Daily Clarion
Kentucky Gazette
Louisville (Ky.) Commercial
Macon (Ga.) Daily Telegraph
Maryland Gazette
Montgomery (Ala.) Advertiser
Montgomery (Ala.) Herald
New Orleans True Delta
New York Daily Tribune
New York Times
Niles' Weekly Register
North Carolina Weekly Standard
Philadelphia American Weekly Mercury
Raleigh (N.C.) News and Observer
Raleigh (N.C.) Progressive Farmer
Raleigh Register and North Carolina State Gazette
Richmond Daily Dispatch
Richmond Dispatch
Richmond Enquirer
Richmond Planet
Richmond Southern Opinion
Richmond State
Star and North Carolina State Gazette
Washington Bee
Western Carolinian (Paris, Ky.)
Wilmington (N.C.) Daily Journal

Wilmington (N.C.) Daily Record
Wilmington (N.C.) Messenger

Colonial and State Supreme Court Reports. 1769–1897.
Alabama
Arkansas
Florida
Georgia
Kentucky
Maryland
Mississippi
Missouri
North Carolina
Tennessee
Texas
Virginia
Washington, D.C.

Published Primary Sources
"Abstracts from Records of Richmond County, Virginia." *William and Mary Quarterly,* 1st ser., 17 (1908): 73–85.
Acts of the General Assembly of the Commonwealth of Virginia. Richmond, 1815–48.
Addams, Jane. "Respect for Law." *Independent* 53 (Jan. 3, 1901): 18–20.
"An Anti-Lynching Crusade in America Begun." *Literary Digest* 9 (Aug. 11, 1894): 421–22.
Archives of Maryland. Baltimore: Maryland Historical Society, 1883–1972.
Avary, Myrta Lockett. *Dixie After the War: An Exposition of Social Conditions Existing in the South, During the Twelve Years Succeeding the Fall of Richmond.* 1906. Reprint, New York: Negro Universities Press, 1969.
Bassett, John Spencer. "Stirring Up the Fires of Race Antipathy." *South Atlantic Quarterly* 2 (October 1903): 297–305.
Berlin, Ira, ed. *The Black Military Experience. Freedom: A Documentary History of Emancipation, 1861–1867,* ser. 2. New York: Cambridge University Press, 1982.
Billings, Warren M., ed. *The Old Dominion in the Seventeenth Century: A Documentary History of Virginia, 1606–1689.* Chapel Hill: University of North Carolina Press, 1975.
"The Black Crime of Europa." *Voice of the Negro* 1 (August 1904): 304. Reprint, *The Black Experience in America: Negro Periodicals in the United States, 1840–1960.* New York: Negro Universities Press, 1969.

Blassingame, John W., ed. *Slave Testimony: Two Centuries of Letters, Speeches, Interviews, and Autobiographies*. Baton Rouge: Louisiana State University Press, 1977.

Bourke, Charles Francis. "The Committee of Twenty-Five." *Collier's Weekly* 22 (Nov. 26, 1898): 5, 16.

Bruce, John Edward. "The Blood Red Record: A Review of the Horrible Lynchings and Burning of Negroes by Civilized White Men in the United States" (1901). In *The Selected Writings of John Edward Bruce: Militant Black Journalist*, edited by Peter Gilbert. New York: Arno Press and New York Times, 1971.

Bruce, Philip A. *The Plantation Negro as a Freeman: Observations on His Character, Condition, and Prospects in Virginia*. New York: G. P. Putnam's Sons, 1889.

———. *The Rise of the New South*. Philadelphia: George Barrie and Sons, 1905.

Buckingham, J. S. *The Slave States of America*. 1842. Reprint, New York: Negro Universities Press, 1968.

Burroughs, Nannie H. "Miss Burroughs Replies to Mr. Carrington." *Voice of the Negro* 2 (February 1905): 106–7. Reprint, *The Black Experience in America: Negro Periodicals in the United States, 1840-1960*. New York: Negro Universities Press, 1969.

Campbell, Sir George. *White and Black: The Outcome of a Visit to the United States*. 1879. Reprint, New York: Negro Universities Press, 1969.

Candler, Allen D., ed. *Colonial Records of Georgia*. Atlanta: State Printers, 1904–16.

Carroll, Charles. *The Negro a Beast; or, In the Image of God*. St. Louis, Mo.: American Book and Bible House, 1900.

Catterall, Helen Tunnicliff, ed. *Judicial Cases Concerning American Slavery and the Negro*. Washington, D.C.: Carnegie Institute, 1926–37.

Chambers, William. *American Slavery and Colour*. 1857. Reprint, New York: Negro Universities Press, 1968.

Chesnut, Mary Boykin. *Mary Chesnut's Civil War*. Edited by C. Vann Woodward. New Haven: Yale University Press, 1981.

Chesnutt, Charles. *The Marrow of Tradition*. 1901. Reprint, Ann Arbor: University of Michigan Press, 1969.

Clark, R. H., T. R. R. Cobb, and D. Irwin. *Code of the State of Georgia*. Atlanta: John H. Seals, 1861.

Clark, Walter, ed. *State Records of North Carolina*. Winston and Goldsboro: State Printers, 1895–1906.

———. "The True Remedy for Lynch Law." *American Law Review* 28 (1894): 801–7.

Cocke, William, ed. *Hanover County Chancery Wills and Notes*. Columbus, Va.: Cocke, 1940.

Constitution of the State of North Carolina, Together with the Ordinances and Resolutions of the Constitutional Convention. Raleigh, 1868.

Cook, Joseph. "New Black Codes at the South." *Our Day* 12 (July 1893): 35–57.

Cooper, Anna Julia. *A Voice from the South by a Black Woman of the South.* 1892. Reprint, New York: Oxford University Press, 1988.

[Croly, David Goodman, and George Wakeman]. *Miscegenation: The Theory of the Blending of the Races, Applied to the American White Man and Negro.* New York: n.p., 1863.

Daniels, Josephus. *Editor in Politics.* Chapel Hill: University of North Carolina Press, 1941.

De Forest, John William. *A Union Officer in the Reconstruction.* Edited by James H. Croushore and David Morris Potter. New Haven: Yale University Press, 1948.

Debates and Proceedings of the Convention Which Assembled at Little Rock, January 7th, 1868. Little Rock, Ark.: 1868.

Delany, Sarah, and A. Elizabeth Delany, with Amy Hill Hearth. *Having Our Say: The Delany Sisters' First Hundred Years.* New York: Kodansha International, 1993.

Dennett, John Richard. *The South as It Is: 1865–1866.* 1865–66. Reprint, edited by Henry M. Christman. New York: Viking, 1965.

Dickenson, Richard B., comp. *Entitled! Free Papers in Appalachia Concerning Antebellum Freeborn Negroes and Emancipated Blacks of Montgomery County, Virginia.* Washington, D.C.: National Genealogical Society, 1981.

Directory of Richmond, Va. Richmond: J. L. Hill, 1897.

Dixon, Thomas, Jr. *The Leopard's Spots.* New York: Doubleday, Page, 1902.

Dixon, William Hepworth. *New America.* London: Hurst and Blackett, 1867.

Dodge, David. "The Free Negroes of North Carolina." *Atlantic Monthly* 57 (January 1886): 20–30.

Douglass, Frederick. "The Future of the Colored Race." *North American Review* 142 (May 1886): 437–40.

———. "Introduction to the Reason Why the Colored American Is Not in the World's Columbian Exposition" (1892). In *The Life and Writings of Frederick Douglass,* edited by Philip S. Foner. New York: International Publishers, 1955.

———. "Lessons of the Hour" (1894). In *The Frederick Douglass Papers,* edited by John W. Blassingame and John R. McKivigan. New Haven: Yale University Press, 1992.

———. "Lynch Law in the South." *North American Review* 155 (July 1892): 17–24.

————. "Lynching Black People Because They Are Black." *Our Day* 13 (July–August 1894): 298–306.

————. "The Negro Problem" (1890). In *The Frederick Douglass Papers,* edited by John W. Blassingame and John R. McKivigan. New Haven: Yale University Press, 1992.

Du Bois, W. E. B. *The Autobiography of W. E. B. Du Bois: A Soliloquy on Viewing My Life from the Last Decade of Its First Century.* New York: International Publishers, 1968.

————. *The Black Man and the Wounded World* (n.d.). In *The World of W. E. B. Du Bois: A Quotation Sourcebook,* edited by Meyer Weinberg. Westport, Conn.: Greenwood, 1992.

————. *Dusk of Dawn: An Essay Toward an Autobiography of a Race Concept.* New York: Harcourt, Brace, 1940.

————. "The Negro and Crime." *Independent* 51 (May 18, 1899): 1355–57.

————. "A Pageant in Seven Decades: 1868–1938." In *Pamphlets and Leaflets by W. E. B. Du Bois,* edited by Herbert Aptheker. White Plains, N.Y.: Kraus-Thomson, 1986.

————. "Rape." *The Crisis: A Record of the Darker Races* 18 (May 1919): 12–13.

————. "The Reminiscences of W. E. B. Du Bois." New York: Columbia University Oral History Research Office, 1960.

Easterby, J. H., ed. *The South Carolina Rice Plantation, as Revealed in the Papers of Robert F. W. Allston.* Chicago: University of Chicago Press, 1945.

Elliott, E. N., ed. *Cotton Is King, and Pro-Slavery Arguments.* 1860. Reprint, New York: Johnson Reprint, 1968.

Felton, Mrs. W. H. [Rebecca Latimer]. "The Negro, as Discussed by Mr. Andrew Sledd." *Atlanta Constitution,* Aug. 3, 1902.

Fontaine, James. *Memoirs of a Huguenot Family.* Translated and compiled by Ann Maury. New York: George P. Putnam, 1853.

Formwalt, Lee W. "Notes and Documents: A Case of Interracial Marriage During Reconstruction." *Alabama Review* 45 (1992): 216–24.

Fortune, T. Thomas. *Black and White: Land, Labor, and Politics in the South.* 1884. Reprint, New York: Arno Press and New York Times, 1968.

"The Frightful Experience of Julius Gardner of Arkansas." In *The Black Man's Burden; or, The Horrors of Southern Lynchings,* by Irenas J. Palmer. Olean, N.Y.: Olean Evening Herald Print, 1902.

Fulkerson, H. S. *The Negro: As He Was, As He Is, As He Will Be.* Vicksburg, Miss.: Commercial Herald, 1887.

Gordon, Loulie M. "How Shall the Women and the Girls in Country Districts Be Protected? A Symposium Secured by Mrs. Loulie M. Gordon." *Atlanta Constitution,* Apr. 23, 1899.

Graham, D. A. "Some Facts About Southern Lynchings" (1899). In *The Voice of Black America: Major Speeches by Negroes in the United States, 1797–1971*, edited by Philip S. Foner. New York: Simon and Schuster, 1972.

Green, Ely. *Ely: Too Black, Too White*. Edited by Elizabeth N. and Arthur Ben Chitty. Amherst: University of Massachusetts Press, 1970.

Grimké, Archibald H. "The Sex Question and Race Segregation." 1915. In *The American Negro Academy, Occasional Papers 1–22*. Reprint, New York: Arno Press and New York Times, 1969.

Grimké, Francis J. *The Lynching of Negroes in the South: Its Causes and Remedy*. Washington, D.C., 1899.

Guild, June Purcell, ed. *Black Laws of Virginia*. Richmond: Whittet and Shepperson, 1936.

Hamilton, Adelbert. "Miscegenetic Marriages." *Central Law Journal* 13 (1881): 121–24.

Harris, Mrs. L. H. [Corra]. "A Southern Woman's View." *Independent* 51 (May 18, 1899): 1354–55.

Hayden, Harry. *The Story of the Wilmington Rebellion*. Wilmington, N.C.: Hayden, 1936.

Haygood, Atticus G. "The Black Shadow in the South." *Forum* 16 (October 1893): 167–75.

Hazard, Ebenezer. "The Journal of Ebenezer Hazard in North Carolina, 1777 and 1778." Edited by Hugh Buckner Johnson. *North Carolina Historical Review* 36 (1959): 358–81.

Helper, Hinton Rowan. *Nojoque: A Question for a Continent*. New York: George W. Carleton, 1867.

Hening, William Waller, ed. *The Statutes at Large: Being a Collection of all the Laws of Virginia from the First Session of the Legislature, in the Year 1619*. 1819–23. Reprint, Charlottesville: University Press of Virginia, 1969.

Hoffman, Frederick L. *Race Traits and Tendencies of the American Negro*. New York: MacMillan, 1896.

"How Miss Wells' Crusade Is Regarded in America." *Literary Digest* 9 (July 28, 1894): 366–67.

Howe, Samuel Gridley. *The Refugees from Slavery in Canada West: Report to the Freedmen's Inquiry Commission*. 1864. Reprint, New York: Arno Press and New York Times, 1969.

Huntington, Addie. "Negro Womanhood Defended." *Voice of the Negro* (July 1904): 280–82. Reprint, *The Black Experience in America: Negro Periodicals in the United States, 1840–1960*. New York: Negro Universities Press, 1969.

Hurd, John Codman, ed. *The Law of Freedom and Bondage in the United States*. 1858. Reprint, New York: Negro Universities Press, 1968.

Jacobs, Harriet A. *Incidents in the Life of a Slave Girl, Written by Her-*

self. Edited by Jean Fagan Yellin. Cambridge, Mass.: Harvard University Press, 1987.

Janson, Charles William. *The Stranger in America, 1793–1806.* 1807. Reprint, New York: Press of the Pioneers, 1935.

Journal of the House of Delegates of the Commonwealth of Virginia. 1802–49.

King, Edward. *The Great South: A Record of Journeys.* 1875. Reprint, New York: Arno Press and New York Times, 1969.

Kirk, Rev. J. Allen, D.D. *A Statement of Facts Concerning the Bloody Riot in Wilmington, N.C.* N.p., n.d., North Carolina Collection, Wilson Library, University of North Carolina, Chapel Hill.

Laws of Maryland. Annapolis: Frederick Green, 1791.

Laws of North Carolina. 1823.

Laws of North Carolina. 1831.

Laws of North Carolina. 1838–39.

Laws of Virginia. 1803.

The Lincoln Catechism, Wherein the Eccentricities and Beauties of Despotism Are Fully Set Forth: A Guide to the Presidential Election of 1864. New York, 1864. In *Union Pamphlets of the Civil War, 1861–1865,* edited by Frank Freidel. Cambridge, Mass.: Harvard University Press, 1967.

"Lynching: Its Cause and Cure, by a Resident of North Carolina." *Independent* 46 (Feb. 1, 1894): 132.

Marbury, H., and William Crawford, eds. *Digest of the Laws of the State of Georgia.* Savannah, Ga.: Seymour, 1802.

Meares, Iredell. "The Wilmington Revolution" (ca. 1900). In Edmund Smithwick and Family Papers, NCDAH.

McIlwaine, H. R., ed. *Journals of the House of Burgesses of Virginia.* Richmond: n.p., 1912.

McKelway, A. J. "The Cause of the Troubles in North Carolina." *Independent* 50 (Nov. 24, 1898): 1488–92.

McPherson, Robert G., ed. "Documents: Georgia Slave Trials, 1837–1849." *American Journal of Legal History* 4 (1960): 257–84.

Miller, Kelly. "Possible Remedies for Lynching." *Southern Workman and Hampton School Record* 28 (November 1899): 418–23.

Miscegenation Indorsed by the Republican Party. Campaign Document No. 11. New York: n.p., 1864.

Morgan, A. T. *Yazoo; or, On the Picket Line of Freedom in the South: A Personal Narrative.* 1884. Reprint, New York: Russell and Russell, 1968.

Morgan, John T. "The Race Question in the United States." *Arena* 2 (September 1890): 385–98.

"The Negro Problem: How It Appeals to a Southern Colored Woman." *Independent* 54 (Sept. 18, 1902): 2221–24.

"The Negro Problem: How It Appeals to a Southern White Woman." *Independent* 54 (Sept. 18, 1902): 2224–28.

Neilson, Peter. *Recollections of a Six Years' Residence in the United States of America.* Glasgow: David Robertson, 1830.

[Newcomb, H.] *The "Negro Pew": Being an Inquiry Concerning the Propriety of Distinctions in the House of God, on Account of Color.* 1837. Reprint, Freeport, N.Y.: Books for Libraries Press, 1971.

"The North Carolina Race Conflict." *Outlook* 60 (Nov. 19, 1898): 707-9.

Northen, W. J. "The Negro at the South" (1899). In *Anti-Black Thought, 1863-1925: Disfranchisement Proposals and the Ku Klux Klan,* edited by John David Smith. New York: Garland, 1993.

Olsen, Otto H., ed. "Albion W. Tourgée and Negro Militants of the 1890s: A Documentary Selection." *Science and Society* 28 (1964): 183-208.

———. *The Thin Disguise: Turning Point in Negro History; Plessy v. Ferguson; A Documentary Presentation, 1864-1896.* New York: Humanities Press, 1967.

Pace v. Alabama 106 U.S. 583 (1883).

Page, Thomas Nelson. *The Negro: The Southerner's Problem.* 1904. Reprint, New York: Johnson Reprint, 1970.

Page, Walter H. "The Last Hold of the Southern Bully." *Forum* 16 (November 1893): 303-14.

Plessy v. Ferguson 163 U.S. 537 (1896).

Poe, Clarence H. "Lynching: A Southern View." *Atlantic Monthly* 93 (February 1904): 155-65.

Presley, Samuel C. *Negro Lynching in the South: Treating of the Negro. His Past and Present Condition; Of the Cause of Lynching, and the Means to Remedy the Evil.* Washington, D.C.: Thos. W. Cadick, 1899.

Prince, Oliver, ed. *A Digest of the Laws of the State of Georgia.* Milledgeville, Ga., 1822.

Proceedings and Debates of the Convention of North-Carolina, 1835. Raleigh: n.p., 1863.

"The Race Problem—An Autobiography, by a Southern Colored Woman." *Independent* 56 (Mar. 17, 1904): 586-89.

"Race Troubles in the Carolinas." *Literary Digest* 17 (Nov. 26, 1898): 623-27.

Rankin, John. *Letters on American Slavery, Addressed to Mr. Thomas Rankin, Merchant at Middlebrook, Augusta Co., Va.* Boston: Garrison and Knapp, 1833.

Rawick, George P., ed. *The American Slave: A Composite Autobiography.* 1941. Reprint, Westport, Conn.: Greenwood, 1972.

Redpath, James. *The Roving Editor; or, Talks with Slaves in the Southern States.* New York: A. B. Burdick, 1859.

Reeves, Henry, and Mary Jo Davis Shoaf. *Davidson County North Carolina Will Summaries, 1823-1846.* Lexington, N.C., 1979.

Revised Laws of North Carolina. 1821.

Revised Laws of North Carolina. 1823.

Revised Statutes of North Carolina. 1836–37.

Riley, Jerome R. *The Philosophy of Negro Suffrage.* Hartford, Conn.: American Publishing, 1895.

Ripley, C. Peter, ed. *The Black Abolitionist Papers.* Chapel Hill: University of North Carolina Press, 1992.

[Royall, Anne.] *Sketches of History, Life, and Manners in the United States, by a Traveller.* 1826. Reprint, New York: Johnson Reprint, 1970.

Saunders, William, ed. *Colonial Records of North Carolina.* Raleigh: State Printers, 1886–90.

Schurz, Carl. *Report on the Condition of the South.* 39th Cong., 1st sess., 1865. S. Exec. Doc. 2. Reprint, New York: Arno Press and New York Times, 1969.

Seaman, L. *What Miscegenation Is! What We Are to Expect Now That Mr. Lincoln Is Re-elected.* New York: Waller and Willetts, 1864.

Session Laws of North Carolina. 1807.

Session Laws of North Carolina. 1818.

Simmons, Enoch Spencer. *A Solution of the Race Problem in the South.* Raleigh, N.C.: Edwards and Broughton, 1898.

Sledd, Andrew. "The Negro: Another View." *Atlantic Monthly* 90 (July 1902): 65–73.

Smith, Billy G., and Richard Wojtowicz, comps. *Blacks Who Stole Themselves: Advertisements for Runaways in the Pennsylvania Gazette, 1728–1790.* Philadelphia: University of Pennsylvania Press, 1989.

Smith, Chas. H. "Have American Negroes Too Much Liberty?" *Forum* 16 (October 1893): 176–83.

Smith, Joseph, and Philip Crowl, eds. *Court Records of Prince George's County, Maryland, 1696–1699.* Washington, D.C.: American Historical Association, 1964.

Smith, Reuben S., et al. "Is the Criminal Negro Justly Dealt with in the Courts of the South?" In *Twentieth Century Negro Literature; or, A Cyclopedia of Thought on the Vital Topics Relating to the American Negro,* edited by D. W. Culp. 1902. Reprint, New York: Arno Press and New York Times, 1969.

Smith, William Benjamin. *The Color Line: A Brief in Behalf of the Unborn* (1905). In *Anti-Black Thought, 1863–1925: Racial Determinism and the Fear of Miscegenation Post 1900,* edited by John David Smith. New York: Garland, 1993.

Somerville, Henderson M. "Some Co-operating Causes of Negro Lynching." *North American Review* 177 (October 1903): 506–12.

Stearns, Charles. *The Black Man of the South and the Rebels; or, The Characteristics of the Former, and the Recent Outrages of the Latter.* 1872. Reprint, New York: Negro Universities Press, 1969.

Sterling, Dorothy, ed., *We Are Your Sisters: Black Women in the Nineteenth Century.* New York: W. W. Norton, 1984.

Terrell, Mary Church. "Lynching from a Negro's Point of View." *North American Review* 178 (June 1904): 853–68.

———. "The Progress of Colored Women." *Voice of the Negro* 1 (July 1904): 291–94. Reprint, *The Black Experience in America: Negro Periodicals in the United States, 1840–1960.* New York: Negro Universities Press, 1969.

Third Annual Message of W. W. Holden. Raleigh, N.C.: n.p., 1870.

Thomas, Ella Gertrude Clanton. *The Secret Eye: The Journal of Ella Gertrude Clanton Thomas, 1848–1889.* Edited by Virginia Ingraham Burr. Chapel Hill: University of North Carolina Press, 1990.

Thorne, Jack [David Bryant Fulton]. *Hanover; or, The Persecution of the Lowly: A Story of the Wilmington Massacre.* 1900. Reprint, New York: Arno Press and New York Times, 1969.

Thorpe, Margaret Newbold. "Life in Virginia, by a 'Yankee Teacher.'" Edited by Richard L. Morton. *Virginia Magazine of History and Biography* 64 (1956): 180–207.

Tourgée, Albion Winegar. *A Fool's Errand by One of the Fools.* New York: Fords, Howard and Hulbert, 1880.

———. *The Invisible Empire.* 1880. Reprint, Baton Rouge: Louisiana State University Press, 1989.

Trial of William W. Holden, Governor of North Carolina, Before the Senate of North Carolina. Raleigh: n.p., 1871.

Trowbridge, J. T. *The South: A Tour of Its Battle-Fields and Ruined Cities.* Hartford, Conn.: L. Stebbins, 1866.

Turner, Henry McNeal. "I Claim the Rights of a Man" (1868). In *The Voice of Black America: Major Speeches by Negroes in the United States, 1797–1971,* edited by Philip S. Foner. New York: Simon and Schuster, 1972.

———. "An Emigration Convention" (1893). In *Respect Black: The Writings and Speeches of Henry McNeal Turner,* edited by Edwin S. Redkey. New York: Arno Press and New York Times, 1971.

U.S. Congress. *Congressional Globe.* Washington, D.C., 1864–72.

———. *Congressional Record.* Washington, D.C., 1873–1900.

———. *Report of the Joint Committee on Reconstruction,* 39th Cong., 1st sess., 1865.

———. *Report of the Joint Select Committee to Inquire into the Condition of Affairs in the Late Insurrectionary States.* 42d Cong., 2d sess., 1872. 13 vols. S. Rept. 41, pt. 1.

U.S. Congress. House. *Condition of Affairs in Georgia, pt. 1; Evidence Taken Before Committee on Reconstruction.* 40th Cong., 3d sess., 1868–69. H.R. Misc. Doc. 52.

————. *Testimony Taken by the Sub-Committee of Elections in Louisiana*. 41st Cong., 2d sess., 1869. H.R. Misc. Doc. 154.

U.S. Congress. Senate. *Denial of Elective Franchise in Mississippi*. 44th Cong., 1st sess., 1875–76. S. Rept. 527.

————. *Denial of Elective Franchise in South Carolina*. 44th Cong., 2d sess., 1877. S. Misc. Doc. 48.

————. *Select Committee to Investigate Alleged Outrages in Southern States*. 42d Cong., 1st sess., 1871. S. Rept. 1.

U.S. War Department. *The War of the Rebellion: A Compilation of the Official Records of the Union and Confederate Armies*. Washington, D.C.: Government Printing Office, 1880–1901.

Van Evrie, J. H. *White Supremacy and Negro Subordination; or, Negroes a Subordinate Race, and (So-Called) Slavery Its Normal Condition*. New York: Van Evrie, Horton, 1868.

The Virginia Report of 1799–1800, Touching the Alien and Sedition Laws, Together with the Virginia Resolutions of December 21, 1798. 1850. Reprint, New York: Da Capo Press, 1970.

Waddell, Alfred M. "The North Carolina Race War." *Collier's Weekly* 22 (Nov. 26, 1898): 4–5, 16.

Walker, David. *David Walker's Appeal: To the Coloured Citizens of the World*. 1829. Reprint, New York: Hill and Wang, 1995.

Wells, Ida B. "Bishop Tanner's Ray of Light." *Independent* 44 (July 28, 1892): 1045–46.

————. *Crusade for Justice: The Autobiography of Ida B. Wells*. Edited by Alfreda M. Duster. Chicago: University of Chicago Press, 1970.

————. "Lynch Law in All Its Phases" (1893). In *Ida B. Wells-Barnett: An Exploratory Study of an American Black Woman, 1893–1930*, by Mildred I. Thompson. New York: Carlson, 1990.

————. *A Red Record: Tabulated Statistics and Alleged Causes of Lynchings in the United States, 1892–1893–1894* (1895). Reprinted in Ida B. Wells-Barnett, *On Lynchings*. Salem, N.H.: Ayer, 1991.

————. *Southern Horrors: Lynch Law in All Its Phases* (1892). Reprinted in Ida B. Wells-Barnett, *On Lynchings*. Salem, N.H.: Ayer, 1991.

Wells-Barnett, Ida B. "Lynch Law in America." *Arena* 23 (January 1900): 15–24.

————. *Lynch Law in Georgia*. Chicago: n.p., 1899.

————. "Lynching and the Excuse for It." *Independent* 53 (May 16, 1901): 1133–36.

————. "Lynching: Our National Crime" (1909). In *Ida B. Wells-Barnett: An Exploratory Study of an American Black Woman, 1893–1930*, by Mildred I. Thompson. Brooklyn, N.Y.: Carlson, 1990.

————. *Mob Rule in New Orleans: Robert Charles and His Fight to the Death*.

Chicago: n.p., 1900. Reprinted in Ida B. Wells-Barnett, *On Lynchings*. Salem, N.H.: Ayer, 1991.

West, Henry Litchfield. "The Race War in North Carolina." *Forum* 26 (January 1899): 578–91.

Winston, George T. "The Relation of the Whites to the Negroes." *Annals of the American Academy of Political Science* 18 (July 1901): 105–18.

Wood, Judson P., trans., and John S. Ezell, ed. *The New Democracy in America: Travels of Francisco de Miranda in the United States, 1783–84*. Norman: University of Oklahoma Press, 1963.

Secondary Sources

Alexander, Adele Logan. *Ambiguous Lives: Free Women of Color in Rural Georgia, 1789–1879*. Fayetteville: University of Arkansas Press, 1991.

Alexander, Ann Field. "Black Protest in the New South: John Mitchell, Jr. (1862–1929), and the Richmond *Planet*." Ph.D. diss., Duke University, 1973.

Alpert, Jonathan. "The Origin of Slavery in the United States—The Maryland Precedent." *American Journal of Legal History* 14 (1970): 189–221.

Anderson, Eric. *Race and Politics in North Carolina, 1872–1901: The Black Second*. Baton Rouge: Louisiana State University Press, 1981.

Applebaum, Harvey M. "Miscegenation Statutes: A Constitutional and Social Problem." *Georgetown Law Journal* 53 (1964): 49–91.

Aptheker, Bettina, ed. "Lynching and Rape: An Exchange of Views." San Jose State University Occasional Papers No. 25. New York and San Jose: American Institute for Marxist Studies, 1977.

———. "The Suppression of the *Free Speech*: Ida B. Wells and the Memphis Lynching, 1892." *San Jose Studies* 3 (1977): 34–40.

Aptheker, Herbert. *Anti-Racism in U.S. History: The First Two Hundred Years*. Westport, Conn.: Praeger, 1993.

Arnold, Marybeth Hamilton. " 'The Life of a Citizen in the Hands of a Woman': Sexual Assault in New York City, 1790 to 1820." In *Passion and Power: Sexuality in History*, edited by Kathy Peiss and Christina Simmons. Philadelphia: Temple University Press, 1989.

Ashe, Samuel, Stephen Weeks, and Charles Van Noppen, eds. *Biographical History of North Carolina from Colonial Times to the Present*. Greensboro, N.C.: Van Noppen, 1917.

Ayers, Edward L. *The Promise of the New South: Life After Reconstruction*. New York: Oxford University Press, 1992.

———. *Vengeance and Justice: Crime and Punishment in the Nineteenth-Century American South*. New York: Oxford University Press, 1984.

Bagby, James Morris. "The First Generation of the Shelton Family in Louisa County." *Louisa County Historical Magazine* 11 (1979): 32–37.

Baker, Robert. *Chattooga County: The Story of a County and Its People.* Roswell, Ga.: Historical Publications Division, 1988.

Baldwin, Nell, and A. M. Hillhouse. *An Intelligent Student's Guide to Burke County (Ga.) History.* Waynesboro, Ga., 1956, GDAH.

Bardaglio, Peter W. "Rape and the Law in the Old South: 'Calculated to excite indignation in every heart.'" *Journal of Southern History* 60 (1994): 749–72.

———. *Reconstructing the Household: Families, Sex, and the Law in the Nineteenth-Century South.* Chapel Hill: University of North Carolina Press, 1995.

Bederman, Gail. "'Civilization,' the Decline of Middle-Class Manliness, and Ida B. Wells's Antilynching Campaign (1892–94)." *Radical History Review* 52 (1992): 5–30.

———. *Manliness and Civilization: A Cultural History of Gender and Race in the United States, 1880–1917.* Chicago: University of Chicago Press, 1995.

Belknap, Michael R. *Federal Law and Southern Order: Racial Violence and Constitutional Conflict in the Post-Brown South.* Athens: University of Georgia Press, 1987.

Bender, Thomas. *Community and Social Change in America.* New Brunswick, N.J.: Rutgers University Press, 1978.

Berlin, Ira. *Slaves Without Masters: The Free Negro in the Antebellum South.* New York: Oxford University Press, 1974.

Berry, Mary Frances. "Judging Morality: Sexual Behavior and Legal Consequences in the Late Nineteenth-Century South." *Journal of American History* 78 (1991): 835–56.

———. *Military Necessity and Civil Rights Policy: Black Citizenship and the Constitution, 1861–1868.* Port Washington, N.Y.: National University Publications, 1977.

Berry, Mary Frances, and John W. Blassingame. *Long Memory: The Black Experience in America.* New York: Oxford University Press, 1982.

Billings, Warren M. "The Cases of Fernando and Elizabeth Key: A Note on the Status of Blacks in Seventeenth-Century Virginia." *William and Mary Quarterly,* 3d ser., 30 (1973): 467–74.

Black, Liza E. "'I Am a MAN, a BROTHER Now': Social Constructions of African American Manhood in the Antebellum Era." Unpublished paper, Department of History, University of Washington, 1993.

Blassingame, John W. *The Slave Community: Plantation Life in the Antebellum South.* New York: Oxford University Press, 1979.

Bleikasten, André. *The Most Splendid Failure: Faulkner's* The Sound and the Fury. Bloomington: Indiana University Press, 1976.

Bleser, Carol K. "Southern Planter Wives and Slavery." In *The Meaning of South Carolina History: Essays in Honor of George C. Rogers, Jr.,* edited by David R. Chesnutt and Clyde N. Wilson. Columbia: University of South Carolina Press, 1991.

Blight, David W. *Frederick Douglass' Civil War: Keeping Faith in Jubilee.* Baton Rouge: Louisiana State University Press, 1989.

Bloch, Ruth H. "The Gendered Meanings of Virtue in Revolutionary America." *Signs* 13 (1987): 37–58.

Block, Sharon. "Coerced Sex in British North America, 1700–1820." Ph.D. diss., Princeton University, 1995.

Bolton, Charles C. *Poor Whites of the Antebellum South: Tenants and Laborers in Central North Carolina and Northeast Mississippi.* Durham, N.C.: Duke University Press, 1994.

Breen, T. H. "A Changing Labor Force and Race Relations in Virginia, 1660–1710." *Journal of Social History* 7 (1973): 3–25.

Breen, T. H., and Stephen Innes. *"Myne Owne Ground": Race and Freedom on Virginia's Eastern Shore, 1640–1676.* New York: Oxford University Press, 1980.

Brown, Elsa Barkley. "Negotiating and Transforming the Public Sphere: African American Political Life in the Transition from Slavery to Freedom." *Public Culture* 7 (1994): 107–46.

Brown, Kathleen, M. *Good Wives, Nasty Wenches, and Anxious Patriarchs: Gender, Race, and Power in Colonial Virginia.* Chapel Hill: University of North Carolina Press, 1996.

Brown, Letitia Woods. *Free Negroes in the District of Columbia, 1790–1846.* New York: Oxford University Press, 1972.

Brown, Richard Maxwell. *Strain of Violence: Historical Studies of American Violence and Vigilantism.* New York: Oxford University Press, 1975.

Brown, Steven E. "Sexuality and the Slave Community." *Phylon* 42 (1981): 1–10.

Brundage, W. Fitzhugh. *Lynching in the New South: Georgia and Virginia, 1880–1930.* Urbana: University of Illinois Press, 1993.

———. " 'To Howl Loudly': John Mitchell Jr. and His Campaign Against Lynching in Virginia." *Canadian Review of American Studies* 22 (1991): 325–41.

———. "The Varn Mill Riot of 1891: Lynchings, Attempted Lynchings, and Justice in Ware County, Georgia." *Georgia Historical Quarterly* 78 (1994): 257–80.

Buckley, Thomas E., S.J. "Assessing the Double Standard: Interracial Sex in Virginia, 1800–1850." Paper presented at Pacific Coast Branch, American Historical Association, Maui, Hawaii, 1995.

———. "Unfixing Race: Class, Power, and Identity in an Interracial Family." *Virginia Magazine of History and Biography* 102 (1994): 349–80.

Burke, Peter. "History of Events and the Revival of Narrative." In *New Per-*

spectives on Historical Writing, edited by Peter Burke. University Park: Pennsylvania State University Press, 1992.

————. "Overture: The New History, Its Past and Its Future." In *New Perspectives on Historical Writing,* edited by Peter Burke. University Park: Pennsylvania State University Press, 1992.

Burnard, Trevor. "A Tangled Cousinry? Associational Networks of the Maryland Elite, 1691–1776." *Journal of Southern History* 61 (1995): 17–44.

Burton, Orville Vernon. *In My Father's House Are Many Mansions: Family and Community in Edgefield, South Carolina.* Chapel Hill: University of North Carolina Press, 1985.

Bynum, Victoria E. *Unruly Women: The Politics of Social and Sexual Control in the Old South.* Chapel Hill: University of North Carolina Press, 1992.

Campbell, James, and James Oakes. "The Invention of Race: Rereading *White Over Black.*" *Reviews in American History* 21 (1993): 172–83.

Campbell, Mildred. "Social Origins of Some Early Americans." In *Seventeenth-Century America: Essays in Colonial History,* edited by James Morton Smith. Chapel Hill: University of North Carolina Press, 1959.

Canny, Nicholas P. *The Elizabethan Conquest of Ireland: A Pattern Established, 1565–76.* New York: Harper and Row, 1976.

Carby, Hazel V. "'On the Threshold of Woman's Era': Lynching, Empire, and Sexuality in Black Feminist Theory." In *"Race," Writing, and Difference,* edited by Henry Louis Gates, Jr. Chicago: University of Chicago Press, 1986.

————. *Reconstructing Womanhood: The Emergence of the Afro-American Woman Novelist.* New York: Oxford University Press, 1987.

Carpenter, John A. "Atrocities in the Reconstruction Period." In *Black Freedom/White Violence, 1865–1900,* edited by Donald G. Nieman. New York: Garland, 1994.

Carr, Lois Green. "The Foundations of Social Order: Local Government in Colonial Maryland." In *Town and Country: Essays on the Structure of Local Government in the American Colonies,* edited by Bruce C. Daniels. Middletown, Conn.: Wesleyan University Press, 1978.

Carr, Lois Green, and Russell R. Menard. "Immigration and Opportunity: The Freedmen in Early Colonial Maryland." In *The Chesapeake in the Seventeenth Century: Essays on Anglo-American Society and Politics,* edited by Thad W. Tate and David L. Ammerman. New York: W. W. Norton, 1979.

Carr, Lois G., and Lorena S. Walsh. "The Planter's Wife: The Experience of White Women in Seventeenth-Century Maryland." In *Colonial America: Essays in Politics and Social Development,* edited by Stanley N. Katz, John M. Murrin, and Douglas Greenberg. New York: McGraw-Hill, 1993.

Carr, Lois Green, Russell R. Menard, and Lorena S. Walsh. *Robert Cole's World: Agriculture and Society in Early Maryland*. Chapel Hill: University of North Carolina Press, 1991.

Cashin, Joan E. "A Lynching in War-Time Carolina: The Death of Saxe Joiner." In *Under Sentence of Death: Lynching in the South,* edited by W. Fitzhugh Brundage. Chapel Hill: University of North Carolina Press, 1997.

———. " 'Since the War Broke Out': The Marriage of Kate and William McLure." In *Divided Houses: Gender and the Civil War,* edited by Catherine Clinton and Nina Silber. New York: Oxford University Press, 1992.

Cecil-Fronsman, Bill. *Common Whites: Class and Culture in Antebellum North Carolina*. Lexington: University Press of Kentucky, 1992.

Censer, Jane Turner. " 'Smiling Through Her Tears': Ante-Bellum Southern Women and Divorce." *American Journal of Legal History* 25 (1981): 24–47.

Channing, Steven A. *Crisis of Fear: Secession in South Carolina*. New York: Simon and Schuster, 1970.

Chisholm, Claudia A. "Wyndcroft." *Louisa County Historical Magazine* 10 (1978): 3–9.

Chisholm, Claudia Anderson, and Ellen Gray Lillie. *Old Home Places of Louisa County*. Louisa County Historical Society, [Louisa County, Va.,] 1979.

Clark, Ernest James, Jr. "Aspects of the North Carolina Slave Code, 1715–1860." *North Carolina Historical Review* 39 (1962): 149–64.

Clinton, Catherine. "Bloody Terrain: Freedwomen, Sexuality, and Violence during Reconstruction." In *Half Sisters of History: Southern Women and the American Past,* edited by Catherine Clinton. Durham, N.C.: Duke University Press, 1994.

———. "Caught in the Web of the Big House: Women and Slavery." In *The Web of Southern Social Relations: Women, Family, and Education,* edited by Walter J. Fraser, Jr., R. Frank Saunders, Jr., and Jon L. Wakelyn. Athens: University of Georgia Press, 1985.

———. *The Plantation Mistress: Woman's World in the Old South*. New York: Pantheon, 1982.

———. " 'Southern Dishonor': Flesh, Blood, Race, and Bondage." In *In Joy and in Sorrow: Women, Family, and Marriage in the Victorian South, 1830–1900,* edited by Carol Bleser. New York: Oxford University Press, 1991.

Connor, Robert. *Ante-Bellum Builders of North Carolina*. 1930. Reprint, Spartanburg, S.C.: Reprint Co., 1971.

Cornish, Dudley Taylor. *The Sable Arm: Negro Troops in the Union Army, 1861–1865*. New York: W. W. Norton, 1966.

Cott, Nancy F. "Passionlessness: An Interpretation of Victorian Sexual Ideology, 1790–1850." *Signs* 4 (1978): 219–36.

Coulter, E. Merton. "Four Slaves Trials in Elbert County, Georgia." *Georgia Historical Quarterly* 41 (1957): 237–46.

Crow, Jeffrey J. *The Black Experience in Revolutionary North Carolina.* Raleigh, N.C.: Department of Cultural Resources, Division of Archives and History, 1983.

Cullen, Jim. " 'I's a Man Now': Gender and African American Men." In *Divided Houses: Gender and the Civil War,* edited by Catherine Clinton and Nina Silber. New York: Oxford University Press, 1992.

Davis, Angela Y. *Women, Race, and Class.* New York: Random House, 1981.

Davis, David Brion. *The Problem of Slavery in the Age of Revolution, 1770–1823.* Ithaca, N.Y.: Cornell University Press, 1975.

———. "Terror in Mississippi." *New York Review of Books,* Nov. 4, 1993.

Davis, Fannie Mae. *Douglas County, Georgia: From Indian Trail to Interstate 20.* Roswell, Ga.: W. H. Wolfe Associates, 1987.

Deal, [Joseph] Douglas. "A Constricted World: Free Blacks on Virginia's Eastern Shore, 1680–1750." In *Colonial Chesapeake Society,* edited by Lois Green Carr, Philip D. Morgan, and Jean B. Russo. Chapel Hill: University of North Carolina Press, 1988.

———. "Race and Class in Colonial Virginia: Indians, Englishmen, and Africans on the Eastern Shore During the Seventeenth Century." Ph.D. diss., University of Rochester, 1981.

DeSantis, John. *For the Color of His Skin: The Murder of Yusuf Hawkins and the Trial of Bensonhurst.* New York: Pharos Books, 1991.

Didion, Joan. "Sentimental Journeys." In *After Henry.* New York: Simon and Schuster, 1992.

Dolan, Jay P. *The American Catholic Experience: A History from Colonial Times to the Present.* New York: Doubleday, 1985.

Domínguez, Virginia R. *White by Definition: Social Classification in Creole Louisiana.* New Brunswick, N.J.: Rutgers University Press, 1986.

Drinan, Robert F. "The Loving Decision and the Freedom to Marry." *Ohio State Law Journal* 29 (1968): 358–98.

Du Bois, W. E. B. *Black Reconstruction in America.* New York: Russell and Russell, 1935.

duCille, Ann. "The Blacker the Juice: O. J. Simpson and the Squeeze Play of Race." In *Skin Trade.* Cambridge, Mass.: Harvard University Press, 1996.

Dyer, Frederick H. *A Compendium of the War of the Rebellion.* New York: Thomas Yoseloff, 1959.

Dyer, Thomas G. " 'A Most Unexampled Exhibition of Madness and Brutality': Judge Lynch in Saline County, Missouri, 1859." *Missouri Historical Review* 89 (1995): 269–89, 367–83.

Edmonds, Helen G. *The Negro and Fusion Politics in North Carolina, 1894–1901.* Chapel Hill: University of North Carolina Press, 1951.

Edwards, John C. "Slave Justice in Four Middle Georgia Counties." *Georgia Historical Quarterly* 57 (1973): 265–73.

Edwards, Laura F. *Gendered Strife and Confusion: The Political Culture of Reconstruction.* Urbana: University of Illinois Press, 1997.

———. "Sexual Violence, Gender, Reconstruction, and the Extension of Patriarchy in Granville County, North Carolina." *North Carolina Historical Review* 68 (1991): 237–60.

Egerton, Douglas R. *Gabriel's Rebellion: The Virginia Slave Conspiracies of 1800 and 1802.* Chapel Hill: University of North Carolina Press, 1993.

Ellis, Mary Louise. " 'Rain Down Fire': The Lynching of Sam Hose." Ph.D. diss., Florida State University, 1992.

Epperson, Terrence W. " 'To Fix a Perpetual Brand': The Social Construction of Race in Virginia, 1675–1750." Ph.D. diss., Temple University, 1990.

Escott, Paul D. *Many Excellent People: Power and Privilege in North Carolina, 1850–1900.* Chapel Hill: University of North Carolina Press, 1985.

Evans, William McKee. "From the Land of Canaan to the Land of Guinea: The Strange Odyssey of the 'Sons of Ham.' " *American Historical Review* 85 (1980): 15–43.

Faust, Drew Gilpin. "Altars of Sacrifice: Confederate Women and the Narratives of War." In *Divided Houses: Gender and the Civil War,* edited by Catherine Clinton and Nina Silber. New York: Oxford University Press, 1992.

———. *Mothers of Invention: Women of the Slaveholding South in the American Civil War.* Chapel Hill: University of North Carolina Press, 1996.

Fields, Barbara J. "Ideology and Race in American History." In *Region, Race, and Reconstruction: Essays in Honor of C. Vann Woodward,* edited by J. Morgan Kousser and James M. McPherson. New York: Oxford University Press, 1982.

———. "Slavery, Race and Ideology in the United States of America." *New Left Review* 181 (1990): 95–118.

Finnegan, Terrence. "Lynching and Political Power in Mississippi and South Carolina." In *Under Sentence of Death: Lynching in the South,* edited by W. Fitzhugh Brundage. Chapel Hill: University of North Carolina Press, 1997.

Flanders, Ralph B. "The Free Negro in Ante-Bellum Georgia." *North Carolina Historical Review* 9 (1932): 250–72.

Flanigan, Daniel J. "Criminal Procedure in Slave Trials in the Antebellum South." *Journal of Southern History* 40 (1974): 537–64.

Fletcher, Robert Samuel. *A History of Oberlin College from Its Foundation Through the Civil War.* Oberlin, Ohio: Oberlin College, 1943.

Foner, Eric. *Reconstruction: America's Unfinished Revolution, 1863–1877.* New York: Harper and Row, 1988.

Forbes, Jack D. *Black Africans and Native Americans: Color, Race and Caste in the Evolution of Red-Black Peoples.* New York: Basil Blackwell, 1988.

Ford, Lacy K., Jr. *Origins of Southern Radicalism: The South Carolina Upcountry, 1800-1860.* New York: Oxford University Press, 1988.

Forsyth-Monroe County, Georgia, Sesquicentennial, 1823-1973. [Forsyth and Monroe Counties, Ga.:] Historical Book Committee, 1973.

Fox-Genovese, Elizabeth. *Within the Plantation Household: Black and White Women of the Old South.* Chapel Hill: University of North Carolina Press, 1988.

Fox-Genovese, Elizabeth, and Eugene D. Genovese. "Jurisprudence and Property Relations in Bourgeois and Slave Society." In *Fruits of Merchant Capital: Slavery and Bourgeois Property in the Rise and Expansion of Capitalism.* New York: Oxford University Press, 1983.

Franklin, John Hope. "*The Birth of a Nation:* Propaganda as History." In *Race and History: Selected Essays, 1938-1988.* Baton Rouge: Louisiana State University Press, 1989.

———. *The Free Negro in North Carolina, 1790-1860.* Chapel Hill: University of North Carolina Press, 1943.

———. *Reconstruction: After the Civil War.* Chicago: University of Chicago Press, 1961.

Fredrickson, George M. *The Arrogance of Race: Historical Perspectives on Slavery, Racism, and Social Inequality.* Middletown, Conn.: Wesleyan University Press, 1988.

———. *The Black Image in the White Mind: The Debate on Afro-American Character and Destiny, 1817-1914.* Middletown, Conn.: Wesleyan University Press, 1971.

———. *White Supremacy: A Comparative Study in American and South African History.* New York: Oxford University Press, 1981.

Freehling, William W. *The Road to Disunion: Secessionists at Bay, 1776-1854.* New York: Oxford University Press, 1990.

Friedman, Jean E. *The Enclosed Garden: Women and Community in the Evangelical South, 1830-1900.* Chapel Hill: University of North Carolina Press, 1985.

Friedman, Lawrence M. *A History of American Law.* New York: Simon and Schuster, 1985.

Fry, Gladys-Marie. *Night Riders in Black Folk History.* Knoxville: University of Tennessee Press, 1975.

Gaines, Kevin K. *Uplifting the Race: Black Leadership, Politics, and Culture in the Twentieth Century.* Chapel Hill: University of North Carolina Press, 1996.

Galenson, David W. *White Servitude in Colonial America: An Economic Analysis.* New York: Cambridge University Press, 1981.

Gatewood, Willard B. *Aristocrats of Color: The Black Elite, 1880–1920.* Bloomington: Indiana University Press, 1990.

"Genealogy of the Boarman Family." N.p., n.d. In MHS.

Genovese, Eugene D. " 'Rather be a Nigger than a Poor White Man': Slave Perceptions of Southern Yeomen and Poor Whites." In *Toward a New View of America: Essays in Honor of Arthur C. Cole,* edited by Hans L. Trefousse. New York: Burt Franklin, 1977.

———. *Roll, Jordan, Roll: The World the Slaves Made.* New York: Random House, 1972.

———. "Yeoman Farmers in a Slaveholders' Democracy." *Agricultvral History* 49 (1975): 331–42.

Getman, Karen A. "Sexual Control in the Slaveholding South: The Implementation and Maintenance of a Racial Caste System." *Harvard Women's Law Journal* 7 (1984): 115–52.

Giddings, Paula. "Ida Wells-Barnett." In *Portraits of American Women: From Settlement to the Present,* edited by G. J. Barker-Benfield and Catherine Clinton. New York: St. Martin's Press, 1991.

———. *When and Where I Enter: The Impact of Black Women on Race and Sex in America.* New York: William Morrow, 1984.

Gilmore, Glenda Elizabeth. *Gender and Jim Crow: Women and the Politics of White Supremacy in North Carolina, 1896–1920.* Chapel Hill: University of North Carolina Press, 1996.

Ginzburg, Carlo. "Checking the Evidence: The Judge and the Historian." *Critical Inquiry* 18 (1991): 79–92.

Glatthaar, Joseph T. *Forged in Battle: The Civil War Alliance of Black Soldiers and White Officers.* New York: Penguin, 1990.

Goodman, James. *Stories of Scottsboro.* New York: Pantheon, 1994.

Gordon, Linda. *Woman's Body, Woman's Right: A Social History of Birth Control in America.* New York: Viking, 1976.

Gossett, Thomas F. *Race: The History of an Idea in America.* Dallas, Tex.: Southern Methodist University Press, 1963.

Graham, Michael. "Meeting House and Chapel: Religion and Community in Seventeenth-Century Maryland." In *Colonial Chesapeake Society,* edited by Lois Green Carr, Philip D. Morgan, and Jean B. Russo. Chapel Hill: University of North Carolina Press, 1988.

Griswold, Robert L. "Divorce and the Legal Redefinition of Victorian Manhood." In *Meanings for Manhood: Constructions of Masculinity in Victorian America,* edited by Mark C. Carnes and Clyde Griffen. Chicago: University of Chicago Press, 1990.

———. "The Evolution of the Doctrine of Mental Cruelty in Victorian American Divorce, 1790–1900." *Journal of Social History* 20 (1986): 127–48.

―――. "Law, Sex, Cruelty, and Divorce in Victorian America, 1840–1900." *American Quarterly* 38 (1986): 721–45.

Grossberg, Michael. *Governing the Hearth: Law and the Family in Nineteenth-Century America*. Chapel Hill: University of North Carolina Press, 1985.

―――. "Guarding the Altar: Physiological Restrictions and the Rise of State Intervention in Matrimony." *American Journal of Legal History* 26 (1982): 197–226.

Gunning, Sandra. *Race, Rape, and Lynching: The Red Record of American Literature*. New York: Oxford University Press, 1996.

Gutman, Herbert G. *The Black Family in Slavery and Freedom, 1750–1925*. New York: Random House, 1976.

Guy-Sheftall, Beverly. *Daughters of Sorrow: Attitudes Toward Black Women, 1880–1920*. Brooklyn, N.Y.: Carlson, 1990.

Hahn, Steven. *The Roots of Southern Populism: Yeoman Farmers and the Transformation of the Georgia Upcountry, 1850–1890*. New York: Oxford University Press, 1983.

Hall, Jacquelyn Dowd. " 'The Mind That Burns in Each Body': Women, Rape, and Racial Violence." In *Powers of Desire: The Politics of Sexuality*, edited by Ann Snitow, Christine Stansell, and Sharon Thompson. New York: Monthly Review Press, 1983.

―――. *Revolt Against Chivalry: Jessie Daniel Ames and the Women's Campaign Against Lynching*. Rev. ed. New York: Columbia University Press, 1993.

Hall, Kermit L. *The Magic Mirror: Law in American History*. New York: Oxford University Press, 1989.

Harris, J. William. "Etiquette, Lynching, and Racial Boundaries in Southern History: A Mississippi Example." *American Historical Review* 100 (1995): 387–410.

―――. *Plain Folk and Gentry in a Slave Society*. Middletown, Conn.: Wesleyan University Press, 1985.

Harris, Malcolm H. *History of Louisa County, Virginia*. Richmond, Va.: Dietz Press, 1936.

Harris, W. Stuart. "Rowdyism, Public Drunkenness, and Bloody Encounters in Early Perry County." *Alabama Review* 33 (1980): 15–24.

Hart, Jane Lewis. "Louisa County." In *Our County Origins*, edited by Sally W. Hamilton. [Richmond?] National Society of the Colonial Dames of America in the Commonwealth of Virginia, 1940.

The Heritage of Davidson County. Lexington, N.C.: Genealogical Society of Davidson County, 1982.

Higginbotham, A. Leon, Jr. *In the Matter of Color: Race and the American Legal Process: The Colonial Period*. New York: Oxford University Press, 1978.

Higginbotham, A. Leon, Jr., and Barbara K. Kopytoff. "Property First, Humanity Second: The Recognition of the Slave's Human Nature in Virginia Civil Law." *Ohio State Law Journal* 50 (1989): 511–40.

———. "Racial Purity and Interracial Sex in the Law of Colonial and Antebellum Virginia." *Georgetown Law Journal* 77 (1989): 1967–2029.

Higginbotham, Evelyn Brooks. "African-American Women's History and the Metalanguage of Race." *Signs* 17 (1992): 251–74.

———. "Beyond the Sound of Silence: Afro-American Women in History." *Gender and History* 1 (1989): 50–67.

Higginson, Mary Thacher. *Thomas Wentworth Higginson: The Story of His Life.* 1914. Reprint, Port Washington, N.Y.: Kennikat Press, 1971.

Hillhouse, Albert. *A History of Burke County, Georgia, 1777–1950.* Swainsboro, Ga.: Magnolia Press, 1985.

Hindus, Michael S., and Lynne E. Withey. "The Law of Husband and Wife in Nineteenth-Century America: Changing Views of Divorce." In *Women and the Law: A Social Historical Perspective,* vol. 2, edited by D. Kelly Weisberg. Cambridge, Mass.: Schenkman, 1982.

Hine, Darlene Clark. "Rape and the Inner Lives of Southern Black Women: Thoughts on the Culture of Dissemblance." In *Southern Women: Histories and Identities,* edited by Virginia Bernhard, Betty Brandon, Elizabeth Fox-Genovese, and Theda Perdue. Columbia: University of Missouri Press, 1992.

Hirsch, Arnold R., and Joseph Logsdon, eds. *Creole New Orleans: Race and Americanization.* Baton Rouge: Louisiana State University Press, 1992.

Holt, Bryce R. *The Supreme Court of North Carolina and Slavery.* Durham, N.C.: Duke University Press, 1927.

Holt, Thomas C. " 'An Empire over the Mind': Emancipation, Race, and Ideology in the British West Indies and the American South." In *Region, Race, and Reconstruction: Essays in Honor of C. Vann Woodward,* edited by J. Morgan Kousser and James M. McPherson. New York: Oxford University Press, 1982.

———. "The Lonely Warrior: Ida B. Wells-Barnett and the Struggle for Black Leadership." In *Black Leaders of the Twentieth Century,* edited by John Hope Franklin and August Meier. Urbana: University of Illinois Press, 1982.

Hooks, Bell. *Ain't I a Woman? Black Women and Feminism.* Boston: South End Press, 1981.

Horn, James. "Adapting to a New World: A Comparative Study of Local Society in England and Maryland, 1650–1700." In *Colonial Chesapeake Society,* edited by Lois Green Carr, Philip D. Morgan, and Jean B. Russo. Chapel Hill: University of North Carolina Press, 1988.

———. "Servant Emigration to the Chesapeake in the Seventeenth Century." In *The Chesapeake in the Seventeenth Century: Essays on Anglo-*

American Society and Politics, edited by Thad W. Tate and David L. Ammerman. New York: W. W. Norton, 1979.

Horsman, Reginald. *Josiah Nott of Mobile: Southerner, Physician, and Racial Theorist*. Baton Rouge: Louisiana State University Press, 1987.

———. *Race and Manifest Destiny: The Origins of American Racial Anglo-Saxonism*. Cambridge, Mass.: Harvard University Press, 1981.

Horton, James Oliver. *Free People of Color: Inside the African American Community*. Washington, D.C.: Smithsonian Institution Press, 1993.

Howard, McHenry. "Some Early Colonial Marylanders." *Maryland Historical Magazine* 15 (1920): 319–24.

Huggins, Nathan I. "The Deforming Mirror of Truth: Slavery and the Master Narrative of American History." *Radical History Review* 49 (1991): 25–48.

Hume, Richard L. "Negro Delegates to the State Constitutional Conventions of 1867–69." In *Southern Black Leaders of the Reconstruction Era*, edited by Howard N. Rabinowitz. Urbana: University of Illinois Press, 1982.

Ignatiev, Noel. *How the Irish Became White*. New York: Routledge, 1995.

Jennings, Thelma. " 'Us Colored Women Had to Go Through A Plenty': Sexual Exploitation of African-American Slave Women." *Journal of Women's History* 1 (1990): 45–74.

Johnson, Charles. *Shadow of the Plantation*. Chicago: University of Chicago Press, 1934.

Johnson, Guion Griffis. *Ante-Bellum North Carolina: A Social History*. Chapel Hill: University of North Carolina Press, 1937.

Johnson, Michael P., and James L. Roark. *Black Masters: A Free Family of Color in the Old South*. New York: W. W. Norton, 1984.

Johnston, James Hugo. *Race Relations in Virginia and Miscegenation in the South, 1776–1860*. Amherst: University of Massachusetts Press, 1970.

Jones, Allen W. "The Black Press in the 'New South': Jesse C. Duke's Struggle for Justice and Equality." *Journal of Negro History* 64 (1979): 215–28.

Jones, Jacqueline. *Labor of Love, Labor of Sorrow: Black Women, Work, and the Family from Slavery to the Present*. New York: Basic Books, 1985.

Jordan, Ervin L., Jr. "Sleeping with the Enemy: Sex, Black Women, and the Civil War." *Western Journal of Black Studies* 18 (1994): 55–63.

Jordan, Winthrop D. *Tumult and Silence at Second Creek: An Inquiry into a Civil War Slave Conspiracy*. Rev. ed. Baton Rouge: Louisiana State University Press, 1995.

———. *White over Black: American Attitudes Toward the Negro, 1550–1812*. 1968. Reprint, New York: W. W. Norton, 1977.

Kaplan, Sidney. "The Miscegenation Issue in the Election of 1864." *Journal of Negro History* 34 (1949): 274–343.

Kimmel, Ross M. "The Negro Before the Law in Seventeenth-Century Maryland." M.A. thesis, University of Maryland, 1971.

———. "Slave Freedom Petitions in the Courts of Colonial Maryland" (1979). Typescript, Ross Kimmel Collection, MHR.

King, Andrew J. "Constructing Gender: Sexual Slander in Nineteenth-Century America." *Law and History Review* 13 (1995): 63–110.

Kolchin, Peter. *First Freedom: The Responses of Alabama's Blacks to Emancipation and Reconstruction.* Westport, Conn.: Greenwood, 1972.

———. "Reevaluating the Antebellum Slave Community: A Comparative Perspective." *Journal of American History* 70 (1983): 579–601.

Konkle, Burton Alva. *John Motley Morehead and the Development of North Carolina, 1796–1866.* Philadelphia: William Campbell, 1922.

Kulikoff, Allan. "A 'Prolifick' People: Black Population Growth in the Chesapeake Colonies, 1700–1790." *Southern Studies* 16 (1977): 391–428.

———. " 'Throwing the Stocking': A Gentry Marriage in Provincial Maryland." *Maryland Historical Magazine* 71 (1976): 516–21.

———. *Tobacco and Slaves: The Development of Southern Cultures in the Chesapeake, 1680–1800.* Chapel Hill: University of North Carolina Press, 1986.

Lancaster, Robert. *A Sketch of the Early History of Hanover County, Virginia.* Richmond, Va.: Whittet and Shepperson, 1976.

Laqueur, Thomas. *Making Sex: Body and Gender from the Greeks to Freud.* Cambridge, Mass.: Harvard University Press, 1990.

Lecaudey, Hélène. "Behind the Mask: Ex-Slave Women and Interracial Sexual Relations." In *Discovering the Women in Slavery: Emancipating Perspectives on the American Past,* edited by Patricia Morton. Athens: University of Georgia Press, 1996.

Lee, Harper. *To Kill a Mockingbird.* 1960. Reprint, New York: Warner, 1982.

Leonard, Jacob Calvin. *Centennial History of Davidson County, North Carolina.* Raleigh, N.C.: Edwards and Broughton, 1927.

Leslie, Kent Anderson. *Woman of Color, Daughter of Privilege: Amanda America Dickson, 1849–1893.* Athens: University of Georgia Press, 1995.

Lewis, Jan. *The Pursuit of Happiness: Family and Values in Jefferson's Virginia.* New York: Cambridge University Press, 1983.

Linn, Jo White. *A Holmes Family of Rowan and Davidson Counties, North Carolina.* Salisbury, N.C.: privately published, 1988.

Litwack, Leon F. *Been in the Storm So Long: The Aftermath of Slavery.* New York: Random House, 1979.

———. " 'Blues Falling Down Like Hail': The Ordeal of Black Freedom." In *New Perspectives on Race and Slavery in America: Essays in Honor of*

Kenneth M. Stampp, edited by Robert H. Abzug and Stephen E. Maizlish. Lexington: University Press of Kentucky, 1986.

Lombardo, Paul A. "Miscegenation, Eugenics, and Racism: Historical Footnotes to *Loving v. Virginia.*" *U.C. Davis Law Review* 21 (1988): 421–52.

Madden, T. O., Jr., with Ann L. Miller. *We Were Always Free: The Maddens of Culpeper County, Virginia; A Two-Hundred-Year Family History.* New York: Random House, 1992.

Main, Gloria. "Maryland and the Chesapeake Economy, 1670–1720." In *Law, Society, and Politics in Early Maryland,* edited by Aubrey C. Land, Lois Green Carr, and Edward C. Papenfuse. Baltimore: Johns Hopkins University Press, 1977.

———. *Tobacco Colony: Life in Early Maryland, 1650-1720.* Princeton, N.J.: Princeton University Press, 1982.

Martin, Waldo E., Jr. *The Mind of Frederick Douglass.* Chapel Hill: University of North Carolina Press, 1984.

Maryland Marriages: 1778-1800. Baltimore: Genealogical Publishing, 1979.

McBride, B. Ransom. "Divorces and Separations Granted by Act of North Carolina Assembly from 1790–1808." *North Carolina Genealogical Society Journal* 3 (1977): 43–47.

———. "Divorces, Separations, and Security of Property Granted by Act of the NC Assembly from 1809 through 1830." *North Carolina Genealogical Society Journal* 9 (1983): 43–46.

McCormac, Eugene. *White Servitude in Maryland, 1634-1820.* Baltimore: Johns Hopkins University Press, 1904.

McCurry, Stephanie. *Masters of Small Worlds: Yeoman Households, Gender Relations, and the Political Culture of the Antebellum South Carolina Low Country.* New York: Oxford University Press, 1995.

McFeely, William S. *Frederick Douglass.* New York: W. W. Norton, 1991.

McFerson, Hazel M. " 'Racial Tradition' and Comparative Political Analysis: Notes Toward a Theoretical Framework." *Ethnic and Racial Studies* 4 (1979): 477–97.

McGovern, James R. *Anatomy of a Lynching: The Killing of Claude Neal.* Baton Rouge: Louisiana State University Press, 1982.

McKivigan, John R. "James Redpath, John Brown, and Abolitionist Advocacy of Slave Insurrection." *Civil War History* 37 (1991): 293–313.

McLaurin, Melton A. *Celia: A Slave.* Athens: University of Georgia Press, 1991.

McMillen, Neil R. *Dark Journey: Black Mississippians in the Age of Jim Crow.* Urbana: University of Illinois Press, 1989.

McPherson, James M. *Battle Cry of Freedom: The Civil War Era.* New York: Oxford University Press, 1988.

———. *The Struggle for Equality: Abolitionists and the Negro in the Civil War and Reconstruction.* Princeton, N.J.: Princeton University Press, 1964.

Menard, Russell R. "British Migration to the Chesapeake Colonies in the Seventeenth Century." In *Colonial Chesapeake Society,* edited by Lois Green Carr, Philip D. Morgan, and Jean B. Russo. Chapel Hill: University of North Carolina Press, 1988.

———. "From Servant to Freeholder: Status Mobility and Property Accumulation in Seventeenth-Century Maryland." In *Colonial America: Essays in Politics and Social Development,* edited by Stanley N. Katz, John M. Murrin, and Douglas Greenberg. New York: McGraw-Hill, 1993.

———. "From Servants to Slaves: The Transformation of the Chesapeake Labor System." *Southern Studies* 16 (1977): 355–90.

———. "Immigrants and Their Increase: The Process of Population Growth in Early Colonial Maryland." In *Law, Society, and Politics in Early Maryland,* edited by Aubrey C. Land, Lois Green Carr, and Edward C. Papenfuse. Baltimore: Johns Hopkins University Press, 1977.

———. "The Maryland Slave Population, 1658 to 1730: A Demographic Profile of Blacks in Four Counties." *William and Mary Quarterly,* 3d ser., 32 (1975): 29–54.

Mills, Gary B. "Miscegenation and the Free Negro in Antebellum 'Anglo' Alabama: A Reexamination of Southern Race Relations." *Journal of American History* 68 (1981): 16–34.

———. "Tracing Free People of Color in the Antebellum South: Methods, Sources, and Perspectives." *National Genealogical Society Quarterly* 78 (1990): 262–78.

Mitchell, Reid. *The Vacant Chair: The Northern Soldier Leaves Home.* New York: Oxford University Press, 1993.

Mohr, James C. *Abortion in America: The Origins and Evolution of National Policy.* New York: Oxford University Press, 1978.

Moller, Herbert. "Sex Composition and Correlated Culture Patterns of Colonial America." *William and Mary Quarterly,* 3d ser., 2 (1945): 113–53.

Monroe County Georgia, A History. Forsyth, Ga.: Monroe County Historical Society, 1979.

Moore, Wilbert E. "Slave Law and the Social Structure." *Journal of Negro History* 26 (1941): 171–202.

Morehead, John Motley, 3d. *The Morehead Family of North Carolina and Virginia.* New York: privately published, 1921.

Morgan, Edmund S. *American Slavery, American Freedom: The Ordeal of Colonial Virginia.* New York: W. W. Norton, 1975.

Morgan, Philip D. "British Encounters with Africans and African-Americans, circa 1600–1780." In *Strangers Within the Realm: Cultural Margins of the First British Empire,* edited by Bernard Bailyn and Philip D. Morgan. Chapel Hill: University of North Carolina Press, 1991.

Morris, Thomas D. *Southern Slavery and the Law, 1619–1860.* Chapel Hill: University of North Carolina Press, 1996.

Morrison, Toni, ed., *Race-ing Justice, En-Gendering Power: Essays on Anita Hill, Clarence Thomas, and the Construction of Social Reality.* New York: Pantheon, 1992.

Morton, Patricia. "From Invisible Man to 'New People': The Recent Discovery of American Mulattoes." *Phylon* 46 (1985): 106–22.

Murray, Pauli. *Proud Shoes: The Story of an American Family.* New York: Harper and Brothers, 1956.

Myrdal, Gunnar. *An American Dilemma: The Negro Problem and Modern Democracy.* New York: Harper and Row, 1944.

Nash, A. E. Keir. "Fairness and Formalism in the Trials of Blacks in the State Supreme Courts of the Old South." *Virginia Law Review* 56 (1970): 64–100.

———. "A More Equitable Past? Southern Supreme Courts and the Protection of the Antebellum Negro." *North Carolina Law Review* 48 (1970): 197–242.

———. "Reason of Slavery: Understanding the Judicial Role in the Peculiar Institution." *Vanderbilt Law Review* 32 (1979): 7–218.

National Association for the Advancement of Colored People (NAACP). *Thirty Years of Lynching in the United States, 1889–1918.* New York: NAACP, 1919.

Nicholls, Michael L. "Passing Through This Troublesome World: Free Blacks in the Early Southside." *Virginia Magazine of History and Biography* 92 (1984): 50–70.

Norton, Mary Beth. "Gender and Defamation in Seventeenth-Century Maryland." *William and Mary Quarterly,* 3d ser., 44 (1987): 3–39.

Oakes, James. *Slavery and Freedom: An Interpretation of the Old South.* New York: Random House, 1990.

Oates, Stephen B. *The Fires of Jubilee: Nat Turner's Fierce Rebellion.* 1975. Reprint, New York: Harper Perennial, 1990.

Olsen, Otto H. "The Ku Klux Klan: A Study in Reconstruction Politics and Propaganda." *North Carolina Historical Review* 39 (1962): 340–62.

Omi, Michael, and Howard Winant. *Racial Formation in the United States From the 1960s to the 1980s.* New York: Routledge, 1994.

O'Rourke, Timothy, ed. *Catholic Families of Southern Maryland: Records of Catholic Residents of St. Mary's County in the Eighteenth Century.* Baltimore: Genealogical Publishing, 1985.

Outlaw, Lucius. "Toward a Critical Theory of 'Race.'" In *Anatomy of Racism,* edited by David Theo Goldberg. Minneapolis: University of Minnesota Press, 1990.

Owings, Donnell MacClure. *His Lordship's Patronage: Offices of Profit in Colonial Maryland*. Baltimore: Baltimore Historical Society, 1953.

Painter, Nell Irvin. "Hill, Thomas, and the Use of Racial Stereotype." In *Race-ing Justice, En-Gendering Power: Essays on Anita Hill, Clarence Thomas, and the Construction of Social Reality*, edited by Toni Morrison. New York: Pantheon, 1992.

———. "The Journal of Ella Gertrude Clanton Thomas: An Educated White Woman in the Eras of Slavery, War, and Reconstruction." In *The Secret Eye: The Journal of Ella Gertrude Clanton Thomas, 1848-1889*, edited by Virginia Ingraham Burr. Chapel Hill: University of North Carolina Press, 1990.

———. "Of *Lily*, Linda Brent, and Freud: A Non-Exceptionalist Approach to Race, Class, and Gender in the Slave South." In *Half Sisters of History: Southern Women and the American Past*, edited by Catherine Clinton. Durham, N.C.: Duke University Press, 1994.

———. " 'Social Equality,' Miscegenation, Labor, and Power." In *The Evolution of Southern Culture*, edited by Numan Bartley. Athens: University of Georgia Press, 1988.

———. "Soul Murder and Slavery: Toward a Fully Loaded Cost Accounting." In *U.S. History as Women's History: New Feminist Essays*, edited by Linda K. Kerber, Alice Kessler-Harris, and Kathryn Kish Sklar. Chapel Hill: University of North Carolina Press, 1995.

Palmer, Paul C. "Miscegenation as an Issue in the Arkansas Constitutional Convention of 1868." *Arkansas Historical Quarterly* 24 (1965): 99-119.

Parran, Alice Norris. *Register of Maryland's Heraldic Families*. Baltimore: H. G. Roebuck and Sons, 1935.

Partington, Donald H. "The Incidence of the Death Penalty for Rape in Virginia." *Washington and Lee Law Review* 22 (1965): 43-75.

Pascoe, Peggy. "Miscegenation Law, Court Cases, and Ideologies of 'Race' in Twentieth-Century America." *Journal of American History* 83 (1996): 44-69.

———. "Race, Gender, and Intercultural Relations: The Case of Interracial Marriage." *Frontiers* 12 (1991): 5-18.

Patterson, Orlando. *Slavery and Social Death: A Comparative Study*. Cambridge, Mass.: Harvard University Press, 1982.

Perman, Michael. "Counter Reconstruction: The Role of Violence in Southern Redemption." In *The Facts of Reconstruction: Essays in Honor of John Hope Franklin*, edited by Eric Anderson and Alfred M. Moss, Jr. Baton Rouge: Louisiana State University Press, 1991.

———. *The Road to Redemption: Southern Politics, 1869-1879*. Chapel Hill: University of North Carolina Press, 1984.

Phillips, Roderick. *Putting Asunder: A History of Divorce in Western Society*. New York: Cambridge University Press, 1988.

Powell, Carolyn J. "In Remembrance of Mira: Reflections on the Death of a Slave Woman." In *Discovering the Women in Slavery: Emancipating Perspectives on the American Past,* edited by Patricia Morton. Athens: University of Georgia Press, 1996.

Prather, H. Leon, Sr. *We Have Taken a City: Wilmington Racial Massacre and Coup of 1898.* Rutherford, N.J.: Fairleigh Dickinson University Press, 1984.

Quaife, G. R. *Wanton Wenches and Wayward Wives: Peasants and Illicit Sex in Early Seventeenth-Century England.* New Brunswick, N.J.: Rutgers University Press, 1979.

Quarles, Benjamin. *The Negro in the Civil War.* Boston: Little, Brown, 1953.

Rable, George C. *But There Was No Peace: The Role of Violence in the Politics of Reconstruction.* Athens: University of Georgia Press, 1984.

———. *Civil Wars: Women and the Crisis of Southern Nationalism.* Urbana: University of Illinois Press, 1989.

Raynor, George. *Piedmont Passages IV: People and Places in Old Rowan.* Salisbury, N.C.: Salisbury Printing., 1991.

Reavis, William A. "The Maryland Gentry and Social Mobility, 1637–1676." *William and Mary Quarterly,* 3d ser., 14 (1957): 418–28.

Reed, Ralph E., Jr. "Emory College and the Sledd Affair of 1902: A Case Study in Southern Honor and Racial Attitudes." *Georgia Historical Quarterly* 72 (1988): 463–92.

Riggan, William. *Pícaros, Madmen, Naïfs, and Clowns: The Unreliable First-Person Narrator.* Norman: University of Oklahoma Press, 1981.

Rise, Eric W. *The Martinsville Seven: Race, Rape, and Capital Punishment.* Charlottesville: University Press of Virginia, 1995.

Roark, James L. *Masters Without Slaves: Southern Planters in the Civil War and Reconstruction.* New York: W. W. Norton, 1977.

Roark, James, and Michael Johnson. "Strategies of Survival: Free Negro Families and the Problem of Slavery." In *In Joy and in Sorrow: Women, Family, and Marriage in the Victorian South, 1830-1900,* edited by Carol Bleser. New York: Oxford University Press, 1991.

Roediger, David R. *Towards the Abolition of Whiteness.* London: Verso, 1994.

———. *The Wages of Whiteness: Race and the Making of the American Working Class.* New York: Verso, 1991.

Rogers, W. McDowell. "Free Negro Legislation in Georgia Before 1865." *Georgia Historical Quarterly* 16 (1932): 27–37.

Rosen, Hannah. "Struggles Over 'Freedom': Sexual Violence During the Memphis Riot of 1866." Paper presented at Berkshire Conference on the History of Women, Vassar College, 1993.

Rutman, Darrett B., and Anita H. Rutman. *A Place in Time: Middlesex County, Virginia, 1650-1750.* New York: W. W. Norton, 1984.

Saillant, John. "The Black Body Erotic and the Republican Body Politic, 1790–1820." *Journal of the History of Sexuality* 5 (1995): 403–28.

Salmon, Marylynn. *Women and the Law of Property in Early America*. Chapel Hill: University of North Carolina Press, 1986.

Saville, Julie. *The Work of Reconstruction: From Slave to Wage Labor in South Carolina, 1860–1870*. New York: Cambridge University Press, 1994.

Schama, Simon. *Dead Certainties (Unwarranted Speculations)*. New York: Alfred A. Knopf, 1991.

Schecter, Patricia A. "Unsettled Business: Ida B. Wells Against Lynching; or, How Anti-Lynching Got Its Gender." In *Under Sentence of Death: Lynching in the South*, edited by W. Fitzhugh Brundage. Chapel Hill: University of North Carolina Press, 1997.

Schultz, Mark R. "Interracial Kinship Ties and the Emergence of a Rural Black Middle Class: Hancock County, Georgia, 1865–1920." In *Georgia in Black and White: Explorations in the Race Relations of a Southern State, 1865–1950*, edited by John C. Inscoe. Athens: University of Georgia Press, 1994.

Schwarz, Philip J. "Forging the Shackles: The Development of Virginia's Criminal Code for Slaves." In *Ambivalent Legacy: A Legal History of the South*, edited by David J. Bodenhamer and James W. Ely, Jr. Jackson: University Press of Mississippi, 1984.

———. *Twice Condemned: Slaves and the Criminal Laws of Virginia, 1705–1865*. Baton Rouge: Louisiana State University Press, 1988.

Scott, Anne Firor. *The Southern Lady: From Pedestal to Politics, 1830–1930*. Chicago: University of Chicago Press, 1970.

———. "Women's Perspective on the Patriarchy in the 1850s." In *Half Sisters of History: Southern Women and the American Past*, edited by Catherine Clinton. Durham, N.C.: Duke University Press, 1994.

Shapiro, Herbert. "Afro-American Responses to Race Violence During Reconstruction." In *Black Freedom/White Violence, 1865–1900*, edited by Donald G. Nieman. New York: Garland, 1994.

———. *White Violence and Black Response: From Reconstruction to Montgomery*. Amherst: University of Massachusetts Press, 1988.

Shifflett, Crandall A. *Patronage and Poverty in the Tobacco South: Louisa County, Virginia, 1860–1900*. Knoxville: University of Tennessee Press, 1982.

Shingleton, Royce Gordon. "The Trial and Punishment of Slaves in Baldwin County, Georgia, 1812–1826." *Southern Humanities Review* 8 (1974): 67–73.

Shore, Laurence. "The Poverty of Tragedy in Historical Writing on Southern Slavery." *South Atlantic Quarterly* 85 (1986): 147–64.

Sink, Margaret Jewell, and Mary Green Matthews. *Pathfinders Past and*

Present: A History of Davidson County, North Carolina. High Point, N.C.: Hall, 1972.

Small, Stephen Augustus. "Racial Differentiation in the Slave Era: A Comparative Study of People of 'Mixed-Race' in Jamaica and Georgia." Ph.D. diss., University of California, Berkeley, 1989.

Smead, Howard. *Blood Justice: The Lynching of Mack Charles Parker.* New York: Oxford University Press, 1986.

Smedley, Audrey. *Race in North America: Origin and Evolution of a Worldview.* Boulder, Colo.: Westview, 1993.

Smith, Daniel Blake. *Inside the Great House: Planter Family Life in Eighteenth-Century Chesapeake Society.* Ithaca, N.Y.: Cornell University Press, 1980.

Smith, Daniel Scott, and Michael S. Hindus. "Premarital Pregnancy in America, 1640–1971: An Overview and Interpretation." *Journal of Interdisciplinary History* 4 (1975): 537–70.

Smith, Valerie. "Split Affinities: The Case of Interracial Rape." In *Conflicts in Feminism,* edited by Marianne Hirsch and Evelyn Fox Keller. New York: Routledge, 1990.

Solomon, Mark. "Racism and Anti-Racism in U.S. History." *Science and Society* 57 (1993): 74–78.

Sommerville, Diane Miller. "The Rape Myth in the Old South Reconsidered." *Journal of Southern History* 61 (1995): 481–518.

Spickard, Paul R. "The Illogic of American Racial Categories." In *Racially Mixed People in America,* edited by Maria P. P. Root. Newbury Park, Calif.: Sage, 1992.

Spindel, Donna J. *Crime and Society in North Carolina, 1663–1776.* Baton Rouge: Louisiana State University Press, 1989.

Sproat, John G. "Blueprint for Radical Reconstruction." *Journal of Southern History* 23 (1957): 34–44.

Stampp, Kenneth M. *The Peculiar Institution: Slavery in the Ante-Bellum South.* New York: Random House, 1956.

Stansell, Christine. *City of Women: Sex and Class in New York, 1789–1860.* New York: Alfred A. Knopf, 1986.

Stanton, William. *The Leopard's Spots: Scientific Attitudes Toward Race in America, 1815–59.* Chicago: University of Chicago Press, 1960.

Steckel, Richard H. "Miscegenation and the American Slave Schedules." *Journal of Interdisciplinary History* 11 (1980): 251–63.

Stevenson, Brenda E. "Distress and Discord in Virginia Slave Families, 1830–1860." In *In Joy and in Sorrow: Women, Family, and Marriage in the Victorian South, 1830–1900,* edited by Carol Bleser. New York: Oxford University Press, 1991.

———. *Life in Black and White: Family and Community in the Slave South.* New York: Oxford University Press, 1996.

Stone, Lawrence. "The Revival of Narrative: Reflections on a New Old History." *Past and Present* 85 (1979): 3–24.

Sundquist, Eric. J. *To Wake the Nations: Race in the Making of American Literature.* Cambridge, Mass.: Harvard University Press, 1993.

Sweat, Edward F. "Free Blacks in Antebellum Atlanta." *Atlanta Historical Bulletin* 21 (1977): 64–71.

Taylor, R. H. "Humanizing the Slave Code of North Carolina." *North Carolina Historical Review* 2 (1925): 323–31.

Thelen, David. "Memory and American History." *Journal of American History* 75 (1989): 1117–1129.

Thomas, C. F., Rev. *The Boarmans.* Washington, D.C.: St. Patrick's Rectory, 1934.

Thomas, Keith. "The Double Standard." *Journal of the History of Ideas* 20 (1959): 195–216.

Thompson, Mildred I. *Ida B. Wells-Barnett: An Exploratory Study of an American Black Woman, 1893–1930.* Brooklyn, N.Y.: Carlson, 1990.

Tolnay, Stewart E., and E. M. Beck. *A Festival of Violence: An Analysis of Southern Lynchings, 1882–1930.* Urbana: University of Illinois Press, 1995.

Toplin, Robert Brent. "Between Black and White: Attitudes Toward Southern Mulattoes, 1830–1861." *Journal of Southern History* 45 (1979): 185–200.

Trelease, Allen W. *White Terror: The Ku Klux Klan Conspiracy and Southern Reconstruction.* 1971. Reprint, Baton Rouge: Louisiana State University Press, 1995.

True, Ransom. "The Louisa Economy in the Years, 1765–1812." *Louisa County Historical Magazine* 7 (1975): 19–31, 77–85; 8 (1976): 40–46.

Tucker, David M. "Miss Ida B. Wells and Memphis Lynching." *Phylon* 32 (1971): 112–22.

Tullos, Allen. *Habits of Industry: White Culture and the Transformation of the Carolina Piedmont.* Chapel Hill: University of North Carolina Press, 1989.

Tushnet, Mark V. *The American Law of Slavery, 1810–1860: Considerations of Humanity and Interest.* Princeton, N.J.: Princeton University Press, 1981.

———. "The American Law of Slavery, 1810–1860: A Study in the Persistence of Legal Autonomy." *Law and Society Review* 10 (1975): 169–75.

Ulrich, Laurel Thatcher. *A Midwife's Tale: The Life of Martha Ballard, Based on Her Diary, 1785–1812.* New York: Alfred A. Knopf, 1990.

Vaughan, Alden T. "Blacks in Virginia: Evidence from the First Decade." In *Roots of American Racism: Essays on the Colonial Experience.* New York: Oxford University Press, 1995.

———. "The Origins Debate: Slavery and Racism in Seventeenth-Century

Virginia." In *Roots of American Racism: Essays on the Colonial Experience*. New York: Oxford University Press, 1995.

Wadlington, Walter. "The *Loving* Case: Virginia's Anti-Miscegenation Statute in Historical Perspective." *Virginia Law Review* 52 (1966): 1189–1223.

Walker, Alice. "Advancing Luna—and Ida B. Wells." In *You Can't Keep a Good Woman Down*. New York: Harcourt Brace Jovanovich, 1981.

Walker, Clarence E. "How Many Niggers Did Karl Marx Know? Or, A Peculiarity of the Americans." In *Deromanticizing Black History: Critical Essays and Reappraisals*. Knoxville: University of Tennessee Press, 1991.

Walsh, Lorena. "Community Networks in the Early Chesapeake." In *Colonial Chesapeake Society*, edited by Lois Green Carr, Philip D. Morgan, and Jean B. Russo. Chapel Hill: University of North Carolina Press, 1988.

———. "Servitude and Opportunity in Charles County, Maryland, 1658–1705." In *Law, Society, and Politics in Early Maryland*, edited by Aubrey C. Land, Lois Green Carr, and Edward C. Papenfuse. Baltimore: Johns Hopkins University Press, 1977.

———. "Slave Life, Slave Society, and Tobacco Production in the Tidewater Chesapeake, 1620–1820." In *Cultivation and Culture: Labor and the Shaping of Slave Life in the Americas*, edited by Ira Berlin and Philip D. Morgan. Charlottesville: University Press of Virginia, 1993.

Walters, Ronald G. *The Antislavery Appeal: American Abolitionism After 1830*. Baltimore: Johns Hopkins University Press, 1978.

Warner, Lee H. *Free Men in an Age of Servitude: Three Generations of a Black Family*. Lexington: University Press of Kentucky, 1992.

Watson, Alan. "North Carolina Slave Courts, 1715–1785." *North Carolina Historical Review* 60 (1983): 24–36

Watson, Harry L. "Conflict and Collaboration: Yeoman, Slaveholders, and Politics in the Antebellum South." *Social History* 10 (1985): 273–98.

Wells, Robert V. "Illegitimacy and Bridal Pregnancy in Colonial America." In *Bastardy and Its Comparative History*, edited by Peter Laslett, Karla Oosterveen, and Richard M. Smith. Cambridge, Mass.: Harvard University Press, 1980.

White, Deborah Gray. *Ar'n't I a Woman?: Female Slaves in the Plantation South*. New York: W. W. Norton, 1985.

White, Hayden. *Tropics of Discourse: Essays in Cultural Criticism*. Baltimore: Johns Hopkins University Press, 1978.

White, Walter. *Rope and Faggot: A Biography of Judge Lynch*. 1928. Reprint, New York: Arno Press and New York Times, 1969.

Whites, LeeAnn. "The Civil War as a Crisis in Gender." In *Divided Houses: Gender and the Civil War*, edited by Catherine Clinton and Nina Silber. New York: Oxford University Press, 1992.

———. "Rebecca Latimer Felton and the Problem of 'Protection' in the

New South." In *Visible Women: New Essays on American Activism,* edited by Nancy A. Hewitt and Suzanne Lebsock. Urbana: University of Illinois Press, 1993.

―――. "Rebecca Latimer Felton and the Wife's Farm: The Class and Racial Politics of Gender Reform." *Georgia Historical Quarterly* 76 (1992): 354–72.

Whitfield, Stephen J. *A Death in the Delta: The Story of Emmett Till.* Baltimore: Johns Hopkins University Press, 1988.

Wiecek, William M. "The Statutory Law of Slavery and Race in the Thirteen Mainland Colonies of British America." *William and Mary Quarterly,* 3d ser., 34 (1977): 258–80.

Wiegman, Robyn. "The Anatomy of Lynching." In *American Sexual Politics: Sex, Gender, and Race Since the Civil War,* edited by John C. Fout and Maura Shaw Tantillo. Chicago: University of Chicago Press, 1993.

Wikramanayake, Marina. *A World in Shadow: The Free Black in Antebellum South Carolina.* Columbia: University of South Carolina Press, 1973.

Williams, Mrs. Eddie, and Rose Hargrave Ellis. "Blacks of Yesterday." In *Historical Gleanings of Davidson County, North Carolina.* Heritage Research Committee of Davidson County Bicentennial Committee, ca. 1978.

Williamson, Joel. *The Crucible of Race: Black-White Relations in the American South Since Emancipation.* New York: Oxford University Press, 1984.

―――. *New People: Miscegenation and Mulattoes in the United States.* New York: Free Press, 1980.

Winant, Howard. *Racial Conditions: Politics, Theory, Comparisons.* Minneapolis: University of Minnesota Press, 1994.

Wood, Forrest G. *Black Scare: The Racist Response to Emancipation and Reconstruction.* Berkeley: University of California Press, 1968.

Wood, Peter H. *Black Majority: Negroes in Colonial South Carolina from 1670 Through the Stono Rebellion.* New York: W. W. Norton, 1974.

Woodson, Carter G. "The Beginnings of the Miscegenation of the Whites and Blacks." *Journal of Negro History* 3 (1918): 335–53.

―――. *Free Negro Owners of Slaves in the United States in 1830.* 1924. Reprint, New York: Negro Universities Press, 1968.

―――. *The Negro in Our History.* Washington, D.C.: Associated Publishers, 1922.

Woodward, C. Vann. *Origins of the New South, 1877–1913.* 1951. Reprint, Baton Rouge: Louisiana State University Press, 1971.

Worsham, Nannie. "History of Stroud Community in Monroe County, Georgia." 1958. Typescript, GDAH.

Wriggins, Jennifer. "Rape, Racism, and the Law." *Harvard Women's Law Journal* 6 (1983): 103–41.

Wright, Gavin. *The Political Economy of the Cotton South: Households, Mar-*

kets, and Wealth in the Nineteenth Century. New York: W. W. Norton, 1978.

Wright, George C. *Racial Violence in Kentucky, 1865-1940: Lynchings, Mob Rule, and "Legal Lynchings."* Baton Rouge: Louisiana State University Press, 1990.

Wright, James M. *The Free Negro in Maryland, 1634-1860.* New York: Columbia University Press, 1921.

Wyatt-Brown, Bertram. "Community, Class, and Snopesian Crime: Local Justice in the Old South." In *Class, Conflict, and Consensus: Antebellum Southern Community Studies,* edited by Orville Vernon Burton and Robert C. McMath, Jr. Westport, Conn.: Greenwood, 1982.

———. "The Mask of Obedience: Male Slave Psychology in the Old South." *American Historical Review* 93 (1988): 1228-52.

———. *Southern Honor: Ethics and Behavior in the Old South.* New York: Oxford University Press, 1982.

Young, Mary. "Racism in Red and Black: Indians and Other Free People of Color in Georgia Law, Politics, and Removal Policy." *Georgia Historical Quarterly* 73 (1989): 492-518.

Zack, Naomi. *Race and Mixed Race.* Philadelphia: Temple University Press, 1993.

Index

The Lyre and the Harp

A Comparative Reconsideration of Oral Tradition
in Homer and Old English Epic Poetry

by Ann Chalmers Watts

New Haven and London, Yale University Press, 1969

The ten lines of T. S. Eliot's "The Waste Land," from
Collected Poems 1909–1962, are reprinted on page 121
by permission of Faber and Faber, Ltd., London, and
Harcourt, Brace and World, Inc., New York.

for
Roberta Teale Chalmers
Gordon Keith Chalmers

Acknowledgments

This book is greatly indebted to John Collins Pope who introduced me to Old English literature and who suggested to me that the theory of the oral composition of Old English poetry could bear reconsideration. Both he and Marie Borroff, who directed the dissertation of which the book is a revision, have read the manuscript more than once with patience and attention and have contributed corrections and ideas, small and weighty. Errors of fact or judgment which remain in the final draft are of my own making and none of theirs. To the editors of the Yale Press I am indebted for technical advice and helpful management. For recommendations, probing questions, reading, and helpful discussion my thanks are due Alice Augusta Miskimin, John Oliver Perry, and Terence Leslie Watts. To the latter for his good humor and encouragement during the writing of both dissertation and book I am inarticulately grateful.

A. C. W.

Table of Contents

List of Abbreviations

(Abbreviations, except where preceded by an asterisk, are consistent with those in the *PMLA* bibliography.)

*AJA	*American Journal of Archaeology*
*AJP	*American Journal of Philology*
BGDSL	*Beiträge zur Geschichte der deutchen Sprache und Literatur*
*BT	Joseph Bosworth and T. Northcote Toller, *An Anglo-Saxon Dictionary*, Oxford, 1898; reprinted 1954.
*BTS	T. Northcote Toller, *An Anglo-Saxon Dictionary: Supplement*, Oxford, 1921; reprinted 1955.
*CH	*A Companion to Homer*, ed. Alan B. Wace and Frank H. Stubbings, London, 1962.
CL	*Comparative Literature*
*CP	*Classical Philology*
CQ	*The Classical Quarterly*
*CW	*Classical Weekly*
DA	*Dissertation Abstracts*
EA	*Études anglaises*
EIC	*Essays in Criticism*
ELH	*English Literary History*
ES	*English Studies*
*HSCP	*Harvard Studies in Classical Philology*
JEGP	*Journal of English and Germanic Philology*
LSE	*Lund Studies in English*
MLN	*Modern Language Notes*
MLQ	*Modern Language Quarterly*
MLR	*Modern Language Review*
MP	*Modern Philology*
MS	*Mediaeval Studies*
NM	*Neuphilologische Mitteilungen*
Neophil.	*Neophilologus*
PBA	*Proceedings of the British Academy*

*PL . . .   *Patrologiae cursus completus: series Latina,* ed. Jacques Paul Migne (Paris, 1844–1864)

PMLA . .   *Publications of the Modern Language Association*

PQ . . .   *Philological Quarterly*

RES . . .   *Review of English Studies*

*TAPA . .   *Transactions of the American Philological Association*

TSLL . .   *Texas Studies in Literature and Language*

*UCPCP . .   *University of California Publications in Classical Philology*

UTQ . . .   *University of Toronto Quarterly*

*YCS . . .   *Yale Classical Studies*

ZDA . . .   *Zeitschrift für deutches Altertum und deutche Literatur*

Note: For abbreviations of Old English poems I have used those suggested by Francis P. Magoun, Jr., in his article, "Abbreviated Titles for the Poems of the Anglo-Saxon Poetic Corpus," *Études anglaises,* 7 (1955), 138–46.

The Lyre and the Harp

Introduction

Grendel was envious of many of the joys of men; and the first of these mentioned in *Beowulf* is not a joy of gifts or of ale, but of song:

> Ða se ellengæst   earfoðlice
> þrage geþolode,   se þe in þystrum bad,
> þæt he dogora gehwam   dream gehyrde
> hludne in healle;   þær wæs hearpan sweg,
> swutol sang scopes.   Sægde se þe cuþe
> frumsceaft fira   feorran reccan,
> cwæð þæt se Ælmihtiga   eorðan worhte,
> wlitebeorhtne wang, ...   (86a–93a)

This is a song of creation. The next song Grendel could not possibly hear, since it is a song of his defeat:

> Hwilum cyninges þegn,
> guma gilphlæden,   gidda gemyndig,
> se ðe ealfela   ealdgesegena
> worn gemunde,   word oþer fand
> soðe gebunden;   secg eft ongan
> sið Beowulfes   snyttrum styrian,
> ond on sped wrecan   spel gerade,
> wordum wrixlan;   (867b–74a)

Yet another song is Hrothgar's song, heard secondhand when Beowulf describes to Hygelac the celebrations in the hall of the Danes:

> Þær wæs gidd ond gleo;   gomela Scilding,
> felafricgende   feorran rehte;
> hwilum hildedeor   hearpan wynne,
> gomenwudu grette,   hwilum gyd awræc
> soð ond sarlic,   hwilum syllic spell
> rehte æfter rihte   rumheort cyning;
> hwilum eft ongan   eldo gebunden,
> gomel guðwiga   gioguðe cwiðan,

hildgestrengo;   hreðer inne weoll,
þonne he wintrum frod   worn gemunde.
                    (2105a–14b)

There are several other songs in *Beowulf* and several passing references
to singing. They are all different, but they all seem to have in common
this: there is nothing in these songs to contradict an impression that they
were produced without recourse to the written word and that they were
produced spontaneously. The scop sings of Beowulf's victory too soon
to have memorized a set piece for the occasion; Hrothgar's recollection
of his own youth seems unpremeditated.

Similar observations may be made of the descriptions of singing in the
Homeric poems, whether there is a public singing at length, as when
Demodokos of Phaeacia takes the harp in Book VIII of the *Odyssey,* or
a private habit of song like that of Achilles when he is found singing "of
the glorious deeds of men" at his tent in Book IX of the *Iliad.*

Minstrels and singers in other old poems are common and are very
much a part of what modern readers take to be the "epic scene." Whether
Greek, Anglo-Saxon, Russian, Roman, or Nordic, these singers generally
sing to a musical instrument and appear to sing spontaneously, or at
least without reference to a printed text. The question of how they
composed their songs almost effortlessly presents itself to a reader of
the *Iliad* or *Beowulf* or other old epic poems. Were the songs made
entirely on the spur of the moment? Is the picture of the scop in
Beowulf or of Demodokos in the *Odyssey* representative of the Old
English poet or Homer himself? What exactly does *word oþer fand,
soðe gebunden* mean?

Such questions of how poetries of now forgotten traditions were
composed, of how relevant to their method of composition are their
internal references to song, have of course been pondered as long as any
of these poems have been read. But it is only recently, in the last century,
that these and many other questions have been critically extended and
explored. The great linguistic learning and knowledge of folklore of
many nineteenth-century scholars indirectly influenced the study of ancient methods of composition. It is in our own century that the problem
of compositional method has received exclusive attention in its own
right.

As a separate study the Homeric method of composition received its greatest impetus from the work of the late Milman Parry, who built his theory of oral-formulaic composition upon a thorough inspection of Homeric epithets for gods and heroes. Parry's theory has provided the modern critical approach to any poetry which either is or conceivably has been orally composed. Parry's student Albert Bates Lord studied the living oral poetry of the Yugoslavian Guslars in the Balkan mountains and found Parry's ideas about ancient oral composition borne out in contemporary practice. Other scholars in other literary disciplines have adopted Parry's theory and have explored it or changed it according to its apparent relevance in languages, epic poems, and eras other than Greek, the *Iliad,* and the eighth century B.C. In the field of Old English literature Francis P. Magoun, Jr., later followed by several of his students as well as by other Old English scholars, has applied Parry's theory of oral-formulaic composition to *Beowulf, Caedmon's Hymn, Christ and Satan,* and other Old English poems.

If Parry's original theory and Magoun's application of it are correct, then the Homeric poems and *Beowulf* were composed in much the same way as the songs described within them seem to have been composed: orally, spontaneously. According to Parry's theory and Magoun's adaptation of it, Homer and the *Beowulf*-poet were illiterate singers who, both from their acquaintance with an old tradition and from their own practice, sang long epic songs in strict meter and in conformity to certain rules of syntax or alliteration without the help of letters or word-for-word memorization. These singers depended for their speed and correctness of composition on *formulae,* or ready-made units of speech so syntactically and metrically defined that the singer was aware of them more for their filling out a hexameter (or a half-verse) than for their significance in meaning. These smaller pieces of language, the formulae, are themselves—according to the theory—often members of larger and looser verbal organizations, *formulaic systems.* Both formulae and formulaic systems are smaller units of whole oral *themes,* or certain patterns of narrative events the sequence of which the singer memorizes before he sings his song.

By now, more than thirty years after Lord's studies, the oral art of Yugoslavia is nearly dead, largely because it seems to be incompatible with literacy. Homer and the *Beowulf*-poet are, of course, silent, very much obscured by the texts of their poems that have come down to us. How, then, is one to recognize the oral-formulaic method of composition in written words? By the presence, so argues Parry, of formulae, formulaic systems, and set, traditional themes. The discoveries made possible by Parry's thesis are thus thought to work in two directions: if a poem is orally composed, then it will abound in exactly repeated phrases; if a text abounds in formulae, then it was orally composed. In order to find out whether the text of an old, long poem is formulaic, it is necessary to analyze every line of the text for exactly or almost exactly repeated phraseology. Parry completed many such analyses for Homer; and more recently (1955) Robert Payson Creed, a student of Magoun's, analyzed the complete text of *Beowulf* and gave evidence for a very high degree of formulaic content.

Lord is perhaps the one scholar intimately acquainted with Parry's work who has considered the theory of oral-formulaic composition with the breadth of observation that belongs to a student of comparative literature. In his book *The Singer of Tales* (1960), Lord discusses at length the Homeric and Serbo-Croatian poems in the context of Parry's theory; but he also offers analyses of brief passages from *Beowulf*, the *Song of Roland*, and *Digenis Akritas* and appends opinions about the oral origin of these works. Lord's conviction about *Beowulf* is specific and may be said to represent a "school" of thought among Old English scholars: "The formulaic character of the Old English *Beowulf* has been proved beyond any doubt by a series of analyses [he lists the work of Magoun and Creed] . . . The documentation is complete, thorough, and accurate. This exhaustive analysis is in itself sufficient to prove that *Beowulf* was composed orally" (p. 198).

This critical position is essentially that of Magoun and his students, Creed and Robert Edwin Diamond, and several other Old English scholars on the question of the oral-formulaic composition not only of *Beowulf* but of other Old English poetry. It is not of course a position that has been held unchallenged. Several men—Stevick, Brodeur, and Benson preeminent among them—have expressed their doubts about the method of oral-formulaic analysis and have taken exception to Magoun's conclusions regarding the "totally formulaic" character of *Beowulf*. In general these scholars object to the "Magoun school" because they think that Magoun and his followers have gone too far in proclaiming the oral composition of most Old English poems without adequately considering critical or historical alternatives.

Objections to the theory of oral-formulaic composition in Old English poetry have been presented, for the most part, either briefly or in subordination to other critical considerations. The objections have always been directed at the theory in its Old English form and not at its original Homeric application. As such, none of these objections has been answered by scholars who support or enlarge upon Magoun's work. Perhaps the relative silence of Magoun and his followers toward their challengers is the result of the disparateness of the challenge. It would therefore be helpful, as well as interesting in the cause of debate, to organize any reasonable and reasoned objections to the application of the theory of oral-formulaic composition to Old English poetry.

An objection to so uncompromising a statement as that by Lord quoted above may be offered without meditation: was the oral composition of *Beowulf* as possible in the age of Bede as that of the *Iliad* in the Iron Age of Greece? Yet objections only begin here. If one should study the work of Parry in Homeric studies, of Lord in studies of the Guslars, and then of Magoun and others in Old English poetry, it is at once apparent that Parry's original thesis has suffered metamorphoses of detail in the transition from Greek and Serbo-Croatian to Old English. These metamorphoses have occurred largely without explanation or, when a discreet change is overtly acknowledged, the reasons for it have not been sufficiently explored. These inconsistencies on the part of Magoun and his followers are possibly extended by the Old English scholars' failure to consider whether Old English poetry, so different from Homeric poetry, should be described in the same methodological terms that have been applied to the *Iliad* and the *Odyssey*.

Magoun's first article on the subject of the theory of oral-formulaic composition in Old English poetry is fifteen years old. It has been both important and influential enough to be reconsidered now in the light of its inspiration, of the scholarship it has fostered, and of its appropriateness to Old English poetry. The purpose of this book is to enter into such a consideration.

Because Magoun's work on the subject of oral poetry took its shape from Parry's work in Homeric studies, and because Parry's original theory and Magoun's and others' translation of it to Old English scholarship are dissimilar, it is best to begin with a thorough discussion of Parry's thesis and to describe this thesis specifically in relation to the field in which it was first evolved. Such a discussion necessitates a brief sketch of the multitudinous and perplexing problems that contribute to what is

known as "the Homeric question," but only to the extent that it is necessary by such a sketch to present Parry within his milieu and within a
certain line of scholarship. Only by understanding the details of the
Homeric application of Parry's theory can one perceive what part of that
theory has been changed in its Old English application, or raise the
essential questions of whether these changes are justified or of whether
the whole theory is as suitable an explanation for Hrothgar's scop as it
seems to be for Demodokos. Accordingly the first chapter of this book is
devoted to Homer and Parry; the following chapters attempt to embrace
in detailed discussion and illustration the theory of the oral-formulaic
composition of Old English poetry with considerations of both the Greek
origin of the theory and the appropriateness of its present critical status
in Old English scholarship. These chapters are taken up with Old English poetry itself, with whatever evidence there may be in Old English
poetic style that reveals or does not reveal oral composition. Illustrations
are almost entirely drawn from *Beowulf* and *Elene,* for the sake of contrast and concentration.

Evidence of a secondary nature (such as historically contemporary
references or descriptions of poetic composition in old Germanic civilizations, or analogies to practices in modern illiterate societies), as much
for lack of certainty as for lack of space, is not discussed. The specific
consideration of primary evidence is not intended to be a "solution" to
any of the questions raised throughout the book, but is an exploration
of some critical possibilities in a poetic style and historical moment the
uncertainties of which are too numerous to conform to any but a tentative description.

Chapter One
Milman Parry and Homeric Scholarship

Any new reader of the *Iliad* or the *Odyssey,* whether he reads the Greek or a translation, is soon aware of verbal repetitions ranging in length from a brief phrase or epithet to several lines of description. At first the recurrence of "wine-dark sea," "swift-footed Achilles," or "he spoke winged words," and whole lines about the details of arming or feasting intrude upon the reader's attention; but as he reads more, or rereads, he takes the repetitious language more for granted, unconsciously assigns it to a vague category of "Homeric style," unconsciously allows it to be subsumed within the epic action.

Homer, whether a conglomerate or a single genius, has long occupied men's thoughts with more than language; yet even from the earliest Alexandrian studies his language in its dialectical, syntactical, and stylistic qualities has received a large share of critical concentration. Scholars have long asked: What are those recurring phrases? Why are they there? And they have long answered and at great length: Because the artist, Homer, liked verbal repetitions and used them for an aesthetic purpose; because the Homeric poems are a hodgepodge of a creation whose contributers copied each other's poetic phrases; because the poems were produced within a certain tradition of poetic convention that demanded repetitive language. These answers held sway until Milman Parry published his dissertation, *L'Épithète traditionnelle dans Homère,* in 1928. Parry was the first to argue that the repetitive language in Homer's poetry was a result of metrical necessity, a matter of essential technique, a characteristic of a specific tradition of poetic composition.

Yet Parry, for all the originality of his thesis, was abstracted neither from the centuries of Homeric scholarship that preceded his, nor from his contemporary Homerists, nor, in his later work, from perplexing Homeric problems other than those of language and style. In considering Parry, it is therefore necessary to acknowledge both the scholarship that preceded his and the relationship of his study of style to other matters in the field. Homer is equal to our joy, but greater than all our disciplines put together: a thorough questioning of "wine-dark sea" inevitably compounds questions of Homer's date and dialect, the date of the Trojan War, the introduction of the alphabet into Greece, the authorship of the *Iliad* and the *Odyssey,* and the textual tradition of the poems.

U. von Wilamowitz-Möllendorff, one of the greatest questioners, once remarked: "Die Geschichte des Epos, das ist die Homerische Frage." [1] Needless to say, an account of "the Homeric question" is unnecessary and could not be undertaken here; but even a brief indication of its history should not only place Parry's scholarship in context but should also help to explain the effect of Parry's work upon subsequent studies of the epic poetry of ancient Greece and England.

I

Before Pisistratean Athens (c. 520 B.C.), [2] Homer's only witnesses were the unacknowledged quotations and vague imitations of a few sixth-century poets. In Xenophanes (fl. 530-20 B.C.) and Simonides (c. 556-468 B.C.) are found the earliest surviving records of his name, and in Herodotus (c. 484-24 B.C.) the earliest mention of the *Iliad* and the *Odyssey.* [3] Yet from the period just after the Persian War, references, quotations, and then critical discussions of Homer have survived in great numbers. For the most part the Greeks did not question that Homer existed, a single and inspired author of both the *Iliad* and the *Odyssey,* nor did they doubt that he had predecessors in the art of epic poetry. [4] By the time of Thucydides (c. 460-400 B.C.), however, the unanimity of opinion was strained by varying traditions of poems and recensions. The authorial power of Homer's name began to attract more than the *Iliad* and the *Odyssey* and was held responsible for the *Homeric Hymns* as well; and then, possibly as the Greek city-states grew more self-aware, each claimed for its founder the first recension of the texts: so Athenians praised either Pisistratus or Hipparchus, while the Spartans credited Lycurgus, with this wise act.

1. Quoted by J. A. Davidson, "The Homeric Question," in *CH,* p. 234 (full titles are given in the List of Abbreviations.

2. For summaries of classical opinion upon Homer see Davidson, pp. 234-37; and Sir John L. Myers, *Homer and His Critics* (London, 1958), pp. 20ff.

3. Herodotus, *Histories* v. 67.

4. See Thomas W. Allen, *Homer: the Origins and Transmission* (Oxford, 1924), p. 139.

Thorough literary criticism of the Homeric poems was the invention of scholars in Alexandria during some four centuries (c. 300 B.C.–100 A.D.).[5] It is through their assiduity that the *Iliad* was handed down in 188 texts, the *Odyssey* in 76,[6] and that modern scholars are able to make any assumptions about a previous textual tradition. The earliest known text of Homer, attested by external sources, is sixth century B.C.; the first critical text (according to Plautus and Strabo) was that which Alexander the Great took with him to the wars.[7] The greatest Alexandrian scholiast of Homer was Aristarchus of Samothrace (c. 215–145 B.C.): his recension was from an Athenian manuscript of old and good tradition, and it is from his recension that the modern "vulgate" stems.

Considering the proliferation of manuscripts (both those that have come down to us and the probable many that are lost), as well as the number of famous, lesser known, and anonymous scholiasts, the consistency of the Alexandrian textual tradition in the Homeric poems is truly amazing.[8] By far the majority of scholiasts marked similar lines as spurious and argued them similarly in their notes. Because they faithfully included such lines or passages in their texts, modern textual scholars can survey their choices and compare their designations with ancient quotations. What the Alexandrians tried to forestall were the so-called "long-texts," unwieldy *Iliads* which had flourished in Athens in the fourth century and in Egypt in the third and second centuries B.C., whose bulk was the obvious result of interpolations readily identifiable by their inferior imitation of the Homeric line and by their linguistic and rhetorical "modernisms." It is not difficult to realize why repetitions, even those which they were forced to admit as "Homeric," were anathema to the scholiasts. Their principles of scholarship were less those of aesthetic than of textual criticism, but their achievement in the latter has been surpassed only in the nineteenth and twentieth centuries. Archilochus' principle of ἡ ἐκ τῆς λέξεως λύσις (literally "freeing from the reading") is a modern editor's finest rule.[9]

5. A convenient account of the most important contributions of the Alexandrian scholars is Davidson in *CH*, p. 237, and also his article "The Transmission of the Text," ibid., p. 219.

6. Myres, p. 16.

7. Davidson, "The Transmission of the Text," p. 221. This text was called ἡ ἐκ τοῦ νάρθηκος, since Alexander kept it in a cylinder, νάρθηκος.

8. See Allen, pp. 302–27, "The Origin of the Vulgate."

9. Quoted by James A. Notopoulos in "Continuity and Interconnection in Homeric Oral Composition," *TAPA, 82* (1951), 94.

With the gradual but eventually complete demise of Alexandrian classical scholarship in the third century A.D. came a grand silence in Homeric criticism, a silence which lasted well over a millennium. Manuscripts of the poems and then printed texts and translations appeared with increasing rapidity in the Renaissance; yet until the late seventeenth century critical estimation of Homer concerned itself not with questions of origin or textual tradition but with the broader characteristics of Homeric narrative and style, and with Homer as a repository of all knowledge—geographical, philosophical, and rhetorical.

It was perhaps the Battle of the Books, as it raged in France and England in the 1690s, that first turned European minds to questions of "old" and "new" in the *Iliad* and the *Odyssey* and thence to questions of historical criticism.[10] René Rapin (*Observations*) and Sir William Temple ("Of Poetry") unembarrassedly believed in the Pisistratean recension; other scholars tentatively wondered whether Homer knew all there was to know, whether his knowledge were not local rather than universal. Richard Bentley in *Remarks upon a Late Discourse of Free Thinking* (1713; a reply to an extravagant essay by Antony Collins) emphatically denied Homer intellectual perfection. The greatness of Bentley's essay, however, rests not so much on his quarrel with Collins as on his discovery and demonstration of the digamma, that initial consonant of a pre-Ionic alphabet, unknown to the Alexandrian scholars. Bentley's discovery not only cleared Homer of the onus of many faulty hexameters and vocalic hiatuses, but for the first time in scholarly history challenged the dependability, hence the supremacy, of Alexandrian scholarship.

A little less than a century after Alexandria was found wanting, Homer himself was said to be the conglomerate name of innumerable "singers" whose "lays" were bound together in one manuscript by an appreciative Athenian tyrant. Friedrich August Wolf did not, in fact, initiate the theory of an illiterate and conglomerate Homer; rather he bolstered with linguistic detail, scholarly argument, and theoretical extension the theory of illiteracy that he saw set forth in a general manner by the Englishman, Robert Wood. Wood, who made a hobby of Homer, traveled to Asia Minor and the Aegean Sea in order to compare the

10. Donald M. Foerster's suggestion in *Homer in English Criticism* (New Haven, 1947), p. 10. For details concerning Homeric criticism in the seventeenth and eighteenth centuries, see Foerster, pp. 5–63; Myres, pp. 43–68.

poet's natural descriptions with reality: Homer flourished under the comparison. When he returned to England, Wood presented his thoughts and confirmations in a privately printed (1767) and later published (1769) essay, the posthumous edition of which appeared in 1775 with the title *An Essay on the Original Genius and Writings of Homer, with a Comparative View of the Ancient and Present State of the Troade.* In this book Wood created the "archaeological Homer" and pursued his idea of the poet as a "correct painter"; but it was his final chapter, "On Homer's Language and Learning," that caught Wolf's eye, for it was here that Wood weighed what he took to be the facts and came to a conclusion that Wolf, and later Parry, were to adopt as a premise in entirely different arguments. Wood's declaration of Homer's illiteracy is stated so clearly and humanely that it demands quotation:

> We are not far removed from the age, when great statesmen, and profound politicians, did not know their alphabet. I mention this undoubted fact to lessen the Reader's astonishment at any insinuation, that Homer could neither read nor write. Nor will it appear altogether so paradoxical, if we consider, how much the one is the work of genius, and the other of art. Poetry is found in savage life; and, even there, it is not without those magic powers over our passions, which is the boasted character of its perfect state. But the art of establishing that wonderful intercourse between the senses of hearing and seeing, by means of arbitrary marks, that have no resemblance to the idea, which is by agreement affixed to them, must have been the result of much deep thought and reflection. I am not surprised that antiquity, however fond of tracing every art up to its inventor, should attribute that of Writing to the Gods. If the invention of Printing is ingenious, what shall we say to that of Letters? [11]

But if Homer could not write, and if he lived long before the days of Pisistratus (Homer was thought to have lived c. 1000 B.C.), how did his poems survive? "It is, I own, very striking," was Wood's response to his own question. His answer was the obvious one: Homer's poems survived by oral tradition. This explanation was in print before Wood's *Essay,* as was the comparison between Homer and the recently dis-

---

11. This quotation and those following are from the Dublin 1776 edition, pp. 212–13, 221, 239.

covered Ossian; but Wood understood the significance of what kind of survival was involved, and he described not only how the process could take place but also how it affected Homer's style:

> the oral traditions of a learned and enlightened age will greatly mislead us, if from them we form our Judgment on those of a period, when History had no other resource. . . . nor can we, in this age of Dictionaries, and other technical aids to memory, judge, what her use and powers were, at a time, when all a man could know, was all he could remember. To which we may add, that, in a rude and unlettered state of society the memory is loaded with nothing that is either useless or unintelligible: whereas modern education employs us chiefly on getting by heart, while we are young, what we forget before we are old.

And then, Wood was as sensitive to the characteristics of unlettered poetry as he was to its very ancient existence: "The frequent repetition of entire passages (for which Homer is censured) was not only more natural, but less observable, and therefore less offensive."

Wood's *Essay* enjoyed many editions in England and was immediately popular in Germany, where Friedrich August Wolf, a young and brilliant scholar at Leipzig, read it in the early 1780s.[12] During the same period a French scholar, Villoison, discovered and published *Venetus A,* the earliest known manuscript of the *Iliad,* with all its Alexandrian marginalia. Upon this publication the authority of the "vulgate" text appeared to be somewhat relative, as Wolf was quick to perceive; and it was this proof of Alexandrian arbitrariness, in addition to Wood's ideas, that led Wolf to publish his *Prolegomena ad Homerum* in 1795. The book was intended as a preface to a school-text of the *Iliad,* which did not appear until 1804 and which added little to the currently published texts. Wolf's scholarly energy was almost entirely spent on the *Prolegomena.* There he argued that since *Venetus A* was no older than A.D., and yet was the oldest surviving manuscript, it undoubtedly did not go

12. The first German edition was 1773; second edition, 1778. For information about Wolf and his work, see Davidson, "The Homeric Question," p. 245; and also H. L. Lorimer, "Homer and the Art of Writing: a Sketch of Opinion between 1713 and 1939," *AJA,* 52 (1948), 11–23; Myres, pp. 73–87; Martin P. Nilsson, *Homer and Mycenae* (London, 1933), pp. 2–3; Cedric H. Whitman, *Homer and the Heroic Tradition* (Cambridge, 1958), p. 4.

back to a manuscript with authorial sanction. Homer's poems therefore must have lived on in an illiterate age by oral transmission. Furthermore (and here Wolf pressed a conclusion not considered by Wood) since they were far too long for one man to have memorized for recitation, the *Iliad* and the *Odyssey* must be compositions of many different plots and styles in short poetic lays or rhapsodies. Homer's name may be either indicative of the first poet of the Trojan "myth" or of a school of reciters who freely contributed numerous versions of essentially the same story; the identity of the author does not necessarily matter, since the poems are obviously disjointed and their textual history can be traced with certainty only back to the Pisistratean recension.

Though it soon became evident that Wolf's work contained factual errors (for instance, he thought *Venetus A* a direct descendant of Aristarchus' recension), his arguments were strongly and clearly set forth, and at the time seemed incontrovertible. His book created the "analytic" school of Homeric critics (also called "separatist" and "divisionist"), who in the following century devoted themselves to most learned scrutiny of the "vulgate" text in order to determine the limits of the separate lays and to describe and point out what seemed to them evident and contrasting individualities of style.

Throughout the nineteenth century the analysts held the field of Homeric scholarship:[13] those who opposed their views and believed the *Iliad* and the *Odyssey* to have been written, pen in hand, by one masterly poet in a concentrated and supreme act of continuous creation, could only argue from a vague appeal to "poetic effect." The "unitarians" suffered badly in comparison with their learned enemies, since they presented no argument from facts as tangible as the linguistic evidence marshaled by the greatest of the analysts; until the very end of the century there was not one unitarian whose scholarship was sufficiently rigorous to stand on its own.

Somewhat because of Wolf, but largely because of a learned tradition of linguistic studies, the analytic movement was at first carried on exclu-

13. For summaries and accounts of Homeric scholarship during this period, see especially Paul Cauer, *Grundfragen der Homerkritik* (3d ed. Leipzig, 1923), pp. 487, 561ff., 656ff.; Samuel Eliot Bassett, *The Poetry of Homer,* Sather Classical Lectures (Berkeley, 1938), pp. 11–12; Nilsson, pp. 2–3, 7, 10–11, 12–13; Myres, pp. 91–122, 197ff; Maurice Platnauer, ed., *Fifty Years of Classical Scholarship* (Oxford, 1954), pp. 21–22; Davidson, "The Homeric Question," pp. 249, 251; C. M. Bowra, *Tradition and Design in the Iliad* (Oxford, 1930), p. 42; Whitman, pp. 3–4.

sively by German scholars. Toward the middle of the century English scholars began to contribute criticism of equal caliber, but the school remained ensconced in German universities until after the First World War.

Whatever their nationality, the analysts were unanimous in adopting Wolf's conclusions; but within the school one may distinguish two differing persuasions, two views whose detailed proofs were similar in method but whose main drifts led to different accounts of the origin of the Homeric poems. Chronologically speaking, the first of these views was the *Liedertheorie,* already indicated by Wolf, and presented with great precision of argument by Karl Lachmann (1793–1851), followed by Herder, Steinthall, and others. The second view, which gradually replaced the first, was the "kernel theory," hinted at by Wolf and powerfully argued by Gottfried Hermann in his book *De interpolationibus Homeri* (1832). According to this theory Homer's poems, unlike the *Kalevala* and the Ossianic lays to which they had been compared, represented narrative accretions around an originally brief story. The nucleus or kernel of the *Iliad,* for instance, was often taken to be the story of the "Wrath of Achilles"; around this original and earliest story other episodes concerning the Trojan War began to accumulate until eventually, when the whole came to be written down, the "wrath" was dissipated, often ineffectually, throughout the poem, and was nearly indistinguishable from the stories about Helen and Menelaus, Priam's splendor, and the sailing from Greece. Hermann's work incited many scholars, German, French, and English, among whom some of the more famous were Fick, Bethe, Cauer, Wilamowitz, Grote, Gladstone, Murray, Berand, and, in their early books, Jebb, Leaf, and Croisset. All these men were agreed that "Homer," whether an individual or a school of poets, lived at the beginning of an oral narrative tradition; and most of them drew the conclusion (*non sequitur*) that "Homer's" work represented the best poetry. Hence all accretion was decline, the later interpolations were clumsy, unwieldy, and cancerous growths upon what had originally been fresh, direct, "poetic," self-contained: the present *Iliad,* in Wilamowitz' famous words, was the work of "ein genug begabter Flickpoet." [14]

But beyond this point agreement among scholars of the kernel theory

---

14. Quoted by Davidson, "The Homeric Question," p. 231, from Wilamowitz' book, *Homerische Untersuchungen.*

ceased. Each one tended either to isolate a different nucleus altogether or to define the limits of the "wrath" kernel uniquely—a confusion foretold by Wolf in the resigned remark: "forsitan ne probabiliter quidem demonstrari poterit a quibus locis potissimum nova subtemnia et limbi procedant" (*Praefatio ad Iliadem,* xxviii).

In the end it was largely the absurd extent to which the more important analytic critics proved each other false that led to the unitarian revolution in the twentieth century. This generation of unitarians, beginning with Andrew Lang, was fully equipped linguistically and, by this time, archaeologically, to oppose the analysts on their own ground.

Since the two schools were now concerned with the same evidence, it should be helpful to glance briefly at a few of the minutiae of their witnesses. One of the strongest arguments exploited with excellent erudition by all analysts was based on the dialect of the Homeric poems. The dialect as it now appears in the manuscripts hardly approximates any other text of ancient Greek, including that of Hesiod (possibly the nearest to Homer in time). Homeric vocabulary in content and inflection is predominately Ionic (a dialectal area consisting mostly of the Aegean coast of Asia Minor and outlying islands), with a mixture of Aeolic (i.e. Cypriot and Arcadian) and a mere sprinkling of Attic (the dialect of ancient Athens and of ancient literary Greek). For instance, in Homer the conjunction meaning "yet," "however," always appears in its Aeolic form, αὐτάρ (the Attic is ἀτάρ); σμικρός is the regularly used Ionic form of Attic μικρός ("small," as in *microscopic*); but then, the adverbial conjunctions πῶς, πότε, always occur with the Attic initial consonant, and not as Ionic κῶς, κότε.[15] The inflections of nouns are not consistently of one dialect or another; similarly, verb forms seem to be borrowed from all dialects at different stages of linguistic development. The whole is a language far removed from any actually spoken speech.

Because the amalgamation called the Homeric language presents chronological as well as dialectal strata, the analytic school of criticism leaned heavily upon phonology as a proof of the kernel theory. Thus, since the old Ionic dative plurals ended in -οισι, -αισι, -ησι, passages from the poems that contained such endings were thought to be earlier than those in which endings in the later -οις, -αις, -ης appeared. Similarly, the

15. For many more examples see Allen, p. 100.

use of abstract nouns was proof of later interpolation, as was the use of ὁ for a pronoun rather than for an article.[16]

There were other than linguistic strata in the *Iliad* and the *Odyssey* which also were available for testimony in the kernel theory. With Schliemann's excavations in Troy and Mycenae, scholarly disbelief in an historical Troy was dispelled: Troy did exist, and in a Homeric splendor; there was even evidence that one of the cities on the site had been destroyed in the early twelfth century B.C., the very time at which the ancient Greeks dated the Trojan War.[17] Then too Mycenae, the crown seat of powerful Agamemnon, was demonstrated to be worthy of its twelfth-century king. Schliemann initiated an interest in and a science of archaeology which continues in the present day, but as the diggings proceeded it became clear that as often as the unearthed objects verified Homer, they accused him of no small inaccuracies. In Homer, cremation is the order for the burial of the dead; yet there were the shaft-graves at Mycenae, graves which spoke loudly of an elaborate concentration upon the preservation of the body. Homer's warriors fought with iron as well as with bronze, yet the earth of Troy and the Greek mainland yielded only bronze weapons from decades during and long after the period of the Trojan War. The analysts understandably made use of these archaeological data to define "original" and "interpolated" work in the Homeric poems: all cremations in the *Iliad* (including the stories of the deaths of Patroclus and Hector) were thus suspect; similarly, the numerous battle scenes involving the use or description of iron weapons were demonstrably the additions of nameless rhapsodists who knew neither Homer's truth nor his art.

Thus did the great analysts interpret the available factual evidence, and for half a century their interpretations stood unchallenged. Their sway was so strong that in 1907 a handbook of Greek literature could display the confident observation that "Time, which makes all heresies orthodox, has suppressed the unitarians . . . and all scholars are now Chorizontes" (i.e. separatists).[18] The observation, if ironical today, was false when stated, for two of Andrew Lang's books, *Homer and the Epic* (1893) and *Homer and His Age* (1906), were already in circulation, to

16. Nilsson, pp. 9–10; Cauer, p. 137.

17. For an account of nineteenth-century classical archaeology see Myres, pp. 123–96; Nilsson, pp. 19ff.

18. Wilber Cave Wright, *A Short History of Greek Literature* (New York, 1907), p. 31.

be followed in 1910 by *The World of Homer*. Lang himself was succeeded and supported by other unitarian scholars, among whom were Carl Rothe (*Das Ilias als Dichtung*, 1910), E. Drerup (*Homerische Poetik*, 1921), John A. Scott (*The Unity of Homer*, 1921), Thomas W. Allen (*Homer: the Origins and Transmission*, 1924), W. J. Woodhouse (*The Composition of Homer's Odyssey*, 1930), and C. M. Bowra (*Tradition and Design in the Iliad*, 1930).[19] Each of these made much of the embarrassing fact that, though every analytic scholar of Homer was convinced upon linguistic evidence that the "vulgate" text of the poems represented datable and divisible strata of composition, no two such scholars divided the text or designated the strata with even approximate agreement. John A. Scott was the first to use this argument in a positive fashion by meticulously demonstrating that Aeolic, Ionic, and Attic words, and both archaic and historic inflections, occur at a relatively constant frequency throughout the *Iliad* and the *Odyssey*.[20] At the time, the only explanation for so evenly distributed a dialectal and developmental variation seemed to lie in the history of migrations: for instance the Aeolic civilization, known to be older than the Ionian, settled across the Aegean sometime in the eighth century B.C.; perhaps the absorption of the Aeolic by the Ionic civilization was recorded only in the dialectal mixture of the Homeric texts.[21]

The problems posed by the conflict of archaeological data and the descriptions to be gleaned from Homer continued to be investigated, both indoors and out. But the discoveries of the Attic Prize Jug, with its eighth-century inscription, and of the Hymettus Graffiti marked a definite advance; until these discoveries it had been assumed that the Greek alphabet was not in use earlier than the sixth century B.C. At the same time the references to iron weapons and Phoenician trade in the Homeric poems strongly indicated an eighth-century redactor. These two considerations, combined with logical and sensitive arguments from the unity of artistic design, gradually made an eighth-century Homer seem not only possible but necessary. The analysts' imagined context was also reversed: whereas they had thought of Homer at the beginning of a tradition whose glory was its youth, the unitarians would place Homer

19. For information about twentieth-century unitarians see Nilsson, pp. 19–38; Myres, pp. 241ff.; Whitman, p. 5.

20. *The Unity of Homer* (Berkeley, 1921), pp. 3ff., and see the bibliography.

21. See e.g. the opinions of Allen, pp. 100ff.

at the culmination of a long-flourishing tradition of which he was the finest offspring.

There was yet another bone of contention between the analysts and the unitarians which is worthy of mention: it concerns what Horace once observed: "quandoque bonus dormitat Homerus" (*Ars Poetica, 359*). Analysts advanced a corroborative argument based solely upon internal evidence, that Homer's nodding was in fact not the relaxation of one poet but the separate and unaware wakefulness of several rhapsodists. Thus when Achilles is carefully noted to put down his sword in XXI.17, only to be carrying it a little later in XXI.67, or when Poseidon's horses are celebrated in XIII.23ff., only to leave the battle unnoticed in XV.228, there is clearly more than one poet at work. A far greater contradiction may be observed in the history of Pylaemenes, king of the Paphlagonians: he is killed by Menelaus in V.576 but reappears at his son's funeral in XII.658. The unitarians objected to what seemed to them a disproportionate emphasis upon these "slips." In general they pointed out that the mere neglect of a detail does not constitute a "contradiction" and that Pylaemenes was a forgivable oversight in a poem of 15,693 lines.[22]

To the unitarians of the early twentieth century, the evidence that had occupied the previous generation of Homeric critics was, finally, subservient to the most generous evidence of all—the manifestly artistic unity of the poems. Woodhouse and Scott, concerned respectively with the *Odyssey* and the *Iliad*,[23] enthusiastically guided the student of Homer to an aesthetic enjoyment of the poems through a chapter-by-chapter observation of how the complete works were predicted in their invocations. In their reaction to the analysts' denial of genius to the poems as a whole, the unitarians made, of course, some extravagant statements: a chapter of Scott's book was devoted to a "proof" that Hector is purely Homer's creation, while Woodhouse went to similar lengths to maintain the imaginative uniqueness of Calypso.[24]

These men and other unitarian scholars thought that the poems were

---

22. E.g., Scott, *Unity of Homer*, pp. 140ff. Scott gleefully reminds us that the first edition of *The Newcomes* contains a character who dies and comes to life again. For recent and vigorous consideration of Homeric inconsistencies in order to support the analytic point of view, see Denys L. Page, *The Homeric Odyssey* (Oxford, 1955), and *History and the Homeric Iliad* (Berkeley, 1959).

23. W. J. Woodhouse, *The Composition of Homer's Odyssey* (Oxford, 1930); Scott, *Unity of Homer*.

24. See Scott, pp. 204–39; Woodhouse, pp. 50ff.

recited, at first by Homer in the eighth century and then by a school of rhapsodists trained by Homer; yet at the same time they entertained the assumption of a "text"—never clearly defined—from which the recitations were made.[25] The "text" was simply a last-minute guide for the rhapsodist who was rather more dependent on *memory,* a cerebral faculty utterly neglected by the analytic school of criticism. The unitarians' defense of word-for-word memory as a medium of transmission is not unlike that of Robert Wood, and to his reasoning they added the famous evidence in Xenophon's *Symposium:* " 'My father,' said Nikeratas, 'who wished me to become an educated man, made me learn all of Homer. Consequently I can now recite completely by heart the *Iliad* and the *Odyssey.*' "[26] And then there were numerous examples, even in a literate age, of the phenomenal powers of the human memory, like that of the forge-worker in Birmingham who knew all of Byron by heart and could not be caught mistaken, though he was subjected to many a test.[27]

For both analysts and unitarians the consideration of the repetition of phrases and whole passages in the Homeric poems had been a minor issue. To the analytic scholar such passages represented "borrowings" of one poet from another, and thus the repetitions were but another proof of the multiple authorship of the poems. The unitarians on the other hand recognized in these recurring lines a traditional language, the legacy of earlier, less inspired poets, which Homer used and wielded in the way of genius. Such were the general views; but toward the end of the nineteenth century, beginning with Carl Eduard Schmidt's *Parallel-Homer* (Göttingen, 1885), wherein were recorded all the repetitions of phrase and line, a specific interest in Homer's language gradually occupied the talents of several gifted scholars.

These men,[28] who were Parry's immediate predecessors, closely argued the evidence for the use and implications of the Homeric repetitions (which they called "formulas"), the origin of the dactylic hexameter,

25. See Allen, p. 139; Scott, p. 156; Bowra, pp. 51–52; E. Drerup, *Das fünfte Buch der Ilias* (Paderborn, 1913), p. 421.

26. *Symposium* 3.5, ed. François Ollier (Paris, 1961), my translation.

27. Related in Bowra, p. 49.

28. Particularly: H. Düntzer, *Homerische Abhandlungen* (Leipzig, 1872); J. Wackernagel, *Sprachliche Untersuchen zu Homer* (Göttingen, 1916); K. Meister, *Die Homerische Kunstsprache* (Leipzig, 1921); A. Meillet, *Les Origines indo-européennes des metres grecs* (Paris, 1923).

and the differentiation of the various dialects in the poems. Düntzer came astonishingly close to Parry's discovery of the connection between metrical necessity and the formulaic epithets. Meillet noted that the reiterated noun-epithets in the epics seemed to be "formules fixes;" and he concluded that, since some of these epithets disobeyed metrical rules, they were possibly formulated at a time, long preceding Homer, when the meter itself was more flexible.[29] These hints were strong, but it was Parry who provided both the imagination to characterize these epithets and the observation that led to the irrefutable proof of their status as an orally traditional language.

II

Milman Parry published his doctoral dissertation, *L'Épithète traditionnelle dans Homère,* in Paris in 1928. The book is a document not only of a rich idea and a thorough presentation but also of an elegant method. Starting with the axiom that a Homeric "langue artificielle," if it existed, would be proof of a "langue traditionnelle," Parry demonstrated that the noun-epithets were employed artificially throughout the *Iliad* and the *Odyssey.* By means of a complete catalog of several of the epithets for heroes or gods, as well as for things and places, Parry isolated but one determining condition: the meter, the demands of the dactylic hexameter. Odysseus is not "of many devices" or "long-suffering, god-like" merely by whim: the first phrase, πολύμητις Ὀδυσσεύς, occurs fifty times at the end of a line in Homer, and always fills out the verse from the caesura after the first syllable in the fourth foot: the use of the phrase "of many devices" is determined here by metrical necessity. Similarly the epithet πολύτλας δῖος Ὀδυσσεύς occurs wherever it is necessary to follow a feminine caesura with the name of this particular hero. These noun-epithets, which occur at the ends of lines, may themselves be preceded by formulaic pharses which extend to one of the possible caesuras. To illustrate:

a) To and from the caesura after the first syllable of the fourth foot:

— xx — xx — xx —	xx — x x — —
τὸν δ᾽ ἀπαμειβόμενος προσέφη	πολύμητις Ὀδυσσεύς
then him answering spoke	of many devices Odysseus

29. Meillet, pp. 69–70.

b)   To and from the feminine caesura (after the second syllable of the third foot, if that foot is a dactyl):

— xx — — — x   x — — — x x — —

ὣς φάτο μείδησεν δὲ   πολύτλας δῖος Ὀδυσσεύς

thus spoke smiling   long-suffering, godlike Odysseus.[30]

The first elements of these doubly formulaic lines are used of other heroes and thus are followed by other noun-epithets, the restriction being only that the noun-epithet fulfill the meter x x / — x x / — — or x / — x x / — x x / — — (a spondee may be substituted for any dactyl except in the fifth foot). Similarly the second elements of the two examples could be preceded by other formulae of address, or battle, or of whatever the poet pleased.

So large was the number of noun-epithets and formulaic phrases which Parry investigated and so consistently were these proved to be of metrical efficacy that it seemed they could not possibly be all the creation of one man. Parry concluded therefore that the language of the Homeric poems was totally traditional, the work of generations of oral poets who passed along to each other the tools of their craft, these formulae.

For the next nine years, until his death, Parry continued to work out the implications of his original thesis and to extend his studies to a comparative consideration of Yugoslavian oral poetry, which was still flourishing in the 1930s. In these "field studies" he was aided by his student Albert Bates Lord, who has continued to expound and amplify Parry's ideas to the present day. Since each one of the publications of these two men has contributed specifically to the general picture of the oral technique of composition, it will be convenient here to consider Parry's and Lord's whole description of Homer within that technique rather than to trace the theoretical and practical development from Parry's *L'Épithète* to Lord's *The Singer of Tales* (1960).[31] For the sake of clarity, the consideration presented here will be descriptive rather than critical.

A singer who orally composes an epic poem must, without a moment's thought, make the words and phrases of his narrative conform to some

---

30. These examples and many of a similar nature may be found in *L'Épithète tradition-nelle dans Homère* (Paris, 1928), pp. 13–18.

31. For a chronological list of Parry's and Lord's works, see the Bibliography.

metrical scheme. If this singer were of Homer's time and country he would have to combine phrases to fill out six dactylic feet, for which, in all but the fifth foot, he was able to substitute spondees (the sixth foot is almost always truncated). Although he was not aware of them as such, he was allowed several choices in the position of the caesura and thus he naturally tended to compose a whole verse (one line) out of two phrases separated by the caesura. Further examples of the different caesuras may be helpful:[32]

a) With the masculine caesura (after the first syllable of the third foot):

— x x — x x —   — — xx — x x — x

μῆνιν ἄειδε θεά   Πηληϊάδα Ἀχιλῆος

the wrath sing,   of Peleus' son

goddess,   Achilles

                                              (I.1)[33]

b) With the feminine caesura:

— x   x   — xx — x   x — xx —   xx   — x

ἄνδρά μοι ἔννεπε μοῦσα   πολύτροπον ὃς μάλα πολλὰ

the man for me tell   of many devices, who

about, Muse   evils many . . .

                                              (i.1)

c) With the caesura after the first syllable of the fourth foot:

— xx — xx — — —   x x — x   x — —

Διογενὲς Λαερτιάδη   πολυμήχαν' Ὀδυσσεῦ

(son) of Diogenes   of many devices

Lærtes,   Odysseus

                                              (v. 203)

Singers of other nations, of course, sing according to different rules. The Yugoslavian shepherds, for instance, sing a line of trochaic pen-

32. The examples are from C. M. Bowra, "Metre," in *CH*, p. 20.

33. Large Roman numerals refer to the *Iliad*, small to the *Odyssey*. The Greek texts referred to are *The Iliad of Homer*, ed. Arthur Platt (Cambridge, 1894), and *Homeri Odyssea*, ed. J. la Roche (Leipzig, 1867). Translations of short phrases are my own and are used merely to indicate the significance of the Greek in the Greek sentence order. For larger sections I have quoted Richard Lattimore's translation of the *Iliad* (Phoenix Books, Chicago, 1961) and have depended upon Robert Fitzgerald's translation of the *Odyssey* (Anchor Books, New York, 1963).

tameter with a rigid caesura after the second foot and no possibility of metrical substitution.[34] For example:

Tri je pase	*bio i ubio*
three pashas	he fought and overcame[35]

The circumstantial requirements for the singing of an epic when no written text exists (as it does not among the Yugoslavian shepherds) are obviously such that demand rapid composition. If a singer is to compose a song about the slaying of the Turks, he has time to think only of the direction of his narrative and not to concentrate upon the placement of each word; nor has he any opportunity to retrace his steps and mend a faulty line. His singing is simultaneously his *composition* and his *performance* of that composition.[36] This difficult simultaneity of composition and performance could hardly be achieved did not the singer rely upon two "mechanical" aids. First of all, he has a musical instrument to mark the time: the shepherd uses a gusla, a one-stringed shell; it is assumed that a Homeric singer would have used a lyre, since this instrument is frequently mentioned in connection with oral singing in the *Iliad* and the *Odyssey*. The marking of time in either dactylic hexameter or trochaic pentameter is not problematical since it is possible for both meters to be isochronous.

A steady beat, however, does not determine the pace of the singer's composition. In order to compose with his mind on the story rather than on the language, the singer needs a stock of ready-made phrases that fit specific metrical patterns and specific situations, characters, and events. Such a ready-made phrase is the *formula,* a term which Parry defined as "a group of words which is regularly employed under the same metical conditions to express a given essential idea."[37] Parry explicitly excluded from the status of a "group," and therefore of a formula, expressions of less than four words or five syllables, such as αὐταρ δε ("but however") or βῆ δ'ἴμεν "(when he was gone"), since such brief phrases

34. Lord, *Singer,* pp. 32, 37.

35. Parry, "Whole Formulaic Verse in Greek and South Slavic Epic Song," *TAPA, 64* (1933), 196.

36. See Lord, *Singer,* pp. 13–31, 91ff.; "Homer and Other Epic Poetry," in *CH,* pp. 179–214.

37. *L'Épithète,* p. 16; "Studies in the Epic Technique of Oral Verse-Making I," *HSCP, 41* (1930), 80.

could easily be repeated merely by chance in the natural word order of the sentence.[38] By "essential idea" Parry indicated "c'est ce qui reste après qu'elle a été débarrassée de toute superfluité stylistique."[39] For instance, a regularly employed group of words in the Homeric epics, a group which constitutes a whole line and whose metrical characteristics therefore never change, is ἦμος δ' ἠριγένεια φάνη ῥοδοδάκτυλος Ἠώς (twenty-two times in all in both poems), "When, early born, shone forth rosy-fingered Dawn," the essential idea of which is "When it was dawn." Similarly the essential idea of the noun-epithet πολύτλας δῖος Ὀδυσσεύς is "Odysseus."

That the descriptive part of the epithet is always metrically, and not always artistically, meaningful to the singer is indicated by the fact that different gods or heroes of metrically equivalent names share some epithets. Thus Διώνη (Dione) and Καλυψώ (Calypso) both fill the metrical pattern x / — — /; when the composer added δῖα θεάων ("among divinities") to either name, he possessed a line complete from the feminine caesura to the end. A like portion of verse is given by the equivalent names Διομήδης (Diomedes) or Μενέλαος (Menelaus) preceded by the epithet βοὴν ἀγαθὸς ("good at the war-cry"). Or, if a singer had completed a line up to the masculine caesura, he could finish with κρατερὸς ("very strong"), Διομήδης or Πολυποίτης (Diomedes or Polypoites).[40] Agamemnon led the Greeks to Troy and is often called ἄναξ ἀνδρῶν ("king of men"); yet not only is the epithet applied to him when his actions are cowardly, but it is applied to Αὐγείας (Augeias), Αἰνείας (Aeneas), Εὐφήτης (Euphates), Εὔμηλος (Eumelos), and many others as well, the metrical condition in this case being that the epithet and noun should fill the space from the beginning of the line to the feminine caesura.[41] It will be noticed that all these names of kings of men, excepting Agamemnon, begin with a diphthong, which ensures a long syllable; the two initial short syllables of Agamemnon's name are equivalent to one long syllable. Again, the epithet δῖος ("godlike") appears with the metrically equivalent names Ἀχιλλεύς (Achilles), Ἀγήνωρ (Agenor), Ἐπειγεύς (Epeigeos), Ἐπειός (Epeios),

38. "Studies I," p. 84 n.
39. L'Épithète, p. 16.
40. Ibid., p. 107.
41. Ibid.

Ἐχέρφον (Exerphon), and Ὀρέστης (Orestes), and with any one of them completes a line from the bucolic diaeresis (end of the fourth foot) to the end (— x x / — x).[42] These names must begin with a short syllable, and in order to be short the syllable must be a vowel since the adjectival part of the epithet, διός, ends in a *sigma,* and a following consonant would cause the syllable -ος to lengthen by position, thus destroying the necessary dactyl in the fifth foot.

One of Parry's major discoveries concerning the use of noun-epithets in the Greek epics was what he called the principle of "thrift" or "economy" (in *L'Épithète,* "simplicité"), the principle whereby the singer's collection of traditional phrases was relatively free from those which were equivalent both in measure and in meaning and which were thus replacements for one another.[43] The statistics set forth in Parry's first book are admirably illustrative of the principle: in Homer there are 40 different (i.e. not metrically equivalent) formulae to distinguish 37 different persons; and out of 723 uses of these formulae (including examples in every case of inflection), only 81 of the same metrical value are applied to the same person.[44] Lack of this astonishing economy or thrift may be seen in the phrases θεὰ λευκώλενος Ἥρη ("the goddess, white-armed Hera") and βοῶπις πότνια Ἥρη ("the ox-eyed queen, Hera"), both of which fill the measures x / — — / — x x / — —; or in the metrically equivalent formulae applied to Achilles, ποδάρκης and ποδώκης,[45] both meaning "swift-footed." Such equivalent formulae, however, are rare by comparison with those that describe certain individuals at certain positions in the hexameter line.

Parry made a convenient distinction between "particular epithet" and "generic epithet" (the latter being "l'épithète ornamentale, fixe"):[46] Homer found it useful to employ generic epithets such as διός (godlike) or ἄναξ ἀνδρῶν (leader of men) whenever they helped to complete a line after one of the caesuras; but thrift as Parry defined it is characteristic of the particular epithets, such as κορυθαίολος ("of glancing helm") used only of Hector (thirty-eight times), or ταχύς ("swift") used only of Ajax

---

42. Ibid., pp. 106–07; "Studies I," p. 123.

43. "Studies I," pp. 86–89; see Lord, *Singer,* pp. 50ff., 144.

44. *L'Épithète,* pp. 22, 41.

45. For further examples not listed by Parry, see Page, *History and the Homeric Iliad,* p. 277.

46. *L'Épithète,* p. 25.

(nine times), or εὐρὺ κρείων ("of wide rule") used only of Agamemnon.[47]

In considering the generic epithets Parry came to the conclusion that they had no literally translatable meaning.[48] Ἄναξ ἀνδρῶν appears much too familiarly of too many warriors to mean "king of men"; δῖος of so many mortals loses its significance as "godlike." These epithets, Parry thought, are rather words which in *essential idea* heighten the hero, god, or thing they designate. The same is also true of the particular epithets if they are formulaic: the constant repetition of an epithet diminishes its literal meaning and adds "glow" to the noun it modifies. To the student just beginning to read Homer, the first sight of the adjective ποδώκης summons a vigorous picture of the hero of the *Iliad* ever on the run; by the twenty-fifth occurrence of the word, however, the student, unconsciously perhaps, has merged the adjective with its noun. The literal picture has disappeared, and what is left in its place is the "Achilles-ness" of Achilles. An analogy to the relative neutrality of formulaic epithets exists in our surnames: people answering to Smith, Johnson, or Chambers do not necessarily have anything to do with anvils, John, or the palace rooms. A strong negative proof of vagueness in the meaning of recurring epithets is their well-known tendency to become contradictory (another *Homerus dormitat* for the analysts of the nineteenth century): ships in Homer, if they are not "black-beaked," are nearly always "swift" (θοαί), even when they lie quite motionless on the beach (see X.306, XI.666, XVI.168); the heavens are called "starry" (ἀστερόεντος) in broad daylight (VII.46, ix.527); the phrase γναμπτοῖσι μέλεσσι, "of supple limbs," is usually used of heroes like Odysseus except in one instance where it describes Priam (XXIV.359), a man "bent with age." Parry argued that all such repeated epithets, whether generic or particular, in some sense equal the nouns they modify while they simultaneously indicate the noun's general significance. Thus even at noon

47. Ibid., p. 112.

48. For the following discussion see especially an article, written before Parry's book: I. Berlage's "De vocibus τυκτός, τετυγμένος, ποιητός, ὀικυμενή, Aliis," in *Mnemosyne*, *53* (1925), 289–98, where the author argues for the neutrality of meaning of the words in his title; thus οἰκυμένα πόλις, which we have a habit of translating *urbs incolis instructa*, really means *urbs situm esse; τυκτός is fructus*, not "well made." Also see C. M. Bowra, *Homer and His Forerunners* (Edinburgh, 1955), p. 12; and Frederick M. Combellack, "Milman Parry and Homeric Artistry," *CL, 11* (1959), 193–208, 202–03; Parry, *L'Épithète*, pp. 21, 146–61; and Lord, *Singer*, pp. 65–66.

it is generally characteristic of the heavens to be starry; the ships on the beach have yet the capacity to be swift, just as on or off the beach they are, by description "black-beaked" (μελαίνης); the hero sulking in his tent still retains his Achillean characteristic of being "swift-footed."

Parry saw that much could be learned about an oral technique by comparing Homer's epithets with Virgil's.[49] Few poets have had so literary a mind as had Virgil; and in his great learning he deliberately set out to imitate his Greek master while he wrote and then polished his twelve daily lines of the *Aeneid*. According to Parry, a literate hand is immediately observable in the number of *particularized* epithets (i.e. those which have a direct and important bearing on the situation), which is far greater than the number of generic epithets. Of the particularized epithets, several are used of one hero and are metrically interchangeable, such as *inscius, ignarus,* and *hospitus* of Aeneas. One epithet might be called "literary" since it seems to be copied directly from the *Iliad:*

> Αἰνείας τ᾽ Ἀγχισιάδης καὶ φαίδιμος Ἕκτωρ   (XVII.754)
> *Aeneas Anchisiades et fidus Achates*   (VIII.521)

There are generic epithets to be found in the *Aeneid,* however, the most common being *pater* and *pius*. Yet these are so brief that they fit any part of an hexameter line: of the forty-one instances in which *pius* is used of Aeneas in the nominative, thirty-five have the metrical value x x, and of these, thirty-one occur in the series x x / — — / —. Homer's use of epithets is far more determined in the metrical line and thus far more economical, by necessity. As Parry said in comparing these two great epic poets, one sees "la différence entre le style de Vergile qui se sert de l'épithète uniquement comme d'un artifice de style, et celui d'Homère qui est guidé dans son emploi de l'épithète par le désir de faciliter la versification."[50]

Another interesting and major difference between the styles of Homer and Virgil which Parry noticed while he was counting epithets involves the use of enjambment by the two poets. The extent of Parry's investigation[51] cannot be described here except in a most summary manner. Of

---

49. *L'Épithète,* pp. 35–42.
50. Ibid., pp. 39–40.
51. See Parry, "Studies I," pp. 125–32, and "The Distinctive Character of Enjambment in Homeric Verse," *TAPA, 60* (1929), 200–20; Lord, "Homer, Parry, and Huso," *AJA, 52*

the two epic poets Homer was found to use "unperiodic enjambment" (where the end of the line coincides with a complete thought or with a natural pause in the syntax of the sentence) more frequently than Virgil, whereas he used "necessary enjambment" (where the end of the line coincides with no break in the syntax or sense) very rarely. On the other hand Homer composed whole sequences of lines in a kind of "adding" style, quite often ending a line and a thought together. This observation led to another: namely that in Homer the advance in the narrative, the action, is set forth in the first part of the line (with the division at one of the caesuras), and merely maintained in the second part, only to be pushed ahead in the first part of the succeeding line, and so on. Quite in keeping with this characteristic is the fact that in Homer the second parts of lines are the more formulaic. These formulaic second parts of lines add no action, are complete in themselves, and complete the line after one of the caesuras, thus creating unperiodic enjambment. Virgil, who did not compose in an oral tradition where formulae are indispensable tools, and who did compose somewhat in a visual dimension, made far more use of a caesural conclusion of sentences. Parry is not insensitive to the probability that literate poets hear a phrase before writing it.[52] "Sound is the gold in the ore," and can neither be apprehended by the eye nor represented by the tools of literacy. Blind Milton spoke his epic; almost all poetry has an oral mode of being: the distinction between Homer and Virgil or Milton lies in Homer's strikingly frequent use of repetitive language, his lack of rhetorical variation.

According to Parry's description and hypothesis, a formulaic phrase must be the singer's smallest unit of composition. Since the oral poet performs as he composes, his time is too precious and the meter too inevitable for a word-by-word advancement of the narrative. Nor, in fact, is the formulaic phrase a large enough tool with which to construct a whole epic: the singer depends to an equal extent upon units of composition provided by the *formulaic system* and the *theme*.

One may distinguish two kinds of formulaic phrases: the first itself is unique, irreplaceable, dissimilar to any other phrase, but recurs in a con-

(1948), 34–44, and *Singer,* pp. 142, 145; Bassett, pp. 152ff.; Notopoulos, p. 87; G. S. Kirk, "Studies in Some Technical Aspects of Homeric Style, II: Verse-Structure and Sentence-Structure in Homer," *YCS,* 20 (1966), pp. 105–52; and see pp. 120–23 of this book.
    52. "Studies I," pp. 143ff.

sistent metrical position; the second, consistent in metrical character, has a likeness to other phrases that express a similar idea in similar words. It is the latter sort that may belong to a system, defined by Parry as "a group of phrases which have the same metrical value and which are enough alike in thought and words to leave no doubt that the poet who used them knew them not only as single formulas but also as formulas of a certain type." [53] A critic of oral poetry may measure two factors in a formulaic system, its length and its economy: "the length of a system consists very obviously in the number of formulas which make it up; the thrift of a system lies in the degree to which it is free of phrases which, having the same metrical value and expressing the same idea, could replace one another." [54] Here is one such system:

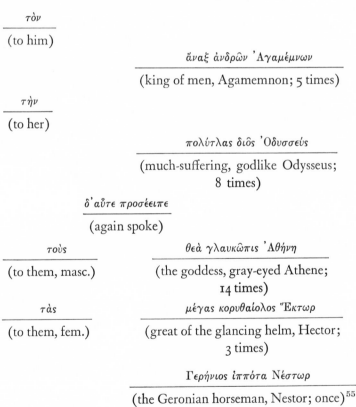

τὸν
(to him)

ἄναξ ἀνδρῶν ᾿Αγαμέμνων
(king of men, Agamemnon; 5 times)

τὴν
(to her)

πολύτλας διὸς ᾿Οδυσσεύς
(much-suffering, godlike Odysseus; 8 times)

δ᾿ αὖτε προσέειπε
(again spoke)

τοὺς
(to them, masc.)

θεὰ γλαυκῶπις ᾿Αθήνη
(the goddess, gray-eyed Athene; 14 times)

τὰς
(to them, fem.)

μέγας κορυθαίολος ῞Εκτωρ
(great of the glancing helm, Hector; 3 times)

Γερήνιος ἱππότα Νέστωρ
(the Geronian horseman, Nestor; once)[55]

53. Ibid., p. 84; Lord, *Singer*, p. 4.
54. "Studies I," p. 86.
55. Parry, "Whole Formulaic Verse," p. 183; see also *L'Épithète*, pp. 118–25.

Parry and Lord in their several publications have pointed out and discussed innumerable formulaic systems in both Homeric and Yugoslavian epic poetry. The particular example just quoted is an extremely useful formulaic system employed for the purpose of letting a named speaker continue a conversation with a speaker whose name is previously known to the audience. The difference between sets of phrases that separately compose a whole line and whole-verse formulae like ἦμος δ'ἠριγένεια φάνη ῥοδοδάκτυλος Ἠώς η ("When, early born, shone forth rosy-fingered Dawn") is clear. The essential idea of the system quoted above is always the same: someone named speaks again to someone previously named. The meter is consistent, as is the syntax. One may describe this formulaic system as the result of a pronoun plus δ'αὖτε προσέειπε, plus a noun epithet that will fill the line from the feminine caesura to the end.

The particular formulaic system just quoted is not only one of many systems, but one of a large number specifically used in situations of address.[56] Just as the δ'αὖτε προσέειπε system is partly composed in its various manifestations of formulaic phrases, so other systems are somewhat a network of formulae per se. Over one such formula within a formulaic system a brief controversy emerged, illustrative, in the end, of Parry's thesis. The formula in question was καὶ μιν φωνήσας ἔπεα πτερόεντα προσηύδα ("And addressing him words winged he spoke"), an introductory phrase occurring 49 times in Homer. Within the formula itself, the phrase ἔπεα πτερόεντα (words winged) is a smaller formula which appears in other verbal contexts no less than 74 times. Stylistically the two words are what Parry called a "fixed metaphor," that is, a word or group of words that, while metaphorical in themselves, are governed so frequently by metrical necessity in the text that their literal meaning is subsumed in their generic meaning.[57] One scholar,[58] however, attempted to demonstrate that the whole-verse formula was used in Homer exclusively to imply emotion or intensity on the part of the speaker. Parry's reply[59] was the observation, absolutely borne out by the texts, that the whole-verse formula belonged to a system and was only used to introduce

56. See Parry, "Whole Formulaic Verse," and Combellack, "Omitted Speech Formulas in Homer," *UCPCP, 12,* No. 4 (1939), 45–46.

57. Parry, "The Traditional Metaphor in Homer," *CP, 28* (1933), esp. p. 38.

58. George M. Calhoun, "The Art of Formula in Homer—ΕΠΕΑ ΠΤΕΡΟΕΝΤΑ," *CP, 30* (1935), 215–27.

59. Parry, "About Winged Words," *CP, 32* (1937), 59–63.

a speech when the names of both speakers were already known to the audience. In short the formulaic system, like the smaller unit, the formula, is a tool of oral composition whose uses are prescribed, it would seem, not on an imaginative but on a mechanical level.

Parry drew a most interesting conclusion regarding the development of formulaic phrases by observing that once a singer was aware of a phrase as a *type,* the representative of the type could well lead him unconsciously to coin new phrases strictly upon the old models. Doubtless the singer would be guided in his analogical manufacture mostly by meter, syntax, and idea, but also by sound: thus Parry conjectured that sound plus meaning was the association in λαίλαπι τύπτων ("in a beating storm") and λαίλαπι θυών ("in a beating wind");[60] but that sound alone associated ὁμοῦ νεφέσσιν ("at the same place in the clouds") with ὁμοῦ νεκύεσιν ("at the same place among the dead"),[61] especially, one may note, since the usual dative plural of νέκυς is νεκύεσσι. Associations made by the ear in a formulaic system are probably rare; in most systems it is assuredly the demands of meter, syntax, and narrative that determine a development, the chronology of the members of which it would be futile to pursue.

Formulae contribute to formulaic systems, and systems to themes, the largest units of composition upon which an oral poet must depend and, perhaps, the simplest to understand. Parry, although he was aware of *themes* as part of the oral epic technique, was more concerned with exact expressions; it was Lord who defined the theme as "a recurrent element of narration or description in traditional oral poetry . . . not restricted, as is the formula, by metrical considerations." [62] A theme may be as brief and exact as the arming of a warrior, the feasting of a guest, the assembling of a council, sailing across the sea; or it may be all-embracing, like an ancient myth, such as the Bear-Son story which lies somewhere behind not only *Beowulf* but also the *Odyssey,* or like a general narrative sequence, such as the Return from the Trojan War.[63] The

---

60. *L'Épithète,* p. 92.

61. "Studies I," p. 140.

62. "Composition by Theme in Homer and South Slavic Epos," *TAPA, 83* (1952), 73; see also *Singer,* pp. 4, 68.

63. For the different epic themes and many related considerations, see C. M. Bowra,

more general theme is what the oral poet must conscientiously memorize, for that is his plan, the direction of his narrative. The "theme by ornamentation" (dressing, eating, arriving, fighting, etc.) is more like formulae and formulaic systems—so much like a conditioned reflex that, without having memorized them on purpose, the trained singer nevertheless produces them from association. As Lord pointed out, a theme may exist for the sake of an epic song (such as the arming of a hero) or may be one theme from the singer's repertory (such as the Return of Agamemnon). This dual existence leads to great inconsistencies among Yugoslavian Guslars when two poets are presumably singing the same song, since each poet perforce entertains different associations. It is important to remember that no theme "belongs" to one or another story: where there is no text, there is no ownership, and the governing principle is fluidity.[64]

It is indeed difficult for a literate people to comprehend the art of an illiterate poet. The techniques of composition in the two societies are of course utterly different. In order to bridge the gap between them, Parry and Lord studied and attempted to define not only the tools of the oral technique—formulae, formulaic systems, and themes—but also the conditions of practice. For Homer we have only the text; for the Guslars, however, Parry and Lord had transcriptions, recording tape, and the *real thing*. If the technique partly determines the style of an oral poet, the conditions of the performance often determine the external character of the poem. A singer is obviously limited by his own physical energy, by the temper of his audience, and by the time he and they are at leisure to spend.[65] Avdo Medjedovitch, the most talented of the Guslars with whom Parry and Lord conversed, was able to sustain oral composition in front of an audience from twenty to forty minutes without a break. In this time he sang 200 to 500 lines.[66] It was noticeable that those places where he chose either to pause for a cup of coffee or to break off entirely

Heroic Poetry (London, 1952), pp. 179–214, 265–66; and Rhys Carpenter, "Argeiphontes: a Suggestion," *AJA, 54* (1950), 177–83. See also Carpenter, *Folktale, Fiction, and Saga in the Homeric Epics* (Berkeley, 1946), pp. 112–35, 139–52; and Lord, *Singer*, pp. 68–69, and "Beowulf and Odysseus," in *Franciplegius*, ed. Jess B. Bessinger and Robert P. Creed (New York, 1965), pp. 86–91.

64. Lord, *Singer*, pp. 94–95; "Homer and Huso II," *TAPA, 69* (1938), 441–42.
65. Notopoulos, p. 81.
66. Lord, "Homer and Huso I," *TAPA, 67* (1936), 107.

had no aesthetic connection with his poem. In fact, a common Yugoslavian formula for continuing an interrupted song is *De bismo, de liostavismo/Malku pjesma o duga zemenia?,* "Where were we, where did we leave our little song of times long past?" [67]

The enthusiasm and leisure of an audience, too, have a great influence upon the singer. When listeners sit in silent attention, the oral poet is much more likely to include an elaborate arming of a hero, or some such "formulaic expansion," than to send the warrior directly into battle; but when the only audience is in the tavern or coffeehouse (usually the case in Yugoslavia) the singer must perform against a constant hum of conversation and a continually changing house. According to Lord, most coffeehouse performances are far better at the beginning, when there is a listeners' agreement, than at the end, when the audience disperses; consequently the beginnings of certain themes and stories are far more *fixed* than are the conclusions, and a singer performs smoothly the introduction to an epic the end of which he actually may not know. For a similar reason, the shorter the song the more stable its narrative sequence; and furthermore the larger themes in a long song tend to form shorter divisible parts that are stable in themselves.[68]

In addition to the oral technique and the conditions incumbent upon performance, the significance of an oral performance is unfamiliar to any *reader* of epic poetry. The absence of a text, let alone a "vulgate," insures the uniqueness of each individual performance of the same song, whether by several singers or at different times in the life of one singer. The art of composition, which is simultaneously the art of performing, in an epic song results invariably in originality; yet the origin of the oral epic lies irrevocably buried in a fairly conservative tradition. Such is the fluidity of the oral tradition that, as Lord remarked,[69] each performance is both the "specific" (i.e. original) and the "generic" (traditional) song.

It is one thing to listen to the Guslar with his songs of 5,000 to 6,000 lines,[70] unquestionably inferior in artistic merit to the *Iliad* and the

67. Ibid., p. 112; see pp. 110–12.

68. Lord, *Singer*, pp. 13–31, 99ff.

69. Ibid., p. 100. For a good analysis of the extent to which an audience may influence an oral poem, see Notopoulos, "Studies in Early Greek Oral Poetry," *HSCP, 68* (1964), pp. 51–54.

70. Lord, "Homer and Huso I," p. 107.

Odyssey, and another to read Homer's epics of 15,693 and 12,110 lines. According to Parry and Lord these discrepancies of both length and excellence all but disappear upon a consideration of the transmission of the epics. Homer's poems, demonstrably oral (according to Parry) in style and arrangement, were at some point in time written down: the question is, how much did transcription affect a poem totally conceived in the oral tradition? In order to discuss the answer, Parry and Lord simulated in twentieth-century Yugoslavia what they took to be the conditions of Homer's Greece: they requested a Guslar to sing while a scribe took down his words.[71] At first the singer felt the awkwardness of a slow pace forced upon him by the scribe; furthermore, since writing has no rhythm, the singer was compelled to put down his gusla, his time-keeper, and as a result some of his lines were metrically faulty. Then again, an audience whose face was ever on his page failed to convey the enthusiasm granted even a coffeehouse singer. The less able Guslars could not overcome these difficulties. The best, however, not only grew accustomed to the new conditions but profited greatly from two unique advantages: time to think ahead and an audience who would hear out the song to its end. The illiterate singer who, for lack of leisure, never changed a phrase once he sang it, could now meditate a choice of phrases in his mind long before the scribe's hand recorded his immediate thought. The results of transcription were consistently longer and better epic songs. The best of the Guslars, Avdo Medjedovitch, consented to a transcription: he sang for two hours in the morning and two in the afternoon, for two weeks, with one week's rest in between, and with coffee-breaks every twenty or thirty minutes, a song of 13,331 lines, which Lord says is his indisputable masterpiece. Other singers who obliged by dictating their songs to Parry and Lord said: "Sung songs are truer [i.e. to the way they heard them], dictated songs are finer!"

Parry and Lord, staunch unitarians, believe that our texts of Homer's poems represent essentially what the poet sang. If Homer himself was involved in the first transcription of the *Iliad* or the *Odyssey,* he was involved in one of two ways: either he wrote the poems or he dictated them to a scribe. Lord[72] has argued strenuously against the first pos-sibility upon the grounds that the creative techniques of a literate and

71. See ibid.; "Homer, Parry, and Huso;" "Homer's Originality: Oral Dictated Texts," *TAPA, 84* (1953), 124–34; *Singer,* pp. 124–38.

72. "Homer's Originality"; *Singer,* pp. 124–38, 149ff.

an illiterate artist are so opposed that it is, and always has been, impossible for an oral poet to compose with pen in hand. Furthermore scholarly chronology places Homer either at the "end" of an oral tradition or at the beginning of a literate one: since he is certainly too good to be identified with the usual early, struggling attempts at literary composition (e.g. Ennius), he must, according to Lord, belong to the height of a long and rich oral habit of making poetry. Lord calls Homer's texts "oral in the second degree," [73] since they are too long to have been transcribed at an actual performance, and of too demonstrably oral a style to have been written by the poet himself. They were rather dictated to a scribe over a period of time.

One scholar has calculated, using Medjedovitch's speed of composition in the coffeehouse as a measure, that a Guslar sings 11.6 lines a minute, and that 350 Serbo-Croatian lines of ten syllables are equal to 233 Homeric lines, or 7.8 lines a minute. At this rate it would take an oral poet 33.5 hours to sing the *Iliad,* and 25.9 to sing the *Odyssey*.[74] When one adds the hours needed for rest and the time needed for transcription, it seems unlikely that the *Iliad* could have been dictated in less than three, the *Odyssey* in less than two, weeks. Though Lord does not speculate upon the conditions under which so lengthy a dictation might have occurred, he does insist that the desire to record the poems in the first place comes from outside the oral tradition, for instance from the literate East, since the conception of texts, of static preservation, is utterly foreign to the oral society's imagination.[75]

While Parry and Lord pursued their thesis concerning the oral nature of Homer's poetry, they could not avoid the many facets of the "Homeric question" that have engrossed scholars ever since Wolf. The learned archaeological conviction of an eighth-century B.C. author they accepted, as well as a late eighth- or early seventh-century date for the introduction of Greek writing. Homeric style, particularly repetitions of brevity and of length, they had brilliantly explained, and from their explanation

73. *Singer,* p. 149.

74. Notopoulos, p. 86. In a later article, Notopoulos slightly changes these figures; see "Studies in Early Greek Oral Poetry," p. 6.

75. *Singer,* pp. 133, 154–57. See Eduard Nielsen, *Oral Tradition: a Modern Problem in Old Testament Introduction,* Studies in Biblical Theology, vol. 2 (London, 1954), 33; S. Gantz, "The Dawn of Literature: Prolegomena to a History of Unwritten Literature," *Osiris,* 7 (1939), 296; Notopoulos, "Studies in Early Greek Oral Poetry," pp. 6–18.

evolved answers to other troublesome problems. These are far too complex to be dealt with justly here, but far too essential to omit from all mention.

The problem of the dialects and of ancient and historical forms, for example, received a plausible elucidation in Parry's hands: since the Greek oral tradition was undoubtedly of great antiquity, and since formulaic phrases are rigidly preserved within their metrical definition, it is not surprising that in the works of a poet who lived at the end of this tradition we should find strata of formulae. The ancient inflections, the Aeolic dialectal forms, have been fossilized by their usefulness to the dactylic hexameter line. Homer's "nodding" could have nearly the same raison d'être, since the oral poet concentrates on the *theme* at hand and lets the formulaic phrases fall in more or less automatically: thus the dead Pylaemenes reappears at his son's funeral in XIII.658 because of the formulaic fixity in metrical definition of μετὰ δέ σφι πατὴρ κίε δάκρυα λείβων ("after him his father walked, tears weeping").[76]

Touching the bristling question of authorship, there was no doubt in Parry's mind: the consistent use of similar epithets for similar heroes is known to indicate consistent authorship, even if the texture of the oral poem is entirely traditional and largely the product of every anonymous singer who has previously composed.[77] In connection with the problem of authorship, both Parry and Lord have been at pains to emphasize the fact that the conventionality of Homer's language was hardly a pejorative characteristic in the eyes of a poet who had no conception of "creative originality," that Olympic height of twentieth-century artistic endeavor; "at no time is [Homer or the singer] seeking words for an idea which has never before found expression, so that the question of originality in style means nothing to him. . . ."[78]

Parry's and Lord's contributions to Homeric studies influenced scholarly opinion concerning many particulars, such as Homeric hiatus and

76. See Berlage, p. 297; Nilsson, *Homer and Mycenae,* pp. 180, 182; Parry, *L'Épithète,* pp. 6–8; *Les Formules et la métrique d'Homère* (Paris, 1928), "The Homeric Gloss," *TAPA,* 59 (1928), and "Studies I," pp. 135ff.; Bowra, *Homer and His Forerunners,* pp. 4–5, 15; L. R. Palmer, "The Language of Homer," in *CH,* pp. 75–178; T. B. L. Webster, *From Mycenae to Homer* (London, 1958), pp. 93–108; Page, *History and the Homeric Iliad,* pp. 218–96.

77. See Parry, *L'Épithète,* pp. 238–40, and Notopoulos, "Studies in Early Greek Oral Poetry," pp. 22–45, where he compares Homer to Hesiod and the anonymous singers of the cyclic epics.

78. Parry, "Studies I," pp. 146–47; Lord, *Singer,* pp. 154–56.

enjambment, the use of the digamma, and artificial lengthening and shortening of syllables, which cannot be discussed here. Their major contribution to the comparative criticism of all early epic poetry, including Homer, was a thorough working description of the oral technique, a description that has revolutionized the pertinent scholarly research and critical thinking in our century as did Wolf's *Prolegomena* for the century after 1795.

III

The revolution was not, however, recognized in 1928, the publication date of Parry's *L'Épithète traditionnelle;* and during the following decade, until the Second World War, Parry's work was very little read on the Continent.[79] In fact, wide awareness or estimation of Parry's thesis and Lord's continuing study has come only during the last decade; the one book which summarizes theory and proof was not published until 1960. This tardy recognition was only partly caused by neglect, for Parry met verbal denunciation from many sides when he came to Harvard University in 1929. The difficulty has been admirably stated by the English scholar, H. T. Wade-Gery:

> The most important assault made on Homer's creativeness in recent years is the work of Milman Parry, who may be called the Darwin of Homeric studies. As Darwin seemed to many to have removed the finger of God from the creation of the world and of man, so Milman Parry has seemed to some to have removed the creative poet from the *Iliad* and the *Odyssey*.[80]

To most unitarians—and Homeric scholars were increasingly unitarian in these years—Parry, though swearing allegiance, seemed to have armed the opposition out of all conscience. Nor was the opposition slow to take advantage. The late Joshua Whatmough of Harvard, one of the few

79. Jan de Vries, in his book *Heroic Song and Heroic Legend* (orig. publ. Utrecht, 1959), mentions formulaic phrases, but without any reference to Parry and, seemingly, without understanding the significance of formulae in an oral tradition (see pp. 20, 31, 51, 142, 153–54). As late as 1942 an American scholar, Eugene G. O'Neill, Jr., published an extremely thorough and most interesting study of how certain words prefer only certain positions in the hexameter line. Although his evidence is of a similar sort, he mentions Parry not at all and depends for an explanation of this regularity of position upon an idea of "pervasion of Form in Greek poetry" (see "The Localization of Metrical Word Types in the Greek Hexameter" [1942], 103–78). *YCS, 8.*

80. *The Poet of the Iliad* (Cambridge, 1952), pp. 38–39.

formidable analysts of the midcentury, convinced upon linguistic evidence alone that "nothing could be more puerile than the notion that the *Iliad* could possibly have been composed by one man," insisted that Parry proved "what was anathema to Parry, . . . that many a composer contributed a part to these immortal epics."[81]

Yet as scholarly discussion of Parry's conception of the oral epic technique has become more widely spread, scholarly acceptance of the thesis in general or in part is now almost taken for granted.[82] Sir Cecil M. Bowra's books are illustrative of a saga of persuasion: in *Tradition and Design in the Iliad* (1930) Parry is mentioned not at all; his ideas are discussed in *Heroic Poetry* (1952), and critically employed in observations on the *Iliad* in *Homer and His Forerunners* (1955). With the exception of Bowra in the last-mentioned book, those scholars who accept Parry as a whole merely state his thesis and set forth his conclusions as fact. Another group of scholars, among whom Lord is preeminent, have followed Parry's direction into territory previously unexposed to his hypothesis[83] and have either reaffirmed his conclusions or have logically extended them.

There yet remain a number of critics, scholars who for the most part seek Homer as a poet, rather than as a poet with a certain technique, or as a poet of archaeological, historical, social, or anthropological facts, or as an example of a "primitive" poet—scholars to whom Parry's thesis seems a mechanical description which falls short of the poetry it is attempting to describe. Among these scholars in turn one may perceive two groups: those who do not consider Parry on his own ground and

81. Joshua Whatmough, "ΩΣΠΕΡ ΟΜΕΡΟΣ ΦΗΕΙ," *AJA, 50* (1948), 45, 50. For the views of a more cautious analyst, see Page, *History and the Homeric Iliad*, pp. 297–340.

82. See books on the epic in general, or concerned with Homeric subjects other than language: Eustace M. W. Tillyard, *The English Epic and Its Background* (London, 1954); H. Monroe Chadwick and N. Kershaw Chadwick, *The Growth of Literature*, Vol. I (Cambridge, 1932); Carpenter; Nilsson; Woodhouse, *The Composition of Homer's Odyssey;* Myres, *Homer and His Critics;* Platnauer, ed., *Fifty Years of Homeric Scholarship.*

83. W. F. Albright, "Some Oriental Glosses on the Homeric Problem," *AJA, 54* (1950), 162–76; George M. Calhoun, "Homeric Repetitions," *UCPCP, 12*, No. 1 (1933), 1–25; Combellack, "Omitted Speech Formulas in Homer"; D. H. F. Gray, "Epithets for Things," *CQ, 40* (1946), 109–21; G. S. Kirk, *The Songs of Homer* (Cambridge, Mass., 1962), and "Homer and Modern Oral Poetry: Some Confusions," *CQ*, N.S. *10* (1960), 271–81; Notopoulos, "The Warrior as an Oral Poet," *CW, 46* (1952), 17–19, "Continuity and Interconnection in Homeric Oral Composition," and "Studies in Early Greek Oral Poetry"; Page, *The Homeric Odyssey* and *History and the Homeric Iliad;* Webster, *From Mycenae to Homer,* esp. chaps. 3, 4, 6, 8.

those who do. The former[84] simply object that Parry's explanation of Homer's language does less than justice to the artistic genius in the language of the poems, and for proof marshal many a phrase to show forth the conscious imagination of the poet. The problem of transmission they settle in various ways: Bassett vaguely urges the force of memory; Gomme wonders whether Homer created the *Kunstsprache;* Greene proposes *hypomnemata* (notes); and Wade-Gery thinks that the Greek alphabet might worthily have been invented for the purpose of recording the *Iliad* and the *Odyssey*.[85] While the objections of these scholars to Parry are reasonable (Yugoslavia, for all the force of analogy, has produced no Homer), they are powerless, since Parry's thickly documented discovery that the repeated phrases in Homer are determined by metrical necessity is in itself incontrovertible fact.

Frederick M. Combellack[86] first recognized that the clash between Parry and those unitarians interested in Homer as a poet, master of tale and language, was a critical dilemma. Parry himself in his first book had remarked the difficulty of praising Homer in modern terms for *le mot juste;*[87] and indeed, as Combellack has been laboring to emphasize, if Parry's description of Homeric style fits the facts, then the favorite critical pastime of seeking the "original," the "comic," the "ironical" phrase in Homer is utterly pointless. Modern theories of authorial irrelevance notwithstanding, part of the function of criticism is still taken to be the elucidation or description of how the weight of an artist's conscious meditation is shadowed forth in the individual words which he chose and kept for his expression. Parry denies the critic of Homer this function.

Combellack proceeded no further than a caveat, but recently two other Homeric scholars, Cedric H. Whitman and Adam Parry, have not only

84. Bassett, *The Poetry of Homer*, pp. 14–19; A. W. Gomme, *The Greek Attitude to Poetry and History* (Berkeley, 1954), pp. 32–33; William Chase Greene, "The Spoken and the Written Word," *HSCP, 60* (1960), 26–29; Wade-Gery, pp. 38ff. See also W. Schadewaldt, *Von Homers Welt und Werk* (Stuttgart, 1951); Jan de Vries, *Heroic Song and Heroic Legend.*

85. Bassett, p. 16; Gomme, p. 34, n. 16; Greene, pp. 30–31; and Wade-Gery, p. 40. Webster inclines to Wade-Gery's view (see *From Mycenae to Homer,* pp. 272ff.).

86. In "Contemporary Unitarians and Homeric Originality," *AJP, 71* (1950), 337–64.

87. Parry, *L'Épithète,* pp. 166ff. But compare the qualifying remarks in Notopoulos, "Studies in Early Greek Oral Poetry," pp. 60–64, and J. B. Hainsworth, "Structure and Content in Epic Formulas: the Question of the Unique Expression," *CQ,* N.S. *14* (1964), 155–64.

recognized the dilemma but have recommended a solution.[88] Each of
them agrees that beside the magnitude of Homeric genius, Parry's explanation of style via the oral epic technique, while undeniably right as
far as it goes, is too mechanical. As Adam Parry said in one of his
earlier studies, Parry's theory of the formulaic method, when critically
employed, is a definition of style and it therefore fails to distinguish
excellencies or to distinguish at all: one may compare a definition of
Elizabethan drama that fails to distinguish Shakespeare from Marlowe
or Shakespeare from Lilly. Adam Parry then proposed that the unit of
artistic expression to consider was not the formula, a metrical prere-
quisite, but the syntactically independent whole or half line, for this is
what Homer might have omitted or substituted for, and yet chose
to include. For instance, when Helen and Priam are on the ramparts of
Troy (in Book III of the *Iliad*) watching the leaders of the two armies,
Priam asks Helen about a certain "Achaian man of power and stature";
she replies that the man is Agamemnon, "widely powerful,/ at the same
time a good king and a strong spear-fighter" (178–79; Lattimore's translation). She could easily have stopped there, but she adds δαὴρ αὖτ'
ἐμὸς ἔσκε κυνώπιδος ἔι ποτ' ἔενγε, "my brother-in-law once, slut that I
am—if that time ever was" (my translation). Helen calls herself κυνῶπις
again in the *Odyssey* (iv.145), but not in such a line as this where only
the last part is formulaic by demonstrable repetition in the 27,000-odd
lines of Homer: the meter could dispense with the line; the poetic
imagination could not dispense with a deft characterization of Helen
of Troy.

Cedric Whitman, whose *Homer and the Heroic Tradition* (1958)
gives new spirit to all the old Homeric questions and adds more besides,
brings true breadth of vision to the particular difficulty of Homer's
poetic language. Whitman absolutely upholds Parry's conviction that
Homer's language was entirely traditional, but objects that, "as in con-
trapuntal music, the rules are strict, but they cannot compose the fugue
by themselves." [89] Whitman gives perspective to the very word *formula*
when he turns to a principle made familiar by Susanne Langer, the
principle that all speech is to some extent formulaic and that "syntax

88. Whitman, *Homer and the Heroic Tradition*; Adam Parry, "Homer and Literary
Criticism," Connecticut Academy of Arts and Sciences, lecture delivered at Yale University, April 4, 1963. Parts of this lecture are included in Parry's article in *YCS, 20* (1966)
mentioned below. See also his earlier article, "The Language of Achilles," *TAPA, 87*
(1956), 1–7.

89. P. 7.

itself is a formula of intelligibility." [90] As syntax is to intelligibility, so the formulae are to the oral poet, the irreducible units with which he must compose. Whitman's new and terse definitions of the formula combine an aesthetic with a functional emphasis: referring to its syntactically consistent order (e.g. adjective plus noun, conjunction plus predicate, etc.), Whitman calls the formula "a semantic unit identified with a metrical demand," an "artificially devised unit of semantic, grammatical, and metrical functions." As such, the formula is already beyond discursive speech and is part of poetry. It is functional in creating the verse because it is "a poetic atom, a fragment of technically transformed speech whose status is already that of art, not logic." [91]

Whitman, like Adam Parry, fully comprehends the difficulty that Milman Parry created for literary criticism of Homer when he removed the possibility of discovering the unique Homer in a striking phrase here or an apt one there. The aptness, Whitman remarks, is probably the genius not so much of Homer as of the style itself.[92] But the very fact of the extensiveness of Homer's vocabulary, and therefore of the formulae that he employs (for, as Parry and Lord were quick to point out, Homer's poetic language is far more formulaic than any comparable to it) is at least proof that Homer could say anything he wished. His was a freedom of imaginative choice which has been blurred in the somewhat deterministic descriptions of Parry and Lord. At this point in his argument Whitman fittingly emphasizes a similarity between the styles of Homer and of Mozart: "based as it is on a developed aristocratic tradition, whose compositional elements are largely formulaic, the eighteenth century manner became in Mozart's hands, through sheer skill of development, a medium of surpassing emotional and artistic authority, whose import is of such intimately combined force and elegance that it is hard to say which predominates." [93]

Again like Adam Parry, Whitman insists that the portions of linguistic units where one may see Homer's individual power are not the formulaic phrases but the whole line or even the whole image.[94] Moreover,

90. *Homer and the Heroic Tradition*, p. 14, and see 91ff.

91. Ibid., pp. 109–10. See also Anne Amory, "The Gates of Horn and Ivory," *YCS, 20* (1966), pp. 3–57. On pp. 35–40 there is pervasive argument for latitude of genius within a conventional style.

92. Ibid., p. 112.

93. Ibid., pp. 112–13.

94. Ibid., p. 110.

Whitman argues, being *functions,* they must be functions of something, in this case, says Whitman, "of the poet's intention." Parry and Lord would strongly object; but Whitman carries the thought further by noticing that the mere inevitability of a formula, such as "and he spoke winged words," strikes and gives pleasure to an audience, and that this inevitability is built up not only by repetition but also by context. On a more complicated level, one may notice that formulae that in themselves are neutral acquire by repetition and context a symbolic weight:[95] for instance, "his armor flashed like fire" is a frequent description of a warrior in battle and, as a phrase, is determined by metrical necessity; but all the repetitions and variations upon this formula linger behind that passage in Book XVIII of the *Iliad* where Achilles paused just before the action of his wrath, and Athene

> swept about his powerful shoulders the fluttering aegis;
> and she, the divine among goddesses, about his head circled
> a golden cloud, and kindled from it a flame far-shining.
> As when a flare goes up into the high air from a city
> from an island far away, with enemies fighting about it
> who all day long are in the hateful division of Ares
> fighting from their own city, but as the sun goes down signal
> fires blaze out one after another, so that the glare goes
> pulsing high for the men of the neighboring islands to see it,
> in case they might come over in ships to beat off the enemy;
> so from the head of Achilleus the blaze shot into the bright air.
>
> (204–14; Lattimore's translation)

Could a poet who did not have his wakeful concentration upon the Trojan's impending doom have made this association with fire merely by means of the oral epic technique? This pattern of imagery must hint at the individual creator's artistic plan, and Whitman reasonably discerns in the lines—the only evidence—the forceful imagination of their author.

In fact, classical scholarship between 1963 and 1967 gives evidence of turning away from a statistical analysis to a critical analysis of the Homeric poems. The change is characterized by a reconsideration of the conclusions drawn from Milman Parry's meticulously collected data by Parry himself and, more especially, by Lord and Notopoulos. J. B. Hainsworth, for example, tries to restrain the definition of the oral

95. Ibid., pp. 7, 115, and see Chap. 7, "Fire and Other Images," pp. 129ff.

formula from Lord's and Notopoulos' broad interpretation.[96] G. S. Kirk in his book, *The Songs of Homer* (Cambridge, 1962), takes exception to Lord's statement that an oral poem must change with each performance, but he otherwise uses Lord's theory of oral poetry in order to consider Homer in detail.[97] Yet in a recent article, "Formular Language and Oral Quality," [98] Kirk seems more cautious. He argues persuasively against Notopoulos' demonstration of the oral composition of the *Homeric Hymns* and postulates literary imitation as an explanation of the Homeric phraseology which fills those poems. At the end of his article, Kirk condemns the easy and imprecise antithesis, *oral poetry* vs. *literary composition,* that is by now common to discussions of oral-formulaic theory; he recommends instead an antithesis between *"natural composition in a formular tradition* (that is, 'oral poetry' in its primary sense) and *deliberate, self-conscious composition in a formular style,* whether with the aid of writing or not." [99] It may be observed in passing that while Kirk's descriptive distinction is a necessary one, the problems of identification of old or anonymous texts remain.

Of major importance to the critical study of Homer and oral theory is Adam Parry's article, "Have We Homer's *Iliad*?" [100] In this essay Adam Parry combines some profound paragraphs on Homer's genius (which he is not afraid to discuss) with fresh and significant criticisms of the "Yugoslavian analogy." His many ideas may be said to take off from a distinction original to Milman Parry's early work but later neglected by him and almost all those who pursued his theories: "That the style [of the Homeric epics] is traditional and therefore *oral* (for composition in performance and not dependent on the use of the written word) may be taken as proved: it is not necessarily proved that our *Iliad* and *Odyssey* were composed orally." [101] Adam Parry rejects Lord's idea that the imposition of a literate culture upon an oral one results in the decline of oral poetry, that a good oral singer who learns to write is incapable of

96. "Structure and Content in Epic Formulae: The Question of the Unique Expression," *CQ, N.S. 14* (1964), 155–64. For strictures upon Hainsworth's article, see Joseph A. Russo, "The Structural Formula in Homeric Verse," *YCS,* 20 (1966), 219–40.

97. See pp. 55–101. Kirk argues for a preservation of the Homeric texts in a pre-literate society by word-for-word memorization.

98. *YCS,* 20 (1966), pp. 155–74. See his references to Notopoulos on pp. 155–56, n. 1, 2.

99. Ibid., p. 174.

100. *YCS,* 20 (1966), 177–216.

101. Ibid., p. 178, n. 4.

writing a good oral poem. As Parry says, Lord's idea is founded upon
Yugoslavian evidence: in the 1930s Lord discovered that those Guslars
who took up writing inevitably wrote poems inferior to the ones they
previously sang. But it does not follow that the decline Lord witnessed
in modern Yugoslavia amounts to a general truth about the relationship
between oral and written poetry in other cultures. As Parry points out,

> When a Yugoslav poet learns how to write, a whole literary cul-
> ture, the culture of the cities of his own country and of what we
> call the civilized world, becomes accessible to him. It is a culture of
> books and newspapers. If he abandons the traditional formulae
> which have enabled him to improvise his heroic narratives, this is
> not necessarily, or even probably, because he is corrupted by a new
> technique. It is because he has become part of a different world, a
> world with new values and new habits of thought (p. 213).

Parry goes on to conjecture that the introduction into Greece of the
Phoenician alphabet would not have represented a cultural change to
the Ionian singer of 725 B.C. He conjectures further that the length and
excellence of the Homeric epics makes their written composition probable: "It seems difficult not to see in the use of writing both the means
and the occasion for the composition, in the improvising style, of poems
which must have transcended their own tradition in profundity as well
as length, just as that tradition itself surpassed all subsequent traditions
of heroic song" (p. 216).

Alexander Pope, whose translation of the *Iliad* was made at the start
of a long era of suspicion of Homeric genius, achieved in his perception
of Homer and Homer's poetry a vision eminently just and penetrating.
In the first place he marked and presented the repetitive language of the
epic poem in a general manner astonishingly emblematic of Milman
Parry's more detailed perception. At a time when French neoclassicists
like D'Aubignac, Madame Dacier, and Boileau[102] tentatively condemned
a stylistic device whose use seemed unnecessary, whose effect cloying,
Pope realized that "to throw his language more out of prose, Homer
seems to have affected the compound epithets. This was a sort of composition peculiarly proper to poetry; not only as it heightened the diction,

---

102. In *Conjectures académiques* (1715), *Iliade* (a translation), and *L'Art poétique*,
respectively. See Donald M. Foerster, *Homer in English Criticism*, pp. 16–17, and Myres,
p. 47.

but as it assisted and filled the numbers with greater sound and pomp." [103]

Furthermore, in ignorance of some Homeric details and of many facts which 250 years have since supplied, Pope yet struck out in his appreciation of Homer a general picture of balance between art and invention in the great epics; for Pope thought that in any work of genius the relationship between art (i.e. technique) and invention was unmistakable: "art is only like a prudent steward that lives on managing the riches of nature." [104] Over the precise designations of Homer's art and Homer's invention Pope and Parry would have disagreed; but in many a brief remark, such as "Homer makes us hearers, and Virgil leaves us readers," [105] Pope saw in the large what Parry proved in the particular.

Parry's particular, the discovery of the oral-formulaic technique of composition, is, quite unintentionally on Parry's part, too mechanical an explanation of Homer's individual invention; but as a description of a method of composition utterly foreign to our literary heritage, it is invaluable to a critic or student of any early epic poetry which may have been composed by that method. Scholars have not been slow to extend the analogy drawn by Parry and Lord between the Guslars and Homer: Lord and Bowra, to mention but two,[106] have considered some of the evidence of a formulaic style in the epic poetry of many nations where the texts are known to have been copied sometime after the composition of the poems.

Still other scholars in other fields have applied Parry's conclusions to the poetry with which they are most familiar. Among the best of these, and certainly the most important to Old English studies, is Francis P. Magoun, Jr., whose articles on Old English poems as oral-formulaic compositions have deservedly excited the interest of numerous students of that literature. His application of Parry's principles and discoveries is worthy of special account, as are the contributions of several scholars whose thoughts were aroused by Magoun's original articles.

103. Pope's translation of the *Iliad*, World's Classics Edition (London, 1959), p. xii.

104. Ibid., p. v.

105. Ibid., p. xi.

106. Lord, *Singer*, pp. 198–221, where he considers *Beowulf*, *The Song of Roland*, and *Digenis Akritas*; and Bowra, *Heroic Poetry*. See Chadwick and Chadwick, *The Growth of Literature*, Vol. 1, and Notopoulos, "Modern Greek Oral Poetry," Ethnic Folkways Library, Album FE 4468 (New York, 1959), pp. 5–29 of the booklet that accompanies the recording.

Chapter Two

Magoun and
Old English Scholarship

The current critical awareness of repeated phrases in Old English poetry may be traced back through vicissitudes of emphasis very similar to those through which the study of the Homeric poetical language has proceeded. Old English scholarship has not the antiquity of the Homeric, yet by the mid-nineteenth century both studies were equally concerned with verbal parallels among poems and with the connection between repetitions and authorship.

This identity of concern is not surprising when one considers that it was the great German scholars of the nineteenth century who founded and impressed with rigor the study of linguistics and who, by necessarily arguing from the past, made the literature of the classical, and especially of the Germanic and of other civilizations, more accessible. Nor is it surprising that men of one age should find generally similar solutions to generally similar problems: as Wilamowitz to the *Iliad*, so Müllenhoff to *Beowulf*.[1] Again, just as the analytic and unitarian schools of Homeric scholarship, depending on their affiliation, understood the repetitions in the Greek poems to be evidence of borrowing or multiple authorship, or of a common poetic language, so the students of Old English poems explained those identical phrases. Adolf Banning, for instance, in his dissertation, *Die epische Formeln im Beowulf* (Marburg, 1886), attempted to prove correct Müllenhoff's division of the poem into "songs" and "interpolations" by listing repeated phrases or words that appeared discretely within the various sections. Better known is the work of Gregor Sarrazin[2] in which evidence is carefully and thoroughly amassed

1. The line is very direct: Müllenhoff was influenced by Lachmann's studies of the *Niebelungenlied;* Lachmann in his studies was influenced by Wolf.
2. First in "Beowulf und Kynewulf," *Anglia, 9* (1886), 515–50, and, with further illustrations, in *Beowulf Studien* (Berlin, 1888), pp. 110–17, 121—24, 124–28. Sarrazin accepted as Cynewulfian the four signed poems, *Riddles, Guthlac, Phoenix, Christ I and III*. When he listed the close parallels between *Beowulf* and *Andreas*, he, like many others

to argue Cynewulf's authorship of *Beowulf* on the basis of the many verbal similarities between that poem and the then commonly accepted "Cynewulf Canon." The further possible significance of the repeated phrases was put forth by Ellen Clune Buttenweiser in *Studien über die Verfasserschaft des Andreas* (Heidelberg, 1889). She expressly warned scholars against accepting verbal parallels as evidence of authorial individuality since, as she clearly demonstrated, so common and ubiquitous are the repeated phrases in Old English poetry that one might well be tempted to think the whole literature the product of a single mind. She accounted for the formulae rather by postulating a common storehouse "des grossen Phrazen- und Wortschatzes der Poesie," available to all poets and used without the stigma of plagiarism.[3]

An important group of nineteenth-century scholars considered the question of poetic repetitions from a larger point of view than that of the scholars noted above. These men thought the repetitions to be a general witness to a common *oral* poetic phraseology doubtless much older than the poems themselves. Again, the course of Old English scholarship is seen to have much in common with Homeric studies; but upon scanning the names—Grimm, Heusler, Sievers, Meyer, ten Brink, as against Schmidt and Düntzer—one is immediately impressed with the greater encouragement given to the conception of an oral poetic phraseology in Old English than in Homeric studies during the nineteenth and very early twentieth centuries. The difference, of course, lies in the accidents of time that put Düntzer 2,600 years from Homer and Sievers 1,100 years from *Beowulf*. Even an unparalleled archaeological activity during the nineteenth century failed to bring Homeric scholars as near to the pre-Attic civilization as Old English scholars found themselves to the old Germanic civilization without lifting a spade. There is nothing close by Homer to compare with Tacitus, and nothing even like the *Heliand*.

Jakob Grimm, through his extensive familiarity with old Germanic literature, first demonstrated the similarity between several Old English poetic phrases and phrases in the *Heliand, Hildebrandslied,* and the Old Norse *Poetic Edda*. In the 1840 edition of *Andreas und Elene* (Cassel)

---

after him, included *Andreas* in the same authorship with the rest. See Thomas Arnold, *Notes on Beowulf* (London, 1898), for a clear account of the *Beowulf-Andreas* question as it seemed after accumulated study at the end of the century.

3. See pp. 60–61.

Grimm argued that these "epische Formeln" appearing so far apart in time and in context must have once had a common origin on common soil before they spread orally to other lands.[4] Scholars were slow to pursue Grimm's lead; further studies of Old English poetic repetitions in the setting of an oral tradition did not appear until the end of the century. In his edition of the *Heliand* (Halle, 1878), Eduard Sievers noted innumerable parallels among Old Saxon, Old High German, Old Norse, and Old English phrases;[5] and following his work came several studies illustrative of the traditional nature of Old English poetic diction.[6] Andreas Heusler and Frederick Klaeber in the early years of the twentieth century contributed studies on the particular epic formulae involved in Old English poetic dialogue and in the introduction of various sections of poetic narrative.[7]

In Old English as in Homeric scholarship, the late nineteenth century saw the end of a German monopoly in rigorous studies of poetic language. In both disciplines too the concern of French, English, and other critics began to be directed to matters of aesthetic importance. In Old English scholarship the study of poetic phrases as a traditional language continued strongly into the twentieth century, often with a larger reference to other literature, such as Slavic, Old French, or Finnish, and with a wider notice of elements other than verbal that characterize the epic poetries of many civilizations.[8] A new kind of consideration of the Old

4. P. xl; see Introduction, pp. xxvi–vii: themes of beasts of battle; xxviii: formulae for military affairs; xl–xliii: examples of epic formulae in OE, ON, OS, and OHG.

5. See "Formelverzeichnis," pp. 391–495.

6. See Otto Hoffmann, *Reimformeln im Westgermanischen* (dissertation, Darmstadt, 1885) (the lists are *passim*); Richard M. Meyer, *Die altgermanische Poesie* (Berlin, 1889); J. Kail, "Über die Parallelstellen in der angelsächsischen Poesie," *Anglia, 12* (1889), 21–40 (vs. Sarrazin's argument for the Cynewulfian authorship of *Beowulf*); Bernhard ten Brink, "Englische Literatur," pp. 510–608 in H. Paul's *Grundriss der germanischen Philologie,* Vol. II (1st ed. Strassburg, 1893); Richard Kistenmacher, *Die wörtlichen Wiederholungen im Beowulf* (dissertation, Greifswald, 1898). Kistenmacher lists not only epic formulae but phrases repeated within the poem at close intervals, as if the poet had them in his ear.

7. Heusler, "Der Dialog in der altgermanischen erzählenden Dichtung," *ZDA, 46* (1902), 189–284; Klaeber, "Studies in the Textual Interpretation of 'Beowulf,'" *MP, 3* (1905–06), 235–65—see pp. 243–47 on the *gefrægn*-formulae, epithets, and others.

8. Note that many of these studies were written after Parry had published his major articles. That Parry's work went so long unnoticed in fields other than those of the classical literatures is a testimony to Lord's and Magoun's perspicacity in making the first documented application of the Parry-Lord thesis to Old English poetry.

See H. Monroe Chadwick, *The Heroic Age* (Cambridge, 1926), esp. p. 78; Chadwick

English poetic formulae, however, appeared beside these continuing studies, a consideration that placed upon the poet conscious responsibility for the repeated phrases within his own poem, even if those phrases seemed to have their origin in an ancient, oral tradition.[9]

In spite of the like concerns and development of Old English and Homeric studies during the period roughly from 1830 to the mid-twentieth century, it is evident that Parry's dissertation and his first papers in the *Harvard Studies in Classical Philology* (1928–31) marked a bolder break with contemporary scholarship than did the publication of Francis P. Magoun, Jr.'s, "The Oral-Formulaic Character of Anglo-Saxon Narrative Poetry" in 1953. The reason was only partly that Parry's studies preceded Magoun's. More important was the habit among Old English scholars of assuming without question that all Old English poetry contained elements of vocabulary and phraseology that originated in some dim but definitely *oral* Germanic past. Proof of such a past was too ready at hand in OS, OHG, and ON poetic forms to be neglected or denied. Furthermore the thorough studies of the Old English metrical system by Sievers, Heusler, and Pope had drawn attention not only to the formulaic nature of some phrases but to the connection between certain formulae and certain rhythmical patterns. One scholar, who as late as 1955 did not seem to be aware of Parry, Lord, or Magoun, became indignant over the lack of any meticulous study of *Beowulf* that would explore the poem's

---

and Chadwick, *The Growth of Literature*, *1*, 553–54, 557, 565–66; C. M. Bowra, *From Virgil to Milton* (London, 1945), pp. 2ff., and *Heroic Poetry*, pp. 30, 40ff., 242–53; Klaeber, ed., *Beowulf and the Fight at Finnsburg* (3d ed., Boston, 1950), especially Introduction, pp. lv, lxi, lxvi–lxvii, cx–cxvii.

And several studies of formulae in Middle English literature: J. P. Oakden, *Alliterative Poetry in Middle English*, Vol. I (Manchester, 1930), Vol. II (Manchester, 1935); J. S. P. Tatlock, "Epic Formulas, Especially in *Lagamon*," *PMLA, 38* (1923), 494–529, and "Lagamon's Poetic Style and Its Relations," *The Manly Anniversary Studies in Language and Literature* (Chicago, 1923), pp. 3–11; E. S. Olszewska, "Illustrations of Norse Formulas in English," *Leeds Studies in English and Kindred Languages, 2* (1933), 76–84, and "The Alliterative Phrases in the Ormulum," *Leeds Studies in English and Kindred Languages, 5* (1936), 50–67; Ruth Crosby, "Oral Delivery in the Middle Ages," *Speculum, 11* (1936), 88–110; R. W. Wilson, *The Lost Literature of Medieval England* (London, 1952), pp. 1–14.

9. E.g. Claes Schaar, *Critical Studies in the Cynewulf Group, LSE*, Vol. XVII (Lund, 1949); Leonard J. Peters, "The Relationship of the Old English *Andreas* to *Beowulf*," *PMLA, 66* (1951), 844–63. A similar study involving themes, not phrases, is that of Adrien Bonjour, "The Techniques of Parallel Description in Beowulf," *RES*, N.S. 2 (1951), 1–10.

obvious grounding in an oral tradition.[10] Homeric scholars, on the other hand, had no such habit of assumption, no such proofs. Parry found all his proof within the *Iliad* and the *Odyssey*. Then, too, *Beowulf*'s author has no name; even if he did, he could not answer Homer poem for poem, fame for fame. Parry shocked many because he was thought to have disenthroned a paragon of genius: the *Beowulf*-poet has never sat so high in as many men's minds.

Nonetheless, the critical act of applying the Parry-Lord thesis to Old English poetry is not therefore to be disparaged. For this perception and achievement Francis P. Magoun, Jr., of Harvard University is given merited praise since, although Lord first subjected a part of *Beowulf* to analysis for oral-formulaic characteristics,[11] it was Magoun who first published such an analysis and who presented it in the context of an Anglo-Saxon civilization.

In the following paragraphs, Magoun's seven pertinent articles are set forth in summary, followed by a description of the work of those students and critics who have pursued his lead with innovations of their own, and by a notice of the few who have opposed a part or the whole of the theory. This somewhat bibliographical presentation precedes a critical one for the purposes of clarity, because, although the study of oral-formulaic poetry is a relatively new one in Old English scholarship, the names, articles, and intricacies of argument are numerous and would be confusing to handle simultaneously. A specific consideration of the points of the controversy appears in Chapters Three and Four.

The articles[12] that Magoun has published on the subject of Old English poetry as oral-formulaic verse are spread out over several years and include not only the initial statement of his thesis, but an exploration of its significance relative to Old English Christian poetry, Old English poetic themes, and the authorship of *Beowulf*. The first and most important article, "The Oral-Formulaic Character of Anglo-Saxon Narrative Poetry" (1953), necessarily begins with a brief account of Parry's and

10. J. C. Van Meurs, "*Beowulf* and Literary Criticism," *Neophil., 39* (1955), 114–30.

11. The *Singer of Tales*, p. 198. Lord says that he analyzed *Beowulf* 1473–87 and showed it to Magoun in 1949 (this statement is corroborated by William Alfred of Harvard University in his preface to his translation of *Beowulf*, in *Medieval Epics* [New York, 1963], p. 10). In *Singer* (1960) Lord carries out systematic analyses of *Beowulf*, *The Song of Roland*, and *Digenis Akritas* (pp. 198–220).

12. See Bibliography.

Lord's definitions for and conclusions about Homer in particular and oral poetry in general. Magoun then quotes from Bede's story of Caedmon and Tacitus' description of the Germans to emphasize the long-lasting unlettered condition of the Germanic peoples and concludes, leaning on previous definitions, that the Germanic poetry on the Continent and in England for the seven centuries preceding Caedmon must have been *oral,* and if oral, then *traditional* and *formulaic.* Magoun next discusses in illuminating detail the first twenty-five lines of *Beowulf,* the text of which is appended to the article with formulae and formulaic systems marked in the text and supporting evidence gathered at the bottom of the page. Magoun selected the opening of the poem because to him it seemed the most likely portion to manifest the marks of individual genius; yet he found it to be nearly 70 per cent formulaic when compared to the surviving corpus of Old English poetry (some 30,000 lines). An analysis of *Christ and Satan* 512-35 (this text is also appended to the article) follows the analysis of *Beowulf,* so that a supposedly untraditional Christian vocabulary and phraseology may be examined against other Old English poetry. Again, the piece under scrutiny Magoun found to be highly formulaic, though not to such an extent as *Beowulf* 1-25. Magoun's explanation for the difference in degree, as well as for the fact that for some of the phrases in *Beowulf* and *Christ and Satan* he could find no parallels, is that the extant material is too limited: he has no doubt that if all Old English poetry had survived, every phrase of it could be demonstrated to be formulaic. Toward the end of this first article Magoun confronts the obvious problems raised by Cynewulf's signed poems. The poems are definitely formulaic, according to the definitions; yet only a literate poet would have enmeshed his runic signature in the lines of his verse. Magoun concludes that Cynewulf must have been raised and trained in the oral tradition and later taught to write, so that he could have "dictated his poems to himself." This possibility led Magoun to conceive of a "transitional period" between a purely oral and a purely literate composition, when men trained as singers also learned to pen their poems. The article closes then with several observations of interest on the subjects of enjambment, intervocalic "h," whole-line formulae, and the pointing of Old English manuscripts.

Magoun's second article, "Bede's Story of Cædman: the Case-History of an Anglo-Saxon Singer" (1955), contains much of the general information about the Parry-Lord thesis that appeared in the previous article. Bede's account of Caedmon is quoted in full in translation. Then follows an analysis of the *Hymn,* the text of which, with the usual markings and assembled evidence, appears at the end of the article. Magoun finds the *Hymn* "made up entirely of formulas or formulaic systems," therefore traditional, therefore not quite so miraculous as Bede would have us think. Doubtless, Magoun argues, Caedmon had been afflicted with stagefright before he had his encouraging dream, but all the while he was assuredly practicing oral poetry by himself out in the fields. His "song" is too smooth and too traditional to be the work of a real novice. This article, like the first one, ends with a reference to Cynewulf and the repeated suggestion that since he was a "lettered singer . . . working in the oral tradition" he could have dictated to himself.

In the same year in which the Caedmon article appeared, Magoun also published "The Theme of the Beasts of Battle in Anglo-Saxon Poetry." Here again he includes some informative material as well as a few remarks on the differences between Homeric and Old English poetry (see Chapter Three). He then gives Lord's definition of a poetic theme in an oral tradition and proceeds to illustrate the Old English poetic theme of "a wolf and/or a raven as beasts attendant on a scene of carnage" in twelve different instances occurring in nine different poems. After examining the illustrations, Magoun concludes that the "beasts of battle" theme was indeed a stock ornament of the Old English singer's repertoire.

Magoun's fourth article, "Two Verses in *Waldere* Characteristic of Oral Poetry" (1958), is less important than his others, but in it he reveals the advances of which a textual critic is capable once he acquires familiarity with the oral-formulaic technique employed by Old English poets in composing their poetry. Magoun examines *Waldere* 18b and 14b (*Ælfheres laf* and *wine Burgenda,* respectively) and finds that, although critics have objected to these lines, they are quite in keeping with what one would expect to find in a traditional song.

Two of Magoun's most recent articles connected with his thesis of a traditional Old English poetry are "*Beowulf A*': a Folk Variant" (1958) and "*Beowulf* B: a Folk Poem on Beowulf's Death" (1963). Relying on the assumption that the *Beowulf* manuscript represents a chance performance or chance performances of oral singers, Magoun argues against a belief in the authorial unity of the poem. He divides *Beowulf* into three parts—A: lines 1–2009a, A': lines 2009b–199, and B: lines 2200–3182. The earlier of these two articles is devoted to the hypothesis that A' was "soldered" into the poem by some "anthologizing scribe" who was proficient in oral composition and who knew a variant account of Beowulf's adventures at Hrothgar's court. This hypothesis is deemed necessary because the contradictions and neglected elements manifest upon comparing A with A' are simply too serious to represent the inconsistencies of a single author. In the next article Magoun draws more heavily upon the characteristics of oral-formulaic verse to argue that *Beowulf* B was "originally" independent of *Beowulf* A. In the first place, oral poets sing in episodes, not in cycles, and the "Return of Beowulf" is cyclic in character. In the second place, the "time gap" between the adventures with the Danes and the adventures with the Geats is too great: if a singer had set out to compose a song cycle on Beowulf, he would, so Magoun is convinced, have included Hygelac's death before *Beowulf* B. Then Magoun notices several idiosyncrasies not common to "Singer A" and "Singer B." For instance, Singer B is much more interested in genealogies and in the Rhineland than is Singer A; Singer B composed five of the six instances of a light A^2 verse ending in *þone* (2007b, 2334b, 2588a, 2959a, 2969b, 3081b); and finally, two conflicting memories of Beowulf's youth are presented in A and B. This final proof, lack of consistency in the portrayal of the hero, Magoun thinks the strongest argument in support of his theory of multiple singers behind the manuscript. He does not think, however, that the three divisions in the poem's composition detract from its aesthetic unity.

Magoun's interest and scholarship have recently been devoted to the Finnish *Kalevala,* a translation of which he published in 1963. As he considered the old Finnish civilization and its folk literature, founded in oral tradition, Magoun discovered some formulae and short themes which Old English poetry and the *Kalevala* have in common. These he pointed out and presented with comments in keeping with his previous convictions about oral poetry in "Some Notes on Old English Poetry," an article in a *Festschrift* for Albert Baugh.

Magoun's initial articles on the subject of an oral tradition in Old English poetry aroused immediate interest and further thought and speculation among students and scholars of the field. Of those whose interest began in their student days, Robert Payson Creed, who studied with Magoun at Harvard, has been the most prolific. His unpublished dissertation, "Studies in the Technique of Composition of the Beowulf Poetry in British Museum Ms. Cotton Vitellius A XV," [13] was the first and so far the only study to subject the whole of *Beowulf* to the sort of formulaic analysis made familiar by Parry, Lord, and Magoun, with this important difference, that only those phrases repeated or echoed within the poem itself are listed as formulae or formulaic systems. Even without drawing upon the rest of Old English poetry for comparison, Creed found that 20 per cent of *Beowulf* consisted of formulae and that another 25 percent was demonstrably formulaic. In his discussion of representative formulae and formulaic systems Creed arranged his evidence according to metrical type, and thereby discovered that whole-verse formulae of the rhythmical types A, D, and E were significantly more common in either half-line than were whole-verse formulae of the B and C types. Creed's discussion is followed by the complete text of *Beowulf* with formulae and formulaic systems clearly marked. The rest of the thesis is taken up with the supporting evidence for the formulae.

Since the completion of his doctorate, Creed has published numerous articles, some of which, though interesting, are of minor importance to the general consideration of the oral tradition because they deal with textual emendations (arrived at through the oral-formulaic method) and one useful formulaic system, the *andswarode* system.[14] Of more weight is the article "The Making of an Anglo-Saxon Poem," [15] where, after some discussion in which he modifies Parry's definition of the formula, Creed goes through the motions of oral composition and ingeniously produces four lines of Old English poetry to match *Beowulf* 356–59. In further articles[16] Creed has considered the special problems that confront the *literary* critic of *oral* poetry and the possible evidence within an oral song of a singer's individual genius.

Another of Magoun's students at Harvard, Robert Edwin Diamond, wrote his dissertation on "The Diction of the Signed Poems of Cynewulf." [17] There he analyzed *Christ II, Elene, Juliana,* and the *Fates of*

13. Harvard University, 1955.

14. See *"Beowulf* 2231a: *sinc-fæt (sohte),"* PQ, *25* (1956), 206–08; "*Genesis* 1316," MLN, *73* (1958), 321–25; "The *Andswarode*-system in Old English Poetry," *Speculum, 32* (1957), 523–28; "Afterword," in Burton Raffel's translation of *Beowulf* (New York, 1963), pp. 123–48.

15. *ELH, 26* (1959), 445–54.

16. "On the Possibility of Criticizing Old English Poetry," TSLL, *3* (1961), 97–106; "A Singer Looks at His Sources," CL, *14* (1962), 44–52.

17. Harvard University, 1953.

the Apostles and found them 42.8 percent formulaic within the Cyne-wulfian authorship and, by a representative test, 62.7 percent formulaic when compared with all Old English poetry. Diamond later published an article[18] in which he suggested various solutions of the particular difficulty posed by a Cynewulf in an oral tradition, redefined the term "formula," and gave an analysis of the *Fates of the Apostles* 1–29. In another article, "Theme as Ornament in Anglo-Saxon Poetry,"[19] Diamond examined the "theme of the sea-voyage" in several Old English poems.

A number of other scholars have concerned themselves more or less intimately with an oral tradition in Old English poetry as a direct result of Magoun's original demonstration. Wayne Albert O'Neil, upon a suggestion in Magoun's first article, scrutinized the Old English elegies for formulaic content and found them highly traditional;[20] and Lewis E. Nicholson thoroughly investigated Old English expanded verses.[21] Much scholarly endeavor has been turned toward an investigation of the ornamental themes of exile, of more beasts of battle, and of the hero on the beach in Old English poetry.[22] Adrien Bonjour in reattacking the subject of the beasts of battle has sought to show that the *Beowulf*-poet alone of all those who sang of the wolf and the raven presented his description with conscientious originality. This consideration has led Bonjour to argue elsewhere[23] that the *Beowulf* poem was written down by a single author and that an oral tradition lies far, not immediately, behind it.

18. "The Diction of the Signed Poems of Cynewulf," *PQ, 38* (1959), 228–41.

19. *PMLA, 76* (1961), 461–68.

20. See "Oral-Formulaic Structure in Old English Poetry," *DA, 21* (1960), 1960; "Another Look at Oral Poetry in the *Seafarer*," *Speculum, 35* (1960), 596–600.

21. "Oral Techniques in the Composition of Expanded Anglo-Saxon Verse," unpublished dissertation, Harvard University, 1958. See also "Oral Techniques in the Composition of Expanded Anglo-Saxon Verse," *PMLA, 78* (1963), 287–92.

22. See Stanley B. Greenfield, "The Formulaic Expression of the Theme of Exile in Anglo-Saxon Poetry," *Speculum, 30* (1955), 200–06; Adrien Bonjour, "*Beowulf* and the Beasts of Battle," *PMLA, 72* (1957), 563–73; David K. Crowne, "The Hero on the Beach: An Example of Composition by Theme in Anglo-Saxon Poetry," *NM, 61* (1960), 362–72. See also Alain Renoir, "Oral Formulaic Theme Survival, *NM, 65* (1964), 70–75; George Clark, "The Traveler Recognizes his Goal: A Theme in Anglo-Saxon Poetry," *JEGP, 54* (1965), 645–59; Albert Bates Lord, "Beowulf and Odysseus," *Franciplegius,* ed. Jess B. Bessinger, Jr., and Robert P. Creed (New York, 1965), pp. 86–91. Donald K. Fry, "The Heroine on the Beach in *Judith*," *NM, 68* (1967), 168–184.

23. See "Poesie héroique du moyen âge et critique littéraire," *Romania, 78* (1957), 243–55; "Beowulf et l'épopée anglo-saxonne," *La Table ronde, 132* (1958), 140–51.

A similar view has been put forward by Jackson J. Campbell in an essay about *The Seafarer*.[24] Both Bonjour and Campbell, however, accept Magoun's application of the Parry-Lord thesis to Old English poetry. An extension of this application into the fields of Old Norse and Middle English has been carried out interestingly and with thoughtful qualifications by Cecil Wood, Ronald A. Waldron, and Albert C. Bough.[25] Randolph Quirk[26] has made a penetrating and much needed study of the possibilities of irony within a system of composition that is oral and therefore traditional.

One of the most far-reaching and important of the articles on oral Old English poetry is William Whallon's "The Diction of Beowulf" (1961).[27] Throughout the article Whallon has drawn attention to the differences between Homeric and Old English poetry not only in meter but in degree of traditional character. In comparing words signifying *shield* and *ship* in Homer and *Beowulf,* Whallon found the Greek far more "economical," according to Parry's definition, than the Old English. Similarly he examined Homer's epithets for Odysseus (where only 9 out of 300 are interchangeable) and the *Beowulf*-poet's epithets for his hero. The later poet provides for every need of meter and alliteration and yet, for an oral poet, is quite superfluous in his epithets. After such observations, Whallon concluded that *Beowulf* is less formulaic than Homer's poems because it appeared sooner in an oral tradition that was diverted from its full development by the arrival in England of Christianity with its learned monks and love of libraries.

In a later qualification of these same ideas[28] Whallon stated that whereas the *Iliad* provides epithets for individuals in a shifting and therefore vague context, *Beowulf* provides epithets for shifting characters in a specific context. The difference he would explain by a mechanical necessity of the long hexameter line: the Greek oral poet filled out a

24. "Oral Poetry in the *Seafarer*," *Speculum, 35* (1960), 87–96.

25. Wood, "The Skald's Bid for a Hearing," *JEGP, 59* (1960), 240–54, and "Concerning the Oral Tradition," *Scandinavian Studies, 34* (1962), 47–53; Waldron, "Oral-Formulaic Technique in Middle English Alliterative Poetry," *Speculum, 32* (1957), 792–804; Baugh, "Improvisation in the Middle English Romances," *Proceedings of the American Philological Society, 103* (1959), 418–54.

26. "Poetic Language and Old English Meter," *Early English and Norse Studies Presented to Hugh Smith,* ed. Arthur Brown and Peter Foote (London, 1963), pp. 150–71.

27. *PMLA, 76* (1961), 309–19. See also his article, "The Idea of God in *Beowulf*," *PMLA, 80* (1965), 19–23.

28. "Formulas for Heroes, in the *Iliad* and in *Beowulf*," *MP, 63* (1965), 95–104.

longer line than did his Old English counterpart, by regularly using the proper names and "individualizing" epithets belonging to his heroes.

The remaining scholars who have considered the possibilities of an oral tradition in Old English poetry have either accepted Magoun's thesis, without qualification or discussion, as useful to their own special research,[29] or, more important, have opposed or very sharply modified the conclusions of Magoun and even of Parry and Lord. The latter group is gaining both in size and influence; but few of the objections set forth by its members have been finally met by Magoun or his "school."

While concerned with other specific problems, James Ross and James L. Rosier[30] have objected, in passing, to the rigidity of the various current definitions of the formula which seem to preclude the possibilities of artistic originality or conscientious irony in a so-called traditional poetry. Kemp Malone and especially Claes Schaar and R. W. V. Elliott[31] have maintained that Magoun's assumption of an unlettered singer is simply irreconcilable with the story in Bede, or with the undeniably literary sources of several of the Old English poems, or with the indubitably literate authors of the signed poems of Cynewulf and of *Maldon*. Further objections have been raised by Alistair Campbell, who has severely taken Parry and Lord to task for the statements that oral poetry *must* be formulaic or vice versa, and who elsewhere has suggested that the elaborately built, long paragraphs of Old English verse seem to bear witness to a design for preservation in writing.[32] One scholar,

---

29. See Jess B. Bessinger, Jr., "*Beowulf* and the Harp at Sutton Hoo," *UTQ, 27* (1958), 148–68; W. P. Lehmann and Takemitsu Tabusa, *The Alliterations of Beowulf* (Austin, Tex., 1958), pp. 2ff.; Alain Renoir, "Point of View and Design for Terror in *Beowulf,*" *NM, 63* (1962), 154–67 (on p. 154 Renoir says that Magoun's theory is "all but generally accepted today"); Robert L. Kellogg, "The South Germanic Oral Tradition," in *Franciplegius,* ed. Jess B. Bessinger, Jr., and Robert P. Creed, pp. 66–67.

30. Ross, "Formulaic Composition in Gaelic Oral Literature," *MP, 57* (1959), 1–12; Rosier, "The Use of Association: Hands and Feet in *Beowulf,*" *PMLA, 78* (1963), 8–14.

31. Malone, "Caedmon and English Poetry," *MLN, 76* (1961), 193–95, and a review of Godfrid Storms' lecture, "Compound Names of Peoples in *Beowulf,* a Study in the Diction of a Great Poet," *ES, 41* (1960), 200–06 (see p. 205); Schaar, "On a New Theory of Old English Poetic Diction," *Neophil., 39–40* (1955–56), 301–05; Elliott, "Form and Image in the Old English Lyrics," *EIC, 11* (1961), 1–10, and "Byrhtnoth and Hildebrand: a Study in Heroic Technique," *CL, 14* (1962), 53–70. And see Kenneth Sisam, *The Structure of Beowulf* (Oxford, 1965), pp. 3(n.), 67.

32. Review of Lord's *The Singer of Tales, MLR, 57* (1962), 75–76; and "Old English

Paull F. Baum, has even argued that the *Beowulf*-poet's style is so "crowded" and his narrative so "convoluted" that the poem must have been "most unsuited for recitation."[33]

All these objections are worthy of answer, yet no one of their authors singly presents such a challenge to Magoun's theory as does Arthur Gilchrist Brodeur in his book *The Art of Beowulf* (Berkeley, 1959). With intimate verbal knowledge of and sensitivity toward *Beowulf* and all Old English poetry, Brodeur has been able to attack the oral-formulaic analysis of poetry on its own ground, namely in a consideration of vocabulary. Brodeur studied closely the compounds to be found in *Beowulf*: of the 903 compounds that he counted, 518 appear in *Beowulf* alone and 578 appear only once in the poem. The high artistic imagination to which these figures point would not be possible in a poem "totally formulaic" (Magoun's phrase used of oral poetry in general). Besides their richness, the compounds in *Beowulf* have a superfluity in relation to the demands of meter and alliteration which, theoretically, should not exist in an entirely traditional poetry. Brodeur further objected that *Beowulf* was too long to have been composed orally, although he thought it possible that the poem was publicly recited. He also brought up the old matter of Cynewulf and observed that the enormous difference in the religious vocabulary of *Beowulf* and *Elene* is but another witness against absolute tradition and in favor of a literate artist. In general, though Magoun's work seemed to him to be helpful, Brodeur considered that the statements setting forth the theory had gone too far when they precluded composition by a person acquainted with letters and by an individual recognizable enough to have left his own stamp upon a poem.

A strongly challenging criticism of Magoun's application of the Parry-Lord thesis to Old English poetry has recently been put forward by Robert D. Stevick in his article, "The Oral-Formulaic Analysis of Old English Verse" (1962).[34] Stevick, who has relied upon Magoun's theory in textual criticism,[35] praised Magoun's work as a "methodological breakthrough," but he thought it had gone too far; in short, he cham-

---

Poetic Style," *English and Medieval Studies Presented to J. R. R. Tolkien* (London, 1962), pp. 13–27.

33. "The *Beowulf*-Poet," *PQ, 39* (1960), 389–99.

34. *Speculum, 37* (1962), 382–89. For a similarly critical but harder-hitting indictment of oral-formulaic theory in Homeric and OE studies, see H. L. Rogers, "The Crypto-Psychological Character of The Oral Formula," *ES, 47* (1966), 89–102.

35. "Emendations of Poetic Texts: *Beowulf* 2523," *MLQ, 20* (1959), 339–43.

pioned Brodeur's objections. Stevick's criticism, however, is quite different from Brodeur's in its scope: Stevick brings a large view to a number of subjects; his breadth and Brodeur's scrutiny well supplement each other. Perhaps to Stevick the most damaging characteristic of the whole oral-formulaic "school" (including classical as well as Old English scholars) is a lack of rigor especially apparent in the definitions—or the lack of them—of the terms "composition," "poem," "song," "singer," and "performance." Stevick has also been the first to point out the discrepancy between the kinds of poetry chosen for analysis by Parry and Lord on the one hand and by Magoun and his followers on the other: all Homeric poetry is epic, whereas the supporting evidence for a passage in *Beowulf* or the *Fates of the Apostles* has been drawn from riddles, elegies, charms, translations from the Latin, and religious meditations. Stevick further observed that the Parry-Lord thesis must remain, after all, analogical in a consideration of Old English poetry, and that as an analogue it needs reconsideration. While he extolled the concept of a "transitional period" between the totally oral and the totally literary, Stevick urged that the stages of such a period be more precisely defined. Finally, he suggested that in our thinking of the oral-formulaic technique of composition in general, we would be helped by analogies to other than a literary art, and he offered contemporary jazz composition as a working comparison.

In a more recent article Stevick considered the familiar *Beowulfian* problem of the relationship between Christian and pre-Christian elements in the poem.[36] Like other scholars before him, he decided that, since the story of the poem would be complete without the Christian references, these references must have been added at some time after the theme and much of the phraseology of the poem had assumed a unified shape. He closely examined three passages for the relative formulaic expression of Christian and "traditional" subject matter, and postulated that the Christian elements entered with the first redaction of the poem to writing, because these elements seem to be expressed in a less formulaic language than are the pre-Christian elements. Stevick argued that his postulation has the virtue of avoiding both the "either-or assumption" on the question of a literate *Beowulf*-poet, and a vague "transitional period" between an oral and a written literature.

An article that may point the way to an important and useful qualifi-

36. "Christian Elements and the Genesis of *Beowulf*," *MP, 61* (1963), 78–89.

cation of Magoun's thesis appeared in 1965 in *Franciplegius,* a volume of essays dedicated to the founder of oral studies in Old English literature. Frederic G. Cassidy in "How Free Was the Anglo-Saxon Scop?"[37] applauds Magoun's work and its present state of being "accepted fact"; but he questions the criterion of repetition which is depended upon by all scholars of oral poetry for identification of formulae. Since much of Old English poetry is lost to us, and since repetition of phrases identifies a poetic formula, it follows that there must lurk many an unidentified formula in the 30,000 lines that have come down to us. Repetition is taken to be a sure means of identification (though Cassidy offers some cautionary remarks on its efficacy); but, repetition failing, Cassidy puts forward the possibly identifying powers of "syntactical patterns or frames" into which fit the words of a half-line. Statistics gathered in the doctoral dissertations of Wayne A. O'Neil and Godfrey L. Gattiker[38] indicate that the Old English half-line has twenty-five different syntactical patterns into ten of which fit 75 percent of all the verses of *Beowulf* and the elegies. From such facts Cassidy argues that not only may modern readers more sensitively discern formulae in Old English verse but the Old English scop was in fact less bound by strictly repeated phrases than the previous studies of oral tradition would imply: "In short, the syntactic frame, very much like Saussure's *langue,* underlies the verbal formula, the *parole,* and furnishes the scop a certain area of freedom within the patterned realm of his discipline."

Because some Old English poetry, unlike any Homeric poetry, affords evidence of literary composition, certain opponents of the "Magoun School" have seized upon such evidence either to dispose of Magoun's theory altogether or to formulate a compromise more satisfying than Magoun's "transitional period" between an oral and a written culture. Larry D. Benson in "The Literary Character of Anglo-Saxon Formulaic Poetry"[39] argues that to say Old English poems are formulaic is to say

37. In *Franciplegius,* pp. 75–85; and see Joseph A. Russo, "The Structural Formula in Homeric Verse," *YCS, 20* (1966), 219–40. See also J. B. Hainsworth, "Structure and Content in Epic Formulas: The Question of the Unique Expression," *CQ,* N.S. *14* (1964), 155–64.

38. See above, n. 20, for O'Neil. For Gattiker, see "The Syntactic Basis of the Poetic Formula in *Beowulf,*" unpublished dissertation, University of Wisconsin, 1962.

39. *PMLA, 81* (1966), 334–41. See also Jackson J. Campbell, "Learned Rhetoric in Old English Poetry," *MP, 73* (1966), 189–201; Gail K. Byerly, "Compounds and Other Elements of Poetic Diction Derived from an Oral-Formulaic Tradition: A Comparison of Aeschylus and the *Beowulf* Poet, *DA, 27* (1966), 1333A (Penn.); Edward J. Wolff,

only that they are Old English. He demonstrates in a close consideration of a few of the *Meters of Boethius* what must be literate composition in formulaic style. Michael Curschmann is more tentative. His article, "Oral Poetry in Mediaeval English, French, and German Literature: Some Notes on Recent Research," [40] besides revealing a bibliographical and linguistic range comparable to that in *The Singer of Tales,* offers in qualified terms some penetrating criticism of oral-formulaic theory in general. In criticizing Parry's and Lord's distinctions between oral and written texts as being inadequate to the facts, Curschmann wonders if in the Old English period there may not have been distinctions between types of poets ("scribe-poet," "writer-poet," "singer-poet") rather than between types of texts ("oral," "written," "transitional"). The question then is, how do we distinguish the writer-poet from the others? At worst, says Curschmann, we cannot distinguish, but

> at best the writer-poet's deliberate use of formulaic language, composition by motifs, and standard patterns, etc. will be recognized as such, and our knowledge of this technique will lead us to a more adequate interpretation of his work. Most Anglo-Saxon texts will in one way or another fall into this group.[41]

That many Old English poems do fall into that group is Stanley B. Greenfield's implicit argument in "The Cannons of Old English Criticism." [42] There he analyzes instances of formulaic language and *variation* in order to prove from poetic context strong possibilities for *le mot juste.*

A major publication on the "Magoun side" is Donald K. Fry's article "Old English Formulas and Systems." [43] Fry's concern is with definitions. After giving a swift but full summary of classical and Old English

---

"Chaucer's Normalized Diction: A Comparison of Recurring Phrases in Chaucer and *Beowulf* to Determine the Validity of the Magoun Thesis," *DA,* 27 (1967), 3022A–23A (Mich. State).

40. *Speculum,* 42 (1967), 36–52. For a bibliographical summary of scholarship in Old and Middle English, see R. F. Lawrence, "The Formulaic Theory and Its Application to English Alliterative Poetry," *Essays on Style and Language,* ed. Roger Fowler (London, 1966), 166–83.

41. Ibid., p. 49.

42. *ELH, 34* (1967), 141–55.

43. *ES,* 48 (1967), 194–204 (the article is a reply to H. L. Rogers' article in the same periodical: see n. 34); and see his companion article, "Old English Formulaic Themes and Type Scenes," *Neophil.,* 52 (1968), 48–54.

scholars' definitions of the formula and the formulaic system, Fry presents his own provocative definitions. He argues that since the rhythm of OE half-lines was evidently irrelevant to the scop, a similarity only of words and syntax determines a formulaic system. A system, furthermore, originates formulae, since the term "formula" implies origin from "schematized diction"[44] or formulaic systems. This means that "the essence of the formula is not repetition, but systematic origin." Fry's new criterion for the identification of Old English formulae answers several of the objections which may be brought against Magoun's thesis. That it does not answer all objections results from Fry's (implied) premise that OE texts were orally composed.

This bibliographical summary should make clear that the recent concern with Old English poetry as a traditional art is a very lively one, one contributed to by several excellent scholars, and one in which agreement has by no means been reached. The survey cannot of course begin to do justice to the details of critical reasoning set forth by these men. A more lengthy discussion therefore follows, in which the Parry-Lord thesis as Magoun and his followers have interpreted it is particularly examined.

44. Ibid., p. 203. The phrase "schematized diction" is Rogers' expression for the diction of OE poems.

Chapter Three

The Imperfect Application

Proponents of the theory of an oral-formulaic composition in ancient verse, whether they be classicists or Old English scholars, find proof of their argument mainly in statistics drawn from the poems themselves but also from the scant notice of an oral tradition contained in contemporaneous documents and from comparisons to the oral compositions of other peoples in other times. History and analogy are important, necessary bolsters to any modern theory of ancient poetry, but are subjects too vast to be taken up in this book. Here and in the following chapter the concern is with the primary evidence, the poetry, and with Magoun's analysis of it.

In applying Parry's theory of oral-formulaic composition to Old English poetry, Magoun may indeed have achieved a "methodological breakthrough," as Robert Stevick calls it; he most certainly did succeed in compelling scholarly attention toward the traditional character of Old English poetic language—a character that was never entirely neglected by students of the poetry but which was rarely scrutinized so closely as Magoun scrutinized it, or considered so inseparably from its meter, except incidentally or for different reasons by men like Sievers and Pope. Yet Magoun's description of Old English poetry as orally composed, or of *Beowulf* as totally formulaic, has elicited criticism from several quarters. This criticism varies greatly in depth and breadth according to the authors' intents, but in its more serious objections it has yet to be answered.

With the exception of Stevick's article,[1] a general plea for exactitude in all facets of the study, the critical objections to Magoun's theory have taken the form of isolated contradictions, queries, qualifications. Several

---

1. "The Oral-Formulaic Analysis of Old English Verse," *Speculum*, 37 (1962), 382–89. See also H. L. Rogers, "The Crypto-Psychological Character of the Oral Formula," *ES*, 42 (1966), 89–102.

scholars have made Cynewulf, always an embarrassment to upholders of the oral-formulaic theory, the image of their objection; many have worried over Parry's definition of a formula; Arthur G. Brodeur concentrated upon what would seem to be an unconventional vocabulary in *Beowulf;* William Whallon remarked important differences between Homeric and Old English poetry; and Larry Benson illustrated the literate use of formulaic language. Such are the more weighty of the criticisms; but strongly and penetratingly as they are presented, they have never been carried back *in toto* to their source, the Parry-Lord thesis. If one considers the work of Parry and Lord, and then considers how Magoun and his followers have utilized methods of criticism originally designed for Homeric poetry, two awkward and unexplained discrepancies appear: first, that the original theory has not been rigorously or consistently applied to Old English poetry although one is given to understand that it has; second, that the practice of analogy has not been adequately questioned or measured by those who believe Old English poetry to be oral in its composition. It is now necessary to set the Old English scholarship beside that of Parry and Lord and to inquire after the appropriate standards. Several of the reservations and objections mentioned below have already been noted, some have not; but each will be offered in the light of the scholarship that inspired Magoun.

The imposition of the Parry-Lord thesis upon Old English poetry as it has been carried out by Magoun and his students presents difficulties both of *equation* and of *distinction.* Certain definitions and procedures that Parry, and to some extent Lord, devised have suffered an unacknowledged change when made to serve Old English poetry. Stevick[2] pointed out the vagueness with which originally exact terms, such as "composition" or "singer," are employed in the new field; but semblance without rigor of equation goes deeper than terms, and the lack of proper attention to fundamental linguistic and metrical differences between Homeric and Old English poetry compounds an initial inexactitude. A most glaring example is the very pedestal of the whole critical theory, the formula.

The formula must be the measure of any poetic language supposed oral in tradition, and therefore its precise definition with its forces of inclusion and exclusion is vital to a study of individual ancient texts. In the context of the oral-formulaic method of composition, Parry, of

2. Ibid., pp. 384, 386.

course, was the first to establish a definition of the formula. From this definition as he applied it to the Homeric poems he evolved other definitions and gathered the other statistics and observations that together comprise his whole theory. The importance of the definition of the formula and what a scholar does with it vis-à-vis a particular poetry cannot be overestimated: by its definition, not only is the degree to which a text may reveal its oral lineage determined, but the definitions of *formulaic system* and *theme* are shaped more or less mechanically, and the scholar's ascertainments of the language, meter, and genre of his subject are called to witness as considerations that must be reasonably consistent with his definition of the formula.

Because of its originating power, it is impossible to discuss the formula and the treatment a certain scholar has given it without keeping in view the same scholar's treatment of the whole theory. Space does not allow for an evenly complete consideration, and such matters as how the definition of the formula affects the definition of the oral theme—one of the more obvious points of the theory, and a study that long anticipated Parry and Magoun—will be omitted in the following paragraphs, while the absorbing questions of language, syntax, verbal association, and meter are included briefly and inseparably from the all-important question of the formula itself. The particular and not so closely related subject of genre follows the treatment of the formula. In the second part of the chapter a specific kind of formula, the epithet, is discussed at length as representative of some of the differences between Greek and Old English poetry.

Here and throughout the book the only Old English poems considered at all in detail are *Beowulf* and *Elene*. Aside from the necessity of limitation, *Beowulf* is chosen because of its length, relatively early date, and overriding importance among the other poems; *Elene* because it is another "long poem" representing a slightly later period and because it was composed by a man who may well have been literate. Length is a desirability in discussions of formulae for obvious statistical reasons, and the two poems are short enough when compared to the *Iliad*'s 15,000-odd lines. If the oral-formulaic tradition existed in Old English poetry and was a tradition upon which time left its mark, then a selection of poems perhaps a century apart in date of composition may be useful. Finally, a Cynewulfian poem, evidently a translation from the Latin, provides an interesting contrast to *Beowulf* within the subject at hand; and runic passages raise questions that must be discussed even if they cannot be settled. One further note: in this and the following chapter the terminology of the oral-formulaic theory is not precisely honored, in spite of Stevick's useful admonition. It is not precisely honored because in Old English poetry it is not precisely proved. Thus the composer of an Old English poem is called a *poet,* his composition a *poem,* with no conditions that the terms indicate literacy or illiteracy. The words *singer* and *song* are also used interchangeably with *poet* and *poem,* but always with quotation marks as trivial witness to the contention that the oral composition of Old English poetry is still an open question.

I

A critical discussion of the oral formula can begin at almost any point, once one has at least agreed that the identifying characteristic of a formula must be the demonstrable fact of repetition. In texts whose exact origin is unknown, whose language and whose artifice we may respond to or understand imperfectly, there is little to dependably mark a formulaic phrase except repetition, whether precise or approximate. Yet considering the large loss of ancient texts of any civilization, is not repetition a superficial means of designating formulae? In his article "How Free Was the Anglo-Saxon Scop?"[3] Frederic G. Cassidy raises this important question in order to penetrate beneath the outward sign to the inner structure of the formula itself, or to that characteristic of formulaic diction which has an identifiable existence independent of the caprice of time, a fire in Alexandria, a horde of church-burning Danes. First arguing from appearances, Cassidy observes that if verbal repetition is to be the criterion for an oral formula, then the Anglo-Saxon scop was restricted in his composition; he had "the freedom to choose, but not greatly to change, formulas." Arguing further and still from outward signs, Cassidy discusses Old English phrases that seem to be formulaic except that the remaining corpus of poetry offers no "proof" via repetition of their formular status.[4] The rest of Cassidy's article is devoted to an ontological argument. A statistical inspection of 8,000 verses of Old English poetry (*Beowulf* and the elegies) has resulted in the discovery

---

3. *Franciplegius,* ed. Jess B. Bessinger, Jr., and Robert P. Creed, pp. 75–85. See p. 60 for a summary of the article. The same question has been raised in relation to Homeric studies by J. B. Hainsworth, "Structure and Content in Epic Formulas: the Question of the Unique Expression," *CQ,* N.S. *14* (1964), 155–64.

4. *Franciplegius,* pp. 75–78.

that all these half-lines fill only 25 syntactical patterns, and that 10 such patterns account for 75 per cent of the 8,000 verses.[5] According to Cassidy, these data leave "no doubt that the syntactical frame was a functioning structural reality"; and he presents charts and figures of his own to describe the 10 major syntactical patterns (e.g. "a stressed adjective or past participle qualifies a stressed noun," "one noun, normally a compound"), and indicates their frequency of use in *Beowulf* and the elegiac poems.[6] Cassidy then argues that the limited number of syntactical frames were themselves tools for oral composition—structural formulae, as it were, of poetic phrases. He sets both frames and phrases within an oral historical development.

> If the ontogeny of the formula recapitulates the phylogeny of Old English verse, it may not be entirely fanciful to reconstruct theoretically the origin of that verse from the nature and use of the oral formula. Each of the latter is a species of which the syntactic frame is the genus, and the genera are the survivors of a process of natural selection.[7]

If the scop could depend upon this limited number of syntactical patterns, then he was indeed free to elaborate or change the individual words of his traditional phrases. Tags and patronymic formulae were a more rigid part of his conventional diction, but only a part. Other phrases he could use where they seemed fitting to his theme.

> It is these that have proved less rigid than some have thought, because, as we now see, all verbal formulas were referable to archetypal syntactic frames: the verbal details could change, not only unstressed elements but even stressed ones as in formulaic systems, within the steadying patterns of the syntax. Most fundamental of all, of course, was the structure of the poetic line with its two alliteratively linked halves, each built on a limited number of established stress patterns. Yet even here the syntactic frame beneath permitted the scop to choose among synonyms for alliteration and to adjust the verse types in various ways. The Anglo-Saxon scop, like any other poet, had to work within the restrictions of his medium. But these were more

5. See above, chap. 2, n. 37.
6. *Franciplegius*, pp. 78–81.
7. Ibid., p. 81.

flexible, less confining, than the "formulaic" idea has seemed to suggest.[8]

Cassidy's article could well be seminal in a much needed reconsideration of the oral formula simply because it raises and attempts to answer an ontological question seldom asked and never, to my knowledge, answered. The criterion of repetition for the determination of the formular status of a poetic phrase is indeed unsatisfactory. The verse *gode gewyrcean* (*Beowulf* 20b) is nowhere repeated in Old English poetry, yet the phrase "feels" formulaic. But dissatisfaction with the conventional designation of formulae is perhaps the better part of Cassidy's article, because his solution actually solves little. The most prolix and undisciplined habit of prose composition in any language will naturally contain the infinite verbal species of finite syntactical genera. Poetry in any language is likely to have fewer syntactical patterns than has prose, because of the selection imposed upon the syntax by poetic form. Twenty-five syntactical patterns, 10 of which account for 75 percent of a typical body of Old English verse, are still not finite enough to designate an oral singer's useful tools. Cassidy himself admits, in a note, that written imitation could not be distinguished from oral verse by means of recognized syntactical frames.[9] Then could not all of *Beowulf*—as long as syntactical frames are the measure—be written? The finite, in linguistic shape, must be more limited than syntactical pattern not only in order that we, in our literate culture, may recognize oral formulaic diction but also in order that such diction may be readily efficacious to (hence identifiable by) the oral singer.

Donald K. Fry also argues against repetition as a determining characteristic of the formula. His article, "Old English Formulas and Systems," [10] offers a thesis and illustrations importantly different from Cassidy's, but it suffers from the same practical flaw: the new criteria do not enable us to distinguish an orally composed text from a text written by a poet using conventional diction. Fry is not concerned with the definition of the oral formula as such, but with specific definitions of the formula and system in Old English poetry. He points out that consistency of rhythmic type is unnecessary to a definition of the formulaic system since we have no proof that the sequence of rhythmic types in

8. Ibid., p. 83.
9. Ibid., p. 85, n. 25.
10. *ES, 48* (1967), 194–204. See pp. 61–2 for a summary of the article.

Old English half-lines is intentional. He then defines the formulaic system as "a group of half-lines, usually related metrically and semantically, which are related in form by the identical relative placement of two elements, one a variable word or element of a compound usually supplying the alliteration, and the other a constant word or element of a compound, with approximately the same distribution of non-stressed elements." [11] Fry gives *heals-beaga mæst, heall-ærna mæst* and *fela feorhcynna, feorhcynna fela* as examples of formulaic systems. He proceeds to derive a definition for the formula from his definition of the system. Since the term "formula" implies origin from "schematized diction," all formulae originate from systems. Strict repetition is therefore not a relevant criterion for the identification of formulae: "to prove that a group of words is a formula, we need only find another recorded group implying a system from which both probably originated." [12] *Heals-beaga mæst* and *heall-ærna mæst* are therefore both formulae since they originated

from a group of words whose systematic pattern is "(noun) (noun) mæst." Groups of words repeated verbatim are merely "the same formula," but verbatim repetition is irrelevant to the definition of the formula, "a group of words, one-half line in length, which shows evidence of being the direct product of a formulaic system." [13] Fry's obliteration of a distinction between formula and formulaic system goes far to describe in a useful way the conventionality of Old English poetic diction; but it does not describe at all the method of composition of Old English poems or of any poetry that consistently employs phrases of a highly traditional character. Indeed, if Fry should catalogue Old English poetic phrases which he thought systematic in origin, he would probably end up with Cassidy's 25 syntactical patterns.[14] As it is, Fry, like Cassidy, presents us with the conventional character of Old English poetic diction, especially with its repetitive syntactical sequences, but not with a demonstrably oral composition. Both Cassidy and Fry, however, believe that Old English poetry was orally composed. The difficulty is

11. Ibid., p. 202.

12. Ibid., p. 204.

13. Ibid.

14. Cf. Fry's system, "(noun) (noun) mæst." The system is, of course, more specific than one of Cassidy's "frames," but still too semantically undefined to give proof of oral language.

ironic, for in Homeric studies the criterion of exact repetition suffices for
the determination of an enormous number of formulae, but in Old English poetry (as Cassidy's and Fry's articles implicitly bear witness) precise repetition of phrases is statistically disappointing.

The criterion of repetition certainly leaves something to be desired,
but in lieu of any other designation that is both evidently and ontologi-
cally superior, it is assumed for the purposes of this discussion that a
phrase which is formulaic is so by virtue of some degree of specific repetition of its syntactical and semantic parts.

Repetition conceded, consideration of the oral formula may continue
arbitrarily at any point; but since the concern here is with Magoun's and
his followers' adaptation of Parry's work, it may be useful to start with
one of the more obvious and influential metamorphoses to which the
formula has been subjected in the change of hands, and a metamorphosis
that well illustrates the problems of equation and distinction attendant
on the transposition of a critical theory from one poetry to another. The
metamorphosis in question is that of *formular length* ("formular" being
a word conveniently used by G. S. Kirk in *The Songs of Homer* to
avoid confusion of "formulaic" with "formulaic system"), and the
change in its determination is representative of the difference between
Parry's work and that of the Old English scholars who depended upon
his Homeric and Serbo-Croatian studies.

Parry's often repeated definition of the formula, "a group of words
which is regularly employed under the same metrical conditions to express a given essential idea," [15] was an entirely workable definition for
his purposes, and one to which he added but a single qualification. His
definition contained no limit upon the size of the "group of words"; but
Parry with little discussion made it quite clear that he did not consider
such necessarily conjunctival or introductory expressions as αὐτὰρ ὁ (although he), ὡς ὁ μεν (but thus), etc., to be formulaic, even though they
were "regularly employed under the same metrical conditions to express
a given essential idea" in the Homeric poems.[16] In a later essay he
rendered the limitation more exact, but again with virtually no discussion: as if such a limitation were only logical, he remarked in a footnote
that he excluded expressions of less than four words or five syllables from

---

15. First stated in *L'Épithète traditionnelle dans Homère*, p. 16; repeated in "Studies in
the Epic Technique of Oral Verse-Making, I," *HSCP, 41* (1930), 84.

16. *L'Épithète*, pp. 23–24.

formular status, lest their repetitions represented merely the natural word order of the whole language and not of a poetic composition.[17] In the same essay Parry further emphasized that although a change of inflection does not affect the formulaic character of a phrase, "any less simple alteration in the word group supposes thought of some length on the part of the poet." [18]

That Parry's restrictions upon the length of a formula were either ignored or changed with inadequate explanation is partly the fault of Lord. In his *Singer of Tales,* where he repeats Parry's definition and otherwise correctly represents the work of his teacher in this particular, Lord silently admits in his analyses of the *Iliad* (lines 1–15) and of *Beowulf* (lines 1473–85) expressions of less than four words or five syllables. Similarly in a recent article summarizing the theory of oral epic poetry, Lord includes in both his Greek and Serbo-Croatian examples expressions that Parry might have thought too brief.[19]

Hence it may be understandable that in his initial, and in some ways most important, article Magoun, also quoting Parry's definition, should nonetheless choose to abandon Parry's restrictions. For Magoun at least did make a choice. Toward the end of that first article, after he had discussed his analysis of *Beowulf* 1–25 in which such expressions as *oþ þæt him* and *on ielde* (Magoun's normalized spelling) are solidly underlined to indicate their formular status, Magoun mentioned in a footnote Parry's limitation upon formular dimension and added without explanation that it was "a restriction that could not be applied to Anglo-Saxon verse." [20] The same absence of explanation and the same inclusion of short expressions were evident in Magoun's next article, "Bede's Story of Cædman: the Case-History of an Anglo-Saxon Singer." But in his third article, a piece devoted to themes rather than to formulae, Magoun at last came to grips with the discrepancy between Parry's practice and his.[21] He first repeated Parry's definition and then maintained that Parry decided not to investigate the formulaic character of single words in

17. "Studies I," p. 84 n.

18. Ibid., pp. 83–84.

19. *The Singer of Tales,* e.g. οὐλομένην, ἐξ οὗ δε, τὰ πρῶτα, p. 143, and þæt ic, wes þu, se mærne, p. 198; see pp. 292–93, 297–330. See also "Homer and Other Epic Poetry," in *CH,* p. 187.

20. "The Oral-Formulaic Character of Anglo-Saxon Narrative Poetry," *Speculum, 28* (1953), 461 n.

21. "The Theme of the Beasts of Battle in Anglo-Saxon Poetry," *NM,* 56 (1955), 81–90.

Homeric poetry because that would be "too overwhelming a task." Such reasoning may be partly true, but it is certainly misleading. Magoun then proceeded with a careful statement regarding the importance of single words or short expressions in the formulaic framework of Old English half-lines:

> In the case of Anglo-Saxon poetry with its short verses (the structural unit) usually with very complicated metrics, the formulaic character of many single words becomes apparent as *sweordum* (*Jud.* 294b), *to willan* (295a) which not only occur under identical metrical conditions but which form obvious portions of A-verses. By the same token the formulaic character of even shorter, rhetorically less conspicuous words appears clearly as *þa* in *þa reordode* (*And.* 415a), *þa hleoðrode* (537a) where, and doubtless in countless other instances, *þa* forms the first measure of a D-verse [sic]. Reversed to *reordode þa, hleoðrode þa* the result is an E-verse where *þa* fills the second measure. . . . In a word, an element as small and insignificant as *þa* is capable of playing an important role formulaically—and metrically.[22]

Magoun's treatment of the formula presents a major break with Parry's criteria for distinguishing the tools of the oral singer; for Magoun relaxed the restrictions upon the formulaic phrase not only out of regard to the special character of Old English or even Germanic poetry but in an attempt to offer a better description of the semantic units from which any epic singer builds his song.

In his redefinition Magoun found unqualified concurrence in the work of his student Robert Creed, who not only considered the formular status of certain single words but included in his doctoral dissertation a thorough listing of what he called "whole measure formulas." Following Pope's thesis pertaining to the B- and C-types of rhythm whereby the first ictus is to be considered the beginning of the second measure, Creed found several repeated word groups of the rhythms / x / or / / x which would tend to corroborate Pope's description. He further discovered that these word groups were conveniently exchanged between types, as / x / between B and D² or / / x between C and D¹. Thus *swa him ær gescod*

---

22. Ibid., pp. 81–82; cf. Magoun's Introduction to his translation of the *Kalevala* (Cambridge, Mass., 1963).

is B-type in 1587b, *Bill ær gescod* is D² in 2777b, in *Beowulf*.[23] The first elements of these rhythmical types are so varied that Creed thought the "singer" must have "felt" only the second measure as a formula. All in all, Creed's statistics are impressive: to give but one example, he counted the same second measure in a B- and D²-type 47 times in 17 different formulaic systems (i.e. different first measures).[24] Like Magoun, however, Creed also argued that Old English poetry was composed in units sometimes smaller than a measure, units such as *þa* in certain verse-types.[25] Then too, the auxiliaries that so often follow infinitives, thereby filling the second measures of A-verses or part of the second measures of C-verses, Creed included in formular status: thus *scolde, wolde, moste, þorfte, comon, þence, cuðe, meahte, dorste,* and the like in auxiliary position would be formulae.[26] According to such definitions as these, Creed underlined *scolde, geong on, eafora, on mode, þa wæs* and similar words or phrases in his complete analysis of the *Beowulf* text. Creed's published work is consistent with the arguments in his dissertation involving the size of the formula. An explicit statement appears in his article "The Making of an Anglo-Saxon Poem," where the formula is allowed to be as large as one-and-a-half lines or "as small as those trisyllabic prepositional phrases which end certain A-verses, or even as small as a single monosyllabic adverb, *if* the adverb makes the whole spoken portion of the measure and thus makes it possible for the singer to compose rapidly." [27]

Robert Diamond, another of Magoun's students to consider the problem of formular dimension, thought the repeated second measures in the B-, C-, D-verses of the Cynewulfian canon to be formulae. The effect on Diamond's figures in his dissertation was astonishing: within the four signed poems he found that repetitions were 42.8 per cent of the whole.[28] Unlike Creed or Magoun, on the other hand, Diamond decided that

23. "Studies in the Techniques of Composition of the Beowulf Poetry in British Museum Ms., Cotton Vitellius A XV" (unpublished dissertation, Harvard University, 1955), pp. 79ff.

24. Ibid., p. 81.

25. Ibid., pp. 92ff.

26. Ibid., pp. 64–70.

27. *ELH, 26* (1959), 446.

28. "The Diction of the Signed Poems of Cynewulf" (unpublished dissertation, Harvard University, 1953), pp. 5–6, 11.

auxiliary disyllables and single adverbs could not be called formulae.[29] In an article that drew upon his dissertation, Diamond offered a redefinition of the formula, specifically the formula in Old English verse: "A formula, then, is a verse, or sometimes only a measure, repeated under similar metrical conditions."[30] In his analysis of a passage from *Fates of the Apostles,* Diamond accordingly underscored measures as well as verses.

Yet another student of Magoun, Lewis E. Nicholson, whose major consideration was the formulaic content of the expanded lines in Old English poetry, has agreed with Diamond in excluding expressions of less than a verse or the second measures of the B-, C-, D-rhythmic types from formulaic classification. He declared that such opening expressions as *oþþæt he, þa wearð, spræc þa,* in Old English expanded lines "can in no way be regarded as formulas."[31]

The greatest difficulty in this matter of formular dimensions lies in its availability for proof of an oral-formulaic technique and therefore of a nonliterary tradition; and the difficulty persists both in the case of Magoun's and Creed's *þa* (or similarly brief expressions) and even in the more conservative limitations set by Diamond and Nicholson. If one is to grant *þa, þa com, þa wæs sweordum, eafora, hildedeor,* and such, formular status in a formulaic tradition, one must attempt to ascertain that so brief expressions are actually metrically defined, and thus truly influential and of a determining character within the compositional unit (in Old English, the half-line or verse); one must also ask whether the "singer" was aware of these expressions just as he was aware of *weox under wolcnum* or *bearn Ecgþeowes,* and discover whether a literate poet would not so employ them or be conscious of them in the same way.

In Homeric as in Old English poetry, the shorter an expression the more variety of position it may have within the compositional unit (in Greek hexameters, the compositional unit is usually taken to be the line or parts of a line defined by various caesuras; there are no "half-lines" in dactylic hexameter) and the more it tends to defy metrical definition or fixity. Yet this fixity, the capability of being "regularly employed under the same metrical conditions," is the essential property of a formula that

29. Ibid., pp. 83–86.

30. "The Diction of the Signed Poems of Cynewulf," *PQ, 38* (1959), 230.

31. "Oral Techniques in the Composition of Expanded Anglo-Saxon Verse," *PMLA, 78* (1963), 288. Note that Donald K. Fry, a proponent of Magoun's theory, fixes formular length in OE at a half-line: "Old English Formulas and Systems," p. 200.

must be fitted into a meter. It is this as much, or possibly more than, the words themselves which determines the ready-made quality of the oral singers' tools. It is metrics and not meaning which dictate that Hector in the nominative shall end the line as φαίδιμος Ἕκτωρ (brilliant Hector), but in the genitive, where his name will not fit the last foot, as Ἕκτορος ἀνδροφόνοιο (Hector man-slaying) or Ἕτορος ἱπποδάμοιο (Hector, master of horses). An expression without metrical definition ceases to be ready-made; in both Greek and Old English, metrics identify the formula.

Now it is obvious that the number of syllables that may be placed in a poetic line without assuming some metrical character is extremely limited, and that its limitation is in close relationship to the language and the rhythm of the poetry involved. The shortest possible number of syllables in the Greek hexameter line is 13, in the Old English whole-line 8: therefore consecutive syllables may sooner take on a metrical character in Old English than in Homeric poetry, and therefore Parry's specific restriction of the formular dimension to four words or five syllables is too severe for the Old English whole-line, and out of the question for the half-line, the Old English unit of composition.

At the same time an expression as brief as *þa* gives no indication of its position in the Old English half-line. If it is considered upon its metrical merits alone it could, theoretically, appear in any of the five major rhythmical frameworks. But since in Old English poetry the rhythm is fashioned of sequences of stressed and unstressed syllables, and since stress confers importance, metrical hierarchy is much in evidence: still considering *þa* in isolation, one may, again theoretically, assume that whatever the rhythmical type of the half-line in which it appears, its adverbial or conjunctive function will probably keep it in an unstressed position. What, in fact, is the position of *þa* in the half-lines of *Beowulf*? According to Klaeber's figures,[32] the adverb begins a "sentence" 87 times and is the second word in a "sentence" 99 times (the third or fourth word, only 4 times); the conjunction almost always appears as the first word of the second half-line. In these initial positions *þa* very frequently contributes to the first element of a B-verse (*þa wæs swigra secg, sunu Ecglafes*, 980) or a C-verse (*þæt hie ne moste, þa Metod nolde*, 706). Often *þa* fills an unstressed syllable in a Sievers-type A₃ (*gewat him ða se hearda mid his hondscole*, 1963) or may appear in the second measure of a B-verse (*ærran mælum, ond se an ða gen*, 2237).

32. *Beowulf and the Fight at Finnsburg*, s.v. *þa*.

The variety of verse-types in which *þa* appears would seem to indicate that it has no determining influence upon the unit of composition. It is, however, the propensity of *þa* to take part in the unstressed element, particularly of B- and C-verses, at or near the beginning of the half-line, that led Magoun and Creed to consider it and slightly longer expressions, like *þa wæs, com þa, gewat þa,* to be formulae. Yet the propensity toward initial position manifest in these expressions is caused not by their metrical character but exclusively by their syntactical character. Quite apart from the influence of syntax upon the hierarchy of words that are likely to receive stress in Old English poetry is the entirely different influence of syntax upon the basic order of words in a sentence. All speech, metaphysically speaking, is formulaic. Most speech, pragmatically speaking, is formulaic to a large and general extent, particularly against the pattern of a sentence. Formulae and sentence patterns necessarily vary from language to language, period to period, style to style. The point is too obvious to belabor; syntactical influence upon Old English *þa* is much the same as its influence upon modern "then." One is inclined to say in rapidly descending order of frequency:

> Then I took down a book and began to read.
> I then took down a book and began to read.
> I took down a book then, and began to read.
> I took down a book and began to read then.

The different sentences convey different styles and tones, of course; but the most neutral, the most narratively common, is certainly the first. The syntactical force operating upon *þa* (or *þa wæs* or *com þa*) was no less strong for the *Beowulf*-poet: adverbial conjunctions introduce sentences and clauses and therefore appear at the beginning of a sentence or a clause. Since the unit of composition in Old English poetry is the half-line, sentences or clauses tend to begin at the beginning of the half-line. Furthermore, since in the syntactical hierarchy *þa* is an unimportant word, it will tend to take its already syntactically determined position in B- and C-verses rather than in A-, D-, and E-verses, except in anacrusis, and it is only to this extent that the word influences the meter in the unit of composition. The extent of that influence, considering the variety of possibilities, is minimal and hence ought to exclude *þa, þa wæs, þær wæs, com þa* and similar expressions from formular status. In such expressions the influence of syntax upon their positions is stronger than their influence upon the rhythm of the half-line: it is a case in which the egg most probably came before the chicken.

The question "Which came first?" no matter what its answer, is intimately involved with the question of what an oral singer "felt" or was conscious of in his use of formulaic expressions. On the one hand, according to the whole character of oral practice as it is described in Lord's *Singer of Tales,* an experienced singer should use formulae without thinking about them, automatically, spontaneously, with never a worry about scansion, while he concentrates on the phrases that lie immediately ahead in his song or on the story itself. It is therefore impossible to judge aright a singer's awareness of a device he is supposed to employ unconsciously. Yet it may be argued that at some time in his period of training, of learning to a point of spontaneity all those formulae, the singer must have been aware of them as grouped words that may be used in a specific place in the poetic line. Moreover a singer in whatever language must employ many expressions of one or two syllables that are necessary syntactically, though of no formulaic character. Creed has not included *he,* for example, or even *nu* plus a pronoun,[33] in a category with *þa* or *þær wæs;* yet *nu* plus a pronoun is strictly comparable to *þa* in its syntactically determined position and in its far from consistent influence upon the rhythm of a half-line. In the end, one must refrain from pronouncements about what the "singer" did or did not "feel" about this or that brief expression. One simply cannot know. It would seem unlikely that *þa* were worth the conscious or unconscious effort of learning by a young singer. It is even more unlikely that a young singer would think of *þa* and of *Beowulf maþelode, bearn Ecgþeowes* in the same terms.

Beside the arguments concerning the syntactical predetermination of adverbial and conjunctive words and phrases like *þa,* or the importance of such phrases to the "singer," is the argument involving a stated difference between oral and literary compositions. The whole Parry-Lord thesis, and particularly expanded discussions by Lord, sets forth the proposition that it is the formula that identifies oral poetry. The proposition is frequently reiterated by Old English scholars upholding the thesis as it pertains to Old English poetry: if a text has a great number of formulae, then it cannot have been composed by a literate poet; if an

---

33. Creed, dissertation, pp. 72, 91. Magoun however includes *nu we* in "Bede's Story of Cædman," *Speculum, 30* (1955), 54.

unwritten song is sung, then it must have a number of formulae. Now *þa,* as representative of its class, is a small matter; but if it is to be called a formula, then it ought to be characteristic of so-called oral texts (any poetic text abounding in formulae) and not characteristic of literary poetic texts. Such is not the case: an inspection of the concordance to the poems of that most literate Elizabethan, Edmund Spenser, reveals that the word *then,* given a partial listing of 102 occurrences, is one of the first three words in a line 74 times. Spenser's pentameters and Alexandrines may deserve the test of a disyllable: the adverb *eftsoones,* which appears 120 times in all, is the first word in the line in 93 appearances, and in 4 other appearances is the second word.[34]

The case for the formular status of various whole measures of different types of verses is much stronger than that for the formular status of *þa* and similar introductory expressions. The second measures of Pope's B- and C-verses, which may be exchanged with the second measures of D²- and D¹-verses, and portions of A-verses, such as *sweordum* and *to willan* (mentioned by Magoun in the paragraph quoted above, p. 72) are expressions that are not placed exclusively by syntax and that are very determining of the rhythms of the half-lines in which they appear. In considering the formulaic propensities of these expressions, one is bound to question again what the "singer" thought of them, and again it is impossible to arrive at an answer. One can perhaps only balance possibilities with what actually appears in a poem.

As it happens, the word *sweordum* occurs only in the first or second measure of an A-verse in *Beowulf* (567a, 586a, 884a), although other inflected forms of the word partake of the second measure of B-verses (1106a, 2193b, 2880b, 1040a). *Hideor,* to mention one of Creed's examples,[35] is a complete second measure of a B- or D²-verse in itself, and as such it always appears in the first half of the line in *Beowulf:* the B-verses are *him þa hildedeor,* 312a, *syþðan hildedeor,* 834a, and *hwilum hildedeor,* 2107a (excluding *hwilum* from the meaningful alliteration); the D²-verses are *hæle hildedeor,* 1646a, 1816a, 3111a, and *heold hildedeor,* 2183a. The only other occurrence of the word in the poem is in the inflected form *hildedeore* (3169b), a complete A-verse. In a similar way the word *hildfreca* in *Beowulf* illustrates an interchanged measure of

---

34. Charles Governor Osgood, *A Concordance to the Poems of Edmund Spenser* (Washington, D.C., 1915); s.v. *then,* pp. 858–59; s.v. *eftsoones,* p. 232.

35. Creed, dissertation, p. 80.

C- and D¹-verse: *fram þam hildfrecan* (2366a) and *hearde hildfrecan*
(2205a). Examples of other compound, trisyllabic words that form the
second measures of two different verse types are not rare in *Beowulf*:
one may mention *æglæca, alwalda, collenferhð, ellenrof, ellorgast,
eorðdraca, freodrihten, goldhroden, quðcyning, heaðorof, hildfruma,
iomeowle, manscaða, þeodcyning,* and the list is not complete. Less numerous but also of the same category are the alternate B-, C-, D-verse
second measures of more than one word, like *ær gescod,* Creed's example
mentioned above.[36] If one considers expressions of fewer than three
syllables, of course, the first or second measures exchanged between
types are overwhelming in number. For illustration, a single category,
referred to above, will suffice: Creed found that auxiliary verbs preceded
by an infinitive were 97 times the second measures of A-verses, 44 times
the second measures of light C-verses in the second half-lines of *Beowulf.*[37]

All these measures of varying rhythmic types, and numerous unmen-
tioned others, have been considered formulæ by those who accept the
Magoun thesis in general. The consideration is based upon the assumption that since such expressions were repeated and all in all seem comparable to the full-verse formulae, then the "singer" must have been just
as aware of them as useful, ready-made semantic units as he was of the
larger repeated phrases. The assumption is probably not one that can
be settled one way or the other. Yet even if one cannot be sure of what
the "singer" felt about these shorter but metrically qualified words or
phrases, one can perhaps argue at a little distance by asking what we,
the readers, feel about them, or what the poet's ancient audience might
have been conscious of as it listened or read.

The question is related to a quality of the formula per se recently
and provocatively discussed by Randolph Quirk.[38] The quality Quirk
emphasized is apparent in his admirable and succinct definition of a
poetic formula, "a habitual collocation, metrically defined." [39] Habit is
mostly the association of two or more objects, and it is characteristic of
a formula that it exists as an association of words whereby one word
suggests the other(s). The formula is thus, in Quirk's words, a "styliza-

36. Ibid.
37. Ibid., pp. 67–70.
38. "Poetic Language and Old English Meter," *Early English and Norse Studies Presented to Hugh Smith,* ed. Arthur Brown and Peter Foote, pp. 150–71.
39. Ibid., p. 150.

tion" of "the expectation that a sequence of words will show lexical congruity, together with (and as a condition of) lexical and grammatical complementarity." [40] For an example Quirk mentions that in Old English the words "wide" and "way" set up a "reciprocal expectancy of each other." [41] The greater part of Quirk's article is concerned rather more with separate words than with formulae and need not be discussed here, but his initial point offers a most useful method of testing the force of a verbal sequence that tends toward the habitual.

No word, except one of whose meaning and syntactical function we are absolutely ignorant, exists in our minds shorn of all association with other words. The mind does not entertain words in dictionary style, but blends their semantic and syntactical significance in some vaguely realized context. It must be understood that here, however, the argument involves finite verbal associations selected from the possibility and existence of all verbal associations in a particular language; it involves a specific *parole,* not the *langue.* Furthermore, "habitual collocations" could not be habitual were it not for their repetitive character within a certain *parole.*

Parry divided the Homeric epithets into three groups: the particular (often fixed), the generic, and the special; or the ones used almost exclusively for a single hero or god, those used of many heroes and gods, and those reserved for unique occasions in the poem (this third group is quantitatively the least important). In the first category of epithets it is immediately apparent that any expectancy created by one word or another usually operates in only one direction: πόδας ὠκὺς (swift-footed) summons Ἀχιλλεύς even outside the context of a bucolic diaeresis in the hexameter line; but upon hearing "Achilles," even supposing it in the x / — x ending of the line, one is at liberty to expect at least three different special and a larger number of generic epithets. Among generic epithets the connections between noun and adjective are even less strong: δῖος (godlike) in the fifth foot certainly does not call to mind a ship, and while the expectancy for either Achilles or Odysseus may be uppermost, seven other heroes may well be the referents since they too have trisyllabic names beginning with a vocalic short syllable followed by a long syllable. Special epithets by definition are not formulae and therefore have no habitual associations. Yet in the first category, the particular

40. Ibid., p. 151.
41. Ibid.

epithets, where the expectancy in one direction is already strong, there are several examples of reciprocal associations: to mention but two, if Agamemnon is the subject, either of the words ἄναξ (leader) or ἀνδρῶν (of men) will call to mind the other; "dawn" and "rosy-fingered" raise a mutual expectancy in a whole-line formula. In formulaic expressions other than particular epithets, reciprocal associations abound: for instance, "brandishing" and "he hurled the long-shadowing spear"; or "winged" and "words" when the speaker has been mentioned in a previous line.

An inspection of Old English repeated phrases, no matter their dimensions, from the point of view of the force of the associations binding them together may decrease the inevitable uncertainty surrounding the question of which expressions the "singer" considered formulaic. Needless to say, this test by association cannot dispel the uncertainty: verbal associations that we are capable of recognizing reach us only through repetition of words or of syntactical patterns; they reach us through reading and are not comparable to the associations experienced by "singer" and original audience via civilization itself, not to mention the then living tradition of Old English poetry. But even a distant consideration of verbal connections may possibly distinguish repeated phrases in a useful manner by revealing that some have greater associative strength than others. Thus, at one extreme, previous argument against the formular status of *þa* would be borne out by its complete lack of lexical association. It raises no expectancy that a certain word or words will follow; a syntactical association exists, but it is only introductory. At the other extreme, no student of Old English poetry would hesitate to supply the second half-line to *Beowulf maþelode,* or the first half-line to *bearn Ecgþeowes;* and the mutual expectation aroused by one phrase toward the other is disappointed in the first instance only three times out of twelve, and in the second instance only once out of ten. The associations binding such a whole-line formula in Old English as this one are certainly enhanced by alliteration.

Repeated phrases comprising a half-line also consist of words mutually predicting one another. Sometimes the prediction is created by alliteration and rhythm alone, as it is among A-verses with double alliteration and the arrangement X (*ond, under, æt,* etc.): *wan under wolcnum, heard under helme, wundur on wealle* (from *Beowulf*); *rice under roderum* (from *Elene*). In this same arrangement a further lexical asso-

ciation is frequently added, that of synonymity or antonymity: *fæhðe
ond fyrene, eafoð ond ellen, lif ond lice, leofes ond laðes, worda ond
worca (Bwf)*; *meðe ond meteleas, werum ond wifum (Ele)*. Still within
the same rhythmical arrangement, the lexical congruity of mere opposition is enough to give some words mutual predictability: so *heofan ond
eorþan (Ele)* or *nean ond feorran, duguðe ond iogoðe (Bwf)*. Sometimes the association, especially when accompanied by alliteration, is of
things related by use or character, such as *billum ond byrnum, frofor ond
fultum, mearum ond madmum, helm ond byrnan (Bwf)*; *soðe ond rihte
(Ele)*. As in Homer, though much less frequently, the mention of an
attribute calls to mind an object as *ece* calls forth *Drihten,* or *longe* calls
forth *hwile (Bwf)*. Much more common, however, are the adjective-noun
pairs which, although they are repeated many times, reflect little reciprocal expectancy: for instance, *deorcum nihtum (Ele)*, *mære þeoden
(Bwf)*.

   In rhythmic types other than A-verses lexical association seems less
apparent, even with the aid of alliteration,[42] but it nevertheless exists.
Among B-verses are *þa wæs sæl ond mæl (Bwf)*, *ond þæt word acwæð
(Ele)*, and certain adverbial phrases where the expectancy aroused by
the first important word does not occur in a reversed direction: for example, *ða wæs forma sið, siððan morgen (æfen) com (Bwf)*; *geond þisne
middangeard (Bwf and Ele)*. In C-, D-, and E-verses, too, examples are
infrequent, but while the sparsity in B-verses may be caused by the difficulty of fitting inflected *X ond X* patterns to the rhythm, the sparsity of
phrases consisting of reciprocally associative elements in the C-, D-, and
E-verses is certainly explained by the tendency of compounds to fill the
important measures of these verses. Especially in C-verses, a compound
whose syllables make the pattern / / x will not usually be brought to
mind by a mere *mid, þa, on, oþþæt,* nor will it presuppose such introductions. Interestingly enough, repeated C-verses in the first half-lines of
Beowulf and *Elene* are likely to be made up of adverbs, prepositions, or
conjunctions in various arrangements, plus a trisyllabic compound; while
the repeated C-verses in the second half-lines of these poems are more
likely to consist of monosyllables and disyllables in any of several orders:
viz., conjunction, verb "to be," monosyllabic adjective, disyllabic noun;

---

42. For instance the only repeated and alliterative half-lines of the B-type in *Beowulf*
(there are none in *Elene*) contain no readily discernible lexical congruity or syntactical
predictability: *wið Grendles gryre, aefter hæleþa hryre, under heofenes hwealf.*

pronoun, monosyllabic pronoun, noun or adverb, disyllabic verb; infinitive with unstressed prefix, auxiliary; or a prepositional phrase. And it is in such arrangements of the second half-lines that one discovers some C-verses whose elements may be said to be somewhat mutually suggestive of each other: for instance, the well-known phrase *þæt wæs god cyning,* with its alliterative variations *an* and *frod* in *Beowulf;* or prepositional phrases of strong lexical association such as *on twa healfe* *(Ele), be sæm tweonum, ofer sealt (wid) wæter (Bwf);* or the few but frequently occurring adverbial clauses, *ær* (or some other adverb) followed by *don, deð* or some form of the preterit *don; hild (deað)* followed by some form of the verb *niman.* There are many other repeated C-verses in the second half-lines of *Beowulf* and *Elene* that fill precisely the same rhythmical and syntactical patterns just described, but which, to the modern reader at least, seem to have little verbal association of formular strength. The elements of *þæs ic wen hæbbe, to hofe sinum (Bwf), on wera corþre (Ele)* have little associative force.

In D- and E-verses, the almost exclusive frames of three- and four-syllable compounds, very few phrases impress one with internal inevitability. Some of those that do, definitely take a large part of their associative strength from alliteration and not a little from context, such as *atol æglæca* in *Beowulf,* and patronymics for the main characters in both poems. The D[2]-verses *har hilderinc* and *hæle hildedeor* are also closely bound, as is perhaps the E-verse *sorhfullne sið.* But the repeated D- and E-verses in *Beowulf* and *Elene* that lack alliteration and can exist by virtue of a single inflected word very rarely exhibit lexical congruity comparable to that of some of the A-verses. The phrase, somewhat expected in context, *word æfter cwæð (spræc)* has mutually anticipating elements, as does an expression that extends the verbal binding of *hild (deað) niman* to the length of a D-verse by compounding the noun: *wældeað fornam;* or by inserting an object: *wig ealle fornam.*

To test the formulaic nature of repeated phrases primarily by what expectation, if any, is raised by their various elements is certainly a method of grave limitation, especially at this distance of time, difference of custom, and without the aid of a complete concordance to Old English poetry. The test gives some indication however of the strength of association that must be present in any formula, and therefore gives some indication of formular dimension in a given context of language and period. It is noticeable that among all the repeated half-lines of *Beowulf* and *Elene,* only the few in the fewer categories described above contain elements that arouse expectation of each other. This fact brings one to the extremely difficult question of whether a single anticipatory element is to be considered a formula in itself. In a half-line any part of which is predictable from the other, how long is the formula? If the formula is shorter than the half-line in question then is any short word or brief pause, repeated itself within unique half-lines in the poem, a formula?

Magoun's and Creed's answer to the last question would probably be yes; others of the school would add qualifications. By Quirk's definition of the formula, however, as by Parry's, the answer would be an unqualified no. Single words (*þa*) manifestly are in themselves no "habitual collocation" nor are they "metrically defined" with anything like the precision necessary to determine their verse-type. The word *sweordum,* which Magoun selected as an example of a formula shorter than a half-line, though considerably closer to being metrically defined than *þa* or other adverbs and conjunctions, is yet free to assume one of several positions in a line. The word *hildedeor* is properly defined metrically: it can only be, in its uninflected state, the second measure of a B- or D²-verse. By itself, however, it is no collocation; and furthermore, though the word may create an expectation of *hæle* with which it appears three times in *Beowulf,* it is four times preceded by some other word or words, namely *hwilum, heold, him þa,* and *siððan.* Or consider the word *singales,* which Creed calls a formula[43] and which in *Beowulf* occurs in no completely repeated half-line: by its form, metrically limited, one may suppose it to be the second measure of a C- or D¹-verse; in fact it contributes the first measure of two E-verses, and the second of a C-verse—*singala seað* (190a), *singales wæg* (1777b), *þa ðe syngales* (1135a). Needless to say, the word by itself forms no associated group.

On the other hand, these longer words, such as *hildedeor* and *singales* and countless other tri- and tetrasyllabic compounds, because of their given rhythmical characteristics in the Old English half-line, could not have been used by a "singer" who did not possess an accurate sense of what measures such words would unavoidably fill. It would therefore seem, according to Parry's definition and indeed any useful definition, that these single words or expressions which do not fill half-lines are actually parts of *formulaic systems.*

43. "On the Possibility of Criticizing Old English Poetry," *TSLL, 3* (1961), 103.

The difference is no quibble: formula and system present distinct degrees of usefulness to the oral singer and of measurement to the twentieth-century reader. To the "singer" the formula is the ready-made filler of a certain narrative and metrical (above all, metrical) context; but the formulaic system is really his own process of analogy and is a more broadly applicable tool than the formula. Parry defines a formulaic system as "a group of phrases which have the same metrical value and which are . . . alike in thought and words." Lord said that it was "a line or half-line constructed on the pattern of formulas." [44] By this definition, *siððan hildedeor* and *hæle hildedeor* truly share a category, and the difference between *swa he oft dyde* and *þa þæt þær dydon* on the one hand and *Beowulf maþelode, bearn Ecgþeowes,* and *billum ond byrnum* on the other is clearly, usefully, and necessarily distinguished.

As the formulaic system or pattern of analogy was a compositional convenience to the "singer" quite distinct from the convenience supplied by the formula, so it represents to the reader of an Old English text some measurement of the oral character of that text quite distinct from that represented by the formula. Parry remarked that in Homer's 27,853 lines there were on the order of 25,000 repetitions (i.e. occurrences of formulae according to Parry's definition).[45] No other poetry, whether it was composed orally or not, is known to have so many repetitions. *Beowulf* and *Elene* of course do not, even by proportional statistics; but the high percentages set forth by Magoun (70 percent) and Creed ("3,000 and more repeated formulae") for *Beowulf,* and Diamond (62.8 percent) for the Cynewulfian poems,[46] would be very much reduced if the differences between a formula and a formulaic system were properly observed after the example of Parry's work with Homer. This failure to clarify the varying forces of two kinds of traditional phraseology may not be disentangled from the failure on the part of the Old English scholars to come to grips with Parry's particular limitations upon formular dimensions: in either case the Old English is said to be like and to be treated similarly to its model, the Greek, and in neither case is it similarly treated. Thus it is that the lack of a rigorous definition

44. Parry, "Studies I," p. 84; *L'Épithète,* p. 7; Lord, *Singer,* p. 4.

45. Cited in Lord, *Singer,* p. 90.

46. Magoun, "Oral-Formulaic Character," pp. 449–50 (if *Beowulf* 1–25 is representative); Creed, "Afterword," in Burton Raffel's translation of *Beowulf* (New York, 1963), p. 129; Diamond, "The Diction of the Signed Poems of Cynewulf," p. 234.

for the formula in Old English poetry has simultaneously permitted *þa* the same status as *bearn Ecgþeowes* and has confused the formula with the formulaic system, a much looser and more variable type of traditional language than is the formula.

From the previous discussion of the failure of an assumed equation between Homeric and Old English poetry and the failure of distinction between formula and formulaic system, a definition of the formula that is suitable to Old English poetry has not emerged. Parry's definition as far as it goes is only reasonable: in any poetry supposed oral one would demand that a formula be a succession of syllables that is repeated at least once in the poem and whose position in the poetic unit of composition, whether line or half-line, is metrically defined. This definition excludes all brief phrases composed of normally unstressed syllables from formular status in Old English poetry since their metrical character is not precisely evident. The difficulty with Parry's definition enters with his qualification that formular dimension be at least four words or five syllables.

The differences between Old English and Greek prosody are both numerous and extremely complex, and it is quite obviously these differences that make Parry's restriction for the Greek formula unworkable in Old English poetry. The subtleties of either the Homeric or Old English line are far too extensive to even attempt to describe here; but a few remarks are pertinent, if only because the Old English scholars who employ Parry's thesis tend to underestimate how completely the *Iliad* and *Beowulf* are disparate in both language and meter. For instance there is a common assumption among these scholars that, while the hexameters of Homer are more "restrictive" than the freer Old English rhythms, the Old English poet had a compensating difficulty to surmount in his observation of strict alliterative patterns, and that the tasks of composing orally in Greek or in Old English are thus somehow "equal." [47] The assumption is doubtless not warranted and for several reasons. In the first place, by the measurement of permissible substitutions alone, the old English prosody allows the "singer" far greater choice, far greater possibility of fitting the syllables correctly than is conceivable in Greek; such scope is all important. The hexameter, of course, allows only five substitutions:

47. See Magoun, "Oral-Formulaic Character," p. 450; Diamond, dissertation, p. 4, and "The Diction of the Signed Poems of Cynewulf," p. 234.

$$\begin{array}{cccccc}
1 & 2 & 3 & 4 & 5 & 6 \\
-\,-/ & -\,-/ & -\,-/ & -\,-/ & -\,\text{xx}/ & -\,- \\
\text{xx} & \text{xx} & \text{xx} & \text{xx} & & \text{x}
\end{array}$$

The flexibility that supports *þæt mihtig God* and *þara þe hit mid mun-dum bewand* (*Bwf* 701a, 1461b) within the same rhythmical type, let alone the entire rhythmical system, must have pressed the Old English "singer" far less than his Homeric counterpart was pressed by the rigidity that permits no more than 17, no fewer than 13 syllables to a line in which the succession of long and short syllables (cf. Old English stressed and unstressed syllables) has a possibility of only two, not five, patterns. And then too the hexameter line is usually longer than two Old English half-lines; even the various poetic feet described by rigidly defined caesuras, which unevenly divide the hexameter line, are longer than the basic rhythmic patterns of Old English verses, and it is probably safe to suppose that the longer a unit of composition a "singer" must fill, the more he will depend on groups of metrically defined words of a fixed significance. Against these severe rules of Greek hexametric com-position, alliteration cannot boast equal difficulties of honoring conven-tion. Indeed, though one cannot be sure, it is not unreasonable to wonder if initial assonance is not more readily available to the ear than is a sense of the time that a syllable takes to be sung in rhythm.

Furthermore there is evidence, though no certain proof, that by Homer's time the dactylic hexameter (inherited perhaps from Indo-European) was quite unnatural to the Greek tongue, precluding as it did the most characteristic succession of syllables within a Greek word, x — .[48] It is little wonder that in both Greek and Latin (structurally related languages) this meter in its artificiality was identified exclu-sively with a highly stylized form of poetry, the epic. When the greatest Greek poets, dramatists, and historians of the fifth century B.C. used hexameters, their purpose was specifically to imitate Homer, to call to mind the *Iliad,* to celebrate epic action; and the Romans, characteristic-ally, did what the Greeks did. The Old English rhythms, on the contrary, are highly suited to the rearrangement that poetry effects upon prose, and seem, from what scanty evidence is available, to have been so from a Proto-Germanic past.[49] Nor is Old English prosody identified with genre

48. See A. Meillet, *Les Origines indo-européennes des mètres grecs,* p. 58.
49. See Winfred P. Lehmann, *The Development of Germanic Verse Form* (Austin, Tex., 1958), pp. 27–30, 93ff.

but serves as much to charm the earth into abundance as to bury Beowulf.

All these typical differences between Homeric and Old English poetic meter and language contribute to the impropriety of transposing to Old English poetry Parry's definition of the formula with his restriction upon formular length. What of Quirk's definition? It too is not without a serious difficulty: according to Parry, ὑπερμενέϊ (overweening), an epithet of Zeus which occurs three times in the same metrical position in the *Iliad,* would be a formula; by Quirk it would be discounted, because although it suggests the idea of Zeus it is never complemented by his name and it thus has no lexical congruity, is no collocation. Now certainly there are whole repeated verses in *Beowulf* and *Elene* that consist of one word only: *hildehlaemmum, heardhicgende, woroldcyninga* (*Bwf*): *leodgebyrga, synwyrcende, forðsnottera* (Ele), to mention a few. While such inflected compounds as these usually fill A- and D¹-verses, in the same category belong the present participial forms of trisyllabic verbs having the stress-pattern x / x in the infinitive; for though these participles appear with a necessary *to,* they in themselves constitute a whole C-verse: for example, in *Beowulf, to gefremmanne* and *to gebidanne* appear twice each. Because these verse-filling words are not in themselves mutually associative groups, are they therefore not formulae?

The question is more easily asked than answered. On the one hand, since the so-called unit of composition in Old English poetry is the half-line and these repeated compounds are half-lines in themselves, then they should be comparable to the portions of hexameter verse defined by the major caesura or to repeated whole-lines in Homer, and these repeated units of composition in Homer are undoubtedly formulae (e.g. "O excellent Atreides, king of men, Agamemnon"; "Then answering him he spoke winged words"; "When, early born, shone forth rosy-fingered Dawn"; "long suffering, god like Odysseus"). On the other hand, no Greek formula that fills a whole-line consists of fewer than five words. The difficulty with the single repeated words of the dimensions of the Old English tetrasyllabic compounds is their seeming lack of relationship to any determining force except alliteration. They may appear in either half-line so long as they do not combine two alliterating stresses; a half-line can theoretically be any one of several different rhythms so that the ready-made verse must always fit metrically; syntax governs them no more than it does most formulae (that is, it is not the main influence). In short, a compound a half-line in length is related only to the other verse in the same line and, barring syntax, it is related only through alliteration. If one inspects this relationship,[50] it is found to follow a pattern no more than does the "rosy-fingered Dawn" line with a preceding or succeeding line in Homer.

Yet in the multisyllabled compounds of Old English, an internal association is often not entirely lacking; and furthermore alliteration, though the only sign of external relationship, is very important. As has been pointed out often in the past, the first or second elements of many Old English compounds are replaceable both in theory and in fact, and their replacement is almost entirely directed not by the meaning (indeed, the meaning is frequently generalized)[51] but by alliteration. Thus, to take a particularly illustrative and well-known example from *Beowulf, woroldcyninga* occurs twice in the poem, once indirectly of Hrothgar (1684b), once indirectly of Beowulf (3180b); *þeodcyninga (-es)* is used once indirectly of Scyld (2a) and once directly of Beowulf (2694b); *heahcyninges* (1039b) describes Hrothgar, *eorðcyninges* (1155b), Finn; *sæcyninga* indirectly refers to Eadgils (2382b); *Frescyninge* describes Daeghrefen's Lord (2503b). It is doubtless no accident that, with one exception, all of these compounded kings occur in the second half-line, where the alliteration is already determined. While none of the adjectives is inappropriate to the man it describes, only *Frescyninge* is really limited in application. *Ðeodcyninga* and *woroldcyninga* are manifestly unspecific, and though *heahcyninges* may seem especially suited to Hrothgar, with whose person and dwelling place the *Beowulf*-poet associates the word *heah,* its particular use could conceivably be fortuitous. Clearly, then, these recurring whole-verse compounds are made up of the same elements as are the two-or-more-word formulae that fill other half-lines. Furthermore an unspecified number of these compounds may owe their shape to a manner of writing two separate words, and a few word-pairs could be compounds in disguise. In a true sense, therefore, a collocation does exist: the simplex elements have relationship to each other; the selection of the first element may govern or be governed by the alliteration of the whole line. The pattern / *-cyninga (-e, -es, -um),* when / is a

50. See for example the lists in Winfred P. Lehmann's *The Alliterations of Beowulf,* and *The Alliterations of the Christ* (Austin, Tex., 1960).

51. See Ernst A. Knock, "Old West Germanic and Old Norse," pp. 14–20 in *Studies in English Philology: a Miscellany in Honor of Fr. Klaeber,* ed. Kemp Malone and Martin B. Rudd (Minneapolis, 1929).

stressed syllable or its equivalent, is a formulaic system within which, if two such patterns are identical, there may be formulae.

Repeated half-lines in which a single compound fills the whole verse should be considered formulae even when the compound is not part of a system with alternating first elements. The genitive plural of *ymbsittend*, for instance, fills two D¹-verses in *Beowulf* (9b, 2734a); and the elements of which the compound is comprised were doubtless inseparable before the time when the poem came into being. In other words, the "singer" did not create from several available simplexes the inner relationship, or "colloquy," of the two parts. Nevertheless he must have been aware, however automatically, that the inflected form of this word must fill a whole normal verse and that it must be compatible with the vocalic alliteration in the whole line. For similar reasons, the C-verses made up of *to* plus the present participial form of a verb whose stress-pattern is x / x could be considered formulaic systems, as a category, and formulae when any specific two or more examples are identical.

In striving for a definition of the formula within the particular context of Old English poetry, one treads dubious ground in including any sequence of important syllables of shorter length than the simplest patterns of the five major whole-verse rhythms. Significant expressions of less than a half-line are limited, but still not defined metrically. Given our ignorance of what the "singer" thought of *hilderinc, singales,* and the like, and our observation of the simultaneous restriction and variety of position, rhythmic type, and alliterative pattern in which they may appear, it would seem fitting to recognize these repeated words not as formulae but as important elements of formulaic systems.

Perhaps then a good working transcription for Old English poetic texts of Parry's definition for the formula would be: a repeated sequence that fills one of Sievers' five basic rhythmical types. A less restricting definition not only fails in consistency but confuses the reasonable distinctions among kinds of recurring expressions which Parry maintained with necessary exactitude. Perhaps the most important observation that a literate audience must make regarding a potentially oral text is that which separates formulaic words or phrases into *formulae* and *formulaic systems.* In terms of the whole concept of oral-formulaic composition, whether by Parry's or Magoun's description, a formula is the most useful tool which a singer may use to make his song. A piece of poetic language entirely ready-made is, in the context of oral composi-

tion, more useful than a pattern of poetic language that the singer variously fills. Thus the predominance of *formulae* in a text is the strongest
evidence of the oral nature of that text. The existence of *formulaic systems* in a text is corroborative evidence, and a consideration of these
systems is extremely telling in a discussion of oral-textual tradition (see
below, pp. 126ff.) Yet without a quantity of indisputable formulae in the
same poetic text, a quantity of formulaic systems—in themselves of
variable shape and closely akin to the systems of words that are language
per se—reveal little of an unquestionable nature about the oral composition of the text. It is therefore essential that a definition for an oral
formula, for whatever language, exclude formulaic systems.

The previous discussion of formular length in Old English poetry
is necessarily concerned with the difference between formulae and formulaic systems in respect of length, and for reasons stated in the discussion the useful distinction to be drawn is contained in the working
definition: a formula is a repeated sequence that fills one of Sievers'
five basic rhythmical types. It remains to note that "repeated sequence"
should be literally understood (as it was by Parry): changes in inflection, tense, number, etc. that do not change the rhythm of the half-line
are permissible, otherwise the repetition must be exact in order to qualify
for formular status. In terms of this understanding of the definition,
monegum mægþum (5a) is exactly repeated in *manigre mægþe* (75a)
and *manigum mægþa* (1771a) in *Beowulf,* and is therefore a formula.
Furthermore it should be noted that the formula should not necessarily
be limited by the half-line but by the skeleton patterns of the five rhythmical types. Thus *ond on weg þanon* (763b), *on weg þanon* (844b), is
a formula in *Beowulf,* as is *ac on mergenne* (565a), *cwæð, he on mergenne* (2939a), or, in *Elene,* the phrase *þurh fyrngewrito* (155a), *ymb
fyrngewritu* (560b). Any expression that comes short of the prescribed
exactitude or length, however, is no formula. Thus it is necessary in any
discussion of *Beowulf's* candidacy for oral-formulaic composition to
designate the renowned opening of the poem a member of a formulaic
system, not a formula, as it is called not only by Magoun and Creed but
by scholars outside the particular argument.[52] This conventional manner

52. Creed, dissertation, p. 200; Magoun, "Oral-Formulaic Character," pp. 453–54:
hwæt plus a pronoun plus *gefrignan* or *gehieran* is said to be a "formula." Klaeber uses
the same word to describe the opening lines of *Beowulf* (*Beowulf and the Fight at Finnsburg,* p. 121).

of introducing a poem or an important section of a poem is ubiquitous
in Old English as it was in classical literature. No two phrases of the
system are similar enough to be formulae, and endless variation on the
system almost seems to be a formal condition of using it. This ingenuity
via convention—if that is what it was to Homer and the *Beowulf*-poet—
is conscious literary imitation in *arma virumque cano* . . . and "Of
Man's First Disobedience. . . ."

In this matter of a definition for the formula in Old English there
remains but one more pursuit of qualification. Are *all* repetitions that
answer the above prescription formulae? Even in the narrow compass
of 30,000 or so lines of Old English poetry, a famous exception comes
immediately to mind: *þæs ofereode, þisses swa mæg.* This whole-line
repetition Magoun included in an illustrative list of Old English whole-
line formulae.[53] Parry was careful to point out that a principal characteristic of the formula in oral poetry is its usefulness as a means of
composition. Oral formulae are not rhetorical but metrical devices; they
are not presented for any special effect but merely to fill out the line.
Hence, as Parry argued, there may be a vast difference between "repeated phrases" and formulae: "Double, double, toil and trouble" is a
phrase repeated for a special effect; "All hail to thee, Macbeth," has an
extra-metrical purpose. Repetitions governed by the rhetorical considerations of refrain, anaphora, polyptoton, and so forth are not the sort depended upon by the oral singer.[54] The repeated line in *Deor* is surely a
refrain, and its presence in the poem is something far from either metrical or thematic necessity. Aesthetic context or rhetorical importance
may also exclude some otherwise suitable expressions from formular
status when the only repetition occurs in noticeable proximity to the
first appearance of the expression.[55] For instance, when Helen loftily
examines Judas' knowledge of the buried Cross, she dismisses his excuse,
Hu mæg ic þæt finden þæt swa fyrn gewearð/wintra gangum, by taunt-

53. "Oral-Formulaic Character," p. 462.

54. Parry, "Studies I," pp. 81–82, 90–117 (a study of repeated phrases in Greek drama
compared to those in Homer).

55. Richard Kistenmacher in his dissertation, *Die wörtlichen Wiederholungen im
Beowulf,* noticed many phrases repeated in proximity to one another and supposed that
the retention in the poet's mind of specific phrases explained the phenomenon. Perhaps
not all pairs of closely following repetitions are to be explained in this way; furthermore,
Kistenmacher defined proximity loosely when he stretched it to over a hundred lines (see
pp. 10–13). See Cassidy, "How Free Was the Anglo-Saxon Scop?" p. 85, n. 27, where this
point is mentioned.

ing him with the Hebrews' accurate knowledge of the Trojan War, a more ancient event, each particular of which they *on gewritu setton* (654b). Judas agrees that his people *þa wiggþræce on gewritu setton* (658b), and his exact repetition of Helen's words may come more of formal argument than of formulaic language. Similarly, Beowulf's repetition of Unferth's taunting words, *ðær git for wlence . . . aldrum neþdon* (508a, 510a), by *þæt wit on garsecg ut/ aldrum neðdon* (537b–38a) intends the defeat of his verbal adversary in his own language. Other kinds of examples admit of argument and it is always risky to search for artistic subtleties, as they are known in the world of literature, in a potentially oral text, since, according to the theory, oral-formulaic composition and a genius for *le mot juste* are mutually exclusive. An oral *Beowulf* is especially troublesome in this matter. It seems likely that the only occurrences of the phrase *sund cunnian* (1426b, 1444b) deliberately emphasize what company Beowulf will join when he plunges into Grendel's mere; the repeated phrase *Denum eallum wearð* (767b, 823b) may intentionally contain Beowulf's struggle with Grendel in a changing register of the Danes' feelings. Other closely following repetitions are far less certainly caused by artistic decision and some, of course, are habitual: even so verse-filling an expression as *wado(-u) weallende(-u)* (546a, 581a) is probably a phrase formulaically inseparable from the allusion to *flod* which accompanies it in both instances.

Finally, in counting formulae, one should at least be aware of a proximate repetition such as *Grendles heafod* (1639b, 1648a), a phrase that occurs only twice and, manifestly, only in *Beowulf*. But the content and form of this particular expression raise another question: how else could a "singer" literally say "Grendel's head"? Must one tabulate as formulae phrases of little or no abstraction whose syntactically given shape and whose concreteness of meaning must be unavoidable in any narrative? The repetition of phrases like *Grendles heafod, manna ænig* (779b, 1416a), *þysses lifes* (197b, 790b, 806b), *to hofe sinum* (1236b, 1507b), is very likely not so much the result of practiced facility in composition as of the very syntactical patterns of the whole language and the random chance of calling a spade a spade. Without a present experience of Old English poetry it is difficult to identify those concrete expressions which a "singer" could not have failed to repeat even if he tried not to. Perhaps one discernible characteristic of some of those expressions is their specificity: the phrase *Grendles heafod* is obviously peculiar to *Beowulf;*

as a "singer's" tool it is highly unadaptable to more than one narrative
and is therefore less likely to have been created by an oral tradition than
is a phrase like *billum ond bordum*.

Because the formula must be the critical point of departure in ascertaining the characteristics of oral-formulaic composition per se, and in
considering any old and often anonymous text in particular, it is essential that the definition of the formula be both reasonable and consistent
both in terms of the general theory and in specific application to a certain
"song." This consistency has not been maintained by Magoun and his
followers in their studies of Old English poetry, and lack of it has led
to inaccurate extensions of the Parry-Lord thesis to *Beowulf* and other
poems. A relaxation of the standards upheld by Parry and an often
simultaneous but unnoticed mutation of these standards has conditioned
much of Magoun's and others' discussion of the formula and, since the
formula is so central to the whole oral theory, their discussion of formulaic systems and themes.

In this consideration of the formula both the Old English scholars'
silent deviation from Parry and the eventual magnitude of what may
initially have seemed a trivial deviation have been pointed out. Magoun's
treatment of the formula absolutely determines his statistics ("70%"),
and of course the statistics are his conclusion. The same is true of Creed
and Diamond and others. If Magoun and his followers had selected a
more consistent definition of the formula in Old English poetry, their
statistics would undoubtedly have been less persuasively conclusive.
Even by rigorous standards, such as those which Parry found workable
in Homeric studies, there are numerous formulae and formulaic systems
in *Beowulf, Elene* and other Old English poems; but Magoun and his
school have somewhat tipped the scales by their looser methods of amass-
ing evidence. The smaller percentages that are obtained from a count
of formulae according to the definition set forth here (and see the next
chapter) neither proves nor disproves the contention that *Beowulf,
Elene* or other poems were composed orally; it merely calls into question
Magoun's conviction that they were so composed. It has seemed to one
scholar that the oral-formulaic composition of Old English poetry is "all
but accepted today," and to Lord that the formulaic character of *Beowulf* "has been proved beyond any doubt." [56] The confidence of such

56. Alain Renoir, "Point of View and Design for Terror in *Beowulf,*" *NM, 63* (1962),
154–67, 154; Lord, *Singer*, p. 198; Cassidy, "How Free Was the Anglo-Saxon Scop?"
p. 75.

statements as these disguises the uncertainty that even the best scholars must acknowledge toward the subject of Old English poetry and how it came into being. Uncertainty does not disappear through relaxed methods of scrutiny, and it is in an attempt to clarify method while admitting uncertainty that a reconsideration of the formula has been undertaken here.

To regard Parry's and Magoun's work in terms of their differing treatments of the formula reveals perhaps the most important difference between their related studies. There are further differences of varying degrees of interest and scope; but of these only one which concerns statistics, and through statistics, genre, is vital to the conception of Old English poetry as oral-formulaic in composition.

Statistics are of great importance in this special study of ancient poetic texts; their power is often gauged as if it were equal to, and at times more than, that of theory. From the very beginning of Parry's scholarship in the field, successors in whatever study have bolstered their statistical conclusions with the inference that if there were more material (more ancient texts) then the percentages of formulaic language in the texts would be much higher, or indeed 100 percent. Magoun, upon this seemingly logical deduction, called all oral poetry "totally formulaic," and other Old English scholars have followed suit.[57] As Ralph Elliott has pointed out, the claim "is not really helpful."[58] It is rather like the proposition that a chimpanzee plus a typewriter would eventually produce all the works of Shakespeare. Beyond a certain point the claim is meaningless, but approaching that point there is some force in the argument. After all, as Parry and others have recognized,[59] it is the

57. Magoun, "Oral-Formulaic Character," p. 446. Magoun understands Lord to have demonstrated "that the characteristic feature of all orally composed poetry is its total formulaic character." Further, pp. 449–50: "Were the surviving corpus [of Old English poetry], say, twice as big, and if, above all, we had other songs of any extent dealing with anything like the same thematic material, there might well be almost nothing in the language here used [i.e. *Beowulf* 1–25] that could not be demonstrated as traditional." Or again, p. 456 (on the comparatively few underlinings in his analysis of *Christ and Satan* 512–35): "[this] can only mean that the surviving corpus of Anglo-Saxon poetry does not happen to contain verses which furnish supporting evidence." See also Magoun, "Cædman," p. 54; Diamond, "The Diction of the Signed Poems of Cynewulf," p. 234 n.; Nicholson, dissertation, p. 1.

58. "Byrhtnoth and Hildebrand: a Study in Heroic Technique," *CL, 14* (1962), 55, n. 10.

59. E.g. Parry, "Studies I," p. 123; Magoun, "Oral-Formulaic Character," p. 450.

repetition in a poetic text of an expression which otherwise fulfills the prescriptions of a formula that calls attention to the formular status of that expression; yet there are numerous phrases in the *Iliad* and other "traditional" poems that are not repeated and that nevertheless may be formulaic. One's means of recognizing their existence in a tradition no longer living is on very shaky grounds once the certitude of repetition is not available. Frederic G. Cassidy's "syntactical frames" and Donald K. Fry's "direct product[s] of formulaic systems" are not precise alternatives. It is not illogical to argue therefore that, given more poetic material of a consistent subject matter (only Magoun remarks this important qualification), some of the extant "unique" phrases would turn out to be formulae. Speculation can attempt to identify a few of these hidden formulae, but it is idle to suppose upon statistical argument alone that infinite text means an infinitely formulaic language. The *Iliad* is five times as long as *Beowulf* and contains not only a greater number of formulae but many more unique expressions as well; Avdo Medjedovitch sang a song slightly longer than the *Odyssey* and far less formulaic in diction.[60] Had many more Old English heroic poems survived, individual phrases and certain kinds of poems might well change their status, and the overall percentages of formulaic content in all Old English poetry would increase, but the number of formulae would fall far short of 100 percent.

The game of statistics with its comparisons and fallacious assumption of a totally formulaic language is in large measure responsible for a second, tacit deviation on the part of Old English scholars from Parry's model study in the matter of poetic genre.[61] Parry and Lord worked entirely with epic poetry, both Homeric and Yugoslavian, for the purpose of illustrating the oral-formulaic method, and considered other poetic forms only by way of contrast; whereas Magoun and all his followers cite supporting evidence for an expression in a particular poem from riddles, charms, prayers, Saints' Lives, lyrics, religious meditations, and heroic poetry. While this difference of procedure is immediately more noticeable than the difference between Parry's and Magoun's treatment of the formula, it is hardly so devastating in effect and may be entirely legitimate. Nevertheless it is worthwhile to raise questions about

60. Lord, "Homer, Parry, and Huso," *AJA*, 52 (1948), 42.

61. Pointed out by Robert Stevick, "The Oral-Formulaic Analysis of Old English Verse," p. 387.

any unacknowledged change that Parry's thesis has undergone in its Old English refashioning.

Both Parry and Lord prefaced their accounts of the formulaic character of the Homeric poems with regretful remarks about the paucity of material—"a mere 27,000 lines from a whole epoch of Greek poetry." [62] Perhaps it is the magical proximity of this number to the Old English readers' familiar "30,000" that made an equation between the two seem likely. At any rate, in his first article Magoun noted "the relatively limited corpus of some 30,000 lines—about the same as the two Homeric poems," [63] and the assumption that equal quantity can represent equal quality has been in force ever since. Parry and Lord, however, very clearly limited the type of poetry which they studied, or they followed the limitations with which the accidents of time presented them. To modern men, Homer seems alone in his era; Hesiod's date is disputed, his subject matter is dissimilar; and the *Homeric Hymns,* some of which may be close to Homer in date, are both too brief and too clouded in obscurity to be really useful.[64] Yet in the very beginning of his studies Parry did not limit his search for formulae to the *Iliad* and the *Odyssey* but considered the lyric poetry, the dramatic, and any other Greek poetry for which a definite proof of literary composition is lacking. His inspection provided the conclusion that "there is very little to learn about the formula outside the epic itself" and that in other forms of Greek as well as modern poetry a repeated phrase is rather "an ornament of verse, not a means of making it." [65] Lord also was keenly aware of the important relationship of meter and consistent subject matter to the use of the formula, and when faced with the superabundance of Yugoslavian Guslar material he restricted himself by the following rule:

> Not only the quantity but also the provenance of the material is of importance for formula analysis. One must work with material of a single singer at a given time, and then outwards by concentric circles to his group, his district, and so forth. Otherwise one uses

---

62. Parry, *L'Épithète,* p. 3; Lord, *Singer,* pp. 142, 158.

63. "Oral-Formulaic Character," p. 449.

64. Notopoulos argued for the common date in "Studies in Early Greek Oral Poetry," *HSCP, 68* (1964), 18–45. G. S. Kirk has recently argued for the literate composition of the "Hymns"; cf. "Formular Language and Oral Quality," *YCS, 20* (1966), 155–74.

65. "Studies I," pp. 114 n., 90–117.

material which is irrelevant to the song and the singer under scrutiny.[66]

In all his work Lord, who listened to many a ballad and drinking song in the Balkan mountains, has admitted only the epic genre to his study of the oral method.

Among Old English scholars involved in the study of oral poetry, only Robert Creed in his dissertation has built the supporting evidence for his analysis of the *Beowulf* text from that poem and no other. The supporting evidence published by Magoun, Diamond, and Nicholson, however, for passages of *Beowulf*, Caedmon, Cynewulf, and Old English expanded lines, is frequently generous, not only because of their broad understanding of what constitutes a formula but because Beowulfian half-lines are to be found in either an identical or echoed phrase in *Juliana, Riddle xxix,* the *Phoenix,* and many other poems; or expressions in *Caedmon's Hymn* turn up also in *Genesis, Beowulf,* the *Wanderer,* and so forth.[67] These "Parallelenstellen" have been recognized, of course, for over a hundred years, and their type is so familiar to any student of the language that no examples are necessary.

Hunting for phrases beyond the unifying limits of a single poem in Old English is fully justified as a means of ramifying evidence if only because, unlike the Greek poetry whose various meters are sometimes characteristic of period, author, and subject matter, almost all Old English poetry is composed according to one rhythmical convention. Furthermore, that the admittedly traditional language of the Old English poems should be shared among different eras, poets, and subjects to the extent now discernible, even without the aid of a concordance, is conveniently and consistently described within and explained by the oral-formulaic theory of composition. The explanation centering on a traditional stock of expressions, appearing in several West Germanic languages, drawn upon by all the poets, was offered by some scholars of the late nineteenth century; in using Parry's thesis, Magoun both seeks to explain the origin of that storehouse and to reveal the hitherto unappreciated extent to which the poetry comprises conventional language.

66. *Singer,* p. 289, n. 11.

67. See Magoun, "Oral-Formulaic Character," pp. 464–65, 466–67; and "Cædman," pp. 54, 62; Diamond, "The Diction of the Signed Poems of Cynewulf," pp. 287ff.; and "Theme as Ornament in Anglo-Saxon Poetry," *PMLA,* 76 (1961), 462–63; Nicholson, "Oral Technique in the Composition of Expanded Anglo-Saxon Verse."

The probable antiquity of a phrase like *hean landes* is readily conceivable. Surely it is reasonable to suppose that a phrase like *longe hwile,* too, has an ancient, perhaps pre-English history of conventional usage, doubtless oral in origin, and one is not surprised to discover the expression in a variety of contexts—epic, Old Testament narrative, Latin Saint's Life, religious meditation, riddle, and Latin short poem (*Bwf* 16a, 2159b; *Dan* 660a; *Jul* 674b; *DrR* 24b; *Rid* 28.9b; *Met* 4.46b). Magoun and his followers only ask that repeated phrases seemingly individual in conception or fortuitous in selection, such as *wilgesiþas* (*Bwf* 23a; *Gen* 2003a) and *ellen fremedon* (*Bwf* 3b; *And* 1208a, *ellen fremman*), be considered in a category with *longe hwile* as the "singer's" stock-in-trade of oral formulae, conned without a pen in hand, heard in any town or on any hillside.

Neither this theory nor an objection to it may be based on absolute proof. There is always the possibility that some of the less common expressions, those occurring only once each in two poems, such as the notorious line *enge anpaðas, uncuð gelad* (*Bwf* 1410; *Exd* 58) or the troublesome array of correspondences between *Beowulf* and *Andreas,* may, all other considerations being equal, represent manuscript borrowing. Until a greater amount of more dependable information about the history of the period, and the poetic conventions which it took for granted, is available, the inclusion of phrases from totally differing poems within the supporting evidence for the formulaic character of one poem cannot be misleading so long as rigorous definitions of the formula and the formulaic system are upheld in practice. In the collection of phrases from Old English poems that are thought to have a Latin origin, it would perhaps be helpful, even necessary, to know whether the expressions submitted for formulaic status closely or literally translate the Latin (e.g. *Elene: leohte bewundene,* 733b, *Acta Cyriaci: luce immensa; Elene: gif hit sie willa þin,* 788b, *Acta Cyriaci: si est voluntas tua*); for the relationship between written word and oral formula thus possibly revealed has important implications for the whole formulaic theory (see Chapter Four, pp. 182ff.).

II

If the Old English scholars concerned with the critical possibilities of Parry's thesis in their own fields neglected to maintain, or to explain why they abandoned, Parry's definitions of the formula and the formulaic system and Parry's consistency of material for supporting evidence, they also without explanation failed to begin their collection of Old English evidence from the formular category whence Parry began his. Slavish imitation is certainly unnecessary, but if the professed adoption into one literary field of methods devised at first in reference to another is mysteriously incomplete, there must be reasons for the partial application that are worthy of assessment. Parry's original and continuing research, the work which first convinced him of the correctness of his theory and which provided him with generous illustration, was an inspection of the Homeric epithets. Magoun and Old English scholars coming after him have concentrated upon any category of repeated phrases. Why? Quite obviously because neither *Beowulf* nor any other Old English poem contains epithets comparable to the Homeric type. Yet one may question whether this difference between, for instance, the *Iliad* and *Beowulf* may not be indicative of, or at least related to, a difference in the origin of their composition or in their oral-formulaic quality.

In Homer the noun-epithet, even though it may have been created for the character of the hero, city, god, or river involved, is in function primarily a means of making the dactylic-hexameter verse. Parry's investigations proved with little room for doubt that it is the metrical, not the lexical, definition of these epithets that is of importance in the composition of the poem, whether one grants that the composition of the poem be a singing of the song or not. The amazing consistency with which certain epithets are used in exclusive portions of the poetic line, the tendency of the inflection of an epithet (governed by the syntax) to determine the metrical value and therefore the selection of the epithet, the thrift of a system of composition which employs 40 different epithets hundreds of times for 37 different gods or heroes, the frequent contradiction or unsuitability which occurs between the literal meaning of an epithet and its context—all these observations of Homer's treatment of epithets marks their metrical above their lexical significance. The given fact of their mechanical usefulness does not diminish the artistic effect of their appearing in the first place. The ships, the man, earth, Olympus, and all become inseparable from their epithets: "swift-footed" is Achilles, "black-beaked" is the ships. The less temporary characteristics of the person or object described are thus kept ever in the foreground, and at the same time the particular style gains elevation by its very propensity toward title-dealing.

Homer, with his abundance of noun-epithets, is also rich in repeated phrases, formulae of every other category, some a whole line long, some whose length depends upon the placement of the various caesuras. The whole-line formulae are common and their numbers revealing, but their size precludes any discoveries about their consistency of position within a hexameter line. The shorter formulae, such as "then answering, he spoke," or "brandishing his long-shadowing spear," are set within the line; but because they are little changed by inflection, because they are not attached to any one hero or event so that their qualities of thrift and scope may be measured, because they do not contradict even slightly the contexts in which they appear, they are a far less rewarding study of the oral-formulaic method than are the noun-epithets which possess all these determinable characteristics.

No poem has ever rivaled either of the Homeric epics in the extent of its formulaic quality (to mention nothing else!); yet Parry and particularly Lord found that the illiterate Guslars of Yugoslavia continually made use of formulae, both noun-epithets and others, in order to sing their songs, and that some, though not all the singers, could approach a thrift of employment comparable to that in the Homeric poems.[68]

Unfortunately for the students of the oral-formulaic method in Old English poetry, the most important kind of evidence supplied by the Homeric epithets is lacking. Formulae of other types are well represented in *Beowulf*, over 400 of whose verses (6%) are substantially repeated within the poem. Yet epithets do exist and their study is well worth the while in what it demonstrates of the difference between what Parry had to work with and what Magoun, using Parry's ideas, had to work with.

First, one may notice generally about epithets in Old English that they more often than not occur without the name, antonomastically, so that they are not noun-epithets at all. Often the hero or person they represent is not even mentioned in the same, the preceding, or the succeeding line. Such is very rarely the case in Homer, where, if the name is not in a phrase with the epithet (the most frequent arrangement), it is at least

---

68. See Lord, *Singer*, pp. 34–53 *passim*. Lord's examples on p. 34 seem to indicate that the epithets are usually nominal.

in close proximity. Homer's constant reiteration of the name with its epithet prevents much possible confusion over who is killing or being killed in the battles, who is speaking, who listening; and the regularity with which a hero is called by his proper name, and not by a pronoun or single adjective, may partially reflect what was at one time an oral delivery of the whole epic, although the metrical value of the noun-epithet is, of course, of greater import than clarity of reference. For the most part the habitual conjunction of proper name with epithet holds the epithet strictly in the position of a modifier. Taken as a whole the formulaic noun-epithet expression has but one meaning, the proper name or the generic noun; taken apart, its epithetical portion cannot be said to have a representative so much as a descriptive, a purely adjectival, force. The "wine-dark sea" *means* "the sea," whether the sea is sky-blue, cold and gray, or glittering; but "wine-dark" does not *stand for* "the sea," and cannot be verbally accepted instead of "the sea." Rather it is attributive: it points toward and raises our expectations of "the sea."

In Old English, however, other expressions are constantly being accepted in place of the proper name and the generic noun, and only partly for the reason that the Old English verse is too short to contain both name and adjective. Rather, the whole system of verbal relationships is far different from that in the *Iliad,* since it is a system characterized by the use of adjectival nouns and *kend heiti*[69] and by the device of variation. The Old English poet or singer, within certain prosodic limitations, used an adjective epithetically of the same person in two different ways: attributively, as in *god guðcyning* (*Bwf* 2563a, referring to Beowulf); and representatively, as in *hæfde se goda* (*Bwf* 205a, meaning Beowulf). The later usage certainly eliminates any need for the proper name, as does the employment of *kend heiti,* or substantive compounds, the base-words of which literally describe the referents. The device of

69. This term is urged by A. G. Brodeur in *The Art of Beowulf* (Berkeley, 1959), p. 18, and App. A, pp. 247–53, in preference to and in distinction from the term "kenning." As he makes clear, the latter term strictly designated a compound expression in which the base term identifies the referent with something it is not: e.g. the ON "tang of the hillside" meaning *grass,* or "oak for the enforced ransom of the otter" meaning *woman;* whereas the more common Old English expressions have base terms which literally signify the referents, as in *yðgewinna* for *ocean.* True kennings in Old English (e.g., *hildennæddre* meaning *arrow*) are rare by comparison to the *kend heiti,* or expressions whose base words literally identify the referents.

variation, so characteristic of Old English poetic style as a whole, is a more important cause of antonomasia in Old English epithets.

Variation, which Brodeur defined as "a double or multiple statement of the same concept or idea in different words with a more or less perceptible shift in stress," [70] is extremely rare in Homer, and is the sign of a grand difference in the spirit of Old English and Homeric styles which is far too complex for complete description here. Suffice it to say that where Homer selected or learned from a traditional stock a few epithets and phrases to belong to a few of his heroes and their surroundings for all time, for the duration of the "song," so that he could proceed from a single statement of their names to a single statement of their actions, the Old English poet selected or learned many more adjectives or nominal expressions than he had heroes with which to match them, so that he could linger over the single idea of the name and the character through the device of multiple statement before proceeding to an action the single idea of which he might again verbally approach from many angles. Where Homer was likely to mention πόδας ὠκὺς Ἀχιλλεύς (swift-footed Achilles), the author of *Beowulf* described his hero as *ealdor ðegna,/ dædcene mon dome gewurþad,/ hæle hildedeor* . . . (1644b–46a). The difference is thus what many have felt it to be, the difference between haste and leisure, action and descriptive meditation, complexity of incident and complexity of qualification. It should be needless to remark that either convention of style in the hands of a good poet or on the lips of a good singer will serve to set forth equally powerful tragedy, or subtle characterization, or will achieve integrity of artistic idea.

The stylistic convention of variation and the use of *kend heiti* and adjectival nouns are largely responsible for the lack in Old English of the noun-epithet groups so ubiquitous in the Homeric epics, and may also influence a second disparity between the appearances of epithets in the two poetries, namely the extent to which the epithets are formulaic and are consistent with the oral-formulaic method of composition. A style that substantially depends upon variation is probably unlikely to evince the economy of the Homeric formulae in its repeated verses, since the whole direction of such a device is, mechanically speaking, toward superfluity. The artist, instead of persisting in the employment of a phrase which will satisfy all occasions of a certain metrical type,

70. Ibid., p. 40.

calls forth a great variety for one occasion, no matter its metrical type. Even though some of the phrases that contribute to Old English variation are demonstrably drawn from a traditional store of phrases, nonetheless many others are not formulaic; and all in all, it seems reasonable to conjecture that a compositional habit like variation would encourage individual inventiveness.

The majority of Old English epithets are different from the Homeric epithets in both antonomastical and variational appearance and in the lack of the usual formulaic qualities; but there are two categorical exceptions: Old English ethnic compounds and patronymic phrases are quite similar to Homeric epithets in general. Ethnic compounds are particularly noticeable in *Beowulf*. In that poem the Danes are mentioned in some form of the word *Dene* 29 times, *Scyldingas* 34 times, and *Ingwina* twice; but they are named 22 further times in the ethnic compounds *Beorht-Dene, East-Dene, Gar-Dene, Hring-Dene, Norð-Dene, Suð-Dene, West-Dene, Ar-Scyldingas, Here-Scyldingas, Sige-Scyldingas,* and *Ðeod-Scyldingas.* Similarly, the Geats appear unadorned *Geatas* or *Wederas* 66 times, but 7 times as *Guð-Geatas, Sæ-Geatas, Weder-Geatas;* and the Swedes as *Sweona* or *Scylfingas* 9 times, as *Guð-Scylfingas* and *Heaðo-Scylfingas* 3 times. Two isolated ethnic-compound names complete the list, *Heaðo-Beardas, Heaðo-Ræmas.* The various first elements of these compounds, with their differing alliterations, have been thought by many scholars to exist for the sake of the alliterating choice. Two scholars however, William Frank Bryan and Godfrid Storms,[71] have pleaded strenuously for the artistic intent of these first elements, arguing that *gear-dagum* in line 1 can hardly explain *Gar-Dene,* that *Beorht-Dene* in 427 and 609 is intended to save face, that the various directional elements are correct where necessary, and so forth. Yet these arguments, since one cannot be sure, are somewhat ex post facto. It is true, by and large, that these ethnic compounds suit their contexts with accuracy, or with subtlety, or with irony, and it is quite possible that the shades of meaning were artistic decisions; the fact remains that *West-Dene* (1578) and *East-Dene* (828) for instance both

71. Bryan, "Epithetic Compound Folk-Names in *Beowulf*," pp. 120–34 in *Studies in English Philology: a Miscellany in Honor of Fr. Klaeber;* Storms, "Compound Names of Peoples in *Beowulf*: a Study in the Diction of a Great Poet," *Openb are Les* (Utrecht, 1951). But cf. the more cautious conclusion by Magoun in "Danes, North, South, East and West, in 'Beowulf'," *Philologies,* ed. Thomas A. Kirby and Henry Bosley Woolf (Baltimore, 1949).

refer to Hrothgar's immediate household. What one finds in these compounds is probably less a matter of delicacy of meaning than of a poet's deft placement of stock epithets, ready-made and available for varying alliterations.

Though only 9 of the above mentioned 31 ethnic compounds are formulae by virtue of repetition, they are otherwise comparable to the Homeric epithets. Like the Greek expressions they are nominal, their first elements are not representative but descriptive, they show signs of being made to build the verse, not the narrative, of the poem. These characteristics are also shared by many patronymic epithets in *Beowulf*, so familiar that they require little illustration. *Sunu Ecgþeowes, bearn Ecgþeowes, mæg Hygelaces,* and *wine Scyldingas, maga Healfdenes, sunu Healfdenes, frean Scyldinga, þeoden Scyldinga, eodor Scyldinga, brego Beorht-Dene,* all of which are formulae, are certainly expressions of the ready-made and useful type to be found among the epithets of Homer. They have no superfluous alliterations and their individual appearances are not demonstrably irreplaceable in significance by other expressions from the same group.

Ethnic compounds and patronymic epithets are but a small part of all the epithets in Old English; and even though they resemble Homeric expressions in their nominal formation, their repetition, and their general suitability, in the quality of thrift they are much more similar to the rest of Old English epithets, whose management seems wasteful when compared to the Greek. This difference in thrift between the Greek and Old English uses of epithets is to be explained largely by the differences between Greek and Old English versification, described above. The Greek dactylic-hexameter line is simply more difficult to fill, especially with oral spontaneity, than is the Old English half-line with its several possible rhythms.

None of the Old English scholars concerned with the oral-formulaic method of composition has yet considered the difference between Homeric and Old English poems evident in the appearances of Greek and Old English epithets, but the matter has been taken up by a classicist. William Whallon, whose dissertation was devoted to a scrutiny of epithets for certain Homeric heroes,[72] published an article called "The

72. See the article published from his dissertation, "The Homeric Epithets," *Yale Classical Studies, 17* (1961), 97–142.

Diction of *Beowulf*,"[73] in which he discussed the disparity between
Homer and *Beowulf* in terms of the epithet. The article has already
been briefly described (see above, pp. 56–57), but it is worthwhile to
expand the description somewhat.

Following Old English scholars, Whallon makes the assumption that
the Greek and Old English prosody are equally difficult of composition,
and he does not dwell upon the distinct problems that they represent.
Though toward the end of the article he notices that the Greek epithets
usually contain the proper name, the Old English epithets, rarely, he
does not attempt to discuss or explain the difference. Instead Whallon
accepts the "kenning" (by which he means *kend heiti*) as the Old
English equivalent of the Homeric epithet, arguing that, like the epithet,
its use involves a "technique based upon frequent and substantial cir-
cumlocution" and therefore that its origin "must reasonably be ascribed
to an oral tradition."[74] Whallon then points out that *Beowulf* has no
comparable ratio to Homer's one in five whole-line repetitions, and
proceeds to illustrate that in shorter expressions too—namely epithets—
Beowulf is far from being formulaic to the same extent as the *Iliad* and
the *Odyssey*. Whallon's persuasive illustrations are comparisons of the
Greek and Old English expressions for "shield," "ship," "sea," and two
epic heroes, Odysseus and Beowulf. In each illustration the Old English
expressions are listed, but only in the last example of the heroes does
Whallon include Greek examples as well as statistics. The figures vary,
but throughout Whallon finds the Old English superabundant, having
many too many expressions that in meter and alliteration are completely
interchangeable, nor among them do all the possibilities of meter and
alliteration begin to be represented. For instance, according to his
count 9 of the 300 Greek epithets for Odysseus are metrically replaceable; whereas at least 19 interchangeable epithets or "kennings" may be
found among the 119 different expressions describing Beowulf (Whallon
omits the heroes' names from his lists). "The difference," he remarks,
"is decisive and vital: the language of *Beowulf* lacks the economy expected from a formulaic language that is highly developed."[75] Further-

73. *PMLA*, 76 (1961), 309–19. See also the more recent article, "Formulas for Heroes
in the *Iliad* and in *Beowulf*, *MP*, 63 (1965), 95–104.
74. "The Diction of *Beowulf*," p. 310.
75. Ibid., p. 318; see pp. 312–18 for lists.

more Whallon notes that whereas Homer abounds in special epithets for individuals so that the formulaic language of his poems has a thrift not only in the low degree of interchangeability among expressions for a certain object or person but also in the discreet number of persons or objects which the expressions describe, *Beowulf* has no such arrangement and its major heroes almost always share any epithet that occurs more than once. Speaking generally, Whallon observes that "some prosodic needs have too many solutions, some have none; a greater neatness, uniqueness and inevitability would appear desirable on the one hand, and a greater amplitude on the other." [76] The conclusion that Whallon very briefly draws from his observations and illustrations is one-sided. Since he believes that "no formulaic language can long maintain a total of superfluous elements that sometimes reaches dozens in 3,000 lines and must be assumed to multiply geometrically in a larger corpus," and that further centuries of practice in a living oral tradition would have "cast many replaceable kennings into oblivion," [77] he argues that *Beowulf* on the basis of its less stereotyped diction may "be taken to represent an earlier stage in the development of an oral poem than do the *Iliad* and the *Odyssey*." [78] This conclusion, following several penetrating observations upon the differences, is disappointing since it finally supports an equation between the two literatures to which the article raised serious objections. Moreover the historical development of oral traditions is obscure at best, and one could reasonably argue against Whallon's position: if time and Homer are to be the measure, there are many indications that an oral tradition had persisted long enough among the Teutonic peoples to bring their poetry to a higher degree of formulaic character than is discoverable in *Beowulf*.

The conclusion and explanations aside, the importance of Whallon's article is its emphasis upon the epithet as a test of the formulaic character of Greek and Old English poetry and its account of the difference between the two poetries. Whallon of course remarked the effect of these differences, not their causes, the disparate prosodies and stylistic conventions. Yet his illustrations are highly worthy of imitation since epithets tell much about a style and since no description of epithets is persuasive without reference to the epithets themselves.

76. Ibid., p. 318.
77. Ibid.
78. Ibid., p. 319.

Illustrations are therefore in order. Although the vastly divergent versification of the dactylic hexameter and the Old English half-line, and the Old English habits of variation, *ƙend heiti,* and adjectival nouns which are not to be found in Homer, cannot be satisfactorily indicated in the charts at the back of this book, they are nevertheless explanations for the differences which the statistics represent. Examples, none of which duplicates those to be found in Whallon, are taken from the *Iliad* and *Beowulf* by arbitrary limitation, and it is taken for granted that a larger or smaller body of poetic evidence would produce similar results.

The four illustrative charts are by no means comprehensive, but represent only the Greek and Old English use of epithets for people and for things. In the first pair of lists the Greek and Old English epithets for Hector and Hrothgar are displayed. Though Agamemnon would be royal and more suitable company for the king of the Danes, his name is a comparatively lengthy one and therefore metrically limited (no matter what the inflection) within the hexameter line. Parry pointed out in his first book that the proportion of a name without, to a name with, an epithet is relative to the length of the name: thus in disyllabic and trisyllabic names with the representative quantities — — (e.g. Hector, Ajax, Here) and x — — (e.g. Achilles, Odysseus, Apollo, Athene), the proportion of a name without to a name with an epithet is one in eight; whereas in the tetrasyllabic names such as Agamemnon, Menelaus, Dimedes (x x — —), the proportion is one in three.[79] In the Old English epic most names are disyllabic, and therefore Hector and Hrothgar make metrically a typical pair.[80] Nor are they otherwise ill-assorted since each is important enough to be his own story, each is or has been a warrior, each leads a life of active virtue such as deserves epithets of approbation.

The second two charts display Homeric and Old English epithets for

79. *L'Épithète,* p. 42.

80. The quantity of names is less important in Old English poetry than in Homeric hexameter but is nonetheless influential. The great number of disyllabic names, when uninflected, make the first and second measures of A-verses; but when they are inflected they make second measures of C- and D¹-verses along with trisyllabic, uninflected names (*Hunlafing,* for instance), as Pope pointed out in *The Rhythm of Beowulf* (2d ed. New Haven, 1966), pp. 358–59. See E. Sievers, "Zur Rhythmik des germanischen Alliterationsverse," *BGDSL,* Vol. 10 (1885), Part 1, pp. 209–314; Part 2, pp. 451–545; sec. 223–42 *passim.*

"swords and spears," or, more precisely, for any pointed weapon wielded by hand or arm, or, by synecdoche, any part of such a weapon that in the poetry becomes a token of the whole. Thus in Old English *bil, ecg, gar, iren, laf, mece, -sceaft, sweord,* and numerous compounds are placed and counted together irrespective of their precise designations; and the Greek αἰχμή (point of spearhead), ἀκωκή (head of spear), ἄορ (sword), βέλος (any sharp missile, such as a dart, spear point, or arrow; the meaning "arrow" is excluded from the list), δόρυ (spear, or wooden shaft of a spear), ἐγχείη or ἔγχος (spear, lance), μελίη (ash spear), ξίφος (sword), ξυστόν (shaft of a spear), χαλκός (adjective meaning "bronze," but nominally descriptive of sword and spear points)—all these Greek words also form one category. This particular genus of weapon is well represented in the *Iliad* and in *Beowulf,* and has not yet been considered as material for the illustration of epithets.

None of the tables could have been arranged without the invaluable aid of Prendergast's and Cook's concordances to the *Iliad* and *Beowulf,*[81] Parry's *L'Épithète traditionnelle,* and the glossary in Klaeber's *Beowulf.* The Greek lists are modeled upon those in Parry's first book; but since Parry collected only the more important epithets for Hector, among other heroes (he did not consider "spears"), and did not illustrate each inflectional variation, the tables here are somewhat more complete than his. It should be borne in mind that Parry based his statistics for particular epithets upon references in both the *Iliad* and the *Odyssey,* while here only the *Iliad* is included.

Some specific directions and pertinent details of information for reading the two sets of charts are necessary. In both the Greek and Old English tables, an adjectival epithet is understood to be a directly modifying adjective, and predicate adjectives are therefore excluded even when these expressions are otherwise similar to an epithet. For instance, in *þæt wæs god cyning* (11b, 2390b), *god cyning* is a predicate adjective,

---

81. Guy Lushington Prendergast, *A Concordance to the Iliad of Homer* (London, 1875).—cf. also Henry Dunbar, *A Complete Concordance to the Odyssey and the Hymns of Homer* (Oxford, 1880)—and, Albert S. Cook, *A Concordance to Beowulf* (Halle,1911). All quotations in Greek are taken from the spellings in Prendergast's concordance; all the Old English quotations are from Klaeber's *Beowulf,* and preserve the spelling, word division, and emendations of his edition, but not his contextual punctuation or his long marks.

For a study of the formulae for Homeric helmets and shields, see D. H. F. Gray, "Homeric Epithets for Things," *CQ, 40* (1946), 114–15.

while in *sweord ær gebræd/ god guðcyning* (2562b–63a), *god guðcyning*
is an epithet. Similarly, *glæd* and *gemyndig* in *beo wið Geatas glæd,
geofena gemyndig* (1173) are not epithets; but the same words qualify in
the phrases *ne hie huru winedrihten wiht ne logon/ glædne Hroðgar*
(862–63a) and *no ðy ær ut ða gen idelhende/ bona blodigtoð, bealwa
gemyndig,/ of ðam goldsele gongan wolde* (2081a–83b). Of course adjectives that describe states of mind, however psychologically representative of the individual (e.g. *geomor sefa*), do not qualify as epithets. A
further exclusion is maintained of those epithets whose referents are
either vague or of elusive importance. Thus the epithets often clustered
in Hrothgar's speeches when the king expounds upon the Good Warrior,
or Sin, or Everyman are discounted, as are the epithets for humanity in
general or in amorphous groups (e.g. *sæliþende, 377b*). When they are
a part of the epithetical phrase, proper names are included in the tables,
and are far more noticeable in the Greek than in the Old English lists.

In all the lists epithetical expressions which are formulaic according
to the definitions are underlined. A number in parentheses which follows
a certain expression, formulaic or not, indicates the number of times the
identical expression is used of the same individual or thing in the same
metrical position in the poem. A second number sometimes follows the
first and is not in parentheses: this stands for the number of individuals
or things, other than the one under consideration, of which the same expression is used. If this second number is preceded by the sign √, the
expression when used of these other individuals or things occurs 90 per
cent of the time in an identical metrical position. Superfluity in the Greek
charts is indicated by an asterisk (*) preceding the expression; in the
Old English charts, by an underlined alliterative letter. The measure of
superfluity in potentially oral-formulaic expressions determines economy,
and is judged, as Parry judged it, on metrical evidence alone, and not
upon meaning.

The arrangement in the Greek charts is first by meter and then by inflection. The whole line and the important caesurae (first to fifth syllable,
masculine caesura, feminine caesura, last three feet, bucolic diaeresis, in
that order) are listed first, followed by pieces of the hexameter line beginning with the first foot. Inflections are indicated by standard abbreviations.

In the Greek tables all phrases are translated. Expressions having
multiple occurrences are listed only once and without line references.

An expression is considered superfluous, or interchangeable with another, when another expression fulfills the same metrical requirements with the same inflection. The nominative and accusative inflections of neuter nouns are not differentiated. Note that in certain metrical positions in the hexameter line, the vocalic initial syllable of a word or phrase may be significant: thus ἔγχεϊ μακρῷ (with a long spear) and δουρί τε μακρῷ (with a long shaft) both appear in the bucolic diaeresis (the last two feet) of the hexameter and both are in the dative case singular; but the expressions do not duplicate each other since one begins with a vowel, the other with a consonant, thus providing for the two different possible endings of a preceding syllable. To avoid hiatus (the vocalic ending of one word followed by the vocalic beginning of another), ἔγχεϊ must be preceded by a consonant; if the "singer" wished to put a dactyl in the fourth foot with a short final, vocalic syllable, he then used δουρί to express the idea of "spear."

In the Old English charts arrangement is by Sievers-types and by inflections. In these charts all expressions, including every occurrence of words for Old English "spears," even identical ones, are written out and accompanied by line and verse references and by an upper-case letter to represent the alliteration of the line. The arrangement of phrases in a division is alphabetical by alliterating letter. An expression is considered superfluous if another expression fulfills the same metrical requirements with the same alliteration and the same inflection. Only in the Old English tables is the number in parentheses sometimes preceded by an asterisk (*): the sign is merely a convenience to point out that the same expression occurs in another verse-type; the numbers are in no way affected. Since several Old English inflections have similar appearances, and since in the Old English tables every appearance of an epithetical expression for Hrothgar or a "spear" is recorded, there would be danger of duplicating counts if each repeated expression were followed by a number. Therefore only the first inflectional occurrence (i.e. vocative, nominative, genitive, dative, and accusative, in that order) of an expression is followed by pertinent data: for instance, the phrase *eodor Scyldina,* a D^1-verse, used of Hrothgar once in the vocative and once in the nominative, is recorded once under both the vocative and the nominative of the D^1-verse; but only after the vocative recording will the number "(2)" be found, indicating that the expression occurs twice in the same metrical position. To discover the numerical data about a phrase not followed by any num-

bers, merely read *up* the table under the particular verse-type. In the
chart for Old English swords and spears, phrases that offer a possibility
of two different entries (e.g. *meces ecgum,* genitive singular or dative
plural) are placed according to the more important word in the phrase
(*ecgum*). Some phrases that are technically predicative in construction
(*ecg wæs iren*) are included because as whole phrases they contribute
metrically, not lexically, to the poem, and because as whole phrases they
are epithetical of a "spear" previously mentioned.

The pertinent data to be gathered from these four charts is perhaps
most conveniently presented by two additional tables, the divisions of
which are self-explanatory (see Tables 1 and 2).

In glancing at these statistics one is immediately struck by the greater
economy and *scope*[82] of the Greek expressions as compared with the Old
English, as well as by the higher formulaic percentages of the Greek
compared with the Old English. True, the *Iliad* is five times the length
of *Beowulf;* but were the two more nearly equal it is reasonable to
assume that, although the specific numbers would change radically,
statistical tendencies would remain roughly similar to those indicated
in the last two tables. The Greek epithets, most particularly the formulaic
epithets, have economy or thrift in that for given metrical and inflectional
limitations there are few interchangeable expressions; scope, in that a
few epithets satisfy a large number of occasions for employment. The
Greek epithets for swords and spears contain a large number of superfluous expressions, but over two-thirds of the occurrences are formulaic.
The Old English expressions on the other hand reveal opposite tendencies. While the use of those epithetical expressions that are formulae
shows little superfluity, and is thus economical, it has little scope: each
Greek formula is numerically twice as useful as each Old English
formula, while other Old English expressions have neither economy nor
scope. Indeed from the numbers gathered here, roughly representative
of the habits of diction in the Greek and Old English poems, it seems
as if the Old English "singer," much as he used traditional language,
delighted in variety of descriptive phraseology and exercised his ingenuity within a decided conventionality of diction in order to make
expressions not for eternal metrical or alliterating situations but for

82. See Parry, *L'Épithète,* pp. 7–8, 22, 41, 48, 50; "Studies I," pp. 86–89, for definitions
and pertinent illustrations of Homeric *economy* and *scope* ("simplicité" and "extension" in
L'Épithète).

Table 1: Numerical Totals of Charts I–IV

	Number of Formulae	Number of Occurrences of Formulae	Number of Phrases Other Than Formulae	Number of Non-Formulaic Occurrences	Number of Superfluous Phrases of Both Types
Epithets for Hector	23	151	25	35	13
Epithets for Hrothgar	16	51	76	81	29
Epithets for Greek Swords and Spears	47	254	45	68	20
Epithets for Old English Swords and Spears	9	23	121	127	14

Table 2: Statistics for Charts I–IV

	Total Number of Expressions	Total Number of Occurrences	Percentage of Formulaic Phrases*	Percentage of Superfluous Phrases*	Percentage of Formulaic Occurrences*	Average Number of Occurrences of Each Expression*
Epithets for Hector	48	186	47.9	27.0	81.1	3.9
Epithets for Hrothgar	92	132	17.4	31.5	38.6	1.4
Epithets for Greek Swords and Spears	92	322	51.1	21.7	79.0	3.5
Epithets for Old English Swords and Spears	130	150	6.9	10.8	15.3	1.2

* Calculated to the nearest decimal place.

fleeting moments of vision. The comparative percentages of formulae in the epithetical phrases would support this possibility, but it must remain conjectural.

Beyond conjecture however is the fundamental difference in the degrees of thrift and scope between the Homeric and Old English poems. Magoun acknowledged a part of this difference but dismissed it somewhat summarily in the words: "The degree of thrift which marks the use of formulas in Homeric verse is scarcely conceivable in the construction of the much more restrictive alliterations of Germanic verse."[83] Whallon devoted an entire and carefully illustrated article to the difference but explained it in terms of historical development. Probably neither Magoun's remark nor Whallon's explanation is as pertinent to what may unquestionably be observed about Homeric and Old English poetry from their texts as is the stylistic explanation preceding the charts of epithets. There is nothing in the alliteration or language or development of Old English poetry actually to prohibit a formular economy and scope, if not comparable to that in the *Iliad,* at least more impressive than it is. The theory that posits a long practice of a thoroughly oral tradition gives, as yet, the most suitable explanation for the thrifty and simultaneously far-reaching use of formulae, including epithets, in Homer. Whether the Old English poetry of the surviving texts was composed by singing or by writing cannot be decided or, unlike the Homeric poems, even argued about upon the evidence of the epithets alone, but it is highly important to observe why not. It was doubtless far more a matter of stylistic convention than of harp or Carolingian script which encouraged what by Homeric standards is a superabundance of Old English epithets. The use of *ƙend heiti* and variation is a statistical spendthrift where epithets are concerned, and the whole direction of such stylistic conventions is toward a *mot juste,* away from a serviceable tool.

This direction is largely responsible for the differing representations of distinct kinds of epithets in Homeric and Old English poetry. Whallon pointed out that *Beowulf* conspicuously lacks particular epithets (epithets used many times of an individual or single thing), and that in Old English even a whole-verse epithet has several referents, such as *mære þeoden,* used seven times of Beowulf, five of Hrothgar, once each

83. "Oral-Formulaic Character," p. 450.

of Heremod and Heardred.[84] Half of Parry's first book was devoted to the illustration of the important particular epithets, most of which are fixed epithets, in the *Iliad* and the *Odyssey*. In Homer no god, goddess, hero, or heroine of any stature or influence is without his or her epithet. Some have more than one to serve various metrical and inflectional requirements.[85] In *Beowulf,* on the contrary, aside from ethnic compounds and patronymics, only God is distinguished by particular epithets, and He has several: *Alwalda* (4 times), *halig* (3), *Metod* (10), *Wealdend* (11), *witig* (4). Of all the other epithets for all the other characters, only five are used more than twice of one person: *strengest* and *wæccende,* three times each of Beowulf; *eodor,* three times of Hrothgar; *hat,* three times of the dragon; and *wita,* three times of the Danes (see Appendix A). In contrast to its few particular epithets, *Beowulf* has several *generic* epithets,[86] which are also frequent in Homeric poetry. In *Beowulf* one finds that Grendel, Grendel's Dam, and the dragon often share epithets descriptive of their common monstrosity or fierceness or their isolation from humanity: epithets such as *æglæca*, sometimes combined with *atol, feond, gast, grim, hetende, manscaða,* and *unhiore*. A number of epithets serve the heroes and rulers in the poem, so that Beowulf, Hrothgar, Hygelac, Offa, Ongentheow, Scyld and others are described by *æþeling, brytta, cyning,* and the like (see Appendix A).

Although very few of the Old English epithets are particular, though many more are generic, by far the majority (over half) are *specific,* or occasional, epithets which occur only once in the poem. Parry gives no figures for the number of such epithets in the *Iliad* and the *Odyssey,* and none appear to be available; but the number is small compared to the particular and generic epithets and is thus consistent with the theory of oral-formulaic composition.[87] It is probably the stylistic device of variation which determines to a certain extent the frequent appearance of the occasional epithet in Old English poetry. Whether a noticeable preponderance of occasional epithets disproves or is irrelevant to the theory of oral composition must remain unclear in a style whose very conventions encourage variety. It is interesting to compare, however, the

---

84. Whallon, "The Diction of Beowulf," p. 318. See also Klaeber, *Beowulf,* p. lxiv, where Onela is not excluded from the list.

85. See Parry, *L'Épithète,* pp. 51–112 passim; "Studies I," p. 124 and n. 1.

86. *L'Épithète,* pp. 106–08, 157.

87. See the discussion in *L'Épithète,* pp. 181–208.

epithets used by a known master of writing. Nicholas Moseley thoroughly studied the epithets in the *Aeneid*,[88] and from his complete listings one may count 532 different epithets, of which 264, or approximately 50 per cent, are used occasionally, a single time of a single person. Now Virgil's language is far less traditional than Homer's and noticeably less so than that of the *Beowulf*-poet or other Old English poets (see above, note 82); but a comparison of his epithets to those in *Beowulf* brings out not only the tendency of both poets to use an epithet on a specific occasion defined aesthetically, instead of in general circumstances defined metrically, but also the fact that the possibilities of such usage were alike open to an author of great learning whose language and tone bear his unmistakable stamp and to an anonymous maker of verse whose ability to write is contested and whose poem contains much traditional phraseology.

That Magoun and other scholars who think that Old English poetry was orally composed should not have adopted Parry's illustrations in imitating Parry's methods is not surprising. The conventionality, the wealth of repeated phrases in Old English, is simply not to be found in epithets but in half-lines of all rhythmical types, syntactical functions, and verbal import. Yet none of these scholars has concerned himself with the implications of that difference between Homer and Old English—that a whole theory of oral composition could reasonably be established upon and could draw illustrations from a rather confined area of Homeric studies, while a similar concentration in Old English could have produced no such theory with no such plausibility. The implications are not that Old English poetry cannot have been orally composed: other tests, proofs, and arguments lie at hand. The implications are that Parry's and Lord's methods of assessing old texts for their kind of origin is not appropriate to Old English poetry. Just as definitions

---

88. *Characters and Epithets: a Study in Virgil's Aeneid* (New Haven, 1926). A table of all the epithets used of various characters can be made from Moseley's lists of epithets (Appendix I, pp. iii–xxvi: list of all the characters with their epithets, line references included; Appendix II, pp. xxix–xlix: alphabetical list of epithets followed by heroes' names). Such a table for Anchises, Aeneas' father, shows a total of 45 epithets used 72 times, with three mutually interchangeable. Percentages are 10% formulaic, 6% superfluous; the number of words per occurrence is 1.3. Figures derived from a study of more important characters, like Aeneas or Turnus, might raise the percentage of formulae (defined in Parry's terms), but not by much. See further A. Gordier, *Études sur le vocabulaire épique dans l'Énéide* (Paris, 1939), pp. 297ff.

must suffer modification when they serve different languages and stylistic habits, so must methods and principles of selection.

The full significance of the modification would necessitate deep and
lengthy discussion; here it is enough to consider but a representative
instance of the contradictions that arise, the trimming and expanding
that is mandatory, if Old English poetry must be subjected to the
methodology of the classicists without qualification. According to the
Parry-Lord thesis, repeated formulae and epithets and formulae of all
kinds are not an end in themselves. They are a means of making verse,
and more, they are a means of making verse rapidly. Parry, and especially Lord, emphasized the practical virtues of a formulaic pattern of
composition and logically argued that the whole system could only have
originated in the necessity of instantaneous, unrehearsed, metrical performance. According to the theory, presumably borne out in practice,
the singer has little or no time in which to think of separate words; he
therefore sings ready-made groups of words automatically and mechanically while his mind concentrates upon the theme or narrative. It is the
story, not the words, which may bare the poet's shaping imagination.
An oral formula is more rigid than an oral theme. Parry went so far as
to say that the slightest change other than one of inflection in a formula
"supposes thought of some length on the part of the poet" in circumstances in which there is no time to think long.[89] Parry's acquaintance
with the circumstances and his knowledge of a vast body of formulae
in Homer and in Serbo-Croatian epic song led him to assert that "at no
time is [the singer] seeking words for an idea which has never before
found expression [i.e. metrical expression], so that the question of originality in style means nothing to him." [90]

"Originality" in old, seemingly oral texts is an extremely complicated
problem and must, in so much inherited silence from the past, remain
obscure. The intimate relationship which Parry discerned between oral
formulae and oral performance, and his conviction that originality of
diction is irrelevant to the habits of a singer pertain in Old English
poetry far less felicitously than they do in Homer and the Yugoslavian
shepherds. It has been shown that the surviving Old English poetic texts
have a vocabulary numerically similar to that of the Homeric texts,[91]

89. "Studies I," pp. 83–84.

90. Ibid., pp. 146–47.

91. 8,157 words compared to some 9,000 in the Homeric poems. The figures are John F.
Madden's in "A Frequency Word Count of Anglo-Saxon Poetry," *MS, 15* (1953), 224–25.

but its distribution is highly uneven. Brodeur in his thorough study of the diction of *Beowulf* has found that more than half of the substantive compounds in the poem (518 out of 903) appear nowhere else in Old English literature.[92] A glance at Appendix A will reveal that over two thirds of the occasional epithets are compounds, substantive and otherwise, and that 40 percent of these are *hapax legomena*.[93] One confronts these facts on the one hand and Parry's thesis on the other. Brodeur argued that the *Beowulf*-poet coined his unusual compounds.[94] That is more than can be known; there is no proof one way or the other. It is certain, however, that a poet who tried to use many words for the nonce was either free from the pressure of rapid composition or was trained in a method of oral composition that has little in common with that described by Parry and Lord. The unknown method may, for instance, have had extensive variations upon formulae, restrictions upon certain repetitions, and a whole schooling of which, at present, it is impossible for scholars to form an accurate idea. Scholars may only observe that the occasional epithets (a single part of diction) in Old English poetry are highly appropriate to their isolated contexts, are far more numerous than the needs of rhythm or alliteration would demand, and are appreciably the most ubiquitous type of adjectival and nominal description. It would seem that such a class of epithets, whether explained by the device of variation or not, would "suppose thought of some length on the part of the poet"; and it is equally likely as unlikely that in these epithets the poet sought "words for an idea which [had] never before found expression." If illustrations of a masterly predilection for *le mot juste*—a predilection which selects *ellensioc* for the dying Beowulf (2787a) and *feorhseoc* (820a) for the dying Grendel—were rare, then they should be as dismissible as Parry thought them to be in Homer. It is the eye-catching preponderance of the individually chosen words which cannot fairly be brought into line with the assumptions of the Parry-Lord thesis, or indeed, with what Magoun and his followers have done with that thesis.

A consideration of Old English epithets in comparison with Homeric epithets is but one means of specifically investigating the pertinent

92. *The Art of Beowulf*, p. 7.

93. The figure was deduced from a perusal of Brodeur's "Appendix B" (*The Art of Beowulf*, pp. 254–71); and the entries for the particular epithetical compounds in *BT;* and Klaeber's index, where any word found only in *Beowulf* is clearly so marked.

94. *The Art of Beowulf*, pp. 6, 11ff.

differences between an ancient Greek text and an ancient Old English text when both show possibilities of having been orally composed. It is a logical investigation to undertake both because Parry's major study was of epithets, from which came the idea of and the illustrations for his theory, and because a comparative study of epithets partly brings to light, partly represents, differences between Homer and Old English poetry that lie far deeper than appropriate definitions for the formula and formulaic system, important though these may be.

The Greek and Old English poetries are diverse in other uncountable qualities which cannot be subsumed under the category of a "singer's" tools, the formula and formulaic system, qualities that are independent and more accessible to twentieth-century readers than contestable degrees of originality to be discovered or found wanting in ancient poems. Studies of these qualities as they appear in Homer and Old English poetry would have much the same purpose and result as the study of the use of epithets in the *Iliad* and *Beowulf:* they would bring to notice and emphasize the extent to which these two poems, two poetic traditions, are dissimilar; they would make unequivocal the precariousness of subjecting dissimilar objects to similar methods of analysis.

Two further examples of these evidently differing rules are useful to consider very briefly as ramifications for the more complete study of epithetical evidence. A comparison of enjambment in Homer with enjambment in Old English poetry, for instance, belies the one-to-one relationship between the two poetries assumed by Magoun and other scholars. Parry, in an article exclusively devoted to the subject of enjambment in Homer,[95] differentiated among three kinds of line-endings: 1) those in which the ending of the sentence or clause coincided with the line-ending, thus producing a full stop ("no enjambment"); 2) those in which a phrase and thought ended with a line-ending, but the thought was added to in the next line ("unperiodic enjambment"); and 3) those in which the line-ending coincided with neither the ending of the thought nor the ending of the phrase ("necessary enjambment"). From an inspection of six groups of 100 consecutive lines each of the *Iliad* and the *Odyssey,* Parry drew the following percentages descriptive of Homeric enjambment:[96]

95. "The Distinctive Character of Enjambment in Homeric Verse," *TAPA,* 60 (1929), 200–20.

96. Ibid., p. 204. For refinements on Parry's arguments and figures, see G. S. Kirk, "Studies in Some Technical Aspects of Homeric Style," *YCS,* 20 (1966), 105–52.

	Iliad	*Odyssey*
No enjambent	48.5%	44.8%
Unperiodic enjambent	24.8%	26.6%
Necessary enjambent	26.6%	28.5%

He found these figures strikingly different from those furnished by the same process from the *Aeneid* and the *Argonauta,* where there are fewer end-stopped lines, half as many lines with unperiodic enjambment, and twice as many with necessary enjambment. These differences seemed to Parry emblematic of differences between oral and literary style: the singer adds phrase to phrase with few conjunctions and few subordinate clauses, and his words tend to pause where his music does—in Homer's case, at the end of the hexameter line; a literate poet with leisure to mull over every word and an eye for punctuation is more likely, so Parry thought, to let his phrase end where his ideas end, regardless of his unit of composition. Homer's verses are not without some degree of enjambment, but when it occurs it rarely has the enforced obliteration of the verse-end which we associate with Shakespearean soliloquies, Milton, Tennyson, and much of modern poetry. For instance, of the first ten lines of *The Waste Land* the "unperiodic enjambment" of 7/8, 8/9, and 9/10 is closer to the Homeric degree of enjambment than is the necessary enjambment of lines 1/2, 2/3, 3/4, 5/6, and 6/7:

> April is the cruelest month, breeding
> Lilacs out of the dead land, mixing
> Memory with desire, stirring
> Dull roots with spring rain.
> Winter kept us warm, covering
> Earth in forgetful snow, feeding
> A little life with dried tubers.
> Summer surprised us, coming over the Starnbergersee
> With a shower of rain; we stopped in the colonnade,
> And went on in sunlight, into the Hofgarten,
> And drank coffee, and talked for an hour.

Aristotle called Homer's style ἡ εἰρομένη λέξις (quoted by Parry; *Rhetoric* 1409a.24; literally "the strung style"; Parry's expression is "the adding style"). It is a style whose usefulness and whose beauty fails to

fit our inherited Aristotelian concepts of stylistic elegance: subtle syntactical subordination, parallel structure in dependent clauses, clausal
antitheses—these may be the attributes of periodic composition, but they
are irrelevant to the equalizing, additive process of unperiodic style.
As Parry said: "The singer has not time for the nice balances and con-
trasts of unhurried thought: he must order his words in such a way that
they leave him much freedom to end the sentence or draw it out as the
story and the needs of the verse demand." [97]

Lord's study of enjambment in the oral epics of the Guslars upholds
Parry's figures and theory. From an analysis of 2,400 lines of Serbo-
Croatian poetry, Lord found, as he expected, that most of the lines were
end-stopped in the true fashion of the oral "adding style" and that only
14.9 percent had necessary enjambment. The last figure is appreciably
lower than the percentage for necessary enjambment in Homer, and
Lord thought it could be explained by the shorter Serbo-Croatian line
(decasyllabic). It seemed to him that "The absence of necessary enjambment is a characteristic of oral composition and is one of the easiest
touch-stones to apply in testing the orality of a poem." [98]

There are few phenomena so familiar to even an elementary student
of Old English poetry as the frequent enjambment between half-line
and half-line, line and line, in most of the poems.

At first blush, the *Beowulf*-poet's versification may seem to be far
less end-stopped than Homer's and therefore closer to Virgil's literary
periodicity; but it is necessary, especially in view of Parry's careful analysis, to distinguish degrees of enjambment. Old English poetic style is of
course capable of any degree: the name lists in *Widsið* [99] are end-
stopped (cf. the catalog of ships in Book II of the *Iliad*), and it is impossible to tell whether the lack of enjambment is the result of subject
matter or style; the *Leiden Riddle* is an exercise in the equation of one
Latin verse to two Old English lines; the *sum* lists in *Elene* (131a–37b)
are perfectly illustrative of ἡ εἰρομένη λέξις; the exclusive stylistic technique of variation belongs structurally to the "adding style." There are
many passages in *Beowulf* whose verse-ends would seem best charac-

97. "The Distinctive Character of Enjambment in Homeric Verse," p. 215.
98. *Singer*, p. 54; see also pp. 131, 145.
99. See Kemp Malone, "Plurilinear Units in Old English Poetry," *RES*, *19* (1943),
201–04. Malone argues that end-stopped versification is characteristic of earlier ("pre-
classic") composition.

terized by the term "unperiodic enjambment," as in 1251ff. (cf. *Ele* 725a–59a, quoted below, pp. 189–90) :

> Sigon þa to slæpe.   Sum sare angeald
> æfenræste,   swa him ful oft gelamp,
> siþðan goldsele   Grendel warode,
> unriht æfnde,   oþ þæt ende becwom,
> swylt æfter synnum.   Þæt gesyne wearþ,
> widcuþ werum,   þætte wrecend þa gyt
> lifde æfter laþum,   lange þrage,
> æfter guðceare;   Grendles modor . . . .

Yet *Beowulf* and more particularly the Christian Cynewulf poems offer many examples of stylistic forethought, of rhetoric in its Aristotelian completeness, so that one may instance parallelism, antithesis, subordinate clauses, and the like, all of which exert pressure toward "necessary enjambment." *Beowulf* 904b–15b and *Elene* 759b–71b (quoted below, pp. 190–91) exhibit verse-endings that when compared to Homeric passages seem balanced rather than strung on, and which would therefore seem to be more characteristic of a kind of composition in which it was possible for the poet to *think of,* as well as *think toward,* the end of his sentences, and to so relate the syntactical structures as to achieve the subordination of some, rather than the listing of all.

The ends of poetic lines then too, like epithets, do not behave the same way in one tradition as in another. A much less important or encompassing difference between Parry's and Lord's scholarly provinces and that of Magoun is quite obvious to the reader of Homeric and Old English poems in translation or in the original: Homer contains many exactly repeated clusters of formulae, line after line made to order for certain themes; but in Old English, where the longest repeated sequence of formulae is three verses, no such clusters occur even though certain themes have multiple appearances. Homer's audience may entertain a security of expectation that when feasts are mentioned in the *Odyssey* the breadbaskets will be forthcoming, and the stools, and the red wine; or when a man is arming in the *Iliad* he will strap on his helmet before he takes up his shield. These and other minor acts, ornamental themes, of rising in the morning, arriving, departing, sailing, recur again and again in Homer and nearly always in the same wording and inner sequence. Similarly, when a speech is delivered by one man to a second to be repeated to a third, it is repeated verbatim, often in precisely reversed order of ideas, as in the famous relay of Agamemnon's message to Achilles in Book IX of the *Iliad;* stories within the poem are told again in phraseology almost identical to the first recounting. In Serbo-Croatian epic song also, according to Lord, formulae cluster about ornamental descriptions and are repeated in sequence nearly word for word.[100] In Old English poetry, however, where ornamental themes recur with many echoes and parallels, phraseology is ever various. Though individual words may suggest or recall an earlier passage about a sea voyage or a battle, rarely is a single verse identical with one that went before. The well-known sailings in *Beowulf* (210–24, 1903–13) share some vocabulary (*famigheals, sund, -næssas, bunden*) but the variation upon the very edges of similarity seems infinite. The discrepancies and omissions apparent in Beowulf's story to Hygelac of his adventures with the Danes (2000ff.), as compared with the poet's story of the same events, are notorious. Magoun considers Beowulf's narrative so far from Homeric consistency that he calls it "*Beowulf* A': a Folk-Variant."[101]

Neither Parry nor Lord assert that clusters of formulae, like formulaic epithets and end-stopped lines, are characteristic of all oral poetry; but comparisons of all these qualities in Homeric and Old English poetry are, taken together, indicative of the centuries and civilizations that separate the *Iliad* from *Beowulf*. Rules for one will not fit the other. Any comparative investigation, whether of epithets or of other verbal arrangements, finally ends not only in a recognition of the distinct characters of the two traditions of poetry but in uncertainty about the oral nature of Old English poetry. Parry and Lord devised certain tests for judging the formulaic content of an old text. Old English poetry, because of its stylistic conventions and meter, seems unsuitable material for those tests. Some of the tests may be modified, such as the requirement for formular status; some may simply be irrelevant, such as the formulaic tendency of epithets characteristic of Homer and Serbo-Croatian oral poetry. In the end one can only decide upon indecision: Parry's and Lord's methods, or Magoun's imperfect application of them, are not adequate to the special qualities of Old English verse; and from such methods, even

---

100. *Singer*, p. 58.

101. See the article by that title in *Arv, 14* (1958), 95–101. Magoun posits an "anthologizing scribe" who knew interesting details of Beowulf's adventures not contained in the transcription represented by lines 1–2000.

applied in modification, it is not at all clear that *Beowulf* or other Old English poems were orally composed, or that they were written down by literate authors.

There is no really workable modification of the Homeric use of epithets for Old English poetry. Old English scholars to date have silently assumed that the Old English equivalent of the thoroughly organized Homeric epithets was the repeated half-lines, and "formulas" in general, where a formula could be as brief as *þa* and as long as three verses. That there are many formulae, even of the more distinguishing definition given earlier in this chapter, cannot be denied; but they are not justly comparable in their multi-syntactical forms, their five rhythmical types, and their diversity of employment, to the strictly modifying, metrically limited, mostly formulaic Homeric epithets. The presence of a highly organized, economical system of formulaic epithets in Homer very strongly supports the theory of oral composition; its absence in *Beowulf* or other poems does not preclude the theory. Unless much more becomes known about the Old English literature lost to us, unless some contemporary description of methods of making verse comes to light, a critical impasse over the origin of Old English poetical composition seems unavoidable.

On the other hand there is no end to useful, if inconclusive and undogmatic, discussion. For instance Homer has no formulaic phraseology comparable to *Beowulf's* *þæt wæs god (an, frod) cyning, billum ond byrnum, grim ond grædig,* or *Elene's a butan ende, soðe ond rihte,* and other numerous repeated phrases of correct formular length and of multiple purpose. The large number of these and shorter repeated phrases Magoun and his followers have taken as evidence of oral-formulaic composition in Old English poetry. It is such phrases as they appear in *Beowulf* and *Elene* that must now be considered in their own category, and without Homeric comparisons.

Chapter Four

Degrees of
Demonstration

Taken together, those scholars who think that Old English poetry was orally composed have demonstrated their theory at least as much as they have described it. Demonstration, following Parry's prototype,[1] consists of an *analysis* of a whole poem or part of one, by which the words and phrases of the poem or passages are compared to other words and phrases within the surviving body of Old English verse, or, more narrowly, to other words or phrases within the poem from which a passage has been selected for inspection. Any identical or nearly similar phrases are listed in the *supporting evidence* for the analysis. Phrases in the poem or passage under scrutiny that are repeated word for word elsewhere are considered formulae and are underscored with a solid line, while phrases recurring in mildly varying forms are considered parts of formulaic systems and are underscored with a broken line. The number of solid and broken lines underscoring a poetic selection naturally determines the scholar's statistics for the formulaic content of the selection; this content itself is of course determined by the scholar's definitions of the formula and formulaic system.

The oral formula and a workable definition for the formula in Old English poetry were discussed at length in the preceding chapter. The definition resulting from the discussion—a repeated phrase of a consistent metrical shape long enough to fill any one of Sievers' five verse-types—proved to be a definition of narrower limits than the definitions that Magoun and others have used for their direction in the recognition of formulae in Old English poetry. It follows then that the stricter definition will allow fewer formulae in a given poem or passage than will the definitions by which Magoun, Creed, Diamond, and Nicholson

1. The first oral-formulaic analysis by Parry occurs in his "Studies in the Epic Technique of Oral Verse-Making, *HSCP*, 41 (1930), 117–29.

(four men most concerned with oral-formulaic analysis) determine their statistics. In order to illustrate the statistical variations produced by the different definitions, it is helpful to acknowledge just which phrases in a long passage of poetry would qualify for formular status according to the limiting definition. A complete list of all the formulae in *Beowulf* and *Elene,* the two poems chosen for concentrated attention here may be found in Appendix B, pages 227ff.

Statistics drawn from lists of formulae in *Beowulf* may be directly compared with statistics of whole-verse formulae compiled by Robert Creed in his complete analysis of *Beowulf*. Creed preceded his analysis with a statistical discussion. He found many more formulae and formulae of more varied length than the ones listed in Appendix B; but when he considered only the whole-verse formulae in *Beowulf,* his resulting statistics were similar to those to be derived from the list in the Appendix.[2]

Table 3: A Comparative Formulaic Analysis of *Beowulf*

Verse-Type	Number of Verses in Poem	Creed's Formulae	Percentage of Type	Recon-sidered Formulae	Percentage of Type
A	2851	666	23.3	595	20.8
B	1047	118	11.4	88	8.4
C	1118	187	16.7	125	11.2
D	853	207	24.4	202	23.6
E	446	45	10.1	43	9.6

According to the numerical totals derived from this chart, Creed finds that roughly 20 percent[3] of the whole-verses in *Beowulf* are formulae, whereas the new definition would give 16.6 percent—a small difference. But the statistical import of two very different definitions of the formula is very clear once Creed includes phrases shorter than the half-line in his lists of formulae, for then he finds that nearly half the verses in *Beowulf*

2. The figures by Creed are taken from p. 390 of his "Studies in the Techniques of Composition of the Beowulf Poetry in British Museum Ms. Cotton Vitellius A XV" (unpublished dissertation, Harvard University, 1955). Note that the numbers of formulae are not of *different* formulae, but of the total number of formulae in a given verse-type. For a detailed table of the formulae in *Beowulf* and *Elene,* see Table 4, pp. 225–26.

3. Actually, 19.2 percent.

are, or contain, formulae;[4] whereas by the stricter definition the figure still stands at 16.6 percent.

Unfortunately it is not convenient to make so detailed a comparison between Diamond's statistics and those derived from the more limiting definition, since Diamond considered Cynewulf's signed poems as a statistical entity; and though he analyzed them separately in his unpublished Harvard dissertation, his numbers and percentages for verse-types represent the four poems as one. If percentages are roughly comparative, however, it may help to point out that Diamond found the signed poems of Cynewulf to be 42.8 percent formulaic within the Cynewulfian corpus;[5] but that *Elene,* according to the more limiting definition of the formula, has verses which are 14.8 percent formulaic within the poem itself.

I

More specific, and therefore more trustworthy, comparisons than those achieved through lists may be made by a consideration of various scholars' analyses of identical poetic passages. Yet since these analyses proceed not only by identification of formulae but also by designation of formulaic systems, it is necessary here to ponder a definition for the formulaic system in Old English poetry and to inquire whether those definitions arrived at by Parry and Lord for application to Greek and Serbo-Croatian poetry, and by Magoun and others for application to Old English, are consonant with the characteristics of Old English verse as we, centuries removed, understand those characteristics to be.

In his first book, *L'Épithète traditionnelle dans Homère,* Parry discussed formulaic systems only obliquely while discussing the complex variety and verbal thrift of the heroic epithets. His formal notice and definition of the formulaic system appears in "Studies in the Epic Technique of Oral Verse-Making, I: Homer and the Homeric Style."[6] The early pages of this essay are taken up with an introduction to and study of the oral formula. Parry noticed that in Homer there were two kinds of formulae, those which have no similarity to any other formula and those which do. He then gave a definition for the formulaic system:

4. See the discussion, pp. 64ff., in his dissertation, and "The Making of an Anglo-Saxon Poem," *ELH,* 26 (1959), 446.

5. "The Diction of the Signed Poems of Cynewulf" (unpublished dissertation, Harvard University, 1953), p. 11.

6. See above, n. 1.

"Any group of two or more such formulas [i.e. similar formulas] make
up a system, and a system may be defined in turn as a group of phrases
which have the same metrical value and which are alike enough in
thought and words to leave no doubt that the poet who used them knew
them not only as single formulas, but also as formulas of a certain
type."[7] As an immediate example of a formulaic system, Parry mentions ἱερὸν πτολίεθρον ἔπερσε ("he destroyed the sacred city"), and ἱερὸν
πτολίεθρον ἑλόντες ("they overpowered the sacred city"). His further and
previously quoted remarks about systems are useful to bear in mind.
Parry considered a formulaic system a "means of measuring the schema-
tization of a poet's style."

> There are in such a measuring two factors, that of length and that of
> thrift. The length of a system consists very obviously in the number
> of formulas which make it up. The thrift of a system lies in the
> degree in which it is free of phrases which, having the same metrical
> value and expressing the same idea, could replace one another.[8]

> . . . the number of repetitions in a style, and the frequency with
> which they are used, bear directly upon the thrift of the diction.[9]

In order to emphasize his remark about the oral poet's recognizing that
some formulae were formulae of a certain type, Parry said: "The repeated use of phrases means not only that the poet is following a fixed
pattern of words; it means equally that he is denying himself all other
ways of expressing the idea."[10] In this particular article all Parry's examples of the formulaic system are like the one quoted above; but in a later
article, "Whole Formulaic Verse in Greek and South Slavic Song,"[11]
he gave many and interesting examples of whole-line formulaic systems,
one of which is reproduced in full above, Chapter One, page 29. That
example, "to (him, her, them) again spoke (epithet) (name of hero or
god)," is strictly comparable to the familiar "(name of hero) *maþelode*
(*bearn, maga, sunu,* etc.) (name of relative or father)" of Old English
poetry. Other illustrations from Homer are numerous, even ones for use
at the close of a speech such as αὐτὰρ ἐπεὶ τό γ᾽ ἄκουσε ("but when this

7. Ibid., p. 84.
8. Ibid., p. 86.
9. Ibid., p. 89.
10. Ibid.
11. *TAPA, 64* (1933), 179–97.

heard") πολύτλας Ὀδυσσεύς ("long-suffering Odysseus"), or Ποσειδάωᾳ ἐνοσίχθον ("Poseidon spear-throwing").[12]

For all his concern, clear definition, and copious examples, Parry's discussion of the formulaic system remains vague beside his discussion of the oral formula. Why the precise definition of the system should be elusive is not difficult to comprehend: a formula by Parry's, and by any truly useful, definition must be a certain length and must exclude all variety save that represented by inflection and extremely minor pronominal and prepositional changes; a system, on the other hand, is variety itself. No laconic description such as Quirk's "a habitual collocation, metrically defined,"[13] will begin to clarify the necessary limits to that variety, if a whole language, if verbal patterns of whatever sort, are not to be called "formulaic systems." Parry's "a group of phrases which have the same metrical value and which are enough alike in thought and words to leave no doubt that the poet who used them knew them not only as single formulas, but also as formulas of a certain type," is more limiting than a completely linguistic definition. At least Parry urges similarity of ideas. Yet who is to say what poet "knew" which formulae as members of a system? There must often be doubt in our minds concerning what an oral singer "knew" or "felt" about phrases so anciently composed as Homer's. Then too, in his practical demonstration Parry seems to leave the door open to undisciplined identification of systems when he qualifies his analysis as follows:

> In the two passages analyzed above I marked with a broken line only those formulas which were like others in rhythm, in parts of speech, and in one important word; but there are more general types of formulas, and one could make no greater mistake than to limit the formulaic element to what is underlined . . . Often one finds the same verse-pattern where the words are different.[14]

It was perhaps in an attempt not only to acknowledge but to exploit the almost necessary vagueness of Parry's definition that Lord presented a needlessly far vaguer definition in his *Singer of Tales*: a formulaic expression, according to Lord, is "a line or half-line constructed in the

---

12. Ibid., p. 187.

13. See "Poetic Language and Old English Meter," in *Early English and Norse Studies Presented to Hugh Smith*, ed. Arthur Brown and Peter Foote, p. 150.

14. "Studies I," p. 133.

pattern of formulas." [15] The difficulty here, of course, lies in the word
"pattern": a rhythmical or syntactical pattern? a pattern of ideas? Lord
apparently did not develop the idea further in discussion; but from his
demonstration, his analysis of *Beowulf* 1473–87, it is quite clear that he
considered rhythmical and syntactical similarity between two phrases to
be sufficient for an assignment of these phrases to a formulaic system.
For instance in his supporting evidence[16] for the second measure of verse
1476b, *hwæt wit geo spræcon,* which he underscored with a broken line,
Lord cited lines "2252, 3126, etc." These lines are respectively *Nah, hwa*
sweord wege (2252b) and *hwa þæt hord strude* (3126b)—lines comparable to the one under consideration only by their rhythmical similarity.
Or again for the verse 1483b, *Higelace onsend,* also underscored with a
broken line, Lord cited "5, 690, 884, etc." These verses are respectively
meodosetla ofteah (5b), *selereste gebeah* (690b), and *Sigemunde ge-*
sprong (884b). Again, they are absolutely similar rhythmically, and here
the grammatical similarity is fairly consistent. Doubtless Lord's conviction that rhythmical similarity alone or rhythmical and syntactical similarity among phrases was sufficient to mark them parts of a formulaic
system was influenced by his reading of Pope's *The Rhythm of Beowulf,*
to which he continually refers throughout his lists of supporting evidence
for *Beowulf* 1473–87 in order to identify correctly the rhythmical type of
every half-line. The references are most helpful and the attention sound;
but it may be questioned whether Lord, seeing the verses grouped in a
certain and necessary way in Pope's book, did not exaggerate the import
of this grouping in the context of a discussion about oral-formulaic diction. It is well known that a few syntactical patterns in Old English
poetry are identified with a certain rhythmical type (see below, pp. 140–
41);[17] what is in question here is the larger number of syntactical
patterns in Old English poetry which may occur in two or more rhythmical types. Lord's identification of system with rhythmical type or with
syntactical sequence alone would seem to imbue the practicing Old English "singer" with a continual and unlikely awareness of Sievers' five
types. An Old English "singer" was most certainly aware of rhythmical
nuances beyond the Sievers terminology, but doubtless not to the extent

15. P. 4.

16. See ibid., pp. 297–301. Note that all Old English quotations within quotations from
Magoun, Lord, Creed, and Diamond are from normalized texts.

17. See also Frederic G. Cassidy, "How Free Was the Anglo-Saxon Scop?" *Franci-*
plegius, ed. Jess B. Bessinger, Jr., and Robert P. Creed.

necessary for a classification of phrases based solely upon rhythmical identity in defiance of syntactical and semantic identity.

Parry's definition of a formulaic system in oral poetry has had little critical reiteration. It simply did not take on the importance of a pedestal for all further description and demonstration and deviation, as did his definition of the formula. Lord repeats all Parry's definitions save this one. The scholars working with analyses of Old English poetry, with the exception of Magoun, have not only neglected Parry's definition of the system but have expressed their own largely in terms of demonstration rather than of description. In that first important article, "The Oral-Formulaic Character of Anglo-Saxon Narrative Poetry," Magoun indeed quotes Parry's definition, but only after his own observation that some formulae, far from being "mere repeats" sometimes "form part of longer formulaic systems used to express the same, or almost the same, idea or used to fit some larger rhythmical-syntactical pattern." [18] The contradiction between this statement and Parry's "same metrical value" is not resolved. Magoun then discusses the formulaic system and gives generous illustrations; but the discussion is brief and does not take account of the kinds of phrases that, in his analysis of *Beowulf* 1–25, Magoun underscores with a broken line. In the discussion of his supporting evidence for the analysis, however, Magoun exemplifies what seems to be a description of the formulaic system in Old English by pointing out for instance that the C-verse *on geardagum* is part of a system expressing the idea "long ago," a system in which the first element of the compound may change according to the requirements of the alliteration, so that one finds *on ærdagum, on ealddagum, on fyrndagum;* similarly, *þæt wæs x cyning* is a system made up of substitutions for the sake of alliteration. Magoun broadens his demonstrative definition excessively, though, when he states that *ymbsittendra* is not only part of a system in which *ymbstandendra* occurs, but also part of a larger system, composed of a first element and present participle, in which one may find *sæliðende, brimliðende, ealiðende, mereliðende,* etc." [19] The implications of this broadened definition are not contemplated.

Yet another, and a farther reaching, definition of the system is possibly embedded in Magoun's discussion of the famous opening of the poem, lines 1a–3b. Here again the definition is no static description

18. *Speculum, 28* (1953), 450.
19. Ibid., pp. 451–52.

which the critic seeks to bolster by textual illustration; it is rather an active illustration, one which evolves out of the illustration, and one which is left inseparable from the action of illustrating. After calling attention to the phrase *hwæt,* plus a pronoun, plus the idea of "hearing" (*hieran,* the more common introductory verb) or "learning" (*frignan,* the less common introductory verb), with which many Old English poems begin, Magoun describes the *Beowulf*-poet's manner of handling conventional diction:

> It will be noticed that the singers ordinarily work in the important verbal idea 'hearing about,' 'learning about' in the course of the first two verses, but the *Beowulf* singer introduced mention of the Spear-Danes (*Gar-Dena*) before proceeding farther. This apparently spoiled his chance of getting in a verb in what appears to be the favored or ordinary position in the first verse. Comparable to Cynewulf in *Ele* 397b, he might in some fashion have worked in a suitable verb in 1b, had there been such a one capable of g-alliteration, but at all events he next called upon one of the several available formulas expressing the idea 'long ago,' already discussed. . . . Thus *gefrugnon* is put off to the fourth verse (2b), while the *hu* of the total phrase *we gefrugnon hu* has to wait for the fifth (3a). The basic formula is all there and the singer has used every scrap of it, though not in what would appear to be the usual way. One might interpret this exceptional treatment as an example of a first-rate singer coping quickly and deftly with an almost awkward situation into which he had got himself, even though the resulting order of words is perhaps not quite natural.[20]

Magoun of course calls the opening of *Beowulf* a formula, not a system, and in his supporting evidence for his analysis of the passage he treats lines 1a–2b as a single unit, a formular one at that, quoting without a saving "cf." openings of other poems which have strong resemblance but not exact similarity. The verse *þrymm gefrugnon* (2b; note that Magoun quotes from normalized texts) is solidly underlined; and for its supporting evidence we are referred to the evidence for lines 1a–2b, where the closest phraseology is *gefrigen habbað* (*Exo* 1) and *hwæt we gefrugnon* (*And* 1; see the chart of Magoun's supporting evidence, below, p. 159). For his other solidly underlined verses or parts of

20. Ibid., pp. 453–54.

verses Magoun is more careful that the repetitions be exact. Hence it would seem as if, although he speaks of "formulas" in discussing *Beowulf* 1–3, Magoun actually had systems in mind. The assumption may well be incorrect: if Magoun really intended "formulas" to categorize these lines, then his definition of formula is unaccountably imprecise and inconsistent with the rest of his article; if, on the other hand, he thought in terms of a formulaic system for lines 1–3, then his implicit definition of a system, though broad, is no broader than that demonstrated in his analysis of *Beowulf* 1–25. At any rate, in the long paragraph just quoted Magoun apparently imagines the Old English singer bound by oral convention to begin his poem *formulaically* in a certain manner. The convention must surely have been binding, whether in literary or in oral practice. Magoun, however, proceeds to picture the singer as an artist who leapt before he looked, one who got himself into "an almost awkward situation" with his *Gar-Dena* before he groped in his mind for a verb of the *hieran, frignan* sort, only to find none, only to come out with his feet miraculously on the ground again two lines later. If Magoun can picture a singer at once so restricted by convention and so free to manage it with "exceptional treatment," he must also conceive of an available *system* of phrases, by reason of their use in *Beowulf* 1–3 associated in idea and more or less associated in grammar.

A definition of the formulaic system in oral poetry defies the precision possible in the definition of the oral formula. That Magoun's definition of a system is vague therefore is not surprising. It seems clear, however, that Magoun does not consider consistent rhythm and grammar to be necessary characteristics of phrases in a system, although he would insist upon a fair consistency of idea. In his analysis of *Beowulf* 1–25, for instance, he considers *feasceaft funden* (7a) part of a system, another member of which he designates as *onfindað feasceaftne* (*And* 181), a phrase strictly comparable neither in rhythm nor in grammatical construction but absolutely comparable in lexical idea.

Robert Creed nowhere discusses the formulaic system in all its manifestations. In his thesis, however, he thoroughly describes and illustrates what he calls "substitution systems" in *Beowulf,* or whole-verse phrases in which the first important element varies, usually because it carries the alliteration.[21] Creed found 452 such substitution systems used in 1,608 verses of *Beowulf* (approximately one quarter of the poem); and 75 per

21. Dissertation, pp. 54–77.

cent of these substitutions he found were dictated by the requirements of alliteration. Creed's examples are far too numerous to quote; a few representative ones may be noted: *þær wæs madma (swylcra) fela* (36b, 2231b); *him on eaxle wearð (læg)* (816b, 1547b); *ne hyrde ic cymlicor (snotorlicor)* (38a, 1842b); *þeod-, heah-, eorð-, weorold-, sæ-, Frescyninge-es-a.* Far less clearly, Creed seems to include other phrases of varying degrees of disparity as parts of formulaic systems. Such are the grammatically and rhythmically similar phrases *healærna mæst* (78a) and *nihtbealwa mæst* (193b), or *magodriht micel* (67a) and *medoærn micel* (69a).[22] In a later article, in noticing the formulaic system *þær* x *sæt,* (e.g. *þær Hroðgar sæt,* 356b), Creed mentions the phrase *þær on wicge sæt,* and comments, "Apparently the singer does not restrict himself to employing the same kind of substitution system." [23] In demonstration, Creed's concept of a formulaic system is consistent with his discussion but goes beyond the discussion. And where it goes beyond, it is consistent with Creed's concept of a formula. Thus a system, like a formula, may also be no longer than a single measure of a verse, especially if the remaining measure of the verse is repeated elsewhere. For example, in his analysis of *Beowulf* 1473–87 Creed underscores the first measure of 1479b with a solid line, the second measure with a broken one: on fæder stæle. The first reference in his supporting evidence for this verse is to line 21, *on fæder bearme, on fæder* being a formula in Creed's terms and *bearme* being part of a formulaic system of which the first unit is such a formula. Creed's other references (lines 35, 214, 896) are rather less pertinent, but stress the C-type rhythm of the verse (see Creed's analysis and supporting evidence, below, page 164).

Of all the scholars concerned with the oral-formulaic analysis of Old English poetry, Robert Diamond is the most explicit about his concept of the formulaic system in its Old English manifestations. Early in his dissertation, Diamond considers the system altogether in its old English setting with no reference to Homer or to Parry. In this setting he distinguishes three types of formulaic systems: 1) phrases in every way similar except that one word has been altered for the sake of alliteration (e.g. *geara gangum* of *Ele* 648a, *Jul* 693a, *Chr* 1035a, becomes *geara hwyrftum* in *Ele* 1b to avoid double alliteration in the off-verse); 2)

22. Ibid., pp. 64–67.
23. "The Making of an Anglo-Saxon Poem," p. 449. With these definitions of the formulaic system in Old English, compare that by Donald K. Fry, quoted on p. 69.

phrases in every way similar except that one word has been altered to suit a particular context ("bracketing phrases," as Diamond calls them, such as *þæm wæs Judas (Simon) nama, Ele* 418, 530); and finally 3) phrases which are "tags" (e.g. *wan under wolcnum*).[24] There is no disparity between Diamond's recognition of these formulaic systems and his demonstrations of them in analyses of Cynewulfian verse, although in his analyses he includes other, shorter phrases whose types he does not discuss.

Magoun, Creed, and Diamond share a technique of designating formulaic systems in their respective analyses that may be somewhat confusing, and which should be noted here, before the merits of their various definitions and general practices are discussed. Because each of these men allows one measure of a verse formular status if it is exactly repeated, in analyses each of them characterizes a system in which but one word, or possibly one measure, is the changeable element by marking the constant word or measure with a solid line and the changeable one with a broken line. To give but brief examples of this practice by each scholar: Magoun marks *Beowulf* 19a thus: Scyldes eafera and cites *Hreðles eafora* (Bwf 2358a) etc., as evidence; Creed marks *Beowulf* 12b: æfter cenned, citing ær acenned (*Bwf* 1356); Diamond marks *Elene* 1260b: nearusorge dreah, citing *Beowulf* 422, *nearoþearfe dreah*. The practice is misleading, first because it confirms a definition of the formula that is not properly conclusive; second because it seems to imply—no doubt unintentionally—that a system may also be as diminutive as a single measure or, in *nearusorge dreah,* as a part of a measure. The first reason is of course controversial ground and has been argued in the preceding chapter, but the second reason involves a confusion which Magoun, Creed, and Diamond do not dispel. No doubt the practice of solidly underscoring and intermittently underscoring parts of the same line descended from Parry himself. He distinguished a formula and a formulaic system in the same hexameter line, as in δ'αὖτε προσέειπε Γερήνιος ἱππότα Νέστωρ ("again spoke the Geranian driver of horses, Nestor"), indicating that the noun-epithet for Nestor appeared only once after δ'αὖτε προσέειπε but was often replaced by noun-epithets for other heroes (Hector, Odysseus, Agamemnon, etc.) that would fill the hexameter from the feminine caesura to the end. It is immediately obvious that

24. Dissertation, pp. 8–10.

δ'αὖτε προσέειπε is a formula, and that if Γερήνιος ἱππότα Νέστωρ were exactly repeated in the whole phrase, it too would be a formula. Both expressions have correct formular length. On the other hand shorter expressions, the constant parts of which were less than four words or five syllables, Parry marked with a broken line, indicating that the formulaic system was represented by the *whole phrase,* not just its changing element—*sorge,* part of the first measure of an E-verse, is hardly rhythmically defined enough to stand on its own as a formula, or even as formulaic. To avoid confusion over just which brief elements constitute a system in a group of brief phrases, it is best to underscore the whole phrase with a broken line. The assumption is, after all, that the "singer" thought not just of a man's having been born (*cenned*) but born in time (*æfter, ær*).

What is an appropriate definition for the formulaic system in Old English poetry? Where is the point at which too nice a precision or too large a breadth in definition becomes less a help than a hindrance? Certainly Lord's definition, "a line or half-line constructed in the pattern of formulas," turns out to be law for great license. Formulae are conceivably of any "pattern"; and even if the outward limits of pattern are discerned as rhythm, or as rhythm plus syntactical sequence (as they are in Lord's demonstrations for Old English poetry), the characteristic of the pattern would seem to be graspable only through analysis, and literary analysis at that. It would be unreasonable to maintain that the similarity between *hwæt wit geo spræcon* and *Nah, hwa sweord wege* would be such as to provide a technically useful compositional device for a singer. There is nothing at all in the relationship of one phrase to the other which should distinguish the composition of an oral singer from that of a lettered poet, which should separate the two phrases in their manner of creation from "O, Harry! thou hast robb'd me of my youth," and "O gentlemen, the time of life is short" (*I Henry IV,* V, ii, iv). In all speech syntactical patterns are too limited in number, too general and common in use; in all kinds of poetry rhythmical conventions are also too narrow in variety, too much a contract among composer, tradition, and audience for syntax or rhythm, singly or together, to proffer the identifying pattern of two or more phrases. It is essential that the meaning of the phrases, their verbal idea, be of a shared and nearly similar sort.

Yet generically similar significance approximated by otherwise differing phrases is not sufficient to characterize a formulaic system. The phrases *wæs se grimma gæst Grendel haten* (*Bwf* 102) and *Beowulf is min nama* (*Bwf* 343b) convey the same kind of information abstracted from any particular compositional method, as do Antony's words about Cleopatra, "Whom everything becomes, to chide, to laugh/ To weep," and Enobarbus' more famous "Age cannot wither her nor custom stale/ Her infinite variety." Furthermore, Old English poetry is so full of synonyms—many of them words not only with the same lexical significance but with what seems at this distance to be the same level of tone, the same stylistic significance—that the very availability of different words to express similar ideas would militate against the identification of formulaic systems if systems comprised merely expressions of single import. For the lexical significance "hero-prince" *Beowulf* alone has *æþeling, beaggyfa, bealdor, beorn, brego, brytta, cyning, dryhten, ealdor, eorl, eðelweard, fengel, frea, fruma, hlaford, leod, ræswa, þengel, and þeoden.*[25] Sir Cecil Maurice Bowra has noted 30 different words for "hall" in *Beowulf,* 26 for "king," 9 for "ship," 17 for "sword," and 23 for "retainers."[26] Naturally, all words in a given lexical category are not truly equivalent; but the presence of numerous synonyms as a predominant stylistic quality of a poetic convention must exclude the possibility of a systematic composition of similar phrases by associations of meaning alone.

The variety of phraseology a poet might use to convey a single and very common idea is strikingly evident in the vast networks of nearly similar expressions that introduce poems and new subjects within poems, or which designate the speaker before or after an address, or which place the action of the poem in time. Some of these networks—loosely called "systems" or even "formulae"—were closely studied long before *L'Épithète* appeared. Andreas Heusler in his article "Der Dialog in der altgermanischen erzählenden Dichtung" (1902)[27] traced numerous expressions accompanying poetic address in several of the Germanic languages, and with great attention to Old High German and Old English. He found that most of these expressions, like most speeches, in Old English begin and/or end where the verse ends. But beyond this simi-

25. See the convenient lists in Otto Jespersen, *Growth and Structure of the English Language* (9th ed. New York, 1938 [first publ. 1905]), p. 53, from which this list has been copied with appropriate omissions.

26. *Heroic Poetry,* p. 244.

27. *ZDA, 46* (1902), 189–284.

larity of significance and position within the line, this group as a whole exhibits the greatest variety: *ond þæt word acwæð, agef him andsware* (*him þa andswarode*), x *maþelode, bearn* (*sunu, maga,* etc.) x *wordum mælde, þa* (pronoun) *spræc* (*þa he to* x *spræc*), *beot* (*hosp-*) *wordum spræc, wordhord* (*modhord*) *onleac, wordlocen* (*ferðlocen*) *onspeon,* and other expressions with *reodian, secgan,* and *andswerian* are a fair sampling of Heusler's lists.[28] Frederic Klaeber studied among other phrases in *Beowulf* the "gefrægn formulae,"[29] of which he found 21 examples in the poem. These he helpfully divided into three groups: those that introduce the poem or sections of the poem; those that point out the moments of action; and those that celebrate things, events, or people. Several of the 21 occurrences of the general type of expression are exact repeats; nevertheless there is great variety within a single poem. In *Beowulf* the most common verbal form of the idea "to hear or learn about" is *mine gefræge,* as in *Ða wæs on morgen mine gefræge* (837; also 776b, 1955b, 2685b, 2837b). Another common form is what Diamond calls a "substitution system," *þa ic on* (*æt*) x *gefrægn, Ða ic æt þearfe* [*gefrægn*] (2694a; also 2484a, 2773a, 575b), or the closely related *Ða ic* (adverb) *gefrægn,* as in *Ða ic snude gefrægn* (2752a; also 74a). A shape of the expression repeated only twice in the poem is *ne hyrde ic cymlicor* (38a; see 1842b; cf. *ne gefrægn ic freondlicor,* 1027a). Yet this precise bias within the general expression is quite differently constructed in *Nænigne ic under swegle selran hyrde* (1197). Two expressions in the plural are roughly comparable in verbal pattern: *hwæt we . . . þrym gefrunon* (1–3) and *þonne yldo bearn æfre gefrunon* (70). The remaining five occurrences of the same idea defy all categories and, except in their shared significance, are unique within the poem: *Hæbbe ic eac geahsod* (433a); *swylcra searoniða secgan hyrde* (582); *þara þe ic on foldan gefrægen hæbbe* (1196); *hyrde ic þæt he ðone healsbeah* (2172a); and *swa hyt gefræge wæs* (2480b).

Is one justified in marshaling all the Old English expressions of hearing or learning about something into one formulaic system in spite of the variety of their rhythmical and syntactical patterns? Parry of course would insist that "the same metrical value" and similar "thoughts and words" be characteristic of any Greek expressions within a single

28. Ibid.; see pp. 253–83.

29. "Studies in the Textual Interpretation of 'Beowulf,' " *MP, 3* (1905–06), 243–45. See also Klaeber, *Beowulf and the Fight at Finnsburg,* "Introduction," p. lxvi.

formulaic system. Are his demands too restrictive for Old English poetry? The answer is no, so long as a formulaic system is conceived, as Parry conceived it, to be a tool of the oral singer. Tools must be recognizable in order to be used: the singer must be able to pick up the handle of a nearly ready-made phrase if he is to use it as something distinguishable from the welter of phrases which comprise language, poetic or not. Single ideas, whether in Homer, Old English, or modern poetry, may assume any number of verbal shapes in which to find their way to and from human comprehension. The expressions in *Beowulf* for hearing or learning about a thing are certainly not infinite (even aside from the fact that any single poem or finished piece must have a finite vocabulary), yet the variety in the whole group of 21 expressions is enough to frustrate the directness with which a singer should seize upon any one set of words, if all these sets of words are supposed to be one sort of tool for oral-formulaic composition.

Nor is the singer's spontaneous election of an almost ready-made expression at all secure if the verbal groups from which he chooses have only rhythm and syntactical sequence in common. Just as the shared idea of "speaking" is not enough to distinguish *Beowulf maþelode* from *he þæt word acwæð* as a compositional tool, so even an astonishingly thorough similarity of rhythm and grammar is too various in the ideas taking such form to offer the singer immediate usefulness. In his book *The Rhythm of Beowulf,* Pope lists for the examples of the D^2 verse-type appearing in the second half-lines, and having the notational value |𝄐𝅘𝅥|𝅘𝅥.𝅮 𝅘𝅥|, twenty verses.[30] Each of these verses is composed of a monosyllabic noun (or adverb, or its equivalent), a monosyllabic adverb or preposition, and a strong verb in the third singular preterit with an unstressed prefix. This conformity of expression is worth quoting in full:

holm up ætbær (519)	*secg eft ongan* (871)
sweg up astag (782)	*Fin eft begeat* (1146)
ceol up geþrang (1912)	*hord eft gesceat* (2319)
hond up abræd (2575)	*lyt eft becwom* (2365)
stefn in becwom (2552)	*frofor eft gelamp* (2941)
sweord ær gemealt (1615)	*helm oft gescær* (1526)
sweord ær gebræd (2562)	*wean oft gehet* (2937)

30. (Rev. ed., New Haven, 1966), p. 363.

bill ær gescod (2777)   *Scyld wel gebearg* (2570)
helm ær gescer (2973)   *hond rond gefeng* (2609)
weard ær ofsloh (3060)

Pope further points out the same syntactical structure in a slightly differing rhythm, for which he lists *mong oft gesæt* (171), *monig oft gecwæð* (857), *gamen eft astah* (1160), *wæter up þurhdreaf* (1619); and, with an adverbial instead of a substantival first element, *þanon eft gewat* (123), *nyðer eft gewat* (3044), and *hider ut ætbær* (3092); and, finally, with two substantives, *sunu deað fornam* (2119).[31] Similar though slightly shorter lists abound of phrases of a consistent rhythmical-syntactical pattern in *Beowulf*. It does not seem likely that a "singer" could be unaware of such consistency when it does occur; but it is perhaps more probable that two phrases such as *helm ær gescer* and *helm oft gescær* would form a far closer association in the singer's mind than would exist among all the phrases quoted above.

Within a given form or significance, then, variety of expression dilutes any quasi ready-made quality a singer's tool ought to possess. Lord's definition of a formulaic system allows a multitude of sins; his practice in the analysis of Old English verse has far too broad a base to be useful in the consideration of that poetry or to be consistent with his work on Homer or with the Yugoslavian Guslars. Magoun's conviction that a system is "used to express the same, or almost the same, idea or used to fit some larger rhythmical-grammatical pattern" may also be a carte blanche for inclusion, and so it is when *æfter cenned, æfter teode,* and *geong acenned* are placed in one systematic category (see Magoun's supporting evidence for *Beowulf* 12b). Creed's concept of the formulaic system enables him to associate as one tool *fromum feohgiftum, no he þære feohgifte,* and *ond æt feohgyftum* (see Creed's supporting evidence for *Beowulf* 21a);[32] and even Diamond admits *æþelinges wæs* and *æþelinges heht* into one type of phraseology.

In writing before Parry of the epic formulae in *Lagamon*, J. S. P. Tatlock in a long footnote gave vent to a complaint about critical inexactitude in the consideration of a certain type of diction.

31. Ibid., p. 364.
32. *Feohgiftum* is solidly underlined in Creed's analysis, but the "cf." in his supporting evidence would seem to indicate the formulaic, not formular, status of the word in his thinking.

There has been much looseness in the use of the term epic formula. Every alliterating phrase, even if repeated in one or more poems, is not a formula; certainly not a mere couple of words, found now together, now some distance apart, still less a mere type of phrase, of which the words vary. There is a clear difference between epic formula and a vague "epic language," or common phrases which happen to be used in narrative poetry . . . Unity and frequency are essential.[33]

Tatlock's idea of formulae is different from the concept here under scrutiny, but his remarking a distinction between "a vague 'epic language'" and a formula, and his remarking an essential unity as well as frequency for the formula, are altogether pertinent to the descriptions and critical demonstrations of the formulaic system by scholars who have analyzed passages of Old English poetry for their oral-formulaic content. The connections pointed out in these analyses, more particularly in the supporting evidence, are often ones of a vague aura of similarity to "oral language," lacking the thorough unity necessary for a formulaic phrase. This thorough unity is a quality that must necessarily comprise the lexical idea, the rhythm, and the syntactical structure of two or more poetic phrases.

The confusion about Old English formulaic systems in theory and practice has, after all, several starting places of uncertainty, all of which have been concisely stated by Frederic G. Cassidy in his article "How Free Was the Anglo-Saxon Scop?" and all of which may be summarized in a need for a definition that limits a phrase rhythmically, syntactically, and semantically. Cassidy's object is to challenge the merit of repetition as an identifying characteristic of the oral formula; but, if we may suppose the challenge withstood (see above, pp. 66ff.), his remarks are pertinent to a discussion of formulaic systems. He points out that we are sure of the formulaic nature of a phrase when the stressed words occur 1) identically, 2) with slightly changed inflections, and 3) with additional or different unstressed words; we are on the other hand less certain of the conventionality of comparable phrases when 1) one of the stressed words is a substitute, 2) the same stressed words occur, but in reversed order, and 3) a changed word order changes the rhythmical

33. "Epic Formulas, Especially in *Lagamon*," *PMLA*, *38* (1923), 494, n. 1.

type.[34] Cassidy's resolution of the uncertainties is the recognition of a limited number of syntactical patterns as formulae—a resolution not helpful to the designation of an oral singer's tools. Yet the types of uncertain classification which he concisely describes may be properly reduced to uncertainties over classification of rhythm, syntax, and lexical significance. A useful definition of the formulaic system in Old English poetry will exert some degree of limitation in all these characteristics, not just in one of them.

For such a definition Parry's statement is excellent, but it is imprecise enough in relation to this specific poetry to warrant extension. The essential demands are more or less present, although consistency of syntactical pattern is not mentioned, but the demands take no specifically Old English shape. The requisite and wanting shape to Parry's definition is supplied by Diamond's threefold description of Old English formulaic systems. Diamond constructed his description without recourse to Parry and, whether aside from or because of this omission, he fails to clarify, or perhaps to limit adequately, matters of rhythm and idea in the systems that he considers. Moreover his description of systems in Old English has only the whole-verse for its sphere, whereas in his analysis of Cynewulfian poetry Diamond apparently admits phrases of less than a verse to formulaic status, just as he (and several others) admits more exactly repeated phrases of a measure in length as Old English formulae.

Perhaps all that is lacking of possible specification of a definition that by the very nature of its object must remain rather loose and tentative is a prescription of formulaic length. Parry's prescription of the necessary similarities between phrases in one system, combined with Diamond's shaping descriptions, still permits a mere *bearme* to appear in an analysis of an Old English text as if it alone represented one member of a system. In consideration of length it seems the obvious course to require of the Old English formulaic system, and for identical reasons, what should be required of the Old English formula: namely that it be at least long enough to fill one of Sievers' five basic rhymical types. This requirement gives to Parry's "same metrical value" a perceptible limiting force:

34. "How Free Was the Anglo-Saxon Scop?" *Franciplegius,* p. 77. Cf. the same kind of query raised by J. B. Hainsworth, "Structure and Content in Epic Formulas: the Question of the Unique Expression," *CQ, N.S. 14* (1964), 155–64; and Donald K. Fry, "Old English Formulas and Systems," *ES, 48* (1967), 194–204.

a phrase shorter by any appreciable degree than the bare skeleton of one of the verse-types is too movable within the Old English verse to be properly useful as a singer's tool. An Old English formulaic system is thus two or more phrases of a similar Sievers' verse-type, syntactical pattern, and lexical significance, which may differ in an important element according to alliterative substitution, or context, or a type of narrative superfluity.

Because a formulaic system in an oral tradition is the embodiment of change, even if it be organized change, no definition for a particular language or poetry can pretend to be independent of illustration for clarity of statement. The definition just set forth, though built of qualifications, leaves room for controversy in principle, let alone controversy in fact; and inevitably there must be phrases, the formulaic degree of which is not with certainty discernible at this distance of time. Perhaps, then, a brief discussion by means of examples will at least reveal the usefulness and the limits of the definition adopted here.[35]

The changing elements in a formulaic system are, according to Diamond: the word in a verse that bears the alliteration of the line and that is changed because of the alliteration; the word, often the most important one in the verse, that is inseparable from its context in the narrative; and finally, the word that is part of a "tag," or phrase which adds nothing to the plot of the poem but which may change for reasons either of alliteration or of context. Needless to say the limits of these classifications are not clearcut and may overlap. Verses that are identical save in the first alliterating element are common in Old English poetry, and of course *Beowulf* and *Elene* offer a fair share of examples. A-verses composed of one word for each measure may have a varied order of the words because of alliteration, as in the frequent *mære þeoden* (12 times in *Beowulf*) which for alliteration on *þ* becomes *þeoden mære* (3 times in *Beowulf*). Because they are each repeated, these phrases are separate formulae, but they are of one formulaic system. The more common type of alliterative substitution, however, affects one element only, as in the A³-verses *gewat him ða se hearda* (*Bwf* 1963a) and *gewat him ða se goda* (*Bwf* 2949a), or in the verses *sorh is geniwod, wroht wæs geniwad,* and *cearu wæs geniwod* (*Bwf* 1322b, 2287b, 1303b). In either of these examples the substituted words have exactly the same rhythmical and

35. Throughout the following discussion of the formulaic system in Old English poetry I am greatly indebted to the suggestions, terminology, and ideas of Marie Borroff.

grammatical character as do those they replace, and more generally they have a similar lexical significance. Note that in the last two examples the changing tense of the verb "to be" is too trivial to affect the formulaic status of the verses.

Examples of alliterative substitution could be easily and needlessly multiplied, but it may be useful to call attention to some which neither reverse the order of the same two elements nor precisely fit the category of, say *ond minra eorla gedryht, mid minra secga gedriht,* and *mid his hæleþa gedryht* (*Bwf* 431b, 633b, 662b). Some substitutions seem to occur specifically to avoid double alliteration in the off-verse. Such a substitution is the *geara hwyrftum* in the first line of *Elene,* which, as Diamond pointed out, replaces the *geara gongum* of *Ele* 648a, *Jul* 693a, and *Chr* 1035a. If the most common sort of alliterative substitution is the replacement of one discreet element by another of the same rhythmical and grammatical character and of nearly the same lexical significance, then the second most frequent change is that of the first elements in compounds, particularly in C- and D^1-verses. Perhaps the longest such substitution system in *Beowulf* is the sevenfold substitution with *-cyning: þeodcyninga (-es), wuldorcyninga, woroldcyninga, sæcyninga, heah-cyninges, eorðcyninges,* and *Frescyninge.* It may well be questioned whether *þeod-, wuldor, worold-, sæ-, heah-, eorð-* and *Fres-,* metrically and syntactically equivalent, approximate a similar lexical significance. As these verses appear in the context of *Beowulf,* one may well equate *wuldor-* and *worold-, þeod-, heah-,* and *eorð-,* and *sæ-* and *Fres-;* but altogether the weight of the simplex elements hardly balances as well as it does in *wroht, sorh,* and *cearu.* Perhaps it is reasonable to suppose on the other hand that the extremely close associative force within the making of these compound words is and was felt to be strong enough to override dissociative differences in meaning. Furthermore the meanings of the first elements are generically within the same class: they are all words that designate a sphere of authority. Certainly no one of the epithets is of unique or subtle importance to its referent. These words, therefore, are in the same formulaic system.

What, if any, may be said to be the limits of a formulaic system characterized by alliterative substitution? Since it is necessary that the substituted element in this kind of system be of a certain rhythmical and syntactical value, whereas its lexical significance is only approximately consistent with the replaced element, then it is in the sphere of meaning where the limits of this formulaic system will seem to fluctuate and will inevitably lead to controversy. The controversy itself must often turn upon an argument over what the "singer" "felt" to be formulaic—an argument incapable of solution. Where either the precise significance of a word or of a composer's awareness of that word is obscure, no rule for the establishment of the limits of a formulaic system can or should be forthcoming. One may only proceed by meditating the possibilities of specific phrases. For instance the expression *þæt wæs god cyning* is a formula in *Beowulf* (11b, 863b, 2390b); it is also part of a formulaic system of alliterative substitution of the adjective: *þa wæs frod cyning* (1306b) and *þæt wæs an cyning* (1885b). If *god, frod,* and *an,* equivalent in rhythm and syntax, are not equivalent in specific lexical significance, they certainly are equivalent in import within the context of the poem where each describes Hrothgar (863b, 1306b, 1885b), where each sets forth the moral state of a king. These phrases, then, form a system. In their supporting evidence for *Beowulf* 11b, both Creed and Magoun appear to extend the system farther: Magoun, by referring to *þæt is soð Metod* (1611b) and *þæt wæs modig secg* (1812b); Creed, by pointing out *næs se folccyning* (2733b). Each of these expressions differs more from the *god, frod, an* phrases than do those phrases among themselves. *þæt is soð Metod* differs in significance (specifically in referent), *þæt wæs modig secg* in rhythmical pattern and significance; *næs se folccyning* in syntactical pattern and significance. To include or not include these phrases within the same formulaic system becomes a question of whether pattern or reference is, or was, felt to be of the greater importance. In confronting this uncertainty perhaps the surest course to take is that which demands consistency of both pattern and at least a generic significance in a formulaic system characterized by alliterative substitution. The point is endlessly debatable, unless unforetold evidence of an objective nature should come to light. In an enforced ignorance, however, it is persuasive of excluding Magoun's and Creed's further illustrations of the system, *þæt wæs god (frod, an) cyning,* to reflect that a "singer" could theoretically say *þæt wæs (is,* etc.) plus any adjective, plus any noun in more than one verse-type, and that he could merely colloquially and prosaically exclaim in such a syntactical pattern. The bare pattern seems too everyday to be identified with the immediacy of a singer's need, unless the pattern itself is identified with a king or a person in the position of mortal authority and with a C-verse.

By this standard of limitation, the formulaic system under discussion would indeed include the hypothetical phrase *þæt wæs til hlaford,* a phrase used by Frederic G. Cassidy to raise questions about conventional criteria for identifying formulae.

It is clear that the lexical significance shared among members of a system is not always exact or specific but is more likely to be generic. Thus the verbal kinship of *god, frod,* and *an* lies in their generically similar designation of a state of moral being. The expression *næs se folc-cyning,* which Creed pointed out to further illustrate the system, not only differs from the *god-frod-an cyning* system in its syntactical organization but in the generic significance of the element, *folc: folc* is no moral state, but an object of government. The adjectives in the other expressions cited by Magoun—*þæt wæs modig secg*—have generically the significance of *god, frod,* and *an;* but the difference of their referents is such as to distinguish them as different tools for instantaneous composition. This difference need not exclude the conjectural possibility of one phrase being the analogical extension of another phrase. Scholars have frequently and plausibly speculated upon the origin of certain religious expressions in Old English poetry: since the expressions often seem to be modeled on more ancient, pagan expressions (as *þæt is soð Metod* seems modeled on *þæt wæs god cyning*), and since the conversion of England took place at a definite time, it is altogether likely that analogical extension made Christian many a pagan phrase. It does not necessarily follow, however, that expressions created upon analogies should properly be considered within the formulaic system of the original expression. The categorical division is that which, in speedy and quasi-automatic composition, would present itself most tangibly, like a tool, to the oral singer. In this case the words referring to a noble, earthly king and to God may be distinct in their associations to form two kinds of ready-made phrases, tools immediately available to the oral composer. Some specific verbal similarity (here, *cyning*), as well as grammatical and metrical similarity, should probably be characteristic of any specific formulaic system.

Formulaic systems comprising alliterative substitutions are of course but one type of system in Old English poetry. A second type described by Diamond is made up of what he calls "bracketing phrases": this kind of system is easier to discern and is capable of greater precision in definition than is the substitution system because its limits of changeability are both narrow and absolute. *Þæm wæs Judas nama (Ele* 418), where *Judas* is replaced by *Simon* in line 530 of the same poem, is an excellent example of the confined fluidity of this kind of Old English formulaic system. The changing element is governed entirely by context, by specific referent, and not by alliteration; it must fill a strictly defined rhythmical and syntactical pattern, but its distinguishing and directing mark is its significance. Because its shape is governed by context, perhaps "bracketing phrase" does not sufficiently describe this type of system. Ronald Waldron in a study of oral formulae in Middle English poetry also considered the pattern typified by *þæm wæs* x *nama,* or "I shall . . . thee . . . telle," etc.; such phrases he called " 'empty' rhythmical-syntactical 'moulds' ready to be filled with meaning."[36] As Marie Borroff has pointed out,[37] these "moulds" are far from being "empty," and it goes somewhat against the psychology of composition to call them so. Although a piece resulting from extensive use of *moulded* phraseology may, to us, appear to be fill-in-the-blank poetry, it is unlikely that the poet or singer inspected his phrases with the kind of scrutiny that leads us to discover certain patterns. Yet Waldron's conception of *moulding* fits the observation better than does *bracketing;* and Waldron himself belies his idea of emptiness by remarking that these patterns are not dependent on narrative and that they are essentially unmmnemonic.[38]

A third and again easily recognizable category of formulaic expressions in Old English is made up of "tags," expressions which, whatever they add to the stylistic tone of the poem, add little or nothing to the mere march of plotted events. It has frequently been noticed that if a young man flourishes and grows, he is bound to do so under the clouds (*weox under wolcnum*); he is also, if in youth, bound to be young in the yards (*geong in geardum*); if powerful, powerful under the skies (*rice under roderum*). Geographical inevitabilities do not account for all Old English "tags"; there are also statements of fact which, both because of frequent repetition and because nothing is built upon their specific lexical import, are superfluous to the narrative as narrative. *Folcum to frofre* is such an expression, as is *þæt wæs god cyning,* a phrase also classified by its alliterative substitutions. In analyzing a passage of Old

---

36. Ronald A. Waldron, "Oral-Formulaic Technique in Middle English Alliterative Poetry," *Speculum, 32* (1957), 797–99.

37. In a private conversation.

38. "Oral-Formulaic Technique," p. 800.

English poetry that contains a "tag" one should probably not hesitate to include in supporting evidence expressions that are dissimilar in syntax. That is, supporting evidence for such an expression as *weox under wolcnum* (*Bwf* 8a) should, strictly speaking, consist of *weox þa under wolcnum* (*Gen* 1702a), *wod under wolcnum* (*Bwf* 714a), *weold under wolcnum* (*Bwf* 1770a), *wand to wolcnum* (*Bwf* 1119a, *to* being an unimportant substitution for *under*), *wriðað under wolcnum* (*Phx* 27a), *awyrde under wolcnum* (*Phx* 247a), *geworden under wolcnum* (*Phx* 247a), *geworden under wolcnum* (*Chr* 266a), and *gewitað under wolcnum* (*Ele* 1277a), or any phrase made up of a verb, a preposition, and *wolcnum,* in an A-verse with alliteration upon *w.* Yet the numerous other phrases similarly constructed, except that their first elements are nouns or adjectives, are fully as superfluous in exactly the same rhythmical and alliterative pattern. Probably the "singer" would use phrases such as *wan under wolcnum* (*Bwf* 651a, *DrR* 55a), *wæter under wolcnum* (*Bwf* 1631a), *waðol under wolcnum* (*Fnb* 8a), *wide under wolcnum* (*Gen* 1950a), etc. with the same awareness of mind in which he used *weox under wolcnum.* The characteristic distinctive to the singer would be the alliteration on *w* of a word in an A-verse preceding the words *under wolcnum.* In any single formulaic system of "tags," however, at least two words, or more than one measure, in the verses should be similar: thus *wan under wolcnum* and *heard under helme,* each formulaic in its own right, should not belong to one formulaic system, although they share the same syntax, rhythm, and stylistic quality.

True, by any of our analyses of these shared qualities, the two phrases are closely related, obviously and formulaically. The only significant difference between them is apparent not so much in the phrases themselves as in the people who perceive them: the illiterate singer on the one hand and, on the other, a reader of the text. Readers never lack the opportunity to reread, to compare; nor do they lack the leisure necessary to comparison. The oral singer, as he is hypothetically described by the Parry-Lord thesis and by Magoun's adaptation of the thesis, and as he was heard to sing in Yugoslavia in the 1930s, has no leisure whatsoever. His composition, as Lord has emphasized, is his performance. His use of phrases must ensure instantaneous results and must therefore be somewhat automatic, even mechanical. It is probably reasonable to suppose, therefore, that the associations among phrases discerned by a reader who has time for large categories are not so intimate or narrow as those discerned by the singer in the very act of singing. The reader has a moment to classify *wan under wolcnum* and *heard under helme* together; the singer in far less than a moment is more likely to have associations that proceed no farther than the necessary alliterating letter and the state of being, or the specific state of being a warrior.

Before considering Magoun's, Creed's, Lord's, and Diamond's analyses of Old English passages for both formulae and formulaic systems, a brief word about the stylistic importance of nearly repeated verses is in order. The subject of style in any poetry, and in some ways especially in a traditional, anonymous poetry, is extremely complex and difficult. Here it is only possible to give an indication of but two characteristics of a no longer practiced style. First and more readily perceived is the elevation of tone achieved primarily through just those phrases that one would underscore in an oral-formulaic analysis of Old English poetry.[39] *Weox under wolcnum* is, of course, a "tag" only to the literality of plot. The courtliness and the epic scope built into the very pedestal of a poem like the *Iliad* or *Beowulf* by a diction inseparably associated with the sway and deaths of heroes is immeasurable.

It is more difficult for us to estimate another characteristic of the traditional diction, namely its specific associative power within one poem, or among several poems judged from an historical point of view. Too much time has intervened for modern critics to avoid entirely the dangers of overly subtle discovery on the one hand and a complete dismissal of individual artistry on the other. Especially because of the poetic composition of the twentieth century it is hard now for a scholar to dissociate like phrases, to forget the fact of the repetition in an old poem, unless he maintains that every expression in the traditional diction has a mechanical, artistically fortuitous direction. Parry certainly, however opposite his intentions, implied in all his studies of Homeric formulae the completely mechanical picture of oral composition: his observations that "the repeated use of phrases means not only that the poet is following a fixed pattern of words, it means equally that he is denying himself all other ways of expressing the idea," and that "at no time" does the singer seek "words for an idea which has never before found expres-

---

39. For an excellent discussion of the elevation of tone via repetitive language, see Marie Borroff, *Sir Gawain and the Green Knight: a Stylistic and Metrical Study* (New Haven, 1962), pp. 6–34; and Bowra, *Heroic Poetry*, p. 244.

sion,"[40] are typical of a mechanical emphasis in Parry's conceptions. Lord, perhaps in an effort to balance the critical misunderstanding which pursued Parry, probably has outdone Parry in his insistence on a singer's dependence on his *tools*. Magoun, too, and to a lesser extent other proponents of the theory of oral-formulaic composition in Old English, have tended to celebrate the statistics to be gleaned from a poetic diction and to neglect other considerations, although such exclusive celebration has certainly not been their intention.

Robert Creed however, in an article entitled "On the Possibility of Criticizing Old English Poetry,"[41] has tried to correct the balance, or at least to confront the critical problem created by Parry's theory. In this essay Creed leaves open the question of the *Beowulf*-poet's literacy but argues strongly that, in spite of the thoroughly formulaic diction of the whole poem, the various repetitions with all their subtle differences now "located" by the modern critic were "intended" by the poet and understood by his audience.[42] He then points out several examples of what he considers to be nearly exact repetitions whose differences contribute to the total meaning of the second occurrence—among them lines 1769a ff. which, he thinks, recall the beginning of the poem:

> Swa ic Hring-Dena   hund missera
> weold under wolcnum   ond hig wigge beleac
> manigum mægþa   geond þysne middangeard,
> æscum ond ecgum,   þæt ic me ænige
> under swegles begong   gesacan ne tealde.

Aside from the difficulty that the old English poet's intentions must be somewhat mysterious to a twentieth-century audience, there is a central difficulty with the position that Creed adopted in his article on criticism. Creed assumes the validity of the theory of oral-formulaic composition in Old English poetry without committing himself on the question of literacy. According to the theory, only an unlettered singer would depend consistently enough upon formulae and formulaic systems to compose a "song" so much a "tissue of formulas" as Creed conceives *Beowulf* to be.[43] Again according to the theory, which Creed follows, no

40. "Studies I," pp. 89, 147.
41. *TSLL, 3* (1961), 97–106.
42. Ibid., esp. p. 101.
43. Ibid., p. 98.

singer, however deftly and imaginatively he uses formulaic phrases to set forth oral themes, uses these phrases in repetition with a sense of an association between occurrences, especially an association that creates new significance via subtle change. In the present incapability of proof one may argue one of two extreme hypotheses, but not both simultaneously. Creed, as a sensitive critic, responds to the inner and outer associations between phrases as he *reads* the Old English poem: it is one thing to so respond, another to maintain at one and the same time that the Old English poet sang his poem in ignorance of letters and yet intended the literary reading of posterity.

Without forming any conclusions, however, where they must be dogmatic to be formed at all, it is worth observing an important difference in the stylistic techniques of Homer and the *Beowulf*-poet (or of any poet of one of the longer Old English poems). This difference has been mentioned before in connection with formulae but is germane to a discussion of repetitive diction, and it is definite enough to be characteristic. Homer has clusters of sequential, exactly repeated formulae for the presentation of certain recurring motifs, such as arming and dining; Old English has no such clusters but exhibits great variety of diction in presenting identical events. On the other hand, both the *Iliad* and *Beowulf* have single words or short formulaic phrases repeated only twice in the whole work in connection with similar occasions or individuals. Some of these repetitions in *Beowulf,* whatever they may have meant to an eighth-century audience or to the poet himself, seem powerful indeed to the modern reader in their urgency toward comparison: Scyld and Beowulf are on an even summit of heroism by the banners that are set over them at their deaths, one on the sea (*segen gyldenne/heah ofer heafod* (47b–48a), one on the land (*segn eallgylden/ heah ofer horde* (2767–68a); the misdeeds of Grendel and a thief assume a haunting similarity of notice and result by the repeated phrase *oð ðæt an ongan* (100b, 2210b); Grendel and the dragon, *gæst* and *Wyrm,* each *yrre cwom* toward the man with whom each fought (2073b, 2669b); the word *unlifigende* (-*es, -ne, -um*) appears five times in the poem, and by the end seems like a knell for the virtuous dead—Heregar (468b), Hondscio (744a), Æschere (1308b, and also, indirectly, 1389a), and Beowulf (2908b). Yet it is more likely than not that all these apparently purposeful and certainly effective repetitions are formulae or are formulaic expressions so attached to the event that their author was aware of them only in the large, as themes, not as detail in diction.

An inspection of slightly longer phrases in recurring themes in Old English poems, however, reveals no such similarity of diction as is to be found in Homer or as the above examples would seem to indicate. Dawns in *Beowulf,* for instance, bring truly new days: *Leoht eastan com,/beorht beacen Godes* (569b–70a); *siþþan morgenleoht/ ofter ylda bearn oþres dogores,/ sunne sweglwered suþan scineð* (604b–06b); *Ða wæs morgenleoht/ scofen ond synded* (917b–18a); *Ða com beorht scacan/ scima ofer sceadwa* (1802b–03a, Klaeber's emendation after Sievers); *Woruldcandel scan,/ sigel suðan fus* (1965b–66a); and compare too the adverbial phrase *þonne dæg lixte* (485b) and the simile *Lixte se leoma, leoht inne stod,/ efne swa of hefene hadre scineð/ rodores candel* (1570a–72a).

Parry's statement that "the repeated use of phrases means not only that the poet is following a fixed pattern of words, it means equally that he is denying himself all other ways of expressing the idea," [44] is in itself open to objection in any context because of the word "equally"; but the statement is ironically pertinent in the reverse to Old English poetry where the variety in the diction seems the result of a deliberate quest, or a deliberate denial of available and exact repetition. What Robert Fitzgerald said of Homeric poetry with his understanding of the subsidiary importance of the mechanical, may also be said, and with more force, of *Beowulf* and other Old English poems: "The formulas give the narrative musical consistency; the innovations keep it alive. The more it is the same, the more it changes." [45]

Furthermore, there is a readily perceptible difference between the styles of *Beowulf* and *Widsith,* perhaps the earliest Old English composition of any length that has survived to modern times. *Widsith's* many end-stopped lines of fine-sounding but rather mechanical catalog may be compared to the catalog of ships at the end of Book II of the *Iliad,* now thought to be the section of that epic least changed from some tradition long preceding Homer. The variety of description and the run-on syntax composed by the *Beowulf*-poet seem indicative of a large degree of creative modification upon an ancient convention of

44. "Studies I," p. 89.

45. Homer, *The Odyssey,* transl. Robert Fitzgerald (New York, 1963), p. 493. See also Tatlock, "Epic Formulas," pp. 515, 516–17; Stanley B. Greenfield, "Syntactic Analysis and Old English Poetry," *NM, 64* (1963), 373–78.

poetic expression. This creative modification would seem to go farther than the analogical extension of *þæt is soð Metod* from *þæt wæs god cyning,* if *Widsith* is at all characteristic of an early, unmodified tradition of composition. It is a modification that seems to be an extensive and intensive imbuing of old, conventional phrases with new meanings, new particular associations within the narrative of the poem. As Kemp Malone has said: "The use of traditional diction is one thing; improvisation is something else again." [46] Whether the artistic meditation supposedly necessary to this apparent creative recasting of traditional elements could take place within a spontaneous oral performance is highly questionable.

II

With its apparently limitless expression for limited objects, Old English poetry is nevertheless highly formulaic. In order to illustrate the controversial degree of its repetitious phraseology, four examples of analyses of poetic passages are presented on pp. 155–180.

---

46. Review of Godfrid Storms' "Compound Names of Peoples in *Beowulf,* a Study in the Diction of a Great Poet," *ES, 41* (1960), 205. See also William Whallon's highly interesting article, "The Idea of God in *Beowulf,*" *PMLA, 80* (1965), 21.

The following examples of oral-formulaic analyses illustrate different scholars' treatments of four passages of poetry, two from *Beowulf* and two from *Elene*. The first passage, *Beowulf* 1–25, appears with Magoun's[a] and then with Creed's[b] analysis, and each example is succeeded by the supporting evidence gathered by each scholar. Magoun of course considered *Beowulf* 1–25 against all surviving Old English poetry; he therefore has underscored the passage more heavily than has Creed, who considered the opening of the poem against only the 6,364 verses of *Beowulf* itself. By the same token, Magoun's supporting evidence is more extensive than is Creed's. If Magoun and Creed differ in the extent of their comparisons, they are in virtual agreement in their definitions of the formula and the formulaic system. Since these definitions are overly inclusive, a reconsidered analysis of Beowulf 1–25, proceeding according to the definitions set forth in this book, is added beneath Magoun's and beneath Creed's analysis. In both cases the scholars' analyses are indicated by straight lines, with solid underscoring for formulae and broken underscoring for formulaic systems, and the reconsidered analysis by wavy lines. Following Magoun's and Creed's supporting evidence is a compilation of reconsidered supporting evidence, again determined according to the definitions discussed above. It should be pointed out that the reconsidered analyses take account of the difference between Magoun's and Creed's scope: that is, the reconsidered analysis of *Beowulf* 1–25, when matched with Magoun, includes all Old English poetry in the field of evidence; when matched with Creed, it refers only to *Beowulf* for the comparison of phrases. The reconsidered supporting evidence for this passage, however, amalgamates the two spheres of discovery.

The other three selections, *Beowulf* 1473–87, *Elene* 1–21, and *Elene* 1256b–76a, are arranged in much the same manner as the first selection, with the reconsidered analyses placed beneath Lord's, Creed's, or Diamond's analyses, and with the pertinent supporting evidence and reconsidered evidence following each passage. Both Lord[c] and Creed[d] analyzed *Beowulf* 1473–87 with reference primarily to that poem; therefore all analyses appear together —Lord's in straight lines, Creed's in heavy lines, and the reconsidered analy-

a. See "The Oral-Formulaic Character of Anglo-Saxon Narrative Poetry," *Speculum,* 28 (1953), 464–65; supporting evidence ibid.

b. See "Studies in the Techniques of Composition of the Beowulf Poetry in British Museum Ms. Cotton Vitellius *A XV*" (unpublished dissertation, Harvard University, 1955), p. 1; supporting evidence on pp. 200–04.

c. See *The Singer of Tales* (Cambridge, Mass., 1960), p. 199; supporting evidence on pp. 297–301.

d. See his dissertation, p. 35; supporting evidence on pp. 300–03.

sis in wavy lines. Diamond analyzed *Elene* 1–21[e] with reference to the four signed poems of Cynewulf (*Christ II, Fates of the Apostles, Juliana,* and *Elene*), and *Elene* 1256b–76a[f] with reference to all Old English poetry. The reconsidered analysis and supporting evidence for the two passages is similarly presented.

The texts quoted appear as they do in Klaeber's edition of *Beowulf* and Gradon's edition of *Elene;*[g] the punctuation, spelling and emendations of these editions are followed not only in the four quoted passages, but in all quoted references to *Beowulf* and *Elene* in the supporting evidence. These editions are selected for convenience, even though Magoun, Creed, Lord, and Diamond all quote from normalized texts and at times prefer a punctuation or even an inflectional ending not favored by Klaeber or Gradon. With the exception of *Judith,* any Old English poems other than *Beowulf* and *Elene* quoted in the supporting evidence are quoted from the Columbia University Press edition of *The Anglo-Saxon Poetic Records,* in six volumes variously edited by George Philip Krapp and Elliott Van Kirk Dobbie.[h] The few references to *Judith* are to the edition by B. J. Trimmer (London, 1952). Contextual punctuation is disregarded in the supporting evidence.

Magoun, Creed, Lord, and Diamond nearly always quote the lines or phrases of poetry to which they refer in their supporting evidence. In order to save space and avoid repetition, these quotations are omitted from the representative lists, and only the line numbers are given. In other respects, these scholars' lists of supporting evidence for the various passages are reproduced verbatim, unless specific omission is indicated. Only Lord's evidence has been severely paraphrased, since it included many descriptions of syntax and rhythm—the latter with precise reference to Pope's *The Rhythm of Beowulf*—which are superfluous in the particular context of this chapter. A tabulation of mere line numbers is, however, not very useful; therefore a general indication of what the references illustrate in common often follows the line numbers and is set off by brackets. Infrequent critical remarks and observations are likewise enclosed in brackets. Creed and Diamond, since they analyzed large portions of Old English poetry in their dis-

e. See "The Diction of the Signed Poems of Cynewulf" (unpublished dissertation, Harvard University, 1953), p. 123; supporting evidence on pp. 177–80.

f. Ibid., pp. 173–74; supporting evidence on pp. 289–93.

g. Frederick Klaeber, *Beowulf and the Fight at Finnsburg* (3d ed. Boston, 1950); the long marks have been omitted. P. O. E. Gradon, ed., *Cynewulf's Elene* (London, 1958); the letters ʒ and Þ are given their modern forms, *g* and *w*.

h. Vol. 1, *The Junius Manuscript,* ed. Krapp (1931); Vol. 2, *The Vercelli Book,* ed. Krapp (1932); Vol. 3, *The Exeter Book,* ed. Krapp and Dobbie (1936); Vol. 5, *The Paris Psalter and the Meters of Boethius,* ed. Krapp (1932); Vol. 6, *The Anglo-Saxon Minor Poems,* ed. Dobbie (1942).

sertations, have used cross-references in their supporting evidence. Here the cross-references are noted with changes in pagination and are then quoted within brackets.

All references made in the reconsidered supporting evidence are quoted in full, unless the phrase to be compared differs only in spelling from the phrase under scrutiny. In the reconsidered evidence for the passages from *Beowulf,* all line numbers refer to that poem unless otherwise noted.

The reconsidered evidence follows Magoun, Creed, Lord, and Diamond in making use of Magoun's suggested abbreviations for all the titles of all the poems in Old English.[i]

Grein's *Sprachsatz* and the Bosworth-Toller *Anglo-Saxon Dictionary*[j] were indispensable in the compilation of the reconsidered supporting evidence for each of the four passages.

I. Beowulf 1–25

Magoun's Analysis

(determined by comparison to
all surviving Old English poetry)

Hwæt, we Gar-Dena   in geardagum,

þeodcyninga   þrym gefrunon,

hu ða æþelingas   ellen fremedon!

    Oft Scyld Scefing   sceaþena þreatum,

5   monegum mægþum   meodosetla ofteah,

egsode earlas,   syððan ærest wearð

i. See Francis P. Magoun, Jr., "Abbreviated Titles for the Poems of the Anglo-Saxon Poetic Corpus," *EA,* 7 (1955), 138–46. Note that Diamond uses *Pho* instead of *Phx* for the *Phoenix,* and Magoun uses *Met* (not *MBo*) for the Meters of Boethius.

j. C. W. M. Grein, *Sprachsatz der angelsächsischen Dichter,* Vol. I (Cassel & Göttingen, 1861); Vol. II (Cassel & Göttingen, 1864); James Bosworth and T. Northcote Toller, *An Anglo-Saxon Dictionary* (Oxford, 1898; repr. 1954); T. Northcote Toller, *An Anglo-Saxon Dictionary: Supplement* (Oxford, 1921; repr. 1955).

feasceaft funden;   he þæs frofre gebad,

weox under wolcnum   weorðmyndum þah,

oð þæt him æghwylc   ymbsittendra

10   ofer hronrade   hyran scolde,

gomban gyldan;   þæt wæs god cyning!

Ðæm eafera wæs   aefter cenned

geong in geardum,   þone God sende

folce to frofre;   fyrenðearfe ongeat,

15   þe hie ær drugon   aldorlease

lange hwile;   him þæs Liffrea,

wuldres Wealdend   woroldare forgeaf,

Beowulf wæs breme   —blæd wide sprang—

Scyldes eafera   Scedelandum in.

20   Swa sceal geong guma   gode gewyrcean

fromum feohgiftum   on fæder bearme,

þæt hine on ylde   eft gewunigen

wilgesiþas,   þonne wig cume,
<u>_____</u>

leode gelæsten;   lofdædum sceal

25   in mægþa gehwære   man geþeôn.
<u>_____</u>

Magoun's Supporting Evidence

1a–2b: *Exo* 1, *And* 1, *FAp* 63, *Ele* 364, 852, *FAp* 23, *Chr* 586 (cp. *Bwf* 2b–3a), *Glc* 108, *Jul* 1, *Ele* 397–98. [none of these is an exact repetition; all illustrate the formulaic system for the introduction of a poem or a new subject].

1b: *XSt* 367, *Wan* 44. Cp. *Chr* 251; *Bwf* 1354, 2233. Note also instrum. use without *on:* *And* 1519; *Ele* 290, 834 (also *Bwf* 2233). Note closely related formulas: *on fyrn-dagum, on ær-dagum,* and *on eald-dagum* (*Chr* 303, *Sft* 1).

2a: *Nom. pl. Gen* 1965; *gen sg. Bwf* 1694; *FAp* 18; *Edw* 34 [the last example is more likely a C-verse: *þæs þe þearf wæs þaes þeodkyninges*].

2b: See 1–2 above for combination of formulas to express the idea of 'having heard or learned long ago.'

3a: *FAp* 3, 85; *Rid* 49, 7. Cp. without def. art. but with a preceding word, usually of light stress *Gen* 1059, 1647, 1868; *Dan* 689; *And* 805, 857.

3b: *And* 1208.

4b: *Jul* 672; cp. *Glc* 902.

5a: *Bwf* 75, 1771.

6b: *Bwf* 1947; cp. 1775; *Ele* 913. Note the more general scheme involving *syþþan* plus a two- or three-syllable word plus verb: *And* 1223; *Ele* 18, 841; *Bwf* 1077, 2124, 1233, 1689.

7a: Cp. *And* 181.

8a: *Gen* 1702; cp. *Bwf* 714; *Phx* 27; *Gen* 1438; *Phx* 247.

8b: *Exo* 258.

9a: *Ele* 865, 885.

9b: *Bwf* 2734, *Ele* 33. Cp. other inflections: *dat. pl. ymbsittendum PPs*

78, 4; 88, 35; *fem. acc. pl. Met* 35, 14 [sic]. Cp. closely related *Gen* 2490 *ymbstandendre;* PPs 140, 4 [sic].

10a: *Gen* 205; *And* 266, 821. Cp. *Bwf* 200; *Ele* 996; *Jul* 675; *Bwf* 1429.

10b: *Dan* 135 [sic]; *Ele* 367; *Met* 9, 45; *Met* 1, 31.

11a: *Gen* 1977b–78a.

11b: *Bwf* 863, 2390. Cp. *Bwf* 1885; *Jul* 224; *Deo* 23; *Wid* 67, and further *Bwf* 1075, 1812 [the last two examples do not express the "same idea" of referent]; *Met* 23, 35 (?), etc.

12a: *Gen* 1188. Note and cp. Bwf 12a–b with *Gen* 1159, 2394.

12b: Cp. *Cæd* 8; *Rid* 40, 44.

13a: *Phx* 355, 647; *Chr.* 201. Cp. *Jul* 35, *Bwf* 2446.

13b: *Dan* 525; cp. *Gen* 1371 [this example is an A-verse].

14a: *Exo* 88; *And* 606; *Ele* 1142 [none of these examples is written out]; *Men* 228; *Ele* 502; *Rid* 39, 19; *Men* 57; *Pa* 50, 148 [the last three examples do not have double alliteration].

15a: *Bwf* 831, 1857 [sic]; *Chr* 615, *Jud* 158.

15b: Cp. *Bwf* 2935; *And* 405. *Ealdorleas* is ordinarily used in the sense "lifeless."

16a: *Bwf* 2159, 2780; *Dan* 660; *DrR* 24; *Jul* 674; *Rid* 28, 9; *Met* 4, 46. For numerous formulas to express a "long" or "short time" cp. *DrR* 70 *gode hwile,* also *micele, lytle, sume hwile,* and with *þrage: ealle, lytle, lange, sume,* also *ænige stunde.*

16b. Cp. *Exo* 271; *Chr* 27.

17a: *Bwf* 183, 1752; *Dan* 14 [sic]; *And* 193, 539.

18a: *Sol* 182; *Dan* 104; *Sol* 238.

18b: *FAp* 6; cp. *Bwf* 1588; *Jul* [sic]; also *Max* I 194.

19a: *Bwf* 897; 1847; *Gen* 1133, 2054; *Met* 26, 36 [sic]; *Men* 136. Cp. also *Gen* 1578, 2834.

19b: *Bwf* 2357; *Gen* 1052. Cp. *Jul* 83.

20a: *Bwf* 1172, 1534; cp. 2066, 2590 [the first three of these examples, although they are C-verses introduced by *swa sceal,* have a verb in the second measure; and the last example is a B-verse].

21b: Cp. *Bwf* 35, *Exo* 375, 896, 214. Note related formula with *fæðm: Bwf* 188; *Max* II 661; *And* 616; *Ele* 765.

22a–b: Cp. *FoM* 60.

22b: See 22a-b, also *Phx* 481.

23a: *Gen* 2003.

25a: *Pre* 74 [here and in *Beowulf* 25a, Magoun reads *gehwæn* for *gehwære*].

Creed's Analysis
(determined by comparison to *Beowulf alone*)

Hwæt, we Gar-Dena   in geardagum,

þeodcyninga   þrym gefrunon,

hu ða æþelingas   ellen fremedon:

Oft scyld Scefing   sceaþena þreatum,

5   monegum mægþum   meodosetla ofteah,

egsode eorlas,   syððan ærest wearð

feasceaft funde;   he þæs frofre gebad,

weox under wolcnum   weorðmyndum þah,

oð þæt him aeghwylc   ymbsittendra

10   ofer hronrade   hyran scolde,

gomban gyldan;   þaet wæs god cyning!

Ðæm eafera wæs   æfter cenned

geong in geardum,   þone God sende

folce to frofgre;   fyrenðearfe ongeat,

15   þe hie ær drugon   aldorlease

lange hwile;   him þæs Liffrea,

wuldres Wealdend   woroldare forgeaf,

Beowulf wæs breme   —blæd wide sprang—

Scyldes eafera   Scedelandum in.

20   Swa sceal geong guma   gode gewyrcean,

fromum feohgiftum   on fæder bearme

þæt hine on ylde   eft gewunigen

wilgesiþas,   þonne wig cume,

leode gelæsten;   lofdædum sceal

25   in mægþa gehwære   man geþeon.

Creed's Supporting Evidence

1a: Cp. 530, 1652; cp. also 1774, 2248; cp. also 942; cp. also 240b [all these examples, including the last, an emendation, contain *hwæt* plus a pronoun, and introduce A³-, B-, or C-verses].

Cp. 601, 1856, 2494 [all are examples with *Gar-Denum* in the second measure of a C-verse]. Cp. also 116, 383, 392, 427, 609, 616, 828, 1069, 1769, 1996; cp. also 783 [all are ethnic-compounds with *-Dene*].

1b: 1343, 2233. Cp. 1451. Note also the more generalized system *on x-dagum (-dæge)* . . . 197, 790, 806, 718, 757, 1062, 3159.

2a: Gen. sg. 2694. Cp. 1039, 1155, 1684, 3180, 2382, 2503.

3a: Cp. 906, 982, 2888, 1244, 1294, 1596, 1804, 2374, 2424 [all examples have *æþeling-e-es-a* in the second measure of C- or D¹-verses]. For *æþelinges-a* as the first measure of E-verses see 33. Cp. also 2708.

5a: Dat. sg. 75, gen. pl. 1771.

6b: 1947. Cp. 1261, 1775.

7b: Cp. 87, 929, 1618, 1779, 2258, 2568, 2736, 3116. Cp. also 400 [with the exception of the last, all examples have *bad* or *gebad* in the second measure of a B-verse whose introductory syllables contain a pronoun].

8a: Cp. 651, 714, 1631, 1770 [excepting 1631, all examples contain a verb].

8b: Cp. 1752. Cp. 1186.

9b: 2734. Cp. 1788, 2015, 2022, 2868 [examples with *heal-* or *fletsitten-dra-um*].

10a: Cp. 200, 1429.

10b: Cp. 85, 230, 704, 832, 910, 1034, 1067, 1070, 1260, 1305, 1449, 1464, 1798, 2056, 2257, 2400, 2421, 2627, 2918, 2974, 2963, 3068 [all examples consist of an infinitive plus a disyllabic form of *scullan,* and with the exception of 910 and possibly of 2400 all examples are A-verses].

11b: 2390, 863. Cp. also 1885. See also 1306. Cp. 2733. Note also the following group of B- C-verses introduced by *þæt wæs (is)* the second measures of which consist of a noun and its modifying adj.: 170, 765, 833, 1075, 1559, 1611, 1691, 1812, 2441. Note also the following group of (miscellaneous) B, C, and A³ verses introduced by *þæt wæs (is, bið)*; 309, 348, 454, 705, 932, 1039, 1388, 1458, 1607, 2129, 2611, 2817, 2999. See also 249. Cp. also 83.

12b: Cp. 1356 (*ær acenned*).

13a: Cp. 2446 (*giong on galgan*). Cp. 1134, 2459. Cp. also 265, 1138 [all these are A-verses ending with a preposition and an inflected form of *geard*].

14a: Cp. 1707. Cp. also 1709, 1961 [examples with *to frofre, to helpe*].

15a: 831, 1858. Cp. also 798, 1966 [the last two examples are C-verses ending in *drugon*].

15b: Cp. 1103, 2935. Cp. also 2761. Cp. also 1587, 1664.

16a: 2159, 2780. Cp. also 54, 114, 1257 (*longe þrage*). Cp. also 1762,

2030, 2097, 2548, 2571 [this last group of examples consists of a disyllabic adjective (accented on the first syllable) and *hwile*].

17a: 183; 1752. Cp. also 1661, 2875 [these are A-verses ending in *Wealdend*].

18b: Cp. 1588.

19a: Cp. 897, 1847, 2358, 2992. See also 189 (*maga Healfdenes*).

19b: Cp. 2357.

20a: Cp. 2590. For *swa sceal* x *don* see 1172. Cp. also 3077 [all these examples contain *swa sceal* in introductory measures of B- and C-verses].

21a: Cp. 1025, 1089 [these are C-verses with *feohgifte-um*].

21b: Cp. 1479. Cp. also 35, 214, 896. Cp. also 188.

23a: Cp. 853 (*ealdgesiðas*).

25a: Cp. 1420, 2033, 2527 [except for the last, which is a D²-verse, these examples are B-verses consisting of at least the genitive of a noun plus an inflected form of *gehwa*].

Reconsidered Supporting Evidence

1b: *Xst* 367a, *Wan* 44a; *þe in geardagum*, *Chr* 251b; *þone on gearda-gum*, *Bwf* 1354a; *swa hy on geardagum*, *Bwf* 2233a. Cf. *in ealddagum*, *Chr* 303a; *waes on ealddagum*, *SFt.* 1a; *swa hine fyrnda-gum*, *Bwf* 1451b; *on fyrndagum*, *And* 1b.

2a: *þeodcyninges* 2694b, *FAp* 18b; *þeodcyningas*, *Gen* 1965a. Cf. —*cyninga-es-e* in *Bwf*: *woroldcyninga* 1684b, 3180b, *heahcyninges* 1039b, *eorðcyninges* 1155b, *sæcyninga* 2382b. *Frescyninge* 2503b.

3:    Cf. *hu þa æðelingas ellen cyðdon*, *FAp* 3.

3a: *FAp* 3a; *ðus ða æðelingas*, *FAp* 85a; *þa æþelingas*, *Rdl* 49, 7a.

3b: *ellen fremman*, *And* 1208b.

4b: *sceaþena þreate*, *Jul* 672b.

5a: *manigre mægþe* 75a, *manigum mægþa* 1771a.

6b: 1947b.

8a: *weox þa under wolcnum*, *Gen* 1702a. Cf. *wod under wolcnum* 714a, *weold under wolcnum* 1770a, *wand to wolcnum* 1119a; *wridað under wolcnum*, *Phx* 27a, *awyrde under wolcnum*, *Phx* 247a; *geworden under wolcnum*, *Chr* 226a; *gewitaþ under wolcnum*, *Ele*

1271a; See also *wan under wolcnum* (*Bwf* 651a, *DrR* 55a), *wæter under wolcnum* (*Bwf* 1631a), *waðol under wolcnum* (*Fnb* 8a), *wide under wolcnum* (*Gen* 1950a).

9b: 2734a, *Ele* 33a; *ymbsittenda, MBo* 25.14a; *ymbsittendum, PPs* 78.4b, 88.35b. Cf. *ymbstandende, PPs* 140.4b; *ymbstandendra, Gen* 2490b.

10a: Cf. *geond hronrade, Gen* 205a; *on hranrade, And* 266a, 634a, 821a. Cf. *ofer swanrade, Bwf* 200a, *Ele* 996b; *on swonrade, Jul* 675a; *on seglrade, Bwf* 1429b.

10b: *Dan* 153b, *MBo.* 9.45b; *hyran sceoldon, Ele* 367b; *hyran sceoldan, MBo* 1.31a.

11a: *Gen* 1978a.

11b: 2390b; *ac þæt wæs god cyning* 863b. Cf. *þæt wæs an cyning,* 1885b; *þæt wæs frod cyning* 1306b; *þæt is soð cyning, Jul,* 224b; *þæt wæs grim cyning, Deo* 23b; *næs þæt sæne cyning, Wds* 67b.

13a: *Phx* 355a, 647a; *geongre in geardum, Chr* 201a.

14a: *Exo* 88a; *folca to frofre, Ele* 502a; *folcum to frofre, Ele* 1142a, *And* 606a, *Chr* 1421a, *Men* 228a.

15a: 831b, 1858b, *XSt* 74b; *þe we ær drugon, Chr* 615b. Cf. *þe ge lange drugon, Jud* 158b.

15b: Cf. *aldorleasne* 1587a, 3003a, with the meaning "lifeless." The word in this sense seems to appear only in *Beowulf*. *Aldorleas* ("*orphanus*") occurs in the *Lindisfarne Gospel of St. John* (see *BT*, s.v. *aldorleas* and *ealdorleas*). Cf. *hlafordlease, Bwf* 2935b, *And* 405b; *ðeodenlease, Bwf* 1103a.

16a: 2159b, 2780a, *Dan* 660a, *Jul* 674b, *DrR* 24b, *Rdl* 28.9, *MBo* 4.46b. Cf. *gode hwile, DrR* 70b; *lytle hwile, Bwf* 2030b, 2097a, *Gen* 486a, *Glc* 423b, 481b, *Sms* 314a, 369b; *læssan hwile, Bwf* 2571b; *monige hwile, Gen* 634a.

17a: 183a, 1752a, *And* 193a, 539a, *Dan* 13a, *XSt* 24a.

18a: Cf. *Saloman wæs bremra, Sms* 182b.

18b: Cf. *hra wide sprong,* 1588b; *lof wide sprang, FAp* 6b; *lead wide sprong, Jul* 585b.

19a: Cf. *Wælses eafera* 897a, *Hreþles eaferan* 1847b, *Hreðles eafora* 2358a, 2992a; *Sethes eafora, Gen* 1133b; *Adames eaforan, Gen* 1682a; *þares afera, Gen* 2054a; *Iobes eafora, MBo* 26.35a; *Zebedes afera, Men* 136a. And cf. in reversed order: *eaforum Ecgwelan, Bwf*

1710a; *eafora Noes, Gen* 1578a; *eafora þares, Gen* 2834b; *aferan Eadweardes, BrB* 7a.

19b: Cf. *Freslondum on,* 2357b; *eastlandum on, Gen* 1052a; *mearclandum on, Exo* 67b; *feorlondum on, Pnt* 10b.

22b: Cf. *long gewunien, Phx* 481b; *lenge gewunian, Jul* 375b.

23a: *Gen* 2003a.

25a: *þa þe her on mægðe gehwære, Pre* 74a.

II. Beowulf 1473–87

Lord's Analysis
Creed's Analysis
(determined by comparison to *Beowulf* alone)

Beowulf maþelode,   bearn Ecgþeowes:

'Geþenc nu, se mære   maga Healfdenes,

1475   snottra fengel,   nu ic eom siðes fus,

goldwine gumena,   hwæt wit geo spræcon,

gif ic æt þearfe   þinre scolde

aldre linnan,   þæt ðu me a wære

forðgewitenum   on fæder stæle.

1480   Wes þu mundbora   minum magoþegnum,

hondgesellum,   gif mec hild nime;

swylce þu ða madmas,   þe þu me sealdest,

Hroðgar leofa,   Higelace onsend.

Mæg þonne on þæm golde ongitan   Geata dryhten,

1485   geseon sunu Hrædles,   þonne he on þæt sinc starað,

þæt ic gumcystum   godne funde

beaga bryttan,   breac þonne moste.

Lord's Supporting Evidence

(Note: Lord sometimes refers to "measures" in terms of the whole line; thus the first half-line contains measures one and two, the second half-line measures three and four.)

1473:   529, 631, 957, 1473 [sic] 1651, 1817, 1999, 2425 . . . Cf. 371, 1321, 456, 499, 2862, 3076.

     1473a: 405, 2510, 2724 . . . Cf. 286, 348, 360, 925, 1215, 1687, 1840.

     1473b: 2177 . . . Cf. 1550, 2367, 2587, 2398. Cf. also 620, 194.

1474:   Cf. 2587, 2011.

     1474a: Cf. 489, 1782, 2747 for the first measure [these examples are A-verses introduced by a verb plus *nu*]; and 762, 675, 2971 [these are A-verses ending in *se* plus a disyllabic, adjectival noun], and lines 2587, and 2011 . . . for the second measure . . .

     1474b: 189, 2143, 1867, and 2011. . . . Cf. also 1465 and 2587.

1475a: 2156. Cf. 1507, 1400, 2345.

1475b: Cf. for the first measure 251, 946 [these are B-verses introduced by *nu ic*], and also 335, 407, and 2527 [B- and C-verses introduced by *ic eom*]. For the second measure cf. 579 and 1794 [A-verses].

1476a: 1171. Cf. 2419, 2584. . . . Cf. also 120, 467.

1476b: Cf. for the first measure 1186 (*hwæt wit to willan*) and 1707 (*freode, swa wit furðum sprǣcon*). For the second measure cf. 2252, 3126, etc. [these last two examples are relevant only in rhythm].

1477:   . . . Cf. 293 (*swylce ic maguþegnas mine hate*).

       1477a: Cf. for the first measure 1822, 2519, and 1185, 2841, 1140, 944 [all examples have *gif* plus a pronoun, introductory A₃-, B-, and C-verses]. For the second measure cf. 1525, 2709 [*æt þeafe* ends these two A-verses], and cf. also 1456, 2694, 1797, and 2801 [examples of *æt (on) þearfe* or *þearfe* in A- and B-verses].

       1477b: For the third measure cf. 2131, 2095, 1823, 1673 etc. [these examples have *þine, -re* as the first measure of A- or D¹-verses]. For the fourth measure cf. 230, 280, 1034, 1067, etc. Out of nineteen cases of *scullan* observed, all but three are in the fourth measure.

1478a: 2443. Cf. also 680, 1524, 2599, 2924, 661, 1469, 1655, etc. [these examples consist of *ealdre* plus a verb, and are all A-verses]. Cf. also such formulas as 1002, 1565 (*aldres orwena*), 1338 *ealdres scyldig*), etc.

1478b: Cf. 313, 1833, 203, 2161 [these examples are C-verses introduced by *þæt* or *þeah* plus a pronoun]. For the fourth measure cf. also 881 (*swa hie a wǣron*), 754 (*no þy ǣr fram meahte*).

1479a: Cf. 1937 (*handgewriþene*), 59 (*forðgerimed*). It is interesting to note the following from other Anglo-Saxon poems: *Gu.* 1107 [sic] *El.* 1267. *Met.* 1052 [*sic*], *El.* 636.

1479b: Cf 1950, 21 [C-verses introduced by a preposition plus *fæder*]; 1114 (*æt hnæfes ade*) . . . Cf. also *Reb* 11 (*on bearna stæl*), *Gen* 1113 (*on leafes stæl*).

1480a: For the first measure cf. 269, 407, 386, 1226 [these examples have *wes* or *beo þu* as introductions to B- or C-verses]. Cf. also such lines as 2946 (*wæs sio swatswaðu/Sweona ond Geata*) and especially 2779 (*þam ðara maðma/mundbora wæs*) . . . For the second measure cf. 349, 373, 3046 etc. [all these have inflected disyllabic compounds as the second measures of C-verses introduced by a verb].

1480b: Cf. the following examples in [1477b] above: 2131, 2095, 1823, and 1673; and in [1477] above: 293. Cf. also 2804, 2797, and for "magoþegn" in the second measure, 2079.

1481a: "Hondgesellum" is a *hapax legomenon* in *Beowulf*. Cf., however, the many instances in which the first half-line is taken up by such a compound: 1495, 1511, 1520, 1526, etc.

1481b: Cf. 452. Cf. also 447, 1491.

1482a: Cf. 293. . . . For the first measure cf. 757, 1156, and 2869, and 2767 [these examples are B- and C-verses introduced by *swylce* plus a pronoun]. For the second measure cf. 2490, and cf. also 2788, 2779, etc. . . .

1482b: . . . the following involve either the verb "sellan" or a pronoun before the verb: 72, 1271, 2182, 2490, 417, and 563. Cf. also 1751, etc.

1483a: Cf. 2745, 1216, 1758, . . . 1854, 1987, 2663. Cf. also 618 (*leodum leofne*) and its opposite 3079 (*leofne þeoden*), etc.

1483b: Cf. 5, 690, 884, etc. [These examples are relevant in rhythm and, with minor qualifications, in syntax]. Cf. also 452 . . .

1484:   Since the rhythmic pattern of the first half-line of this line is found here only, the line as a whole could not be considered as either formula or formulaic, although the second half of the line is a very common formula.

> 1484b: 1831, 2483, 2560, 2576, 2991, and the reverse: 2402, 2901. Cf. also 2419 and 2584 (*goldwine Geata*), etc.

1485:   Since the rhythmic patterns in both halves of this line are rare . . . the line as a whole must be considered nonformulaic.

> 1485a: . . . For the second measure cf. 1847, 2191, 2358, 2992 . . . and 454, which are all cases of the reverse order for the sake of alliteration. [These examples, A-verses and one B-verse, contain the name *Hreðel* as the first or second measure]. Cf. also 2025, and many other formulas with "sunu" as a base: 524, 645, 980, 1009, etc. Cf. also other related rhythmical patterns (D^1) such as 758, etc.

> 1485b: . . . This is the only case of this pattern in *Beowulf,* but cf. also the related patterns 996, 2864. Cf also 2796 and 1603.

1486a: Cf. 260, 378, 556, 571, and 894. [These examples are C-verses whose second measures are compounds in the genitive case.]

1486b: Cf. 2789 (*driorigne fand*), 1810, 1969, 199 [The last three examples have *godne* as the first measure of A-verses.], and for another instance of "funde" in the second measure of the half-line cf. 1415 . . .

1487a: 35, 352 . . .

1487b: Cf. 1177, 894, 3100, 2241 [the last three examples are *brucan moste*], and for the position of "breac" cf. also 1216 and 2162. [In these examples, *bruc* is the first word in an A- and an E-verse.]

Creeds's Supporting Evidence

1473: 529, 631, 957, 1383, 1651, 1817, 1999, 2425.

    1473a: 405, 529, 631, 957, 1383, 1651, 1817, 1999, 2425, 2510, 2724. See also above, 1473.

    1473b: 529, 631, 957, 1383, 1651, 1817, 1999, 2177, 2425. See also above, 1473.

1474: Cp. 2011. Cp. also 2857 [sic].

    1474a: Cp. 762. See also above, 1474.

    1474b: 189, 2143. See also above, 1474.

1475a: 2156. Cp. also 1400.

1476a: 1171, 1602.

1476b: Cp. 1707. See also 1215.

1477a: Cp. 1525, 2694, 2709. Cp. also 1456 [these examples contain *æt þearfe* (*on þearfe*) as vital parts of A- and B-verses].

1477b: 1 sg. 965.

1478a: Gen. 2443.

1478b: See 203 (*þeah he him leof wære*).

1479b: See 21.

1480a: Cp. 2779 (*mundbora wæs*).

1480b: See 293 [I.e. p. 231: Cp. 1405, 1480, 2079. Cp. also 408].

1481a: Cp. 2169, 2596.

1481b: 452.

1482: Cp. 2490.

    1482a: See above, 1482.

    1482b: 3 sg. 2490. Cp. also 1370 (*ær he feorh seleð*).

1483a: See 1216 [i.e. p. 287: 1758. Cp. also 1854, 1987, 2663. Cp. also 1483, 2745].

1483b: Cp. 452. See also 194 (*Higelaces þegn*)

1484a: Cp. 2032 (*mæg þæs þonne ofþyncan*).

1484b: 2560, 2576, 2991, ac. sg. 1831, dat. sg 2483. See also 1050 (*eorla drihten*).

1485b: Cp. 996 (*þara þe on swylc stara∂*).

1486a: Cp. 2453 [sic. 2543a is *gumcystum god*].

1487a: 35, 352.

1487b: Cp. 1177.

Reconsidered Supporting Evidence

1473: 529, 631, 957, 1383, 1651, 1817, 1999, 2425. Cf. *Hro∂gar maþelode, helm Scyldinga*, 371, 456, 1321; *Wiglaf maþelode, Weohstanes sunu*, 2862, 3076; *Unfer∂ maþelode, Ecglafes bearn*, 499.

    1473a: In addition to 1473: 405, 2510, 2724. Cf. in addition to 1473: *Wulfgar maþelode*, 348a, 360a; *Hro∂gar maþelode*, 925a, 1687a, 1840a; *weard maþelode*, 286a; *Wealh∂eo maþelode*, 1215a.

    1473b: In addition to 1473: 2177. Cf. in addition to 1473: *sunu Ecg∂eowes*, 1550b, 2367b, 2398b; *sunu Healfdenes*, 268a, 344b, 645a, 1040b; 1652b, 1699a, 2147a; *sunu Ecglafes*, 590b, 980b, 1808a; *sunu (suna) Ohtheres*, 2380b, 2394b, 2612a; *sunu Beanstanes*, 524a; *sunu Hygelaces*, 2386b; *sunu Wonredes*, 2971b; *maga (mago) Healfdenes*, 189b, 1474b, 1867a, 2011b, 2143b; *mago Ecglafes*, 1465b; *maga Ecg∂eowes*, 2587b; *byre Wihstanes*, 2907b, 3110b.

1474: Cf. *sona me se mæra mago Healfdenes*, 2011; *þæt se mære maga Ecg∂eowes*, 2587.

    1474b: 189b, 2143b; *mago Healfdenes*, 1867a, 2011b. Cf. above, 1473b.

1475a: 2156a. Cf. *wisa fengel*, 1400b; *hringa fengel*, 2345b; *hringa þengel*, 1507a.

1476a: 1171a, 1602a. Cf. *goldwine Geata*, 2419a, 2584a.

1477b: Cf. *minum scolde*, 965b.

1478a: *ealdres linnan*, 2443b.

1481a: Cf. *hondgesteallan,* 2169a, 2596b.

1481b: 452b. Cf. *gif mec deað nimeð,* 447b; *oþðe mec deað nimeð,* 1491b; *se þe hine deað nimeð,* 441b.

1482:   Cf. *ic him þa maðmas þe he me sealde,* 2490.

> 1482b: Cf. *ðe him God sealde,* 1271b, 2182b; *swylc him God sealde,* 72b; *þæs þe him ær God sealde,* 1751b.

1483a: Cf. *Beowulf leofa,* 1216b, 1758b; *Wiglaf leofa,* 2745a; *leofa Beowulf,* 1854b, 1987b, 2663a.

1483b: Cf. *onsend Higelace,* 452a.

1484b: 1831a, 2560b, 2576a, 2991b; *Geata dryhtne,* 2483a. Cf. *dryhten Geata,* 2402a, 2901a.

1487a: 35a, 352a.

1487b: Cf. *bruc þenden þu mote,* 1177b.

III. Elene 1–21

Diamond's Analysis
(determined by comparison to the signed poems of Cynewulf)

þa wæs agangen   geara hwyrftum

tu hund ond þreo   geteled rimes

swylce þrittig eac   þinggemearces

wintra for worulde   þæs þe wealdend God

5   acenned wearð   cyninga wuldor

in middangeard   þurh mennisc heo

soðfæstra leoht;   þa wæs syxte gear

Constantines   caserdomes

þæt he Romwara   in rice wearð

10   ahæfen hildfruma   to hereteman.

Wæs se leodhwata   lindgeborga

eorlum arfæst,   æðelinges weox

rice under roderum;   he wæs riht cyning,

guðwearð gumena.   Hine God trymede

15   mærðum ond mihtum   þæt he manegum wearð

geond middangeard   mannum to hroðer

werþeodum to wræce   syððan wæpen ahof

wið hetendum.   Him wæs hild boden,

wiges woma;   werod samnodan

20   Huna leode   ond Hreðgotan,

foron fyrdhwate   Francan ond Hugas. . . .

Diamond's Supporting Evidence

1a: Cp. *Beo* 2821. The phrase *þa wæs* is a formulaic introduction to A₃-, B-, and C-verses. For other such A₃-verses cp. *Ele* 144; 194; 282; 894, 967; 1043; 1125; *Jul* 32, 237; *Jul* 38; *Jul* 236; *Jul* 287; *Jul* 635 [a list of B- and C-verses introduced by *þa wæs* follows, but is here omitted].

1b: Cf. *Ele* 648, *Jul* 693, *Chr* 1035 (all in the on-verse). A formulaic system with substitution in order to avoid having double alliteration in the off-verse.

2a–b: A formulaic verse-pair. Cp. *Ele* 634 (*tu hund oððe ma geteled rime*).

3a: See *FA* 50a [i.e. p. 109; for the system *swylce* x *eac* . . . cp. *Ele* 3; *Chr* 145; *Dan* 506; *Bru* 19; *Bru* 30; *DRd* 92].

4a: For A-verses ending with the phrase *for weorlde* cp. *Ele* 978; *Jul* 570.

5a–b: A verse-pair formula. *Ele* 178.

    5a: Also *Ele* 775, *Chr* 444.

    5b: Also *Jul* 279; *Chr* 508; *And* 171, 555, 899, 1141 [sic]: *Jud* 155. For a formulaic system with substitution for the sake of alliteration, cp. further *Ele* 186.

6a: *Ele* 774; *Chr* 452, 787.

6b: Cp. *Chr* 721; cp. also *Chr* 657.

7b: See 1a, above.

8a: For this name filling an entire *A*-verse, cp. *Ele* 79, 103, 1007; *Ele* 145.

9a: *Romware* is a formula which gives the second measure of a C-verse. Cp. *Ele* 40; *Ele* 46; *Ele* 59; *Ele* 981.

11a: [Note: this verse is not underlined in Diamond's analysis, although underlining was certainly intended.] A formulaic system of compounds of *hwæt* (inflected) conveying within the limits of the second measure of a C-verse the idea "bold," "brave." The substitutions in the first element of the compounds are for alliteration. Cp. *Ele* 292; *Chr* 385; *Dan* 353 [sic]; *Aza* 67; *Ele* 1178; *And* 8; *Chr* 429; *Exo* 124; *Dan* 357.

12b: The genitive singular of *æðeling* will combine with a monosyllabic third singular preterite verb to form an E-verse. Cp. *Ele* 885; *Ele* 1197.

13a: *Ele* 147, 631. For other A-verses ending with the phrase *under roderum,* cp. *Ele* 46, *Ele* 803; *Ele* 918; *Ele* 1234; *Chr* 484, 526.

13b: For a system of C-verse *þæt wæs* (*is*) x *cyning,* where *x* is a monosyllabic adjective, cp. *Jul* 224; *Bwf* 11, 2390; *Bwf* 863; *Bwf* 1885; *Deo* 23. Cp. also *MBo* 26, 35.

15b: See *FAp* 52a [i.e. p. 109; cf. *Ele* 15, 501; *And* 960].

16a: See *FAp* 7b [i.e. p. 99: *Ele* 434, 917; *Chr.* 105, 698, 1046; *And* 224, 345, 701, 1323, 1372, 1718; *Exo* 2, 48, 286; *Dan* 105; *Pho* 4; *MPs* 58,13, 137,6, 144,2. Cp. *Ele* 6, 774, *Chr* 452, 787, *XSt* 438, 474; *And*

1502; *Pho* 640; *Ele* 16, 1176; *Chr* 644; *XSt* 271, 582; *Glc* 501; *Pho* [sic]; *Bwf* 75, 1771; *Wan* 75; *Gfm* 28 *DrR* 104; *Pra* 32; *Jul* 3].

16b: See *FAp* 95b [i.e. p. 117: *Jul* 416]. A noun in the dative case (or an adjective used as a noun) will combine with the phrase *to hroðre* (*hroðor*) to make an A-verse. Cp. *Ele* 16; *Ele* 1159; *Chr* 623; *Chr* 414; *Bwf* 2448.

18a: *Bwf* 3004, *Jul* 663.

19a: *Jul* 576.

19b: *Ele* 60. For a formulaic system with substitution for the sake of alliteration, cp. *Ele* 55.

20a: *Ele* 128.

21a: See *FAp* 12a [i.e p. 101: *Bwf* 1641, 2476]. *Fierdhwæt* (inflected) is a formula which gives the second measure of either a C- or a D-verse. Cp. the C-verses *Ele* 1178; *And* 8; and the D-verse *Ele* 21.

Reconsidered Evidence

1b: Cf. *geara gongum, Ele* 648a, *Jul* 693a.

2b: *geteled rime, Ele* 634b.

5:    *Ele* 178.

   5a: In addition to 5, above: *Ele* 775a, *Chr* 444a.

   5b: In addition to 5, above: *Jul* 279b. Cf. *beorna wuldor, Ele* 186b.

6a: *Ele* 774b; *Chr* 452a, 787a.

6b: Cf. *ond þær mennisc hiw, Chr* 721b; cf. *in monnes hiw, Chr* 657a.

8a: *Constantinus, Ele* 79a, 103a, 1007a; *Constantino, Ele* 145a.

13a: *Ele* 147a, 631a. Cf. *rincas under roderum, Ele* 46a; *swylce rec under roderum, Ele* 803a; *ræd under roderum, Ele* 918a; cf. *rode under roderum, Ele* 1234a; cf. *folc under roderum, Chr.* 484b, 526b.

13b: Cf. *þæt is soð cyning, Jul* 224b.

15b: *þæt he manegum wearð, Ele* 501b. Cf. *þær manegum wearð, FAp* 52a.

16a: *Ele* 1176a, *Chr* 644b. Cf. *ofer middangeard, Ele* 434a, 917a, *Chr* 698a, *FAp* 7b; *in middangeard,* see above, 6a; *se geond middangeard, Jul* 3b.

16b: Cf. *dugoðum to hroðer, Ele* 1159a. Cf. *weormum to hroðre, FAp* 95b.

18a: *wið hettendra, Jul* 663a.

19a: *wiges womum, Jul* 576a.

19b: *Ele* 60b. *Cf. mægen samnode, Ele* 55b.

20a: *Ele* 128a.

IV. Elene 1256b–76a

Diamond's Analysis
(determined by comparison to
all surviving Old English poetry)

A wæs sæcg oð ðæt
cynssed cearwelmum, ᚳ drusende
þeah he in medohealle maðmas þege,
aeplede gold. ᚣ gnornode,
ᚾ gefera nearusorge dreah,
enge rune þær him ᛖ fore
milpaðas mæt, modig þrægde,
wirum gewlenced, ᚹ is geswiðrad,
gomen æfter gearum, geogoð is gecyrred,
ald onmedla. ᚢ wæs geara
geogoðhades glæm; nu synt geardagas
æfter fyrstmearce forð gewitene,
lifwynne geliden swa ᛚ toglideð,

flodas gefysde.   ⊦ æghwam bið

1270   læne under lyfte;   landes frætwe,

gewitaþ under wolcnum   winde geliccost

þoonne he for hæleðum   hlud astigeð,

wæðeð be wolcnum,   wedende færeð,

ond eft semninga   swige gewyrðeð

1275   in nedcleofan   nearwe geheaðrod,

þream forþrycced; . . .

Diamond's Supporting Evidence

1257b: Any trisyllabic form of *drusian* is a formula which gives the second measure of a D-verse. Cp. *Glc* 1379; *Bwf* 1630. [But this is not true of *Glc* 1061a, *drusendne hyge* (an E-verse) or *Pho* 268a, *forþon he drusende* (a C-verse).]

1258a: Cp. *Wid* 55, *GfM* 69; *Wan* 27; *Bwf* 638.

1258b: For a formulaic system with substitution for the sake of alliteration, cp. *Jul* 687.

1259a: *Jul* 688, *Pho* 506. [Note: this verse is not underlined in Diamond's analysis.]

1259b: The preterite of *gnornian* (or, indeed, of any second-class weak verb with a long root vowel) is a formula which gives the second measure of a D-verse. Cp. *Glc* 429; *Bwf* 1117; *Gen* 770. [This is not true of *Xst* 279a, *swa gnornedon* (a C-verse).]

1260b: Cp. *Bwf* 422.

1263b: See 698b, above (i.e. p. 249: Cp. *Ele* 1263b; *Ele* 917].

1264a: For another A-verse ending with the phrase *æfter gearum* cp. *Pho* 258.

1264b: See 1060b, above [i.e. p. 276; see 503b above. Cp. also *Ele* 1264; *And* 36 (*hyge wæs oncyrred*)]. [*Ele* 503b is an A-verse.]

1266a: For a formulaic system with substitution in order to avoid double alliteration in the off-verse, cp. *Jul* 168.

1266b: *gear-dagas* is a formula which gives the second measure of a C-verse. Cp. *MPs* 89, 10.

1267a: See 1033a, above [i.e. p. 275: *Ele* 1267, *And* 133, *Pho* 223].

1268b: Cp. *FAp* 102.

1269a: *Chr* 985.

1270a: *Glc* 120. For A-verses ending with the phrase *under lyfte, cp. Pho* 39; *And* 420; *Glc* 761; *Glc* 1289; *Glc* 1308; *Chr* 219; *Rid* 84, 31. The phrase is as colorless as *on geardum* and seems to have been used merely to fill an A-verse.

1270b: *Pho* 150, 508; *Glc* 1282. For a formulaic system with substitution for the sake of alliteration, cp. *Chr* 805, *MPa* 101, 22; *Pan* 48; *Pho* 257; *Men* 207.

1271a: For A-verses ending with the phrase *under wolcnum,* cp. *Chr* 226; *Chr* 588; *Gen* 1058; *Gen* 1231; *Gen* 1438; *Gen* 1702; *Gen* 1950; *Pho* 27; *Pho* 247; *Bwf* 651; *And* 837; *Glc* 1280; *DRd* 55; *Bwf* 714, 1631, 1770, *Fin* 8; *And* 93; *MBo* 1, 76; 7, 26; *Sol* 103. The phrase is as colorless as *under lyfte* or *on geardum* and seems to have been used merely to fill out an A-verse.

1271b: *Gelic* (inflected) is a formula which gives the second measure of an A-verse and the last syllable of the first measure, with a noun in the dative as the rest of the first measure. Cp. *XSt* 162; *MPs* 182, 5; *Ele* 1320; *MPs* 65,5; *Bwf* 218; *And* 497; *Pho* 585; *Run* 11; *MBo* 20; 211, 217; *MPs* 103, 3; *Bwf* 1608; *Bwf* 727; *MPs* 101, 3; *MPs* 26.2; *Pho* 302; *Pho* 610; *XSt* 306; *MPs* 123, 3; *And* 953; *MPs* 57, 6; *And* 1145; *Dan* 345 [sic]; *MBo* 25, 18 [exceptions to the consistency of this observation are *Sol* 312b, *slæp bið deaðe gelicost,* and *Phx* 424a, is *þon gelicast*].

1272a: For other A-verses ending with the phrase *for(e) hæleðum,* cp. *Exo* 252, *Chr* 669. For related phrases (*fore rincum, for weorodum*) . . . . see *FAp* 11a, 55a. [These lists are omitted.]

1273b: A present participle will combine with *færeþ* to make an E-verse. Cp. *MBo* 20, 216; *Rid* 3, 48.

1274a: See 1109a, above [i.e. p. 280: *Jul* 242, 614 (*ða cwom semninga*)

. . . Cp. *Ele* 1274; *Chr* 491; *Bwf* 644, 1640; *Chr* 899; *Wha* 27; *And* 464; *And* 820; *MPs* 63, 4; *MPs* 72, 15; *Rid* 40, 10].

1275a: See 711b, above [i.e. p. 250: *niedclifan* is a formula which gives the second measure of a C-verse. Cp. *Ele* 1275; *Jul* 240].

1276a: *Glc* 1198; *Jul* 520; *Chr* 1445.

Reconsidered Evidence

1258a: *on meoduhealle*, *GfM* 69a; *þone þe in meoduhealle*, *Wan* 27a; *in meoduhealle*, *Wid* 55b. Cf. *on þisse meoduhealle*, *Bwf* 638a.

1258b: Cf. *beagas þegon*, *Jul* 687b.

1259a: *Phx* 506b, *Jul* 688a. Note the similarity of *þeah he in meoduhealle maðmas þege,/æplede gold* (*Ele* 1258a–59a) and *ofer beorsetle beagas þegon,/æpplede gold* (*Jul* 687a–88a).

1260b: Cf. *nearoþearfe dreah*, *Bwf* 422b.

1262a: Cf. *mæton milpaðas*, *Exo* 171a. The phrase may well be formulaic; but the sequence of words, the different rhythm, may just as well be the deliberate choice of the "singer."

1263a: Cf. *wire geweorþad*, *Rdl* 71.5. *Gewlencan* is recorded elsewhere only in prose (see *BT*, s.v.). In the context of *Elene* it seems too loaded with particular meaning to be linked in formular status with this phrase from the *Riddle*.

1263b: Cf. *mægen wæs geswiðrod*, *Ele* 698b; *min is geswiðrod*, *Ele* 917b.

1264a: Cf. *gomel æfter gearum*, *Phx* 258a.

1264b: Cf. *nama wæs gecyrred*, *Ele* 1060b.

1266a: Cf. *geoguðhades blæd*, *Jul* 168b.

1267a: *Ele* 1033a, *Phx* 223a, *And* 133a.

1267b: *MBo* 10.52b; *forðgewitena*, *Glc* 1134b; *forðgewitenum*, *Bwf* 1479a.

1268b: *efne swa* ⸽ *toglideð*, *FAp* 102b.

1269a: *flodas afysde*, *Chr* 985a.

1270a: *Glc* 120a. Cf. *leaf under lyfte*, *Phx* 39a. Cf. *lufað under lyfte*, *Glc* 761a; *tolysed under lyfte*, *Glc* 1289a; *belifd under lyfte*, *Glc* 1308a; *lærde under lyfte*, *And* 420a. Cf. *eorl under lyfte*, *Chr* 219b; *þæs þe under lyfte*, *Rdl* 84.31.

1270b: *Phx* 150b, 508a; *Glc* 1282a. Cf. *eorþan frætwe*, *PPs* 101.22a; *eorþan frætwa*, *Chr* 805a; *eorþan frætwum*, *Pan* 48b; *foldan frætuwa*, *Men* 207a, *Phx* 257a.

1271a: See note *8a* of *Beowulf*, pp. 164–65.

1271b: Cf. *wedere gelicost*, Dan 346b; *fugole gelicost*, And 497b, Bwf 218b, Phx 585b; *wættre geliccost*, And 953b; *wexe gelicost*, And 1145b; *attre gelicost*, XSt 162a; *ligge gelicost*, Bwf 727a; *ise gelicost*, Bwf 1608b; *stane gelicast*, Phx 302b; *hweole gelicost*, MBo 20.211a, 217a, *wuhta gelicost*, MBo 25.18b; *wætere gelicost*, PPs 57.6; *earne gelicast*, PPs 102.5b; *englum gelice*, Ele 1320a; *eorðan gelice*, PPs 65.5b; *hyde gelice*, PPs 103.3b; *smece gelice*, PPs 101.3a; *sunnan gelice*, XSt 306b, Phx 601b; *wætre gelice*, PPs 123.3b.

1273b: Cf. *winnende fareð*, Rdl 3.48b; *scriðende færeð*, MBo 20.216b; but cf. *farað feohtende*, Rdl 3.46a

1275a: Cf. *ond of nydcleofan*, Ele 711b; *in þam nydclafan*, Jul 240a.

1276a: Glc 1198a; *þream forþrycte*, Jul 520a; *þream biþrycton*, Chr 1445a.

These four groups of analytic information, like the charts of epithets and formulae, may be statistically abridged by a smaller table, so that the differences between the results of two distinct sets of definitions of formula and system may be comprehended at a glance.

		Number of Verses	Number of Verses Underscored	Percentage of Verses Underscored
I.	Magoun's Analysis	50	37	74
	Reconsidered Analysis	50	26	52
	Creed's Analysis	50	28	56
	Reconsidered Analysis	50	15	30
II.	Lord's Analysis	30	29	97
	Creed's Analysis	30	25	83
	Reconsidered Analysis	30	15	50
III.	Diamond's Analysis	42	24	57
	Reconsidered Analysis	42	16	38
IV.	Diamond's Analysis	40	23	58
	Reconsidered Analysis	40	19	48

The most conservative of these scholars, Robert Diamond, is of course statistically closest to results obtained by applying the definitions of the formula and formulaic system set forth in this paper. The divergences between these results and those urged by Magoun, Creed, and Lord, however—divergences from 50 to 20 percent—are not only significant but dramatic. They are such as to make objections to Magoun's theory of oral-formulaic composition in Old English poetry more than objections to degree. All poetry is to some extent of and for the ear. The difference between texts whose origin was recitation by an illiterate singer and those composed pen in hand by a literate poet must be in the percentage of repetitive language. It is reasonable to argue, as a few scholars have, that Magoun and his followers have gone too far, and to take exception to the degree of formulaic texture that he and others discover in Old English poetry; it is also reasonable to argue that a significant lowering of the degree of formulaic content may necessitate a significant revision or qualification of the theory itself, that a difference in degree causes enough difference in kind to leave the critical question of oral composition open beyond any conclusion that is not fundamentally tentative. Compared with the burden of proof compiled with consistency and circumspection by Parry for the Homeric poems and by Lord for the Serbo-Croatian poems, the proof amassed by Magoun, Creed, Diamond, Nicholson, and others less concerned is too thin, and especially too permissive, to enable Old English scholars to support the Parry-Lord thesis in Old English poetry as logically as it may be supported in Greek and Serbo-Croatian poetry. If statistics are arrived at by methods similar to Parry's, statistics for the Old English poems themselves are simply not conclusive. The primary evidence is not enough from which to form a picture of the illiterate singer and the whole psychology of his composing in his oral art.

III

If primary evidence is inconclusive, secondary evidence in other ways is equally so. The involved problems of archaeology, contemporary accounts, the history of writing, and the critical value of analogy are far beyond the scope of this book; yet it is necessary to consider a few matters of secondary pertinence here because of the nature of the evidence used in oral-formulaic analyses. These matters may be said to have one problematical center, Cynewulf; and it is in relation to Cynewulf and scholarly treatment of Cynewulf that they will be discussed.

For the purposes of a general exposition of the oral-formulaic theory of composition in Old English poetry, any one of the longer signed poems of Cynewulf offers a good and illustrative companion to *Beowulf,* and it is for this reason and for its apparent attachment to learning that *Elene,* rather than, say, *Genesis* or *Christ and Satan* was chosen for specific consideration in this and the preceding chapter. *Elene,* like *Juliana* and the *Fates of the Apostles* is a fairly close translation of a Latin prose original; and like these other poems and *Christ II, Elene* concludes with a runic signature of the poet Cynewulf's name. Yet for all this bias toward the literate, the Cynewulfian poems are, according to Robert Diamond's thoroughly documented dissertation, highly formulaic. According to Magoun's method of substantiating the theory, these poems are so highly formulaic that they must have been orally composed. The near apothegm, established by Parry and emphasized by Lord, is that if a text abounds in formulae then it is of oral composition, and if a song is orally composed then it abounds in formulae. The corollary then understood by both Parry and Lord was that only an illiterate singer could compose an oral poem.

Yet there was Cynewulf who, aside from an apparent Latinity, certainly knew how to spell and certainly made his poems of traditional phraseology. This potential dilemma for criticism was first attacked by Magoun, and his solution has been both confronted and reiterated by all who accept his theory, and even by some mild dissenters. Only Lord has spoken out against Magoun's solution. According to the bare possibilities of the textual evolution of poems, 1) either a poet writes his own poem, or 2) he dictates it to a machine, or 3) he dictates it to a scribe. If a poem was orally composed many centuries ago, then the first two possibilities are presumed closed. Indeed the whole argument of Parry and Lord and some other classical scholars has favored the third possibility for the "first text" of the Homeric poems. The argument is based both upon historical study and upon, one may say, a psychology of composition. Archaeological and paleontological evidence, as it is understood at the present time, would place Homer and the first "classical" Greek writing in the same century—the eighth B.C. Then too, it seems by proof of analogy that an oral poet (that is, a singer brought up within and proficient in the oral tradition of poetic composition), once he has learned letters not only loses his skill in rapid oral composition but never attains a literary skill of any dependability. Homer is thought too fine and developed to be the beginning of a written tradition rather than the end, and apex, of an oral one.

With Cynewulf, however, the fact of literacy is hardly arguable. How then, did he compose, formulae and all? Magoun both saw and began to answer this question in his first essay on the oral-formulaic technique.

> Mention of Cynewulf raises a question concerning the relation between lettered persons and orally composed poetry. Not all Anglo-Saxon Christian poetry needs to have been composed by lettered singers [Magoun has not previously stated that composers of this Christian poetry were or were not literate]—witness the story of Cædman. Any good unlettered singer who had translated for, or expounded to, him the *Apocryphal Gospel of St. Matthew and St. Andrew* could easily have composed *Andreas*. But Cynewulf was surely a lettered person, else how could he have conceived a plan to assure mention of his name in prayers by means of runic signatures which depend upon a knowledge of spelling and reading for their

efficiency? If, however, the narrative parts of his poems prove on testing to be formulaic, one must assume that those parts at least he composed in the traditional way. That he subsequently got them written down, whether dictating to himself, as it were, or to another person—possibly a more convenient procedure—is beside the point. In any event there would be no conflict with, or contradiction to, tradition.[47]

In a later article Magoun supposes that a singer like Caedmon, presumably illiterate, learned the narratives of his songs by listening to his literate friends, the monks; whereas "A lettered singer, say Cynewulf, writing in the oral tradition—probably the only way an Anglo-Saxon could conceive of composing narrative verse—might, of course, dictate to himself, though this would presumably be an uncommon if not awkward procedure." [48] All of Magoun's further remarks on this subject have carried assumptions that learning and literacy are not incompatible with the oral composition of poetry. In comparing Old English Christian poetry disadvantageously with Old English heroic poetry, he mentions the "careless care and giddy cunning of most lettered poets writing isochronous verse";[49] and his thoughts about some passages in *Beowulf* demand a hypothetical "anthologizing scribe." [50]

The basic concept of a "transition period" during which "transitional texts" would be produced was formulated by Bowra, and to some extent by Wade-Gery, as an escape from the Homeric illiteracy imposed by Parry's thesis.[51] Homeric scholars are not troubled by a Cynewulf. In Old English studies, the hypothesis of a transitional text, a text *written* by a *singer,* seems all the more necessary a solution to paradoxical premises. As a solution it has been accepted as a matter of course by those who, for the most part, accept Magoun's theory of the oral-formulaic composition of Old English poetry.[52] Adrien Bonjour has written

47. "The Oral-Formulaic Character of Anglo-Saxon Narrative Poetry," *Speculum, 28* (1953), 460–61.

48. "Bede's Story of Cædman," *Speculum, 30* (1955), 60.

49. "Some Notes on Old English Poetry," in *Studies in Medieval Literature in Honor of Albert Croll Baugh,* p. 281.

50. "Beowulf B: a Folk Poem on Beowulf's Death," *Early English and Norse Studies Presented to Hugh Smith,* p. 131.

51. For Bowra's first application of this concept to Old English poetry, see *Heroic Poetry,* p. 241.

52. E.g. William Whallon, "The Diction of *Beowulf," PMLA, 76* (1961), 311; Jackson K. Campbell, "Oral Poetry in the *Seafarer," Speculum, 35* (1960), 88; John C. Mac-

of the concept of a transitional period (productive of transitional texts)
as if it were a matter of inevitability: after suggesting that the first Old
English religious poems of the first clergy were oral chants, he goes on
to say,

> C'est d'ailleurs à cette époque, ou à peu près, que l'intervention de
> l'écriture tend à modifier la situation et crée un stade de transition
> où des chanteurs, tout en continuant de composer dans le style tradi-
> tionnelle, sont aussi parfois des lettres et commencent à s'aider de
> la plume. Nous y reviendrons puisque le *Beowulf* est à notre avis,
> du moins tel qu'il nous est parvenu, précisément un témoignage de
> ce stade intermédiaire.[53]

Bonjour continues by arguing not only that the learned and lettered poet
composed in the traditional style but that by doing so he did not change
the style. As for Cynewulf, he could only have *written* the runic passages: "Et pourtant ils offrent tous les traits caractéristiques du style
formulaire!"[54]

The suppositions, both mentioned and inferred, in the concept of
transitional periods and transitional texts were not truly scrutinized in
print until the publication of Lord's *The Singer of Tales* in 1960. In an
earlier article Lord considered the subject,[55] but in his book he takes a
definite stand against the probability—one may say the psychological
probability—of such a hybrid form of composition as that hypothetically
produced by a literate man writing worthy oral poetry. Lord presents his
objections strongly and carefully; and because the implications of a
"transitional text" have not been fully explored by Old English scholars,
Lord's objections need reiteration. In his discussion of writing and the
oral tradition,[56] Lord described the characteristics of the oral-dictated
text, that is, the song sung slowly by an illiterate singer to a scribe. Lord
insists these are not "transitional texts," or texts thought up by "diplo-
matic Homerists who on the one hand cannot deny the oral nature of

---

Galliard, "The Complex Art of *Beowulf*," a review of Brodeur's *The Art of Beowulf*, in
MP, 59 (1961–62), 277–78.

53. "Beowulf et l'épopée anglo-saxonne," *La Table ronde*, *132* (1958), 141. See also
Bonjour, "Poésie héroïque du moyen âge et critique littéraire," *Romania*, *78* (1957),
252–53, where Bonjour supposes *Beowulf* to be midway between an oral and a literary
composition.

54. "Beowulf et l'épopée," p. 184.

55. "Homer's Originality: Oral Dictated Texts," *TAPA*, *84* (1953), 129–31.

56. *Singer*, pp. 124–38.

the Homeric poems and, on the other, cannot tolerate the unwashed illiterate." Lord then mentions the attractiveness of the idea to certain medieval scholars, and queries whether it is possible for a text to be *written* by an oral poet, or for a poet to think two such different ways simultaneously. Lord meets his own query: "I believe that the answer must be in the negative, because the two techniques are, I submit, contradictory and mutually exclusive." [57] This statement attaches a footnote of further emphasis:

> I thus return to the conviction . . . It seems to me that there can be no compromise or middle ground, although there will be lots of texts that may *look* transitional, cases in which we simply do not have enough information to tell.[58]

Lord, however, thinks it only inevitable that between oral and literary periods of compositional practice there should be a *period* of "transition," and he seems to admit into the realm of possibility the young singer who learned to write in his old age.[59] "Transitional texts" in Magoun's conception do, of course, exist. Lord has watched some of these "autograph texts," as he calls them, made before his eyes. Yet without fail, Lord insists, such texts do injustice to both singer and song because of the mixed traditions, and only inferior works are forthcoming. In direct reference to *Beowulf*, Lord, less uncompromising in his position, is still consistent:

> Analysis of *Beowulf* indicates oral composition. The corpus of Anglo-Saxon poetry is so small that it is scarcely possible for us to know its tradition well enough to assert that *Beowulf* breaks away from that tradition of formula and theme. It seems to be more logical to assume that a text so analyzed belongs to the category of oral dictated texts unless one has sufficient evidence from the tradition itself on which to base a judgment that it is "transitional." [60]

Both Lord's adamant reservation about "transitional texts" and his thought about "transitional periods" should be reformed in the light of Adam Parry's cogent and imaginative argument on the subject (see above, pp. 43–44). It now seems clear that the inferior poems which Lord

57. Ibid., p. 129.
58. Ibid., p. 289, n. 9.
59. Ibid., pp. 129–30; see also 134, 149.
60. Ibid., p. 200.

explained by a theory of compositional incompatibility may more reasonably be explained by a theory of cultural incompatibility. Adam Parry persuasively argues that whereas literacy to a modern Guslar means journalese and not a literary preservation of an epic past, the change in Homer's time from singing to writing poetry would have entailed no such devastating change. The argument renders ineffectual Lord's theory that oral and literary practices productive of good poems are mutually exclusive.

Leaving aside the problem of the degree of cultural change a literate culture imposes on an oral one, it is only logical to assume that during any such change there must be a "transitional period" in which "transitional texts" (poems written by singers) are conceivable. Once Lord's objections are dispelled, the difficulty with the theory of "transitional texts" is not its reasonableness, but its practicality. When the period of transition is in the largely unknown past, how are we to identify an orally composed text? How are we to distinguish the methods of composition of extremely conventional styles in times and places where either oral or literary composition is possible? In such cases "transitional texts" could be poems written in oral style as well as poems sung in literary style, and such distinctions are of course meaningless.

For Cynewulf, however, the distinctions are not meaningless. In the first place, his poetry is less formulaic than Magoun and Diamond have argued. In the second place, the conception of Cynewulf as a singer and writer of good "oral poetry" is less probable than a conception of a learned poet writing in a traditional, conventional diction which doubtless had its origin in oral song, but which had a literary continuance in manuscripts and was changed thereby (long before Cynewulf's time) into a far from "totally formulaic" poetic language. Cynewulf is nothing if not a learned poet, and the degree of his learning has been either neglected or underrated. Magoun and others dwell upon the runes, his signature against illiteracy, against completely oral composition. Magoun supposes the "narrative parts" of Cynewulf's poems to be "composed in the traditional way," that is, orally.

All existing evidence, sparse and equivocal as it is, makes Magoun's position strained if not untenable. Most scholars place Cynewulf in the ninth century and locate him either in Mercia or Northumbria.[61] It is

61. For a full discussion of scholarly debate upon the time, identity, and geographical setting of Cynewulf, see Kenneth Sisam, "Cynewulf and His Poetry," *PBA, 18* (1932),

well known that writing was in use in England from 597 onward. Thus at least two centuries of literacy precede the likeliest span of Cynewulf's life. True, this literacy was confined by class and by occupation. Yet Homer lived, so far as is known, in no comparable ferment of letters and learning. Then too, and most important, Cynewulf wrote poems that translate certain Latin sources so closely that, even though the rendering into Old English is not word for word, even though extensive interpolations occur, there can be little question that his eye or finger were not on some page of prose as he composed the isochronous, traditional verse that was the only poetic form in ninth-century England. It is not impossible to imagine, though it involves some contorted pictures, that a learned monk would read the *Acta Cyriaci,* the *Acta Sanctorum,* or from Gregory, to an illiterate singer, named Cynewulf, who would fashion the Latin prose into Old English verse as he listened. Yet the closeness of such work, one should suppose, would be suffocating to forethought; and in their relation to the Latin, Cynewulf's clauses in *Elene* have direction and look ahead.

The texts of *Elene* and the *Acta Cyriaci,* appearing in the *Acta Sanctorum* for May 4th, have been edited conveniently together so that any interested student may contemplate the attachment of poem to prose.[62] It is well known that Cynewulf, far from submitting to the tyranny of a source, freely digressed from the Latin *Acta,* notably in the passages about the battle between the Romans and the Huns, the sea voyage, and, of course, in the epilogue. For all these descriptions and meditative excursions, however, the narrative substance of *Elene,* like that of *Juliana,*[63] imitates the Latin not only in sequence of action but in phrasing. Because Cynewulf's apparent knowledge of Latin has received less attention from scholars interested in the oral-formulaic tradition in Old English poetry than has Cynewulf's runic signature, it is useful for proper emphasis to examine some Latin and Old English side by side. A passage fairly close to the Latin has been chosen for illustration: Judas' prayer in *Elene* 725–801.[64]

303–31. See also P. O. E. Gradon, *Cynewulf's Elene* (London, 1958); "Introduction," pp. 22–23. Relevant to my argument is Larry Benson's, "The Literary Character of Anglo-Saxon Formulaic Poetry," *PMLA, 81* (1966), 334–41.

62. E.g. Charles W. Kent, ed., *Elene* (Boston, 1889).

63. See James M. Garret, "The Latin and Anglo-Saxon *Juliana,*" *PMLA,* N.S. 7 (1899), 279–99.

64. The Latin text of the *Acta Cyriaci* is taken from Kent's edition of *Elene,* pp. 45–48.

725 Dryhten Hælend, þu ðe ahst doma geweald
ond þu geworhtest þurh þines wuldres miht
heofon ond eorðan ond holmþræce,
sæs sidne fæðm samod ealle gesceaft,
ond þu amæte mundum þinum
730 ealne ymbhwyrft ond uprador
ond þu sylf sitest, sigora waldend
ofer þam æðelestan engelcynne
þe geond lyft farað leohte bewundene,
mycle mægenþrymme; ne mæg þær manna gecynd
735 of eorðwegum up geferan
in lichoman mid þa leohtan gedryht,
wuldres aras; þu geworhtest þa
ond to þegnunge þinre gesettest,
halig ond heofonlic; þara on hade sint
740 in sindreame syx genemned
þa ymbsealde synt mid syxum eac
fiðrum, gefrætwad; fægere scinaþ;
þara sint feower þe on flihte a
þa þegnunge þrymme beweotigaþ
745 fore onsyne eces deman,
singallice singaþ in wuldre
hædrum stefnum heofoncininges lof,

Deus, Deus, qui fecisti
coelum et terram,

qui palmo metisti coelum
et pugno terram mensurasti;
qui sedes super currum Cherubin,
et ipsa sunt volantia in
aeris cursibus luce immensa,
ubi humana natura transire
non potest;

quia tu es qui fecisti ea
ad ministerium tuum:
sex animalia, quae habent
senas alas;

quatuor quidem ex ipsis
quae volant, ministran-
tia et incessabili
voce

woða wlitegaste ond þas word cweðaþ
clænum stefnum—þam is Ceruphin nama—
750 "Halig is se halga heahengla God,
weoroda wealdend; is ðæs wuldres ful
heofun ond eorðe ond eall heahmægen
tire getacnod;" syndon tu on þam,
sigorcynn on swegle þe man Seraphin
755 be naman hateð; he sceal Neorxnawang
ond lifes treo legene sweorde
halig healdan. Heardecg cwacaþ,
beofaþ brogdenmæl ond bleom wrixleð
grapum gryrefæst; þæs ðu, God dryhten,
760 wealdest widan fyrhð ond þu womfulle,
scyldwyrcende, sceaðan of radorum
awurpe, wonhydige; þa sio werge sceolu
under heolstorhofu hreosan sceolde
in wita forwyrd þær hie in wylme nu
765 dreogaþ deaðcwale in dracan fæðme
þeostrum forþylmed. He þinum wiðsoc
aldordome; þæs he in ermðum sceal
ealra fula ful fah þrowian,
þeowned þolian. Þær he þin ne mæg
770 word aweorpan, is in witum fæst

clamantia,

"Sanctus, Sanctus, Sanctus,"
Cherubin vocantur;

duo autem ex his posu-
isti in Paradiso
custodire lignum vitae,
quae vocantur Seraphin.

Tu autem dominaris
omnium, quia tua factura
sumus, qui incredibiles
Angelos profundo tartaro
tradidisti; et ipsi sunt
sub fundo abyssi a
draconum foetore cruci-
andi,

et tuo praecepto contra-
dicere non possunt.

ealre synne fruma susle gebunden.
Gif þin willa sie, wealdend engla,
þæt ricsie se ðe on rode wæs
ond þurh Marian in middangeard
775 acenned wearð in cildes had,
þeoden engla—gif he þin nære,
sunu synna leas næfre he soðra swa feala,
in woruldrice, wundra gefremede
dogorgerimum no ðu of deaðe hine
780 swa þrymlice, þeoda wealdend,
aweahte for weorodum gif he in wuldre þin
þurh ða beorhtan bearn ne wære—
gedo nu, fæder engla, forð beacen þin;
swa ðu gehyrdest þone halgan wer,
785 Moyses on meðle þa ðu, mihta God,
gehywdest þam eorle on þa æðelan tid
under beorhhliðe ban Iosephes
swa ic þe, weroda Wyn, gif hit sie willa þin,
þurh þæt beorhte gesceap biddan wille
790 þæt me þæt goldhord gasta scyppend
geopenie þæt yldum wæs
lange behyded. Forlæt nu, lifes Fruma,
of ðam wangstede wynsumne up,

Et nunc, Domine, si tua
voluntas est regnare
filium Mariae, qui miss-
us est a te
(nisi autem fuisset ex te,
tantas virtutes fecisset;

nisi vero tuus puer esset,
non suscitares eum a
mortuis)

fac nobis, Domine, prodigium
hoc; et sicut
exaudisti famulum tuum
Moysen, et ostendisti ei
ossa patris nostri Ioseph;
ita et nunc, si est
voluntas tua,
ostende nobis occultum
thesaurum:
et fac
ab eodem loco

        under radores ryne, rec astigan
795 lyftlacende; ic gelyfe þe sel
     ond þy fæstlicor ferhð staðelige,
     hyht untweondne on þone ahangnan Crist
     þæt he sie soðlice sawla nergend,
     ece ælmihtig, Israhela cining,
800 walde widan ferhð wuldres on heofenum
     a butan ende ecra gestealda.

fumum odoris aromatum et

suavitatis ascendere:

ut et ego credam cruci-

fixo Christo,

quia ipse est Rex Israel,

et nunc et in secula seculorum.

Both the nature and the extent of poetic imitation is here so close that to place Cynewulf in the context of Lord's *Singer of Tales* becomes an act of forced imposition. There is of course no proof one way or the other; yet it seems more reasonable to assume that Cynewulf did indeed compose the narrative parts of his poems "in the traditional way"—not, as Magoun meant by that phrase, orally, or under no influence of a literary kind, but as a man of letters writing within the only poetic convention that existed in the vernacular in his time. This was a convention that in almost every quality, whether rhythmical or grammatical or formulaic, carried the weight of an old, undoubtedly pre-English tradition whose regulations were not only prescription but habit. After all, Bede wrote a death song.

Cynewulf's runic signatures, as all scholars have recognized, cannot avoid signifying the alphabetical habit of a literate author. The use of these letters in his poems is far from the Continental, third-century origin of runes,[65] and even from their earliest preserved appearance in England on the Franks Casket and the Ruthwell Cross.[66] In Cynewulf, the letters are not purely magical nor at all epigraphical, but seem to reflect a ninth-century interest in "antiquarian curiosities." [67] As Elliott says in his book *Runes: an Introduction*:

> At some stage, clearly, a live popular tradition of the epigraphic use of runes coupled with magico-ritualistic beliefs and practises became, in part at least, "bookish." Cynewulf's acrostic use of runes to spell his name, the runic *Riddles,* and the cryptic runic message in the Anglo-Saxon poem, *The Husband's Message,* lie somewhere along this road. They still echo, just as the Icelandic poems and sagas do, something of the genuine runic usages of earlier generations—their mystery, secrecy, concealment . . .[68]

An association between runic knowledge and the knowledge of books is securely joined in *Riddle 42,* lines 5b–8a:

65. See H. Monroe Chadwick and N. Kershaw Chadwick, *The Growth of Literature, 1,* 476, 478; R. Derolez, *Runica Manuscripta* (Brussels, 1954), pp. xivff.; Bruce Dickens, ed., *Runic and Heroic Poems of Old Teutonic Peoples* (Cambridge, 1915), pp. 1–4; Ralph W. V. Elliott, *Runes: an Introduction* (Manchester, 1959), pp. 3ff.

66. Dickens, p. 3; Elliott, pp. 37, 42; R. H. Hodgkin, *A History of the Anglo-Saxons* (3d ed. Oxford, 1959), *1,* 362.

67. On the learned and on the Continental and scriptorial interest in runes in the ninth and tenth centuries, see Dickens, pp. 4–5; Elliott, pp. 42–44; Sisam, pp. 311, 320–21; Gradon, p. 23.

68. Elliott, p. 43.

Ic on flette mæg
þurh runstafas   rincum secgan,
þam þe bec witan,   bega ætsomne
naman þara wihta.

Robert Diamond has demonstrated that the four runic passages in
Cynewulf's poems are as a whole just as formulaic (even slightly more
so) as the narrative parts of the same poems. The narratives of at least
two of the signed poems are variously liberal and close translations of
Latin prose; the runic signatures represent not only an act of literacy in
themselves but are one with a literary Continental tradition of acrostic
signature and request for prayer;[69] Cynewulf's poetry, according to the
sample reconsidered analyses above, has a formulaic content roughly
comparable to the formulaic content of *Beowulf*. These statements are
based if not entirely then to a persuasive extent upon demonstrable facts.
The likely conclusion to be drawn from them is that Cynewulf, a literate poet, composed a highly conventionalized poetry; or, to put it nega-
tively, that the poetry to which Cynewulf's name is attached was not
composed by an oral-formulaic method such as that described by Parry,
Lord, and Magoun.

69. See Gradon, p. 23; Elliott, p. 42; Sisam, pp. 320–21; and Elliott, "Cynewulf's Runes
in *Juliana* and *The Fates of the Apostles*," ES, 34 (1953), 202–03.

Conclusion

The "Cynewulf problem" can be looked upon as symptomatic of the too great lengths to which Magoun and others have applied the Parry-Lord thesis to Old English poetry. In a more restrained form, Magoun's thesis is essential and revealing; pushed to its present extent, it becomes unnecessary and somewhat obstructive. The thesis has directed a needed emphasis upon the formulaic diction of Old English poems and upon the oral origin of poetic formulae: thus far the thesis is sound, but where it reaches farther, it overreaches. It overreaches at both ends, as it were, in the translation of a workable theory for one literature to another and in the application of the theory so translated. On the one hand, Magoun and his followers, while professing to adopt, have not consistently adopted the major parts of Parry's thesis, or they have not explained or discussed those changes they thought must be made. Neither have they considered adequately the Homeric and Old English differences of language, time, and poetical form. Furthermore, in the other direction, those who accept Magoun's thesis have pushed it to include Cynewulf, to include what would seem to be its antithesis.

These objections to the extent to which Magoun and other scholars have imposed the idea of the oral-formulaic composition of Old English poetry are not meant to imply that some opposite theory is "correct." The methods of the composition of Old English poetry in the eighth century are not known. Therefore the objection summarized in the paragraph above and discussed at length throughout the preceding chapters amounts to a statement that Magoun's theory is not consistent enough, either internally or with what little is known of Old English civilization, to be accepted—as it has been by some—as an indubitably factual description. The (total) formulaic character of *Beowulf* has not been "proved beyond any doubt by a series of analyses." The documentation is not "complete, thorough, and accurate." The "exhaustive analysis" is not "in itself sufficient to prove that Beowulf was composed orally." [1] An opposite theory of the literary composition of *Beowulf,* or *Genesis,* or *The Ruin,* is as open to inconsistencies and misapplications as Magoun's

1. The phrases in quotation are Lord's; see *The Singer of Tales,* p. 198.

theory. Ignorance at this point is giant ignorance, because we must stand aloof.

If the formulaic analysis of Old English texts is not in itself sufficient witness to an oral-formulaic method of composition, the secondary evidence supplied by historical documents and critical analogy is too limited and contradictory to either support or condemn Magoun's theory. A consideration of Cynewulf's Latinity produces a strong argument for his literacy. It is tempting to ask, if Cynewulf could *write* formulae, could not the *Beowulf*-poet also? The question must be offered tentatively. Caedmon, thanks to Bede, is somewhat known to us; Cynewulf, in spite of his desire, less so; the *Beowulf*-poet, not at all.

Once we leave the texts in order to consider secondary evidence about ancient poetry, we are on uncertain ground, especially in Anglo-Saxon studies where just enough is known to make the whole seem ambiguous. Yet no theory of the habit of artistic composition of past ages should ever be conceived without reference to whatever history can offer, whether through archaeology, contemporary documents, or analogical information. Among the scholars who uphold the theory of oral-formulaic composition of Old English poetry, Magoun has bolstered his position with historical references; and, needless to say, much of the persuasive strength of the Parry-Lord thesis concerning Homer comes from analogical comparisons to Yugoslavian shepherds. Yet it is a rare argument from Anglo-Saxon history that goes justly unchallenged, and the Yugoslavian analogy, being no more than an analogy, should not be expected to reveal a Bulkan Homer. Magoun finds in Caedmon his ready-made evidence, but the *Meters of Boethius* provide Benson with evidence against Magoun's theory.[2] The discussion here has necessarily been devoted to an appraisal of the theory of oral-formulaic composition in Old English poetry as it is relevant to the poetry, the primary and most important evidence. The rest is far beyond either the art or the scope of this book.

The primary evidence itself presents profound difficulties to anyone who seeks to ascertain the means of its composition. Unsatisfactory as it is, there seems to be no better evidence for the oral composition of ancient poetry than a high degree of formular phraseology. The degree must

2. See Francis P. Magoun, Jr., "The Story of Cædman: the Case-History of an Anglo-Saxon Singer," *Speculum, 30* (1955), 49–53; and Larry D. Benson, "The Literary Character of Anglo-Saxon Formulaic Poetry," *PMLA, 81* (1966), 334–41.

vary from language to language, verse-form to verse-form, and must be determined in each case; but even though the untold loss of early poetical manuscripts must make the criterion of exactly repeated phraseology a rough gauge at best, still no other criterion comes as near to identifying for us the difference between phrases selected for their metrical efficacy and phrases not so selected. The rough gauge is hardly good enough to be useful. Adam Parry wonders in a reasonable way whether Homer did not, after all, write the *Iliad* and the *Odyssey*.[3]

Adam Parry's point that the whole Parry-Lord thesis set out to be a description not of a compositional method, but of a style, is a most important one.[4] The formulaic analysis of Old English texts may characterize what is on the page but not the means by which it got there. This distinction is of paramount importance to the study of any old poetry less formulaic than Homer—that is, all un-Homeric poetry. In fact, the question "if Cynewulf could write formulae, could not the *Beowulf*-poet also?" implies the larger question raised in Chapter 4 (see p. 187), "how can we identify oral texts?" According to the arguments set forth at length in this book, the degree of formular phraseology in *Beowulf* and *Elene* is small by Homeric standards. At what point does a small degree of formular content become conventional diction in a literary composition as opposed to formular phraseology in an oral composition?

Analyzed by the means now at hand, most Old English poetic texts yield no certain answer to this question. *Elene,* which is probably a literary composition, is less formulaic than *Beowulf,* whose method of composition is unknown. In the face of our present ignorance in such matters, the most fruitful course of study would seem to be one which acknowledges the unknowns for what they are and proceeds with what we know—the texts. To the description of the poetic style of these texts Francis P. Magoun, Jr., has made an invaluable contribution. The extreme to which he and others have pushed his theory should not prevent scholars from inquiring about the complex connections between styles and methods of composition; nor should it prevent readers of Old English from reading the poems as if the possibilities of artistic intention had not been fallacious.

3. "Have We Homer's *Iliad*?", YCS, 20 (1966), 216 (and see the discussion of the article in this book, pp. 43–44). Cf. R. F. Lawrence, "The Formulaic Theory and Its Application to English Alliterative Poetry," *Essays on Style and Language,* ed. Roger Fowler, 166–83; p. 175.

4. *Ibid.,* p. 178, n. 4.

Appendix A

Epithets
in *Beowulf*

The following list is arranged alphabetically according to the spellings but
without the long marks in Klaeber's glossary (pages 293–441 of his *Beowulf
and the Fight at Finnsburg,* 1950). Pertinent emendations are those in Klaeber's text. All epithets are given in the nominative case, precisely as they are
in Klaeber's glossary—e.g. the reading *aldorlease* appears as (*e*)*aldorleas*
directly after the word *ealdorgewinna.* Except for the patronymic epithets and
ethnic compounds, epithets are listed as single words only, not as phrases,
even though two single epithets often make one epithetical phrase (e.g. *atol
aglæca*). Groups of individuals are designated by their nationality (Danes,
Geats), though at times they form a specific part and are not representative
of their nation. Groups of particular evil spirits, however, be they the Nicers
associated with Breca, or the sea monsters, demons, and forces of chaos,
cohorts of Grendel, are gathered together under the general heading "monsters." Comparatives and superlatives of adjectives are listed under the positive forms of the words, including irregular adjectives. Verbal adjectives with
the prefix *ge-* are listed according to the base word.

A # preceding a word indicates that only in *Beowulf* is the word to be
found in Old English; evidence is taken from Klaeber's glossary. An asterisk,
*, is placed before words that are used other than epithetically in the poem
(e.g. as predicate adjectives), or are used of things, or of so vague, so general,
or so minor a being (e.g. mankind, sailors, Hrothgar's messenger, the thief
of the barrow) that they have little significance in a list of definite persons.
All indefinite adjectives and adjectives of number are omitted (e.g *aenig,
fea*). The list as a whole has three sections: epithets consisting of a single
word, patronymics, and ethnic compounds. Numbers in parentheses immediately following a name represent the number of times the individual or group
is described by the epithet in question.

Appendix A

Single-Word Epithets

			Total Number of Occurrences	Total Number of Persons[a] Involved
#	*æfengrom:*	Grendel (1)	1	1
	Ælmihtig:	God (1)	1	1
#	*ælwiht:*	monsters (1)	1	1
#*	*ærfæder:*	Wihstan (1)	1	1
#*	*ærgod:*	Æschere (1), Beowulf (1), Hrothgar (1)	3	3
*	*æþele:*	Beowulf (1), Ecgtheow (1), Hrothgar (1)	3	3
*	*æþeling:*	Æschere (1), Beowulf (9), Dæghrefn (1), Hrothgar (1), Hygelac (1), Scyld (1), Sigemund (1), Wiglaf (1)	16	8
	Agend:	God (1)	1	1
	agendfrea:	Beowulf (1)	1	1
	aglæca:	dragon (5), Grendel 13, monsters (1)	19	3
#	*aglæcwif:*	Grendel's Dam (1)	1	1
	Alwalda:	God (4)	4	1
	andsaca:	Cain (1), Grendel (1)	2	2
	angenga:	Grendel (2)	2	1
	anhaga:	Beowulf (1)	1	1
#	*anhar:*	Hrothgar (1)	1	1
	anhydig:	Beowulf (1)	1	1
	anræd:	Beowulf (2)	2	1
	Anwalda:	God (1)	1	1
	atelic:	Grendel (1)	1	1
*	*atol:*	dragon (1), Grendel (4), Grendel's Dam (1)	6	3

a. Groups are considered collectively, as one person. Numbers appearing in parentheses signify application of one epithet to two persons.

			Total Number of Occurrences	Total Number of Persons Involved
	attorsceaða:	dragon (1)	1	1
#	*aþumswearas:*	Hrothgar and Ingeld (1)	1	(1)
*	*bana:*	dragon (1), Finn (1), Grendel (1), Hygelac (1)	4	4
	beadorinc:	Hnaef (1)	1	1
	beaggyfa:	Hnæf (1)	1	1
	beaghroden:	Wealhtheow (1)	1	1
	bealdor:	Beowulf (1), Hygelac (1)	2	2
#	*bealohycgende:*	Beowulf and dragon (1)	1	(1)
*	*bearn:*	Beowulf (10), Danes and Geats (1), Eadgils (1), Eanmund (1), Frisians (2), Geats (3), Grendel (1), Heardred (1), Heorogar (1), Herebeald and Hæthcyn (1), Heremod (1), Hrethric (1), Hrothgar (1), Sigemund (1), Unferth (1)	27	13 (2)
	gebeaten:	Hygelac (1)	1	1
	bedæled:	Grendel (2)	2	1
*	*befeallen:*	Danes (1)	1	1
#	*beodgeneat:*	Danes (1)	1	1
*	*beorn:*	Æschere (2), Beowulf (3)	5	2
#	*beorncyning:*	Hygelac (1)	1	1
#	*beorscealc:*	Danes and Geats (1)	1	(1)
*	*bereafod:*	dragon (2)	2	1
*	*berofene:*	Ongentheow's Wife (1)	1	1
	beswæled:	dragon (1)	1	1
*	*betlic:*	Hygelac (1)	1	1
*	*bitere:*	Geats (1)	1	1
*	*biwenede:*	Danes and Geats (1)	1	(1)

		Total Number of Occurrences	Total Number of Persons Involved
#	*blædagande:*	Danes and Geats (1)	1	(1)
#	*blædfæst:*	Æschere (1)	1	1
	blodfag:	Ingeld (1)	1	1
#	*blodigtoð:*	Grendel (1)	1	1
	blondenfeax:	Danes (1), Hrothgar (2), Ongentheow (1)	4	3
	boldagend:	Danes (1)	1	1
*	*gebolgen:*	Beowulf (1), Geats (1)	2	2
	bolgenmod:	Grendel (1), Heremod (1)	2	2
#	*bordhæbbend:*	Geats (1)	1	1
	brego:	Hrothgar (2), Offa (1)	3	2
#	*bregorof:*	Hygelac (1)	1	1
#	*brimwisa:*	Ongentheow (1)	1	1
#	*brimwylf:*	Grendel's Dam (2)	2	1
*	*broðor:*	Abel (1), Æschere (1), Herebeald (1), Hnæf (1), Ohthere (1), Wonreding (1)	6	6
*	*bryd:*	Ongentheow's Wife (1)	1	1
	brytta:	Hrothgar (3), Hygelac (3), Scyld (1)	7	3
	gebunden:	Hrothgar (1)	1	1
*	*byre:*	Hrethric and Hrothmund (1), Wiglaf (1)	2	1 (1)
#	*ceasterbuend:*	Danes (1)	1	1
*	*cempa:*	Dæghrefn (1), Beowulf (4), Hondscioh (1), Offa (1), Wihstan (1)	8	5
*	*cene:*	Danes (1)	1	1
*	*ceorl:*	Danes (1), Geats (1)	2	2
*	*cniht:*	Hrethric and Hrothmund (1)	1	(1)
	collenferhð	Beowulf (2)	2	1

			Total Number of Occurrences	Total Number of Persons Involved
	cræftig:	Eomer (1), Unferth (1)	2	2
*	*cuma:*	Beowulf (1)	1	1
*	*cumene:*	Geats (2)	2	1
*	*cuð*	Beowulf (1)	1	1
#	*cwealmcuma:*	Grendel (1)	1	1
	cwen:	Hildeburh (1), Modthrytho (1), Onelea's Queen (1), Wealtheow (5)	8	4
*	*cyning:*	Beowulf (6), Finn (1), Heorogar (1), Hrethric (1), Hrothgar (6), Hygelac (3), Onela (1), Scyld (1)	20	8
#	*cyningbald:*	Geats (1)	1	1
#	*kyningwuldor:*	God (1)	1	1
#	*dædcene:*	Beowulf (1)	1	1
	dædfruma:	Grendel (1)	1	1
#	*dædhata:*	Grendel (1)	1	1
	deal:	Geats (1)	1	1
#	*deaðfæge:*	Grendel (1)	1	1
	deaðscua:	Grendel (1)	1	1
#	*deaðwerig:*	Æschere (1)	1	1
	Demend:	God (1)	1	1
*	*deofol:*	monsters (2)	2	1
*	*deogol:*	Grendel (1)	1	1
	deor:	Grendel (1), Modthrytho (1)	2	2
*	*deorc:*	Grendel (1)	1	1
*	*deore:*	Beowulf (1), Danes (1), Modthrytho (1)	3	3
	deorsta:	Æschere (1)	1	1
*	*dohtor:*	Freawaru (1), Hildeburh (2), Hrethel's Daughter (1), Hygd		

		Total Number of Occurrences	Total Number of Persons Involved
	(2), Hygelac's Daughter (1), Wealhtheow (1)	8	6
# *dolsceaða:*	Grendel (1)	1	1
* *druncen:*	Unferth (2)	2	1
# *dryhtbearn:*	Ingeld (1)	1	1
dryhten:	Beowulf (1), God (14), Hæthcyn (1), Hrothgar (2), Hygelac (5)	29	5
* *dryhtguma:*	Beowulf (1), Danes (2), Danes and Geats (1)	4	2 (1)
* *dryhtlic:*	Wealhtheow (1)	1	1
* *duquð:*	Danes (4), Danes and Geats (4), Geats (3), Franks (1)	12	3 (1)
* *dyrne:*	monsters (1)	1	1
* *eacen:*	Beowulf (1)	1	1
* *eafera:*	Beow (2), Beowulf (1), Grendel (1), Hygelac (3), Ohthere and Onela (1), Sigemund (1)	9	5 (1)
* *eald:*	Beowulf (2), dragon (1), Grendel (1), Hrethel (1), Hrothgar (2), Hygelac (1), Ongentheow (1)	9	7
yldra:	Æschere (1), Heorogar (1)	1	1
yldesta:	Beowulf (2), Herebeald (1)	3	2
ealdfæder:	Ecgtheow (1)	1	1
ealdgesið:	Danes (1)	1	1
# *ealdgewinna:*	Grendel (1)	1	1
ealdhlaford:	Beowulf (1)	1	1
# *Ealdmetod:*	God (1)	1	1
ealdor:	Beowulf (2), Hrothgar (4), Hygelac (2), Scyld (1)	9	4

			Total Number of Occurrences	Total Number of Persons Involved
	ealdorgewinna:	dragon (1)	1	1
	(e)aldorleas:	Danes (1) ("lordless")	1	1
#	*ealdorleas:*	Beowulf (1), Grendel (1) ("lifeless")	1	2
	(e)aldorþegn:	Æschere (1)	1	1
*	*ealgearo:*	Danes and Geats (1)	1	(1)
	eam:	Fitele (1)	1	1
*	*earm:*	Beowulf (1), Geats (1)	1	2
*	*earmsceapen:*	Grendel (1)	1	1
	eaxlgestealla:	Æschere (1), Danes (1)	2	2
*	*ece:*	God (16)	16	1
	egesfull:	Ongentheow (1)	1	1
*	*egeslic:*	dragon (1)	1	1
#	*ellengæst:*	Grendel (1)	1	1
*	*ellenrof:*	Beowulf (1)	1	1
#	*ellensioc:*	Beowulf (1)	1	1
#	*ellorgast:*	Grendel (1), Grendel and Grendel's Dam (1), Grendel's Dam (2)	4	2 (1)
	eodor:	Hrothgar (3)	3	1
*	*eorl:*	Beowulf (4), Danes (5), Danes and Geats (2), Geats (6), Wiglaf (2)	19	4 (1)
#	*eorlweorod:*	Geats (1)	1	1
	eorðcyning:	Finn (1)	1	1
#	*eorðdraca:*	dragon (2)	2	1
*	*eoten:*	Grendel (1)	1	1
*	*eþelweard:*	Beowulf (1), Hrothgar (1)	2	2
*	*fæder:*	God (3), Ongentheow (1)	4	2
	fæderenmæg:	Abel (1)	1	1

			Total Number of Occurrences	Total Number of Persons Involved
*	*fæge:*	Danes and Geats (1), Grendel (1)	3	1 (1)
	fægen:	Geats (1)	1	1
#	*gefægnod:*	Grendel's Dam (1)	1	1
	fæmne:	Freawaru (2)	2	1
*	*fæst:*	Beowulf (2), dragon (1)	3	2
*	*fag:*	Beowulf (2), dragon (1), Wonreding (1) ("blood-stained")	4	3
*	*fah:*	Breca (1), Cain (1), Grendel (2), monsters (1) ("hostile")	5	4
*	*feasceaft:*	Eadgils (1)	1	1
#	*felafridgende:*	Hrothgar (1)	1	1
#	*felageomor:*	Ongentheow (1)	1	1
#	*felamodig:*	Geats (2)	2	1
#	*fengel:*	Beowulf (1), Hrothgar (3)	4	2
*	*feond:*	dragon (3), Grendel (12), Grendel and Grendel's Dam (1), Grendel's Dam (1), monsters (1)	18	4 (1)
	feondscaða:	monsters (1)	1	1
#	*feorbuend:*	Geats (1)	1	1
	feorhbona:	Hæthcyn (1)	1	1
#	*feorhgeniðla:*	Beowulf (1), Geats (1), Grendel (1)	3	3
#	*feorhseoc:*	Grendel (1)	1	1
#	*feorrancund:*	Beowulf (1)	1	1
#	*ferhðfrec:*	Finn (1)	1	1
#	*ferhðgeniðla:*	dragon (1)	1	1
*	*feða:*	Danes and Geats (1)	1	(1)
#	*feþecempa:*	Beowulf (1)	1	1

			Total Number of Occurrences	Total Number of Persons Involved
	feðegest:	Geats (1)	1	1
#	*fifelcyn:*	monsters (1)	1	1
	fletsittend:	Danes (1), Danes and Geats (1)	2	1 (1)
#	*fletwerod:*	Danes (1)	1	1
*	*geflymed:*	Grendel (1)	1	1
*	*folc:*	Danes (4), Geats (7)	11	2
	folcagend:	Geats (1)	1	1
#	*folccwen:*	Wealhtheow (1)	1	1
	forðgewiten:	Beowulf (1)	1	1
	frea:	Beowulf (6), God (2), Hrothgar (9)	17	3
	freadrihten:	Hrothgar (1)	1	1
#	*freawine:*	Herebeald (1), Hygelac (2)	3	2
	freca:	Beowulf (1)	1	1
*	*frecne:*	Beowulf (1), dragon (1)	2	2
	fremde:	monsters (1)	1	1
	freodrihten:	Beowulf (1), Hrothgar (1)	2	2
	freolic:	Wealhtheow (2)	2	1
*	*freond:*	Eadgils (1), Heremod (1)	2	2
	freoðuwebbe:	Modthrytho (1)	1	1
#	*freowine:*	Hrothgar (1)	1	1
#	*friðusibb:*	Wealhtheow (1)	1	1
*	*frod:*	Æschere (1), Beowulf (2), dragon (1), Hrothgar (4), Ongentheow (2), Wihstan (1)	11	6
*	*frofor:*	Beowulf (1)	1	1
*	*from:*	Geats (1)	1	1
	frumgar:	Beowulf (1)	1	1
*	*fultum:*	Beowulf (1)	1	1

		Total Number of Occurrences	Total Number of Persons Involved
*	*fus:*	Danes and Geats (1)	1	(1)
#	*fylwerig:*	Grendel (1)	1	1
*	*fyrdhwæt:*	Geats (1)	1	1
#	*fyrdraca:*	dragon (1)	1	1
	frydwyrðe:	Beowulf (1)	1	1
*	*gefysed:*	Beowulf (1), dragon (1)	2	2
	gædeling:	Eanmund (1)	1	1
	galgmod:	Grendel's Dam (1)	1	1
*	*gamol:*	Beowulf (6), Danes (1), Ecgtheow (1), Healfdene (1), Hrothgar (5), Ongentheow's Wife (1)	15	7
	gamolfeax:	Hrothgar (1)	1	1
#	*garwiga:*	Wiglaf (2)	2	1
#	*garwigend:*	Beowulf (1)	1	1
*	*gast:*	Grendel (4), monsters (1)	5	2
#	*gastbona:*	Grendel (1)	1	1
*	*gearo:*	Danes (2), dragon (1), Geats (2)	5	3
#	*gearofolm:*	Grendel (1)	1	1
*	*geatolic:*	Hrothgar (1)	1	1
	gebroðor:	Hrethric and Hrothmund (1)	1	(1)
	gedryht:	Geats (1)	1	1
	gefæg:	Beowulf (1)	1	1
*	*gemyndig:*	Beowulf (1), Beowulf and Hygelac (1), dragon (1), Grendel (1), Wealhtheow (1)	5	4 (1)
*	*geogoð:*	Danes (3), Danes and Geats (1), Hrethric and Hrothmund (1)	5	1 (2)
#*	*geomeowle:*	Ongentheow's Wife (1)	1	1

		Total Number of Occurrences	Total Number of Persons Involved
*	geong: Beow (1), Freawaru (1), Hygelac (1), Offa (1), Wihlaf (4)	8	5
#	geoscæftgast: monsters (1)	1	1
*	gesið: Danes (2), Geats (3)	5	2
*	gesund: Geats (1)	1	1
	getrum: Danes (1)	1	1
	gewittig: Beowulf (1)	1	1
*	gifre: Grendel's Dam (1)	1	1
#	gilphlæden: Beowulf (1)	1	1
*	gist: Beowulf (2), dragon (1), Geats (2), Hengest (1), monsters (1)	7	5
*	glæd: Danes (1), Hrothgar (1), Hrothulf (1), Ingeld (1)	4	4
#	glædman: Hrothgar (1)	1	1
#	gledegesa: dragon (1)	1	1
*	god: Beowulf (13), Hrethric and Hrothmund (1), Hrothgar (4), Hygelac (1), Ongentheow (1), Scyld (1)	21	5 (1)
*	betst: Beowulf (3), Hnæf (1)	4	2
*	selest: Æschere (1), Geats (2), Hrothgar (1), Offa (1), Ongentheow (1)	6	5
	goldgyfa: Beowulf (1)	1	1
	goldhroden: Freawaru (1), Modthrytho (1), Wealhtheow (2)	4	3
	goldwine: Beowulf (2), Hrothgar (3)	5	2
	goldwlanc: Beowulf (1)	1	1
*	grædig: Grendel (1), Grendel's Dam (1)	2	2

		Total Number of Occurrences	Total Number of Persons Involved
*	*gram:*	Beowulf (1), Beowulf and Grendel (1), monsters (1) — 3	2 (1)
*	*grim:*	Breca (1), dragon (1), Grendel (2), Grendel's Dam (2) — 6	4
	grimlic:	dragon (1) — 1	1
	gromheort:	Grendel (1) — 1	1
#	*grundhyrde:*	Grendel's Dam (1) — 1	1
#	*grundwyrgen:*	Grendel's Dam (1) — 1	1
	gryrebroga:	dragon (1) — 1	1
#	*gryrefah:*	dragon (1) — 1	1
#	*gryregiest:*	dragon (1) — 1	1
	gryrelic:	Grendel's Dam (1), monsters (1) — 2	2
*	*guma:*	Beowulf (3), Danes (4), Geats (2), Grendel (1), Hrothgar (1), Wiglaf (1) — 12	6
#	*gumdryhten:*	Beowulf (1) — 1	1
#	*gumfeða:*	Danes (1) — 1	1
	guðcyning:	Beowulf (4), Hrothgar (1), Hygelac (1) — 6	3
#	*guðfloga:*	dragon (1) — 1	1
	guðfreca:	dragon (1) — 1	1
#	*guðreow:*	Beow (1) — 1	1
*	*guðrinc:*	Beowulf (2), Hengest (1) — 3	2
	guðrof:	Hrothgar (1) — 1	1
#	*guðsceaða:*	dragon (1) — 1	1
#	*guðwerig:*	Grendel (1) — 1	1
#	*guðwiga:*	Hrothgar (1) — 1	1
*	*hæft:*	Grendel (1) — 1	1
	hægsteald:	Geats (1) — 1	1

			Total Number of Occurrences	Total Number of Persons Involved
*	*hæle(ð):*	Beowulf (3), Geats (1), Wiglaf (1)	5	3
*	*hæþen:*	Grendel (1)	1	1
*	*hal:*	Beowulf (1)	1	1
	halig:	God (3)	3	1
#	*hamweorðung:*	Hygelac's Daughter (1)	1	1
#*	*handgestealla:*	Geats (1)	1	1
#	*handscolu:*	Geats (1)	1	1
*	*har:*	Beowulf (1), Hrothgar (2)	3	2
*	*hat:*	dragon (3)	3	1
*	*heah:*	Healfdene (1)	1	1
	heahcyning:	Hygelac (1)	1	1
#	*healsgebedda:*	Onela's Queen (1)	1	1
#*	*healsittend:*	Danes (1)	1	1
#	*healðegn:*	Geats (1)	1	1
*	*hean:*	Grendel (2)	2	1
*	*heap:*	Danes (2), Geats (4)	6	2
*	*heard:*	Beowulf (6), Eofor (1), Geats (1), Sigemund (1), Swedes (1), Unferth (1)	11	6
#	*heardhycgende:*	Geats (2)	2	1
#	*hearmscaða:*	Grendel (1)	1	1
#	*heaþodeor:*	Beowulf (1), Beowulf and Grendel (1)	2	1 (1)
*	*heaðogrim:*	dragon (1)	1	1
	heaþoliðend:	Geats (2)	2	1
#	*heaðomære:*	Geats (1)	1	1
	heaðorinc:	Beowulf (1), Geats (1), Hæthcyn (1)	3	3
	heaþorof:	Beowulf (1), Danes and Geats (1), Hygelac (1)	3	2 (1)

			Total Number of Occurrences	Total Number of Persons Involved
#	heaðosioc:	Beowulf (1)	1	1
*	helm:	Beowulf (2), Eadgils (1), God (1), Hrothgar (3), Hygelac (1)	8	5
	helmberend:	Geats (1)	1	1
#	heoroblac:	Ongentheow (1)	1	1
*	heorodreorig:	Beowulf (1)	1	1
	heorogifre:	Grendel's Dam (1)	1	1
*	heorogrim:	Beowulf (1)	1	1
#	heorowearh:	Grendel (1)	1	1
*	heoroðgeneat:	Danes (1), Geats (3)	4	2
	hererinc:	Beowulf (1)	1	1
	herewisa:	Beowulf (1)	1	1
	hetelic:	Grendel (1)	1	1
	hettend:	Grendel and Grendel's Dam (1), Swedes (1)	2	1 (1)
	higerof:	Beowulf (1)	1	1
	higeþihtig:	Hondscioh (1)	1	1
	hildedeor:	Beowulf (5), Geats (1), Hrothgar (1), Wiglaf (1)	8	4
#	hildemecg:	Geats (1)	1	1
	hilderinc:	Beowulf (3), Geats (1), Grendel (1), Hrothgar (1)	6	4
#	hildewisa:	Beowulf (1)	1	1
	hildfreca:	Beowulf (1), Swedes (1)	2	2
	hildfruma:	Beowulf (2), Hrothgar (1)	3	2
	hildlata:	Geats (1)	1	1
	hiofende:	Geats (1)	1	1
#	hioroweallende:	dragon (1)	1	1
*	hlaford:	Beowulf (4), Hrothgar (1)	5	2
	hlafordleas:	Geats (1)	1	1

			Total Number of Occurrences	Total Number of Persons Involved
	hleo:	Beowulf (4), Hrothgar (4), Hygelac (2)	10	3
*	*hold:*	Hrothgar (1)	1	1
#	*hondgesella:*	Geats (1)	1	1
*	*hordweard:*	dragon (4), Hrothgar (1)	5	2
*	*hremig:*	Beowulf (1), Grendel (1)	2	2
*	*hreoh:*	Beowulf (1)	1	1
	hreomod:	Hrothgar (1)	1	1
#	*hringboga:*	dragon (1)	1	1
	hror:	Beowulf (1)	1	1
	hwæt:	Beowulf (1), Danes (2), Geats (2), Heoroweard (1), Wiglaf (1)	7	5
*	*hyrde:*	Beowulf (3), Dæghrefn (1), dragon (3), Sigemund's dragon (1), Grendel (1), Grendel and Grendel's Dam (1), God (1), Hrothgar (2), Hygelac (1)	14	8 (1)
	hyse:	Beowulf (1)	1	1
	idelhende:	Grendel (1)	1	1
*	*ides:*	Hildeburh (1), Grendel's Dam (2), Wealhtheow (2)	5	3
#	*infrod:*	Hrethel (1), Hrothgar (1)	2	2
#	*ingenga:*	Grendel (1)	1	1
#	*inwitgæst:*	dragon (1)	1	1
#	*irenþreat:*	Geats (1)	1	1
	lacende:	dragon (1)	1	1
	læt:	Beowulf (1)	1	1
*	*laf:*	Geats (1)	1	1
#	*lagucræftig:*	Beowulf (1)	1	1
#	*landfruma:*	Scyld (1)	1	1

			Total Number of Occurrences	Total Number of Persons Involved
#	*langtwidig:*	Beowulf (1)	1	1
*	*lað:*	Breca (1), dragon (3), Grendel (4), Grendel's Dam (1)	9	4
#	*laðgeteona:*	Grendel (1), monsters (1)	2	2
*	*leas:*	Grendel (1)	1	1
#	*leasceawere:*	Geats (1)	1	1
*	*leod:*	Beowulf (9), Geats (2), Hrothgar (2), Swedes (1), Wiglaf (1), Wulfgar (1)	16	6
#	*leodcyning:*	Beow (1)	1	1
	leodfruma:	Hrothgar (1)	1	1
	leodgebyrgea:	Hrothgar (1)	1	1
	leodsceaða:	Grendel (1)	1	1
	leof:	Æschere (1), Beow (1), Beowulf (12), Breca (1), Hondscioh (1), Hrothgar (1), Scyld (1), Wiglaf (1)	19	8
	leofest:	Beowulf (1)	1	1
	leoflic:	Wiglaf (1)	1	1
	lidman:	Geats (1)	1	1
#	*lifbysig:*	Grendel (1)	1	1
	Liffrea:	God (1)	1	1
*	*lifigende:*	Beowulf (2), Modthrytho (1)	3	2
#	*ligdraca:*	dragon (2)	2	1
#	*ligegesa:*	dragon (1)	1	1
#	*lindgestealla:*	Beowulf (1)	1	1
#	*lindhæbbend:*	Danes (1), Geats (1)	2	2
#	*lindwiga:*	Wiglaf (1)	1	1
	liðend:	Geats (1)	1	1
#	*lyftfloga:*	dragon (1)	1	1

			Total	*Total*
			Number of	*Number of*
			Occurrences	*Persons*
				Involved
*	*mæg:*	Beowulf (7), Danes (1), Eanmund (1), Eofor (1), Eomer (1), Frisians (1), Geats (3), Grendel (1), Grendel's Dam (2), Hæthcyn (1), Heremod (2), Heorogar (1), monsters (1), Offa (1), Wihstan (1), Wiglaf (1)	26	16
*	*mægen:*	Danes (1), Geats (1) ("military force")	1	2
	mægwine:	Hygelac (2)	2	1
*	*mære:*	Beowulf (10), Eadgils (1), Grendel (1), Heremod (1), Hondscioh (1), Hrothgar (9), Modthrytho (1), Scyld (1), Wealhtheow (1)	26	9
	mærost:	Sigemund (1)	1	1
	maga:	Beowulf (2), Grendel (1), Hrothgar (3), Wiglaf (1)	7	4
	mage:	Grendel's Dam (1)	1	1
	mago:	Hrothgar (2), Unferth (1)	3	2
#	*magodriht:*	Danes (1)	1	1
	magorinc:	Geats (1)	1	1
#	*manfordædla:*	monsters (1)	1	1
	manscaða:	dragon (1), Grendel (2), Grendel's Dam (1)	4	3
*	*gemearcod:*	Cain (1)	1	1
#	*mearcstapa:*	Grendel (1), Grendel and Grendel's Dam (1)	2	1 (1)
#	*meredeor:*	Breca (1)	1	1
#	*merefara:*	Beowulf (1)	1	1
#	*merefisc:*	Breca (1)	1	1
	mereliðend:	Geats (1)	1	1

		Total Number of Occurrences	Total Number of Persons Involved
#	*merewif:*	Grendel's Dam (1)	1	1
	Metod:	God (10)	10	1
*	*micel:*	Danes (1), monsters (1) ("great," "large")	2	2
*	*mæst:*	Beowulf (1) ("greatest")	1	1
	mihtig:	Greca (1), God (4), Grendel's Dam (2)	7	3
	modgiomor:	Geats (1)	1	1
*	*modig:*	Beowulf (5), Geats (1), Wiglaf (1)	7	3
	modiglic:	Geats (1)	1	1
	modor:	Grendel's Dam (7), Ongentheow's Wife (1)	8	2
*	*mon:*	Æschere (1), Beowulf (21), Danes (1), Geats (3), Hrothgar (1), Hygelac (1), Offa (1)	29	7
*	*mondryhten:*	Beowulf (6), Hygelac (2)	8	2
*	*mundbora:*	dragon (1)	1	1
*	*nacod:*	dragon (1)	1	1
	nefa:	Beowulf (1), Eomer (1), Hygelac (2), Sigemund (1)	5	4
	neðende:	Beowulf (1)	1	1
#	*niðdraca:*	dragon (1)	1	1
	niðgæst:	dragon (1)	1	1
	niðheard:	Beowulf (1)	1	1
#	*nydgestealla:*	Fitela and Sigemund (1)	1	(1)
	ofermægen:	Franks (1)	1	1
	ordfruma:	Ecgtheow (1)	1	1
	oretmecg:	Danes (1), Geats (2)	3	2
	oretta:	Beowulf (2)	2	1

			Total Number of Occurrences	Total Number of Persons Involved
	orwena:	Beowulf (1), Grendel (1)	2	2
	rædbora:	Æschere (1)	1	1
	Rædend:	God (1)	1	1
	ræswa:	Healfdene (1)	1	1
	randwiga:	Æschere (1), Beowulf (1)	2	2
#	*renweard:*	Beowulf and Grendel (1)	1	(1)
#	*reoc:*	Grendel (1)	1	1
	reþe:	Beowulf (1), Beowulf and Grendel (1), Grendel (1)	3	2 (1)
	rice:	Æschere (1), Beowulf (1), Danes (1), Hrothgar (2), Hygelac (2)	7	5
*	*rinc:*	Beowulf (1) Danes (2), Eofor (1), Grendel (1), Hondscioh (1), Hrothgar (1)	7	6
*	*rof:*	Beowulf (4), Grendel (1)	5	2
	rumheort:	Hrothgar (2)	2	1
	rumwita:	Æschere (1)	1	1
#	*sæcyning:*	Geats (1)	1	1
	sæd:	Beowulf (1)	1	1
	sædeor:	monsters (1)	1	1
#	*sædraca:*	monsters (1)	1	1
*	*sæliðend:*	Geats (1)	1	1
	saeman:	Geats (2)	2	1
#	*sæmeþe:*	Geats (1)	1	1
	særinc:	Geats (1)	1	1
	sarigferð:	Wiglaf (1)	1	1
	sarigmod:	Geats (1)	1	1
	sawolleas:	Æschere (1), Beowulf (1)	2	2
	scamiende:	Geats (1)	1	1

			Total Number of Occurrences	Total Number of Persons Involved
#	*sceadugenga:*	Grendel (1)	1	1
*	*scealc:*	Beowulf (1)	1	1
*	*sceaþa:*	Geats (2), Grendel (1)	3	2
*	*sceotend:*	Danes (1), Danes and Geats (1)	2	1 (1)
*	*scir:*	God (1)	1	1
#	*scirham:*	Geats (1)	1	1
#	*scyldfreca:*	Beowulf (1)	1	1
*	*scyldig:*	Grendel (2), Ingeld (1)	1	2
#	*scynscaþa:*	Grendel (1)	1	1
	searohæbbend:	Geats (1)	1	1
*	*secg:*	Beowulf (9), Geats (2), Grendel (1), Grendel's Dam (1), Unferth (1), Wiglaf (2)	16	6
#	*selegyst:*	Grendel's Dam (1)	1	1
*	*selerædend:*	Danes (1)	1	1
#	*seleþegn:*	Beowulf (1)	1	1
#	*seleweard:*	Beowulf (1)	1	1
	sellic:	dragon (1), monsters (1)	2	2
	seoc:	Beowulf (2), Geats (1)	3	2
#	*sibæðeling:*	Beowulf and Wiglaf (1)	1	(1)
	sibbegedriht:	Danes (1), Geats (1)	2	2
*	*sid:*	Geats (1)	1	1
	sigedrihten:	Hygelac (1)	1	1
	sigefolc:	Danes and Geats (1)	1	(1)
	sigehreþig:	Beowulf (1), God (1), Wiglaf (1)	3	3
	sigerof:	Hrothgar (1)	1	1
	sigeþeod:	Geats (1)	1	1
#	*sigoreadig:*	Beowulf (2)	2	1

			Total Number of Occurrences	Total Number of Persons Involved
*	*sincgifa:*	Beowulf (1), Hrothgar (1)	2	2
#	*sinhere:*	Swedes (1)	1	1
	sinnig:	Grendel's Dam (1)	1	1
	siðfrom:	Geats (1)	1	1
*	*slæpend:*	Danes (1), Hondscioh (1)	2	2
	snel:	Wulf (1)	1	1
	snellic:	Geats (1)	1	1
*	*snotor:*	Beowulf (1), Danes (1), Geats (2), Hrothgar (4), Wiglaf (1)	9	5
*	*sorhful:*	Grendel's Dam (1)	1	1
*	*soð:*	God (1)	1	1
	Soðcyning:	God (1)	1	1
#	*stearcheort:*	Beowulf (1), dragon (1)	2	2
*	*stille:*	dragon (1)	1	1
	stiðmod:	Beowulf (1)	1	1
	strengel:	Beowulf (1)	1	1
	strengest:	Beowulf (1)	1	1
	suhtergefæderan:	Hrothgar and Hrothulf (1)	1	(1)
*	*sunu:*	Beowulf (3), Breca (1), Eadgils (2), Eanmund (1), Finn (1), Heardred (1), Hrothgar (8), Hygelac (1), Ingeld (1), Unferth (3), Wiglaf (5), Wulf (1)	28	12
*	*swæs:*	Danes (2), Geats (2)	4	2
*	*geswenced:*	Grendel (1)	1	1
#	*sweordfreca:*	Beowulf (1)	1	1
*	*swiðferhð:*	Beowulf (1), Geats (1), Heremod (1)	3	3
#*	*swiðhicgende:*	Hrothgar and Hrothulf (1)	1	(1)

			Total Number of Occurrences	Total Number of Persons Involved
	swiðmod:	Beowulf (1)	1	1
	synscaða:	Grendel (1)	1	1
	teoh:	Geats (1)	1	1
*	*til:*	Halga (1), Wiglaf (2)	3	2
	tireadig:	Beowulf (1)	1	1
	tirfæst:	Hrothgar (1)	1	1
#	*tirleas:*	Grendel (1)	1	1
#	*treowloga:*	Geats (1)	1	1
	tydre:	Geats (1)	1	1
*	*þegn:*	Beowulf (4), Danes (1), Geats (1), Hengest (1), Ingeld (1), Wiglaf (2)	10	6
	þengel:	Beowulf (1)	1	1
	þeod:	Danes (2), Danes and Geats (1), monsters (1)	4	2 (1)
	þeodcyning:	Beowulf (3), Hrothgar (1), Ongentheow (2)	6	3
*	*þeoden:*	Beowulf (15), Heremod (1), Hnaef (1), Hrothgar (13), Hygelac (2), Ingeld (1), Onela (1), Scyld (1)	35	8
#	*þeodenleas:*	Danes (1)	1	1
	þeodscaða:	dragon (2)	2	1
	geþungen:	Wealtheow (1)	1	1
	þristhydig:	Beowulf (1)	1	1
*	*þrydlic:*	Beowulf (1)	1	1
#	*þryðswyð:*	Beowulf (1), Hrothgar (1)	2	2
	þyle:	Unferth (2)	2	1
	þyrs:	Grendel (1)	1	1
#	*uhtfloga:*	dragon (1)	1	1
#	*uhtsceaða:*	dragon (1)	1	1

			Total Number of Occurrences	Total Number of Persons Involved
#	*umborwesende:*	Hrothulf (1), Scyld (1)	2	2
*	*unbliðe:*	Geats (1), Hrothgar (1)	2	2
*	*uncuð:*	Grendel (1)	1	1
#	*unfrod:*	Wiglaf (1)	1	1
	unfrom:	Beowulf (1)	1	1
*	*unheore:*	dragon (1), Grendel's Dam (1)	2	2
#	*unhlitme:*	Hengest (1)	1	1
	unleof:	Geats (1)	1	1
*	*unlifigende:*	Æschere (1), Beowulf (1), Heorogar (1), Hondscioh (1)	4	4
	unrot:	Geats (1)	1	1
	unsynnig:	Beowulf (1)	1	1
	unwrecen:	Herebeald (1)	1	1
*	*wæccende:*	Beowulf (3)	3	1
*	*wæfre:*	Grendel's Dam (1)	1	1
#	*wægbora:*	monsters (1)	1	1
#	*wælgast:*	Grendel (1), Grendel's Dam (1)	2	2
	wælreow:	Hrothgar (1)	1	1
	wæpnedmon:	Beowulf (1)	1	1
	wealaf:	Danes (2)	2	1
	Wealdend:	God (11)	11	1
*	*weard:*	Beowulf (1), dragon (5), Hrothgar (2)	8	3
	welþungen:	Hygd (1)	1	1
#	*weoroddrædend:*	Finn (1)	1	1
*	*weorð:*	Beowulf (1)	1	1
*	*geweorðad:*	Beowulf (1), Offa (1)	2	2

		Total Number of Occurrences	Total Number of Persons Involved
*	*wer:* Beowulf (3), Danes and Geats (3), Geats (1), Grendel (1), Geats and Swedes (1)	9	3 (2)
	werga: Grendel (2)	2	1
	wergend: Geats (1)	1	1
	gewergad: Wiglaf (1)	1	1
	werede: Geats (2)	2	1
	werig: Beowulf (2), Geats (1)	3	2
	werigmod: Beowulf (1), Grendel (1)	2	2
*	*werod:* Danes (2), Geats (2), monsters (1)	5	3
	widcuð: Beowulf (1)	1	1
#	*widfloga:* dragon (1)	1	1
*	*wif:* Freawaru (1), Grendel's Dam (2), Hildeburh (1), Wealtheow (2)	6	4
*	*wiga:* Beowulf (1)	1	1
*	*wigend:* Danes (2), Geats (3)	5	2
#	*wigfreca:* Hygelac (1)	1	1
#*	*wigfruma:* Hrothgar (1)	1	1
#	*wiggeweorþad:* Beowulf (1)	1	1
#	*wigheap:* Danes (1)	1	1
*	*wiht:* dragon (2), Grendel (1)	3	2
	wildeor: monsters (1)	1	1
	wilgeofa: Beowulf (1)	1	1
*	*wine:* Beowulf (3), Danes (1), Geats (1), Hrothgar (7), Ingeld (1), Scyld (1), Unferth (1)	15	7
*	*winedryhten:* Beowulf (2), Hrothgar (2)	4	2
	wineleas: Eanmund (1)	1	1

			Total Number of Occurrences	Total Number of Persons Involved
	winemæg:	Danes (1)	1	1
*	*wis:*	Beowulf (3), Hrothgar (3), Hygd (1)	7	3
	wisa:	Beowulf (1)	1	1
	wisfæst:	Wealhtheow (1)	1	1
#	*wishycgende:*	Beowulf (1)	1	1
*	*wita:*	Danes (3)	3	1
	witig:	God (4)	4	1
*	*wlonc:*	Beowulf (1), dragon (1), Grendel's Dam (1)	3	3
#	*wohbogen:*	dragon (1)	1	1
#	*wollentear:*	Geats (1)	1	1
*	*won:*	Grendel (1)	1	1
	wonsaeli:	Grendel (1)	1	1
	wræcmæcg:	Eadgils and Eanmund (1)	1	(1)
*	*wrað:*	Grendel (2), monsters (1)	3	2
*	*wrecca:*	Eanmund (1), Hengest (1)	2	2
	wrecend:	Grendel's Dam (1)	1	1
	Wuldurcyning:	God (1)	1	1
	wund:	Beowulf (1), Danes and Frisians (1), dragon (1), monsters (1)	4	3 (1)
	wunderlic:	monsters (1)	1	1
	wyrm:	dragon (18), Sigemund's dragon (3), monsters (1)	22	3
	wyrmcynn:	monsters (1)	1	1
*	*wyrsa:*	Hygelac (1)	1	1
*	*ymbsittend:*	monsters (1)	1	1
*	*yrre:*	Beowulf (2), dragon (1), Grendel (1), Grendel's Dam (1)	5	4
#	*yrremod:*	Grendel (1)	1	1

Appendix A

PATRONYMIC EPITHETS

(listed alphabetically by character)

Æschere: *Yrmenlafes yldra broþor* (1)

Beow: *Scyldes eafora* (1), *Beowulf Scyldinga* (1)

Beowulf: *bearn Ecgþeowes* (10), *maga Ecgþeowes* (1), *sunu Ecgþeowes* (2), *Geata cempa* (2), *Beowulf Geata* (2), *Geata
leod* (7), *dryhten Geata* (1), *Geata dryhten* (1), *Geat* (4),
Guð-Geata leod (1), *Hreþles eafora* (1), *mæg Hygelaces*
(5), *Hygelaces þegn* (3), *freca Scyldinga* (1), *Wedera
helm* (2), *Wedera leod* (2), *Wedera þeoden* (3), *Weder-
Geata leod* (1)

Breca: *Sunu Beanstanes* (1)

Dæghrefn: *Huga cempa* (1)

Eadgils: *sunu Ohtheres* (1)

Eadgils and
   Eanmund: *Ongenþeowes eaforan* (1)

Eomer: *nefa Garmundes* (1), *Hemminges mæg* (1), *bona Ongenþeowes* (1)

Finn: *Folcwaldan sunu* (1)

Freawaru: *dohtor Hroðgares* (1)

Grendel: *deaðcwealm Denigea* (1)

Grendel's Dam: *Grendles modor* (7), *Grendles mage* (1)

Hæthcyn: *Hæðcyn Hreðling* (1)

Heardred: *nefa Hererices* (1), *sunu Hygelaces* (1)

Heorogar: *leod Scyldina* (1), *bearn Healfdenes* (1)

Hildeburh: *Hoces dohtor* (1)

Hnæf: *Hnæf Scyldinga* (1), *Finnes eafora* (1), *hæleð Healfdene*
(1)

Hrethel: *Hreðel Geata* (1)

Hrothgar: *maga (mago) Healfdenes* (5), *sunu Healfdenes* (8), *bearn
Healfdenes* (1), *dryhtbearn Dena* (1), *wine Deniga* (1),
aldor Dena (1), *Deniga frea* (3), *brego Beorht-Dene* (1),
aldor East-Dena (1), *eodur Ingwina* (1), *frea Ingwina*
(1), *eodor Scyldinga* (2), *frea Scyldinga* (4), *gamela Scylding* (2), *helm Scyldinga* (3) *leod Scyldinga* (2), *þeoden
Scyldinga* (2), *wine Scyldinga* (5)

Hygd: *Hæreðes dohtor* (2)

Hygelac: *Hygelac Geata* (1), *Geata dryhten* (2), *dryhten Geata* (3), *Geata cyning* (1), *goldwine Geata* (2), *Hygelac Hreðling* (1), *Hreðles eafora* (3), *sunu Hrædles* (1), *dryhten Wedera* (1)

Ingeld: *sunu Froda* (1), *þeoden Heaðo-Bearda* (1)

Offa: *Hemminges mæg* (1)

Onela: *helm Scylfinga* (1)

Ongentheow: *Frescyning* (1), *faeder Ohtheres* (1), *gamela Scylfing* (2)

Scyld: *Scyld Scefing* (1), *wine Scyldinga* (1)

Sigemund: *Wælses eafora* (1), *Wælsing* (1)

Unferth: *Ecglafes bearn* (1), *mago Ecglafes* (1), *sunu Ecglafes* (3), *ðyle Hroðgares* (1)

Wealhtheow: *cwen Hroðgares* (1), *ides Helminga* (1), *ides Scyldinga* (1)

Wiglaf: *Wihstanes sunu* (3), *sunu Wihstanes* (2), *byre Wigstanes* (2), *leod Scylfinga* (1)

Wulf: *Wulf Wonreding* (1), *sunu Wonredes* (1)

Wulfgar: *Wendla leod* (1)

Ethnic Compound Names for the Danes, the Geats, and the Swedes

Danes: *Beorht-Dene* (1), *Gar-Dene* (4), *Hring-Dene* (3), *East-Dene* (2), *Norð-Dene* (1), *Suð-Dene* (2) *West-Dene* (2); *Ar-Scyldinga* (2), *Here-Scyldinga* (1), *Sige-Scyldinga* (2), *þeod-Scyldinga* (1)

Geats: *Guð-Geatas* (1), *Sæ-Geatas* (2), *Weder-Geatas* (4)

Swedes: *Guð-Scylfinga* (1), *Heaðo-Scylfinga* (2)

Table 4: Tabulation of Epithets

Total number of epithets (excluding ethnic compounds)	561
Total number of uses of epithets	1584
Total number of epithets used once for a single subject	352 (62.7% of 561)

Total number of
epithetical words found only in *Beowulf*   170 (30.3%
                                                                  of 561

Total number of epithetical words
found only in *Beowulf* that are used once of one subject   137 (38.9%
                                                                  of 352

Total number of patronymic epithets   95

Total number of uses of patronymic epithets   172

Total number of patronymic epithets used once of one subject 63 (36.6%
                                                                  of 172)

    The accuracy of these figures is neither assured nor important, for they are undoubtedly influenced by contestable MS. readings, the untold loss of Old English literature, and changeable definitions of Old English compounds. The approximate figures, however, indicate the tendencies of the *Beowulf*-poet's use of diction, as much as any figures can measure any element of style, any element beyond statistics. The figures represent an epithetical diction employed largely for single moments of description, for unique occasions or moods in the narrative; and use of this diction may suppose "thought of some length on the part of the poet." Whether the poet's thought would have held his hand pausing too long on the harp string for composition to proceed with the alacrity and confidence necessary to oral performance is an open question. That there must be a difference in the compositional methods of an Old English "singer," and a Guslar and Homer himself may be strongly argued to the point where it becomes shortsighted to apply the same critical tests to and draw the same critical conclusions from the works of the one certain singer of modern times and the works of two possible singers of long ago.

Appendix B

Formulae in
Beowulf and *Elene*

The following lists of formulae in *Beowulf* and *Elene* are arranged according to Sievers' five rhythmical types (D^2 is differentiated for convenience) by half-lines and by line numbers in the order in which they occur in the poems. The half-line categories are the on-verses containing double alliteration (a), the on- and off-verses containing only one important alliterating syllable (a-b), and the off-verses, or phrases which appear only in the second half-line in *Beowulf* or in *Elene* (b). A numerical table of the formulae in both poems precedes the lists. The lists of formulae are intended to be complete. The accompanying lists of formulaic systems, however, are illustrative rather than exhaustive. These appear after the formulae in the pertinent rhythmical categories.

If a certain formula is itself part of a system, the system is listed in parentheses beside the formula and is introduced by "cf."; phrases having some similarity to the formula, yet not a systematic similarity, are also listed in parentheses but are introduced by "further," and if they are of a different rhythmic type, the necessary indication is given in brackets. For instance, *hæle hildedeor* is a formula occurring three times in *Beowulf* and is demonstrably part of a system of D^2 verses with double alliteration; the word *hildedeor* also contributes to B-verses and, when inflected, to an A-verse. All this information is thus presented: *hæle hildedeor* 1646a, 1816a, 3111a (cf. *heold hildedeor* 2183a; further *him þa hildedeor* 312a, *siþðan hildedeor*, 834a, *hwilum hildedeor* 2107a [B], *hildedeore*, 3169b [A]). When a formula or a formulaic system of a certain rhythmical type bears comparison with a formula or a system of another type, cross-references to the pertinent rhythmical type, half-line, and line number are given. The formula *ealdres orwena* (*Beowulf* 1002a, 1565a), a D^1 verse of the first half-line, may be compared to the formula *ealdres scyldig,* an A-verse of either half-line, and the comparison is represented: *ealdres orwena,* 1002a, 1565a (see *ealdres scyldig,* A^{a-b}, 1338a). Formulae of the same system are listed together.

The lists by rhythmical categories in *Beowulf* and *Elene* are each succeeded by lists of whole-line or three-verse formulae and formulaic systems whose single verses are already listed separately according to their rhythmical character. These verses are indicated in the lists of regular formulae and formulaic systems by means of an asterisk placed before the line number of the verse. A further list of miscellaneous brief expressions follows that of the whole-line formulae in *Beowulf* and is merely for the purposes of comparison. References are made to it in the lists of regular formulae in *Beowulf*. There is no such list of brief expressions for *Elene*.

Throughout the lists the only differences between comparable phrases that are not observed in recording are spelling differences. A phrase will appear as it is spelled in its first occurrence in the text. Contextual punctuation is disregarded. All spellings and emendations are those of Klaeber's third edition of *Beowulf* (*Beowulf and the Fight at Finnsburg,* 1950) and P. O. E. Gradon's edition of *Elene* (*Cynewulf's Elene,* 1958). Only proper names are capitalized; long marks are omitted in citations from Klaeber's text; and the letters ʒ and þ in citations from *Elene* appear in their modern forms, *g* and *w*.

The formulae in the lists are, of course, repeated phrases. If for any reason the poet's use of a repetition seems rhetorical or otherwise not strictly gov-

TABLE 5: FORMULAE IN BEOWULF AND ELENE

Beowulf

Verse-Type	A-Verse	A- and B-Verses	B-Verse	Total *
A	136	310	149	595
B	8	22	58	88
C	2	60	63	125
D¹	28	105†	54	187
D²	11	0	4	15
E	9	10	24	43

* total number of formulae: 1053, or 16.6% of the poem
† 69 of these are verses containing proper names

Elene

Verse-Type	A-Verse	A- and B-Verses	B-Verse	Total *
A	42	56	58	156
B	3	48	23	74
C	0	58	18	76
D¹	12	34	18	64
D²	2	0	0	2
E	4	4	12	20

* total number of formulae: 392 or 14.8% of the poem

erned by an efficacy of versemaking, the point is argued in a footnote to the formula in question.

These notes call attention only to rather obviously questionable formulae. The line between repetition for the sake of rhetoric or by syntactical necessity on the one hand and repetition for the sake of versemaking on the other is often amorphous, and in such cases the benefit of the doubt is given to the "oral formula" without discussion. Even those verses that seem to be repeated for reasons other than those of versemaking are included statistically as if they were oral formulae.

The lists could not have been made without the help of the following: Albert S. Cook, *A Concordance to Beowulf* (Halle, 1911); Richard Kistenmacher, *Die wörtlichen Wiederholungen im Beowulf* (Greifswald, 1898); John Collins Pope, *The Rhythm of Beowulf* (rev. ed. New Haven, 1966); Eduard Sievers, "Zur Rhythmik des germanischen Alliterationsverse," *BGDSL, 10* (1885).

Metrical classifications are meant to be consistent with those of Pope. Reference is made to *The Rhythm of Beowulf* where the appropriate classification seems debatable.

BEOWULF

Formulae of the A-Verses

FORMULAE OF THE FIRST HALF-LINE (A^a)

monegum mægþum 5a *manigre mægþe** 75a, *monegum mægþa** 1771a.

wuldres Wealdend 17a, 183a, 1752a.

swæse gesiþas 29a, 2040a, 2518a, *swæsra gesiða* 1934a.

beaga bryttan 35a, 352a, 1487a.

billum ond byrnum 40a, *bill ond byrnan* 2621a (see below, Brief Expressions, 1).

madma mænigo 41a, 2143a (cf. *manegum maðmum* 2103a).

secgan to soðe 51a, *secge ic þe to soðe* 590a.

swefan æfter symble 119a, *swefeþ æfter symle* 1008a.

grim ond grædig 121a, 1499a.

æþeling ærgod 130a, 1329a, 2342a.

lað ond longsum 134a, 192a. (See the preceding half-lines, 133b and 191b.)

fæhðe ond fyrene 137a, 248a, *fæhðe ond fyrena,* 879a. (Cf. *fyrene ond fæhðe* 153a.)

secg on searwum 249a, 2700a, *secgas on searwum* 2530a.

wǽpnum geweorðad 250a, 331a (cf. *since gewurþad,* A^b, 1038b; see below, Brief Expressions, 2).

worda ond worca 289a, *wordum ne worcum* 1100a, *wordum ond weorcum* 1833a.

lixte se leoma 311a, 1570a.

bugon þa to bence 327a, 1013a.

heard under helme 342a, 404a, 2539a.

wordum wrixlan 366a, 874a.

hynðo on Heorote 475a, 593a (further *heardra hynða* 166a, alliterates with Heorot).

golde gegyrwed 553a, *golde gegyrede* 1028a, 2192a.

eafoð ond ellen 602a, 902a, 2349a.

frofor ond fultum 698a, *frofre ond fultum* 1273a.

dreamum bedæled 721a, *dreame bedæled* 1275a.

lif wið lice 733a, 2423a, *lif of lice* 2743a, *life ond lice* 2571a.

sawle secan 801a, *sawol secean* 2820a (further *secean sawle hord* 2422a).

hæfde be honda 814a, *hæfen on handa* 3023a.

earm ond eaxle 835a, 972a.

hatan heolfre 849a, 1423a.

iren ærgod 989a, 2586a.

fylle gefægon 1014a, *fylle gefægnod* 1333a.

wicga ond wæpna 1045a, *wicgum ond wæpnum* 2395a.

hordweard hæleþa 1047a, 1852a.

mearum ond madmum 1048a, 1898a, *meara ond maðma* 2166a.

leofes ond laþes 1061a, 2910a.

gomenwudu greted 1065a, *gomenwudu grette* 2108a.

morþorbealo maga 1079a, 2742a.[1]

goldwine gumena 1171a, 1476a, 1602a.

self mid gesiðum 1313a, *selfa mid gesiðum* 1924a.

ecg wæs iren 1459a, 2778a.

ealdsweord eotenisc 1558a, 2616a, 2979a[2] (cf. *ealdsweord eacen* 1663a).

hæleðum to helpe 1709a, 1961a, *hæleþa to helpe* 1830a.

maþma gemænra 1784a, *maþmas gemæne* 1860a.

wide geweorðod 1959a, *wide weorðeð* 2913a.

---

1. See Pope, p. 257.
2. Ibid.

elne geeodon 1967a, 2917a, *elne geeode* 2676a.

eorlscipe efnde 2133a, 3007a, *eorlscype efne* 2535a, *eorlscipe efnan* 2622a.

hildehlæmmum 2201a, *hildehlemma* 2351a, 2544a.

feorhbealo frecne 2250a, 2537a.

dryncfæt deore 2254a, 2306a.

fyre befangen 2274a, 2595a.

gledum forgrunden 2335a, 2677a.

freawine folca 2357a, 2429a.

goldwine Geata 2419a, 2584a.

æghwæs unrim 2624a, 3135a.

wundur on wealle 2759a, *wundur under wealle* 3103a (cf. *wundur æfter wundre* 931a, *wræte under wealle* 3060a).

gomel on giohðe 2793a, 3095a.

FORMULAIC SYSTEMS OF THE FIRST HALF-LINE (A^a)

heah ofer heafod 48a, *heah ofer horde* 2768a (both expressions describe *segn;* see *segen glydenne,* D^{1a-b}, 47b).

Heorogar ond Hroðgar 61a, *Hroðgar ond Hroþulf* 1017a, *Hreðric ond Hroðmund* 1189a, *Herebeald ond Hæðcyn* 2434a.

wiges weorðmynd 65a, *wigena weorðmynd* 1559a.

sinc æt symle 81a, *geaf me sinc ond symbel* 2431a.

ana wið eallum 145a, *ealle buton anum* 705a, *an æfter eallum* 2268a, *an æfter anum* 2461a.

wan under wolcnum 651a, *won to wolcnum* 1374a; *wand to wolcnum* 1119a, *weox under wolcnum* 8a, *wod under wolcnum* 714a; *wæter under wolcnum* 1631a, *weold under wolcnum* 1770a.

freogan on ferhþe 948a, *ferhðum freoge* 3176a.

feonda feorum 1152a, *freonda feorum* 1306a.

gang ofer grundas 1404a, *glad ofer grundas* 2073a.

ðeodne æt þearfe 1525a, *þegnes þearfe* 1797a, *þegn æt ðearfe* 2709a.

mærða gemyndig 1530a, *mærða gemunde* 2678a.

adl ne yldo 1736a, *þæt þec adl oððe ecg* 1763a, *adl oþðe iren* 1848a.

hond ond heard sweord 2509a, *helmas ond heard sweord* 2638a.[3]

feoll on fedan 2919a, *feoll on foldan* 2975a (see the preceding half-lines, 2918b and 2974b).

3. Ibid., p. 259.

FORMULAE OF THE FIRST AND SECOND HALF-LINES $\left(A^{a-b}\right)$

lange hwile 16a, 2159b, 2780a.

hringedstefna 32b, 1897b, *hringedstefnan* 1131a.

þeodgestreonum 44a, *þeodgestreona* 1218a.

longe þrage 54b, 114a, 1257b.

earfoðlice 86b, 1636a, 1657a, 2303a, 2822a, 2934b.

ece Drihten 108a, *ecean Dryhtne* 1692a, 1779a, 2330b.

mære þeoden 129b, 1046b, 1715a, *mærne þeoden* 201a, 1598a, 2384a, 2788b, 3141b, *mærum þeodne* 345a, 1992a, 2572a, *mæres þeodnes* 797a.

wergan gastas 133a, 1747b.

husa selest 146a, 285b, 658b, 935a.

weana ȝehwylcne 148b, *weana ȝehwylces* 1396a (see below, Brief Expressions, 3).

duguþe ond geoguþe 160b, 621a, 1674a.

Geata leoda 205b, *Geata leode* 260b, 362b, 1213b, 2318b, 2927a, 3137b, 3178b, *Geatena leode* 443b, *Geata leodum* 1856a, 1930b (see *Weder-Gaeta leod,* E^{a-b}, 1492b).

findan mihte 207a, *findan meahton* 1156b, 2373b, 3162b, *findan meahte* 2870b (see below, Brief Expressions, 3).

Wedera leode 225a, 3156b, *Wedera leodum* 697b, 1894b, *Wedra leoda* 2900b (see *Weder-Geata leod,* E^{a-b}, 1492b).

guðgewædo 227a, *guðgewædu* 2617b, 2730a, 2851a, 2871b, *guðgewæda* 2623b.

byrnum werede 238a, 2529b.

heorðgeneatas 261b, 1580b, 2180a, 3179b, *heorðgeneatum* 2418b.

Deniga frean 271a, 359a, 1680b.

deorcum nihtum 275b, 2211a.

arum healdan 296a, 1182a, *arum heolde* 1099a.

leofne mannan 297b, 1943b, 2127a, 3108a, *leofra manna* 1915b, *leofes mannes* 1994a, 2080a, 2897a.

oretmecgas 332a, 363b, 481b.

bordgeneatas 343a, 1713b.

þeoden mærne 353a, 2721a, *þeodnas mære* 3070a.

feorran cumene 361b, 1819a.

angan dohtor 375a, 2997b.

Deniga leodum 389a, 1323a, 1712b, *Denigea leode* 696a, 2125b (cf. *leode Deniga* 599a).

þanon he gesohte 463a, 520a.

folce Deniga 465b, *folces Deniges* 1582a.

gumena ængum 474a, 2416b, *gumena ænig* 3054a.

beore druncne 480b, *beore druncen* 531a.

bidan woldon 482b, *bidan wolde* 1494a, 2308a.

aldrum neþdon 510a, 538a, *aldre geneþan* 1469b, *ealdre geneðde* 2133b.[4]

hildebille 557a, 1520a, 2679a.

siþes werig 579a, *siðes wergum* 1794b.

dæd gefremede 585b, 940b, *dædum gefremed* 954a.

folces hyrde 610a, 1832a, 1849a, 2644b, 2981a.

æfenræste 646a, 1252a.

hildegeatwe 674b, *hildegeatwa* 2362a.

Beowulf Geata 676a, 1191a.

guþgeweorca 678a, 981b, 1825a.

sona þæt onfunde 750a, 1497a.

manna ænig 779b, *manna ængum* 1461a (see below, Brief Expressions, 1).

ealde lafe 795b, 1688a.

ellenmærþum 828a, 1471a.

worn gemunde 870a, 2114b.

ellendædum 876a, 900a.

brucan moste 894b, 2241a, 3100b (see below, Brief Expressions, 3).

ærran mælum 907b, 2237a.

feorhgeniðlan 969a, 1540a, 2933b.

hilderinces 986b, *hilderince* 1495a, 1576a, *hilderinca* 3124a (see *har hilderinc*,
  D²ᵃ, 1307a).

yrfelafe 1053a, 1903a.

sincgestreonum 1092b, *sincgestreona* 1226a.

fættan goldes 1093a, 2246a, *fættan golde* 2102a.

arum heolde 1099a, *arum healdan* 1182a.

hildeleoman 1143b, 2583a.

nean ond feorran 1174a, 2317b (cf. *feorran ond nean* 839b).

---

4. *aldrum neþdon* 510a, 538a. Perhaps the second occurrence of the phrase in proximity to the first reflects the intended rhetoric of a *flit*. Beowulf is repeating in a more glorious context Unferth's words, which had had scornful implications. There are other, doubtless similarly constructed, repetitions in their two speeches (cf. 512b and 539b, 428a and 545a).

nyhstan siðe 1203b, 2511a.

breostgewædu 1211a, 2162a.

hafast þu gefered 1221a, 1855a.

Grendles modor 1258b, 1282a, 1538b, 2118b, 2139b.

eaxlgestealla 1326a, *eaxlgesteallan* 1714a.

hafelan weredon 1327a, *hafelan werede* 1448b.

ealdres scyldig 1338a, 2061a (cf. *morðres scyldig* 1683a, *synnum scildig* 3071b; further *ealdres orwena*, D¹ᵃ, 1002a).

ealdgestreonum 1381a, *ealdgestreona* 1458b.

worolde lifes 1387a, 2343a.

Grendles magan 1391a, *Grendeles maga* 2006b, *Grendeles mægum* 2353b (see Hemmingesmæg, Eᵇ, 1944b).

ic hit þe gehate 1392a, *ic hit þe þonne gehate* 1671a.

yðgewinnes 1434a, *yðgewinne* 2412a.

snottra fengel 1475a, 2156a.

aldre linnan 1478a, *ealdres linnan* 2443b.

Geata dryhten 1484b, 1831a, 2560b, 2576a, 2991b, *Geata dryhtne* 2483a.

æfter þæm wordum 1492a, 2669a.

biden wolde 1494a, 2308a (further *biddan wille*, 427b).

ær he þone grundwong *1496a, *þæt he þone grundwong* *2770a.

deorum madme 1528a, *deore maðmas* 2236a, 3131a.

feþecempa 1544a, 2853a.

aldorleasne 1587a, 3003a.

blondenfeaxe 1594b, *blondenfeaxum* 1873a, *blondenfexa* 2962a.

Grendles heafod 1639b, 1648a.⁵

þæt la mæg secgan 1700a, 2864a (see the preceding lines, 1698b f. and 2862b f.).

mægenes wynnum 1716b, 1887a.

eorþan wynne 1730b, 2727a.

side rice 1733a, 2199a.

niowan stefne 1789a, 2594a.

gamela Scylding 1792a, 2105b.

meces ecge 1812a, *meces ecgum* 2614a, 2939a.

Hreþles eaferan 1847b, *Hreðles eafora* 2358a, 2992a.

---

5. *Grendles heafod* 1639b, 1648a. This phrase probably owes its formulaic status far more to syntax than to facility of versemaking, especially since these two appearances within ten lines of each other are the only ones in the poem.

hordgestreonum 1899b, *hordgestreona* 3092a.

Hæreþes dohtor 1929a, 1981b.

geongum cempan 1948b, 2044b, *geongan cempan* 2626a.

lifgesceafta 1953a, 3064a.

laðan cynnes 2008a, 2354a.

rices hyrde 2027a, 3080a.

lytle while 2030b, 2097a.

wealdan moston 2038b, 2984b, *wealdan moste* 2574a, *wealdan ne moste* 2827b
    (further *gif he wealdan mot* 442b, [B]; see below, Brief Expressions, 3).

dyrnum cræfte 2168a, *dyrnan cræfte* 2290a.

hondgesteallan 2169a, 2596b.

uferan dogrum 2200b, 2392a.

fiftig wintra 2209a, 2733a (cf. *þusend wintra* 3050a).

sylfes willum 2222a, 2639b.

leoda duguðe 2238a, 2945a.

fæted wæge 2253b, 2282a.

eacencræftig 2280a, 3051b.

Wedera þioden 2336a, 2786b, 3037a, *Wedra ðeodnes* 2656a.

hames niosan 2366b, 2388a.

dryhten Geata 2402a, 2901a.

orleghwila 2427a, *orleghwile* 2911a.

gomela Scylfing 2487b, 2968a.

gumena gehwylcne 2516b, *gumena gehwylcum* 2859a (see below, Brief Expressions, 3).

middelnihtum 2782a, 2833a.

FORMULAIC SYSTEMS OF THE FIRST AND SECOND HALF-LINES $(A^{a–b})$

wæs min fæder 262a, *gesloh þin fæder* 459a, *þone þin fæder* 2048a.

witena welhwylc 266a, *witena gehwylcum* 936b.

wen' ic þæt ge for wlenco 338a, *ðær git for wlence* 508a, *siþðan he for wlenco* 1206a.

beo ðu on ofeste 386a, *bio nu on ofeste* 2747a, *heo wæs on ofste* 1292a, *ar wæs on ofoste* 2783a (further *ic on ofoste gefeng* 3090b [B]).

duguð unlytel 498a, *torn unlytel* 833a, *dom unlytel* 885b.

hwæþereme gesælde 574a, *hwæþre him gesælde* 890a (see below, Brief Expressions, 3).

gespræc þa se goda 675a, *gemunde þa se goda* 758a.

hwearf þa bi bence 1188a, *hwearf þa be wealle* 1573a (further *hwearf þa hrædlice* 356a [C]).

eode þa to setle 1232a, *ga nu to setle* 1782a.

næfne he wæs mara 1353a, *buton hit wæs mara* 1560a (see below, Whole-Line Formulaic Systems).

gewat him ða se hearda 1963a, *gewat him ða se goda* 2949a (see below, Whole-Line Formulaic Systems).

FORMULAE OF THE SECOND HALF-LINE (A^b)

leofne þeoden 34b, 3079b.

forð onsendon 45b, *forð onsended* 2266b.

men ne cunnon 50b, 162b.

wica neosan 125b, 1125b.

oft gefremede 165b, *oft gefremedon* 2478b, *eft gefremede* 135b.

gretan moste 168b, *gretan moton* 347b (cf. *gretan nolde* 803b, *gretan sceolde* 2421b, *gretan dorste* 2735b; see below, Brief Expressions, 3).

geoce gefremede 177b, *geoce gefremman* 2674b.

mægenes strengest *196b, *mægene strengest* *789b.

þysses lifes *197b, *790b, 806b.

secean wolde 200b, 645b (see below, Whole-Line Formulaic Systems).

snotere ceorlas 202b, 416b, 1591b.

beorhte frætwe 214b, *beorhte frætwa* 896b (further *beorhte randas* 231b).

oþres dogeres 219b, 605b.

Gode þancedon 227b, 1626b, *Gode þancode* 625b, 1397b.

gearwe ne wisson 246b, *gearwe ne wiston* 878b.

Ecgþeow haten 263b, 373b.^6

wide geond eorþan 266b, 3099b.

secean cwomon 268b, *secean come* 1597b (see below, Whole-Line Formulaic Systems).

secgan hyrdon 273b, *secgan hyrde* 582b, 875b, 1346b.

colran wurðaþ 282b, *colran weorðað* 2066b (see below, Whole-Line Formulaic Systems).

samod ætgædere 329b, 387b, 729b, 1063b (see below, Whole-Line Formulaic Systems).

6. See Pope, p. 329.

leode mine 415b, 1336b, 1345b.

wine min Beowulf 457b, 1704b.[7]

middangearde 504b, 751b (see *geond þisne middangeard,* Bᵇ, 75b; further, hypermetric, *mon on middangearde* 2996a).

helpe gefremede 551b, 1552b.

laðgeteonan 559b, *laðgeteone* 974b.

aldre gedigest 661b, *ealdre gedigde* 1655b (cf. *feore gedigde* 578b, *niða gedigde* 2350b, *guða gedigde* 2543b).

manna cynnes 701b, 712b, 735b, *manna cynne* 810b, 914b, 1725b (see below, Whole-Line Formulaic Systems).

anra gehwylces 732b, *anra gehwylcnum* 784b (see below, Brief Expressions, 3).

forman siðe 740b, 2286b (see *ne wæs þæt forma sið,* Bᵇ, 716b).

mine gefræge 776b, 837b, 1955b, 2685b, 2837b.

ænige þinga 791b, 2374b, 2905b.

eal gemenged 848b, 1593b.

heardan clammum 963b, *heardum clammum* 1335b.

helm ond byrnan 1022b, 2868b, *helm ond byrne* 1629b (see below, Brief Expressions, 1).

since gewurþad 1038b, 1450b (see *wæpnum geweorðad,* Aᵃ, 250a; see below, Brief Expressions, 2).

eorla drihten 1050b, 2338b.

eþgesyne 1110b, 1244b.

Beowulf leofa 1216b, 1758b.

hringed byrne 1245b, *hringde byrnan* 2615b (see below, Brief Expressions, 1, and Whole-Line Formulaic Systems).

þegne monegum 1341b, 1419b.

ende gebidan 1386b, 2342b.

wide gesyne 1403b, 2316b, 2947b, 3158b.

sawolleasne 1406b, 3033b.

strenge getruwode 1533b, 2540b.

witig Drihten 1554b, 1841b.

Hroðgar gretan *1646b, 2010b, *Hroðgar grette* *1816b.

þinra leoda 1673b, *þine leode* 2095b (cf. *leodum þinum* 1708b; see below, Whole-Line Formulaic Systems).

eagum starige 1781b, *eagum starede* 1935b.

7. Ibid., p. 331.

eft to leodum 1804b, 2368b.

godne tealde 1810b, *gode tealde* 2641b, *godne ne tealdeon* 2184b.

leofa Beowulf 1854b, 1987b.

oþres swiðor 1874b, *oðrum swiðor* 2198b.

hringnet bæron 1889b, *hringnet beran* 2754b.

gomelra lafe 2036b, *gomele lafe* 2563b.

hindeman siðe 2049b, 2517b.

syllan wolde 2160b, 2729b.

wisse he gearwe 2339b, 2725b.

hord ond rice 2369b, 3004b (further *folc ond rice* 1179a).

Sweona ond Geata 2472b, 2946b.

oðre siðe 2670b, 3101b.

minum leodum 2797b, 2804b.

ende gefered 2844b, *ende gefere* 3063b.

bugan sceolde 2918b, 2974b.

FORMULAIC SYSTEMS OF THE SECOND HALF-LINE (A^b)

swa wæter bebugeð 93b, *swa sæ bebugeð* 1223b.

soð ic talige 532b, *wen ic talige* 1845b.

cearu wæs geniwod 1303b, *sorh is geniwod* 1322b, *wroht wæs geniwad* 2287b.

Formulae of the B-Verses

FORMULAE OF THE FIRST HALF-LINE (B^a)

wið Grendles gryre 384a, *on Grendles gryre* 478a.

under heofones hwealf 576a, 2015a.

æfter hæleþa hryre 2052a, 3005a (see below, Whole-Line Formulaic Systems).

wæs þæs wyrmes wig 2316a, *ne him þæs wyrmes wig* 2348a.

FORMULAE OF THE FIRST AND SECOND HALF-LINES (B^a–b)

se þe on handa bær 495a, *sum on handa bær* 3124b.

gegrette þa 652a, 2516a.

ða him Hroðgar gewat 662a, *ond him Hroþgar gewat* 1236b.

hu mihtig God 701a, 1725a (see below, Whole-Line Formulaic Systems).

næfre he on aldordagum 718a, *swylce he on ealderdagum* 757a.[8]

on feonda geweald 808a, 903a.

8. Ibid., p. 281.

under swegles begong 860a, 1773a.

he to healle geong 925b, *þæt to healle gang* 1009a (see below, Brief Expressions, 3).

heht ða eorla hleo 1035a, 2190a.

þæt him hildegrap 1446a, *ac him hildegrap* 2507a.

þæt wæs yðgeblond 1593a, *wæron yðgebland* 1620a (further *þannon yðgeblond* 1373a).

ond þegna gehwylc 1673a, *ond þegna gehwam* 2033a (see below, Whole-Line Formulaic Systems).

FORMULAIC SYSTEMS OF THE FIRST AND SECOND HALF-LINES (B^{a-b})

þonne yldo bearn 70a, *ofer ylda bearn* 605a (further *ylda bearnum* 150a [A]; *wið Eotena bearn* 1088a, *þæt he Eotena bearn* 1141a, *swa hyne Geata bearn* 2184a; *þæt þæt ðeodnes bearn* 910a, *ond hæleða bearna* 2224a [A]; *þara þe gumena bearn* 878a, *gumena bearna* 1367a [A], *niþða bearna* 1005b [A]).

under Heorotes hrof 403a, *under geapne hrof* 836b, *under beorges hrof* 2755b.

þær wæs hæleða dream 497b, *þær wæs hæleþa hleahtor* 611a.

þe æt fotum sæt 500a, *æt fotum sæt* 1166a (hypermetric) (cf. *ðær on wicge sæt* 286b; further *unbliðe sæt* 130b [E], *þær Hroðgar sæt* 356b, *þær se goda sæt* 1190b, *he gewergad sæt* 2852b, *modgiomor sæt* 2894b [E]; see below, Whole-Line Formulaic Systems).

ond syþðan witig God 685b, *nefne him witig God* 1056a.

þa wæs sæl ond mæl 1008b (further *sæla ond mæla* 1611a [A]).

gif he þæt eal gemon 1185b, *feor eal gemon* 1701b, *se ðe eal geman* 2042b, *ic þæt eall gemon* 2427b (further *ic þe þæs lean geman* 1220b, *ic ðæt mæl gemon* 2633a).

ond wunden gold 1193a, *þa wæs wunden gold* 3134a (further *wundnum golde* 1382a [A]).

he under rande gecranc 1209b, *he æt wige gecrang* 1337b, *heo on flet gecrong* 1568b, *ac in campe gecrong* 2505a (see *oþðe on wæl crunge* 635b, C^b).

swa Wedra helm 2462b, *forwrat Wedra helm* 2705a.

þa ic on morgne gefrægn 2484a, *ða ic æt þearfe gefrægn* 2694b, *ða ic on hlæwe gefrægn* 2773a.

FORMULAE OF THE SECOND HALF-LINE (B^b)

syððan ærest wearð 6b, 1947b.

him wæs geomor sefa 49b, 2419b (see *him bið grim sefa* 2043b, C^b systems).

geond þisne middangeard *75b, *1771b (see *middangeardes,* A^b, 504b).

oð ðæt an ongan 100b, 2210b.

he him ðæs lean forgeald 114b, 1584b.

undyrne cuð 150b, 410b.

hine fyrwyt bræc 232b, 1985b, 2784b.

þæt ænig oðer man 503b, *ðonne ænig oðer man* 534b (see *þonne ænig man oðer,* C^b, 1353b; see below, Brief Expressions, 1).

swa hit gedefe wæs 561b, 1670b.

ond þæt word acwæð 654b, 2046b (see *fea worda cwæð,* E^b, 2246b).

in sele þam hean 713b, 1984b, *to sele þam hean* 919b, *on sele þam hean* 1016b.

ne wæs þæt forma sið 716b, *næs þæt forma sið* 1463b.

ða he gebolgen wæs 723b, 1539b, 2550b, *þæt he gebolgen wæs* 2220b.

þær he meahte swa 762b, *ðær hie meahton swa* 797b.

he under harne stan 887b, *under harne stan* 2553b, 2744b (cf. *ofer harne stan* 1415a).

ða hie se fær begeat 1068b, *þa hyne se fær begeat* 2230b.

siþðan morgen com 1077b, 2103b, 2124b (cf. *siþðan morgen bið* 1784b, *syþðan æfen cwom* 1235b, *oð ðæt æfen cwom* 2303b, *oþ þæt ende bicwom* 1254b, *oð ðæt niht becwom* 2116b).

ða wæs forma sið 1527b, 2625b (see *forman siðe,* A^b, 740b).

ond hine þa heafde becearf 1590b, *ond ic hæfde becearf* 2138b.

þe is wide cuð 2135b, *ac wæs wide cuð* 2923b (cf. *þæt wæs yldum cuð* 705b; see *undyrne cuð,* B^b, 150b).

næs ic fæge þa gyt 2141b, *næs he fæge þa git* 2975b.

ne byð him wihte ðy sel 2277b, *næs him wihte ðe sel* 2687b.

he þæt sone onfand 2300b, 2713b.

næs ða long to ðon 2591b, 2845b (further *ne wæs hit lenge þa gen* 83b).

ðe us ðas beagas geaf 2635b, *þe us beagas geaf* 3009b.

FORMULAIC SYSTEMS OF THE SECOND HALF-LINE (B^b)

him on bearme læg 40b, *him on eaxle læg* 1547b.

þær wæs hearpan sweg 89b, *nis þær hearpan sweg* 2458b, *nalles hearpan sweg* 3023b.

wæs þæs gewin to strang 133b, *wæs þæt gewin to swyð* 191b (cf. *wæs sio hond to strong* 2684b).

þa him wæs manna þearf 201b, *þær ðe bið manna þearf* 1835b.

mid his eorla gedriht 357b, *ond minra eorla gedryht* 431b, *mid minra secga gedryht* 633b, *mid his hæleþa gedryht* 662b, *mid þinra secga gedriht* 1672b.

hine halig God 382b, *ond halig God* 1553b.

swa him se hearda bebead 401b, *swa se rica bebead* 1975b.

nu ic þus feorran com 430b, *se þe ær feorran com* 825b (see *feorran cumene,* A^a–b, 361b).

þe þa deað fornam 488b, *ealle hie deað fornam* 2236b, *ðe hyne swylt fornam* 1436b, *þara ðe þær guð fornam* 1123b, *hyne wyrd fornam* 1205b, *ac hyne ecg fornam* 2772b (further *ecga fornamon* 2828b [A]; see *gif mec deað nimeð,* C^b, 447b, and *heaðoræs fornam,* D^2b systems, 557b).

no he wiht fram me 541b, *no ic wiht fram þe* 581b.

þæs ðe hire se willa gelamp 626b (further *willa gelumpen* 824b [A]).

drace morðre swealt 892b, *oð þæt he morþre swealt* 2782b.

to widan feore 933b, *ne seah ic widan feorh* 2014b.

nalles for ealdre mearn 1442b, *nalas for fæhðe mearn* 1537b.

se ðe flode begong 1497b, *ofer floda begang* 1826b.

ond þa þas worold ofgeaf 1681b, *þara ðe þis lif ofgeaf* 2251b (see *gumdream ofgeaf,* D^2, 2469a).

þær he worna fela 2003b, *se ðe worna fela* 2542b.

syððan Hygelac læg 2201b, *syððan Heardred læg* 2388b.

no þon lange wæs 2423b, *þær he longe wæs* 3082b (cf. *þær he longe sceal* 3108b).

nelle ic beorges weard 2524b, *þa he biorges weard* 3066b.

þa he of ealdre gewat 2624b, *him of hræðre gewat* 2819b.

Formulae of the C-Verses

FORMULAE OF THE FIRST HALF-LINE (C^a)

æfter deaðdæge 187a, 885a.

geond widwegas 840a, 1704a.

FORMULAE OF THE FIRST AND SECOND HALF-LINES (C^a–b)

in geardagum 1b, *þone on geardagum* 1354a, *swa hy on geardagum* 2233a.

þe hie ær drugon 15a, 831b, 1858b (see below, Whole-Line Formulaic Systems).

on bearm scipes 35b, *bær on bearm scipes* 896a (cf. *on bearm nacan* 214a).

to gefremmanne 174b, 2644a.

þa Metod nolde 706b, 967b.

ond on weg þanon 763b, *on weg þanon* 844b.

be sæm tweonum 858b, 1297b, *1685b, *1956b.

geseon moste 961b, 1998b, *geseon moston* 1628b, 1875b (see below, Brief Expressions, 3 and Whole-Line Formulaic Systems).

swa sceal man dôn 1172b, 1534b (cf. *swa sceal mæg dôn* 2166b; further, *swa he nu git deð* 1058b, *swa he nu gen deð* 2859b, *swa he oft dyde* 444b, *swa he nu gyt dyde* 956b, *swa ic ær dyde* 1381b, *ðonne ic gyt dyde* 1824b, *swa he ær dyde* 1891b, *swa þu ær dydest* 1676b, *swa hie oft ær dydon* 1238b, *þa ðæt þær dydon* 3070b).

to hofe sinum 1236b, 1507b.

on hreon mode 1307b, 2581b.

þonne hniton feþan 1327b, 2544b.

þonne ænig man oðer 1353b, 1560b (see below, Whole-Line Formulaic Systems; see *þæt ænig oðer man,* B^b, 503b; see below, Brief Expressions, 1).

abroten hæfde 1599b, *abroten hæfdon* 2707b.

on flett gâð 2034b, *on flet gâð* 2054b (further *on flet teôn* 1036b, *on flet boren* 1647b).

gedon wolde 2090b, 2186b

on Hronesnæsse 2805b, *to Hronesnæsse* 3136b.

FORMULAIC SYSTEMS OF THE SECOND HALF-LINE (C^b)

cwæð he guðcyning 199b, *him þæs guðkyning* 2335b, *þa gen guðcyning* 2677b, *þæt se guðcyning* 3036b (see *geongne guðcyning,* D^{1a} systems, 1969a).

þeah he him leof wære 203b (further *þeah him leof ne wæs* 2467b [B]).

het hine wel brucan 1045b (further *het hyne brucan well* 2812b [B]).

swylc scolde eorl wesan 1328b, *swylc sceolde secg wesan* 2708b.

wolde hyre mæg wrecan 1339b, *wolde hire bearn wrecan* 1546b.

him bið grim sefa 2043b, *mæs him hreoh sefa* 2180b, *him wæs sefa geomor* 2632b (see *him wæs geomor sefa,* B^b, 49b).

þa wæs dæg sceacen 2306b, *ða wæs eall sceacen* 2727b, *þa wæs winter scacen* 1136b.

Formulae of the D-Verses

FORMULAE OF THE FIRST HALF-LINE (D^{1a})

heard hondlocen 322a, 551a.

heardhicgende 394a, 799a.

brego Beorht-Dena 427a, 609a.

wado weallende 546a, *wadu weallendu* 581a.

atol æglæca 592a, 732a, 816a (cf. *ac se æglæca* 159a).

aldres orwena 1002a, 1565a (see *ealdres scyldig*, A^(a–b), 1338a).

morðorbealo maga 1079a, 2742a.

wyrsan wigfrecan 1212a, 2496a.

locene leoðosyrcan 1505a, 1890a.

frome fyrdhwate 1641a, 2476a.

feorhbealo frecne 2250a, *feorhbealu frecne* 2537a.

hwate helmberend 2517a, 2642a.

geongum garwigan 2674a, 2811a.

ne sohte searoniðas 2738a, *sohte searoniðas* 3067a.

FORMULAIC SYSTEMS OF THE FIRST HALF-LINE (D^(1a))

fyrdsearu fuslicu 232a, *fyrdsearo fuslic* 2618a [A].

geongne quðcyning 1969a, *god guðcyning* 2563a (cf. *leof leodcyning* 54a, *sigora Soðcyning* 3055a; see *cwæð he quðcyning*, C^b systems, 199b).

FORMULAE OF THE FIRST HALF-LINE (D^(2a))

þryðlic þegna heap 400a, 1628a.

har hilderinc 1307a, 3136a (see *hilderinces*, A^(a–b), 986b).

forbarn brodenmæl 1616a, 1667a.

hæle hildedeor *1646a, *1816a, 3111a (cf. *heold hildedeor* 2183a; further *him þa hildedeor* 312a, *siþðan hildedeor* 834a, *hwilum hildedeor* 2107a [B], *hildedeore* 3169b [A]).

eald eþelweard 1702a, 2210a.

FORMULAIC SYSTEMS OF THE FIRST HALF-LINE (D^(2a))

seon sibbegedriht 387a, *swefan sibbegedriht* 729 (see below, Whole-Line Formulaic Systems).

eode eorla sum 1312a, *eode eahta sum* 3123a.[11]

awræc wintrum frod 1724a, *warað wintrum frod* 2277a (further *þonne he wintrum frod* 2114a [B]).

FORMULAE OF THE FIRST AND SECOND HALF-LINES (D^(1a–b))

þeodcyninga 2a, *þeodcyninges* 2694b (cf. *wuldurcyninga* 2795a; see *Þeod-*

11. See Pope, p. 312.

Scyldingas, D^{1a-b}, 1019a, *worold-cyninga,* D^{1b} 1684b; *hæfde Kyningwuldor* 665a [C]).

ymbsittendra 9b, 2734a.

wine Scyldinga 30b, 148a, 170b, 1183a, 2026b, 2101b, *winum Scyldinga* 1418a (further *ic þæs wine Deniga* 350b [C]).

segen gyldenne 47b, 1021a (cf. *segn eallgylden* 2767b; further *swyn ealgylden* 1111b).

selerædende 51b, 1346a.

maga Healfdenes 189b, 1474b, 2143b, *mago Healfdenes* 1867a, 2011b (cf. *mago Ecglafes* 1465b, *mago Ecgðeowes* 2587b; see *Grendles magan,* A^{a-b}, 1391a; see below, Whole-Line Formulaic Systems).

lindhæbbende 245b, *lindhabbendra* 1402a.

sunu Healfdenes 268a, 344b, 645a, 1040b, 1652a, 1699a, 2147a (cf. *sunu Beanstanes* 524a, *sunu Hygelaces* 2386a, *sunu Wonredes* 2971b; further *gladum suna Frodan* 2025b; *Healfdenes sunu* 1009b [E], *geseon sunu Hradles* 1485a [C], *sunu Ecgbeowes,* D^{1b}, 1550b, *suna Ohtheres,* D^{1a-b}, 2380b; see below, Whole-Line Formulaic Systems).

frean Scyldinga 291a, 351a, 500b, 1166a (hypermetric) (cf. *frean userne,* D^{1b}, 3002b, *frean Ingwina* 1319a; further *Deniga frean,* A^{a-b} 271a; see below, Whole-Line Formulaic Systems).

foldbuendum 309b, *foldbuende* 1355a

Wulfgar maþelode 348a, 360a.

Hroðgar maþelode *371a, *456a, 925a, *1321a, 1687a, 1840a.

Beowulf maþelode 405a, *529a, *631a, *957a, *1383a, *1473a, *1651a, *1817a, *1999a, *2425a, 2510a, 2724a.

eodor Scyldinga 428a, 663a (cf. *eodor Ingwine* 1044a).

unlifigende 468b, *unlyfigendes* 744a, *unlyfigendne* 1308b, *unlifigendum* 1389a, 2908b.

bearn Healfdenes 469a, 1020b (cf. *bearn Ecgðeowes,* D^{1b}, 529b; further *Ecglafes bearn* 499b, *Ongenðiowes bearn* 2387b [E]).

sunu Ecglafes 590b, 980b, 1808a (cf. *sunu Healfdenes,* D^{1a-b}, 268a, *sunu Ecgðeowes,* D^{1b}, 1550b).

Sige-Scyldinga 597b, *Sige-Scyldingum* 2004a.

mæg Hygelaces 737a, 758b, 813b, 914a, 1530b (cf. *mæg Alfheres* 2604a; further *sunu Hygelaces* 2386b, *Hemminges mæg,* E^{b}, 1944b).

feorh ealgian 796b, 2655b, 2668a.

sið Beowulfes 872a, 1971a (further *wæs him Beowulfes sið* 501b [E]).

swiðhicgende 919a, 1016a.

hwate Scyldingas 1601a, 2052b (cf. *hwate scyldwigan* 3005b; see below, Whole-Line Formulaic Systems).

felamodigra 1637a, 1888b.

leod Scyldinga 1653a, 2159a (cf. *leod Scylfinga* 2603b; further *Weder-Geata leod,* E^b, 1492b).

þeoden Scyldinga 1675a, 1871a.

fletsittendum 1788a, *fletsittende* 2022b.

heoþoliðende 1798a, *heaðoliðendum* 2955a.

inwitniþas 1858a, *inwitniða* 1947a (see below, Whole-Line Formulaic Systems).

healsittendra 2015b, *healsittendum* 2868a.

suna Ohtheres 2380b, 2612a, *sunu Ohtheres* 2394b (cf. *sunu Healfdenes,* D^{1a-b}, 268a).

Wægmundinga 2607b, 2814a.

Wiglaf maþelode 2631a, *2862a, *3076a (cf. *weard maþelode* 286a, *Unferð maþelode* 499a, *Wealhðeo maþelode* 1215a).

FORMULAIC SYSTEMS OF THE FIRST AND SECOND HALF-LINES (D^{1a-b})

feond mancynnes 164b (further *nancynnes feond* 1276a [E]; see below, Brief Expressions, 2).

onsend Higelace 452a (further *Hygelace onsend* 1483b [D^2]).

sorh is me to secganne 473a, *wundor is to secganne* 1724b.

FORMULAIC SYSTEMS OF THE FIRST AND SECOND HALF-LINES (D^{2a-b})

þanon eft gewat 123b, alliteration on *þ* (further *þanon eft gewiton* 853a [B], alliteration on *e*).

seah on enta geweorc 2717b, *eald enta geweorc* 2774a (further *Welandes geweorc* 455b, *giganta geweorc* 1562b).

FORMULAE OF THE SECOND HALF-LINE (D^{1b})

fela missera 153b, 2620b.

fea þingian 156b, *fea þingode* 470b.

secg wisade 208b, *þa secg wisode* 402b.

andswarode 258b, 340b (see below, Whole-Line Formulaic Systems).

helm Scyldinga *371b, *456b, *1321b (cf. *helm Scylfinga* 2381b; further *swa Wedra helm,* B^{a-b} systems, 2462b).

cnihtwesende 372b, 535b.

wean ahsodon 423b, *wean ahsode* 1206b.

Ar-Scyldinga 464b, *Ar-Scyldingum* 1710b.

bearn Ecgþeowes *529b, *631b, *957b, *1383b, *1473b, *1651b, *1817b, *1999b, 2177b, *2425b (cf. *bearn Healfdenes,* D^{1a-b}, 469a).

Godes andsacan 786b, *Godes andsaca* 1682b.

wundor sceawian 840b, 3032b (cf. *gang sceawian* 1391b, *wong sceawian* 1413b, *dracan sceawian* 2402b, *hord sceawian* 2744a, *þær sceawian* 3008b).

last weardian 971b, *last weardode* 2164b.

wæl reafodon 1212b, *wæl reafode* 3027b.

samod ærdæge 1311b, 2942b (further *samod ætgædere,* A^b, 329b).

sund cunnian 1426b, 1444b.[12]

hund missera 1498b, 1769b.

sunu Ecgbeowes 1550b, 2367b, 2398b (cf. *sunu Healfdenes,* D^{1a-b}, 268a; further *bearn Ecgðeowes,* D^{1b}, 529b).

woroldcyninga 1684b, 3180b (cf. *þeodcyninga,* D^{1a-b}, 2a, *eorðcyninges* 1155b, *heahcyninges* 1039b, *sæcyninga* 2383b, *Frescyninge* 2503b; further *ge-ongne guðcyning,* D^{1a} systems, 1969a, *ða ic ðe, beorncyning,* 2148a [C]).

heorodreorigne 1780b, 2720b.

sunu Wihstanes 2752b, 3120b.

byre Wihstanes 2907b, 3110b.

frean userne 3002b, 3107b (cf. *frean eowerne* 2537b; further *frean Scyldinga,* D^{1a-b}, 291a).

FORMULAIC SYSTEMS OF THE SECOND HALF-LINE $\left(D^{1b}\right)$

last sceawedon 132b, *hæl sceawedon* 204b, *hand sceawedon* 983b, *weras scea-wedon* 1440b, *gold sceawode* 2793b.

þeod ealgearo 1230b, *beorh eallgearo* 2241b.

FORMULAE OF THE SECOND HALF-LINE $\left(D^{2b}\right)$

Denum eallum wearð 767b, 823b (cf. *Denum eallum wæs* 1417b).[13]

andlean forgeald 1541b, 2094b.

---

12. *sund cunnian* 1426b, 1444b. The phrase may purposefully link Beowulf, known to be a great swimmer, with the *wyrmas ond wildeor* of Grendel's mere.

13. See Pope, p. 362. *Denum eallum wearð* 767b, 823b. The repetition contains Beowulf's struggle against Grendel: before the fight, the Danes have *ealuscerwen,* afterward, their *willa.*

FORMULAIC SYSTEMS OF THE SECOND HALF-LINE (D²ᵇ)

word æfter cwað 315b, *word æfter spræc* 341b (further *þæt word acwæð* 41038—Lyre & Harp

heaþoræs fornam 577b, *wældeað fornam* 695b, *wig ealle fornam* 1080b, *sunu deað fornam* 2119b, *guðdeað fornam* 2249b (further *þe þa deað fornam,* Bᵇ systems, 488b, *gif mec deað nimeð,* Cᵇ, 447b).

seleræste gebeah 690b, *fletræste gebeag* 1241b.

welhwylc gecwæð 874b, *æghwylc gecwæð* 987b.

lig ealle forswealg 1122b, *lic eall forswealg* 2080b.

helm oft gescær 1526b, *helm ær gescer* 2973b.

gæst yrre cwom 2073b, *wyrm yrre cwom* 2669b.

hreðer inne weoll 2113b, *breost innan weoll* 2331b (cf. *hreðer æðme weoll* 2593b; further *geofon yþum weoll* 515b, *swat yþum weoll* 2693b, *holm storme weoll* 1131b, *holm heolfre weoll* 2138a, *flod blode weol* 1422a).

Formulae of the E-Verses

FORMULAE OF THE FIRST HALF-LINE (Eᵃ)

sorhfullne sið 512a, 1278a, 1429a.

heoþosteapa helm 1245a, *heoðsteapne helm* 2153a (see below, Whole-Line Formulaic Systems).

gimfæste gife *1271a, *ginfæstan gife* *2182a.

sigoreadig secg 1311a, 2352a.

FORMULAE OF THE FIRST AND SECOND HALF-LINES (Eᵃ⁻ᵇ)

irena cyst 673a, 802b, 1697a.

æþelinges bearn 888a, *æþelinga bearn* 1408b, 2597a, 3170a (further *þonne yldo bearn,* Bᵃ⁻ᵇ systems, 70a).

Weder-Geata leod 1492b, 1612b, 2551a (cf. *Guð-Geata leod* 1538a *Geatmecga leod* 829a; further *wlanc Wedera leod,* D² 341a, *þæt wæs Wendla leod* 348b [B]; see *leod Scyldinga,* D¹ᵃ⁻ᵇ, 1653a).

FORMULAIC SYSTEMS OF THE FIRST AND SECOND HALF-LINES (Eᵃ⁻ᵇ)

nihtlongne fyrst 528a, *fif nihta fyrst* 545a.[14]

searowundor seon 920a, *niðwundor seon* 1365b (further *metodsceaft séon* 1180a [A]).

feorbennum seoc 2740a, *sexbennum seoc* 2904a.

14. *nihtlongne fyrst* 528a, *fif nihta fyrst* 545a. See n. 4.

FORMULAE OF THE SECOND HALF-LINE (E^b)

undyrne cuð 150b, 410b (further *þe is wide cuð*, B^b systems, 2135b).

Hygelaces ðegn 194b, 1574b, 2977b.

sidfæþmed scip 302b, *sidfæþme scip* 1917b.

wigendra hleo 429b, 899b, 1972b, 2337b.

werod eall aras 651b, 3030b.[15]

Beowulfe wearð 818b, 2842b.

Hemminges mæg 1944b, 1961b (further *mæg Hygelaces*, D^{1a-b}, 737a, *Grendeles maga*, A^{a-b}, 2006b).

fea worda cwæð 2246b, 2662b (further *ond þæt word acwæð*, B^b, 654b, *word æfter cwæð*, D^{2b} systems, 315b).

Weoxstanes sunu 2602b, *2862b, *3076b (cf. *Folcwaldan sunu* 1089b; further *Weohstan bana* 2613b, *sunu Healfdenes*, D^{1a-b}, 268a).

FORMULAIC SYSTEMS OF THE SECOND HALF-LINE (E^b)

weorðmyndum þah 8b, *weorðmynda dæl* 1752b.

blæd wide sprang 18b, *hra wide sprong* 1588b.

æþelinga gedriht 118b, *æðelinga gestreon* 1920b (further *mid his eorla gedriht*, B^b systems, 357b).

wræclastas træd 1352b, *meodowongas træd* 1643b, *græsmoldan træd* 1881b.

andlangne dæg 2115b, *ondlonge niht* 2938b.

wyrd ungemete neah 2420b, *deað ungemete neah* 2728b.

Deficient Verses

secg betsta 947a, 1759a[16] (further *ðegn betestan* 1871b).

Three-Verse and Whole-Line Formulae

manigre (-um) mægþe geond þisne middangeard (75, 1771).

mægenes strengest/on þæm dæge þysses lifes (196b–97. *mægene strengest/ on þæm dæge þysses lifes* 789b–90 (cf. 806).

Hroðgar maþelode helm Scyldinga 371, 456, 1321.

Beowulf maþelode bearn Ecgþeowes 529, 631, 957, 1383, 1473, 1651, 1817, 1999, 2425.

swiðhicgende to sele þam hean 919, *swiðhicgende on sele þam hean* 1016.

gimfæste gife ðe him God sealde 1271, *ginfæstan gife þe him God sealde* 2182.

---

15. See Pope, p. 370.
16. Ibid., pp. 319–20 where the reading *secg betesta* is suggested.

ær he þone grundwong ongytan mehte 1496, *þæt he þone grundwong ongitan meahte* 2770.

hæle hildedeor Hroðgar gretan 1646, *hæle hildedeor Hroðgar grette* 1816.

ðæm (þone) selestan be sæm tweonum 1685, 1956.

Wiglaf maðelode Weohstanes sunu 2862, 3076.

Whole-Line Formulaic Systems

se wæs moncynnes mægenes strengest/on þæm dæge þysses lifes 196–197, *se þe manna wæs mægene strengest/on þæm dæge þysses lifes* 789–780.

him se yldesta andswarode 258, *him þa ellenrof andswarode* 340.[17]

sunu Healfdenes secean cwomon 268, *sunu Healfdenes secean wolde* 645.

swa we soþlice secgan hyrdon 273, *ac he soðlice sægde ofer ealle* 2899.

ond þa cearwylmas colran wurðaþ 282, *æfter cearwælmum colran weorðað* 2066.

seon sibbegedriht samod ætgædere 387, *swefan sibbegedriht samod ætgædere* 729.

þe æt fotum sæt frean Scyldinga 500, *æt fotum sæt frean Scyldinga* 1166a (hypermetric).

þæt mihtig God manna cynnes 701, *hu mihtig God manna cynne* 1725.

inwidsorge þe hie ær drugon 831, *inwitniþas þe hie ær drugon* 1858.

heaþosteapa helm hringed byrne 1245, *heaðosteapne helm hare byrnan* 2153.

næfne he wæs mara þonne ænig man oðer 1353, *buton hit wæs mare þonne ænig man oðer* 1560.

geþenc nu se mære maga Healfdenes 1474, *sona me se mære mago Healfdenes* 2011, *þæt se mære maga Ecgðeowes* 2587.

swylce þu ða madmas þe þu me sealdest 1482, *ic him þa maðmas þe he me sealde* 2490.

þæs þe hi hyne gesundne geseon moston 1628, *þæs ðe ic ðe gesundne geseon moste* 1998.

ond þegna gehwylc þinra leoda 1673, *ond þegna gehwam þara leoda* 2033.

gewat him ða se hearda mid his hondscole 1963, *gewat him ða se goda mid his gædelingum* 2949.

---

17. *him se yldesta andswarode* 258, *him þa ellenrof andswarode* 340. Although the verses of these lines are formulaic in their own right, the whole-line repetition may purposefully lend formularity to the verbal challenges with which the hero is greeted in the land of the Danes before he has even spoken his name (343b).

æfter hæleþa hryre hwate Scyldungas 2052, *æfter hæleða hryre hwate Scyld-*
  wigan 3005.

no ðy ær suna sinum syllan wolde 2160, *nu ic suna minum syllan wolde* 2729.

Brief Expressions

Most of the consistent elements in these expressions are too short to be
formulaic in any proper sense. They are rather patterns of syntax or of rhythm
or of both, and as such may be interestingly compared to the most rigid collocations of formulæ and formulaic systems.

I. EXPRESSIONS IDENTIFIED ONLY BY LEXICAL ASSOCIATION

ful oft: in its adverbial sense, *ful* always occurs with *oft: ful oft*
                     gebeotedon 480a, *ful oft ic for læssan* 951a, *swa him ful*
                     oft gelamp 1252b.

banhus: this word occurs twice in the poem: *banhus gebræc*
                     2508a, *oð þæt he ða banhus gebrocen hæfde* 3147.

nipan: the verb appears only twice: *nipende niht* 547a, *oþ ðe*
                     nipende niht ofer ealle 649.

gidd wrecan: *gidd* is used in the idiom as much as it is used apart
                     from it: *gid oft wrecen* 1065b, *ic þis gid be þe/awræc*
                     wintrum frod 1723b–24a, *gyd æfter wræc* 2154b, *þonne*
                     he gyd wrece 2446b, *wordgyd wrecan* 3172a.

armor: vaguely similar phrases and even some formulae are
                     built by the listings of two or more pieces of armor:
                     isernbyrnan,/helm of hafelan, sealde his hyrsted sweord
                     . . . 671b–72, *helm ond byrnan;/ mære maðþumsweord*
                     . . . 1022b–23a, *heaþosteapa helm, hringed byrne,/*
                     þrecwudu þrymlic 1245–46a, *sweord swate fah swin*
                     ofer helme/ecgum dyhtig . . . heardecg togen/sweord
                     ofer setlum, sidrand manig/ . . . helm ne gemunde,/
                     byrnan side . . . 1286–87a, 1288b–89, 1290b–91a, *helm*
                     ond byrne 1629b, *heaðosteapne helm, hare byrnan,/*
                     guðsweord geatolic 2153–54a, *brunfagne helm, hringde*
                     brynan, ealdsweord etonisc 2615–17a, *helmas ond heard*
                     sweord 2638a, *urum sceal sweord ond helm,/byrne*
                     ond beaduscrud 2659b–60a, *goldfahne helm,/beah ond*
                     byrnan 2811b–12a, *helm ond byrnan* 2868b, *ealdsweord*
                     eotenisc entiscne helm . . . 2979, *irenbyrnan,/heard*
                     swyrd hilted, ond his helm somod 2986b–87, *helmum*
                     behongen, hildebordum,/beorhtum byrnum 3139–40a.

ænig mon: the common association of these words is an important element of several verse-types: *manna ænig* 779b, *manna ængum* 1461a, *þæt ænig oðer man* 503b, *ne inc ænig mon* 510b, *ðonne ænig oþþer man* 534b, *næfre ic ænegum men* 655a, *þæt ðær ænig mon* 1099b, *ne ðær ænig mon* 2297b, *þonne ænig man oðer* 1353b, 1560b.

wen ic þæt: *wen ic þæt ge for wlenco* 338a, *wen ic þæt he wille* 442a, *wene ic þæt he mid gode* 1184a; further *wende þæs ylcan,/þæt he lytel fæc* 2239b-40a (*wenan* takes several other constructions).

2. CERTAIN WORDS PROMINENTLY BUT NOT EXCLUSIVELY IDENTIFIED WITH CERTAIN VERSE-TYPES

gebad: the preterit third singular of *gebidan* ends a B-verse six out of nine times: *he þæs frofre gebad* 7b, *fela ic laþes gebad* 929b, *se þe ær æt sæcce gebad* 1618b, *þæs ðe ic on aldre gebad* 1779b, *sio æt hilde gebad* 2258b, *þone ðe oft gebad* 3116a; further *gebad wintra worn* 264a, *licsar gebad* 815b, *dreamleas gebad* 1720b.

geweorðod: the preterit participle of *geweorðian* always forms the second element of an A-verse in the poem; *wæpnum geweorðad* 250a, 331a, *since gewurþad* 1038b, 1450b, *dome gewurþad* 1645b, *wide geweorðod* 1959a, *breost geweorðod* 2176b.

moncyn: inflected forms of this word may be exemplary of the way the syllabic sequence / / x fits not only the expected C- and D^1-verses, but fills other measures as well; *mancynne fram* 110b, *feond mancynnes* 164b, *se wæs moncynnes* 196a, *mancynnes feond* 1276a, *ealles moncynnes* 1955a, *ac he mancynnes* 2181a.

sand: only the dative singular of this word appears in the poem, and it fills only the second measure of A-verses: *sund wið sande* 213a, *nacan on sande* 295b, *þa wæs on sande* 1896a, *sælde to sande* 1917a, *sylf æfter sande* 1964a, *fundon ða on sande* 3033a.

3. WORDS AND EXPRESSIONS THAT CONTRIBUTE TO CERTAIN VERSE-TYPES ACCORDING TO A CERTAIN SYNTAX

gegan: this infinitive appears three times in the poem, always followed by the preterit singular of an auxiliary verb, thus making a C-verse: gegan wolde 1277b, *gegan dorste* 1462b, *gegan þenceð* 1535b; further *gegan hæfdon* 2630b (past participle of *gan*).

gehwylc: every inflection of this word in the poet contributes to the second measure of an A-verse in a partitive genitive construction: *cynna gehwylcum* 98a, *weana gehwelcne* 148b, *weana gehwylces* 1396a, *rinca gehwylcum* 412b, *anra gehwylces* 732b, *cenra gehwylcum* 768b, *anra gehwylcum* 784b, *ecga gwhwylcre* 805a, *witena gehwylcum* 936b, *secga gehwylcum* 996a, *dogra gehwylce* 1090a, *mæla gehwylce* 2057b, *yfla gehwylces* 2094a, *torna gehwylces* 2189b, *fyra gehwylcne* 2250b, *morna gehwylce* 2450b, *gumena gehwylcne* 2516b, *gumena gehwylcum* 2859a, *eorla gehwylcum* 2891a; further *ðin ofer þeoda gehwylce* 1705a (hypermetric).

gangan: the preterit third singular of this verb usually occurs in the final measure of B-verses following a syntactical pattern of (conjunction or adverb), noun, and prepositional phrase; *he to healle geong* 925b, *þæt to healle gang* 1009a, *þa heo to fenne gang* 1295b, *ær hie to setle geong* 2019b, *þær on innan giong* 2214b, *he ofer willan giong* 2409b, *ða se æðeling giong* 2715b, *se ðe on orde geong* 3125b: further *nu ðu lungre geong* 2743b (imp.), *gang ða æfter flore* 1316a, *geong sona to* 1785b.

hraþe: the adverb is used in several different constructions and verse-types, but three times it introduces A$_3$ verses and is followed by a prepositional phrase: *hraþe wæs to bure* 1310a, *hræþe wearð on yðum* 1437a, *hraþe wæs æt holme* 1914a; further *hraðe wæs gerymed* 1975a.

hwæt: the interjection followed by a pronoun occurs six times in the poem and is part of a formulaic system for introductory and emphatic statements: *hwæt we GarDena* 1a: *hwæt þu worn fela* 530a; *hwæt þæt secgan mæg* 942b: *hwæt we þe þas sælac* 1652a: *hwæt me þæs on eþle* 1774a, *hwæt hyt ær on ðe* 2248b.

hwæþre: in all but three of its appearances this adverb is followed by a pronoun and introduces A$_3$-, B-, and C-verses; *hwæþre me gefeþe wearð* 555b, *hwæþere me gesælde*

574a, *hwæþere ic fara feng* 578a, *hwæþre him gesælde* 890a, *hwæþere he his folme forlet* 970b, *hwæþre he gemunde* 1270a, *hwæþer him Alwalda* 1314a, *hwæþere him on ferhþe greow* 1718b, *hwæþre him sio swiðre* 2098a, *hwæðre he hine on folce* 2377a, *hwæðre him God uðe* 2874b.

hyrde ic þæt: *hyrde ic þæt . . .* 62a, *hyrde ic þæt þam frætwum* 2163a, *hyrde ic þæt he ðone healsbeah* 2172a.

magan: forms of the verb frequently occur with an infinitive in the same half-line and, no matter what the syntactical order, with one exception, make A- and C-verses. *Magan* plus infinitive, A₃-verses: *mæg þonne on þæm golde ongitan* 1484a, *þæt la mæg secgan* 1700a, 2864a, *mæg þæs þonne ofþyncan* 2032a, *ne mihte ða forhabban* 2609a, *ne meahton we gelæran* 3079a; C-verses: *a mæg God wyrcan* 930b, *ne mæg ic her leng wesan* 2801b. Infinitive plus *magan,* monosyllabic forms, B-verses: *ðær þu findan miht* 1378b; C-verses: *hwæt þæt secgan mæg* 942b, *þæs þe þincean mæg* 1341a; disyllabic forms, A-verses: *sceðþan ne meahte* 243b, *habban ne mihte* 462b, *fleotan meahte* 542b, *hebban mihte* 656b, *frecne ne meahte* 1032b, *findan mihte* 207a, 2870b, *findon meahton* 1156b, 2373b, 3162b, *bitan ne meahton* 1454b *ðurhfon ne mihte* 1504b, *hrinan ne mehte* 1515b, *forberan ne mehte* 1877b, *helpan ne meahte* 2340b, *hatian ne meahte* 2466b; C-verses: *ongytan mehte* 1496b, 2770b, *ongytan mihton* 308b, *belean mihte* 511b, *geseon mihte* 571b, 1078b, *geseon meahton* 648b, *tobrecan meahte* 780b, *þurteon mihte* 1140b, *forwrecan meahte* 1919b, *onsacan mihte* 2954b.

motan: like those of *magan,* the forms of this verb when accompanied by an infinitive frequently contribute to A- and C-verses, with one exception (similar observations could be made of *scyllan, willan,* etc.). Monosyllabic, B-verse: *gif he wealdan mot* 442b; disyllabic, A-verses: *gretan moste* 168b, *gretan moton* 347b, *brucan moste* 894b, 2241a, 3100b, *agan moston* 1088b, *scyran moste* 1939b, *wealdan moste* 2574a, *wealdan moston* 2038b, 2984b, *bringan moste* 2504b, *wealdan ne moste* 2827b, *hrinan ne moste* 3053a; C-verses: *geseon moste* 961b, 1998b, *geseon moston* 1628b, 1875b.

wiht:
wihte

in 18 of its 20 occurrences this word is part of a negative construction, and in 11 of those 18 the syntactical pattern *wiht* (plus *ne*) plus a verb makes A-verses exclusively: *wihte gewendan* 186b, *wiht ne logon* 862b, *wiht gefeohtan* 1083b, *wihte ne scepede* 1514b, *wiht gewyrcan* 1660a, *wihte gebettest* 1991b, *wihte ne grette* 1995b, *wihte ne meahte* 2464b, *wiht onwendan* 2601a, *wihte ne wene* 2923a.

Elene

Formulae of the A-Verses

FORMULAE OF THE FIRST HALF-LINE (A^a)

rice under roderum 13a, 147a, 631a (cf. *rincas under roderum* 46a, *swylce rec under raderum* 803a, *ræd under roderum* 918a, *rode under roderum* 1234a).

hergum to hilde 32a, *herge to hilde* 52a.

wæpnum to wigge 48a, *wæpen æt wigge* 1188a.

egesan geaclad 57a, 1128a.

hlude for hergum 110a, 406a.

wigge geweorðod 150a, *wigge weorðod* 1195a.

halig under hrusan 218a, 625a, 842a (cf. *halig under heofenum* 975a, *hord under hrusan* 1091a).

werum ond wifum 236a, 1221a (further *þara þe wif oððe wer* 508a [B]).

þriste on geþanca 267a, *þristra geþonca* 1286a.

cwoman in þa ceastre 274a, *cuman in þa ceastre* 1204a.

sundor asecað 407a, *sundor asecean* 1018a.

leohtne geleafan 491a, *leohte geleafan* 1136a.

folce to frofre 502a, *folcum to frofre* 1142a.

lifes lattiow 520a, 898a.

fæste on fyrhðe 570a, *fæst on ferhðe* 1036a.

meðe ond meteleas 612a, 698a.

Elene for eorlum 620a, 1197a (see below, Whole-Line Formulae).

hæleðum to helpe 679a, 1011a.

gasta geocend 682a, 1076a.

a butan ende 801a, 893a (further *yrmðu butan ende* 952a).

FORMULAIC SYSTEMS OF THE FIRST HALF-LINE (A^a)

to flote fysan 226a, *flodas gefysde* 1269a.

wende hine of worulde 440a, *gewended to wuldre* 1046a.

halig ond hefonlic 739a further *halig heofonlic gast* 1144a [D^2]).

breostum onbryrded 1094a (further *inbryrded breostsefa* 841a [D^2]).

wuldres wynne 1039a (further *on wuldres wyn* 1089a [B]).

gewitað under wolcnum 1271a, *wæðeð be wolcnum* 1273a.

FORMULAE OF THE FIRST AND SECOND HALF-LINES (A^{a-b})

Constantines 8a, *Constantinus* 79a, 103a, 1007a, *Constantino* 145a.[18]

Huna leode 20a, 128a.

urigfeðera 29a, 111a.

ofstum myclum 44b, 102b, 999a.

sigores tacen 85a, *sigores tacne* 184b.

hildenædran 119b, 141a.

þa wæs gesyne 144a, *þær wæs gesyne* 264a.

lærde wæron 173a, 191a.

leodgebyrga 203a, *leodgebyrgean* 556a.

to widan feore 211a, 1321b, *on widan feore* 1288b.

collenferhðe 247a, 378a, 848a.

caseres bodan 262b, 551a.

reccan cuðon 281b, 284a.[19]

wordum negan 287b, *wordum genegan* 385a.

deman ongunnon 303a, 311a.[20]

18. *Constantines* 8a, 103a, 145a, 1007a. One may object that this Latin name did not achieve but had formular status thrust upon it.

19. *reccan cuðon* 281b, 284a (cf. *þurh rihte æ* 281a, *þa ðe Mosses æ* 283b). The repetition is the statement and fulfillment of an order (see 276), much like the repetitious description and utterance of a wish or command in Homer, in fairy stories, and so forth (e.g. "There was once a woman who wished for a very little child; but she did not know where she could procure one. So she went to an old witch and said, 'I do so very much wish for a little child! Can you not tell me where I can get one?' "—*Thumbelina*). Cf. *Elene* 700b and 712b, 1087a and 1100a.

20. *deman ongunnon* 303a, 311a. Several of the speeches in *Elene* are unmistakably well wrought of phrases whose significance is primarily rhetorical and dependent on the debate (see for instance in this address by Elene the deft oppositions, *lige wið soðe, leoht wið þystrum,/ aeft wið are*, 307a–08a). In such discourse, repetitions may not be merely functional in the making of the verse. By this particular repetition, Elene emphasizes the temerity (so it seems to her) of the Jews' judgment.

sigora dryhten 346a, *sigora dryhtne* 1139a.

hwæt we þæt gehyrdon *364a, *hwæt we ðæt hyrdon* *670a, *852a (cf. *nu ðu meaht gehyran* 511a, *þæt ðu gehyre* 442a, *næfre we hyrdon* 538a, *æfre hyrdon* 572b, *þa ðæt gehyrde* 709a, *swa ðu gehyrdest* 784a).

geomormode 413a, 555b.

ðeoden engla 487a, 776a, 857b.

torngeniðlan 568a, 1306a.

hæleðum cuðan 661a, 671a.[21]

dogorrimum 705a, 779a.

heofon ond eorðan 727a, *heofun ond eorðe* 752a.

niwan stefne 1060a, 1127a.

gastes mihtum 1069b, 1099a.

nerigend fira 1077a, 1172a.

FORMULAIC SYSTEMS OF THE FIRST AND SECOND HALF-LINES (A^{a-b})

wordum ond bordum 24b, *bordum ond ordum* 235a (further *berað bord ond ord* 1186a [D^2]).

þe þæt gefrugnon 172a, *þara þe gefrugnen* 1013a.

wordes cræftig 419a, further *wordes cræftige* 3146 [E].

FORMULAE OF THE SECOND HALF-LINE (A^b)

cyninga wuldor *5b, *178b.

garas lixtan 23b, 125b.

hreopan friccan 54b, 550b.

stundum wræcon 121b, 232b.

gastgerynum 189b, 1147b.

rodora waldend 206b, 482b.

wergðu dreogan 211b, 951b.

hyded wære 218b, *hydde waron* 1107b.

beboden hæfde 224b, 412b.

wordgeryno 289b, 323b.

bote gefremede 299b, *bote gefremaþ* 515b (further *wundra gefremede* 363a, *dæd gefremedon* 386b, *þe we gefremedon* 402a).

21. *hæleðum cuðan* 661a, 671a. This is one of several repetitions which bind the speeches of Elene and Judas. It contributes so much to the verbal contest that it seems more than metrically efficacious: half a victory lies in using an opponent's very words in order to argue him down.

secgan cunnon 317b, *secgan cunnen* 376b.

halige rune 333b, 1168b.

wordum mælde 351b, *wordum mældon* 537b.

mæste hæfdon 381b, *mæste hæbben* 408b.

soðe ond rihte 390b, 663b.

þeoda waldend 421b, 780b.

fæderas usse 425b, 458b.

sawla nergend 461b, 798b.

selest þince *532b, *selost þuhte* *1164b.

riht getæhte 601b, *ryhte getæhteð* 1074b.

anforlete 630b, 946b.

Criste to willan 678b, 1010b (cf. *drihtne to willan* 193b).

up forlæten 700b, *up forlete* 712b.²²

seolf gecneowe 708b, *seolf gecnawen* 807b.

biddan wille 789b, 813b.

larum na hyrdon 838b, *larum hyrdon* 1209b.

miclum geblissod 839b, 875b.

syððan wunodest 949b, *siððan wunode* 1027b.

FORMULAIC SYSTEMS OF THE SECOND HALF-LINE (Aᵇ)

weordes breahtme 39b, *heriges beorhtme* 205b.

laðode wæron 383b (further *þa hie laðod wæron* 556b [C]).

witgan sungon 561b (further *be ðam se witga sang* 1188b [B]).

Formulae of the B-Verses

FORMULAE OF THE FIRST HALF-LINE (Bᵃ)

þurh gastes gife 199a, 1057a, 1156a.

FORMULAE OF THE FIRST AND SECOND HALF-LINES (Bᵃ⁻ᵇ)

acenned wearð *5a, *178a, 775a (further *cenned wurde* 336b [A]).

in middangeard 6a, *geond middangeard* 16a, *ofer middangeard* 434a.

ond þæt halige treo 107b, *swa þæt halige treo* 128b, *hwær þæt halige trio* 429a, *ymb þæt halige treo* 442b, *þurh þæt halige treo* 840b.

þurh fyrngewrito 155a, *ymb fyrngewritu* 560b (further *frod fyrngewritu* 431a [D²]).

---

22. *up forlæten* 700b, *up forlete* 712b. See n. 19.

on rode treo, 206a, 855a.

on Creca land 250a, 262a, 998a.

ymb lytel fæc 272a, 383a (cf. *ond swa lytlum fæce* 959b).

to Hierusalem 273a, *in Ierusalem* 1055a.

in cildes had 336a, 775b.

ond þæt word gecwæð 338a, 344a, 440b, 938a, *he þæt word gecwæð* 1190b.

ic up ahof 353a, *ond up ahof* 878b.

þurh snyttro cræft 374a, *ond snyttro cræft* 1171b.

swa him sio cwen bebead 378b, 715b, *þa sio cwen bebead* 979b, 1017a.

ahangen wæs *445a, *718a.

ðe þone ahangnan cyning 453a, *þone ahangnan cyning* 933a.

hwæt eow þæs on sefan *532a, *hwæt him þæs on sefan* *1164a.

ymb þæt lifes treow 664a, *be ðam lifes treo* 706b, *þær þæt lifes treo* 1026b
   (cf. *ymb þæt mære treo* 214a, *þurh þæt wlitige treo* 165b, *æfter þam
   wuldres treo*, B[b] 827b; see *wliti wuldres treo*, D[2a] Systems, 89a).

on Calvarie 672a, 1010a, 1097b.

oð þa nigoðan tid 869a, *wæs þa nigoðe tid* 873b.

FORMULAIC SYSTEMS OF THE FIRST AND SECOND HALF-LINES (B[a–b])

fram þam engan hofe 712a, *in þam engan ham* 920a.[23]

ic frumþa God 345a, *syððan him frymða god* 502b.

FORMULAE OF THE SECOND HALF-LINE (B[b])

þa se casere heht 42b, *hie se casere heht* 998b (further *ond þa his modor het*
   214b).

he wæs sona gearu 85b, *ac wæs sona gearu* 222b.

þurh his wuldres miht 295b, *þurh þines wuldres miht* 726b.

ond for eorlum spræc *332b, *404b.

þurh halige bec *364b, *670b, *852b.

hio sio cwen ongan 384b, *þa sio cwen ongan* 558b, 1204b.

ðam wæs Iudas nama *418b, *586b (cf. *ðam wæs Symon nama* 530b, *þam
   wæs Sachius nama* 437b).

hwær sio halige rod 720b, *þær sio halige rod* 1011b.

---

23. *fram þam engan hofe* 712a, *in þam engan ham* 920a. The first phrase refers to
the pit into which Elene caused Judas to be thrown; the second refers to hell. In his
speech, the devil identifies his evil with Judas' former conduct. There is a possibility,
though only a possibility, that the "narrow house" is one means of that identification.

æfter þam wuldres treo 827b, *be ðam wuldres treo* 866b (cf. *ond þæt halige treo,* B^{a-b}, 107b).

to þære haligan byrig 1005b, 1053b, 1203b.

FORMULAIC SYSTEMS OF THE SECOND HALF-LINE (B^b)

sume wig fornam 131b, *sume drenc fornam* 136b.^{24}

swa hit siððan gelamp 271b, *swa hit eft gelamp* 1154b.

butan þec nuþa 539b, *butan her nuþa* 661b.

ofer þæt fæge hus 880b, *þurh þæt fæcne hus* 1236b.

Formulae of the C-Verses

FORMULAE OF THE FIRST AND SECOND HALF-LINES (C^{a-b})

on neaweste 67a, 873a.

þam casere 70a, 212b.

on fyrhðsefan 98a, 213a, 316a, 849a, 894b, 1078a.

on herefelda 126a, *ofer herefeldas* 269a.

þa wisestan 153b, 323a, *þa þa wisestan* 169a.

be þam sigebeacne 168b, 1256a (further *sigebeacen soð* 887a [E], *selest sigebeacna* 974a [D^1]).

of byrgenne 186a, *in byrgenne* 484a.

on Godes bocum 204b, 290a.

to Iudeum 216a, *mid Iudeum* 328a, 1202a (further *geond Iudeas* 278a [D^1]).

ofer lagofæsten 249a, 1016a

on wera corþre 304b, 543a.

be ðam sigebeame 420b, 444a, 665b, 860b (further *selest sigebeama* 1027a [D^1]).

in fyrndagum 425a, *on fyrndagum* 528b.

on woroldrice 456b, *in woruldrice* 778a, 1048a.

be naman haten 505a, *be naman hateð* 755a.

geþrowade 563b, 858a, *geþrowedon* 854a (cf. *on ðam þrowode* 421a, *þæt geþrowade* 519a).

Iudas hire ongen þingode 609a, 667a.

24. *sume wig fornam* 131b, *sume drenc fornam* 136b. The phrases are certainly formulaic, but their close association in the poem comes of a conscientiously contrived "Sum-passage."

25. *Iudas hire ongen þingode* 609a, 667a. Both verses are followed by the alliterating *gehðu* in the second half-lines, and indeed, the phrase is used of Judas after Elene delivers her cruelest threat and then her cruelest accusation.

hie ðæt ofstlice 713a, *þa þæt ofstlice* 1196a.

ofer þam æðelestan 733a, *mid þam æðelestum* 1024a.

of eorðwegum 735a, *on eorðwege* 1014a.

geopenie 791a, *geopenigean* 1101a.

of ðam wangstede 793a, *on þam wangstede* 1103a.

on twa halfe 954b, 1179a.

to bisceope 1056a, *to þam bisceope* 1072a.

FORMULAIC SYSTEMS OF THE FIRST AND SECOND HALF-LINES (C^{a–b})

hio him andsware 166a, *him on andsware* 642b.

fram blindnesse 299a, *ða ge blindnesse* 389a.

þæt we fæstlice 427a, *ond þy fæs tlicor* 796a (see below, Whole-Line Formulaic Systems).

FORMULAE OF THE SECOND HALF-LINE (C^b)

geteled rimes 2b, *geteled rime* 634b.

swa hio him to sohte 325b, *þæs hio him to sohte* 568b.

nu ge raþe gangaþ 372b, *ge nu hraðe gangað* 406b.

ne we eare cunnon 399b, *nu ge geare cunnon* 531b.

on þysse folcscere 402b, *in þære folcscere* 967b.

ond geflitu ræran 443b, *geflitu rærdon* 953b.

on gewritu setton 654b, 658b.[26]

on gewritum cuðed 826b, *on gewritum cyðan* 1255b.

in þæs weres breostum 966b, 1037b.

FORMULAIC SYSTEMS OF THE SECOND HALF-LINE (C^b)

on hwæðre geare nyste 719b, *ne ful gere wiste* 859b (further *ic wat geare* 914b, *wite ðu þe gearwor* 945b [A], *nysse ic gearwe* 1239b [A]).

Formulae of the D-Verses

FORMULAE OF THE FIRST HALF-LINE (D^{1a})

beorna beaggifa 100a, *beorna beaggifan* 1198a.

frod fyrnweota 343a, 438a.

gidda gearosnottor *418a, *giddum gearusnottorne* *586a.

soð sunu meotudes 461a, 564a (further *on to suna metudes* 1318b [C]).

26. *on gewritu setton* 654b, 658b. See n. 21.

weras wonsælige 478a, *werum wansæligum* 977a.

eallum eaðmedum 1087a, 1100a.[27]

FORMULAIC SYSTEMS OF THE FIRST HALF-LINE (D^{1a})

hofon herecombul 25a, *hebban heorucumbul* 107a.

sægdon sigerofum 190a (further *sigerof sægde* 437a [A]).

sohton searoþancum 414a, *snotter searuþancum* 1189a.

elnes anhydig 828a, *eorlas anhydig* 847a (further *elnes oncyðig* 724a).

selest sigebeacna 974a, *selest sigebeama* 1027a.

hattost heaðowelma 579a, *hat heofodwylm* 1132a [D^2] (further *in hatne wylm* 1297b [B], *of ðam heaðuwylme* 1305a [C].

FORMULAE OF THE FIRST HALF-LINE (D^{2a})

wealdest widan fyrhð 760a, *walde widan ferhð* 800a.

FORMULAIC SYSTEMS OF THE FIRST HALF-LINE (D^{2a})

wlitig wuldres boda 77a, *wliti wuldres treo* 89a (further *þurh þæt wlitige treo* 165b, *ond þæt halige treo*, B^{a-b}, 107b).

lange legere fæst 722a, *lic legere fæst* 882a.

FORMULAE OF THE FIRST AND SECOND HALF-LINES (D^{1a-b})

deareðlacende 37a, *dareðlacendra* 651a.

byrnwiggendra 224a, *byrnwigendum* 235b.

wuldorcyninge 291b, 962a, 1304a, *wuldorcyninges* 1321a (further *cyninga wuldor*, A^b, 5).

Elene maþelode *332a, *404a, 573a, 604a, 642a, 685a.

deophycggende 352a, 881a.

synwyrcende 395a, 943a.

undearninga 405a, 620b.

rædþeahtende 449a, 868a.

sigebearn Godes 481a, 862a, 1146a.

Iudas maðelade 627a, 655a, 806a.

stiðhycgende 683a, 716b.

FORMULAIC SYSTEMS OF THE FIRST AND SECOND HALF-LINES (D^{1a-b})

radorcyninges 624b, *rode rodercininges* 1074a (further *radorcyninges beam* 886b [E]).

27. *eallum eaðmedum* 1087a, 1100a. See n. 19.

FORMULAE OF THE SECOND HALF-LINE (D^{1b})

werod samnodan 19b, *werod samnodon* 60b.

ham eft þanon 143b, 148b.

cyning ælmihtig 145b, 865b, 1090b.

forþsnottera 379b, *forðsnoterne* 1052b.

ferhð staðelien *427b, *ferhð staðelige* *796b.

ageaf andsware 455b, 462b, 662b.

Gode þancode 961b, 1138b.

gife unscynde 1200b, 1246b (further *dom unscynde* 365b).

FORMULAIC SYSTEMS OF THE SECOND HALF-LINE (D^{1b})

andsæc fremede 472b, *wiðersæc fremedon* 569b.

Formulae of the E-Verses

FORMULAE OF THE FIRST HALF-LINE (E^{a})

wisdomes gewitt 357a, 1190a.

lacende lig 580a, 1110a.

FORMULAE OF THE FIRST AND SECOND HALF-LINES (E^{a-b})

Romwara cyning 62a, 129b.

Iudea cyn 209a, 836a.

FORMULAIC SYSTEMS OF THE FIRST AND SECOND HALF-LINES (E^{a-b})

tireadig cyning 104a, *tireadig cwen* 605a.

FORMULAE OF THE SECOND HALF-LINE (E^{b})

Godes agen bearn 179b, 422b, 1076b.

heofonrices weard 197b, *445b, *718b.

caseres mæg 330b, 669b.

fulwihtes bæð 490b, 1033b.

andwyrde agifan 545b, *andwyrde ageaf* 619b.

FORMULAIC SYSTEMS OF THE SECOND HALF-LINE (E^{b})

hlæfdige us 400b, *hlæfdige min* 656b.

Whole-Line Formulae

acenned wearð cyninga wuldor 5, 178.

Elene maþelade ond for eorlum spræc 332, 404.

Hwæt we þæt gehyrdon þurh halige bec 364, *hwæt we þæt hyrdon þurh halige bec* 670, 852.

gidda gearosnotor ðam wæs Iudas nama 418, *giddum gearusnotterne þam wæs Iudas nama* 586.

ahangen wæs heofonrices weard 445, 718.

hwæt eow þæs on sefan selest þince 532, *hwæt him þæs on sefan selost þuhte* 1164.

Whole-Line Formulaic Systems

þæt we fæstlice ferhð staðelien 427, *ond þy fæstlicor ferhð staðelige* 796.

Selected Bibliography

Allen, Thomas William, *Homer: the Origins and Transmission,* Oxford, Clarendon Press, 1924.

Bassett, Samuel Eliot, *The Poetry of Homer,* Sather Classical Lectures, Berkeley, University of California Press, 1938.

Berlage, I., "De vocibus Τυκτός, Τετυγμενός, Ποιητός, Οἰκυμένη, aliis," *Mnemosyne, 53* (1925).

Benson, Larry D., "The Literary Character of Anglo-Saxon Formulaic Poetry," *PMLA, 81* (1966), 334–41.

Bessinger, Jess B., Jr., and Robert P. Creed, eds., *Franciplegius,* New York, New York University Press, 1965.

Bethurum, Dorothy, "Stylistic Features of Old English Laws," *MLR, 27* (1932), 263–79.

Bonjour, Adrien, "Poésie héroïque du moyen âge et critique littéraire," *Romania, 78* (1957), 243–55.

——, "Beowulf et l'épopée anglo-saxonne," *La Table ronde, 132* (1958), 140–51.

Borroff, Marie, *Sir Gawain and the Green Knight: a Stylistic and Metrical Study,* New Haven, Yale University Press, 1962.

Bosworth, Joseph, and T. Northcote Toller, *An Anglo-Saxon Dictionary,* Oxford, Oxford University Press, 1898; reprinted 1954.

Bowra, Sir Cecil Maurice, *Tradition and Design in the Iliad,* Oxford, Clarendon Press, 1930.

——, *From Virgil to Milton,* London, Macmillan Co., 1945.

——, *Heroic Poetry,* London, Macmillan Co., 1952.

——, *Homer and His Forerunners,* Edinburgh, Nelson & Co., 1955.

——, "Metre," in *CH,* pp. 19–25.

Brodeur, Arthur Gilchrist, *The Art of Beowulf,* Berkeley, University of California Press, 1959.

Brown, Arthur, and Peter Foote, eds., *Early English and Norse Studies Presented to Hugh Smith,* London, Methuen and Co., 1963.

Bryan, William Frank, "Epithetic Compound Folk-Names in *Beowulf,*" in *Studies in English Philology: a Miscellany in Honor of Fr. Klaeber,* ed. Kemp Malone and Martin B. Rudd (Minneapolis, University of Minnesota Press, 1929), pp. 120–34.

Calhoun, George M., "Homeric Repetitions," *UCPCP, 12,* No. 1 (1933), 1–14.

———, "The Art of Formula in Homer—ΕΠΕΑ ΠΤΕΡΟΕΝΤΑ," *CP, 30* (1935), 215–27.

Campbell, Alistair, A review of Lord's *Singer of Tales, MLR, 57* (1962), 75–76.

———, "Old English Poetic Style," in *English and Medieval Studies Presented to J. R. H. Tolkien,* ed. Norman Davis and C. L. Wrenn (London, Allen & Unwin, 1962), pp. 13–27.

Campbell, Jackson J., "Oral Poetry in the *Seafarer,*" *Speculum, 35* (1960), 87–96.

Carpenter, Rhys, *Folktale, Saga, and Fiction in the Homeric Epics,* Berkeley, University of California Press, 1946.

Cassidy, Frederic G., "How Free Was the Anglo-Saxon Scop?" in *Franciplegius,* ed. Jess B. Bessinger and Robert P. Creed (New York, New York University Press, 1965), pp. 75–85.

Cauer, Paul, *Grundfragen der Homerkritik,* 3d ed. Leipzig, S. Hirzel, 1923.

Chadwick, Hector Monroe, *The Heroic Age,* Cambridge, Cambridge University Press, 1926.

———, and N. Kershaw Chadwick, *The Growth of Literature,* Vol. I, Cambridge, Cambridge University Press, 1932.

Chambers, Raymond Wilson, *Beowulf: an Introduction to the Study of the Poem with a Discussion of the Stories of Offa and Finn,* Cambridge, Cambridge University Press, 1929.

———, *Man's Unconquerable Mind,* London, J. Cape, 1939.

Combellack, Frederick M., "Omitted Speech Formulas in Homer," *UCPCP, 12* No. 4 (1939), 43–56.

———, "Contemporary Unitarians and Homeric Originality," *AJP, 71* (1950), 337–64.

———, "Milman Parry and Homeric Artistry," *CL, 11* (1959), 193–208.

Cook, Albert Stanburrough, *A Concordance to Beowulf,* Halle, M. Niemeyer, 1911.

Cordier, A., *Études sur le vocabulaire épique dans L'Énéide,"* Paris, Société d'éditions "Les belles lettres," 1939.

Creed, Robert Payson, "Studies in the Techniques of Composition of the Beowulf Poetry in British Museum Ms. Cotton Vitellius A XV," unpublished Ph.D. dissertation, Harvard University, 1955.

———, "The *Andswarode*-System in Old English Poetry," *Speculum, 32* (1957), 523–28.

———, "The Making of an Anglo-Saxon Poem," *ELH, 26* (1959), 445–54.

———, "On the Possibility of Criticizing Old English Poetry," *TSLL, 3* (1961), 97–106.

———, "A Singer Looks at his Sources," *CL, 14* (1962), 44–52.

Curschmann, Michael, "Oral Poetry in Mediaeval English, French and German Literature: Some Notes on Recent Research," *Speculum, 42* (1967), 36–52.

Davidson, J. A., "The Transmission of the Text," in *CH*, pp. 215–33. "The Homeric Question," in *CH*, pp. 234–66.

Diamond, Robert Edwin, "The Diction of the Signed Poems of Cynewulf," unpublished Ph.D. dissertation, Harvard University, 1953.

——, "The Diction of the Signed Poems of Cynewulf," *PQ, 38* (1959), 228–41.

——, "Theme as Ornament in Anglo-Saxon Poetry," *PMLA, 76* (1961), 461–68.

Dobbie, Elliott Van Kirk, *see* Krapp, George Philip.

Elliott, Ralph Warren Victor, *Runes: an Introduction,* Manchester, Manchester University Press, 1959.

Fitzgerald, Robert, trans., *The Odyssey,* New York, Anchor Books, 1963.

Foerster, Donald M., *Homer in English Criticism,* New Haven, Yale University Press, 1947.

Fry, Donald K., "Old English Formulas and Systems," *ES, 48* (1967), 194–204.

Gantz, S., "The Dawn of Literature, Prolegomena to a History of Unwritten Literature," *Osiris, 7* (1939), 261–522.

Gomme, Arnold Wycombe, *The Greek Attitude to Poetry and History,* Berkeley, University of California Press, 1954.

Gradon, P. O. E., ed., *Cynewulf's Elene,* London, Methuen and Co., 1958.

Gray, D. H. F., "Homeric Epithets for Things," *CQ, 40* (1946), 109–21.

Greene, William Chase, "The Spoken and the Written Word," *HSCP, 66* (1960), 23–59.

Greenfield, Stanley B., "Stylistic Analysis and Old English Poetry," *NM, 64* (1963), 373–78.

Grein, C. W. M., *Sprachsatz der angelsächsischen Dichter,* Cassel und Göttingen, Vol. 1, 1861; Vol. 2, 1864.

Grimm, Jakob, ed., *Andreas und Elene,* Cassel, 1840.

Heusler, Andreas, "Der Dialog in der altgermanischen erzählenden Dichtung," *ZDA, 46* (1902), 189–284.

Hodgkin, R. H., *A History of the Anglo-Saxons,* 3d ed., Oxford, Oxford University Press, 1959, Vols. 1 and 2.

Homer, *The Iliad,* ed. Arthur Platt, Cambridge, 1894.

——, *Homeri Odyssea,* ed. J. La Roche, Leipzig, 1867.

Jespersen, Otto, *Growth and Structure of the English Language,* 9th ed. New York, Anchor Books, 1938

Kail, J., "Über die Parallelstellen in der angelsächsischen Poesie," *Anglia, 12* (1889), 21–40.

Kent, Charles W., ed., *Elene,* Boston, 1889.

Kirk, Geoffrey Stephen, *The Songs of Homer,* Cambridge, Cambridge University Press, 1962.

———, "Homer and Modern Oral Poetry: Some Confusions," *CQ,* N.S. *10* (1960), 271–81.

———, "Formular Language and Oral Quality," *YCS, 20* (1966), 155–74.

Kistenmacher, Richard, *Die wörtlichen Wiederholungen im Beowulf,* Greifswald, 1898.

Klaeber, Frederick, "Studies in the Textual Interpretation of 'Beowulf,'" *MP, 3* (1905–06), 235–65.

———, ed., *Beowulf and the Fight at Finnsburg,* 3d ed., Boston, D. C. Heath and Co., 1950.

Krapp, George Philip, and Elliott Van Kirk Dobbie, eds., *The Anglo-Saxon Poetic Records,* 6 vols. New York, Columbia University Press, 1932–53. Vol. 1, *The Junius Manuscript,* ed. Krapp (1931); Vol. 2, *The Vercelli Book,* ed. Krapp (1932); Vol. 3, *The Exeter Book,* ed. Krapp and Dobbie (1936); Vol. 5, *The Paris Psalter and the Meters of Boethius,* ed. Krapp (1932); Vol. 6, *The Anglo-Saxon Minor Poems,* ed. Dobbie (1942).

Lattimore, Richard, trans., *The Iliad of Homer,* Chicago, University of Chicago Press, 1961.

Leach, MacEdward, ed., *Studies in Medieval Literature in Honor of Albert Croll Baugh,* Philadelphia, University of Pennsylvania Press, 1962.

Lehmann, Winfred P., *The Development of Germanic Verse Form,* Austin, Texas University Press, 1958.

Lord, Albert Bates, "Homer and Huso I: The Singer's Rests in Greek and South Slavic Heroic Song," *TAPA, 67* (1936), 106–13.

———, "Homer and Huso II: Narrative Inconsistencies in Homeric and Oral Poetry," *TAPA, 69* (1938), 439–45.

———, "Homer and Huso III: Enjambment in Greek and South Slavic Heroic Song," *TAPA, 79* (1948), 113–24.

———, "Homer, Parry, and Huso," *AJA, 52* (1948), 34–44.

———, "Composition by Theme in Homer and South Slavic Epos," *TAPA, 83* (1952), 71–80.

———, "Homer's Originality: Oral Dictated Texts," *TAPA, 84* (1953), 124–34.

———, *The Singer of Tales,* Cambridge, Harvard University Press, 1960.

———, "Homer and Other Epic Poetry," in *CH,* pp. 179–214.

Lorimer, H. L., "Homer and the Art of Writing: a Sketch of Opinion between 1713 and 1939," *AJA, 52* (1948), 11–23.

———, *Homer and the Monuments,* London, Macmillan, 1950.

Madden, John F., "A Frequency Word Count of Anglo-Saxon Poetry," *MS, 15* (1953), 221–25.

Magoun, Francis P., Jr., "The Oral-Formulaic Character of Anglo-Saxon Narrative Poetry," *Speculum, 28* (1953), 446–65.

———, "Bede's Story of Cædman: the Case-History of an Anglo-Saxon Singer," *Speculum, 30* (1955), 49–53.

———, "The Theme of the Beasts of Battle in Anglo-Saxon Poetry," *NM, 56* (1955), 81–90.

———, "Abbreviated Titles for the Poems of the Anglo-Saxon Poetic Corpus," *EA, 7* (1955), 138–46.

———, "Beowulf A': a Folk Variant," *Arv, 14* (1958), 95–101.

———, "Some Notes on Old English Poetry," in *Studies in Medieval Literature in Honor of Albert Croll Baugh,* ed. MacEdward Leach (Philadelphia, University of Pennsylvania Press, 1962), pp. 272–83

———, "Beowulf B: a Folk Poem on Beowulf's Death," in *Early English and Norse Studies Presented to Hugh Smith,* ed. Arthur Brown and Peter Foote (London, Methuen and Co., 1963), pp. 127–40.

Malone, Kemp, "Plurilinear Units in Old English Poetry," *RES, 19* (1943), 201–04.

———, and Martin B. Rudd, eds., *Studies in English Philology: a Miscellany in Honor of Fr. Klaeber,* Minneapolis, University of Minnesota Press, 1929.

Meillet, Antoine, *Les Origines indo-européennes des mètres grecs,* Paris, Les presses universitaires de France, 1923.

Moseley, Nicholas, *Characters and Epithets: a Study in Virgil's Aeneid,* New Haven, Yale University Press, 1926.

Myres, Sir John L., *Homer and His Critics,* ed. D. Gray, London, L. Routeledge, 1958.

Nicholson, Lewis Edward, "Oral Techniques in the Composition of Expanded Anglo-Saxon Verse," unpublished Ph.D. dissertation, Harvard University, 1958.

———, "Oral Techniques in the Composition of Expanded Anglo-Saxon Verse," *PMLA, 78* (1963), 287–92.

Nielsen, Eduard, *Oral Tradition: a Modern Problem in Old Testament Introduction,* Studies in Biblical Theology, Vol. 2, London, SCM Press, 1954.

Nilsson, Martin P., *Homer and Mycenae,* London, Methuen and Co., 1933.

Notopoulos, James A., "Continuity and Interconnection in Homeric Oral Composition," *TAPA, 82* (1951), 81–101.

———, "The Warrior as Oral Poet," *CW, 46* (1952), 17–19.

———, "Modern Greek Oral Poetry," Ethnic Folkways Library, booklet accompanying Album FE 4468, New York, 1959.

———, "Studies in Early Greek Oral Poetry," *HSCP, 68* (1964), 1–77.

Oakden, James Parker, *Alliterative Poetry in Middle English,* Manchester, Manchester University Press, Vol. 1, 1930; Vol. 2, 1935.

Page, Denys L., *The Homeric Odyssey,* Oxford, 1955.

———, *History and the Homeric Iliad,* Berkeley, University of California Press, 1959.

Palmer, L. R., "The Language of Homer," in *CH,* pp. 75–178.

Parry, Adam, "Homer and Literary Criticism," Connecticut Academy of Arts and Sciences, lecture delivered at Yale University, April 4, 1963.

———, "Have We Homer's Iliad?", *YCS, 20* (1966), 177–216.

Parry, Milman, *L'Épithète traditionnelle dans Homère,* Paris, Société d'éditions "Les belles lettres," 1928.

———, *Les formules et la métrique d'Homère,* Société d'Éditions "Les belles lettres," Paris, 1928.

———, "The Homeric Gloss," *TAPA, 59* (1928), 235–37.

———, "The Distinctive Character of Enjambment in Homeric Verse," *TAPA, 60* (1929), 200–20.

———, "Studies in the Epic Technique of Oral Verse-Making, I: Homer and the Homeric Style," *HSCP, 41* (1930), 73–147.

———, "Studies in the Epic Technique of Oral Verse-Making, II: the Homeric Language as the Language of Oral Poetry," *HSCP, 42* (1932), 1–50.

———, "The Traditional Metaphor in Homer," *CP, 28* (1933), 30–43.

———, "Whole Formulaic Verse in Greek and South Slavic Epic Song," *TAPA, 64* (1933), 179–97.

———, "About Winged Words," *CP, 32* (1937), 59–63.

Prendergast, Guy Lushington, *A Concordance to the Iliad of Homer,* London, 1875.

Platnauer, Maurice, ed., *Fifty Years of Classical Scholarship,* Oxford, Blackwell, 1954.

Pope, Alexander, trans., *Iliad,* World's Classics Edition, London, Oxford University Press, 1959.

Pope, John Collins, *The Rhythm of Beowulf,* rev. ed. New Haven, Yale University Press, 1966.

Quirk, Randolph, "Poetic Language and Old English Meter," in *Early Eng-*

lish and Norse Studies Presented to Hugh Smith, ed. Arthur Brown and Peter Foote (London, Methuen and Co., 1963), pp. 150–71.

Rogers, H. L., "The Crypto-Psychological Character of Oral Formula," *ES, 47* (1966), 89–102.

Schaar, Claes, *Critical Studies in the Cynewulf Group,* Vol. 17, in *LSE,* Lund, 1949.

Schipper, Jacob, ed., *Bede's Historia Ecclesiastica Gentis Anglorum,* Leipzig, 1899.

Scott, John Adams, *The Unity of Homer,* Berkeley, University of California, 1921.

Sievers, Eduard, ed., *Heliand,* Halle, 1878.

———, "Zur Rhythmik des germanischen Alliterationsverse," *BGDSL,* Vol. 10 (1885), Part 1, pp. 209–314, Part 2, pp. 451–545.

Sisam, Kenneth, "Cynewulf and His Poetry," *PBA, 18* (1932), 303–31.

Stevick, Robert D., "The Oral-Formulaic Analysis of Old English Verse," *Speculum, 37* (1962), 382–89.

———, "Christian Elements and the Genesis of *Beowulf,*" *MP, 61* (1963), 79–89.

Storms, Godfrid, "Compound Names of Peoples in *Beowulf:* a Study in the Diction of a Great Poet," *Openb are Les,* Utrecht, 1951.

Stubbings, Frank H., *see* Wace, Alan B.

Tatlock, J. S. P., "Epic Formulas, Especially in *Lagamon,*" *PMLA, 38* (1923), 494–529.

———, "Lagamon's Poetic Style and Its Relations," in *The Manly Anniversary Studies in Language and Literature* (Chicago, University of Chicago Press, 1923), pp. 3–11.

Tillyard, Eustace M. W., *The English Epic and Its Background,* London, Chatto and Windus, 1954.

Toller, T. Northcote, *An Anglo-Saxon Dictionary: Supplement,* Oxford, Oxford University Press, 1921; reprinted 1955.

Trimmer, B. J., ed., *Judith,* London, Methuen and Co., 1952.

Wace, Alan B., and Frank H. Stubbings, eds., *A Companion to Homer,* London, Macmillan, 1962.

Wade-Gery, H. T., *The Poet of the Iliad,* Cambridge, Cambridge University Press, 1952.

Waldron, Ronald A., "Oral-Formulaic Technique in Middle English Alliterative Poetry," *Speculum, 32* (1957), 792–804.

Webster, T. B. L., *From Mycenae to Homer,* London, Methuen & Co., 1958.

Whallon, William, "The Homeric Epithets," *YCS, 17* (1961), 97–142.

———, "The Diction of *Beowulf,*" *PMLA, 76* (1961), 309–19.

————, "Formulas for Heroes in the *Iliad* and in *Beowulf*," MP, *63* (1965), 95–104.

Whatmough, Joshua, ΩΣΠΕΡ ΟΜΕΡΟΣ ΦΗΕΙ   *AJA, 50* (1948), 45–50.

Whitelock, Dorothy, *The Audience of Beowulf*, Oxford, Oxford University Press, 1951.

Whitman, Cedric H., *Homer and the Heroic Tradition*, Cambridge, Harvard University Press, 1958.

Woodhouse, William John, *The Composition of Homer's Odyssey*, Oxford, Clarendon Press, 1930.

Index of Subjects and Authors

This index is not complete. References confined to bibliographical notes are omitted. Lists of general references to Homer, the *Iliad,* the *Odyssey,* and Milman Parry are partial. Old English poems other than *Beowulf* and *Elene* are omitted. General references to those two poems and to Francis P. Magoun, Jr., occur so frequently, that their pagination would encompass all but Chapter 1.

The Rhythm of Beowulf

An Interpretation of the Normal and Hypermetric Verse-Forms in Old English Poetry

by John Collins Pope

This book expounds a new theory of Old English metric, with special reference to *Beowulf*. Like the pronunciation of the final e in Chaucer, the use of "initial rests" before certain types of lines brings out the order essential to competent verse. Specifically, these rests make it possible to adjust the varied syllabic patterns of Old English poetry as defined by Sievers to a basic rhythmic pattern consisting of two measures of 4/8 time for each normal half-line and two measures of 4/4 time for each hypermetric half-line. The rests point to the accompaniment of the harp as the necessary condition of their development and preservation.

The book presents a critique of the theories of Sievers, Leonard, and Heusler, sets forth the new theory, and finally illustrates it by recording the resultant rhythm of extended passages. An appendix contains notes on the text of *Beowulf* and a catalogue of all the rhythmic variations in the normal half-lines of the poem. Musical notation is employed as the most accurate of the familiar methods of indicating rhythm.

For the 1966 printing, a complete line index was compiled, and a new Preface brings certain details in the application of the theory up to the present.

cloth $7.50; paper $2.45